FUNDAMENTALS OF DATABASE SYSTEMS

Titles of Related Interest

FUNDAMENTALS OF DATABASE SYSTEMS

Ramez Elmasri
Department of Computer Science
University of Houston

Shamkant B. Navathe
Database Systems Research and Development Center
Department of Computer and Information Sciences
University of Florida

The Benjamin/Cummings Publishing Company, Inc.
Redwood City, California • Fort Collins, Colorado
Menlo Park, California • Reading, Massachusetts • New York
Don Mills, Ontario • Wokingham, U.K. • Amsterdam • Bonn
Sydney • Singapore • Tokyo • Madrid • San Juan

Sponsoring Editor: Alan R. Apt
Associate Editor: Mark McCormick
Production Editor: Mary B. Shields
Text and Cover design: Hal Lockwood
Copy Editor: Mary Prescott
Composition: Graphic Typesetting Service/Coordinator: Sharon Squires
Typesetter: Rebecca Herren

Cover Art: "Sandstone". Original hand pulled limited edition serigraph by Tetsuro Sawada. Image size, 35" × 22-3/4". Edition size, 60.
With thanks to Galerie de Metropolitan, La Jolla, CA. Exclusive Sawada publisher and distributor: Buschelen/Mowatt Fine Arts Ltd. 111-1445 West Georgia Street, Vancouver, Canada V6G 2T3.

The basic text of this book was designed using the Modular Design System, as developed by Wendy Earl and Design Office Bruce Kortebein.

Library of Congress Cataloging-in-Publication Data

Elmasri, Ramez.
  Fundamentals of database systems.

  Bibliography: p. 751
  Includes indexes.
  1. Data base management. 2. Data base design. I. Navathe, Sham. II. Title.
QA76.9.D3E57   1989   005.74   88–35001

ISBN 0-8053-0145-3

   FGHIJ-MU- 93210

The Benjamin/Cummings Publishing Company, Inc.
390 Bridge Parkway
Redwood City, California 94065

To my wife Amalia,
my parents Aziz and Dora,
and
my children Ramy, Riyad, and Katrina
R.E.

To my wife, Aruna
for everything
S.B.N.

Preface

The purpose of this book is to introduce the fundamental concepts necessary for the design, use, and implementation of database systems. Our presentation stresses the fundamentals of database modeling and design, the languages and facilities provided by database management systems, and the techniques for implementing database systems. The book is meant to be used as a textbook for a one or two semester course in database systems at the junior, senior, or graduate levels, and as a reference book. We assume that readers are familiar with elementary programming and data structuring concepts, and have some exposure to basic computer organization. To keep the book as self-contained as possible we discuss a few elementary topics that some readers may be familiar with; for example, the discussion on characteristics of disk storage devices in Chapter 4 and the summary of tree data structures necessary for the understanding of indexing in Chapter 5.

We have chosen to start the book with the presentation of the concepts at both ends of the database spectrum—the conceptual modeling concepts and the physical file storage techniques. We believe that these concepts are essential to achieving a good understanding of database systems. For students who have already taken a course on file organization techniques, parts of Chapters 4 and 5 could be assigned as reading material to review file organization concepts. Chapter 3, which covers conceptual modeling using the Entity-Relationship (ER) model, provides an important conceptual understanding of data. However, it may be left out, or covered later if the instructor so wishes.

Key Features of the Book

We would like to point out several key features of *Fundamentals of Database Systems*. These are the following:

1. Coverage of data models: We offer comprehensive coverage of the relational, network, and hierarchical data models. In addition, we include in-depth presenta-

tions of the ER model (Chapter 3) and semantic modeling concepts (Chapter 15). We also discuss object-oriented and functional data modeling concepts in Chapter 15. In Chapter 12, we present the similarities and differences among the classical data models. We also show how an ER schema can be mapped to relational, network, or hierarchical schemas, and continue the mapping procedure in Chapter 15 to include advanced semantic modeling concepts. We have tried to keep the individual chapters as self-contained as possible. This modular organization will enable instructors to select the chapters they wish to cover, and to cover them in their preferred order. In particular, the ER model and the three data models presented in Part II—the relational, network, and hierarchical models—can be taught in any order. The instructor may choose not to cover some of these data models at all without sacrificing continuity.

2. Examples: We use the same example of a COMPANY database throughout the book so the reader can compare the different approaches using the same database application. The COMPANY database was structured in a way to illustrate the fine points of the various data models and query languages. The same set of queries is demonstrated with different languages, and queries are labelled for easy cross referencing. Several additional example databases are introduced in the exercises.

3. Flexibility: Because it is very difficult to cover all the data models in depth in a single course, we present each model individually without reference to the other models. Individual instructors may cover their preferred models in their favorite order. In addition, file organization concepts may be covered in depth early on in a course, left out entirely, or presented later. The simplified dependency chart below shows which chapter sequences can be covered following the introductory chapters 1 and 2. (Later chapters are not included on the dependency chart to maintain simplicity.)

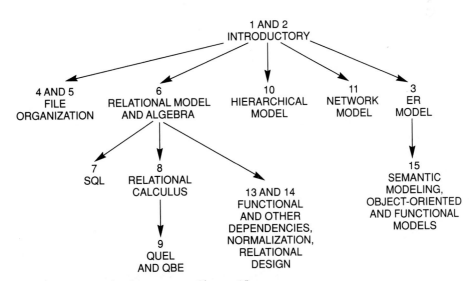

Dependency Chart for chapters up to Chapter 15.

4. Concepts before systems: We cover the conceptual aspects of each major approach to database management before we give examples of real database management systems. This approach is pedagogically sound because systems are often in a state of flux whereas basic concepts are more stable. We have found that our students grasp the concepts better when they are presented independently of real systems, which often have their own idiosyncracies. Chapter 23 provides coverage of several commercial DBMSs, including a relational, a hierarchical, a network, and an object-oriented system. In Chapter 23, we discuss the similarities and differences between the concepts presented earlier and their implementation in the actual systems. This material can be integrated into the course wherever the instructor feels is appropriate.

5. Coverage of database design techniques and DBMS system implementation concepts: Database design techniques, both theoretical and practical, are covered in Part III. Implementation concepts and techniques for query optimization, concurrency control, recovery, security, and integrity are covered in Part IV. The functions of the DBMS catalog/data dictionary are discussed in Chapter 17. The concept of a database transaction is introduced in Chapter 19.

6. State-of-the-art coverage: Coverage of recent advances in database systems is included. Semantic modeling and object-oriented concepts are presented in Chapter 15. Distributed databases are covered in Chapter 21. Chapter 22 includes a discussion of a number of recent advances in database technology and applications, such as expert database systems, knowledge bases, multi-media databases, databases for engineering design, and office information systems.

7. Class testing and comprehensive reviewing: The notes and various drafts upon which this book is based have been class tested over the past three years at both the University of Houston and University of Florida. The text has been thoroughly reviewed by numerous database systems experts who provided many suggestions that contributed to major improvements over the course of three drafts of the book.

Contents of *Fundamentals of Database Systems*

PART I describes the basic concepts necessary for a good understanding of database design and implementation. The first two chapters introduce databases, their typical users, and DBMS concepts and architecture. In Chapter 3, we discuss the conceptual design of databases using the concepts of the Entity-Relationship (ER) model. Chapters 4 and 5 show how database files are organized at the physical storage level. Chapter 4 describes the primary methods of organizing files of records on disk; Chapter 5 describes indexing techniques for files, including B-tree and B$^+$-tree data structures.

PART II describes the data models and languages used in the majority of current commercial database systems. These models are the relational, network, and hierarchical data models. The material on the relational model is covered in several chapters—Chapters 6 through 9—because it is becoming the preferred model, both in industry and for formalizing database issues in academic research. We cover in detail the formal relational algebra and calculus, as well as a number of significant commercial relational languages that have been implemented—SQL, QUEL, and QBE. The hierarchical and network data models are covered in Chapters 10 and 11, respectively, independently of specific DBMSs. Chapter 12 compares the data models and corresponding DBMSs based on their modeling concepts, languages, integrity constraints, and storage structures, and also shows how to convert the conceptual design of a database schema in the ER model into relational, network, or hierarchical schemas.

PART III covers database design. First, we cover the formalisms, theory, and algorithms developed for relational database design in Chapters 13 and 14. This material includes functional and other types of dependencies and normal forms for relations. Step by step intuitive normalization is presented in Chapter 13, and formal relational design algorithms are given in Chapter 14. Chapter 15 discusses data abstraction and semantic data modeling concepts, and briefly compares these to knowledge representation techniques. The ER model is extended to incorporate these ideas, leading to the enhanced-ER (EER) data model. The concepts presented include subclasses, specialization, generalization, and categories. We also describe the object-oriented and functional approaches to data modeling. Chapter 16 presents an overview of the different phases of the database design process for medium-sized and large organizations, and also discusses physical database design issues pertinent to relational, network, and hierarchical DBMSs.

PART IV discusses techniques used in the implementation of database management systems (DBMSs). Chapter 17 describes implementation of the DBMS catalog, which is a vital part of any DBMS. Chapter 18 presents the techniques used for processing and optimizing queries specified in a high-level database language. Chapter 19 introduces the concept of a transaction and discusses concurrency control and recovery techniques for multi-user DBMSs. Chapter 20 discusses techniques for specifying and maintaining database security constraints and semantic integrity constraints.

PART V includes two chapters. In Chapter 21, we discuss distributed databases, where the database and the DBMS are distributed over many sites connected via a communication network. With powerful workstations and high speed communication networks, truly distributed databases are becoming viable. Chapter 22 surveys the trends in database technology and includes discussions of several emerging database applications and technologies, including expert database systems, databases for computer-aided design applications, multi-media databases, and office information systems.

Finally, PART VI describes some characteristics of several representative commercial DBMSs. The DBMSs surveyed include IBM's DB2 relational system, the IMS hierarchical system, and Cullinet's IDMS network system. We also present features of the Vbase DBMS as an example of an object-oriented system.

Guidelines for Using *Fundamentals of Database Systems*

There are many different ways to teach a database course. The chapters in Part I and II can be used in an introductory course on database systems in the order they are given or in the preferred order of each individual instructor. Selected chapters may be left out, and the instructor can add other chapters from the rest of the book, depending on the emphasis of the course. For an emphasis on system implementation techniques, selected chapters from Part IV can be used. For an emphasis on database design, chapters from Parts III can be used. Examples to illustrate the use of specific systems can be included from Part VI.

For a single-semester course, based on this book, some chapters can be assigned as reading material. Chapters 4, 5, 12, 16, 17, and 22 can be considered for such reading assignments. The book can also be used for a two-semester sequence. The first course, "Introduction to Database Systems," at the sophomore, junior, or senior level, could cover most of Chapters 1 to 13. The second course, "Database Design and Implementation Techniques," at the senior or first year graduate level, can cover the remaining chapters, and any chapters left out from the first course. Part V can serve as introductory material for additional topics the instructor may wish to cover. Chapters from Part VI can be used selectively in either semester, and material describing the DBMS at the local institution can be covered in addition to the material in the book.

Acknowledgements

It is a great pleasure for us to acknowledge the assistance and contributions of a large number of individuals to this effort. First and foremost, we owe a great deal to our editor Alan Apt for his persistent personal interest in the project from its inception and his constant encouragement. He was able to solicit comments from an eminent array of database professionals, and provided crucial feedback that influenced the contents and organization of the book.

Many individuals have reviewed the outlines and various drafts of the manuscript for *Fundamentals of Database Systems*. We are very grateful to Scott Downing, Dennis Heimbigner, Julia Hodges, Yannis Ioannidis, Jim Larson, Per-Ake Larson, Rahul Patel, David Stemple, and Kyu-Young Whang, who have reviewed one or more drafts of the manuscript. They provided us with many helpful and insightful comments that influenced the final manuscript. In particular, we are indebted to Jim Larson who provided pages of constructive criticism on every chapter. Dennis Heimbigner's comments contributed to the final contents of several chapters, and in particular to the order of presentation of relational algebra operations in Chapter 6. Kyu-Young Whang's comments on Chapters 18 and 19 were very helpful. We would like to acknowledge the influence of Rafi Ahmed, Scott Downing, and Julia Hodges on Chapter 8, and Yannis Ioannidis on Chapter 9.

In addition to our main reviewers, we would like to thank several persons who reviewed our proposed outline or drafts of individual chapters of the book. These include Don Batory, Dennis McLeod, Nicholas Roussopoulos, Michael Stonebraker, and Frank Tompa. We are also grateful to Tim Andrews of Ontologic, and Vic Ghorpadey, Sam Greenlaw, and Jeff Scherb of Cullinet who reviewed the material on their respective commercial systems in Chapter 23. Any bugs that remain in the manuscript are, of course, the responsibility of the authors.

Ramez Elmasri used the drafts of various chapters numerous times as class notes at the University of Houston for the undergraduate database course COSC 3380 (and its predecessor course COSC 4320). In addition, selected chapters were used in the graduate course COSC 6340. We are grateful to the students' comments on the manuscript. Unfortunately, we did not keep track of the names of students who provided feedback on the earlier drafts of the book. We would like to mention Christopher Lewis, Xing-Fang Lin, Srinivas Pyda, Ed Smelko, and Yu-Tung Wu, who looked at more recent drafts. Ramez Elmasri would also like to acknowledge the influence of students at the Institute for Retraining in Computer Science, where he taught the database course for two summers. Discussions with the students, particularly Joe Bergin and Wadi Juredeini, clarified some of the concepts presented in Chapters 13 and 14.

Sham Navathe used drafts of various chapters for his course CIS 6120 at the University of Florida. Students taking the course provided very useful feedback. We would particularly like to mention Subhasis Das, Mike Dybevick, Seong Geum, C.K. Luo, Jackie Morie, David Noden, Terry Sullivan, Mridul Tandon, and J.J.Yu. Many graduate students working with Navathe provided technical and editorial comments during the later revisions. We particularly thank Arunkumar Balaraman, Ajay Budhraja, Aloysius Cornelio, Dinesh Desai, Sunit Gala, Sunil George, Stephan Grill, K. Kamalakar, Sumant Pal, Sangam Pant, Bhavani Ravichandran, Prabhakar Satya, Yogesh Sridhare, and Arun Thakore.

Rajeev Kumar helped immensely in manuscript preparation for Chapters 22 and 23. Sharon Grant provided assistance in manuscript preparation and secretarial help throughout. Mohan Pillalamarri helped in index preparation. John Gibbs provided precious assistance with writing style during the early stages of the project. We would also like to thank Colleen Dunn, Mark McCormick, Mary Shields, and Mary Ann Telatnick of Benjamin Cummings Publishing Company.

Finally, Ramez Elmasri would like to thank his parents for their continuous encouragement and support, and his wife Amalia and children Ramy, Riyad, and Katrina who endured through the course of development of the book. Sham Navathe would like to thank his grandparents and parents for their encouragement and support throughout his career, and his wife Aruna and children Manisha and Amol for their sacrifice and patience during the project.

R.E.
S.B.N.

Brief Contents

Contents

PART II   DATABASE MODELS AND LANGUAGES   133

PART III   DATABASE DESIGN   353

PART IV   SYSTEM IMPLEMENTATION TECHNIQUES   487

FUNDAMENTALS
OF DATABASE
SYSTEMS

BASIC CONCEPTS

CHAPTER 1

Databases and Database Users

1.1 Introduction

Databases and database technology are having a major impact on the growing use of computers. It is fair to say that databases will play a critical role in almost all areas where computers are used, including business, engineering, medicine, law, education, and library science, to name a few. The word "database" is in such common use that we must begin by defining what a database is. Our initial definition is quite general.

A **database** is a collection of related data.* By **data,** we mean known facts that can be recorded and that have implicit meaning. For example, consider the names, telephone numbers, and addresses of all the people you know. You may have recorded this data in an indexed address book, or you may have stored it on a diskette using a personal computer and software such as DBASE III or Lotus 1-2-3. This is a collection of related data with an implicit meaning and hence is a database.

The above definition of database is quite general; for example, we may consider the collection of words that make up this page of text to be related data and hence a database. However, the common use of the term database is usually more restricted. A database has the following implicit properties:

- A database is a logically coherent collection of data with some inherent meaning. A random assortment of data cannot be referred to as a database.

---

*We will use the word *data* in both singular and plural, which is common in database literature. Context will determine whether it is singular or plural. In standard English, data is used only as the plural; datum is used as the singular.

- A database is designed, built, and populated with data for a specific purpose. It has an intended group of users and some preconceived applications in which these users are interested.

- A database represents some aspect of the real world, sometimes called the **miniworld**. Changes to the miniworld are reflected in the database.

In other words, a database has some source from which data are derived, some degree of interaction with events in the real world, and an audience that is actively interested in the contents of the database.

A database can be of any size and of varying complexity. For example, the list of names and addresses referred to earlier may have only a couple of hundred records in it, each with a simple structure. On the other hand, the card catalog of a large library may contain half a million cards stored under different categories—by primary author's last name, by subject, by book title, and the like—with each category organized in alphabetic order. A database of even greater size and complexity may be that maintained by the Internal Revenue Service to keep track of the tax forms filed by taxpayers of the United States. If we assume that there are 100 million taxpayers and each taxpayer files an average of five forms with approximately 200 characters of information per form, we would get a database of $100*(10^6)*200*5$ characters (bytes) of information. Assuming the IRS keeps the past three returns for each taxpayer in addition to the current return, we would get a database of $4*(10^{11})$ bytes. This huge amount of information must somehow be organized and managed so that users can search for, retrieve, and update the data as needed.

A database may be generated and maintained manually or by machine. Of course, in this book we are mainly interested in computerized databases. The library card catalog is an example of a database that may be manually created and maintained. A computerized database may be created and maintained either by a group of application programs written specifically for that task or by a database management system.

A **database management system** (DBMS) is a collection of programs that enables users to create and maintain a database. The DBMS is hence a *general-purpose* software system that facilitates the processes of defining, constructing, and manipulating databases for various applications. **Defining** a database involves specifying the types of data to be stored in the database, along with a detailed description of each type of data. **Constructing** the database is the process of storing the data itself on some storage medium that is controlled by the DBMS. **Manipulating** a database includes such functions as querying the database to retrieve specific data, updating the database to reflect changes in the miniworld, and generating reports from the data.

Note that it is not necessary to use general-purpose DBMS software for implementing a computerized database. We could write our own set of programs to create and maintain the database, in effect creating our own *special-purpose* DBMS software. In either case—whether we use a general-purpose DBMS or not—we usually have a considerable amount of software to manipulate the database in addition to the database itself. The database and software are together called a **database system**. Figure 1.1 illustrates the above ideas.

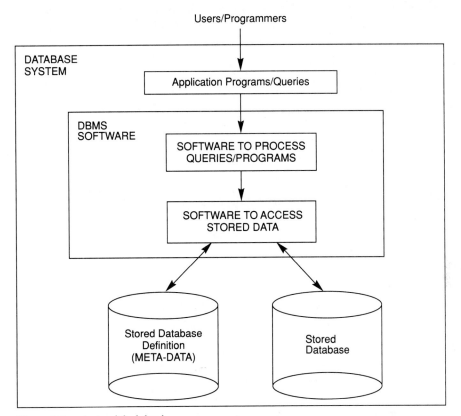

Figure 1.1   A simplified database system environment.

1.2   An Example

Let us consider an example that most readers may be familiar with—a database for maintaining information concerning students, courses, and grades in a university environment. Figure 1.2 shows the database structure and a few sample data for such a database. The database is organized as five files, where each file stores data records of the same type.* The STUDENT file stores data on each student, the COURSE file stores data on each course, the SECTION file stores data on each section of a course, the GRADE_REPORT file stores the grades that students receive in the various sections they completed, and the PREREQUISITE file stores the prerequisites of each course.

To *define* this database, we must specify the structure of the records of each file by specifying the different types of **data elements** to be stored in each record. In Figure 1.2 each STUDENT record includes data to represent the student's Name, StudentNumber, Class (freshman, sophomore, ...), and Major (math, computer science, business, ...); each COURSE record includes data to represent the CourseName, CourseNumber,

---

*We will define files and records more formally in Chapter 4.

STUDENT	Name	StudentNumber	Class	Major
	Smith	17	1	COSC
	Brown	8	2	COSC

COURSE	CourseName	CourseNumber	CreditHours	Department
	Intro to Computer Science	COSC1310	4	COSC
	Data Structures	COSC3320	4	COSC
	Discrete Mathematics	MATH2410	3	MATH
	Database	COSC3380	3	COSC

PREREQUISITE	CourseNumber	PrerequisiteNumber
	COSC3380	COSC3320
	COSC3380	MATH2410
	COSC3320	COSC1310

SECTION	SectionIdentifier	CourseNumber	Semester	Year	Instructor
	85	MATH2410	Fall	86	King
	92	COSC1310	Fall	86	Anderson
	102	COSC3320	Spring	87	Knuth
	112	MATH2410	Fall	87	Chang
	119	COSC1310	Fall	87	Anderson
	135	COSC3380	Fall	87	Stone

GRADE_REPORT	StudentNumber	SectionIdentifier	Grade
	17	112	B
	17	119	C
	8	85	A
	8	92	A
	8	102	B
	8	135	A

Figure 1.2   Example of a database

CreditHours, and Department (the department that offers the course); and so on. We must also specify a **data type** for each data element within a record. For example, we can specify that Name of STUDENT is a string of alphabetic characters, StudentNumber of STUDENT is an integer, and Grade of GRADE_REPORT is a single character from the set {A, B, C, D, F, I}. We may also use a coding scheme to represent a data item. For example, in Figure 1.2 we represent the Class of a STUDENT as 1 for freshman, 2 for sophomore, 3 for junior, 4 for senior, and 5 for graduate student.

To *construct* the database, we store data to represent each student, course, section, grade report, and prerequisite as a record in the appropriate file. Note that records in the various files may be related to one another. For example, the record for "Smith" in the

STUDENT file is related to two records in the GRADE_REPORT file that specify Smith's grades in two sections. Similarly, each record in the PREREQUISITE file relates two course records: one representing the course and the other representing the prerequisite. Most medium-sized and large databases include many types of records and have many relationships among the records.

Database *manipulation* involves querying and updating. Examples of queries are "retrieve the transcript (a list of all courses and grades) of Smith"; "list the names of students who took the section of the Database course offered in Fall 1987 and their grades in that section"; and "what are the prerequisites of the Database course?" Examples of updates are "change the class of Smith to Sophomore"; "create a new section for the Database course for this semester"; and "enter a grade of A for Smith in the Database section of last semester." These informal queries and updates must be specified precisely in the database system language before they can be processed.

1.3   Characteristics of the Database Approach versus the Traditional File Processing Approach

A number of characteristics distinguish the database approach from the traditional approach of programming with files. In traditional **file processing** each user defines and implements the files needed for a specific application. For example, one user, the grade reporting office, may keep a file on students and their grades. Programs to print a student's transcript and to enter new grades into the file are implemented. A second user, the accounting office, may keep track of students' fees and their payments. Although both users are interested in data about students, each user maintains separate files—and programs to manipulate these files—because each requires some data not available from the other user's files. This redundancy in defining and storing data results in wasted storage space and in redundant efforts to maintain common data up-to-date.

In the database approach, a single repository of data is maintained that is defined once and then accessed by various users. The main characteristics of the database approach versus the file processing approach are the following.

1.3.1   Self-contained Nature of a Database System

A fundamental characteristic of the database approach is that the database system contains not only the database itself but also a complete definition or description of the database. This definition is stored in the system **catalog,** which contains information such as the structure of each file, the type and storage format of each data item, and various constraints on the data. The information stored in the catalog is called **meta-data** and describes the structure of the primary database (Figure 1.1).

The catalog is used by the DBMS software and occasionally by database users who need information about the database structure. The DBMS software is not written for any specific database application and hence must refer to the catalog to know the structure of the files in a specific database, such as the type and format of data it will access. The DBMS software must work equally well with *any number of database applications*—for example, a university database, a banking database, or a company database—as long as the database definition is stored in the catalog.

In traditional file processing, data definition is typically part of the application programs themselves. Hence, these programs are constrained to work with only *one specific database* whose structure is declared in the application programs. For example, a PASCAL program may have file variables declared in it; a PL/I program will have file structures specified with DCL (declare) statements; and a COBOL program has Data Division statements to define its files. Whereas file processing software can access only one specific database, DBMS software can access many different databases by extracting the database definitions from the catalog and using these definitions to correctly access any one of those databases.

In our example of Figure 1.2 the DBMS would store in the catalog the definitions of all the files shown. Whenever a request is made to access, say, the Name of a STUDENT record, the DBMS software would refer to the catalog to determine the structure of the STUDENT file and the position and size of the Name data item within a STUDENT record. The DBMS would then access the database to retrieve or update the name of a student. By contrast, in a typical file processing application, the file structure and, in some cases, the exact location of Name within a STUDENT record are already coded within each program that accesses this data item. In fact, these programs may not even refer to the name of a data item, such as Name of STUDENT, but only to the position and size of the data item within a record, as illustrated in Figure 1.3.

1.3.2 Insulation between Programs and Data

In traditional file processing, the structure of data files is embedded in the access programs, so any changes to the structure of a file may require *changing all programs* that access this file. By contrast, DBMS access programs are written independently of any specific files. The structure of data files is stored in the DBMS catalog separately from the access programs. We call this property **program-data independence**. For example, a file access program may be written in such a way that it can access only STUDENT records of length 42 characters (Figure 1.3). If we want to add another piece of data to each STUDENT record, say the Birthdate, such a program will no longer work and must be changed. By contrast, in a DBMS environment we just need to change the description of STUDENT records in the catalog; no programs are changed. The next time a DBMS program refers to the catalog, the new structure of STUDENT records will be accessed and used.

data item name	starting position in record	length in characters (bytes)
Name	1	30
StudentNumber	31	4
Class	35	4
Major	39	4

STUDENT record length = 42 bytes

Figure 1.3   Storage format for a STUDENT record

1.3.3   Data Abstraction

A DBMS should provide users with a **conceptual representation** of data that does not include many of the details of how the data is stored. A **data model** is a type of data abstraction that is used to provide this conceptual representation. The data model uses logical concepts, such as objects, their properties, and their interrelationships, which may be easier for most users to understand than computer storage concepts. Hence, the data model *hides* storage details that may not be of interest to most database users.

For example, consider Figure 1.2. In a file processing application, each file may be defined by its record length—the number of characters (bytes) in each record—and each data item may be specified by its starting byte within a record and its length in bytes. The STUDENT record would be represented as shown in Figure 1.3. A typical database user may not be concerned with where each data item is within a record or what its length is; the user is only concerned that when a reference is made to Name of STUDENT, the correct value is returned. A conceptual representation of the STUDENT record should not be concerned with such details but only with the name of each data item, as shown in Figure 1.2. Many other details of file storage organization—such as the access paths specified on a file—can be hidden from database users by the DBMS; we will discuss storage details in Chapters 4 and 5.

In the database approach the detailed structure and organization of each file is stored in the catalog. The database users refer to the conceptual representation of the files, and the DBMS extracts the details of file storage from the catalog when needed by the DBMS software. There are many data models that can be used to provide this data abstraction to database users. A major part of this book is devoted to presenting various data models and the concepts they use to abstract the representation of data.

1.3.4   Support of Multiple Views of the Data

A database typically has many users, each of whom may require a different perspective or **view** of the database. A view may be a subset of the database or it may contain **virtual** data that is derived from the database files but is not explicitly stored. A multiuser DBMS whose users have a variety of applications must provide facilities for defining multiple views. For example, one user of the database of Figure 1.2 may be interested only in the transcript of each student; the view for this user is shown in Figure 1.4(a). A second user, who is interested only in checking that students have taken the prerequisites of each course they register for, may require the view shown in Figure 1.4(b).

The above four characteristics are most important in distinguishing a DBMS from traditional file processing software. In Section 1.6 we discuss additional functions that characterize a DBMS. First, we categorize the different types of persons who work in a database environment.

1.4   Actors on the Scene

For a small personal database, such as the list of addresses discussed in Section 1.1, one person will typically define, construct, and manipulate the database. However, many persons are involved with the design, use, and maintenance of a large database—for

(a)

TRANSCRIPT	StudentName	StudentTranscript				
		CourseNumber	Grade	Semester	Year	SectionId
	Smith	COSC1310	C	Fall	87	119
		MATH2410	B	Fall	87	112
	Brown	MATH2410	A	Fall	86	85
		COSC1310	A	Fall	86	92
		COSC3320	B	Spring	87	102
		COSC3380	A	Fall	87	135

(b)

PREREQUISITES	CourseName	CourseNumber	Prerequisites
	Database	3380	COSC3320
			MATH2410
	Data Structures	3320	COSC1310

Figure 1.4 Two views of the sample database in Figure 1.2. (a) The student transcript view. (b) The course prerequisites view.

instance, where a DBMS is being used to manage a database for a few hundred users. In this section we identify the people whose job involves the day-to-day use of a large database; we call them the "actors on the scene" and discuss what they do. In Section 1.5 we consider people who may be called "workers behind the scene;" those who work to maintain the database system environment, but are not actively interested in the database itself.

1.4.1   Database Administrators

In any organization where many persons use the same resources, there is a need for a chief administrator to oversee and manage these resources. In a database environment, the primary resource is the database itself and the secondary resource is the DBMS and related software. Administering these resources is the responsibility of the **database administrator (DBA)**. The DBA is responsible for authorizing access to the database and for coordinating and monitoring its use. The DBA is accountable for problems such as breach of security or poor system response time. In large organizations, the DBA is assisted by a staff that helps in carrying out these functions.

1.4.2   Database Designers

Database designers have the responsibility for identifying the data to be stored in the database and for choosing appropriate structures to represent and store this data. These tasks are mostly undertaken before the database is actually implemented. It is the responsibility of database designers to communicate with all prospective database users in order to understand their requirements, and come up with a design that meets these requirements. In many cases, the designers are on the staff of the DBA and may continue on with other responsibilities after the database design is completed. Database designers typically interact with each potential group of users and come up with a **view** of the database that meets the data and processing requirements of this group. These views are then analyzed and integrated with the views of other user groups. The final database design must be capable of supporting the requirements of all user groups.

1.4.3 End Users

These are the persons whose job requires access to the database for querying, updating, and generating reports; the database primarily exists for their use. There are several categories of end users:

- **Casual end users** occasionally access the database, but they may need different information each time they access it. They may use a sophisticated database query language to specify their requests and are typically middle- or high-level managers or other occasional browsers.

- **Naive or parametric end users** make up a sizable portion of database end users. Their main job function revolves around querying and updating the database using standard types of queries and updates—called **canned transactions**—that have been carefully programmed and tested. We are all accustomed to dealing with several types of such users. Bank tellers check balances and post withdrawals and deposits. Reservation clerks for airlines, hotels, and car rental companies check availability for a given request and make reservations. These users constantly perform database retrievals and updates. Data entry clerks are a special category of such users who enter new information into the database.

- **Sophisticated end users** include engineers, scientists, business analysts, and others who thoroughly familiarize themselves with the facilities of the DBMS so as to meet their complex requirements.

A typical DBMS provides multiple facilities to access a database. Naive end users need to learn very little about the facilities provided by the DBMS; they have only to understand the types of standard transactions designed and implemented for their use. Casual users learn only a few facilities that they may use repeatedly. Sophisticated users try to learn most of the DBMS facilities in order to achieve their complex requirements.

1.4.4 System Analysts and Application Programmers

System analysts determine the requirements of end users, especially naive and parametric end users, and develop specifications for transactions that meet these requirements. **Application programmers** implement these specifications as programs, then test, debug, document, and maintain these programs. These analysts and programmers should be familiar with the full range of capabilities provided by the DBMS to accomplish their tasks.

1.5 Workers behind the Scene

In addition to those who design, use, and administer a database, there are others who are associated with the design, development, and operation of the DBMS *software and system environment*. These persons are typically not interested in the database itself. We call them the workers behind the scene, and they include the following categories.

1.5.1   DBMS *Designers and Implementers*

These are persons who design and implement the DBMS as a software package. A DBMS is a complex software system and is made of many components or **modules,** including modules for implementing the catalog, query language, interface processors, data access, and security. The DBMS must interface with other system software, such as the operating system and compilers for various programming languages. Design and implementation of all these DBMS modules and interfaces are the jobs of the DBMS designers and implementers.

1.5.2   *Tool Developers*

Tools are software packages that facilitate database system design and use and help in improving performance. Tools are not part of the DBMS software but are optional packages that are often purchased separately. They include packages for database design, performance monitoring, natural language or graphical interfaces, prototyping, simulation, and test data generation. Tool developers include persons who design and implement such tools. In many cases, independent software vendors develop and market such tools.

1.5.3   *Operators and Maintenance Personnel*

These are the persons responsible for the actual running and maintenance of the hardware and software environment for the database system.

The above categories of workers behind the scene are instrumental in making the database system available to end users. However, they typically do not use the database for their own purposes. We will examine databases mainly from the perspective of the end users, administrators, designers, and analysts/programmers in Parts II and VI of the book. In Part III we discuss database design, and in Part IV we examine DBMS implementation techniques. Part I discusses general principles that are useful to most types of database users, and Part V discusses novel database applications.

1.6   Intended Uses of a DBMS

In this section we discuss the intended uses of a DBMS and the capabilities a good DBMS should possess to meet these intended uses. Current commercial DBMSs incorporate these capabilities to varying degrees, but an ideal DBMS would include all of them. The DBA must utilize these capabilities to accomplish a variety of objectives related to the design, administration, and use of a large multiuser database. In our discussion, we will compare the DBMS approach with the traditional file processing approach. Many of the capabilities discussed below are not provided by traditional file systems.

1.6.1   *Controlling Redundancy*

In traditional file processing every user group maintains its own files for handling its data processing applications. For example, consider the university database example of Section 1.2; two groups of users could be the course registration personnel and the accounting office. In the traditional approach, each group independently keeps files on students. The accounting office also keeps data on registration and related billing information, whereas the registration office keeps track of student courses and grades. Much of the data is stored twice: once in the files of each user group. Additional user groups may further duplicate some or all of the same data in their own files.

This **redundancy** in storing the same data multiple times leads to several problems. First, there is a need to perform a single logical update—such as entering data on a new student—multiple times: once for each file where student data is recorded. This leads to *duplication of effort*. Second, *storage space is wasted* on storing the same data repeatedly, which may be serious for large databases. A third and more serious problem is that files that represent the same data may become *inconsistent*. This may happen because an update is applied to some of the files but not to others. Even if an update—such as adding a new student—is applied to all the appropriate files, the data concerning the student may be inconsistent because the updates are applied independently by each user group. For example, one user group may enter a student's birthdate erroneously as JAN-19-1968, whereas the other user groups enter the correct value of JAN-29-1968. The result is that the birthdate of the same student is **inconsistent** among the various files.

In the database approach we integrate the views of different user groups during database design. For consistency, we should have a database design that stores each logical data item—such as a student's name or birthdate—in *only one place* in the database. This does not permit any inconsistency, and it also saves storage space. In some cases, **controlled redundancy** may be useful. For example, we may want to store StudentName and CourseNumber redundantly in the GRADE_REPORT file, as shown in Figure 1.5(a), because whenever we retrieve GRADE_REPORT data we want to retrieve the student name and course number along with the grade, student number, and section identifier. By placing all the data that we retrieve together in one file, we do not have to search multiple files to collect this data. In such cases, the DBMS should have the capability to **control** this redundancy so as to prohibit inconsistencies among the files. This may be done by automatically checking that the StudentName-StudentNumber values in any GRADE_REPORT record in Figure 1.5(a) match one of the Name-StudentNumber values of a STUDENT record (Figure 1.2). Similarly, the SectionIdentifier-CourseNumber values in GRADE_REPORT can be checked against SECTION records. Such checks can be specified to the DBMS during database design and automatically enforced by the DBMS whenever the GRADE_REPORT file is updated. Figure 1.5(b) shows a GRADE_REPORT record that is inconsistent with the STUDENT file of Figure 1.2, which may be entered erroneously if the redundancy is not controlled.

1.6.2 Sharing of Data

A multiuser DBMS, as its name implies, must allow multiple users to access the database at the same time. This is essential if data for multiple applications is to be integrated and maintained in a single database. The DBMS must include **concurrency control** software to ensure that several users trying to update the same data do so in a controlled manner so that the result of the updates is correct. An example is when several reservation clerks try to assign a seat on an airline flight; the DBMS should ensure that each seat be accessed by only one clerk at a time for assignment to a passenger. Another mechanism that sup-

(a)

GRADE_REPORT	StudentNumber	StudentName	SectionIdentifier	CourseNumber	Grade
	17	Smith	112	MATH2410	B
	17	Smith	119	COSC1310	C
	8	Brown	85	MATH2410	A
	8	Brown	92	COSC1310	A
	8	Brown	102	COSC3320	B
	8	Brown	135	COSC3380	A

(b)

GRADE_REPORT	StudentNumber	StudentName	SectionIdentifier	CourseNumber	Grade
	17	Brown	112	MATH2410	B

Figure 1.5   Redundant storage of data items among files. (a) Including the StudentName and CourseNumber in the GRADE_REPORT file. (b) A GRADE_REPORT record that is inconsistent with the STUDENT records in Figure 1.2 (in Figure 1.2 the Name of student number 17 is Smith, not Brown).

ports the notion of data sharing in a multiuser DBMS is the facility for defining a **user view,** which is used to specify the portion of a database that is of interest to a particular user group. Examples of user views on the database of Figure 1.2 are shown in Figure 1.4.

1.6.3   Restricting Unauthorized Access

When multiple users share a database, it is likely that some users are not authorized to access all information in the database. For example, financial data is often considered confidential, and hence only authorized persons should be allowed to access such data. In addition, some users may be permitted only to retrieve data, whereas others are allowed to both retrieve and update. Hence, the type of access operation—retrieval or update—can also be controlled. Typically, users or user groups are given account numbers protected by passwords, which they can use to gain access to the database. A DBMS should provide a **security and authorization** subsystem, which is used by the DBA to create accounts and specify account restrictions. The DBMS should then enforce these restrictions automatically. Notice that we can apply similar controls to the DBMS software. For example, only the DBA's staff may be allowed to use certain **privileged** software, such as the software for creating new accounts. Similarly, parametric users may be allowed to access the database only through the canned transactions developed for their use.

1.6.4   Providing Multiple Interfaces

Because many types of users, with varying technical knowledge, use a database, a DBMS should provide a variety of user interfaces. The types of interfaces include query languages for casual users, programming language interfaces for application programmers, forms for parametric users, menu-driven interfaces for naive users, and natural language interfaces.

1.6.5   Representing Complex Relationships among Data

A database may include a variety of data that are interrelated in many ways. Consider the example shown in Figure 1.2. The record for Brown in the STUDENT file is related to four records in the GRADE_REPORT file. Similarly, each SECTION record is related to one COURSE record as well as a number of GRADE_REPORT records—one for each student who completed that section. A DBMS must have the capability to represent a variety of complex relationships among the data as well as to retrieve and update related data in an easy and efficient manner. This is essential whenever a user needs to identify and process data related by complex relationships.

1.6.6   Enforcing Integrity Constraints

Most database applications will have certain **integrity constraints** that must hold on the data. The simplest type of integrity constraint is to specify a data type for each data item. For example, in Figure 1.2 we may specify that the value of the Class data item within each STUDENT record must be an integer between 1 and 5 or that the value of the Name data item must be a string of no more than 30 alphabetic characters. Most DBMSs have facilities for defining the data types of data items and for checking that data items in a record match the specified data types.

There are more complex types of constraints. One type of constraint that occurs frequently is to specify that a record in one file must be related to records in other files. For example, in Figure 1.2 we can specify that "every SECTION record must be related to a COURSE record." Another type of constraint specifies uniqueness constraints on data items, such as "every COURSE record must have a unique value for CourseNumber." These constraints are derived from the meaning or **semantics** of the data and the miniworld it represents. It is the responsibility of the database designers to specify integrity constraints during database design. Some constraints can be specified to the DBMS and automatically enforced. Other constraints may have to be checked by update programs or at the time of data entry. Current DBMSs are somewhat limited in the types of constraints they can enforce automatically.

Note that a data item may be entered erroneously but still satisfy the specified integrity constraints. For example, if a student receives a grade of A but a grade of C is entered in the database, the DBMS cannot discover this error automatically because C is a valid value for the Grade data type. Such data entry errors can only be discovered manually (when the student receives the grade and complains) and corrected later by updating the database. However, a grade of X can be automatically rejected by the DBMS because X is not a valid value for the Grade data type.

1.6.7   Providing Backup and Recovery

A DBMS must provide facilities for recovering from hardware or software failures. The **backup and recovery** subsystem of the DBMS is responsible for recovery. For example, if the computer system fails in the middle of a complex update program, the recovery subsystem is responsible for making sure that the database is restored to its state before the program started executing. Alternatively, the recovery subsystem could ensure that the program is resumed from the point at which it was interrupted so that its full effect is recorded in the database.

1.7   Additional Advantages of the Database Approach

In addition to the issues discussed in the previous section, there are other advantages to the database approach. We discuss some of these here.

1.7.1   Potential for Enforcing Standards

The database approach permits the DBA to define and enforce standards among database users in a large organization. This facilitates communication and cooperation among various departments, projects, and users within the organization. Standards can be defined for names and formats of data elements, display formats, report structures, terminology, etc. The DBA can enforce standards in a centralized database environment more easily than in an environment where each user group has control of its own files and software.

1.7.2   Flexibility

It may be necessary to change the structure of a database as requirements change. For example, a new user group may emerge that needs additional information not currently in the database. We may need to add a new file to the database or just extend the data elements in an existing file. Some DBMSs allow such changes to the structure of the database without affecting most of the existing application programs.

1.7.3   Reduced Application Development Time

A prime selling feature of the database approach is that developing a new application—such as the retrieval of certain data from the database for printing a new report—takes very little time. Designing and implementing a new database from scratch may take more time than writing a single specialized file application. However, once a database is up and running, it generally takes substantially less time to create new applications using DBMS facilities. The time to develop a new application using a DBMS is estimated to be one-sixth to one-fourth of that when using a traditional file system because of the easy-to-use interfaces available with a DBMS. Hence, whenever many new applications are expected to be developed during the lifetime of a database, it is more cost effective to use a DBMS.

1.7.4   Availability of Up-to-Date Information

A DBMS makes the database available to all users. As soon as one user's update is applied to the database, all other users immediately see this update. This availability of up-to-date information is essential for many applications, such as reservation systems or banking databases, and is made possible by the concurrency control and recovery subsystems of a DBMS.

1.7.5 Economies of Scale

The DBMS approach permits consolidation of data and applications, thus reducing the wasteful overlap between activities of data processing personnel in different projects or departments. This makes it possible for the whole organization to invest in more powerful processors, storage devices, or communication gear than could be obtained if single departments had to purchase their own equipment separately and at the same time reduces overall costs of operation and management.

1.8 When Not to Use a DBMS

In spite of the advantages listed above, there are situations where using a DBMS may represent unnecessary overhead costs as compared to traditional file processing. The overhead of using a DBMS is due to the following:

- High initial investment and possible need for additional hardware.
- Generality that a DBMS provides for defining and processing data.
- Overhead for providing security, concurrency control, recovery, and integrity functions.

Additional problems may arise if the database designers and DBA do not properly design the database or if the database systems applications are not implemented properly. If the DBA does not administer the database system properly, security and integrity may be compromised. Because of the overhead of using a DBMS and the potential problems of improper administration, it may be preferable to use regular files under the following circumstances:

- The database and applications are simple, well defined, and not expected to change.
- There are stringent real-time requirements for some programs that may not be met because of DBMS overhead.
- Multiple access to data is not required.

1.9 Summary

In this chapter we defined a database as a collection of related data, where data means recorded facts. A typical database represents some aspect of the real world and is used for specific purposes by one or more groups of users. A DBMS is generalized software for implementing and maintaining a computerized database. The database and software together form a database system. We presented four important characteristics that distinguish the database approach from traditional file processing applications:

- Existence of a catalog or data dictionary.
- Program-data independence.

Summary continued on page 20.

DATABASE SYSTEMS: A BRIEF TIME CAPSULE

	Event	Significance
Pre-1960's		
1945	Magnetic tapes developed (the first medium to allow searching).	Replaced punch card and paper tape.
1957	First commercial computer installed.	
1959	McGee proposed the notion of generalized access to electronically stored data.	
1959	IBM introduced the Ramac system.	Read data in a nonsequential manner, and access to files became feasible.
The 60's		
1961	The first generalized DBMS—GE's Integrated Data Store designed by Bachman; wide distribution by 1964. Bachman popularized data structure diagrams termed record types and set types.	This terminology formed the basis of the Network Data Model developed by the Conference on Data Systems and Languages Database Task Group. (CODASYL DBTG).
1965–70	• Generalized File Management Systems developed. Concurrently, IBM developed the Hierarchical Model.	Provided two-level organization of data.
	• Information Management System developed to solve aerospace design and production problems.	
	• IMS DB/DC (database/data communication) System was the first large-scale DB/DC system.	Supported network views on top of the hierarchies.
	• Dodd at GM developed extensions to PL/1 called APL (associative programming language).	
	• SABRE, developed by IBM and American Airlines.	Allowed multi-user access to data involving a communication network.
	• Credit Reporting System by TRW experienced nationwide use.	
The 70's		
	Database technology experienced rapid growth.	A number of commercial systems followed the CODASYL DBTG proposal, but none fully implemented it. Examples include the IDMS system by B. F. Goodrich, Honeywell's IDS II, UNIVAC's DMS 1100, Burroughs's DMS-II, CDC's DMS-170, Phillips's PHOLAS, and Digital's DBMS-11. Some either restricted implementations of the DBTG approach or developed their own network models. Several integrated DB/DC systems were also implemented such as

		Cincom's TOTAL plus ENVIRON/1 System. DBMS developed as an academic discipline and a research area.
1970	The relational model is developed by Ted Codd, an IBM research fellow, followed by normalization process.	Identifies the problems of insertion, deletion, and updates; allows research to become formalized.
1971	CODASYL Database Task Group Report.	
1972	ACM Special Interest Group on Management of Data (SIGMOD) organized the first international conference.	
1975	Very Large Data Base Foundation organized the first international conference.	
1976	International Federation of Information Processing Society's Working Group 2.6 organized international conference.	

1976
- Entity-relationship (ER) model introduced by Chen.
- **Research projects in the 70's:** System R (IBM), INGRES (University of California, Berkeley), System 2000 (University of Texas, Austin), Socrate Project (University of Grenoble, France), ADABAS (Technical University of Darmstadt, W. Germany).
- **Query Languages developed in the 70's:** SQUARE, SEQUEL (SQL), QBE, QUEL.

The 80's

Micro-DBMS family is developed.

Allowed end user to define the data and manipulate it with flexibility and ease. They lack multiview/multiaccess support and insulation between programs and data (data independence).

1983	ANSI/SPARC survey revealed >100 relational systems had been implemented by the beginning of the 80's [Schmidt 83].	

1985
- Preliminary SQL standard published.
- Business world influenced by "Fourth Generation Languages"
- Proposal for Network Definition Language (NDL) made by ANSI.
- **Current trends:** Distributed DBMSs, Expert Database Systems, Object-oriented DBMSs, Extendible DBMSs

Generated complete application programs starting from a high level nonprogrammer language interface.

Summary, continued from page 17.

- Data abstraction.
- Support of multiple user views.

We then discussed the main categories of database users, or the "actors on the scene":

- Database designers and administrators.
- End users.
- Application programmers and system analysts.

In addition to database users, there are several categories of support personnel, or "workers behind the scene," in a database environment:

- DBMS designers and implementers.
- Tool developers.
- Operators and maintenance personnel.

Then we presented a list of capabilities that should be provided by the DBMS software to the DBA, database designers, and users to help them in administering, designing, and using a database:

- Controlling redundancy.
- Sharing of the database.
- Restricting unauthorized access.
- Providing multiple interfaces.
- Representing complex relationships among data.
- Enforcing integrity constraints.
- Providing backup and recovery.

We listed some additional advantages of the database approach over traditional file processing systems:

- Potential for enforcing standards.
- Flexibility.
- Reduced application development time.
- Availability of up-to-date information to all users.
- Economies of scale.

Finally, we discussed the overhead of using a DBMS and discussed some situations where it may not be advantageous to use a DBMS. In the next chapter we discuss the architecture of a DBMS and introduce the concepts and terminology that we need in succeeding chapters.

Review Questions

1.1. Define the following terms: data, database, DBMS, database system, database catalog, program-data independence, user view, DBA, end user, canned transaction.

1.2. What are the three main types of actions involving databases? Briefly discuss each.

1.3. Discuss the main characteristics of the database approach and how it differs from traditional file systems.

1.4. What are the responsibilities of the DBA and the database designers?

1.5. What are the different types of database end users? Discuss the main activities of each.

1.6. Discuss the capabilities that should be provided by a DBMS.

Exercises

1.7. Give some informal queries and updates that you would expect to apply to the database shown in Figure 1.2.

1.8. What is the difference between controlled and uncontrolled redundancy? Illustrate with examples.

1.9. Give all the relationships among the records of the database shown in Figure 1.2.

1.10. Give some additional views that may be needed by other user groups for the database shown in Figure 1.2.

1.11. Give some examples of integrity constraints that you think should hold on the database shown in Figure 1.2.

Selected Bibliography

The March 1976 issue of ACM *Computing Surveys* is an introduction to DBMSs. In this issue, Sibley (1976) and Fry and Sibley (1976) provide a good perspective on how databases evolved from traditional file processing. Many database textbooks provide a discussion of the material presented here and in Chapter 2, including Wiederhold (1983), Ullman (1982), Date (1986), and Korth and Silberschatz (1986), among others.

DBMS Concepts and Architecture

In this chapter we discuss in more detail many of the concepts and issues that were introduced in Chapter 1. We also present the terminology that we use throughout this book. We start by discussing data models and defining the concepts of schemas and instances, which are fundamental to the study of database systems. We then discuss the following topics:

- DBMS architecture and data independence.
- Different types of interfaces and languages provided by a DBMS.
- The database system software environment.
- Classification of DBMSs.

2.1 Data Models, Schemas, and Instances

One of the fundamental characteristics of the database approach is that it provides some level of data abstraction by hiding details of data storage that are not needed by most database users. A data model is the main tool for providing this abstraction. A **data model** is a set of concepts that can be used to describe the structure of a database.* By *structure of a database*, we mean the data types, relationships, and constraints that should hold on the data. Most data models also include a set of **operations** for specifying retrievals and updates on the database.

---

*Sometimes the word "model" is used to denote a database description, or schema—for example, "the marketing data model." We will not use this interpretation.

2.1.1   Categories of Data Models

Many data models have been proposed. We can categorize data models based on the types of concepts they provide to describe the database structure. **High-level** or **conceptual** data models provide concepts that are close to the way many users perceive data, whereas **low-level** or **physical** data models provide concepts that describe the details of how data is stored in the computer. Concepts provided by low-level data models are generally meant for computer specialists, not for typical end users. Between these two extremes is a class of **implementation** data models, which provide concepts that may be understood by end users but that are not too far removed from the way data is organized within the computer. Implementation data models hide some details of data storage but can be implemented on a computer system in a direct way.

High-level data models use concepts such as entities, attributes, and relationships. An **entity** is an object that is represented in the database. An **attribute** is a property that describes some aspect of an object. **Relationships** among objects are easily represented in high-level data models, which are sometimes called **object-based** models because they mainly describe objects and their interrelationships. We will present the Entity-Relationship model, which is a popular high-level data model, in Chapter 3.

Implementation data models are the ones used most frequently in current commercial DBMSs and include the three most widely used data models—relational, network, and hierarchical. Part II of the book describes these models, their operations, and their languages. They represent data using record structures and hence are sometimes called **record-based** data models.

Physical data models describe how data is stored in the computer by representing information such as record formats, record orderings, and access paths. An **access path** is a structure that makes the search for particular database records much faster. We will discuss physical storage techniques and access structures in Chapters 4 and 5.

2.1.2   Schemas and Instances

In any data model it is important to distinguish between the *description* of the database and the *database itself*. The description of a database is called the **database schema**. A database schema is specified during database design and is not expected to change frequently. Most data models have certain conventions for diagrammatically displaying schemas specified in the data model. A displayed schema is called a **schema diagram.** Figure 2.1 shows a schema diagram for the database shown in Figure 1.2, which displays the structure of each file but not the actual records. We call each object in the schema—such as STUDENT or COURSE—a **schema construct**.

A schema diagram displays only *some aspects* of a schema, such as the names of files and data items, and some types of constraints. Other aspects are not specified in the schema diagram; for example, Figure 2.1 shows neither the data type of each data item nor the relationships among the various files. Many types of constraints are not represented in schema diagrams; for example, a constraint such as "students majoring in computer science must take COSC1310 before the end of their sophomore year" is quite difficult to represent.

The actual data in a database may change relatively frequently; for example, the database shown in Figure 1.2 changes every time we add a new student or enter a new

STUDENT

Name	StudentNumber	Class	Major

COURSE

CourseName	CourseNumber	CreditHours	Department

PREREQUISITE

CourseNumber	PrerequisiteNumber

SECTION

SectionIdentifier	CourseNumber	Semester	Year	Instructor

GRADE_REPORT

StudentNumber	SectionIdentifier	Grade

Figure 2.1   Schema diagram for the database of Figure 1.2

grade for a student. The data in the database at a particular moment in time is called a **database instance** (or **occurrence** or **state**). Many database instances can correspond to a particular database schema. Every time we insert or delete a record, or change the value of a data item, we change one instance of the database into another instance.

The distinction between database schema and database instance is very important. When we **define** a new database, we only specify its database schema to the DBMS. At this point, the corresponding database instance is the "empty instance" with no data. We get the "initial instance" of the database when the data is first **loaded.** From there on, every time an update operation is applied to the database, we get another database instance. The DBMS is partially responsible for ensuring that *every* instance of the database satisfies the structure and constraints specified in the schema. Hence, specifying a correct schema to the DBMS is extremely important, and the schema must be designed with the utmost care. The DBMS stores the schema in the DBMS catalog so that DBMS software can refer to the schema whenever it needs to. The schema is sometimes called the **intension,** and a database instance is sometimes called an **extension** of the schema.

2.2   DBMS Architecture and Data Independence

Three important characteristics of the database approach, listed in Section 1.3, are: (a) insulation of programs and data (program-data independence), (b) support of multiple user views, and (c) use of a catalog to store the database description (schema). In this section we specify an architecture for database systems, called the **three-schema architecture,*** which was proposed to help achieve these characteristics. We then discuss the concept of data independence.

---

*This is known as the ANSI/SPARC architecture after the committee that proposed it (Tsichritzis and Klug 1978).

2.2.1   The Three-Schema Architecture

The goal of the three-schema architecture, illustrated in Figure 2.2, is to separate the user applications and the physical database. In this architecture, schemas can be defined at the following three levels:

1. The **internal level** has an **internal schema,** which describes the physical storage structure of the database. The internal schema uses a physical data model and describes the complete details of data storage and access paths for the database.

2. The **conceptual level** has a **conceptual schema,** which describes the structure of the whole database for a community of users. The conceptual schema is a global description of the database that hides the details of physical storage structures and concentrates on describing entities, data types, relationships, and constraints. A high-level data model or an implementation data model can be used at this level.

3. The **external** or **view level** includes a number of **external schemas** or **user views**. Each external schema describes the database view of one group of database users. Each view typically describes the part of the database that a particular user group is interested in and hides the rest of the database from that user group. A high-level data model or an implementation data model can be used at this level.

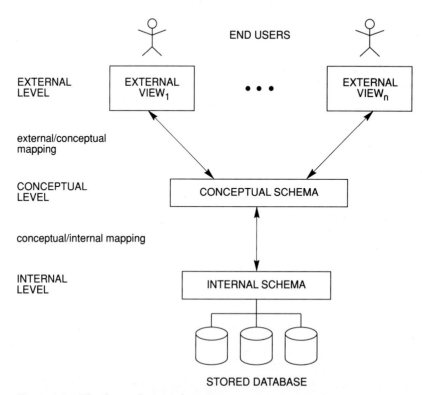

Figure 2.2   The three-schema architecture

Most DBMSs do not separate the three levels completely. For example, many DBMSs will include some physical level details in the conceptual schema. However, other DBMSs fit in the general framework of the three-schema architecture. In most DBMSs that support user views, external schemas are specified in the same data model used at the conceptual level. Some DBMSs allow different data models to be used at the conceptual and external levels.

Notice that the three schemas are only descriptions of data; the only data that *actually exists* is at the physical level. In a DBMS based on the three-schema architecture, each user group refers only to its own external schema. Hence, the DBMS must transform a request specified on an external schema into a request on the conceptual schema, then into a request on the internal schema for processing on the stored database. If the request is a database retrieval, the data extracted from the stored database must be reformatted to match the user's external view before it is presented to the user. The processes of transforming requests and results between levels are called **mappings**. These mappings may be time consuming, so some DBMSs—especially those that run on microcomputers and are meant to support small databases—do not support external views. Even in such systems, a certain amount of mapping is necessary to transform requests between the conceptual and internal levels.

2.2.2 Data Independence

The three-schema architecture can be used to explain the concept of **data independence,** which can be defined as the capacity to change the schema at one level of a database system without having to change the schema at the next higher level. We can define two types of data independence:

1. **Logical data independence** is the capacity to change the conceptual schema without having to change external schemas or application programs. We may change the conceptual schema to expand the database by adding a new record type or data item, or to reduce the database by removing a record type or data item. In the latter case, external schemas that refer only to the remaining data should not be affected. For example, the external schema of Figure 1.4(a) should not be affected by changing the GRADE_REPORT file in Figure 1.2 to that in Figure 1.5(a). Only the view definition and the mappings need be changed in a DBMS that supports logical data independence.

2. **Physical data independence** is the capacity to change the internal schema without having to change the conceptual (or external) schemas. Changes to the internal schema may be needed because some physical files are reorganized—for example, by creating additional access structures—to improve the performance of retrieval or update. If the same data as before remains in the database, we should not have to change the conceptual schema. For example, providing an access path to improve retrieval of SECTION records (Figure 1.2) by Semester and Year should not require a query such as "list all sections offered in Fall 1986" to be changed, although the query should be executed more efficiently by the DBMS by utilizing the new access path.

Whenever we have a multiple-level DBMS, its catalog must be expanded to include information on how to map requests and data among the various levels. The DBMS uses additional software to accomplish these mappings by referring to the mapping information in the catalog. Data independence is accomplished because when we change the schema at some level, we can leave the schema at the next higher level unchanged and change only the mapping between the two levels. Application programs referring to the higher-level schema need not be changed. Hence, the three-schema architecture can make it easier to have true data independence. However, the two levels of mappings create an overhead when compiling or executing a query or program, leading to inefficiencies in the DBMS. Because of this, few DBMSs have implemented the full three-schema architecture.

2.3   Database Languages and Interfaces

In Section 1.4 we discussed the variety of users supported by a DBMS. The DBMS must provide appropriate languages and interfaces for each category of users. In this section we discuss the types of languages and interfaces provided by a DBMS and the user categories targeted by each interface.

2.3.1   DBMS *Languages*

Once the design of a database is completed and a DBMS is chosen to implement the database, the first order of the day is to specify conceptual and internal schemas for the database and any mappings between the two. In many DBMSs where no strict separation of levels is maintained, one language, called the **data definition language** (DDL), is used by the DBA and database designers to define both schemas. The DBMS will have a DDL compiler whose function is to process DDL statements to identify descriptions of the schema constructs and to store the schema description in the DBMS catalog.

In DBMSs with a clear separation between the conceptual and internal levels, the DDL is used to specify the conceptual schema only. Another language, the **storage definition language** (SDL), is used for specifying the internal schema. The mappings between the two schemas could be specified in either one of these languages. We will assume that only the DDL is used to specify the database, except where specific reference is made to an SDL.

For a true three-schema architecture we would need a third language, the **view definition language** (VDL), to specify user views and their mappings to the conceptual schema. Most systems that support external views either provide a variation of the DDL or extend the DDL with statements for view definition.

The DDL language statements may be embedded in a general-purpose programming language, or they may be compiled separately. In the former case, DDL statements must be identified as such within the program so they can be extracted and processed by the DDL compiler. Once the schema is compiled and the database is populated with data, users must have some means for manipulating the database. Typical manipulations include retrieval, insertion, deletion, and modification of the data. The DBMS provides a **data manipulation language** (DML) for these purposes.

There are two main types of DMLs. A **high-level** or **nonprocedural** DML can be used on its own to specify complex database operations in a concise manner. Many DBMSs allow high-level DML statements either to be entered interactively from a terminal or to be embedded in a general-purpose programming language. In the latter case, DML statements must again be identified as such within the program so they can be processed by the DBMS.

A **low-level** or **procedural** DML *must* be embedded in a general-purpose programming language. This type of DML typically retrieves individual records from the database and processes each record separately. Hence, it needs to make use of programming language constructs, such as looping, to retrieve and process each individual record from a set of records. Low-level DMLs are also called **record-at-a-time** DMLs because of this property. High-level DMLs can specify and retrieve many records in a single DML statement and are hence called **set-at-a-time** or **set-oriented** DMLs. A query in a high-level DML often specifies *what* data is to be retrieved rather than *how* to retrieve the data; hence, such languages are also called **declarative**.

Whenever DML commands, whether high-level or low-level, are embedded in a general-purpose programming language, that language is called the **host language** and the DML is called the **data sublanguage**. On the other hand, a high-level DML used in a stand-alone interactive manner is called a **query language**. In general, both retrieval and update commands of a high-level DML may be used interactively and are hence considered part of the query language.*

Casual end users typically use a high-level query language to specify their requests, whereas programmers use the DML in its embedded form. For naive and parametric users, there usually are **user-friendly interfaces** for interacting with the database, which can also be used by casual users or others who do not want to learn the details of a high-level query language. We discuss these types of interfaces next.

2.3.2 DBMS *Interfaces*

User-friendly interfaces provided by a DBMS may include the following:

Menu-based Interfaces

These interfaces present the user with lists of options, called **menus,** that lead the user through the formulation of a request. Menus do away with the need to memorize the specific commands and syntax of a query language; rather, the query is composed step by step by picking options from a menu list that is displayed by the system.

Graphical Interfaces

A graphical interface will typically display a schema to the user in diagrammatic form. The user can then specify a query by manipulating the diagram. In many cases, graphical interfaces are combined with menus. Most graphical interfaces will use a **pointing device,** such as a mouse or light pen, to pick certain parts of the displayed schema diagram.

---

*According to the meaning of the word "query" in English, it should really only be used to describe retrievals, not updates.

Forms-based Interfaces

A forms-based interface displays a **form** to the user. The user can fill out all entries in a form to insert new data, or the user can fill certain entries and the DBMS will retrieve matching data to fill the remaining entries. Forms are usually designed and programmed for naive users as interfaces to canned transactions. Many DBMSs have special languages, called forms specification languages, that help programmers to specify such forms.

Natural Language Interfaces

These interfaces accept requests written in English or some other language and attempt to "understand" and process them. A natural language interface usually has its own "schema," which is similar to the database conceptual schema. The interface refers to the words in its schema as well as a set of standard words in interpreting the request. If the interpretation is successful, the interface generates a high-level query corresponding to the natural language request and submits it to the DBMS for processing; otherwise, a dialogue is started with the user to clarify the request.

Interfaces for Parametric Users

Parametric users, such as bank tellers, often have a small set of operations that they perform repeatedly. The systems analysts and programmers will usually design and implement a special interface for a known class of naive users. Usually, a small set of abbreviated commands is included, with the goal of minimizing the number of keystrokes for each request. For example, function keys in a terminal may be programmed to initiate the various commands. This allows the parametric user to proceed as quickly as possible. Such interfaces can be called command languages.

Interfaces for the DBA

Most database systems will have certain privileged commands that can be used only by the DBA's staff. These include commands for creating accounts, setting system parameters, granting account authorization, changing a schema, and reorganizing the storage structure of a database file.

2.4   The Database System Environment

A DBMS is a complex software system. In this section we discuss the types of software components that constitute a DBMS and the types of computer system software with which the DBMS interacts.

2.4.1   *DBMS Component Modules*

Figure 2.3 illustrates the typical DBMS components.The database and the DBMS catalog are usually stored on disk. Access to the disk is controlled primarily by the *operating sys-*

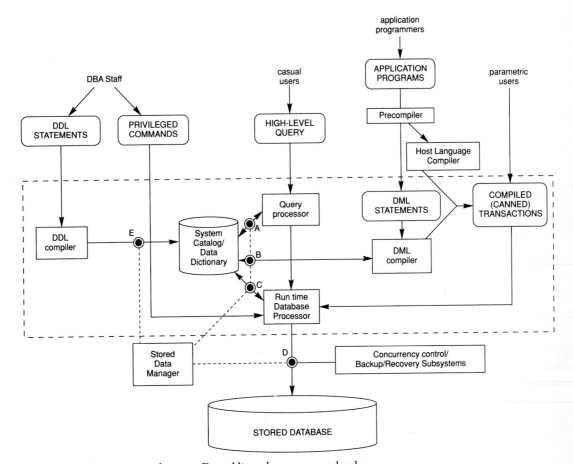

Figure 2.3 Components of a DBMS. Dotted lines show access under the control of the stored data manager.

tem (OS), which schedules disk input/output. A higher-level **stored data manager** module of the DBMS controls access to DBMS information stored on disk, whether it is part of the database or the catalog. The dotted lines and the points marked A, B, C, D, and E in Figure 2.3 illustrate accesses under the control of this stored data manager. The stored data manager may use basic OS services for carrying out low-level data transfer between the disk and computer main storage but controls other aspects of data transfer, such as handling buffers in main memory. Once the data is in main memory, it can be processed by other DBMS modules. Alternatively, the DBMS can rely on the OS for all disk access if the OS file subsystem provides adequate facilities.

The **DDL compiler** processes schema definitions, specified in the DDL, and stores descriptions of the schemas in the DBMS catalog. The catalog includes information such as the names of files, data items, storage details of each file, mapping information among schemas, and constraints. DBMS software modules that need to look up this information must access the catalog.

The **run time database processor** handles database accesses at run time; it receives retrieval or update operations and carries them out on the database. Access to disk goes through the stored data manager. The **query processor** handles high-level queries that are entered interactively, where the user expects the query results right away. It parses and analyzes a query, then generates calls to the run time processor for executing the request.

The **precompiler** extracts DML commands from an application program written in a host programming language. These commands are sent to the DML **compiler** for compilation into object code for database access. The rest of the program is sent to the host language compiler. The object codes for the DML commands and the rest of the program are linked, forming a canned transaction whose executable code includes calls to the run time database processor. As discussed earlier, canned transactions are used by parametric or naive users and are typically invoked via user-friendly interfaces such as menus or forms.

Figure 2.3 is not meant to describe a specific DBMS; rather, we use it to illustrate typical DBMS modules. The DBMS interacts with the operating system when disk accesses—to the database or the catalog—are needed. If the computer system is shared by many users, the OS will schedule DBMS disk access requests and DBMS processing along with other processes. The DBMS also interfaces with compilers for general-purpose host programming languages. User-friendly interfaces can be provided to help any of the user types shown in Figure 2.3 in specifying their requests.

2.4.2   Database System Utilities

In addition to the software modules described above, most DBMSs will have **database utilities** that help the DBA in running the database system. Common utilities have the following types of functions:

Loading: A loading utility is used to load existing data files—such as text files or sequential files—into the database. Usually, the current (source) format of the data file and the desired (target) database file structure are specified to the utility, which will then automatically reformat the data and store it in the database.

Backup: A backup utility creates a backup copy of the database, usually by dumping the entire database on tape. The backup copy can be used to restore the database in case of catastrophic failure.

File reorganization: This utility can be used to reorganize a database file into a different file organization to improve performance.

Report generation: These utilities are used to format reports by controlling spacing, including headers and footers, doing totals or data summaries, performing computations on the data, and so on.

Performance monitoring: Such a utility will monitor database usage and provide statistics to the DBA. The DBA uses the statistics for decisions such as reorganizing files to improve performance.

Other utilities may be available for sorting of files, data compression, monitoring of users, and other functions. Another utility that can be quite useful in large organizations is an expanded **data dictionary system**. In addition to storing catalog information such as schemas and constraints, the data dictionary stores other information such as design decisions, usage standards, application program descriptions, and user information. This information can be accessed *directly* by users and the DBA when needed. A data dictionary utility is similar to the DBMS catalog except that it includes a wider variety of information and is accessed mainly by users rather than by the DBMS software. A combined catalog/data dictionary, which is accessed by both users and the DBMS software, is called a **data directory** or an **active** data dictionary. A data dictionary that is accessed by users and the DBA but not by the DBMS software is called **passive**.

The DBMS also needs to interface with **communications software,** whose function is to allow users at locations remote from the database system site to access the database through computer terminals, such as CRT monitors, or through their local micro- or minicomputers. These are connected to the database site through data communications hardware such as phone lines, long-haul networks, or satellite communication. Many commercial database systems have communication packages that work with the DBMS. The integrated DBMS and data communications system is called a **DB/DC** system.

2.5   Classification of Database Management Systems

The main criterion used to classify DBMSs is the **data model** on which the DBMS is based. The data models used most often in current commercial DBMSs are the relational, network, and hierarchical models. Some recent DBMSs are based on conceptual or object-oriented models. We will categorize DBMSs as **relational, network, hierarchical,** and **others**.

Another criterion used to classify DBMSs is the **number of users** supported by the DBMS. **Single-user** systems support only one user at a time, and are mostly used with personal computers. **Multiuser** systems include the majority of DBMSs and support many users concurrently.

A third criterion is the **number of sites** over which the database is distributed. Most DBMSs are **centralized,** meaning that their data is stored at a single computer site. A centralized DBMS can support multiple users, but the DBMS and database themselves reside totally at a single computer site. A **distributed DBMS (DDBMS)** can have the actual database and DBMS software distributed over many sites connected by a computer network. **Homogeneous DDBMSs** use the same DBMS software at multiple sites. A recent trend is to develop software to access several autonomous preexisting databases stored under **heterogeneous** DBMSs. This leads to a **federated DBMS** (or **multidatabase system**), where the participating DBMSs are loosely coupled and have a degree of local autonomy (see Chapter 21).

A fourth criterion is the **cost** of the DBMS. The majority of DBMS packages cost between $10,000 and $100,000. Single-user low-end systems that work with microcomputers cost between $100 and $3000. At the other end, a few elaborate packages cost between $100,000 and $300,000.

We can also classify a DBMS on the basis of the **types of access path** options available for storing files. One well-known family of DBMSs is based on inverted file structures. Finally, a DBMS can be **general purpose** or **special purpose**. When performance is a prime consideration, a special-purpose DBMS can be designed and built for a specific application and cannot be used for other applications. Many airline reservations and telephone directory systems are special-purpose DBMSs.

Let us briefly discuss the main criterion for classifying DBMSs: the data model. The **relational** data model represents a database as a collection of tables, which look like files. The database in Figure 1.2 is shown in a manner very similar to a relational representation. Most relational databases have high-level query languages and support a limited form of user views. Usually, the conceptual and internal schemas are not distinguishable, and a single DDL is used to describe all aspects of the database structure. We discuss the relational model and its languages and operations in Chapters 6 to 9.

The **network** model represents data as record types and also represents a limited type of 1:N relationship, called a set type. Figure 2.4 shows a network schema diagram for the database of Figure 1.2, where record types are shown as rectangles and set types are shown as labeled directed arcs. The network model, also known as the CODASYL DBTG model,* has an associated record-at-a-time language that must be embedded in a host programming language. The model and language were specified in detail in several reports, which have undergone revisions in recent years. Most network DBMSs do not implement the full capabilities specified in these reports. We present the network model and its language in Chapter 11.

The **hierarchical** model represents data as hierarchical tree structures. Each hierarchy represents a number of related records. There is no standard language for the hierarchical model, although most hierarchical DBMSs have record-at-a-time languages. We discuss the hierarchical model in Chapter 10.

In the next chapter we present the concepts of the Entity-Relationship model, a popular high-level conceptual data model that is often used in database design. We compare these four data models in Chapter 12. In Chapter 23, we discuss some DBMSs based on these models.

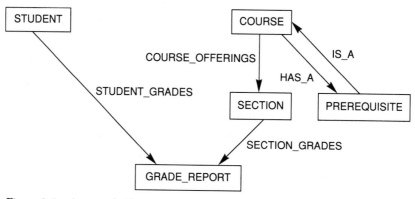

Figure 2.4   A network schema

---

*CODASYL DBTG stands for Computer Data Systems Language Data Base Task Group, which is the committee that specified the network model and its language.

2.6 Summary

In this chapter we introduced the main concepts used in database systems. We defined what a data model is and distinguished three main categories of data models:

- High-level or conceptual data models.
- Record-based or implementation data models.
- Low-level or physical data models.

We distinguished the schema, or description of a database, from the database itself. The schema does not change very often, whereas the database changes every time data is inserted, deleted, or modified. We called each occurrence of the database a database instance or state. We then described the three-schema DBMS architecture, which allows three schema levels:

- External schemas describe the views of different user groups.
- A conceptual schema is a high-level description of the whole database.
- An internal schema describes the database storage structures.

A DBMS that cleanly separates the three levels must have mappings between the schemas to transform requests and results from one level to the next. Most DBMSs do not separate the three levels completely. We used the three-schema architecture to define the concepts of logical and physical data independence, which are fundamental aspects of the database approach.

In Section 2.3 we discussed the main types of languages that DBMSs support. A data definition language (DDL) is used to define the database conceptual schema. In some DBMSs, the DDL also defines user views and storage structures, whereas in other DBMSs separate languages (VDL, SDL) exist for specifying views and storage structures. The DBMS compiles all schema definitions and stores them in the DBMS catalog. A data manipulation language (DML) is used for specifying database retrievals and updates. DMLs can be high-level (nonprocedural) or low-level (procedural). A high-level DML can be embedded in a host programming language or can be used as a stand-alone language; in the latter case it is often called a query language. Low-level DMLs are always embedded in a host programming language.

We discussed different types of interfaces provided by DBMSs, and the types of DBMS users with which each is associated. We then discussed the database system environment, typical DBMS software components, and DBMS utilities for helping users and the DBA in performing their tasks.

Finally, we classified DBMSs according to data model, number of users, number of sites, cost, types of access paths, and generality. The main classification of DBMSs is based on the data model. We briefly discussed the three main data models used in current commercial DBMSs.

Review Questions

2.1. Define the following terms: data model, database schema, database instance, internal schema, conceptual schema, external schema, data independence, DDL, DML,

SDL, VDL, query language, host language, data sublanguage, database utility, active data dictionary, passive data dictionary, catalog.

2.2. Discuss the three main categories of data models.

2.3. What is the difference between a database schema and a database instance?

2.4. Describe the three-schema architecture. Why do we need mappings between the different schema levels? How do different schema definition languages support this architecture?

2.5. What is the difference between logical data independence and physical data independence? Which is easier to accomplish? Why?

2.6. What is the difference between procedural and nonprocedural DMLs?

2.7. Discuss the different types of user-friendly interfaces and the types of users who would typically use each.

2.8. What other computer system software does a DBMS interact with?

2.9. Discuss some types of database utilities and their functions.

Exercises

2.10. Think of different users for the database of Figure 1.2. What types of applications would each user need? To which user category would each belong and what type of interface would they need?

2.11. Choose a database application that you are familiar with. Design a schema and show a sample database for that application using the notation of Figures 2.1 and 1.2. What type of additional information and constraints would you like to represent in the schema? Think of several users for your database and design a view for each.

Selected Bibliography

Many database textbooks provide a discussion of the various database concepts presented here, including Wiederhold (1983), Ullman (1982), Date (1986), and Korth and Silberschatz (1986). Tsichritzis and Lochovsky (1982) provide a detailed discussion of data models and their languages. Tsichritzis and Klug (1978) and Jardine (1977) present the three-schema architecture, which was first suggested in the CODASYL DBTG report (1971) and later in an American National Standards Institute (ANSI) report (1975). Uhrowczik (1973) summarizes the features of data dictionary/directory systems and Weldon (1981) discusses database administration.

CHAPTER 3

Data Modeling Using the Entity-Relationship Model

In this chapter we present the basic data modeling concepts of the **Entity-Relationship** (ER) model, which is a high-level conceptual data model. The ER model concepts are designed to be closer to users' perception of data and are not meant to describe the way in which data will be stored in the computer. In Section 2.1 we defined a **data model** as a group of concepts that help us specify the structure of a database and a set of associated operations for specifying retrievals and updates on the database. In this chapter, to keep the presentation somewhat simple, we discuss only the structuring concepts of the ER model.

At the present time, the ER model is used mainly during the process of database design. It is expected that a class of commercial DBMSs based directly on the ER model or other high-level data models will be available in the near future. Such DBMSs, whenever they are ready, will have the capacity to implement directly a database described by a high-level conceptual schema. In this chapter we do not consider this use of the ER model; rather, we concentrate on its use as a tool for database modeling and design.

This chapter is organized as follows. In Section 3.1 we discuss the role of conceptual data models in database design. We introduce an example database application in Section 3.2 to illustrate the use of the ER model concepts. This example database is also used in subsequent chapters. In Section 3.3 we present the concepts of the ER model; then we present the diagrammatic technique for displaying an ER schema in Section 3.4. Section 3.5 shows how schema constructs are named. Section 3.6 discusses some of the problems associated with representing high-order relationship types, and Section 3.7 is a summary.

37

3.1   High-Level Conceptual Data Models and Database Design

Figure 3.1 shows a simplified description of the database design process. The first step shown is **requirements collection and analysis**. During this step, the database designers interview prospective database users to understand and document their data require-

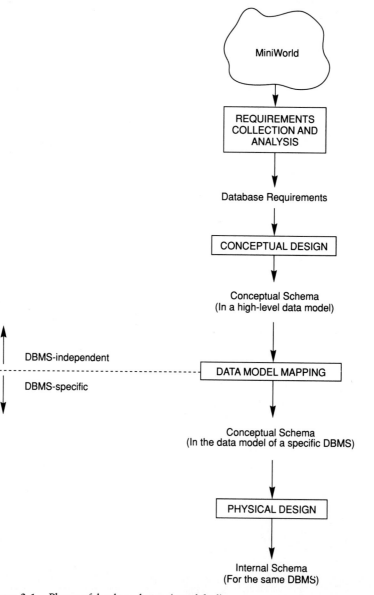

Figure 3.1   Phases of database design (simplified)

ments. The result of this step is a set of users' requirements written down in a concise way. These requirements should be specified in as detailed and complete a form as possible.

Once all requirements are collected and analyzed, the next step is to create a **conceptual schema** for the database using a high-level conceptual data model. This step is called **conceptual database design**. The conceptual schema is a concise description of the data requirements of the users and includes detailed descriptions of the data types, relationships, and constraints; these are expressed using the concepts provided by the high-level data model. Because these concepts do not include any implementation details, they are usually easier to understand and can be used to communicate with nontechnical users. This high-level conceptual schema can also be used to make sure that all users' data requirements are met and that the requirements do not include any conflicts. In addition, the database designers can concentrate on specifying the properties of the data without being concerned with storage details. This makes it easier to come up with a good conceptual database design.

The next step in database design is the actual implementation of the database using a commercial DBMS. Most current commercial DBMSs use an implementation data model, so the conceptual schema is transformed from the high-level data model to the implementation data model. This step is called **data model mapping,** and its result is a conceptual schema in the implementation data model of the DBMS. Finally, the last step is the **physical database design** phase, during which we specify the internal storage structures and file organizations for the database. We will discuss the database design process in more detail in Chapter 16.

3.2   An Example

In this section we describe an example database, called COMPANY that we use to illustrate the process of database design. We list the data requirements for the database here and then create its conceptual schema step-by-step as we introduce the modeling concepts of the ER model. The COMPANY database keeps track of a company's employees, departments, and projects. Suppose that after the requirements collection and analysis phase, the database designers stated the following description of the "miniworld"—the part of the company to be represented in the database:

1. The company is organized into departments. Each department has a name, a number, and an employee who manages the department. We keep track of the start date when that employee started managing the department. A department may have several locations.

2. A department controls a number of projects, each of which has a name, a number, and a single location.

3. We store each employee's name, social security number, address, salary, sex, and birth date. An employee is assigned to one department but may work on several projects, which are not necessarily controlled by the same department. We keep track of the number of hours per week that an employee works on each project.

We also keep track of the direct supervisor of each employee.

4. We want to keep track of the dependents of each employee for insurance purposes. We keep each dependent's name, sex, birth date, and relationship to the employee.

3.3   ER Model Concepts

We now present the concepts of the ER model. In Section 3.3.1 we introduce the concepts of entities and their attributes. We then discuss entity types and key attributes in Section 3.3.2. In Section 3.3.3 we discuss relationship types and their structural constraints. We discuss weak entity types in Section 3.3.4 and then demonstrate the use of the ER concepts in designing the COMPANY database in Section 3.3.5.

3.3.1   Entities and Attributes

The basic object that the ER model represents is an **entity,** which is a "thing" in the real world with an independent existence. An entity may be an object with a physical existence—a particular person, car, house, or employee—or it may be an object with a conceptual existence—a company, a job, or a university course. Each entity has particular properties, called **attributes,** that describe it. For example, an employee entity may be described by the employee's name, age, address, salary, and job. A particular entity will have a **value** for each of its attributes. These attribute values that describe each entity become a major part of the data stored in the database.

Figure 3.2 shows two entities and the values of their attributes. The employee entity e_1 has four attributes: Name, Address, Age, and HomePhone; their values are "John Smith", "2311 Kirby, Houston, Texas 77001", "55", and "713-749-2630", respectively. The company entity c_1 has three attributes: Name, Headquarters, and President; their values are "Sunco Oil", "Houston", and "John Smith", respectively.

Some attributes can be divided into smaller subparts with independent meanings of their own. For example, the Address attribute of the employee entity shown in Figure 3.2 can be subdivided into StreetAddress, City, State, and Zip, with the values "2311 Kirby",

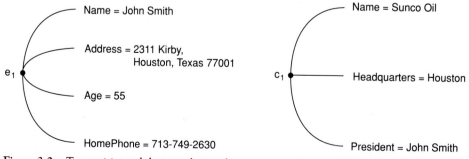

Figure 3.2   Two entities and their attribute values

"Houston", "Texas", and "77001". An attribute that is composed of several more basic attributes is called **composite,** whereas attributes that are not divisible are called **simple** or **atomic** attributes. Composite attributes can form a hierarchy; for example, Street-Address can be further subdivided into three simple attributes, Number, Street, and ApartmentNumber, as shown in Figure 3.3. Another example of a composite attribute is the name of a person, which can be subdivided into FirstName, MiddleInitial, and LastName. The value of a composite attribute is the concatenation of the values of the simple attributes that form it.

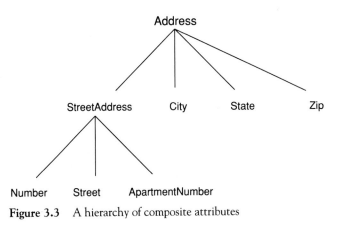

Figure 3.3 A hierarchy of composite attributes

Composite attributes are useful when a user sometimes refers to the composite attribute as a unit but at other times refers specifically to its components. If we refer to the composite attribute only as a whole, there is no need to subdivide it into component attributes. If we never need to refer to the individual components of an address (Zip, Street, and so on) we just keep the whole address as a simple attribute.

Most attributes have a single value for a particular entity; such attributes are called **single-valued**. For example, a person entity has one value for Age, so Age is a single-valued attribute of person. In some cases an attribute can have a set of values for the same entity, for example, a Colors attribute for a car or a CollegeDegrees attribute for a person. Cars with one color will have a single value, whereas two-tone cars need two values for Colors. Similarly, one person may not have any college degree, another person may have one, and a third person may have two or more degrees, so different persons can have different *numbers of values* for the CollegeDegrees attribute. Such attributes are called **multivalued**. A multivalued attribute may have lower and upper bounds on the number of values for an individual entity. For example, the Colors attribute of a car may have between one and five values if we assume that a car can have at most five colors.

In some cases two (or more) attribute values are related, for example, the Age and BirthDate attributes of a person. For a particular person entity, the value of Age can be determined from the current (today's) date and the value of that person's BirthDate. The Age attribute is hence called a **derived attribute** and is said to be **derivable from** the BirthDate attribute. Some attribute values can be derived from *related entities;* for example, an attribute NumberOfEmployees of a department entity can be calculated by counting the number of employees related to (working for) that department.

In some cases a particular entity may not have any applicable value for an attribute. For example, the ApartmentNumber attribute of an address applies only to addresses that are in apartment buildings and not to other types of residences such as single-family homes. Similarly, a CollegeDegrees attribute applies only to persons with college degrees. For such situations, a special value called **null** is created. An address of a single-family home would have null for its ApartmentNumber attribute, and a person with no college degree would have null for CollegeDegrees. Null can also be used if we do not know the value of an attribute for a particular entity, for example, if we do not know the home phone of "John Smith" in Figure 3.2. The meaning of the former type of null is *not applicable*, whereas the meaning of the latter is *unknown*.

3.3.2   Entity Types, Value Sets, and Key Attributes

A database will usually contain groups of entities that are similar. For example, a company employing hundreds of employees may want to store similar information concerning each of the employees. These employee entities share the same attributes, but each entity will have its own value(s) for each attribute. Such similar entities define an **entity type,** which is a set of entities that have the same attributes. For most databases we can identify many entity types. Each entity type is described by a name and a list of attributes. Figure 3.4 shows two entity types, named EMPLOYEE and COMPANY, and a list of attributes for each. A few individual entities of each type are illustrated, along with values of their attributes. In Figure 3.4 the attribute values for each entity are listed in the same order as the attributes.

The entity type description is called the **entity type schema** and specifies a common structure shared by individual entities of that type. The schema specifies the entity type name, the name and meaning of each of its attributes, and any constraints that

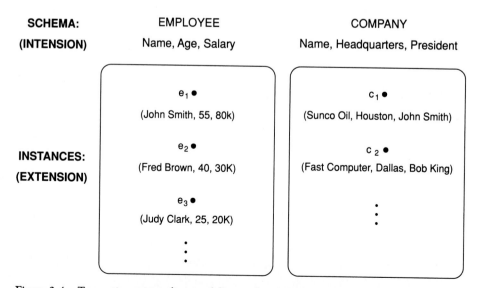

Figure 3.4   Two entity types and some of the member entities

should hold on the individual entities. The set of individual entity instances at a particular moment in time is called an **extension** of the entity type. The schema does not change often because it describes the structure of individual entities. The extension may change often; for example, every time we add or remove an entity from the entity type, we get a different extension.

Key Attributes of an Entity Type

An important constraint on the entities of an entity type is the **key** or **uniqueness** constraint on attributes. An entity type usually has an attribute whose values are distinct for each individual entity. Such an attribute is called a **key attribute,** and its values can be used to identify each entity uniquely. The Name attribute is a key of the COMPANY entity type in Figure 3.4, because we do not allow two companies to have the same name. For the PERSON entity type, a typical key attribute is SocialSecurityNumber, because we know that every person has a distinct value for this attribute. Sometimes several attributes together can form a key, meaning that the *combination* of the attribute values must be distinct for each individual entity. A set of attributes with the above property can be grouped into a composite attribute, which becomes a key attribute of the entity type.

Specifying that an attribute is a key of an entity type means that the above uniqueness property must hold on *every extension* of the entity type. Hence, it is a constraint that prohibits any two entities from having the same value for the key attribute at the same time. It is not the property of a particular extension but is a constraint on *all extensions* of the entity type. This key constraint, and other constraints we discuss later, is derived from the properties of the miniworld that the database represents.

Some entity types have *more than one* key attribute. For example, each of the VehicleID and Registration attributes of the entity type CAR (Figure 3.5) is a key in its own right. The Registration attribute is an example of a composite key formed from two simple component attributes, RegistrationNumber and State, neither of which is a key on its own. This is because two cars from different states can have the same value for RegistrationNumber.

Value Sets (Domains) of Attributes

Each simple attribute of an entity type is associated with a **value set** (or **domain**), which specifies the set of values that may be assigned to that attribute for each individual entity. In Figure 3.4, if the range of ages allowed for employees is between 16 and 70, we specify the value set of the Age attribute of EMPLOYEE to be the set of integer numbers between 16 and 70. Similarly, we can specify the value set for the Name attribute as the set of strings of alphabetic characters separated by blank characters, and so on.

Mathematically, an attribute A of entity type E whose value set is V can be defined as a **function** from E to the power set* of V:

$$A : E \rightarrow P(V)$$

---

*The **power set** $P(V)$ of a set V is the set of all subsets of V.

CAR
Registration(RegistrationNumber, State), VehicleID, Make, Model, Year, {Color}

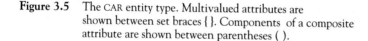

car₁ ●

((ABC 123, TEXAS), TK629, Ford Mustang, convertible, 1986, {red, black})

car₂ ●

((ABC 123, NEW YORK), WP9872, Nissan Sentra, 2-door, 1985, {blue})

car₃ ●

((VSY 720, TEXAS), TD729, Chrysler LeBaron, 4-door, 1987, {white, blue})

.
.
.

Figure 3.5   The CAR entity type. Multivalued attributes are shown between set braces { }. Components of a composite attribute are shown between parentheses ( ).

We refer to the value of attribute A for entity e as A(e). The above definition covers both single-valued and multivalued attributes, as well as nulls. A null value is represented by the empty set. For single-valued attributes, we restrict A(e) to be a singleton* for each entity e in E. We do not place any restrictions on multivalued attributes. For a composite attribute A, the value set V is the cartesian product of $P(V_1)$, $P(V_2)$, ..., $P(V_n)$, where V_1, V_2, ..., V_n are the value sets of the simple component attributes that form A:

$$V = P(V_1) \text{ X } P(V_2) \text{ X } \cdots \text{ X } P(V_n)$$

Note that composite and multivalued properties of attributes can be nested in an arbitrary way. We can describe arbitrary nesting by grouping components of a composite attribute between parentheses ( ) and separating them with commas, and by displaying multivalued attributes between braces { }. For example, if a person can have more than one residence and each residence can have multiple phones, an attribute AddressPhone for a PERSON entity type can be specified as shown in Figure 3.6.

Initial Conceptual Design of The COMPANY Database

We can now define the entity types for the COMPANY database described in Section 3.2. We will define several entity types and their attributes here, then *refine* our design in the next section after we introduce the concept of a relationship. According to the require-

---

*A singleton set is a set with only one element (value).

```
{AddressPhone( {Phone(AreaCode,PhoneNumber)},
Address(StreetAddress(Number,Street,ApartmentNumber),
City,State,Zip) ) }
```

Figure 3.6 A multivalued composite attribute with multivalued and composite components

ments listed in Section 3.2, we can identify four entity types—one corresponding to each of the four items in the specification:

1. An entity type DEPARTMENT with attributes Name, Number, Locations, Manager, and ManagerStartDate. Locations is the only multivalued attribute. We can specify that each of Name and Number is a key attribute, because we do not expect any two departments to have the same Name or the same Number.

2. An entity type PROJECT with attributes Name, Number, Location, and ControllingDepartment. Each of Name and Number is a key attribute.

3. An entity type EMPLOYEE with attributes Name, SSN (for social security number), Sex, Address, Salary, BirthDate, Department, and Supervisor. Both Name and Address may be composite attributes; however, this was not specified in the requirements. We must go back to the users to see if any of them will refer to the individual components of Name—FirstName, MiddleInitial, LastName—or of Address.

4. An entity type DEPENDENT with attributes Employee, DependentName, Sex, BirthDate, and Relationship.

So far, we did not represent the fact that an employee can work on several projects nor did we represent the number of hours per week an employee works on each project. This fact is listed as part of requirement 3 in Section 3.2, and we can represent it by a multivalued composite attribute of EMPLOYEE called WorksOn and call its simple components (Project, Hours). Alternatively, we can represent it as a multivalued composite attribute of PROJECT called Workers with simple components (Employee, Hours). We choose the first alternative in Figure 3.7, which shows a schema for each of the entity types described above. The Name attribute of EMPLOYEE is shown as a composite attribute, presumably after consulting with the users.

It is important to have a simple key attribute for each entity type whenever possible. In some cases, if we get a complex composite key attribute, it may be an indication that we should break up the entity type into several ones, where each has a smaller number of attributes. Of course, in some cases it is not possible to meet this criterion.

In Figure 3.7 there are several *implicit relationships* among the various entity types. In fact, whenever an attribute of one entity type refers to another entity type, some relationship exists. For example, the attribute Manager of DEPARTMENT refers to an employee who manages the department; the attribute ControllingDepartment of PROJECT refers to the department that controls the project; the attribute Supervisor of EMPLOYEE refers to another employee—the one who supervises this employee; the attribute Department of EMPLOYEE refers to the department for which the employee works; and so on. In the ER model, these references should not be represented as attributes but as **relationships,** which we define in the next section. We will refine our COMPANY

DEPARTMENT
Name, Number, {Locations}, Manager, ManagerStartDate

PROJECT
Name, Number, Location, ControllingDepartment

EMPLOYEE
Name (FName, MInit, LName), SSN, Sex, Address, Salary,
BirthDate, Department, Supervisor, {WorksOn (Project, Hours)}

DEPENDENT
Employee, DependentName, Sex, BirthDate, Relationship

Figure 3.7   Preliminary Design of Entity Types for the database
described in Section 3.2. Multivalued attributes are
shown between set braces { }. Components of a composite attribute are shown between parentheses ( ).

database schema to represent relationships explicitly in Section 3.3.5. It is common *ini-tially* to represent some relationships as attributes during conceptual schema design and then to convert these attributes into relationships as the design progresses and is better understood.

3.3.3   Relationships, Roles, and Structural Constraints

In most databases there will be many entity types. In addition to the attribute values of the entities that belong to those entity types, we are interested in relationships among the entities. For example, in Figure 3.2 the entities c_1 and e_1 are related because e_1 is the president of company c_1.

Relationship Types and Relationship Instances

A **relationship type** R among n entity types $E_1, E_2, ..., E_n$ is a set of associations among entities from these types. Mathematically, R is a set of **relationship instances** r_i, where each r_i is an n-tuple of entities $(e_1, e_2, ..., e_n)$, and each entity e_j in r_i is a member of en-tity type E_j, $1 \le j \le n$. Hence, a relationship type is a mathematical relation on $E_1, E_2, ..., E_n$, or alternatively it can be defined as a subset of the Cartesian product $E_1 \times E_2 \times \cdots \times E_n$. Each of the entity types $E_1, E_2, ..., E_n$ is said to **participate** in the relationship type R, and similarly each of the individual entities $e_1, e_2, ..., e_n$ is said to participate in the rela-tionship instance $r_i = (e_1, e_2, ..., e_n)$.

Informally, each relationship instance r_i in R is an association of entities, where the association includes exactly one entity from each participating entity type. Each such relationship instance r_i represents the fact that the entities participating in r_i are related together in some way in the corresponding miniworld situation.

For example, consider a relationship type WORKS_FOR between the two entity types EMPLOYEE and DEPARTMENT, which associates each employee with the department the employee works for. Each relationship instance in WORKS_FOR associates one employee

EMPLOYEE WORKS_FOR DEPARTMENT

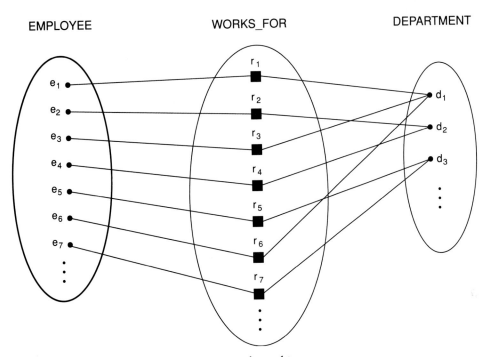

Figure 3.8 Some instances of the WORK_FOR relationship

entity and one department entity. Figure 3.8 illustrates this example, where each relationship instance r_i is shown connected to the employee and department entities that participate in r_i. In the miniworld represented by Figure 3.8, employees e_1, e_3, and e_6 work for department d_1; e_2 and e_4 work for d_2; and e_5 and e_7 work for d_3.

Degree of a Relationship Type

The **degree** of a relationship type is the number of participating entity types. Hence, the WORKS_FOR relationship type is of degree two. A relationship type of degree two is called **binary** and of degree three is called **ternary**. An example of a ternary relationship type is SUPPLY, shown in Figure 3.9, where each relationship instance r_i associates three entities—a supplier s, a part p, and a project j—whenever s supplies part p to project j. Relationships can be of any degree, but the ones that occur most commonly are binary relationships.

In general, a ternary relationship type represents more information than three binary relationship types. For example, consider the three binary relationship types CAN_SUPPLY, USES, and SUPPLIES. Suppose that CAN_SUPPLY, between SUPPLIER and PART, includes an instance (s, p) whenever supplier s *can supply* part p (to any project); USES, between PROJECT and PART, includes an instance (j, p) whenever project j *uses* part p; and SUPPLIES, between SUPPLIER and PROJECT, includes an instance (s, j) whenever supplier s *supplies some part* to project j. The existence of three relationship instances (s, p), (j, p), and (s, j) in CAN_SUPPLY, USES, and SUPPLIES, respectively, does not necessarily imply that

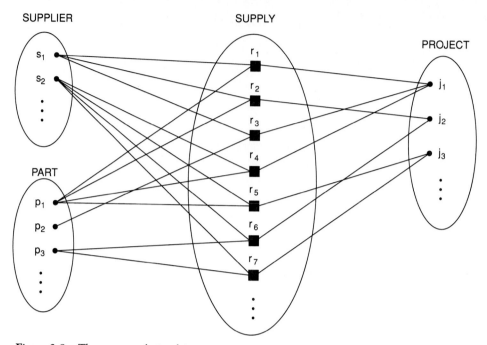

Figure 3.9   The ternary relationship SUPPLY

an instance (s, j, p) exists in the ternary relationship SUPPLY! This has been called the **connection trap** and is discussed further in Section 3.5.

Relationships as Attributes

It is sometimes convenient to think of a relationship type in terms of attributes, as we discussed at the end of the previous section. Consider the WORKS_FOR relationship type of Figure 3.8. One can think of an attribute called Department of the EMPLOYEE entity type whose value for each employee entity is the *department entity* that the employee works for. Hence, the value set for this Department attribute is the *set of all DEPARTMENT entities*, which is the DEPARTMENT entity type. In fact, this is what we did in Figure 3.7 when we specified the attributes of the entity type EMPLOYEE for the COMPANY database. However, when we think of a binary relationship as an attribute, we always have two options. In this example, the alternative is to think of a multivalued attribute Employees of the entity type DEPARTMENT whose values for each department entity is the *set of employee entities* who work for that department. The value set of this Employees attribute is the EMPLOYEE entity type. Either of these two attributes—Department of EMPLOYEE or Employees of DEPARTMENT—can represent the WORKS_FOR relationship type. If both are represented, they are constrained to be inverses of each other.*

---

*This concept of representing relationship types as attributes is used in a class of data models called **functional data models** (see Section 15.4.2).

Role Names and Recursive Relationships

Each entity type that participates in a relationship type plays a particular **role** in the relationship. The **role name** signifies the role that a participating entity from the entity type plays in each relationship instance. For example, in the WORKS_FOR relationship type, EMPLOYEE plays the role of employee or worker and DEPARTMENT plays the role of department or employer. The choice of role name is not always straightforward. For the relationship type in Figure 3.9, it is hard to come up with simple role names.

Role names are not necessary in relationship types where all the participating entity types are distinct. However, in some cases the *same* entity type participates more than once in a relationship type in *different roles*, in such cases the role name becomes essential in order to distinguish the meaning of each participation. Such relationship types are called **recursive,** and Figure 3.10 shows an example. The SUPERVISION relationship type relates an employee to a supervisor where both employee and supervisor entities are members of the same EMPLOYEE entity type. Hence, the EMPLOYEE entity type *participates twice* in SUPERVISION: once in the *role of supervisor* and once in the *role of supervisee*. Each relationship instance r_i in SUPERVISION associates two employee entities e_j and e_k, one of which plays the role of supervisor and the other the role of supervisee. In Figure 3.10, the lines marked "1" represent the supervisor role, and those marked "2" represent the supervisee role; hence, e_1 supervises e_2 and e_3; e_4 supervises e_6 and e_7; and e_5 supervises e_1 and e_4.

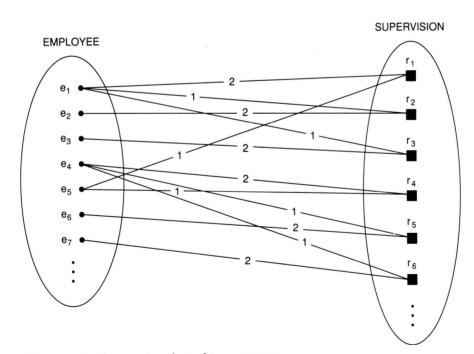

Figure 3.10 The recursive relationship SUPERVISION— EMPLOYEE plays two roles of supervisor (1) and supervisee (2)

Constraints on Relationship Types

Relationship types usually have certain constraints that limit the possible combinations of entities participating in relationship instances. These constraints are determined from the miniworld situation that the relationships represent. For example, in Figure 3.8, if the particular company represented has a rule that an employee works for exactly one department, then we would like to describe this constraint in the schema. We can distinguish two main types of relationship constraints that occur relatively frequently: cardinality ratio and participation.

The **cardinality ratio** constraint specifies the number of relationship instances that an entity can participate in. The WORKS_FOR binary relationship type DEPARTMENT: EMPLOYEE is of cardinality ratio 1:N, meaning that each department entity can be related to numerous employee entities (numerous employees work for a department) but an employee entity can be related to only one department (an employee works for only one department). Common cardinality ratios for binary relationship types are 1:1, 1:N, and M:N.

An example of a 1:1 binary relationship type between DEPARTMENT and EMPLOYEE is MANAGES (Figure 3.11), which relates a department entity to the employee who manages that department. This relationship is 1:1 if we know that an employee can manage only one department and that a department has only one manager. The relationship type WORKS_ON (Figure 3.12) between EMPLOYEE and PROJECT is of cardinality ratio M:N if we know that an employee can work on several projects and that several employees can work on a project.

The **participation constraint** specifies whether the existence of an entity depends on its being related to another entity via the relationship type. There are two types of participation constraints, total and partial, which we illustrate by example. If a company

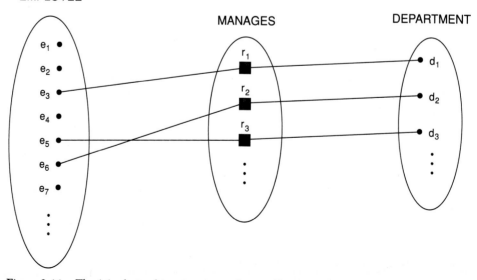

Figure 3.11   The 1:1 relationship MANAGES, with partial participation of EMPLOYEE and total participation of DEPARTMENT

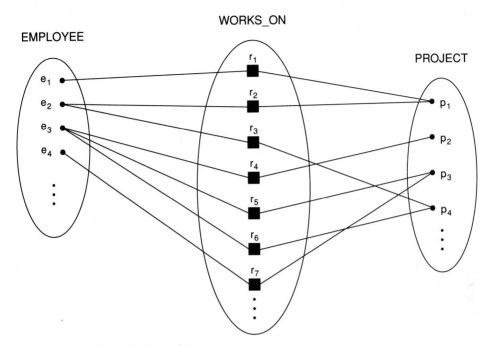

Figure 3.12   The M:N relationship WORKS_ON

rule states that *every* employee must work for a department, then an employee entity can exist only if it participates in a WORKS_FOR relationship instance (Figure 3.8). The participation of EMPLOYEE in the WORKS_FOR relationship type is called **total,** meaning that every entity in "the total set" of employee entities must be related to a department entity via WORKS_FOR. Total participation is sometimes called **existence dependency.** In Figure 3.11 we do not expect every employee to manage a department, so the participation of EMPLOYEE in the MANAGES relationship type is **partial,** meaning that *some* or "part of the set of" employee entities are related to a department entity via MANAGES, but not necessarily all.

We will refer to the cardinality ratio and participation constraints taken together as the **structural constraints** of a relationship type. There is a simpler way of specifying structural constraints, although it may not be as intuitive as separating them into cardinality ratio and participation constraint. We can associate a pair of integer numbers (min, max) with each participation of an entity type E in a relationship type R, where $0 \leq$ min $\leq$ max and max ≥ 1. The numbers mean that for each entity e in E, e must participate in at least min and at most max relationship instances in R *at all times.* Note that in this method min = 0 implies partial participation, whereas min > 0 implies total participation. The advantage of using this method is that it is more precise, and we can use it easily to specify structural constraints for relationship types *of any degree.*

Attributes of Relationship Types

Relationship types can also have attributes, similar to those of entity types. For example, we may want to record the number of hours per week that an employee works on a project; this can be kept with each relationship instance in WORKS_ON, so we need to include an attribute Hours for the WORKS_ON relationship type of Figure 3.12. Another example is to include the date on which a manager started managing a department via an attribute StartDate for the MANAGES relationship type of Figure 3.11.

Notice that attributes of 1:1 or 1:N relationship types can be included as attributes of one of the participating entity types. For example, the StartDate attribute for the MANAGES relationship can be an attribute of either EMPLOYEE or DEPARTMENT—although conceptually it belongs to MANAGES. This is because MANAGES is a 1:1 relationship, so every department or employee entity participates in at most one relationship instance. Hence, the value of the StartDate attribute can be determined separately either by the participating department entity or by the participating employee (manager) entity.

For a 1:N relationship type, a relationship attribute can be included *only* as an attribute of the entity type at the N side of the relationship. For example, in Figure 3.8, if the WORKS_FOR relationship also has an attribute StartDate that indicates when an employee started working for a department, this attribute could be included as an attribute of EMPLOYEE. This is because the relationship is 1:N so each employee entity participates in at most one relationship instance in WORKS_FOR. Hence, the participating employee entity alone can determine the value of StartDate. In both 1:1 and 1:N relationship types, the decision as to where a relationship attribute should be placed—as a relationship type attribute or as an attribute of a participating entity type—is determined subjectively by the schema designer.

If the value of an attribute is determined by the *combination of participating entities* in a relationship instance, and not by any single one, then the attribute *must* be specified as a relationship attribute. This condition applies to attributes of M:N relationship types because entities from either participating entity type can participate in numerous relationship instances. An example is the Hours attribute of the M:N relationship WORKS_ON (Figure 3.12); the number of hours an employee works on a project is determined by an employee-project combination and not separately by either.

3.3.4   Weak Entity Types

Some entity types may not have any key attributes of their own. This implies that we may not be able to distinguish between some entities because the combinations of values of their attributes can be identical. Such entity types are called **weak entity types**. Entities belonging to a weak entity type are identified by being related to specific entities from another entity type in combination with some of their attribute values. We call this other entity type the **identifying owner,** and we call the relationship type that relates a weak entity type to its owner the **identifying relationship** of the weak entity type. A weak entity type always has a *total* participation constraint (existence dependency) with respect to its identifying relationship, because it may not be possible to identify a weak entity without an owner entity. However, not every existence dependency results in a weak entity type.

For example, consider the entity type DEPENDENT, related to EMPLOYEE, which is used to keep track of the dependents of each employee via a 1:N relationship. The attributes of DEPENDENT are DependentName (the first name of the dependent), Birth-Date, Sex, and Relationship (to the employee). Two dependents of distinct employees may have the same values for DependentName, BirthDate, Sex, and Relationship, but they are still distinct entities. They are identified as distinct entities only after determining the employee entity to which each is related. Each employee entity is said to **own** the dependent entities related to it.

A weak entity type has a **partial key,** which is the set of attributes that can uniquely identify weak entities related to *the same owner entity.* In our example, if we assume that no two dependents of the same employee ever have the same name, then the attribute DependentName of DEPENDENT is the partial key.

Weak entity types can sometimes be represented as composite, multivalued attributes. In the above example we could specify a composite multivalued attribute Dependents for EMPLOYEE, whose simple component attributes are DependentName, BirthDate, Sex, and Relationship; this attribute could replace the weak entity type DEPENDENT. The choice of which representation to use is made by the database designer. One criterion we can use is to choose the weak entity type representation if the weak entity type has many attributes and participates independently in relationship types other than its identifying relationship type.

In general, any number of levels of weak entity types can be defined; an owner entity type may itself be a weak entity type. In addition, a weak entity type may have more than one identifying entity type and an identifying relationship type of degree higher than two, as we illustrate in Section 3.6.

3.3.5 *Refining the* ER *Design for the* COMPANY *Database*

We can now refine the database design of Figure 3.7 by changing the attributes that represent relationships into relationship types. The cardinality ratio and participation constraint of each relationship type are determined from the requirements listed in Section 3.2. If it is not possible to determine some cardinality ratio or dependency from the requirements list, then we must go back to the users to determine these structural properties.

In our example, we specify the following relationship types:

1. MANAGES, a 1:1 relationship type between EMPLOYEE and DEPARTMENT. EMPLOYEE participation is partial. DEPARTMENT participation is not clear from the requirements. We go back to the users, who say that a department must have a manager at all times, which implies total participation. The attribute StartDate is assigned to this relationship type.

2. WORKS_FOR, a 1:N relationship type between DEPARTMENT and EMPLOYEE. Both participations are total.

3. CONTROLS, a 1:N relationship type between DEPARTMENT and PROJECT. Participation of PROJECT is total, whereas that of DEPARTMENT is determined to be partial after consultation with the users.

4. SUPERVISION, a 1:N relationship type between EMPLOYEE (in the supervisor role) and EMPLOYEE (in the supervisee role). Both participations are determined to be partial after the users indicate that not every employee is a supervisor and not every employee has a supervisor.

5. WORKS_ON, determined to be an M:N relationship type with attribute Hours after the users indicate that a project can have several employees working on it. Both participations are determined to be total.

6. DEPENDENTS_OF, a 1:N relationship type between EMPLOYEE and DEPENDENT, which is also the identifying relationship for the weak entity type DEPENDENT. Participation of EMPLOYEE is partial, whereas that of DEPENDENT is total.

After specifying the above six relationship types, we remove the attributes that have become redundant from Figure 3.7. These include Manager and ManagerStartDate from DEPARTMENT; ControllingDepartment from PROJECT; Department, Supervisor, and WorksOn from EMPLOYEE; and Employee from DEPENDENT. It is important to have the least possible redundancy when we design the conceptual schema of a database. If some redundancy is desired at the storage level or at the user view level, it can be introduced later as discussed in Section 1.6.1. The conceptual schema designers should concentrate on specifying the data structures and constraints that match the database requirements in the best possible way.

It is quite useful to display a schema in diagrammatic form, as we discussed in Section 2.1.2. In the next section we present diagrammatic conventions to display an ER schema. We display the COMPANY database schema in Figure 3.13 using this notation, which is called an ER **diagram**.

3.4   Entity-Relationship (ER) Diagrams

In Figures 3.8 to 3.12 we have represented entity types and relationship types by displaying their extensions—the individual entities and relationship instances. In ER diagrams the emphasis is on representing the schemas rather than the instances. This is more useful because a database schema rarely changes whereas the extension may change frequently. Also, the schema is usually easier to display than the extension of a database because it is much smaller.

Figure 3.13 displays the COMPANY ER **database schema** for our example database as an ER diagram. Entity types such as EMPLOYEE, DEPARTMENT, and PROJECT are shown in rectangular boxes. Relationship types such as WORKS_FOR, MANAGES, CONTROLS, and WORKS_ON are shown in diamond-shaped boxes attached to the participating entity types with straight lines. Attributes are shown in ovals and each attribute is attached to its entity type or relationship type by a straight line. Component attributes of a composite attribute are attached to the oval representing the composite attribute, as illustrated by the Name attribute of EMPLOYEE. Multivalued attributes are shown in double ovals, as illustrated by the Locations attribute of DEPARTMENT. Key attributes have their names underlined. Derived attributes are shown in dotted ovals, as illustrated by the NumberOf Employees attribute of DEPARTMENT.

Weak entity types are distinguished by placing them in double rectangles and placing their identifying relationship in double diamonds, as illustrated by the DEPENDENT entity type and the DEPENDENTS_OF identifying relationship type. The partial key of the weak entity type is underlined with a dotted line.

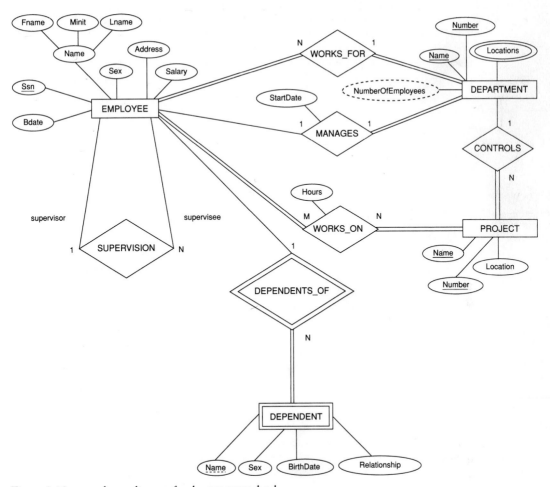

Figure 3.13 ER schema diagram for the COMPANY database
described in Section 3.2

In Figure 3.13 the cardinality ratio of each binary relationship type is specified by attaching a 1, M, or N on each participating edge. The cardinality ratio of DEPARTMENT:EMPLOYEE in MANAGES is 1:1, whereas it is 1:N for DEPARTMENT:EMPLOYEE in WORKS_FOR, and M:N for WORKS_ON. The participation constraint is specified by a single line for partial participation and double lines for total participation (existence dependency). Hence, the participation of EMPLOYEE in WORKS_FOR is total (every employee must work for a department), whereas the participation of EMPLOYEE in MANAGES is partial (not every employee manages a department).

In Figure 3.13 we show the role names for the SUPERVISION relationship type because the EMPLOYEE entity type plays both roles in that relationship. Note that the cardinality is 1:N from supervisor to supervisee because each employee, in the role of supervisee, has at most one direct supervisor, whereas an employee in the role of supervisor can supervise zero or more employees.

Figure 3.14 shows the same COMPANY database schema with all the role names displayed. We also use the alternative notation for displaying structural constraints of relationship types by displaying two integers (min, max) next to each line that represents the participation of an entity type in a relationship type. As discussed in Section 3.3.3, this technique is more general and applies to relationship types of any degree. Figure 3.15 summarizes the conventions for ER diagrams.

3.5 Naming of Schema Constructs

The choice of names for entity types, attributes, relationship types, and particularly roles is not always straightforward. One should choose names that convey as much as possible the meanings attached to the different constructs in the schema. We choose to use *singu-*

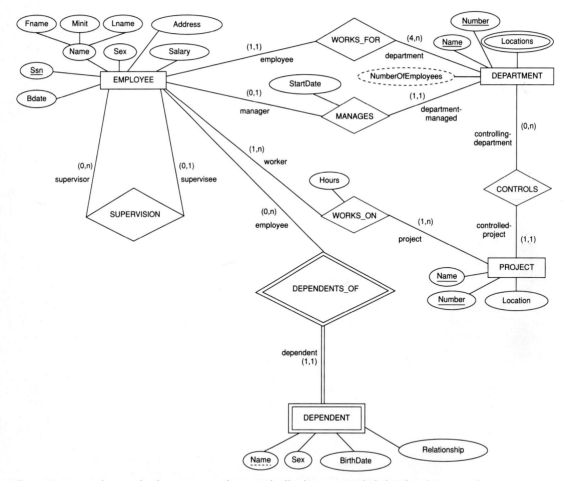

Figure 3.14   ER diagram for the COMPANY schema with all role names included and with structural constraints on relationships specified using the alternate notation (min, max)

Symbol | Meaning

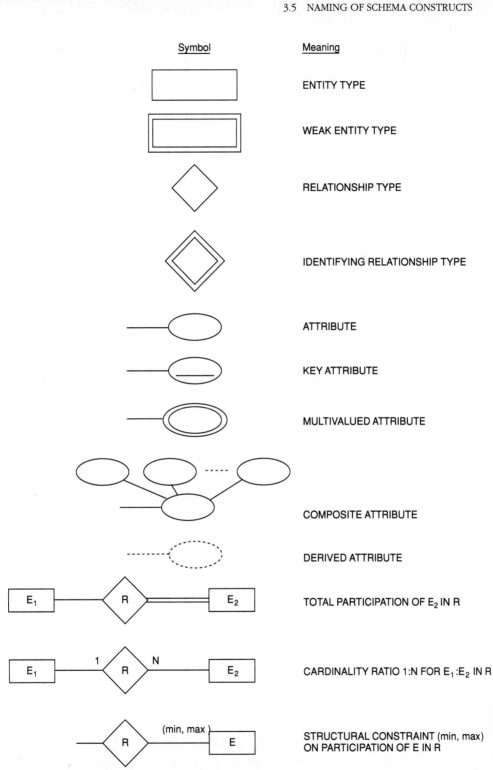

ENTITY TYPE

WEAK ENTITY TYPE

RELATIONSHIP TYPE

IDENTIFYING RELATIONSHIP TYPE

ATTRIBUTE

KEY ATTRIBUTE

MULTIVALUED ATTRIBUTE

COMPOSITE ATTRIBUTE

DERIVED ATTRIBUTE

TOTAL PARTICIPATION OF E_2 IN R

CARDINALITY RATIO 1:N FOR E_1:E_2 IN R

STRUCTURAL CONSTRAINT (min, max) ON PARTICIPATION OF E IN R

Figure 3.15 Summary of ER diagram notation

lar names for entity types rather than plural ones because the entity type name applies to each individual entity belonging to that entity type. In our ER diagrams we will use the convention that entity type and relationship type names are in uppercase letters, attribute names are capitalized, and role names are in lowercase letters. We have already used this convention in Figures 3.13 and 3.14.

The ER modeling concepts we presented thus far—entity types, relationship types, attributes, keys, structural constraints—can model a wide variety of database applications. However, some applications—especially newer ones such as databases for engineering design or for artificial intelligence applications—require additional concepts if we want to model them with greater accuracy. We will discuss these advanced modeling concepts in Chapter 15. In the next section we discuss some common problems that arise when modeling relationship types of degree higher than two.

3.6   Relationship Types of Degree Higher Than Two

In Section 3.3.3 we defined the **degree** of a relationship type as the number of participating entity types and called a relationship type of degree two **binary** and of degree three **ternary**. The ER diagram notation for a ternary relationship type is shown in Figure 3.16(a), which shows the schema for the SUPPLY relationship type that was displayed at the extension level in Figure 3.9. In general, a relationship type R of degree n will have n edges in an ER diagram, one connecting R to each participating entity type.

Figure 3.16(b) shows an ER diagram for the three binary relationship types CAN_SUPPLY, USES, and SUPPLIES. As we discussed in Section 3.3.3, these three are not equivalent to the ternary relationship type SUPPLY. It is often tricky to decide whether a particular relationship should be represented as a relationship type of degree n or broken down into several relationship types of smaller degrees. The designer must base this decision on the semantics or meaning of the particular situation being represented.

Another example is shown in Figure 3.16(c). The ternary relationship type OFFERS represents information on instructors offering courses during particular semesters; hence, it includes a relationship instance (i, s, c) whenever instructor i offers course c during semester s. The three binary relationship types shown in Figure 3.16(c) have the following meaning:

- CAN_TEACH relates a course to the instructors who *can teach* that course.
- TAUGHT_DURING relates a semester to the instructors who taught *some course* during that semester.
- OFFERED_DURING relates a semester to the courses offered during that semester *by any instructor*.

In general, these ternary and binary relationships represent different information but certain constraints should hold among the relationships. For example, a relationship instance (i, s, c) should not exist in OFFERS *unless* an instance (i, s) exists in TAUGHT_DURING, an instance (s, c) exists in OFFERED_DURING, and an instance (i, c) exists in CAN_TEACH. However, the reverse is not always true; we may have instances (i, s), (s, c), and (i, c) in the three binary relationship types with no corresponding instance (i, s, c) in OFFERS. Under certain *additional constraints* the latter may hold, for

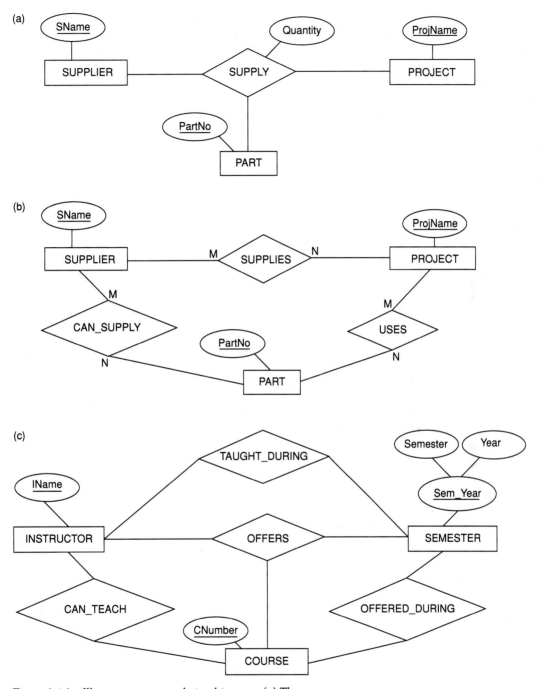

Figure 3.16 Illustrating ternary relationship types. (a) The ternary relationship type SUPPLY. (b) Three binary relationship types that are not equivalent to the ternary relationship type SUPPLY. (c) Another example of ternary versus binary relationship types.

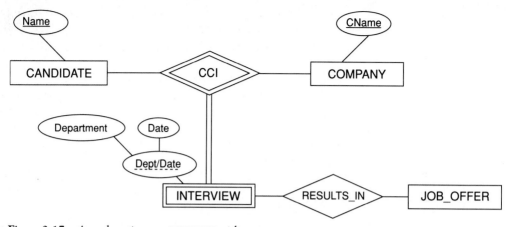

Figure 3.17   A weak entity type INTERVIEW with a ternary
identifying relationship type

example, if the CAN_TEACH relationship is 1:1 (an instructor can teach one course and a course can be taught by only one instructor). The schema designer must analyze each specific situation to decide which of the binary and ternary relationship types are needed.

Notice that it is possible to have a weak entity type with a ternary (or n-ary) identifying relationship type. In this case, the weak entity type can have *several* owner entity types. An example is shown in Figure 3.17. Also, the (min, max) cardinality ratios are applicable to n-ary relationships.

3.7   Summary

In this chapter we presented the modeling concepts of a high-level conceptual data model, the Entity-Relationship (ER) model. We started by discussing the role that a high-level data model plays in the database design process and then presented an example set of database requirements. We then defined the basic ER model concepts of entities and their attribute values. These concepts are used at the instance or "extension" level. We discussed null values, then presented the various types of attributes, which can be nested arbitrarily:

- Simple or atomic.
- Composite.
- Multivalued.

We also briefly discussed derived attributes. We then discussed the ER model concepts at the schema or "intension" level:

- Entity types.
- Attributes and their value sets.
- Key attributes.

• Relationship types.

• Participation roles of entity types in relationship types.

We presented two methods for specifying the structural constraints of relationship types. The first method distinguished two types of structural constraints:

• Cardinality ratios (1:1, 1:N, M:N for binary relationships).

• Participation constraints (total, partial).

Alternatively, a more general method of specifying structural constraints is to specify minimum and maximum numbers (min, max) on the participation of each entity type in a relationship type. This applies to relationship types of any degree. We then discussed weak entity types and the related concepts of owner entity types, identifying relationship types, and partial key attributes.

ER schemas can be represented diagrammatically as ER diagrams. We showed how to design an ER schema for the COMPANY database by first defining the entity types and their attributes and then refining the design to include relationship types. We displayed the ER diagram for the COMPANY database schema. Finally, we discussed ternary and higher-degree relationship types and the circumstances under which they are distinguished from a set of binary relationship types.

Review Questions

3.1. Discuss the role of a high-level data model in the database design process.

3.2. List the various cases where use of a null value would be appropriate.

3.3. Define the following terms: entity, attribute, attribute value, relationship instance, composite attribute, multivalued attribute, derived attribute, key attribute, value set (domain).

3.4. What is an entity type? Explain the difference between an entity and an entity type.

3.5. Explain the difference between an attribute and a value set.

3.6. What is a relationship type? Explain the difference between a relationship instance and a relationship type.

3.7. What is a participation role? When is it *necessary* to use role names in the description of relationship types?

3.8. Describe the two alternatives for specifying structural constraints on relationship types. What are the advantages and disadvantages of each?

3.9. Under what conditions can an attribute of a binary relationship type be moved to become an attribute of one of the participating entity types?

3.10. When we think of relationships as attributes, what are the value sets of these attributes? What class of data models is based on this concept?

3.11. What is meant by a recursive relationship type? Give some examples of recursive relationship types.

3.12. When is the concept of weak entity useful in data modeling? Define the terms owner entity type, weak entity type, identifying relationship type, and partial key.

3.13. Can an identifying relationship of a weak entity type have degree greater than two? Give examples.

3.14. Discuss the conventions for displaying an ER schema as an ER diagram.

3.15. Discuss the conditions under which a ternary relationship type can be represented by a number of binary relationship types.

Exercises

3.16. Consider the following set of requirements for a university database that is used to keep track of students' transcripts. This is similar but not identical to the database shown in Figure 1.2:

   a. The university keeps track of each student's name, student number, social security number, current address and phone, permanent address and phone, birthdate, sex, class (freshman, sophomore, ..., graduate), major department, minor department (if any), and degree program (B.A., B.S., ..., Ph.D.). Some user applications need to refer to the city, state, and zip of the student's permanent address and to the students' last name. Both social security number and student number have unique values for each student.

   b. Each department is described by a name, department code, office number, office phone, and college. Both name and code have unique values for each department.

   c. Each course has a course name, description, code number, number of semester hours, level, and offering department. The value of code number is unique for each course.

   d. Each section has an instructor, semester, year, course, and section number. The section number distinguishes different sections of the same course that are taught during the same semester/year; its values are 1, 2, 3, ..., up to the number of sections taught during each semester.

   e. A grade report has a student, section, and grade.

   Design an ER schema for this application, and draw an ER diagram for that schema. Specify key attributes of each entity type and structural constraints on each relationship type. Note any unspecified requirements, and make appropriate assumptions to make the specification complete.

3.17. Composite and multivalued attributes can be nested to any number of levels. Suppose we want to design an attribute for a STUDENT entity type to keep track of previous college education. Such an attribute will have one entry for each college previously attended, and this entry is composed of college name, start and end dates, degree entries (degrees awarded at that college, if any), and transcript entries (courses completed at that college, if any). Each degree entry is formed of degree name and the month and year the degree was awarded, and each transcript entry is formed of a course name, semester, year, and grade. Design an attribute to hold this information. Use the conventions of Figure 3.6.

3.18. Show an alternative design for the attribute described in Exercise 3.17 that uses only entity types (including weak entity types if needed) and relationship types.

3.19. Consider the ER diagram of Figure 3.18, which shows a simplified schema for an airline reservations system. Extract from the ER diagram the requirements and constraints that resulted in this schema. Try to be as precise as possible in your requirements and constraints specification.

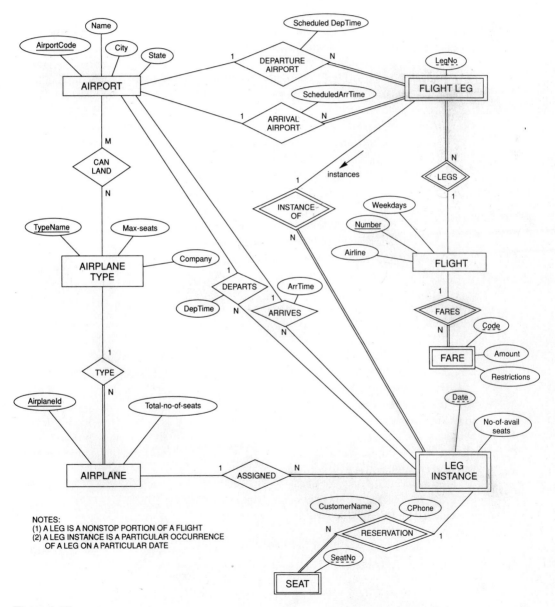

Figure 3.18

3.20. In Chapters 1 and 2 we discussed the database environment and users. We can consider many entity types to describe such an environment, such as DBMS, stored database, DBA, and catalog/data dictionary. Try to specify all the entity types that can fully describe a database system and its environment; then specify the relationship types among them and draw an ER diagram to describe such a general database environment.

3.21. A trucking company called TRUCKERS is responsible for picking up shipments for warehouses of a retail chain called MAZE BROTHERS and delivering the shipments to individual retail store locations of MAZE BROTHERS. Currently there are 6 warehouse locations and 45 retail stores of MAZE BROTHERS. A truck may carry several shipments during a single trip, which is identified by a Trip#, and delivers those shipments to multiple stores. Each shipment is identified by a Shipment# and includes data on shipment volume, weight, destination, etc. Trucks have different capacities for both the volumes they can hold and the weights they can carry. The TRUCKERS company currently has 150 trucks, and a truck makes 3 to 4 trips each week. A database—to be used by both TRUCKERS and MAZE BROTHERS—is being designed to keep track of truck usage and deliveries and to be used for scheduling trucks to provide timely deliveries to stores. Design an ER schema diagram for the above application. Make any assumptions you need but state them clearly.

3.22. A database is being constructed to keep track of the teams and games of a sports league. A team has a number of players, not all of whom participate in each game. It is desired to keep track of the players participating in each game for each team, the positions they played in that game, and the result of the game. Try to design an ER schema diagram for this application, stating any assumptions you make. Choose your favorite sport (soccer, baseball, football, ...).

Selected Bibliography

The Entity-Relationship model was introduced by Chen (1976), and related work appears in Schmidt and Swenson (1975), Wiederhold and Elmasri (1979), and Senko (1975). Since then numerous modifications to the ER model have been suggested. We have incorporated some of these in our presentation. Structural constraints on relationships are discussed in Abrial (1974), Elmasri and Wiederhold (1980), and Lenzerini and Santucci (1983). Multivalued and composite attributes are incorporated in the ER model in Elmasri, Weeldreyer, and Hevner (1985). A conference for the dissemination of research results related to the ER model has been held regularly since 1979. The conference has been held in Los Angeles (ER 1979, ER 1983), Washington D.C. (ER 1981), Chicago (ER 1985), Dijon, France (ER 1986), and New York City (ER 1987). The next conference is scheduled for Rome, Italy, in 1988.

CHAPTER 4

Record Storage and Primary File Organizations

4.1 Introduction

The collection of data that makes up a computerized database must be physically stored on some computer **storage medium**. The DBMS software can then retrieve, update, and process this data as needed. Computer storage media form a *storage hierarchy* that includes two main categories:

- Primary storage. This category includes storage media that can be operated on directly by the computer central processing unit (CPU), such as the computer main memory and smaller but faster cache memories. Primary storage usually provides fast access to data but is of limited storage capacity.

- Secondary storage. Secondary storage devices include magnetic disks, tapes, and drums and are usually of larger capacity, lower cost, and provide slower access to data than primary storage. Data in secondary storage cannot be processed directly by the CPU; it must be copied into primary storage for processing.

Databases typically store large amounts of data that must persist over long periods of time. The data is accessed and processed repeatedly during this period. This contrasts with the notion of data structures that persist for only a limited time during program execution, which is common in programming languages. Most databases are stored permanently on **disk** secondary storage for the following reasons:

- Generally, databases are too large to fit entirely in main memory.

- The types of circumstances that cause permanent loss of stored data occur less frequently for disk secondary storage than for primary storage. Hence, we refer to disk—and other secondary storage devices—as **nonvolatile storage,** whereas main memory is often called **volatile storage**.

65

• The cost of storage per unit of data is an order of magnitude less for disk than for primary storage.

New technologies are emerging, such as optical disk storage and cheaper and larger main memories, as well as special-purpose database-oriented hardware. These technologies may provide viable alternatives to the use of magnetic disks in the future. However, for the present time, it is important to study and understand the properties and characteristics of magnetic disks and the way data files can be organized on disk in order to design effective databases with acceptable performance.

Magnetic tapes are frequently used as a storage medium for backing up the database because the cost of storage on tape is even less than for disk. However, access to data on tape is quite slow. Data stored on tapes may be **off-line;** that is, human intervention by an operator to load a tape may be needed before this data becomes available. However, disks are **on-line** devices that can be directly accessed at any time.

In this and the following chapter we describe the techniques used to store large amounts of structured data on disk. These techniques are important for database designers, the DBA, and implementers of a DBMS. Database designers and the DBA must know the advantages and disadvantages of each storage technique when they design, implement, and operate a database on a specific DBMS. The DBMS will usually have several options available for organizing the data, and the process of **physical database design** involves choosing the particular data organization techniques that best suit the given aplication requirements from among the available options. DBMS system implementers must study data organization techniques so that they can implement them efficiently and thus provide the DBA and users of the DBMS with sufficient options for various uses of the DBMS.

Typical database applications need only a small portion of the database at a time for processing. Whenever a certain portion of the data is needed, it must be located on disk, copied to main memory for processing, and then re-written to the disk if the data is changed. The data stored on disk is organized as **files** of **records**. Each record is a collection of data values that can be interpreted as facts about entities, their attributes, and their relationships. Records should be stored on disk in a manner that makes it possible to locate them efficiently whenever needed.

In Section 4.2 we describe disk storage devices and their characteristics and also briefly describe tape storage devices. Section 4.3 discusses the technique of double buffering, which is used to speed up retrieval of multiple disk blocks. In Section 4.4 we discuss the various ways in which records of a file can be formatted and stored on disk. In Section 4.5 we present the various types of operations that are typically applied to records of a file. These include operations for locating, copying, and updating of records. We then present three primary methods for organizing records of a file on disk. Unordered records are discussed in Section 4.6, ordered records in Section 4.7, and hashed records in Section 4.8. We discuss the advantages and disadvantages of each technique with respect to the various types of file operations.

Section 4.9 very briefly discusses files of mixed records, which are used to physically implement relationships among records. In Chapter 5 we discuss techniques for creating access structures, called indexes, that speed up searching for and retrieval of records. These techniques involve storage of auxiliary data besides the records themselves.

4.2   Secondary Storage Devices

In this section we describe some characteristics of magnetic disk and magnetic tape devices. The reader who has studied these devices before may just browse through this section.

4.2.1   Hardware Description of Disk Devices

Magnetic disks are used for storing large amounts of data. The most basic unit of data on the disk is a single **bit** of information. By magnetizing an area on disk in certain ways, it can represent a bit value of either 0 (zero) or 1 (one). To code information, bits are grouped into **bytes** (or **characters**). Byte sizes are typically 4 to 8 bits, depending on the computer and the device. We assume one character is stored in a single byte and use the terms byte and character interchangeably. The **capacity** of a disk is the number of bytes it can store, which is usually very large. We refer to disk capacities in kilobytes (Kbyte or 1000 bytes), megabytes (Mbyte or 1 million bytes), and gigabytes (Gbyte or 1 billion bytes). Small floppy disks used with microcomputers typically hold from 400 Kbytes to 1.2 Mbytes, hard disks for micros typically hold from 10 to 30 Mbytes, and large disk packs used with minicomputers and mainframes have capacities that range up to a few Gbytes.

Whatever the capacity, disks are all made of magnetic material shaped as a thin circular disk (Figure 4.1a) and protected by a plastic or acrylic cover. A disk is **single-sided** if it stores information on only one of its surfaces and **double-sided** if both surfaces are used. To increase storage capacity, disks are assembled into a **disk pack** (Figure 4.1b), which may include as many as 30 surfaces. Information is stored on a disk surface in concentric circles of *small width*, each having a distinct diameter. Each circle is called a **track**. For disk packs, the tracks with the same diameter on the various surfaces are called a **cylinder** because of the shape they would form if connected in space. The concept of a cylinder is important because data stored on the same cylinder can be retrieved much faster than if it were distributed among different cylinders.

Each track typically stores the same amount of information, so bits are packed more densely on the smaller-diameter tracks. The number of tracks on a disk ranges up to 800, and the capacity of a track typically ranges from 4 to 50 Kbytes. Because a track usually contains a large amount of information, it is divided into smaller blocks or sectors. The division of a track into **sectors** is hard-coded on the disk surface and cannot be changed. Sectors subtend a fixed angle at the center (Figure 4.2), and not all disks have their tracks divided into sectors. The division of a track into equal-sized **blocks** is set by the operating system during disk **formatting** (or **initialization**). Block size is fixed during initialization and cannot be changed dynamically. Typical disk block sizes range from 512 to 4096 bytes. A disk with sectors often has the sectors further subdivided into blocks. Blocks are separated by fixed-size **interblock gaps,** which include specially coded control information written during disk initialization. This information is used to determine which block on the track follows each interblock gap.

A disk is called a *random access* addressable device. Transfer of data between main memory and disk takes place in units of blocks. The **hardware address** of a block—a

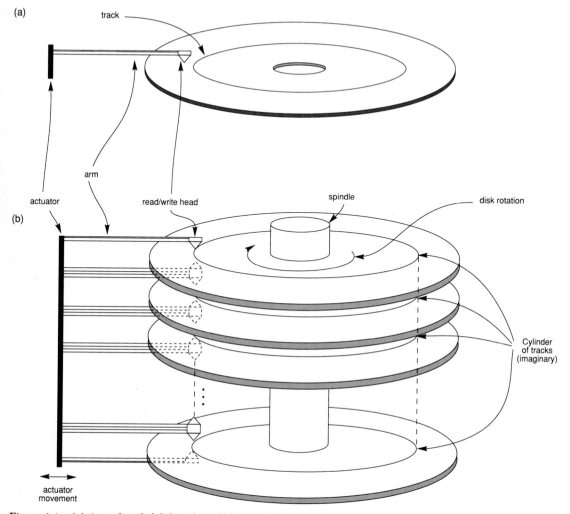

Figure 4.1   (a) A single-sided disk with read/write hardware.
(b) A disk pack with read/write hardware.

combination of a surface number, track number (within the surface), and block number (within the track)—is supplied to the disk input/output (I/O) hardware. The address of a **buffer**—a contiguous reserved area in main storage that holds one block—is also provided. For a **read** command the block from disk is copied into the buffer, whereas for a **write** command the contents of the buffer are copied into the disk block. Sometimes we transfer several contiguous blocks, called a **cluster,** as a unit. In this case the buffer size is adjusted to match the number of bytes in the cluster.

The actual hardware mechanism that reads or writes a block is the disk **read/write head,** which is part of a system called a **disk drive**. A disk or disk pack is mounted in the disk drive, which includes a motor that rotates the disks. A read/write head includes an electronic component attached to a **mechanical arm**. For disk packs with multiple sur-

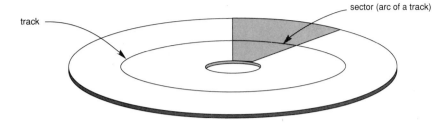

Figure 4.2 A group of sectors that subtend the same angle

faces there are several read/write heads—one for each surface (Figure 4.1b). All arms are connected to an **actuator,** which is attached to another electrical motor that moves the read/write heads in unison and positions them precisely over the cylinder of tracks specified in a block address.

Disk drives for hard disks rotate the disk pack continuously at a constant speed. For a floppy disk, the disk drive begins to rotate the disk whenever a particular read or write request is initiated and ceases rotation soon after the data transfer is completed. Once the read/write head is positioned on the right track and the block specified in the block address moves under the read/write head, the electronic component of the read/write head is activated to transfer the data. For read, the read/write head senses the magnetic orientation of the bits on the disk surface and transfers them to the buffer in main memory. For write, the data from the buffer is transferred to the I/O device, and electrical signals are issued by the read/write head to magnetize the bits on the disk surface appropriately.

Some disk units have fixed read/write heads, with as many heads as the number of tracks. These are called **fixed-head** disks, whereas disk units with an actuator motor are called **movable-head** disks. For fixed-head disks, a track or cylinder is selected by electronically switching to the appropriate read/write head rather than by actual mechanical movement, which is much faster. However, the cost of the additional read/write heads is quite high. Hence, fixed-head disks are not commonly used.

To transfer a disk block given its address, the disk drive must first mechanically position the read/write head on the correct track. The time it takes to do this is called the **seek time**. Following that, there is a delay—called the **rotational delay** or **latency**—until the beginning of the block rotates into position under the read/write head. Finally, some time is needed to transfer the data; this is called the **block transfer time**.

Hence, the total time to locate and transfer an arbitrary block given its address is the sum of the seek time, rotational delay, and block transfer time. The seek time and rotational delay are usually much larger than the block transfer time. To make the transfer of multiple blocks more efficient, it is common to transfer several consecutive blocks on the same track or cylinder. This eliminates the seek time and rotational delay for all but the first block and can result in substantial saving in time when numerous contiguous blocks are transferred. Usually, the disk manufacturer provides a **bulk transfer rate** to calculate the time it takes to transfer consecutive blocks. Appendix A contains a more complete discussion of these and other disk parameters.

The time to locate and transfer a disk block is in the order of milliseconds, usually ranging from 15 to 60 msec. For contiguous blocks, locating the first block takes from 15 to 60 msec, but transferring subsequent blocks may take 1 to 2 msec each. Many search techniques attempt to take advantage of consecutive retrieval of blocks when searching for data on disk. In any case, a transfer time in the order of milliseconds is considered quite high compared to the time it takes to process data in main memory by current CPUs. Hence, locating data on disk is **a** *major bottleneck* in database applications. The file structures we discuss here and in Chapter 5 attempt to *minimize the number of block transfers* needed to locate and transfer the required data.

4.2.2 Magnetic Tape Storage Devices

Disks are **random access** secondary storage devices, because an arbitrary disk block may be accessed "at random" once we specify its address. Magnetic tapes are **sequential access** secondary storage devices; to access the nth block on tape, we must first read the preceding n – 1 blocks. Data is stored on reels of high-capacity magnetic tape, somewhat similar to audio or video tapes but larger. A **tape drive** is required to read the data from or write the data to a **tape reel**. Usually, each group of bits that form a byte are stored across the tape, and the bytes themselves are stored consecutively on the tape. A tape reel is mounted manually on the tape drive whenever data stored on that reel is needed. Libraries of tape reels are kept in a computer installation. Two tape reels are usually mounted on the tape drive—the data tape and an empty takeup reel. After the tape has been used, it is rewound to its reel and removed so other data tapes can be mounted.

A read/write head is used to read or write data on tape. Data records on tape are also stored in blocks, although the blocks may be substantially larger than those for disks and interblock gaps are also quite large. With typical tape densities of 1600 to 6250 bytes per inch, a typical interblock gap* of 0.6 inches corresponds to 960 to 3750 bytes of wasted storage space. For better space utilization it is customary to group many records together in one block.

The main characteristic of a tape is that we must access the data blocks in **sequential order**. To get to a block in the middle of a reel of tape, we must mount the tape and then read through it until the required block gets under the read/write head. For this reason, tape access can be slow and tapes are not used to store on-line data. However, tapes serve a very important function—that of **backing up** the database. One reason for backup is to keep copies of disk files in case the data is lost because of a disk crash, which can happen if the disk read/write head touches the disk surface because of mechanical malfunction. For this reason, disk files are periodically copied to tape. Tapes can also be used to store excessively large database files. Database files that are seldom used or outdated but are required for historical record keeping can be **archived** on tape.

4.3   Buffering of Blocks

When several blocks need to be transferred from disk to main memory and we know all the disk addresses beforehand, we can arrange to have several buffers in main memory to

---

*Called interrecord gaps in tape terminology.

speed up the transfer. While one buffer is being read or written, the CPU can process data in the other buffer. This is possible because an independent disk input/output processor usually exists which, once started, can proceed to transfer a data block between memory and disk independent of and in parallel with CPU processing.

Figure 4.3 illustrates how two processes can proceed in parallel. Processes A and B are running **concurrently** in an **interleaved** fashion, whereas processes C and D are running **concurrently** in a **simultaneous** fashion. When a single CPU controls multiple processes, simultaneous execution is not possible. However, the processes can still run concurrently in an interleaved way. Buffering is most useful when processes can run concurrently in a simultaneous fashion, either because a separate disk I/O processor is available or because multiple processors exist.

Figure 4.4 illustrates how reading and processing can proceed in parallel when the time to process a disk block in memory is less than the time to read the next block and fill a buffer. The CPU can start processing a block once its transfer to main memory is completed, while at the same time the disk I/O processor reads and transfers the next block into a different buffer. This technique is called **double buffering** and can also be used to write a continuous stream of blocks from memory to the disk.

When we use buffering, we can take advantage of continuously reading or writing data on consecutive disk blocks, which saves the seek time and rotational delay as discussed in Section 4.2.1. Moreover, data is kept ready for processing, thus reducing the waiting time in the programs.

4.4 Placement of File Records on Disk

In this section we define the concepts of records, record types, and files. Then we discuss the different techniques for placing file records on disk.

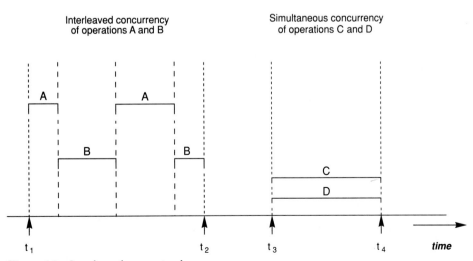

Figure 4.3 Interleaved versus simultaneous concurrency

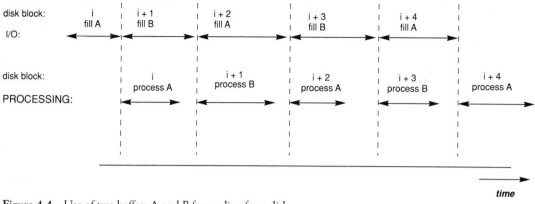

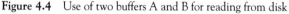

Figure 4.4   Use of two buffers A and B for reading from disk

4.4.1   Record Types

Data is usually stored in the form of **records**. Each record consists of a collection of related data **values** or **items,** where each value is formed of one or more bytes and corresponds to a particular **field** of the record. Records usually describe entities, their
attributes, and their relationships. For example, an EMPLOYEE record represents an employee entity, and each field value in the record specifies some attribute or relationship
of that employee, such as NAME, BIRTHDATE, SALARY, or SUPERVISOR. A collection of field
names and their corresponding data types constitutes a **record type** or **record format**
definition. A **data type,** associated with each field, specifies the type of values a field
can take.

The data type of a field is usually one of the standard data types used in programming. These include numeric (integer, long integer, or real number), string of characters
(fixed length or varying), Boolean (having 0 and 1 or TRUE and FALSE values only), and
sometimes specially coded **date** data types. The number of bytes required for each data
type is fixed for a given computer system. An integer may require 4 bytes, a long integer
8 bytes, a real number 4 bytes, a Boolean 1 byte, a date 4 bytes (to code the date into an
integer), and a fixed-length string of k characters k bytes. Variable-length strings may require as many bytes as there are characters in each field value. For example, an EMPLOYEE
record type may be defined—using PASCAL notation—as follows:

RECORD TYPE NAME	FIELD NAMES	DATA TYPES
type EMPLOYEE = record	NAME	: packed array [1..30] of character;
	SSN	: packed array [1..9] of character;
	SALARY	: integer;
	JOBCODE	: integer;
	DEPARTMENT	: packed array [1..10] of character
end;		

4.4.2   Files, Fixed-Length Records, and Variable-Length Records

A **file** is a *sequence* of records. In many cases, all records in a file are of the same record
type. If every record in the file has exactly the same size (in bytes), the file is said to be

made up of **fixed-length** records. If different records in the file may have different sizes, the file is made up of **variable-length** records.

A file may have variable-length records for several reasons:

- The file records are of the same record type but one or more of the fields are of varying size (**variable-length fields**). For example, the NAME field of the EMPLOYEE file may be declared as a variable-length string of characters rather than defined as a fixed-length string with as many characters as there are in the longest NAME value.

- The file records are of the same record type but one or more of the fields may have multiple values for individual records; such a field is called a **repeating field** and a group of values for the field is often called a **repeating group**. An example is a CAR_COLOR field of a CAR file.

- The file records are of the same record type but one or more of the fields are **optional**; that is, they may have values for some but not all of the file records (**optional fields**). For example, in an EMPLOYEE file, records for secretarial employees may have values for the fields TYPING_SPEED, SECRETARY_GRADE, and EQUIPMENT_CODE, whereas other employee records do not have values for these optional fields.

- The file contains records of *different record types* and hence of varying size (**mixed file**). This would occur if related records of different types were placed together; for example, the GRADE_REPORT records of a particular student may be placed following that STUDENT's record.

The fixed-length EMPLOYEE records (Figure 4.5a) have a record size of 71 bytes. In a file of fixed-length records, every record has the same fields and field lengths are fixed, so we can tell the starting byte position of each field relative to the starting position of the record. This facilitates locating field values by programs that access such files.

Notice that it is possible to represent a file that logically should have variable-length records as a fixed-length records file. For example, in the case of optional fields we could have *every field* included in *every file record* but store a special null value if no value exists for that field. For a repeating field, we could allocate as many spaces in each record as the maximum number of values that the field can take. For example, we could allocate five spaces for the CAR_COLOR field of a CAR file if a car record can have at most five color values. In either case, space is wasted when certain records do not have values for all the physical spaces provided in each record. Below, we discuss other options for formatting records of a file of variable-length records.

In the case of *variable-length fields*, each record has a value for each field, but we do not know the exact length of some field values. To determine the bytes within a particular record that represent each field, we can use special **separator** characters—which do not appear in any field value (such as ? or % or $)—to terminate variable-length fields (Figure 4.5b).

A file of records with optional fields can be formatted in different ways. If the total number of fields for the record type is large but the number of fields that actually appear in a typical record is small, we can include in each record a set of <field-name, field-value> pairs rather than just the field values. In Figure 4.5c three types of separator characters are used, although we could use the same separator character for the first two

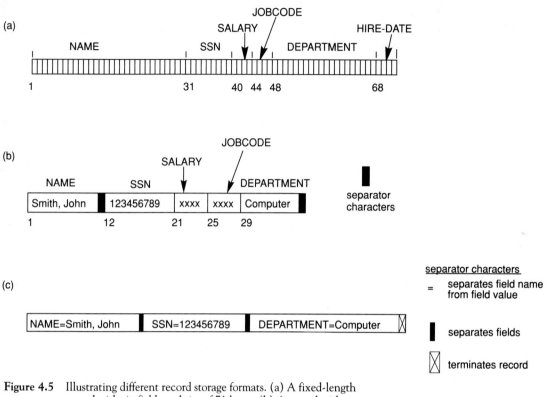

Figure 4.5 Illustrating different record storage formats. (a) A fixed-length record with six fields and size of 71 bytes. (b) A record with two variable-length fields and three fixed-length fields. (c) A variable-field record with three types of separator characters.

purposes—separating the field name from the field value and separating a field from the next field. A more practical option is to assign a short **field type**—say, an integer number—to each field and include in each record a sequence of <field-type, field-value> pairs rather than <field-name, field-value> pairs.

A *repeating field* needs one separator character to separate the repeating values of the field and another to indicate termination of the field. Finally, for a file that includes *records of different types*, each record is preceded by a **record type** indicator. As we can see, programs that process files of variable-length records need to be more complex than those for fixed-length records, where the starting position and size of each field are known and fixed.

4.4.3 Record Blocking and Spanned versus Unspanned Records

The records of a disk file must be allocated to disk blocks because a block is the unit of data transfer between disk and memory. When the block size is larger than the record size, each block may contain numerous records, although some files may have unusually large record sizes that cannot fit in one block. Suppose the block size is B bytes. For a file of fixed-length records of size R bytes with B ≥ R we can fit bfr = ⌊(B/R)⌋ records per block, where the ⌊(x)⌋ *function* rounds the value x down to the next integer. The value bfr is called the **blocking factor** for the file. In general, R may not divide B exactly, so we have some unused space in each block equal to

B – (bfr * R) bytes

To utilize this space, which is not large enough to store a whole record, we can store part of a record on one block and the rest on another block. We place a **pointer** at the end of the first block to point to the block with the remaining part of the record in case it is not the next consecutive block on disk. This organization, occasionally used with variable-length records, is called **spanned,** because a record can span more than one block. Whenever a record is larger than a block, we *must* use a spanned organization.

If we do not allow records to cross block boundaries, the organization is called **unspanned**. This is often used with fixed-length records having B ≥ R because it makes each record start at a known location in the block, simplifying record processing. For variable-length records, either a spanned or unspanned organization can be used. If the average record size is large, it is advantageous to use spanning; otherwise the lost space in each block may be considerable. Figure 4.6 illustrates spanned versus unspanned organization.

For variable-length records or spanned organization, each block may store a different number of records. In this case, the blocking factor bfr represents the *average* number of records per block for the file. We can use bfr to calculate the number of blocks b needed for a file of r records:

b = ⌈(r/bfr)⌉ blocks

where the ⌈(x)⌉ *function* rounds the value x up to the next integer.

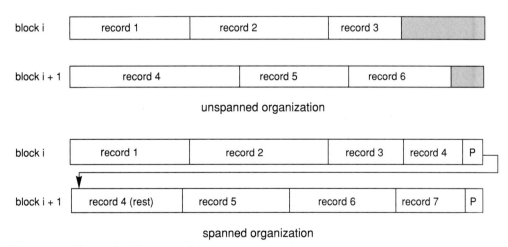

Figure 4.6 Spanned and unspanned organization

Practically all secondary storage devices use some form of record blocking for the following two main reasons:

- Blocking reduces the number of data transfer operations required to transfer a file between memory and the secondary storage device. These operations are expensive—for example, because of the seek time and rotational delay of a disk. To read an unblocked file of 1000 records, we need 1000 data transfers. With a blocking factor of 10, the same file would require 100 data transfers—one for each block.

- Blocking reduces the number of interblock gaps. In the above example, if records were unblocked, we would need 999 interrecord gaps, whereas with blocking we need only 99 interblock gaps. Hence, blocking increases the useful storage capacity of the secondary storage device.

4.4.4   Allocating File Blocks on Disk

There are several standard techniques for allocating the blocks of a file on disk. In **contiguous allocation** the file blocks are allocated to consecutive disk blocks. This makes reading the whole file very fast using double buffering but makes it difficult to expand the file. In **linked allocation** each file block contains a pointer to the next file block. This makes it easy to expand the file but makes it slow to read the whole file. A combination of the two allocates **clusters** of consecutive disk blocks, and the clusters are linked together. Clusters are sometimes called segments or extents. Another possibility is to use **indexed allocation,** where one or more **index blocks** contain pointers to the actual file blocks. It is also common to use combinations of the above techniques.

4.4.5   File Descriptors

A **file header** or **file descriptor** contains information about a file that is needed by the programs that access the file records. This includes information to determine the disk addresses of the file blocks as well as record format descriptions. The latter include field lengths and order of fields within a record for fixed-length unspanned records and field type codes, separator characters, and record type codes for variable-length records.

To search for a record on disk, one or more blocks are copied into main memory buffers. Programs then search for the desired record or records within the buffers utilizing the information in the file header. If the address of the block that contains the desired record is not known, the search programs must do a **linear search** through the file blocks. Each file block is copied into a buffer and searched until either the record is located or all the file blocks have been searched unsuccessfully. This can be very time consuming for a large file. The goal of a good file organization is to locate the block that contains the desired record with a few block transfers.

4.5   Operations on Files

Operations on files are usually grouped into **retrieval** operations and **update** operations. The former do not change any data in the file but only locate certain records so that their field values can be examined and processed. The latter change the file by insertion or deletion of records or modification of field values. In either case, we may have to **se-lect** one or more records for retrieval, deletion, or modification based on a **selection cri-terion,** which specifies conditions that the desired record or records must satisfy.

Consider an EMPLOYEE file with fields NAME, SSN, SALARY, JOBCODE, and DEPARTMENT. A simple selection criterion may involve an equality condition on some field value, for example, (SSN = '123456789') or (DEPARTMENT = 'Research'). More complex conditions can involve other types of comparison operators, such as > or ≥; an example is (SALARY ≥ 30000). The general case is to have an arbitrary Boolean expression on the fields of the file as the selection criterion.

Most file systems search for records based on simple conditions only. A complex selection criterion must be decomposed by the DBMS (or the programmer) to extract a simple **search criterion,** which can be used to locate the records on disk. Each located record is then checked for satisfying the full selection criterion. For example, we may extract the search criterion (DEPARTMENT = 'Research') from the selection criterion ((SALARY ≥ 30000) AND (DEPARTMENT = 'Research')); each record satisfying (DEPART-MENT = 'Research') is located then tested to see if it also satisfies (SALARY ≥ 30000).

When several file records satisfy a search criterion, only the *first*—with respect to the physical sequence of file records—is located. Other records satisfying the search criterion need additional operations to locate them. The record of the file last located by the system is designated as the **current record** of the file. Subsequent search operations commence from this record and locate the *next* record in the file satisfying the search criterion.

Actual operations for locating and accessing file records vary from system to system. Below, we present a set of representative operations. We assume that high-level programs, such as DBMS software programs, are attempting to access the records using these commands, so we sometimes refer to **program variables**.

- *Find (or Locate)*—Searches for the first record satisfying a search criterion. Transfers the block containing that record into a main memory buffer (if it is not already there). The record is located in the buffer and becomes the current record of the file. Sometimes different verbs are used to indicate whether the located record is to be retrieved or updated.

- *Read (or Get)*—Copies the current record from the buffer to a program variable or work area in the user program. This command may also advance the current record pointer to the next record in the file.

- *FindNext*—Searches for the next record in the file satisfying the search criterion. Transfers the block containing that record into a main memory buffer (if it is not already there). The record is located in the buffer and becomes the current record of the file.

- *Delete*—Deletes the current record of the file and (eventually) updates the file on disk to reflect the deletion.

- *Modify*—Modifies some field values for the current record of the file and (eventually) updates the file on disk to reflect the modification.

- *Insert*—Inserts a new record in the file by locating the block where the record is to be inserted, transferring that block into a main memory buffer (if it is not already there), writing the record into the buffer, and (eventually) writing the buffer to disk to reflect the insertion.

The above are called **record-at-a-time** operations because each operation applies to a single record. In some file systems, additional **set-at-a-time** higher-level operations may be applied to a file. Examples of some of these are:

- *FindAll*—Locates *all* the records in the file that satisfy a search criterion.
- *FindOrdered*—Retrieves all the records in the file in some specified order.
- *Reorganize*—As we shall see, some file organizations require periodic reorganization. This operation starts the reorganization process. An example is to reorder the file records by sorting them on a specified field.

Other operations are needed to prepare the file for access (Open) and to indicate that we are done with using the file (Close).

At this point, it is worthwhile to note the difference between the terms "file organization" and "access method." The latter is commonly used on IBM and other systems; for example, ISAM and HDAM are abbreviations for indexed sequential access method and hierarchical direct access method. A **file organization** refers to the organization of the data of a file into records, blocks, and access structures; this includes the way records are distributed on the storage medium and interlinked. An **access method,** on the other hand, consists of a group of programs that allow operations—such as those listed above—to be applied to a file. In general, it is possible to apply several different access methods to a file organization. Some access methods, though, can be applied only to files organized in certain ways. For example, we cannot apply an indexed access method to a file without an index (see Chapter 5).

Usually, we expect to use some search criteria more than others. In addition, some files may be **static,** meaning that update operations are rarely performed; other more **volatile** files may change frequently, so update operations are constantly applied to the file. A successful file organization should perform as efficiently as possible the operations we expect to *apply frequently* to the file. For example, consider the EMPLOYEE file described above, which stores the records for current employees in a company. We expect to insert new records (when employees are hired), delete records (when employees leave the company), and modify records (say, when an employee's salary is changed). Deleting or modifying a record requires a selection criterion to identify a particular record or set of records. Retrieving one or more records also requires a selection criterion. The expected users of the file should know how they intend to locate an employee record for retrieval or update, whether by NAME, SSN, or some other criterion.

If users expect mainly to apply a search criterion based on SSN, then we must choose a file organization that facilitates locating a record given its SSN value. We may physically order the records by SSN value or define an index on SSN (see Chapter 5). Suppose a second application uses the file to generate employee paychecks and requires that paychecks be grouped by department. For this application it is best to store all employee records having the same department value contiguously, packing them into blocks and perhaps ordering them by name within each department. However, this conflicts with ordering the records by SSN values. If possible, we should choose an organization that allows both operations to be done efficiently. Unfortunately, in many cases there may not be an organization that allows us to implement efficiently all needed operations on a file. For example, some file organizations make retrieval on some search criteria very efficient but make updating more expensive. In such cases we may choose some compromise organization that is not best for either operation but allows each to be performed reasonably; or we may choose an organization that is best for the operation we expect to apply most frequently.

In the following sections and in Chapter 5 we discuss different methods for organizing records of a file on disk. Several general techniques are frequently used to create access methods, such as ordering, hashing, and indexing. In addition, there are general techniques for handling insertions and deletions that work with many file organizations. In Section 4.6 we present the unordered records file organization; then we discuss files of ordered records in Section 4.7. Section 4.8 discusses file organizations based on hashing. Indexing techniques, which are organizations that store additional information on disk to speed up the search process, are discussed in Chapter 5.

4.6 Files of Unordered Records

In this simplest and most basic organization, records are placed in the file in the order in which they are inserted. New records are inserted at the end of the file. Such an organization is called a **heap** or **pile** file.* Unordered records are used when we want to collect and store data records for use in the future but do not yet know exactly how we will use them. Also, this organization is used with additional access paths, such as the secondary indexes discussed in Chapter 5.

Inserting a new record is *very efficient;* the last disk block of the file is copied into a buffer, the new record is added, and the block is then **rewritten** back to disk. The address of the last file block is kept in the file header. However, searching for a record on any search criterion involves a **linear search** through the file block by block, an expensive procedure. If only one record satisfies the search criterion, then, on the average, we will read into memory and search half the file blocks before we find the record. For a file of b blocks, this requires searching (b/2) blocks on the average. If several records satisfy the search criterion, we must read and search all b blocks in the file.

To delete a record, we must first search for it. Once it is found, the block containing the record will be in a buffer in main memory. We must delete the record from the buffer and then **rewrite the block** back to the disk. This leaves extra unused space in the disk block. Deleting a large number of records in this way results in wasted storage space. Another technique used for record deletion is to have an extra byte or bit, called a **deletion marker,** stored with each record. We delete a record by setting the deletion marker to a certain value. A different value of the marker indicates a valid (not deleted) record. If a deletion marker is used, search programs consider only valid records in a block when conducting their search. Both these deletion techniques require periodic **reorganization** of the file to claim the unused space of deleted records. During reorganization, the file

---

*Some file systems such as Digital Equipment Corporation's VAX RMS (Record Management Services) call this organization a sequential file.

blocks can be accessed consecutively and records are packed whenever unused space exists in a block. After such a reorganization, the blocks are filled to capacity once more. Another possibility is to use the space of deleted records when inserting new records, although this requires keeping track of empty locations and may increase insertion time.

We can use either spanned or unspanned organization for an unordered file and either fixed-length or variable-length records. Modifying a variable-length record may require deleting the old record and inserting a modified record because the modified record may not fit in its old space on disk.

To read all records in order of the values of some field, we first sort the records of the file in order of the required field, usually by creating a sorted copy of the file. Sorting is an expensive operation for a large disk file. Special **external sorting** techniques are used. A common method is a variation of the merge sort technique. First, the records within each block are sorted. Then sorted blocks are merged to create groups of sorted records each the size of two blocks. Each such group of sorted records is sometimes called a **run**. Following that, runs of two blocks are merged to form runs of four blocks, and so on until the final run is the completely sorted file.

For a file of unordered *fixed-length records* using *unspanned blocks* and *contiguous allocation*, it is straightforward to access any record by its **position** in the file. If the file records are numbered 0, 1, 2, ..., r − 1 and the records in each block are numbered 0, 1, ..., bfr − 1, where bfr is the blocking factor, then the ith record of the file is located in block (i div bfr) of the file, and is the (i mod bfr)th record in that block. Such a file is often called a **relative file*** because records can easily be accessed by their relative position in the file. Accessing a record by its position does not help locate a record based on a search criterion; however, it facilitates the construction of access paths on the file, such as the indexes discussed in Chapter 5.

4.7 Files of Ordered Records

We can physically order the records of a file on disk based on the values of one of their fields—called the **ordering field** of the file. This leads to an **ordered** or **sequential** file.** If the ordering field is also a **key field** of the file—a field guaranteed to have a unique value in each record—then the field is also called the **ordering key** for the file. Figure 4.7 shows an ordered file with NAME as the ordering key field (assuming employees have distinct names).

Ordering the records gives some advantages over unordered files. First, reading the records in order of the ordering field values becomes extremely efficient since no sorting is required. Also, finding the next record from the current one in order of the ordering field usually requires no additional block accesses because the next record will be in the same block as the current one (unless the current record is the last one in the block). A third advantage is that using a search criterion based on the value of an ordering key

---

*For example, VAX RMS (Record Management Services) calls this organization a relative file.
**Some file systems, such as Digital Equipment Corporation's VAX RMS system, use the term sequential file to denote the unordered file described in Section 4.6.

	NAME	SSN	BIRTHDATE	JOB	SALARY	SEX
block 1	Aaron, Ed					
	Abbott, Diane					
			⋮			
	Acosta, Marc					
block 2	Adams, John					
	Adams, Robin					
			⋮			
	Akers, Jan					
block 3	Alexander, Ed					
	Alfred, Bob					
			⋮			
	Allen, Sam					
block 4	Allen, Troy					
	Anders, Keith					
			⋮			
	Anderson, Rob					
block 5	Anderson, Zach					
	Angeli, Joe					
			⋮			
	Archer, Sue					
block 6	Arnold, Mack					
	Arnold, Steven					
			⋮			
	Atkins, Timothy					

⋮

	NAME	SSN	BIRTHDATE	JOB	SALARY	SEX
block n-1	Wong, James					
	Wood, Donald					
			⋮			
	Woods, Manny					
block n	Wright, Pam					
	Wyatt, Charles					
			⋮			
	Zimmer, Byron					

Figure 4.7   Some blocks of an ordered (sequential) file of EMPLOYEE records with NAME as the ordering field

field results in faster access by using the binary search technique, which is an improvement over linear search although it is not often used for disk files.

Binary search for disk files can be done on the blocks rather than on the records. Suppose the file has b blocks numbered 1, 2, ..., b, the records are ordered by ascending value of their ordering key field, and we are searching for a record whose ordering key field value is K. Assuming that disk addresses of the file blocks are available in the file header, binary search can be described by Algorithm 4.1. Binary search usually accesses $\log_2(b)$ blocks whether the record is found or not, an improvement over linear search, where on the average (b/2) blocks are accessed when the record is found and b blocks are accessed when the record is not found.

> **ALGORITHM 4.1**   Binary search on an ordering key of a
> disk file

```
l ← 1; u ← b; (* b is the number of file blocks*)
while (u > l) do
    begin i ← (l + u) div 2;
    read block i of the file into the buffer;
    if K < ordering field value of the first record in the block
    then u ← i - 1
    else if K > ordering field value of the last record in the block
        then l ← i + 1
        else if the record with ordering field value = K is in the buffer
            then goto found
            else goto notfound;
    end;
goto notfound;
```

A search criterion involving the conditions $>$, $<$, $\geq$, and $\leq$ on the ordering field is quite efficient because the physical ordering of records means that all records satisfying the condition are contiguous in the file. For example, referring to Figure 4.7, if the search criterion is (NAME < 'F')—where < means alphabetically before—the records satisfying the search criterion are those from the beginning of the file up to the first record that has a NAME value starting with the letter 'F'.

Ordering does not provide any advantages for random or ordered access of the records based on values of a *nonordering field* of the file. In these cases we do a linear search for random access, and to access the records in order based on a nonordering field it is preferable to sort the file on that field.

Inserting and deleting records are expensive for an ordered file because the records must remain physically ordered. To insert a new record, we must find its correct position in the file based on its ordering field value and then make space in the file to insert the record in that position. For a large file this can be very time consuming because, on the average, half the records of the file must be moved to make space for the new record. This means that half the file blocks must be read and rewritten after moving records among them. For record deletion the problem is less severe if we use deletion markers and reorganize the file periodically. However, if we physically delete the record from the file we have to move subsequent records to fill its location, which would make deletion as expensive as insertion.

One option for making insertion more efficient is to keep some unused space in each block for new records. However, once this space is used up, the original problem resurfaces. Another frequently used method is to create a temporary *unordered* file called an **overflow** or **transaction** file. With this technique, the actual ordered file is called the **main** or **master** file. New records are inserted at the end of the overflow file rather than in their correct position in the main file, thus saving the excessive time needed to move records around.

Periodically, the overflow file is merged with the master file during file reorganization. Insertion becomes very efficient but at the cost of increased complexity in the search algorithm. The overflow file must by searched using linear search if, after the binary search, the record is not found in the main file. For applications that do not require the most up-to-date information, overflow records can be ignored when searching.

Modifying a field value of a record depends on two factors: the search criterion to locate the record and the field to be modified. If the search criterion involves the ordering key field, we can locate the record using binary search; otherwise we must do a linear search. A nonordering field can be modified by changing the record and rewriting it in the same physical location on disk—assuming fixed-length records. On the other hand, modifying the ordering field means that the record can change its position in the file, which requires a deletion of the old record followed by an insertion of the modified record.

Reading the file records in order of the ordering field is quite efficient if we ignore the records in overflow, because we can read the blocks consecutively using double buffering. To include the records in overflow, we must merge them in their correct positions; in this case, we can first reorganize the file, then read its blocks sequentially. To reorganize the file, we first sort the records in the overflow file, then merge them with the master file. We also remove the records marked deleted during the reorganization.

Ordered files are not used often in database applications unless an additional access path, called a primary index, is included with the file. This further improves the random access time on the ordering key field. We will discuss indexes in Chapter 5.

4.8   Hashing Techniques

Another primary file organization is hashing, which provides very fast access to records on certain search criteria. This organization is usually called a **hash** or **direct** file.* The search criterion for fast access must be an equality condition on a single field, called the **hash field** of the file. Often, the hash field is also a key field of the file, in which case it is called the **hash key** of the file. The idea behind hashing is to provide a function h, called a **hash function** or **randomizing function,** which is applied to the hash field value of a record and yields the *address* of the disk block in which the record is stored. A search for the record within the block can be carried out in a main memory buffer. For most records, we need only a single block access to retrieve that record.

*In the VAX RMS file system of Digital Equipment Corporation, the term **direct access** refers to accessing a relative file by record position.

Hashing is also used as an internal data structure within a program whenever we need a small temporary file of records that we access exclusively using the value of one field. We first describe the use of hashing for internal files in Section 4.8.1 and then show how we modify it to store external files on disk in Section 4.8.2. In Section 4.8.3 we discuss techniques for extending hashing to dynamically growing files; these techniques include linear hashing, dynamic hashing, and extendible hashing.

4.8.1   Internal Hashing

For internal files, we usually implement hashing by using an array of records. Suppose the array index range is from 0 to $M - 1$ (Figure 4.8a); then we have M **slots** whose addresses correspond to the array indexes. We choose a hash function that transforms the hash field value into an integer between 0 and $M - 1$. One common hash function is the $h(K)$ = K **mod M** function, which returns the remainder of an integer hash field value K after division by M; this value is then used for the record address.

Noninteger hash field values can be transformed to integers before applying the mod function. For character strings, we can use the numeric codes associated with characters in the transformation, for example, by multiplying those code values. For a hash field whose data type is a string of 20 characters, Algorithm 4.2a can be used to calculate the hash address. We assume that the code function returns the numeric code of a character and that we are given a hash field value K of type array [1..20] of char.

ALGORITHMS 4.2   Illustrating some simple hashing algorithms. (a) Applying the mod hash function to a character string. (b) Collision resolution by open addressing.

```
a)  temp ← 1;
    for i ← 1 to 20 do temp ← temp * code(K[i]);
    hash_address ← temp mod M;

b)  i ← hash_address;
    if location i is occupied
      then begin i ← (i + 1) mod M;
            while (i ≠ hash_address) and location i is occupied
                  do i ← (i +1) mod M;
            if (i = hash_address) then all positions are full
                        else new_hash_address ← i;
    end;
```

Other hashing functions can be used. One technique, called **folding,** involves applying an arithmetic function such as addition or a logical function such as "exclusive or" to different portions of the hash field value to calculate the hash address. Another technique involves picking some digits of the hash field value—for example, the third, fifth, and eighth digits—to form the hash address. The problem with most hashing functions is that they do not guarantee that distinct values will hash to distinct addresses, because the **hash field space**—the number of possible values a hash field can take—is usually much larger than the **address space**—the number of available addresses for records. The hashing function maps the hash field space to the address space.

A **collision** occurs when the hash field value of a new record being inserted hashes to an address that already contains a different record. We must insert the new record in

(a)

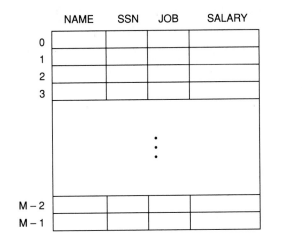

(b)

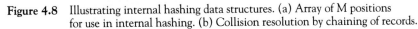

- null pointer = −1
- overflow pointer refers to position of
  next record in linked list

Figure 4.8   Illustrating internal hashing data structures. (a) Array of M positions
for use in internal hashing. (b) Collision resolution by chaining of records.

some other position since its hash address is occupied. The process of finding another
position in which to insert the new record is called **collision resolution**. There are numerous methods for collision resolution, including the following:

- *Open addressing*—Proceeding from the occupied position specified by the hash
  address, we check the subsequent positions in order until an unused (empty) position is found. Algorithm 4.2b may be used.

- *Chaining*—For this method, we must keep a number of overflow locations, usually by extending the array with a number of overflow positions. In addition, a pointer field is added to each record location. We resolve a collision by placing the new record in an unused overflow location and setting the pointer of the occupied hash address location to the address of that overflow location. We maintain a linked list of overflow records for each hash address, as shown in Figure 4.8b.
- *Multiple hashing*—We may apply a second hash function if the first results in a collision. If we get another collision, we may use open addressing or apply a third hash function and then use open addressing if necessary.

Each collision resolution method will require its own algorithms for insertion, retrieval, and deletion of records. The algorithms for chaining are the simplest. Deletion algorithms for open addressing are rather tricky. Knuth (1973) and other data structures textbooks discuss hashing algorithms in more detail.

The goal of a good hashing function is to distribute the records uniformly over the address space so as to minimize collisions while not leaving many unused locations. Simulation and analysis studies have shown that it is usually best to keep a hash table between 70 and 90% full so that the number of collisions remains low and we do not waste too much space. Hence, if we expect to have r records to store in the table, we should choose M locations for the address space such that (r/M) is between 0.7 and 0.9. It may also be useful to choose a prime number for M since it has been demonstrated that this distributes the hash addresses better over the address space when the mod hashing function is used. Other hash functions may require M to be a power of 2.

4.8.2   External Hashing

Hashing for disk files is called **external hashing**. We can modify the hashing method to suit the characteristics of disk storage by taking advantage of the fact that data records are stored in blocks on disk rather than separately in single locations. We call each block a **bucket**. Sometimes a cluster of blocks rather than a single block is used for a bucket. Rather than specifying an address for each single record, we specify a **bucket address**. Usually, the hashing function provides a relative bucket number rather than an absolute block address for the bucket. A table maintained in the file header can provide the corresponding disk block addresses, as illustrated in Figure 4.9

The collision problem is less severe with buckets because as many records as will fit in a bucket can hash to the same bucket address without causing problems. However, we must have provisions for the case where a bucket is filled to capacity and a new record being inserted hashes to that bucket. We can use a variation of chaining by maintaining a pointer in each bucket to a linked list of overflow records for the bucket, as shown in Figure 4.10. The pointers in the linked list should be **record pointers,** which include both a block address and a relative record position within the block.

Although hashing provides the fastest possible access for retrieving an arbitrary record given the value of its hash field, it is not very useful when other applications are required of the same file unless additional access paths are constructed. For example, if we require the retrieval of records in order of their hash field values, hashing is not very suitable, since the majority of good hash functions do not maintain records in order of

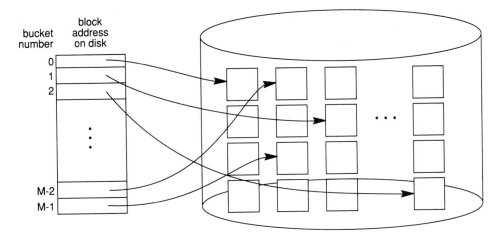

Figure 4.9 Matching bucket numbers to disk blocks

hash field values. Some hash functions can maintain the order of records by hash field values in the file to some extent. A simple example is to take the leftmost three digits of an invoice number field as hash address and keep the records sorted by invoice number within each bucket. Another example is to use an integer hash key directly as an index to a relative file if the hash key values fill up a particular interval; for example, if employee numbers in a company are assigned as 1, 2, 3, ... up to the number of employees, we can use the identity hash function that maintains order; unfortunately, this does not occur often.

Another drawback of hashing is the fixed amount of space allocated to the file. Suppose we allocate M buckets for the address space and let m be the maximum number of records that can fit in one bucket; then at most m*M records will fit in the allocated space. If the number of records turns out to be substantially less than m*M, we have a lot of unused space allocated to the file. On the other hand, if the number of records increases to substantially more than m*M, numerous collisions will result and retrieval will be slowed down because of the long lists of overflow records. In either case, we may have to change the number of blocks allocated and redistribute the records among the buckets using a different hashing function. Newer file organizations based on hashing allow the number of buckets to vary dynamically; we discuss some of these techniques in Section 4.8.3.

In regular external hashing, searching for a record given a value of some field other than the hash field is as expensive as in the case of an unordered file—we must do a linear search. Record deletion can be implemented by removing the record from its bucket. If the bucket has an overflow chain, we can move one of the overflow records into the bucket to replace the deleted record in the block. If the record to be deleted is already in overflow, we simply remove it from the linked list. Note that removing an overflow record means we should keep track of empty positions in overflow. This is easily done by maintaining a linked list of unused overflow locations.

Modifying a field value of a record depends on two factors: the search criterion to locate the record and the field to be modified. If the search criterion is an equality com-

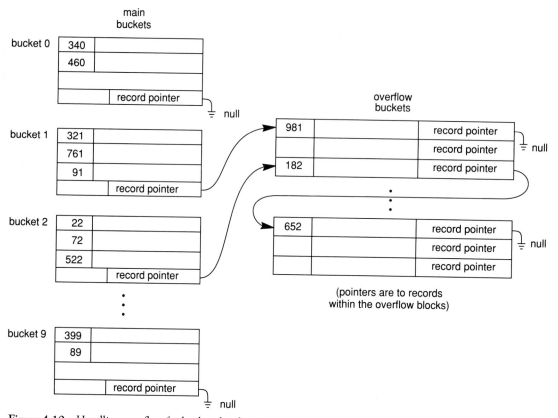

Figure 4.10   Handling overflow for buckets by chaining

parison on the hash field, we can locate the record efficiently using the hashing function; otherwise we must do a linear search. A nonhash field can be modified by changing the record and rewriting it in the same physical location on disk—assuming fixed-length records. On the other hand, modifying the hash field means that the record can move to another bucket, which requires a deletion of the old record followed by an insertion of the modified record.

4.8.3   Hashing Techniques That Allow Dynamic File Expansion

A major drawback of the hashing scheme discussed above is that the hash address space is fixed. Hence, it is difficult to expand or shrink the file dynamically. The schemes described in this section attempt to remedy this situation. The first two schemes—dynamic hashing and extendible hashing—store an access structure in addition to the file, and hence are similar to indexing (Chapter 5). The main difference is that the access structure is based on the values that result after applying the hash function to the search field. In indexing, the access structure is based on the value of the search field itself. The third technique—linear hashing—does not require any additional access paths.

These hashing schemes take advantage of the fact that the result of the hashing function is usually a nonnegative integer and hence can be represented as a binary number. The access structure is built on the **binary representation** of the result of applying the hashing function to the hash field value of a record, which is a string of **bits**. We call this the **hash value** of a record. Records are distributed among buckets based on the values of the leading bits in their hash values.

Dynamic Hashing

In dynamic hashing the number of buckets is not fixed as in regular hashing but grows or diminishes as needed. The file can start with a single bucket; once that bucket is full, and a new record is inserted, the bucket **overflows** and is split into two buckets. The records are distributed among the two buckets based on the value of the first bit of their hash values. All records whose hash values start with a 0 bit are stored in one bucket, and all those whose hash values start with a 1 bit are stored in the other bucket.

At this point, a binary tree structure called a **directory** (or **index**) is built, which has two types of nodes:

- **Internal nodes** guide the search; each has a left pointer corresponding to a 0 bit and a right pointer corresponding to a 1 bit.
- **Leaf nodes** hold a pointer to a bucket—a bucket address. Figure 4.11 illustrates a directory and the buckets of the data file.

ALGORITHM 4.3   Illustrating the search procedure for dynamic hashing

```
h ← hash value of record;
t ← root node of directory;
i ← 1;
while t is an internal node of the directory do
  begin
  if the iᵗʰ bit of h is a 0
    then t ← left son of t
    else t ← right son of t;
  i ← i + 1
  end;
search the bucket whose address is in node t;
```

The search for a record proceeds as in Algorithm 4.3. The directory can be stored on disk blocks if it becomes large; otherwise, it can be stored in main memory. If the directory does not fit in one block, it is distributed over two or more levels. Note that directory entries are quite compact. Each internal node holds a tag bit to specify the type of node, plus the left and right pointers. A parent pointer may also be needed. Each leaf node holds a bucket address. Special representations of binary trees can be used to reduce the space needed by left, right, and parent pointers of internal nodes. In general, if a directory of x levels is stored on disk, we need x + 1 block accesses to retrieve a bucket.

If a bucket overflows, it is split into two, and the records are distributed based on the next significant bit in their hash value. For example, if a new record is inserted into the bucket for records whose hash values start with 10—the fourth bucket in Figure 4.11—and causes overflow, then all records whose hash value starts with 100 are placed in the first split bucket and the second bucket contains those whose hash value

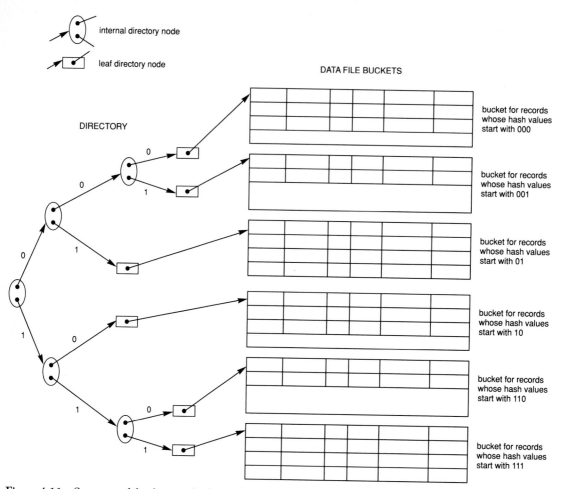

Figure 4.11   Structure of the dynamic hashing schema

starts with 101. The directory is expanded with a new internal node to reflect the split; this node points to two leaf nodes that point to the two buckets. The levels of the binary tree can then expand dynamically.

If the hash function distributes the records uniformly, the directory tree will be balanced. Buckets can be combined if one becomes empty or if the total number of records in two neighboring buckets can fit in a single bucket. In this case, the directory loses an internal node and the two leaf nodes are combined to a single leaf node that points to the new bucket. The levels of the binary tree can shrink dynamically.

Extendible Hashing

In extendible hashing a different type of **directory**—an array of 2^d bucket addresses—is maintained, where d is called the **global depth** of the directory. The first (high-order) d bits of a hash value determine a directory entry, and the address in that entry determines the bucket in which the corresponding records are stored. However, there does not have to be a distinct bucket for each of the 2^d directory locations. Several directory locations with the same first d' bits for their hash values may contain the same bucket address if all the records that hash to these locations fit in a single bucket. A **local depth** d'—stored with each bucket—specifies the number of bits on which the bucket contents are based. Figure 4.12 shows a directory with global depth d = 3.

The value of d can be increased or decreased by one at a time, thus doubling or halving the number of entries in the directory. Doubling is needed if a bucket using the full d bits for identification overflows. Halving occurs if none of the buckets needs the full d bits for identification. Most record retrievals will require two block accesses, one to the directory and the other to the bucket.

To illustrate bucket splitting, suppose a new record is inserted in the bucket for the records whose hash values start with 01—the third bucket in Figure 4.12 causing overflow. We distribute the records among two buckets; the first contains all records whose hash value starts with 010 and the second contains those whose hash value starts with

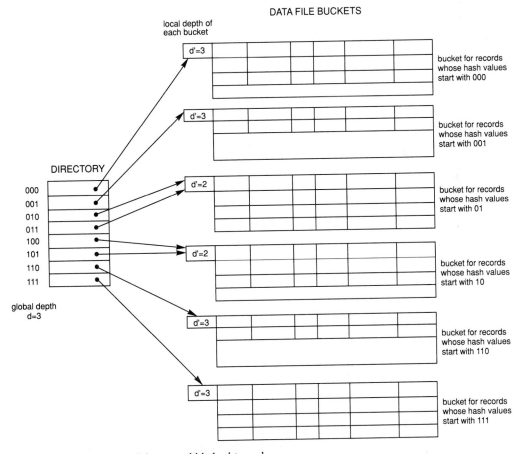

Figure 4.12 Structure of the extendible hashing scheme

011. Now the two directory locations for 010 and 011 point to the two new distinct buckets. Before the split, they pointed to the same bucket that contained all records whose hash value started with 01. The local depth d' of the two new buckets is one more than the local depth of the old bucket; in our example, the new local depth becomes 3.

If a bucket that overflows and is split had a local depth equal to the global depth of the directory, then the size of the directory must be doubled because we must now use an extra bit to distinguish the buckets. For example, if the bucket for records whose hash value starts with 111 in Figure 4.12 overflows, the two new buckets need a directory with global depth $d = 4$ because the two buckets are now addressed as 1110 and 1111, and hence their local depths are both 4. The directory size is hence doubled, and each of the other original locations in the directory is split into two locations, both of which have the same pointer as that in the original location.

Linear Hashing

The idea behind linear hashing is to allow a hash file to expand and shrink its number of buckets dynamically *without* needing a directory. Suppose the file starts with M buckets numbered 0, 1, ..., M − 1 and uses the mod hash function $h(K) = K \bmod M$; this hash function is called the initial hash function h_0. Overflow because of collisions is still handled by chaining. However, when a collision does occur leading to an overflow record in *any* file bucket, the *first* bucket in the file, bucket 0, is split into two buckets—the original bucket 0 and a new bucket M at the end of the file. The records originally in bucket 0 are distributed among the two buckets based on a different hashing function $h_1(K) = K \bmod 2M$. Any records that hashed to bucket 0 based on h_0 will hash to either bucket 0 or bucket M based on h_1; this is necessary for linear hashing to work.

As further collisions leading to overflow records occur, additional buckets are split in the *linear* order 1, 2, 3, ... If enough overflows occur, all file buckets are split, so the records in overflow are redistributed into regular buckets using the function h_1 via a *delayed split* of their buckets. We do not need any directory—only a value n is needed to determine which buckets have been split. For retrieving a record with hash key value K, we first apply the function h_0 to K; if $h_0(K) < n$, we then use the function h_1 on K because the bucket is already split. Initially, $n = 0$, indicating that the function h_0 applies to all buckets; n grows linearly as buckets are split.

When $n = M$, all the original buckets have been split and the hash function h_1 applies to all records in the file. At this point, n is reset to 0 (zero), and any new collisions causing overflow lead to the use of a new hashing function $h_2(K) = K \bmod 4M$. In general, a sequence of hashing functions $h_j(K) = K \bmod (2^j M)$ is used, where j = 0, 1, 2, ... ; a new hashing function h_{j+1} is needed whenever all the buckets 0, 1, ..., $(2^j M) - 1$ have been split and n is reset to 0. The search for a record with hash key value K is given by Algorithm 4.4.

Buckets that have been split can also be combined back if the load of the file falls below a certain threshold. In general, the file load l can be defined as $l = r/(bfr*N)$, where r is the current number of file records, bfr is the maximum number of records that can fit in a bucket, and N is the current number of file buckets. Blocks are combined linearly and n is decremented appropriately. In fact, the file load can be used to trigger

ALGORITHM 4.4   Illustrating the search procedure for linear
hashing

```
if n = 0
    then m ← hⱼ(K) (* m is the hash value of record with hash key K *)
    else   begin
             m ← hⱼ(K);
             if m<n then m ← hⱼ₊₁ (K)
           end;
search the bucket whose hash value is m (and its overflow, if any);
```

both splits and combinations; in this manner the file load can be kept within a desired range. Splits can be triggered when the load exceeds a certain threshold, say 0.9, and combinations can be triggered when the load falls below another threshold, say 0.7.

4.9   Files of Mixed Records

The file organizations we studied so far assume that all records of a particular file are of the same record type. The records could be of EMPLOYEEs, PROJECTs, STUDENTs, or DEPARTMENTs, but each file contains records of only one type. In most database applications we encounter situations where there are numerous types of entities that are interrelated in various ways, as we saw in Chapter 3. Relationships among records in various files can be represented by **connecting fields**. For example, a STUDENT record can have a connecting field MAJORDEPT whose value gives the name of the DEPARTMENT in which the student is majoring. This MAJORDEPT field *refers* to a department entity, which should be represented by a record of its own in the DEPARTMENT file. If we want to retrieve field values from two related records, we must retrieve one of the records first. Then we can use its connecting field value to retrieve the related record in the other file. Hence, relationships are implemented by **logical field references** among the records in distinct files.

File organizations in hierarchical and network DBMSs implement relationships among records as **physical relationships** realized by physical contiguity of related records or by physical pointers. These file organizations allow a single file to have records of more than one type so that records of different record types can be physically related. If a particular relationship is expected to be used very frequently to retrieve related records of different types, implementing the relationship physically can increase the efficiency of retrieving related records. There are two main organizations for mixed files—**hierarchical files** and **ring files**. We will discuss these in Chapters 10 and 11 when we present the hierarchical and network data models. We use a simple example here to illustrate each type of organization.

Figure 4.13a illustrates how a file of mixed records implements relationships by physical contiguity. This is an example of a hierarchical file. A COURSE record is followed by its PREREQUISITE records. This is followed by each SECTION record of the course along with its own related records of types STUDENT and INSTRUCTOR. Each SECTION record is in turn followed by an INSTRUCTOR record (who taught the course) followed by a sequence of STUDENT records (one for each student who completed the course).

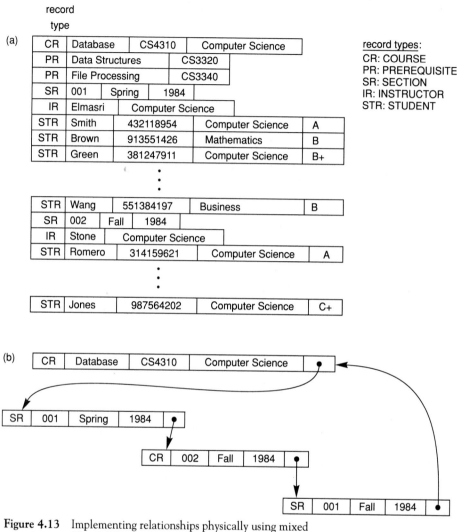

record types:
CR: COURSE
PR: PREREQUISITE
SR: SECTION
IR: INSTRUCTOR
STR: STUDENT

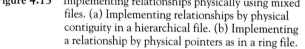

Figure 4.13 Implementing relationships physically using mixed files. (a) Implementing relationships by physical contiguity in a hierarchical file. (b) Implementing a relationship by physical pointers as in a ring file.

To distinguish the records in a mixed file, each record has—in addition to its field values—a **record type** field, which specifies the type of record. This is typically the first field in each record and is used by the system software to determine the type of record it is about to process. Using the catalog information, the DBMS can determine the fields of that record type and their sizes in order to interpret the record data.

Figure 4.13b shows how relationships may be implemented by pointers; a record of type COURSE points to a linked list of records of type SECTION related to it. Usually, a pointer back to the COURSE is placed in the last record in the linked list—hence the term ring file.

4.10   Summary

In this chapter we started by discussing the characteristics of secondary storage devices. We concentrated on magnetic disks because they are used most often to store on-line database files. Data on disk is stored in blocks, and accessing a disk block is expensive because of the seek time, rotational delay, and block transfer time. Double buffering can be used when accessing consecutive disk blocks to reduce block access time.

We discussed different ways of storing records of a file on disk. Records of a file are grouped into disk blocks and can be of fixed length or variable length, spanned or unspanned, same record type or mixed. We discussed the file header, which describes the record formats and keeps track of the disk addresses of the file blocks. Information in the file header is used by system software accessing the file records.

We then presented a set of typical commands for accessing individual file records and discussed the concept of the current record of a file. We discussed how complex record selection criteria are transformed into search conditions that are used to locate records in the file.

Three primary file organizations were discussed: unordered, ordered, and hashed. Unordered files require a linear search to locate records, but record insertion is very simple. We discussed the deletion problem and the use of deletion markers.

Ordered files improve the time to read records in order of the ordering field. The time to search for an arbitrary record given the value of its ordering field is also reduced if binary search is used. However, maintaining the records in order makes insertion very expensive, and the technique of using an overflow file to reduce the cost of record insertion was discussed. Overflow records are merged with the master file periodically during file reorganization.

Hashing provides very fast access to an arbitrary record of a file given the value of its hash field. The most suitable method for external hashing is the bucket technique, with one or more contiguous blocks corresponding to each bucket. Collisions causing bucket overflow are usually handled by chaining. Access on any nonhash field is slow; so is sequential access of the records on any field. We then discussed hashing techniques that allow the file to expand and shrink dynamically, including dynamic, extendible, and linear hashing.

Finally, we briefly discussed files of mixed records—hierarchical files and ring files, which implement relationships among records of different types physically as part of the storage structure.

Review Questions

4.1. What is the difference between primary and secondary storage?

4.2. Why are disks and not tapes used to store on-line database files?

4.3. Define the following terms: disk, disk pack, track, block, cylinder, sector, interblock gap, read/write head.

4.4. Discuss the process of disk initialization.

4.5. Discuss the mechanism used to read data from or write data to the disk.

4.6. What are the components of a block address?

4.7. Why is accessing a disk block expensive? Discuss the time components involved in accessing a disk block.

4.8. How does double buffering improve block access time?

4.9. What are the different reasons for having variable-length records? What type of separator characters are needed for each?

4.10. Discuss the different techniques for allocating file blocks on disk.

4.11. What is the difference between a file organization and an access method?

4.12. What is the difference between a selection criterion and a search criterion?

4.13. What are the typical record-at-a-time operations for accessing a file? Which of these depend on the current record of a file?

4.14. Discuss the different techniques for record deletion.

4.15. Discuss the advantages and disadvantages of using an (a) unordered file, (b) ordered file, and (c) regular hash file with buckets and chaining. Which operations can be efficiently performed on each of these organizations and which operations are expensive?

4.16. Discuss the different techniques for allowing a hash file to expand and shrink dynamically. What do you think are the advantages and disadvantages of each?

4.17. What are mixed files used for? What are the two main types of mixed files and in what type of DBMS is each used?

Exercises

4.18. Consider a disk with the following characteristics (these are not parameters of any particular disk unit): block size B = 512 bytes, interblock gap size G = 128 bytes, number of blocks per track = 20, number of tracks per surface = 400. A disk pack consists of 15 double-sided disks.

  a. What is the total capacity of a track and what is its useful capacity (excluding interblock gaps)?

  b. How many cylinders are there?

  c. What are the total capacity and the useful capacity of a cylinder?

  d. What are the total capacity and the useful capacity of a disk pack?

  e. Suppose the disk drive rotates the disk pack at a speed of 2400 rpm (revolutions per minute); what are the transfer rate in bytes/msec and the block transfer time btt in msec? What is the average rotational delay rd in msec? What is the bulk transfer rate (see Appendix A)?

  f. Suppose the average seek time is 30 msec. How much time does it take (on the average) in msec to locate and transfer a single block given its block address?

  g. Calculate the average time it would take to transfer 20 random blocks and compare it with the time it would take to transfer 20 consecutive blocks using double buffering to save seek time and rotational delay.

4.19. A file has r = 20,000 STUDENT records of *fixed length*. Each record has the following fields: NAME (30 bytes), SSN (9 bytes), ADDRESS (40 bytes), PHONE (9 bytes), BIRTHDATE (8 bytes), SEX (1 byte), MAJORDEPTCODE (4 bytes), MINORDEPTCODE (4 bytes), CLASSCODE (4 bytes, integer), and DEGREEPROGRAM (3 bytes). An additional byte is used as a deletion marker. The file is stored on the disk whose parameters are given in Exercise 4.18.

    a. Calculate the record size R in bytes.

    b. Calculate the blocking factor bfr and the number of file blocks b assuming an unspanned organization.

    c. Calculate the average time it takes to find a record by doing a linear search on the file if (i) the file blocks are stored contiguously and double buffering is used and (ii) the file blocks are not stored contiguously.

    d. Assume the file is ordered by SSN; calculate the time it takes to search for a record given its SSN value by doing a binary search.

4.20. Suppose only 80% of the STUDENT records have a value for PHONE, 85% for MAJORDEPTCODE, 15% for MINORDEPTCODE, and 90% for DEGREEPROGRAM and we use a variable-length record file. Each record has a 1-byte *field type* for each field occurring in the record, plus the 1-byte deletion marker and a 1-byte end-of-record marker. Suppose we use a *spanned* record organization, where each block has a 5-byte pointer to the next block (this space is not used for record storage).

    a. Calculate the average record length R in bytes.

    b. Calculate the number of blocks needed for the file.

4.21. Consider a sequential file on *magnetic tape* with CUSTOMER records. Each record is 400 bytes and includes a customer Number, Name, Address, Phone, etc. There are 1000 customer records.

    a. What is involved in adding 5 new customer records to the file?

    b. What is involved in adding a new variable-length field of maximum size 20 bytes to each record in the file?

    c. With a tape density of 6400 bytes per inch and gaps of 3/4 inch each, calculate how much space is occupied on the tape and the percentage of the space occupied by data records if (i) no blocking is used, (ii) the blocking factor is 10, and (iii) the blocking factor is 32.

    d. Each customer has roughly 100 transactions (orders, payments, returns, etc.) per year. Suggest two alternatives for keeping the transaction data associated with each customer master record. You may embed this data in the master file or keep additional files.

4.22. A PARTS file with Part# as hash key includes records with the following Part# values: 2369, 3760, 4692, 4871, 5659, 1821, 1074, 7115, 1620, 2428, 3943, 4750, 6975. The file uses 8 buckets, numbered 0 to 7. Each bucket is one disk block and holds two records. Load these records into the file in the given order using the hash function h(K) = K mod 8. Calculate the average number of block accesses for a random retrieval on Part#.

4.23. Load the records of Exercise 4.22 into expandable hash files based on (i) dynamic hashing and (ii) extendible hashing. Show the structure of the directory at each step. For extendible hashing, show the global and local depths at each stage.

4.24. Load the records of Exercise 4.22 into an expandable hash file using linear hashing. Start with a single disk block using the hash function $h_0 = K \bmod 2^0$ and show how the file grows and the hash functions change as the records are inserted. Assume blocks are split whenever an overflow occurs, and show the value of n at each stage.

4.25. Compare the file commands listed in Section 4.5 to those available on a file access method you are familiar with.

4.26. Suppose we have an unordered file of fixed-length records that uses an unspanned record organization. Specify algorithms for insertion, deletion, and modification of a file record. State any assumptions you make.

4.27. Suppose we have an ordered file of fixed-length records and an unordered overflow file to handle insertion. Both files use unspanned records. Specify algorithms for insertion, deletion, and modification of a file record and for reorganizing the file. State any assumptions you make.

4.28. Can you think of techniques other than an unordered overflow file that can be used to make insertion in an ordered file more efficient?

4.29. Suppose we have a hash file of fixed-length records and overflow is handled by chaining. Specify algorithms for insertion, deletion, and modification of a file record. State any assumptions you make.

4.30. Can you think of techniques other than chaining to handle bucket overflow in external hashing?

4.31. Write program code that can be used to access individual fields of records under each of the following circumstances. For each case, state the assumptions you make concerning pointers, separator characters, etc. Also, determine the type of information needed in the file header for your code to be completely general in each case.

   a. Fixed-length records with unspanned blocking.

   b. Fixed-length records with spanned blocking.

   c. Variable-length records with variable-length fields and spanned blocking.

   d. Variable-length records with repeating groups and spanned blocking.

   e. Variable-length records with variable fields and spanned blocking.

   f. Variable-length records that allow all three cases in c, d, and e.

Selected Bibliography

Wiederhold (1983) has a detailed discussion and analysis of secondary storage devices and file organizations. Other textbooks, listed in the bibliography at the end of Chapters 1 and 2, include discussions of the material presented here. Most data structures textbooks discuss hashing in more detail, including Knuth (1973), which has a complete discussion of hash functions and collision resolution techniques as well as their performance comparison. Knuth also discusses in detail techniques for sorting external files.

Morris (1968) is an early paper on hashing. Dynamic hashing is due to Larson (1978) and extendible hashing is described in Fagin et al. (1979). Linear hashing is described by Litwin (1980), and its predecessor technique of virtual hashing is described in Litwin (1978). Bachman (1969) discusses ring files.

Several textbooks have appeared whose main topic is file organizations and access methods, including those by Claybrook (1983), Smith and Barnes (1987), Miller (1987), and Livadas (1989).

CHAPTER 5

Index Structures for Files

In Chapter 4 we described three primary methods for organizing records of a file on disk—as unordered, ordered, and hashed records. Of these, only dynamic hashing and extendible hashing require additional data structures—the directories—to be stored on disk to speed up retrieval of the desired records. In general, hashing methods allocate more space than is strictly necessary and utilize a computational procedure—the hashing function—to make access on the hash field very efficient. The techniques we discuss in this chapter require additional data structures, called **indexes,** to be stored on disk. Indexes make the search for records based on certain fields, called the **indexing fields,** more efficient. Indexes can themselves be considered as *auxiliary* files whose only purpose is to speed up record access. We will refer to the actual file that contains the data records as the **data** or **main** file to distinguish it from the index.

We describe different types of single-level indexes—primary, secondary, and clustering—in Section 5.1. In Section 5.2 we show how the single-level indexes can themselves be viewed as ordered files, and we describe the concept of multilevel indexes. We describe B-trees and B^+-trees, which are commonly used to implement dynamically changing multilevel indexes, in Section 5.3.

5.1 Types of Indexes

The idea behind an index access structure is similar to that behind the indexes used commonly in textbooks. A textbook index lists important terms at the end of the book in alphabetic order. Along with each term, a list of page numbers where the term appears is given. We can search the index to find a list of *addresses*—page numbers in this case—and use these addresses to locate the term in the textbook by *searching* the specified pages. The alternative, if no other guidance is given, is to sift slowly through the whole textbook word by word to find the term we are interested in, which corresponds to doing a linear search on a file. Of course, most books do have additional information, such as chapter and section titles, which can help us find a term without having to search through the whole book. However, the index is the only exact indication of where each term occurs in the book.

An index is usually defined on a single field of a file, called an **indexing field**. The index typically stores each value of the index field along with a list of pointers to all disk blocks that contain a record with that field value. The values in the index are ordered so that we can do a binary search on the index. The index file is much smaller than the data file, so searching the index using binary search is reasonably efficient. Multilevel indexing does away with the need for binary search at the expense of creating indexes to the index itself! Multilevel indexing is discussed in Section 5.2.

There are several types of indexes. A **primary index** is an index specified on the *ordering key field* of an ordered file of records. Recall from Section 4.7 that an ordering key field is used to *physically order* the file records on disk, and every record has a *unique value* for that field. If the ordering field is not a key field—that is, several records in the file can have the same value for the ordering field—another type of index, called a **clustering index,** can be used. Notice that a file can have *at most one* physical ordering field, so it can have at most one primary index or one clustering index, *but not both.* A third type of index, called a **secondary index,** can be specified on any *nonordering* field of a file. A file can have several secondary indexes in addition to its primary access method. In the next three subsections we discuss these three types of indexes.

5.1.1 Primary Indexes

A **primary index** is an ordered file whose records are of fixed length with two fields. The first field is of the same data type as the ordering key field of the data file, and the second field is a pointer to a disk block—a block address. The ordering key field is called the **primary key** of the data file. There is one **index entry** (or **index record**) in the index file for each *block* in the data file. Each index entry has the value of the primary key field for the *first* record in a block and a pointer to that block as its two field values. We will refer to the two field values of index entry i as <K(i), P(i)>.

To create a primary index on the ordered file shown in Figure 4.7, we use the NAME field as primary key, because that is the ordering key field of the file (assuming that each value of NAME is unique). Each entry in the index will have a NAME value and a pointer. The first three index entries would be:

<K(1) = (Aaron,Ed), P(1) = address of block 1>
<K(2) = (Adams,John), P(2) = address of block 2>
<K(3) = (Alexander,Ed), P(3) = address of block 3>

Figure 5.1 illustrates this primary index. The total number of entries in the index will be the same as the *number of disk blocks* in the ordered data file. The first record in each block of the data file is called the **anchor record** of the block, or simply the **block anchor.*** A primary index is an example of what is called a **nondense index** because it includes an entry for each disk block of the data file rather than for *every record* in the data file. A **dense index,** on the other hand, contains an entry for every record in the file.

---

*We can use a scheme similar to the one described here with the last record in each block, rather than the first, as the block anchor.

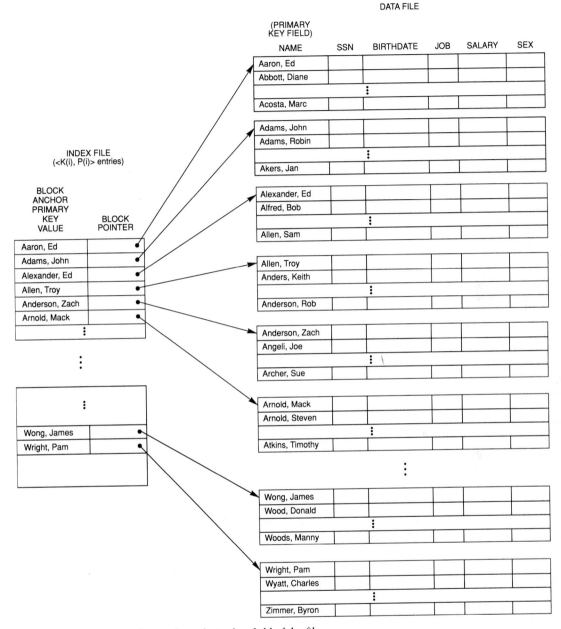

Figure 5.1 Primary index on the ordering key field of the file shown in Figure 4.8

The index file for a primary index needs substantially fewer blocks than the data file for two reasons. First, there are *fewer index entries* than there are records in the data file because an entry exists for each whole block of the data file rather than for each record. Second, each index entry is typically *smaller in size* than a data record because it has only two fields, so more index entries than data records will fit in one block. A binary search on the index file will hence require fewer block accesses than a binary search on the data file.

A record whose primary key value is K will be in the block whose address is P(i), where $K(i) \leq K < K(i + 1)$. The ith block in the data file contains all such records because of the physical ordering of the file records on the primary key field. Hence, to retrieve a record given the value K of its primary key field, we do a binary search on the index file to find the appropriate index entry i, then retrieve the data file block whose address is P(i). Notice that the above formula would not be correct if the data file was ordered on a *nonkey field* that allows multiple records to have the same ordering field value. In that case the same index value as that in the block anchor could be repeated in the last records of the previous block. Example 1 illustrates the saving in block accesses when using an index to search for a record.

EXAMPLE 1: Suppose we have an ordered file with r = 30,000 records stored on a disk with block size B = 1024 bytes. File records are of fixed size and unspanned with record length R = 100 bytes. The blocking factor for the file would be bfr = $\lfloor (B/R) \rfloor$ = $\lfloor (1024/100) \rfloor$ = 10 records per block. The number of blocks needed for the file is b = $\lceil (r/bfr) \rceil$ = $\lceil (30,000/10) \rceil$ = 3000 blocks. A binary search on the data file would need approximately $\lceil (\log_2 b) \rceil$ = $\lceil (\log_2 3000) \rceil$ = 12 block accesses.

Now suppose the ordering key field of the file is V = 9 bytes long, a block pointer is P = 6 bytes long, and we construct a primary index for the file. The size of each index entry is R_i = (9 + 6) = 15 bytes, so the blocking factor for the index is bfr_i = $\lfloor (B/R_i) \rfloor$ = $\lfloor (1024/15) \rfloor$ = 68 entries per block. The total number of index entries r_i is equal to the number of blocks in the data file, which is 3000. The number of blocks needed for the index is hence b_i = $\lceil (r_i/bfr_i) \rceil$ = $\lceil (3000/68) \rceil$ = 45 blocks. To perform a binary search on the index file would need $\lceil (\log_2 b_i) \rceil$ = $\lceil (\log_2 45) \rceil$ = 6 block accesses. To search for a record using the index, we need one additional block access to the data file for a total of 6 + 1 = 7 block accesses—an improvement over binary search on the data file, which required 12 block accesses.

A major problem with a primary index—as with any ordered file—is insertion and deletion of records. We already discussed this in Section 4.7. With a primary index, the problem is compounded because if we attempt to insert a record in its correct position in the data file, we not only have to move records to make space for the new record but also have to change some index entries because moving records will change the anchor records of some blocks. We can use an unordered overflow file, as discussed in Section 4.7, to reduce this problem. Another possibility is to use a linked list of overflow records for each block in the data file. This is similar to the method of dealing with overflow records described with hashing in Section 4.8.2. We can keep the records within each block and its overflow linked list sorted to improve retrieval time. Record deletion can be handled using deletion markers.

5.1.2   Clustering Indexes

If records of a file are physically ordered on a nonkey field that *does not have a distinct value* for each record, that field is called the **clustering field** of the file. We can create a different type of index, called a **clustering index,** to speed up retrieval of records that have the same value for the clustering field. This differs from a primary index, which requires that the ordering field of the data file have a *distinct value* for each record.

A clustering index is also an ordered file with two fields; the first field is of the same type as the clustering field of the data file and the second field is a block pointer. There is one entry in the clustering index for each *distinct value* of the clustering field, containing that value and a pointer to the *first* block in the data file that has a record with that value for its clustering field. Figure 5.2 shows an example of a data file with a clustering index. Note that record insertion and record deletion still cause considerable problems

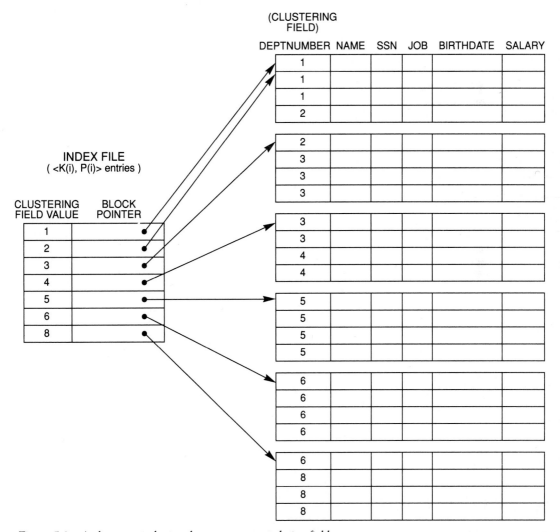

Figure 5.2 A clustering index on the DEPTNUMBER ordering field of an EMPLOYEE file

because the data records are physically ordered. To alleviate the problem of insertion, it is common to reserve a whole block for *each value* of the clustering field; all records with that value are placed in the block. If more than one block is needed to store the records for a particular value, additional blocks are allocated and linked together. This makes insertion and deletion relatively straightforward. Figure 5.3 shows this scheme.

A clustering index is another example of a *nondense* index because it has an entry for every *distinct value* of the indexing field rather than for every record in the file.

5.1.3   *Secondary Indexes*

A **secondary index** also is an ordered file with two fields, and, as in the other indexes, the second field is a pointer to a disk block. The first field is of the same data type as some *nonordering field* of the data file. The field on which the secondary index is constructed is called an **indexing field** of the file, whether its values are distinct for every record or not. There can be *many* secondary indexes, and hence indexing fields, for the same file.

We first consider a secondary index on a key field—a field having a *distinct value* for every record in the data file. Such a field is sometimes called a **secondary key** for the file. In this case there is one index entry for *each record* in the data file, which has the value of the secondary key for the record and a pointer to the block in which the record is stored. A secondary index on a key field is a **dense** index because it contains one entry for each record in the data file.

We again refer to the two field values of index entry i as $<K(i), P(i)>$. The entries are **ordered** by value of $K(i)$, so we can use binary search on the index. Because the records of the data file are *not* physically ordered by values of the secondary key field, we cannot use block anchors. That is why an index entry is created for each record in the data file rather than for each block as in the case of a primary index. Figure 5.4 illustrates a secondary index on a key attribute of a data file. Notice that in Figure 5.4 the pointers $P(i)$ in the index entries are *block pointers*, not record pointers. Once the appropriate block is transferred to main memory, a search for the desired record within the block can be carried out.

A secondary index will usually need substantially more storage space than a primary index because of its larger number of entries. However, the *improvement* in search time for an arbitrary record is much greater for a secondary index than it is for a primary index, because we would have to do a *linear search* on the data file if the secondary index did not exist. For a primary index, we could still use binary search on the main file even if the index did not exist because the records are physically ordered by the primary key field. Example 2 illustrates the improvement in number of blocks accessed when using a secondary index to search for a record.

EXAMPLE 2:   Consider the file of Example 1 with r = 30,000 fixed-length records of size R = 100 bytes stored on a disk with block size B = 1024 bytes. The file has b = 3000 blocks as calculated in Example 1. To do a linear search on the file, we would require b/2 = 3000/2 = 1500 block accesses on the average.

Suppose we construct a secondary index on a nonordering key field of the file that is V = 9 bytes long. As in Example 1, a block pointer is P = 6 bytes long, so each index

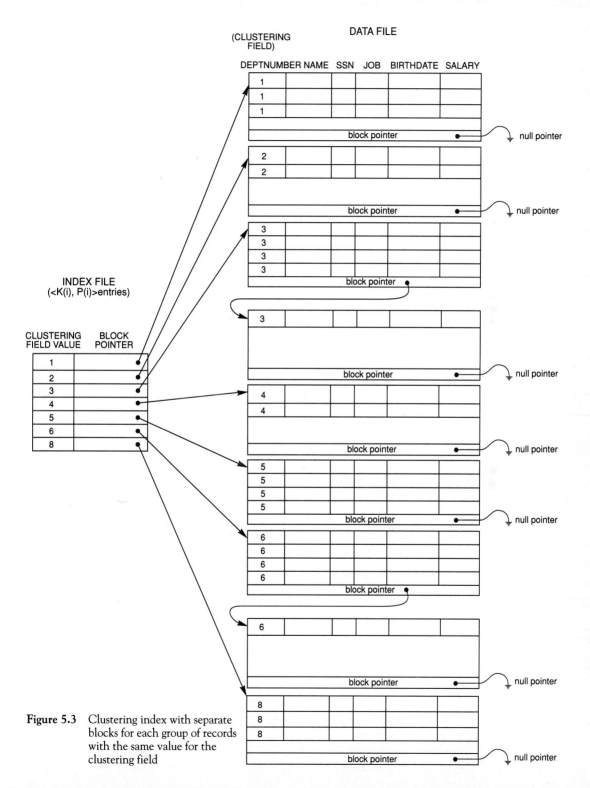

Figure 5.3 Clustering index with separate blocks for each group of records with the same value for the clustering field

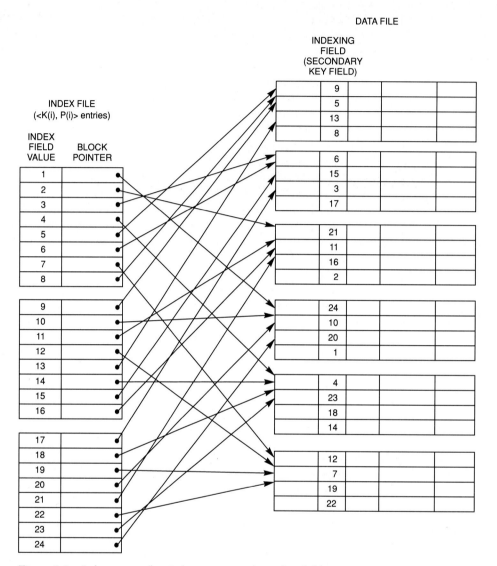

Figure 5.4 A dense secondary index on a nonordering key field of a file

entry is $R_i = (9 + 6) = 15$ bytes, and the blocking factor for the index is $bfr_i = \lfloor (B/R_i) \rfloor = \lfloor (1024/15) \rfloor = 68$ entries per block. In a dense secondary index such as this, the total number of index entries r_i is equal to the *number of records* in the data file, which is 30,000. The number of blocks needed for the index is hence $b_i = \lceil (r_i/bfr_i) \rceil = \lceil (30,000/68) \rceil = 442$ blocks. Compare this to the 45 blocks needed by the nondense primary index in Example 1.

A binary search on this secondary index needs $\lceil (\log_2 b_i) \rceil = \lceil (\log_2 442) \rceil = 9$ block accesses. To search for a record using the index, we need an additional block access to the data file for a total of 9 + 1 = 10 block accesses—a vast improvement over the 1500 block accesses needed on the average for a linear search.

We can also create a secondary index on a *nonkey field* of a file. In this case numerous records in the data file can have the same value for the indexing field. There are several options for implementing such an index:

- Option 1 is to include several index entries with the same K(i) value—one for each record. This would be a dense index.

- Option 2 is to have variable-length records for the index entries, with a repeating field for the pointer. We keep a list of pointers <P(i,1), ..., P(i,k)> in the index entry for K(i)—one pointer to each block that contains a record whose indexing field value equals K(i). In either option 1 or option 2, the binary search algorithm on the index must be modified appropriately.

- Option 3, which is used commonly, is to keep the index entries themselves at a fixed length and have a single entry for each index field value, but create an extra level of indirection to handle the multiple pointers. In this scheme, which is nondense, the pointer P(i) in index entry <K(i), P(i)> points to a *block of record pointers*; each record pointer in that block points to one of the data file records with a value K(i) for the indexing field. If some value K(i) has too many records, so that their record pointers cannot fit in a single disk block, a linked list of blocks can be used. This technique is illustrated in Figure 5.5. Retrieval via the index requires an additional block access because of the extra level, but the algorithms for searching the index and, more important, for insertion of new records in the data file are straightforward. In addition, retrievals on complex selection conditions may be handled by referring to the pointers without having to retrieve many unnecessary file records (see Exercise 5.16).

Notice that a secondary index provides a **logical ordering** on the records by the indexing field. If we access the records in order of the entries in the secondary index, we get them in order of the indexing field.

5.1.4   Summary

To conclude this section, we summarize the discussion on index types in two tables. Table 5.1 shows the index field characteristics of each of the types of indexes discussed—primary, clustering, and secondary. Table 5.2 summarizes the properties of each type of index by comparing the number of index entries and specifying which indexes are dense and which use block anchors of the data file. In the next section we discuss multilevel indexing.

5.2   Multilevel Indexes

The indexing schemes we described thus far involve an ordered index file. Binary search is applied to the index to locate a record (or records) in the file having a specific index field value. Binary search requires approximately $(\log_2 b_i)$ block accesses for an index

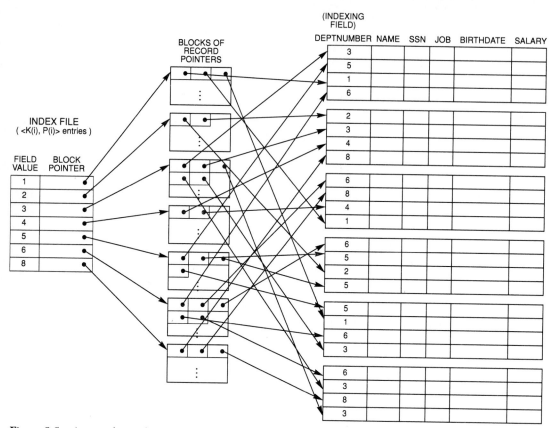

Figure 5.5 A secondary index on a nonkey field implemented using one level of indirection so that index entries are fixed length and have unique field values

with b_i blocks because each step of the algorithm reduces the part of the index file that we continue to search by a factor of 2. This is why we take the log function to the base 2. The idea behind a **multilevel index** is to reduce the part of the index that we continue to search by bfr_i, the blocking factor for the index, which in most cases is larger than 2. Hence, the search space is reduced much faster. The value bfr_i is called the **fan-out** of the multilevel index, and we will refer to it by the symbol **fo**. Searching a multilevel index requires approximately ($\log_{fo} b_i$) block accesses, which is less than for binary search if the fan-out is larger than 2.

A multilevel index considers the index file, which we will refer to now as the **first** (or **base) level** of a multilevel index, as an *ordered file* with a *distinct value* for each K(i). Hence we can create a primary index for the first level; this index to the first level is called the **second level** of the multilevel index. Because the second level is a primary index, we can use block anchors so that the second level has one entry for *each block of*

Table 5.1   Types of Indexes

	Ordering Field	**Nonordering Field**
Key field	Primary index	Secondary index (key)
Nonkey field	Clustering index	Secondary index (nonkey)

Table 5.2   Properties of Index Types

		Properties of Index Type		
		Number of (First Level) Index Entries	**Dense or Nondense**	**Block Anchoring on the Data File**
Type of Index	Primary	Number of blocks in data file	Nondense	Yes
	Clustering	Number of distinct index field values	Nondense	Yes/no[a]
	Secondary (key)	Number of records in data file	Dense	No
	Secondary (nonkey)	Number of records[b] or Number of distinct index field values[c]	Dense or Nondense	No

[a]Yes if every distinct value of the ordering field starts a new block, no otherwise.
[b]For option 1.
[c]For options 2 and 3.

the first level. The blocking factor bfr_i for the second level—and all subsequent levels—is the same as that for the first-level index because all index entries are the same size, each having one field value and one block address. If the first level has r_1 entries and the blocking factor—which is also the fan-out—for the index is $bfr_i = fo$, then the first level will need $\lceil (r_1/fo) \rceil$ blocks, which will be the number of entries r_2 needed at the second level of the index.

We can repeat the above process for the second level. The **third level,** which is a primary index for the second level, has an entry for each second-level block, so the number of third-level entries is $r_3 = \lceil (r_2/fo) \rceil$. Notice that we need a second level only if the first level uses more than one block of disk storage, and, similarly, we need a third level only if the second level uses more than one block. We can repeat the above process until

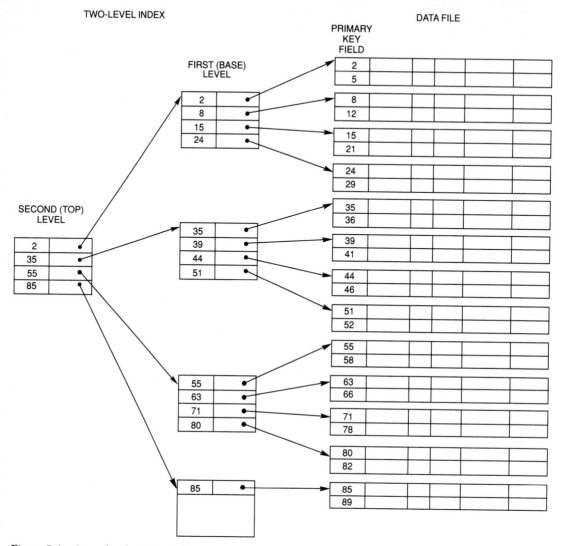

Figure 5.6   A two-level primary index

all the entries of some index level t fit in a single block. This block at the tth level is called the **top** index level.* Each level reduces the number of entries at the previous level by approximately a factor of fo—the index fan-out—so we can use the formula $1 \leq (r_1/((fo)^t))$ to calculate t. Hence, a multilevel index with r_1 first-level entries will have approximately t levels, where $t = \lceil (\log_{fo}(r_1)) \rceil$.

The multilevel scheme described here can be used on any type of index, whether it is a primary, clustering, or secondary index, as long as the first-level index has *distinct*

---

*The numbering scheme for index levels used here is the *reverse* of the way levels are commonly defined with tree data structures. In tree data structures, t is referred to as level 0 (zero), t − 1 is level 1, etc.

values for K(i) and fixed-length entries. Figure 5.6 shows a multilevel index built over a primary index. Example 3 illustrates the improvement in number of blocks accessed when a multilevel index is used.

EXAMPLE 3: Suppose the dense secondary index of Example 2 is converted into a multilevel index. We calculated the index blocking factor bfr_i = 68 index entries per block, which is also the fan-out fo for the multilevel index. The number of first-level blocks b_1 = 442 blocks was also calculated.

The number of second-level blocks will be $b_2 = \lceil (b_1/fo) \rceil = \lceil (442/68) \rceil = 7$ blocks, and the number of third-level blocks will be $b_3 = \lceil (b_2/fo) \rceil = \lceil (7/68) \rceil = 1$ block. Hence, the third level is the top level of the index, and t = 3. To access a record by searching the multilevel index, we need to access one block at each level plus one block from the data file, so we need t + 1 = 3 + 1 = 4 block accesses. Compare this to Example 2, where 10 block accesses were needed when a single-level index and binary search were used.

Notice that we could also have a multilevel primary index, which would be nondense. Exercise 5.10c illustrates this case, where we *must* access the data block from the file before we can determine whether the record being searched for is in the file. For a dense index, this can be determined by accessing the first index level without having to access a data block because there is an index entry for *every* record in the file.

Algorithm 5.1 outlines the search procedure for a record in a data file using a nondense multilevel primary index with t levels. We refer to entry i at level j of the index as $<K_j(i), P_j(i)>$ and search for a record whose primary key value is K. We assume that any overflow records are ignored. If the record is in the file, there will be some entry at level 1 with $K_1(i) \leq K < K_1(i + 1)$ and the record will be in the block of the data file whose address is $P_1(i)$. Exercise 5.15 discusses modifying the search algorithm for other types of indexes.

ALGORITHM 5.1   Searching a nondense multilevel primary
index with t levels

```
p ← address of top level block of index;
for j ← t step − 1 to 1 do
      begin
      read the index block (at jth index level) whose address is p;
      search block p for entry i such that Kⱼ(i) ≤ K < Kⱼ(i + 1) (if Kⱼ(i) is the
            last entry in the block, it is sufficient to satisfy Kⱼ(i) ≤ K);
      P ← Pⱼ(i)
      end;
read the data file block whose address is p;
search block p for record with key = K;
```

As we have seen, a multilevel index further reduces the number of blocks accessed when searching for a record given its indexing field value. However, we are still faced with the problems of dealing with index insertions and deletions because all index levels are *physically ordered files*. To retain the benefits of using multilevel indexing while reducing index insertion and deletion problems, a multilevel index that leaves some space in

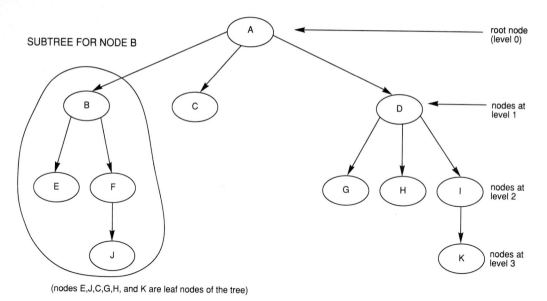

Figure 5.7   A tree data structure

each of its blocks for inserting new entries is used. This is called a **dynamic multilevel index** and is often implemented using data structures called B-trees and B$^+$-trees. We discuss these techniques in the next section.

5.3   Dynamic Multilevel Indexes Using B-Trees and B$^+$-Trees

B-trees and B$^+$-trees are special cases of the well-known tree data structure. We introduce very briefly the terminology used in discussing tree data structures. In general, a **tree** data structure is formed of **nodes**. Each node in the tree, except for a special node called the **root,** has one **parent** node and several—zero or more—**child** nodes. The root node has no parent. A node that does not have any child nodes is called a **leaf** node; a nonleaf node is called an **internal** node. The **level** of a node is defined as one more than the level of its parent, with the level of the root node being zero.* A **subtree** of a node consists of that node and all its **descendent** nodes—its child nodes, the child nodes of its child nodes, etc. A precise recursive definition of a subtree is that it consists of a node n and the subtrees of all the child nodes of n. Figure 5.7 illustrates a tree data structure. The root node is A, and its child nodes are B, C, and D. Nodes E, J, C, G, H, and K are leaf nodes.

Usually, we display a tree with the root node at the top, as shown in Figure 5.7. One way to implement a tree is to have as many pointers in each node as the number of its child nodes. Each pointer points to one of these child nodes. In some cases, a parent

---

*This standard definition of level of a tree node, which we use throughout Section 5.3, is different from the one we gave for multilevel indexes in Section 5.2.

pointer is also stored in each node. In addition to pointers, a node usually has some kind of information stored in it. When a multilevel index is implemented as a tree structure, this information includes the values of the indexing field of the file that are used to guide the search for a particular record.

In Section 5.3.1, we introduce search trees and then discuss B-trees, which can be used as dynamic multilevel indexes to guide the search for records in a data file. B-tree nodes are kept between 50% and 100% full, and pointers to the data blocks are stored in both internal nodes and leaf nodes of a B-tree structure. In Section 5.3.2 we discuss B$^+$-trees, a variation of B-trees where pointers to the data blocks of a file are stored only in leaf nodes; this can lead to fewer levels or higher-capacity indexes, as we shall see. We also outline search and insertion procedures for a B$^+$-tree.

5.3.1   Search Trees and B-Trees

A search tree is a special type of tree used to guide the search for a record given the value of one of its fields. The multilevel indexes discussed in Section 5.2 can be thought of as a variation of a search tree. Each node in the multilevel index has as many as fo pointers and fo key values, where fo is the index fan-out. The index field values in each node guide us to the next node, until we reach the data file block that contains the required records. By following a pointer, we restrict our search at each level to a subtree of the search tree and ignore all nodes not in this subtree.

Search Trees

A search tree is slightly different from a multilevel index. A **search tree** of order p is a tree such that each node contains *at most* $p - 1$ search values and p pointers in the order $<P_1, K_1, P_2, K_2, ..., P_{q-1}, K_{q-1}, P_q>$, where $q \leq p$, each P_i is a pointer to a child node (or a null pointer), and each K_i is a search value from some ordered set of values. All search values are assumed to be unique.* Figure 5.8 illustrates a node of a search tree. Two constraints must hold at all times on the search tree:

1. Within each node, $K_1 < K_2 < \cdots < K_{q-1}$.
2. For all values X in the subtree pointed at by P_i, we have $K_{i-1} < X < K_i$ for $1 < i < q$, $X < K_i$ for $i = 1$, and $K_{i-1} < X$ for $i = q$ (see Figure 5.8).

Whenever we search for a value X, we follow the appropriate pointer P_i according to the formulas in condition 2 above. Figure 5.9 illustrates a search tree of order $p = 3$ and integer search values. Notice that some of the pointers P_i in a node may be **null** pointers. We can use a search tree as a mechanism to search for records stored in a disk file. The values in the tree can be the values of one of the fields of the file, called the **search field** (same as the index field if a multilevel index guides the search). Each value in the tree is associated with a pointer to the record in the data file having that value. Alternatively, the pointer could be to the disk block containing that record. The search tree itself can be stored on disk by assigning each tree node to a disk block. When a new

---

*This restriction can be relaxed but then the following formulas must be modified.

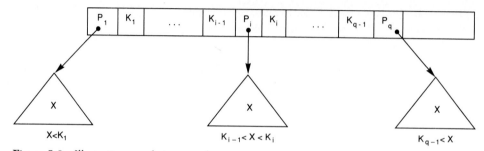

Figure 5.8   Illustrating a node in a search tree

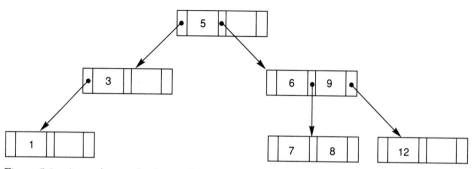

Figure 5.9   A search tree of order p = 3

record is inserted, we must update the search tree by including the search field value of the new record and a pointer to the new record in the search tree.

Algorithms are necessary for insertion and deletion of search values into the search tree while maintaining the above two constraints. In general, these algorithms do not guarantee that a search tree is **balanced,** meaning that all of its leaf nodes are at the same level.* Keeping a search tree balanced is important because it guarantees that no nodes will be at very high levels and hence require many block accesses during tree search. Another problem with search trees is that record deletion may leave some nodes in the tree nearly empty, thus wasting storage space and unnecessarily increasing the number of levels.

B-Trees

The B-tree, which is a search tree with some additional constraints on it, solves both of the above problems to some extent. These constraints ensure that the tree is always balanced and that the space wasted by deletion, if any, never becomes excessive. The algorithms for insertion and deletion, though, become more complex in order to maintain these constraints. However, the majority of insertions and deletions are simple processes;

---

*The definition of balanced is different for *binary* trees. Balanced binary trees are known as AVL trees.

they become complicated only under special circumstances, namely whenever we attempt an insertion into a node that is already full or a deletion from a node that makes it less than half full.

More formally, a **B-tree** of order p, when used as an access structure on a *key field* to search for records in a data file, can be defined as follows:

1. Each internal node in the B-tree (Figure 5.10a) is of the form

$$<P_1, <K_1, Pr_1>, P_2, <K_2, Pr_2>, ..., <K_{q-1}, Pr_{q-1}>, P_q>$$

   where $q \leq p$. Each P_i is a **tree pointer**—a pointer to another node in the B-tree. Each Pr_i is a **data pointer**—a pointer to a block in the data file that contains a record with search key field value equal to K_i.

2. Within each node, $K_1 < K_2 < \cdots < K_{q-1}$.

3. For all search key field values X in the subtree pointed at by P_i, we have

   $K_{i-1} < X < K_i$ for $1 < i < q - 1$, $X < K_i$ for $i = 1$, and $K_{i-1} < X$ for $i = q$
   (see Figure 5.10a).

4. Each node has at most p tree pointers.

5. Each node, except the root and leaf nodes, has at least $\lceil (p/2) \rceil$ tree pointers. The root node has at least two tree pointers unless it is the only node in the tree.

6. A node with q tree pointers, $q \leq p$, has $q - 1$ search key field values (and hence $q - 1$ data pointers).

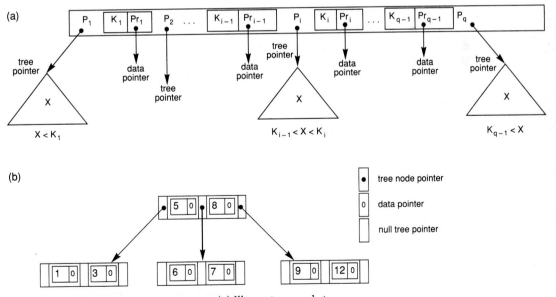

Figure 5.10 Illustrating B-tree structures. (a) Illustrating a node in a B-tree with q – 1 search values. (b) A B-tree of order p = 3. The values were inserted in the order 8,5,1,7,3,12,9,6.

7. All leaf nodes are at the same level. Leaf nodes have the same structure as internal nodes except that all their *tree pointers* P_i are **nil**.

Figure 5.10b illustrates a B-tree of order p = 3. Note that all search values K in the B-tree are unique because we assumed that it is used as an access structure on a key field of the file. If we use a B-tree on a nonkey field of a file, where numerous records can have the same value for the search field, we must change the definition of the file pointers Pr_i. In this case, rather than pointing directly to a file block, each Pr_i points to a block—or linked list of blocks—that contain pointers to the file records themselves. This extra level of indirection is similar to Option 3, discussed in Section 5.2.3, for secondary indexes that are constructed on a nonkey field of a file.

A B-tree starts with a single root node (which is also a leaf node) at level 0 (zero). Once the root node is full with p − 1 search key values and we attempt to insert another entry in the tree, the root node is split into two nodes at level 1. Only the middle value is kept in the root node, and the rest of the values are split as evenly as possible and moved to the other two nodes. In general, when a nonroot node is full and a new entry is inserted into it, that node is split into two nodes at the same level, and the middle entry is moved to the parent node along with two pointers to the split nodes. If the parent node is full, it is also split in the same way. Splitting can propagate all the way to the root node, creating a new level whenever the root is split. We will not discuss algorithms for B-trees in detail here; rather, we outline search and insertion procedures for B^+-trees in the next section. Exercise 5.17 concerns adapting the B^+-tree procedures to B-trees.

If deletion of a value makes a node less than half full, it may be combined with its neighboring nodes, and this can also propagate all the way to the root. Hence, deletion can cause reduction of the tree levels. It has been shown by analysis and simulation that after performing numerous random insertions and deletions on a B-tree, the nodes are approximately 69% full when the number of values in the tree stabilizes. This is also true of B^+-trees. If this happens, then node splitting and combining will occur only rarely, so insertion and deletion become quite efficient. At the same time, if the number of values grows, the tree will expand without a problem, although splitting of nodes may occur, so some insertions will take more time. Example 4 illustrates how we may calculate the order p of a B-tree stored on disk.

EXAMPLE 4: Suppose the search field is V = 9 bytes long, the disk block size is B = 512 bytes, and a block pointer is P = 6 bytes. Each B-tree node can have *at most* p tree pointers, p − 1 data pointers, and p − 1 search key field values (Figure 5.10a). These must fit into a single disk block if each B-tree node is to correspond to a disk block. Hence, we must have:

$$(p * 6) + ((p - 1) * (6 + 9)) \leq 512$$
$$\text{or } (21 * p) \leq 527$$

We can choose p to be the largest value that satisfies the above inequality, which gives p = 25.

In general, a B-tree node may have additional information needed by the algorithms that manipulate the tree. This information can include the number of entries in the node q and a pointer to the parent node. Hence, before we do the above calculation for p, we should reduce the block size by the amount of space needed for all such information. Next, we illustrate how to calculate the number of blocks and levels for a B-tree.

EXAMPLE 4a: Suppose the search field of Example 4 is a nonordering key field, and we construct a B-tree on this field. We assume that each node of the B-tree is 69% full. Each node, on the average, will have $p*0.69 = 25*0.69$ or approximately 17 pointers and hence 16 search key field values. The **average fan-out** $fo = 17$. We can start at the root and see how many values and pointers exist on the average at each subsequent level:

root:	1 node	16 entries	17 pointers
level 1:	17 nodes	272 entries	289 pointers
level 2:	289 nodes	4624 entries	4913 pointers
level 3:	4913 nodes	78,608 entries	83,521 pointers

At each level, we calculated the number of entries by multiplying the total number of pointers at the previous level by 16, the average number of entries in each node. Hence, for the block size, pointer size, and search key field size given above, a two-level B-tree holds up to $4624 + 272 + 16 = 4912$ entries on the average; a three-level B-tree holds up to 83,520 entries on the average.

Notice that if a node is full, it can hold 25 pointers and 24 key values. Hence, a one-level B-tree with all its nodes full to capacity would hold $25*24 + 24 = 624$ entries; for two levels the maximum is $25*25*24 + 624 = 15,624$ entries. For three levels the maximum is $25*25*25*24 + 15,624 = 390,624$ entries. However, it is *extremely unlikely* that all the nodes of a B-tree would be filled to capacity under random insertions and deletions.

5.3.2 B⁺-Trees

Most implementations of a dynamic multilevel index use a variation of the B-tree data structure called a **B⁺-tree**. In a B-tree, every value of the search field appears once at some level in the tree along with a data pointer. In a B⁺-tree, data pointers are stored *only at the leaf nodes* of the tree; hence, the structure of leaf nodes is different from the structure of internal nodes. The leaf nodes have an entry for *every* value of the search field, along with a data pointer to the block that contains this record if the search field is a key field. For a nonkey search field, the pointer will point to a block containing pointers to the data file records, creating an extra level of indirection.

The leaf nodes of the B⁺-tree are usually linked together to provide ordered access on the search field to the records. These leaf nodes are similar to the first (base) level of an index. Internal nodes of the B⁺-tree correspond to the other levels of the index. Some search field values from the leaf nodes are repeated in the internal nodes of the B⁺-tree to guide the search. The structure of the *internal nodes* of a B+-tree of order p (Figure 5.11a) is as follows:

1. Each internal node is of the form

   $<P_1, K_1, P_2, K_2, ..., P_{q-1}, K_{q-1}, P_q>$

   where $q \leq p$ and each P_i is a **tree pointer**.

2. Within each internal node, $K_1 < K_2 < ... < K_{q-1}$.

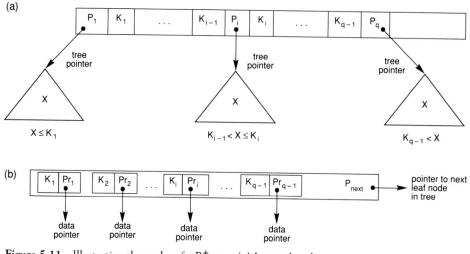

Figure 5.11   Illustrating the nodes of a B^+-tree. (a) Internal node
of a B^+- tree with $q - 1$ search values. (b) Leaf node
of a B^+-tree with $q - 1$ search values.

3. For all search field values X in the subtree pointed at by P_i, we have $K_{i-1} < X \leq K_i$ for $1 < i < q$, $X \leq K_i$ for $i = 1$, and $K_{i-1} < X$ for $i = q$ (see Figure 5.11a).

4. Each internal node has at most p tree pointers.

5. Each internal node, except the root, has at least $\lceil (p/2) \rceil$ tree pointers. The root node has at least two tree pointers if it is an internal node.

6. An internal node with q pointers, $q \leq p$, has $q - 1$ search field values.

The structure of the *leaf nodes* of a B^+-tree of order p (Figure 11.5b), is as follows:

1. Each leaf node is of the form

$$< <K_1, Pr_1>, <K_2, Pr_2>, ..., <K_{q-1}, Pr_{q-1}>, P_{next}>$$

where $q \leq p$, each Pr_i is a data pointer, and P_{next} points to the next *leaf node* of the B^+-tree.

2. Within each leaf node, $K_1 < K_2 < \cdots < K_{q-1}$, $q \leq p$.

3. Each Pr_i is a **data pointer** that points to a file block containing the record whose search field value is K_i (or to a block of record pointers that point to records whose search field value is K_i if the search key field is not a key).

4. Each leaf node has at least $\lfloor (p/2) \rfloor$ values.

5. All leaf nodes are at the same level.

Notice that both leaf nodes and internal nodes have the same number of pointers and values. However, the pointers in internal nodes are *tree pointers* that point to blocks that are tree nodes, whereas the pointers in leaf nodes are *data pointers* that point to the data file blocks—except for the P_{next} pointer, which is a tree pointer that points to the next leaf node. Notice that a P$_{previous}$ pointer can also be included. Because entries in the internal nodes of a B$^+$-tree include search values and tree pointers without any data pointers, more entries can be packed into an internal node of a B$^+$-tree than for a similar B-tree. For the same block (node) size, the order p will be larger for the B$^+$-tree than for the B-tree, as we illustrate in Example 5. This can lead to fewer B$^+$-tree levels, improving search time.

EXAMPLE 5:   To calculate the order p of a B$^+$-tree, suppose the search field is V = 9 bytes long, the block size is B = 512 bytes, and a block pointer is P = 6 bytes, as in Example 4. An internal node of the B$^+$-tree can have up to p tree pointers and p − 1 search field values; these must fit into a single block. Hence, we have:

$$(p * 6) + ((p - 1) * 9) \leq 512$$
$$\text{or } (15 * p) \leq 521$$

We can choose p to be the largest value satisfying the above inequality, which gives p= 34. This is larger than for the B-tree, resulting in a larger fan-out and more entries in a B$^+$-tree internal node than in the corresponding B-tree. The leaf nodes of the B$^+$-tree will have the same number of values and pointers, except that the pointers are data pointers and a next pointer.

As with the B-tree, we may need additional information—to implement the insertion and deletion algorithms—in each node. This information can include the type of node, internal or leaf, the number of current entries in the node q, and pointers to the parent and sibling nodes. Hence, before we do the above calculation for p, we should reduce the block size by the amount of space needed for all such information. The next example illustrates how we can calculate the number of entries in a B$^+$-tree.

EXAMPLE 5a: Suppose we construct a B$^+$-tree on the field of Example 5. To calculate the approximate number of entries of the B$^+$-tree, we assume that each node is 69% full. Each node on the average will have 34*0.69 or approximately 23 pointers and hence 22 values. Hence, the **average fan-out** fo = 23. A four-level tree will have the following average number of entries at each level:

root:	1 node	22 entries	23 pointers
level 1:	23 nodes	506 entries	529 pointers
level 2:	529 nodes	11,638 entries	12,167 pointers
leaf level:	12,167 nodes	267,674 entries	

For the block size, pointer size, and search field size given above, a two-level B$^+$-tree holds up to 11,638 entries on the average and a three-level B$^+$-tree up to 267,674 entries on the average. Compare these to the 4912 and 83,520 entries for the corresponding B-tree in Example 4a.

Search, Insertion, and Deletion with B$^+$-Trees

Algorithm 5.2 outlines the procedure for searching for a record using the B$^+$-tree as access structure. Algorithm 5.3 illustrates the procedure for inserting a record in a file with a B$^+$-tree access structure. We now illustrate insertion and deletion with an example.

ALGORITHM 5.2   Searching for a record with search field value K using a B^+-tree

```
n ← block containing root node of B⁺-tree;
read block n;
while (n is not a leaf node of the B⁺-tree) do
    begin
    q ← number of tree pointers in node n;
    if K ≤ n.K₁ (*n.kᵢ refers to the iᵗʰ search field value in node n*)
        then n ← n.P₁ (*n.Pᵢ refers to the iᵗʰ tree pointer in node n*)
        else if K > n.K_{q-1}
                then n ← n.P_q
                else begin
                        search node n for an entry i such that n.K_{i-1} < K ≤ n.Kᵢ;
                        n ← n.Pᵢ
                        end;
    read block n
    end;
search block n for entry (Kᵢ,Prᵢ) with K = Kᵢ; (* search leaf node *)
if found
    then read data file block with address Prᵢ and search for record
    else record with search field value K is not in the data file;
```

ALGORITHM 5.3   Inserting for a record with search field value K in a B^+-tree of order p.

```
n ← block containing root node of B⁺-tree;
read block n; set stack S to empty;
while (n is not a leaf node of the B⁺-tree) do
    begin
    push address of n on stack S;
        (*stack S holds parent nodes that are needed in case of split*)
    q ← number of tree pointers in node n;
    if K ≤ n.K₁ (*n.Kᵢ refers to the jᵗʰ search field value in node n*)
        then n ← n.P₁ (*n.Pᵢ refers to the iᵗʰ tree pointer in node n*)
        else if K > n.K_{q-1}
                then n ← n.P_q
                else begin
                        search node n for an entry i such that n.K_{i-1} < K ≤ n.Kᵢ;
                        n ← n.Pᵢ
                        end;
    read block n
    end;
search block n for entry (Kᵢ,Prᵢ) with K = Kᵢ; (*search leaf node n*)
if found
    then record already in file--cannot insert
    else (*insert entry in B⁺-tree to point to record*)
    begin
    create entry (K,Pr) where Pr points to file block containing new record;
    if leaf node n is not full
```

```
        then insert entry (K, Pr) in correct position in leaf node n
        else
        begin (*leaf node n is full with p−1 entries--is split*)
        copy n to temp (*temp is an oversize leaf node to hold extra entry*);
        insert entry (K, Pr) in temp in correct position;
            (*temp now holds p entries of the form (Kᵢ, Prᵢ)*)
        new ← a new empty leaf node for the tree;
        j ← ⌈(p/2)⌉;
        n ← first j entries in temp (up to entry (Kⱼ,Prⱼ)); n.Pₙₑₓₜ ← new;
        new ← remaining entries in temp; K ← Kⱼ;
(*now we must move (K,new) and insert in parent internal node
  --however, if parent is full, split may propagate*)
        finished ← false;
        repeat
        if stack S is empty
          then (*no parent node--new root node is created for the tree*)
          begin
          root ← a new empty internal node for the tree;
          root ← <n, K, new>; finished ← true;
          end
        else
          begin
          n ← pop stack S;
          if internal node n is not full
                then
                begin (*parent node not full--no split*)
                insert (K, new) in correct position in internal node n;
                finished ← true
                end
                else
                begin (*internal node n is full with p tree pointers--is split*)
                copy n to temp (*temp is an oversize internal node*);
                insert (K,new) in temp in correct position;
                    (*temp now has p+1 tree pointers*)
                new ← a new empty internal node for the tree;
                j ← ⌊(p/2)⌋;
                n ← entries up to tree pointer Pⱼ in temp;
                    (*n contains <P₁, K₁, P₂, K₂, ..., Pⱼ₋₁, Kⱼ₋₁, Pⱼ >*)
                new ← entries from tree pointer Pⱼ₊₁ in temp;
                    (*n contains < Pⱼ₊₁, Kⱼ₊₁, ..., Kₚ₋₁, Pₚ, Kₚ, Pₚ₊₁ >*)
                K ← Kⱼ
            (*now we must move (K,new) and insert in parent internal node*)
                end
          end
        until finished
      end;
end;
```

Figure 5.12 illustrates insertion of records in a B^+-tree of order p = 3. First, the root is the only node in the tree, so it is also a leaf node. As soon as more than one level is created, the tree is divided into internal nodes and leaf nodes. Note that *every value must exist at the leaf level*, because all data pointers are at the leaf level. However, only some values exist in internal nodes to guide the search. Note also that every value appearing in an internal node also appears as *the rightmost value* in the subtree pointed at by the tree pointer to the left of the value. This fact is important for deletion.

When a *leaf node* is full and a new entry is inserted there, the node **overflows** and must be split. The first j = $\lceil (p/2) \rceil$ entries in the original node are kept there and the remaining entries moved to a new leaf node. The jth search value is replicated in the parent internal node, and an extra pointer to the new node is created in the parent. These must be inserted in the parent node in their correct sequence. If the parent internal node is full, the new value will cause it to overflow also, so it must be split. The entries in the internal node up to P_j—the jth tree pointer after inserting the new value and pointer, where j = $\lfloor (p/2) \rfloor$—are kept, while the jth search value is *moved* to the parent, not replicated. A new internal node will hold the entries from P_{j+1} to the end of the entries in the node (see Algorithm 5.3). This splitting can propagate all the way up to create a new root node and hence a new level for the B^+-tree.

Figure 5.13 illustrates deletion from a B^+-tree. When an entry is deleted, it is always removed from the leaf level. If it happens to occur in an internal node, it must also be removed from there. In the latter case, the value to its left in the leaf node must replace it in the internal node, because it is now the rightmost entry in the subtree. Deletion may cause **underflow** by reducing the number of entries in the leaf node to below the minimum required. In this case we try to find a **sibling** leaf node—a leaf node directly to the left or to the right of the node with underflow—that is more than half full. If we find such a sibling, we can **redistribute** the entries among the node and its sibling so that both are at least half full; otherwise, the node is merged with one of its siblings and the number of leaf nodes is reduced. A common method is to try redistributing entries with the left sibling; if this is not possible, an attempt to redistribute with the right sibling is made. If this is not possible either, the three nodes are merged into two leaf nodes. In the latter case, underflow may propagate to **internal** nodes because one fewer tree pointer and search value are needed. This can propagate and reduce the tree levels.

Notice that implementing the insertion and deletion algorithms may require parent and sibling pointers for each node, or for the use of a stack as in Algorithm 5.3. Each node should also include the number of entries in it and its type (leaf or internal). Another alternative is to implement insertion and deletion as recursive procedures.

Variations of B-Trees and B^+-Trees

To conclude this section, we briefly mention some variations of B-trees and B^+-trees. In some cases, constraint 5 on the B-tree (or B^+-tree), which requires each node to be at least half full, can be changed to require each node to be at least two-thirds full. In this case the B-tree has been called a **B*-tree**. In general, some systems allow the user to choose a **fill factor** between 0.5 and 1.0, where the latter means that the B-tree (index) nodes are to be completely full. In addition, some systems allow the user to spec-

INSERTION SEQUENCE: 8, 5, 1, 7, 3, 12, 9, 6

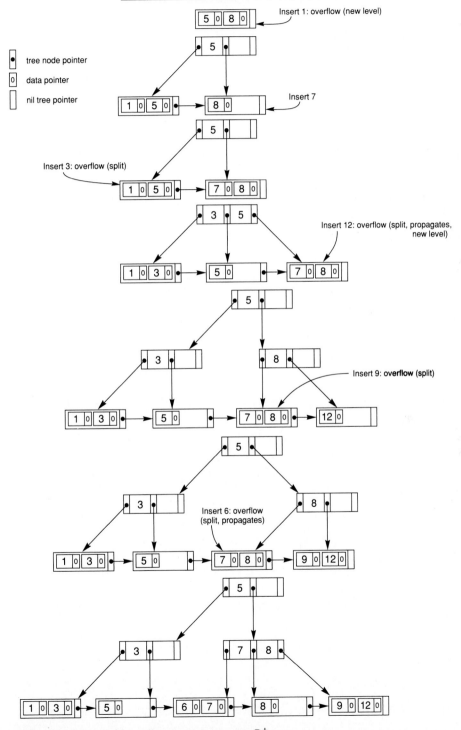

Figure 5.12   Example to illustrate insertion in a B⁺-tree

DELETION SEQUENCE: 5, 12, 9

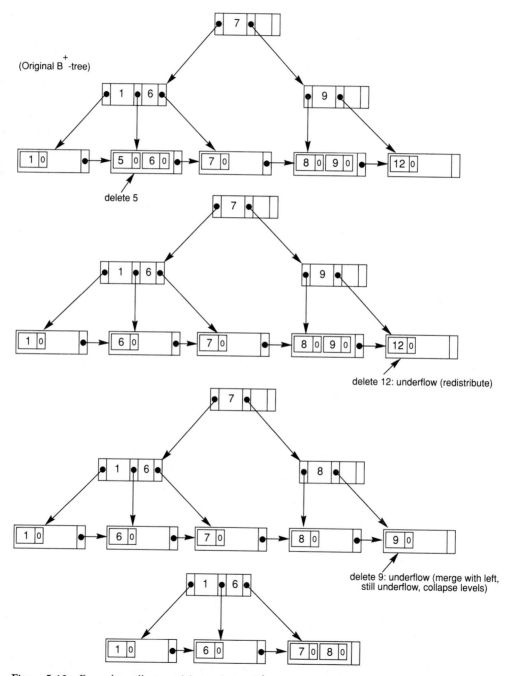

Figure 5.13 Example to illustrate deletion from a B⁺-tree

ify two fill factors for a B^+-tree, one for the leaf level and one for the internal nodes of the tree. When the index is first constructed, each node is filled up to approximately the fill factors specified. In the next section we discuss a number of file systems that use indexing variations.

5.4   Discussion

In many systems, an index is not an integral part of the data file but can be created and discarded dynamically. That is why it is often called an access structure. Whenever we expect to access frequently a file based on some search criterion involving a particular field, we can request the DBMS to create an index on that field. Usually, a secondary index is created to avoid physical ordering of the records in the data file on disk.

The main advantage of secondary indexes is that, theoretically at least, they can be created in conjunction with *virtually any record organization*. Hence, a secondary index could be used to complement other primary access methods such as ordering or hashing, or could even be used with mixed hierarchical and ring files. To create a B^+-tree secondary index on some field of a file, we must go through all records in the file to create the entries at the leaf level of the tree. These entries are then sorted and filled according to the specified fill factor while at the same time the other index levels are created.

It is more expensive and much harder to create primary indexes and clustering indexes dynamically, because the records of the data file must be physically sorted on disk in order of the indexing field. However, some systems allow users to create these indexes dynamically on their files by first sorting the files and then creating the index.

It is common to use a primary or secondary index to enforce a *key constraint* on the index field of a file. While searching the index to insert a new record, it is straightforward to check at the same time whether another record in the file—and hence in the tree—has the same value for the index field. If so, the insertion can be rejected.

A file that has a secondary index on every one of its fields is often called a **fully inverted file**. Because all indexes are secondary, new records are inserted at the end of the file, so the data file itself is an unordered (heap) file. The indexes are usually implemented as B^+-trees, so they are updated dynamically to reflect insertion or deletion of records.

Another common file organization is an ordered file with a multilevel primary index on its ordering key field. Such an organization is often called an **indexed sequential file** and is commonly used in business data processing. Insertion is handled by some form of overflow file that is merged periodically with the data file. The index is recreated during file reorganization.

IBM's **indexed sequential access method** (ISAM) has a two-level index that is closely related to the organization of the disk. The first level is a cylinder index, which has the key value of an anchor record for each cylinder of a disk pack and a pointer to the track index for the cylinder. The track index has the key value of an anchor record for each track in the cylinder and a pointer to the track. The track can then be searched sequentially for the desired record or block. Another IBM method, the **virtual storage access method** (VSAM), is somewhat similar to the B^+-tree access structure.

5.5   Summary

In this chapter we presented file organizations that involve additional access structures, called indexes, to improve the efficiency of retrieval of records from a data file. These access structures can be used *in conjunction with* the primary file organizations discussed in Chapter 4, which are used to organize the file records themselves on disk.

We first discussed three types of single-level indexes: primary, secondary, and clustering. Each index is specified on a field of the file. Primary and clustering indexes are constructed on the physical ordering field of a file, whereas secondary indexes are specified on nonordering fields. The field for a primary index must also be a key of the file, whereas it is a nonkey field for a clustering index. A single-level index is an ordered file and is searched using binary search. We showed how multilevel indexes can be constructed to improve the efficiency of searching an index.

We then showed how multilevel indexes can be implemented as B-trees and B^+-trees, which are dynamic structures that allow an index to expand and shrink dynamically. The nodes (blocks) of these index structures are kept between half full and completely full by the insertion and deletion algorithms. Nodes are usually 69% full, allowing space for insertions without having to reorganize the index for the majority of insertions. B^+-trees generally can hold more entries in their internal nodes than B-trees, so they may have fewer levels or hold more entries than a corresponding B-tree.

It is important to note that many combinations of the above organizations can be used. For example, secondary indexes are often used with hierarchical and ring files, as well as with unordered and ordered files. Secondary indexes can also be created for hash files and dynamic hash files.

Review Questions

5.1. Define the following terms: indexing field, primary key field, clustering field, secondary key field, block anchor, dense index, nondense index.

5.2. What are the differences between primary, secondary, and clustering indexes? How do these differences affect the way in which the indexes are implemented? Which of the indexes are dense and which are not?

5.3. Why can we have at most one primary or clustering index on a file, but several secondary indexes?

5.4. How does multilevel indexing improve the efficiency of searching an index file?

5.5. What is the order p of a B-tree? Describe the structure of B-tree nodes.

5.6. What is the order p of a B^+-tree? Describe the structure of both internal and leaf nodes of a B^+-tree.

5.7. How does a B-tree differ from a B^+-tree? Why is a B^+-tree usually preferred as an access structure to a data file?

5.8. What is a fully inverted file?

5.9. What is an indexed sequential file?

Exercises

5.10. Consider a disk with block size B = 512 bytes. A block pointer is P = 6 bytes long, and a record pointer is P_R = 7 bytes long. A file has r = 30,000 EMPLOYEE records of *fixed length*. Each record has the following fields: NAME (30 bytes), SSN (9 bytes), DEPARTMENTCODE (9 bytes), ADDRESS (40 bytes), PHONE (9 bytes), BIRTH-DATE (8 bytes), SEX (1 byte), JOBCODE (4 bytes), SALARY (4 bytes, real number). An additional byte is used as a deletion marker.

a. Calculate the record size R in bytes.

b. Calculate the blocking factor bfr and the number of file blocks b, assuming an unspanned organization.

c. Suppose the file is *ordered* by the key field SSN and we want to construct a *primary index* on SSN. Calculate (i) the index blocking factor bfr_i (which is also the index fan-out fo), (ii) the number of first-level index entries and the number of first-level index blocks, (iii) the number of levels needed if we make it a multilevel index, (iv) the total number of blocks required by the multilevel index, and (v) the number of block accesses needed to search for and retrieve a record from the file—given its SSN value—using the primary index.

d. Suppose the file is *not ordered* by the key field SSN and we want to construct a *secondary index* on SSN. Repeat the previous exercise (c) for the secondary index and compare with the primary index.

e. Suppose the file is *not ordered* by the nonkey field DEPARTMENTCODE and we want to construct a *secondary index* on DEPARTMENTCODE using option 3 of Section 5.1.3, with an extra level of indirection that stores record pointers. Assume there are 1000 distinct values of DEPARTMENTCODE and that the EMPLOYEE records are evenly distributed among these values. Calculate (i) the index blocking factor bfr_i (which is also the index fan-out fo), (ii) the number of blocks needed by the level of indirection that stores record pointers, (iii) the number of first-level index entries and the number of first-level index blocks, (iv) the number of levels needed if we make it a multilevel index, (v) the total number of blocks required by the multilevel index and the blocks used in the extra level of indirection, and (vi) the approximate number of block accesses needed to search for and retrieve *all* records in the file having a specific DEPARTMENTCODE value using the index.

f. Suppose the file is *ordered* by the nonkey field DEPARTMENTCODE and we want to construct a *clustering index* on DEPARTMENTCODE that uses block anchors (every new value of DEPARTMENTCODE starts at the beginning of a new block). Assume there are 1000 distinct values of DEPARTMENTCODE and that the EMPLOYEE records are evenly distributed among these values. Calculate (i) the index blocking factor bfr_i (which is also the index fan-out fo), (ii) the number of first-level index entries and the number of first-level index blocks, (iii) the number of levels needed if we make it a multilevel index, (iv) the total number of blocks required by the multilevel index, and (v) the number of block accesses needed to search for and retrieve all records in the file having a specific DEPARTMENTCODE value using the clustering index (assume that multiple blocks in a cluster are either contiguous or linked by pointers).

g. Suppose the file is *not* ordered by the key field SSN and we want to construct a B^+-tree access structure (index) on SSN. Calculate (i) the order p of the B^+-tree, (ii) the number of leaf-level blocks needed if blocks are approximately 69% full (rounded up for convenience), (iii) the number of levels needed if internal nodes are also 69% full (rounded up for convenience), (iv) the total number of blocks required by the B^+-tree, and (v) the number of block accesses needed to search for and retrieve a record from the file—given its SSN value—using the B^+-tree.

h. Repeat part (g) but for a B-tree rather than a B^+-tree. Compare your results for the B-tree and the B^+-tree.

5.11. A PARTS file with Part# as key field includes records with the following Part# values: 23, 65, 37, 60, 46, 92, 48, 71, 56, 59, 18, 21, 10, 74, 78, 15, 16, 20, 24, 28, 39, 43, 47, 50, 69, 75. Suppose the search field values are inserted in the given order in a B+-tree of order p = 4; show how the tree will expand and what the final tree looks like.

5.12. Repeat Exercise 5.11 but use a B-tree of order p = 4 instead of a B^+-tree.

5.13. Suppose the following search field values are deleted in the given order from the B^+-tree of Exercise 5.11; show how the tree will shrink and show the final tree. The deleted values are 65, 75, 43, 18, 20, 92, 59, 37.

5.14. Repeat Exercise 5.13 but for the B-tree of Exercise 5.12.

5.15. Algorithm 5.1 outlines the procedure for searching a nondense multilevel primary index to retrieve a file record. Adapt the algorithm for each of the following cases:

a. A multilevel secondary index on a nonkey nonordering field of a file. Assume that option 3 of Section 5.1.3 is used, where there is an extra level of indirection that stores pointers to the individual records with the corresponding index field value.

b. A multilevel secondary index on a nonordering key field of a file.

c. A multilevel clustering index on a nonkey ordering field of a file.

5.16. Suppose several secondary indexes exist on nonkey fields of a file, implemented using option 3 of Section 5.1.3; for example, we could have secondary indexes on the fields DEPARTMENTCODE, JOBCODE, and SALARY of the EMPLOYEE file of Exercise 5.10. Describe an efficient way to search for and retrieve records satisfying a complex selection condition on these fields, such as (DEPARTMENTCODE = 5 AND JOBCODE = 12 AND SALARY > 50,000) using the record pointers in the indirection level.

5.17. Adapt Algorithms 5.2 and 5.3, which outline search and insertion procedures for a B^+-tree, to a B-tree.

5.18. It is possible to modify the B^+-tree insertion algorithm to delay the case where a new level is produced by checking for a possible *redistribution* of values among the leaf nodes. Figure 5.14 illustrates how this could be done for our example of Figure 5.12; rather than splitting the leftmost leaf node when 12 is inserted, we do a *left redistribution* by moving 7 to the leaf node to its left (if there is space in this node). Figure 5.14 shows how the tree would look when redistribution is considered. It is also possible to consider *right redistribution*. Try to modify the B$^+$-tree insertion algorithm to take redistribution into account.

5.19. Outline an algorithm for deletion from a B$^+$-tree.

5.20. Repeat Exercise 5.19 for a B-tree.

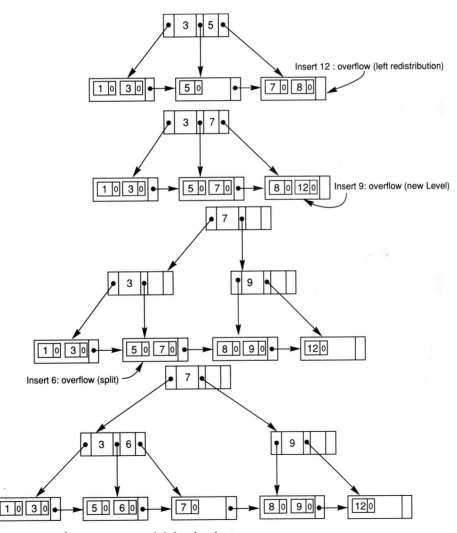

Figure 5.14   B$^+$-tree insertion with left redistribution

Selected Bibliography

Nievergelt (1974) discusses the use of binary search trees for file organization. Bayer and McCreight (1972) define B-trees, and Comer (1979) provides a survey of B-trees and their variations and history. Knuth (1973) provides detailed analysis of many search techniques, including B-trees and their variations. Wirth (1972) and Smith and Barnes (1987) provide search, insertion, and deletion algorithms for B-trees. Larson (1981) analyzes index-sequential files, and Held and Stonebraker (1978) compare static multilevel indexes with B-tree dynamic indexes. Lehman and Yao (1981) discuss concurrent access to B-trees. The books by Wiederhold (1983), Smith and Barnes (1987), and Ullman (1982), among others, discuss many of the techniques described in this chapter.

DATABASE MODELS AND LANGUAGES

CHAPTER 10
The Hierarchical Data Model

CHAPTER 11
The Network Data Model

CHAPTER 12
Comparison of Data Models

CHAPTER 6

The Relational Data Model and Relational Algebra

The relational model of data was introduced by Codd (1970). Among the three data models we present in Part II, it has the simplest and the most uniform data structures and is the most formal in nature. We will discuss various aspects of the relational model in several chapters because there is more conceptual material to cover on the relational model than on the other two data models we discuss in Part II—the hierarchical and network models.

We begin this chapter by defining the modeling concepts of the relational model in Section 6.1. We also discuss constraints specified on relational databases and relational update operations. In Section 6.2 we present the relational algebra, which is a collection of operations for manipulating relations. We discuss additional operations for relational databases in Section 6.3. Section 6.4 contains examples of relational queries and Section 6.5 provides a summary.

6.1 Relational Model Concepts

The relational model represents the data in a database as a collection of relations. Informally, each relation resembles a table or, to some extent, a simple file. For example, the database of files shown in Figure 1.2 is considered to be in the relational model. However, there are important differences between relations and files, as we shall soon see.

When a relation is thought of as a **table** of values, each row in the table represents a collection of related data values. These values can be interpreted as a fact describing an entity or a relationship instance. The table name and column names are used to help in interpreting the meaning of the values in each row of the table. For example, the first table of Figure 1.2 is called STUDENT because each row represents facts about a particular student entity. The column names—Name, StudentNumber, Class, Major—specify how to interpret the data values in each row based on the column each value is in. All values in a column typically are of the same data type.

In relational database terminology, a row is called a *tuple*, a column name is called an *attribute*, and the table is called a *relation*. The data type describing the types of values that can appear in each column is called a domain. We now define these terms—domain, tuple, attribute, and relation—more precisely.

6.1.1 Domains, Tuples, Attributes, and Relations

A **domain** D is a set of atomic values. By **atomic** we mean that each value in the domain is indivisible as far as the relational model is concerned. A common method of specifying a domain is to specify a data type from which the data values forming the domain are drawn. It is also useful to specify a name for the domain to help in interpreting its values. Some examples of domains follow:

- USA_phone_numbers: The set of valid 10-digit phone numbers in the USA.
- Local_phone_numbers: The set of valid 7-digit phone numbers within a particular area code.
- Social_security_numbers: The set of valid 9-digit social security numbers.
- Names: The set of names of persons.
- Grade_point_averages: Possible values of computed grade point averages; a value between 0 and 4.
- Employee_ages: Possible ages of employees of a company; a value between 16 and 70 years old.
- Academic_departments: The set of academic departments in a university. Such as Computer Science, Economics, and Physics.

The above are logical definitions of domains. A **data type** or **format** is also specified for each domain. For example, the data type for the domain USA_phone_numbers can be declared as a character string of the form (ddd)ddd-dddd, where each d is a numeric (decimal) digit and the first three digits form a valid telephone area code. The data type for Employee_ages is an integer number between 16 and 70. For Academic_departments, the data type is the set of character strings that is a valid department name or code.

As we can see, a domain is given a name, data type, and format. Additional information for interpreting the values of a domain can also be given; for example, a numeric domain such as Person_weights should have the units of measurement—pounds or kilograms—specified. Next, we define the concept of a relation schema, which describes the structure of a relation.

A **relation schema** R, denoted by $R(A_1, A_2, ..., A_n)$, is a set of attributes $R = \{A_1, A_2, ..., A_n\}$. Each **attribute** A_i is the name of a role played by some domain D in the relation schema R. D is called the **domain** of A_i and is denoted by $dom(A_i)$. A relation schema is used to *describe* a relation; R is called the **name** of this relation. The **degree of a relation** is the number of attributes n of its relation schema.

An example of a relation schema for a relation of degree 7, which describes university students, is the following:

STUDENT(Name, SSN, HomePhone, Address, OfficePhone, Age, GPA)

For this relation schema, STUDENT is the name of the relation, which has seven attributes. We can specify the following domains for some of the attributes of the STUDENT relation: dom(Name) = Names, dom(SSN) = Social_security_numbers, dom(HomePhone) = Local_phone_numbers, dom(OfficePhone) = Local_phone_numbers, dom(GPA) = Grade_point_averages.

A **relation** (or **relation instance**) r of the relation schema R(A_1, A_2, ..., A_n), also denoted by r(R), is a set of n-tuples r = {t_1, t_2, ..., t_m}. Each **n-tuple** t is an ordered list of n values t = <v_1, v_2, ..., v_n>, where each value v_i, $1 \le i \le n$, is an element of dom(A_i) or is a special **null** value. The terms relation **intension** for the schema R and relation **extension** for a relation instance r(R) are also commonly used.

Figure 6.1 shows an example of a STUDENT relation, which corresponds to the STUDENT schema specified above. Each tuple in the relation represents a particular student entity. We display the relation as a table, where each tuple is shown as a row and each attribute corresponds to a column header to indicate a role or interpretation of the values in that column. Null values represent attributes whose values are unknown or do not exist for some individual STUDENT tuples.

The above definition of a relation can be *restated* as follows: A relation r(R) is a **subset of the Cartesian product** of the domains that define R.

$$r(R) \subseteq (\text{dom}(A_1) \text{ X } \text{dom}(A_2) \text{ X } \cdots \text{ X } \text{dom}(A_n))$$

The Cartesian product specifies all possible combinations of values from the underlying domains. Hence, if we denote the number of values or **cardinality** of a domain D by $|D|$, then, assuming all domains are finite, the total number of tuples in the Cartesian product would be

$$|\text{dom}(A_1)| * |\text{dom}(A_2)| * \cdots * |\text{dom}(A_n)|$$

Out of all these possible combinations, a relation instance at a given time—the **current relation instance**—reflects only the valid tuples that represent a particular state of the real world. In general, as the state of the real world changes, so does the relation by

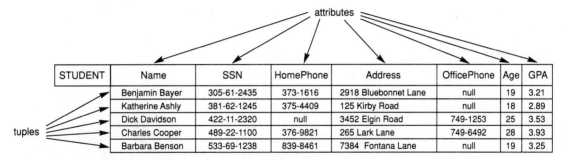

Figure 6.1   The attributes and tuples of a relation STUDENT

being transformed to another relation instance. However, the schema R is relatively static and does *not* change except very infrequently—for example, by adding an attribute to represent new information that was not originally stored in the relation.

It is possible for several attributes to *have the same domain*. The attributes indicate different **roles,** or interpretations, for the domain. For example, in the STUDENT relation the same domain Local_phone_numbers plays the role of HomePhone, referring to the "home phone of a student," and OfficePhone, referring to the " office phone of the student."

6.1.2   Characteristics of Relations

The definition of relations given above implies certain characteristics that make a relation different from a file or a table. We discuss some of these characteristics in this section.

Ordering of Tuples in a Relation

A relation is defined as a *set* of tuples. Mathematically, elements of a set have *no order* among them; hence, tuples in a relation do not have any particular order. However, in a file, records are physically stored on disk so there always is an order among the records. This ordering indicates first, second, i^{th}, and last records in the file. Similarly, when we display a relation as a table, the rows are displayed in a certain order.

The reason that tuple ordering is not part of a relation definition is that a relation attempts to represent facts at a logical or abstract level. Many logical orders can be specified on a relation; for example, tuples in the STUDENT relation of Figure 6.1 could be logically ordered by values of Name, SSN, Age, or some other attribute. The definition of a relation does not specify any order—there is *no preference* for one logical ordering over another. Hence, the relation displayed in Figure 6.2 is considered *identical* to the one shown in Figure 6.1. When a relation is implemented as a file, then a physical ordering may be specified on the records of the file.

Ordering of Values within a Tuple

According to the definition of a relation given above, an n-tuple is an *ordered list* of n values, so ordering of values in a tuple—and hence of attributes in a relation schema definition—is important. However, at a logical level, the order of attributes and attribute

STUDENT	Name	SSN	HomePhone	Address	OfficePhone	Age	GPA
	Dick Davidson	422-11-2320	null	3452 Elgin Road	749-1253	25	3.53
	Barbara Benson	533-69-1238	839-8461	7384 Fontana Lane	null	19	3.25
	Charles Cooper	489-22-1100	376-9821	265 Lark Lane	749-6492	28	3.93
	Katherine Ashly	381-62-1245	375-4409	125 Kirby Road	null	18	2.89
	Benjamin Bayer	305-61-2435	373-1616	2918 Bluebonnet Lane	null	19	3.21

Figure 6.2   The same relation STUDENT of Figure 6.1 with a different order of rows

values are *not* really important as long as the correspondence between attributes and values is maintained.

An **alternative definition of a relation** can be given, making the ordering of values in a tuple *unnecessary*. In this definition a relation r of relation schema R = {A_1, A_2, ..., A_n} is a finite set of **mappings** r = {t_1, t_2, ..., t_m}, where each tuple t_i is a mapping from R to D, and D is the union of the attribute domains; that is, D = dom(A_1) $\cup$ dom(A_2) $\cup$ ··· $\cup$ dom(A_n). In this definition, $t(A_i)$ must be in dom(A_i) for $1 \leq i \leq n$ for each mapping t in r. Each mapping t_i is called a tuple.

According to this definition, a **tuple** can be considered as a **set** of (<attribute>, <value>) pairs, where each pair gives the value of the mapping from an attribute A_i to a value v_i from dom(A_i). The ordering of attributes is *not* important because the attribute name appears with its value. Under this definition, the two tuples shown in Figure 6.3 are identical. This makes sense at an abstract or logical level, since there really is no preference to having one attribute value appear before another in a tuple.

When a relation is implemented as a file, the attributes can be physically ordered as fields within a record. We will continue to use the first definition of relation, where the values within tuples *are ordered*, because it simplifies much of the notation. However, it is important to note that the alternative definition given here is logically a better and more general definition of tuples and relations than the first one.

Values in the Tuples

Each value in a tuple is an **atomic** value; that is, it is not divisible into components within the framework of the relational model. Hence, composite and multivalued attributes (see Chapter 3) are not allowed. Much of the theory behind the relational model was developed with this assumption in mind, which is called the **first normal form** assumption. Multivalued attributes must be represented by separate relations, and composite attributes are represented only by their simple component attributes. Recent research in the relational model attempts to remove these restrictions by using the concept of **non-first normal form** or **nested** relations.

The values of some attributes within a particular tuple may be unknown or may not apply to this particular tuple. A special value, called **null,** is used for these cases. For example, in Figure 6.1 some student tuples have null for their office phones because they do not have an office. Another student has a null for home phone presumably because either he does not have a home phone or he has one but we do not know it. In general, we can have *several types* of null values, such as "value unknown," "attribute does not apply to this tuple," or "this tuple has no value for this attribute." Some implementations

t = < (Name ,Dick Davidson),(SSN, 422-11-2320),(HomePhone,null),(Address, 3452 Elgin Road), (OfficePhone ,749-1253),(Age ,25),(GPA ,3.53)>

t = < (Address,3452 Elgin Road),(Name,Dick Davidson),(SSN, 422-11-2320),(Age ,25), (OfficePhone ,749-1253),(GPA,3.53),(HomePhone,null)>

Figure 6.3 Two identical tuples when order of values is not part of the definition of a relation

actually devise different codes for different types of null values. Incorporating different types of null values into the relational model operations has proved difficult and a full discussion is outside the scope of this book.

Interpretation of a Relation

The relation schema can be interpreted as a declaration or a type of **assertion**. For example, the schema of the STUDENT relation of Figure 6.1 asserts that, in general, a student entity has a Name, SSN, HomePhone, Address, OfficePhone, Age, and GPA. Each tuple in the relation can then be interpreted as a **fact** or a particular instance of the assertion. For example, the first tuple in Figure 6.1 asserts the fact that there is a STUDENT whose name is Benjamin Bayer, SSN is 305-61-2435, Age is 19, and so on.

Notice that some relations may represent facts about *entities* whereas other relations may represent facts about *relationships*. For example, a relation schema MAJORS (StudentSSN, DepartmentCode) asserts that students major in academic departments; a tuple in this relation relates a student to his or her major department. Hence, the relational model represents facts about both entities and relationships *uniformly* as relations.

An alternative interpretation of a relation schema is as a **predicate;** in this case, the values in each tuple are interpreted as values that *satisfy* the predicate. This interpretation is quite useful in the context of logic programming languages, such as PROLOG, because it allows the relational model to be used within these languages. We discuss this further in Section 22.3.

6.1.3   Relational Model Notation

We will use the following notation in our presentation:

- A relation schema R of degree n is represented as $R(A_1, A_2, ..., A_n)$.
- An n-tuple t in a relation r(R) is represented as $t = <v_1, v_2, ..., v_n>$, where v_i is the value corresponding to attribute A_i. We use the following notation to refer to **component values** of tuples:
  - $t[A_i]$ refers to the value v_i in t for attribute A_i.
  - $t[A_u, A_w, ..., A_z]$, where $A_u, A_w, ..., A_z$ is a list (or set) of attributes from R, refers to the subtuple of values $<v_u, v_w, ..., v_z>$ from t corresponding to the attributes specified in the list.
- The letters Q, R, S denote relation names.
- The letters q, r, s denote relation instances.
- The letters t, u, v denote tuples.
- In general, the name of a relation such as STUDENT indicates the current set of tuples in that relation—the *current relation instance*—whereas STUDENT(Name, SSN, ...) refers to the relation schema.
- Attribute names are sometimes qualified with the relation name to which they belong, for example, STUDENT.Name or STUDENT.Age.

Consider the tuple t = <'Barbara Benson', '533-69-1238', '839-8461', '7384 Fontana Lane', null, 19, 3.25> from the STUDENT relation in Figure 6.1; we have t[Name] = <'Barbara Benson'>, and t[SSN, GPA, Age] = <'533-69-1238', 3.25, 19>.

6.1.4   Key Attributes of a Relation

A relation is defined as a *set of tuples*. By definition, all elements of a set are distinct; hence, all tuples in a relation must also be distinct. This means that no two tuples can have the same combination of values for *all* their attributes. Usually, there are other **subsets of attributes** of a relation schema R with the property that no two tuples in any relation instance r of R should have the same combination of values for these attributes. Suppose we denote one such subset of attributes by SK; then for any two distinct tuples t_1 and t_2 in a relation instance r of R, we have:

$$t_1[SK] \neq t_2[SK]$$

Any such set of attributes SK is called a **superkey** of the relation schema R. Every relation has at least one superkey—the set of all its attributes. A **key** K of a relation schema R is a superkey of R with the additional property that removing any attribute A from K leaves a set of attributes K' that is not a superkey of R. Hence, a key is a *minimal superkey*; a superkey from which we cannot remove any attributes.

For example, consider the STUDENT relation of Figure 6.1. The attribute set {SSN} is a key of STUDENT because we know that no two student tuples will ever have the same value for SSN. Any set of attributes that includes SSN—for example, {SSN, Name, Age}—is a superkey. However, the set {SSN, Name, Age} is not a key of STUDENT because removing Name or Age or both from the set still leaves us with a superkey.

The value of a key attribute can be used to identify uniquely a tuple in the relation. For example, the SSN value 305-61-2435 identifies uniquely the tuple corresponding to Benjamin Bayer in the STUDENT relation. Notice that a set of attributes being a key is a property of the relation schema; it is a constraint that should hold on *every* relation instance of the schema. A key is determined from the meaning of the attributes in the relation schema. Hence, the property is *time invariant*; it must still hold when we insert new tuples in the relation. For example, we should not designate the Name attribute of the STUDENT relation in Figure 6.1 as a key, because there is no guarantee that two students with identical names will never exist.*

In general, a relation schema may have more than one key. In this case, each of the keys is called a **candidate key**. For example, the CAR relation in Figure 6.4 has two candidate keys: LicenseNumber and EngineSerialNumber. It is common to designate one of the candidate keys as the **primary key** of the relation. This is the candidate key whose values are used to *identify* tuples in the relation. We use the convention that the attributes that form the primary key of a relation schema are <u>underlined</u>, as shown in Figure 6.4. Notice that when a relation schema has several candidate keys, the choice of one to become primary key is arbitrary; however, it is usually better to choose a primary key with a single attribute or a small number of attributes.

6.1.5   Relational Database Schemas and Integrity Constraints

So far, we have discussed single relations and relation schemas. A relational database usually contains many relations, with tuples in those relations related together in various ways. In this section we define a relational database and relational database schema and

---

*Names are sometimes used as keys, but then some artifact—such as appending an ordinal number—must be used to distinguish any identical names.

CAR	LicenseNumber	EngineSerialNumber	Make	Model	Year
	Texas ABC-739	A69352	Ford	Mustang	85
	Florida TVP-347	B43696	Oldsmobile	Cutlass	83
	New York MPO-22	X83554	Oldsmobile	Delta	79
	California 432-TFY	C43742	Mercedes	190-D	82
	California RSK-629	Y82935	Toyota	Camry	86
	Texas RSK-629	U028365	Jaguar	XJS	85

Figure 6.4   The CAR relation with two candidate keys: License-Number and EngineSerialNumber

discuss two basic integrity constraints that, together with key constraints discussed in Section 6.1.4, may be considered an *integral part* of the relational data model.

Definition of a Relational Database Schema and Relational Database

A **relational database schema** S is a set of relation schemas S = {R_1, R_2, ..., R_m} and a set of **integrity constraints** IC. A **relational database instance** DB of S is a set of relation instances DB = {r_1, r_2, ..., r_m} such that each r_i is an instance of R_i and such that the r_i's satisfy the integrity constraints specified in IC. Figure 6.5 shows a relational database schema that we call COMPANY, and Figure 6.6 shows a relational database instance corresponding to the COMPANY schema. We use this schema and database in this chapter and in Chapters 7 through 9 for developing example queries in different relational languages. When we refer to a relational database, we implicitly include its schema and instance.

Observe that in Figure 6.5 the DNUMBER attribute in both DEPARTMENT and DEPT_ LOCATIONS stands for the same real world concept—the number given to a department. That same concept is called DNO in EMPLOYEE and DNUM in PROJECT. We will allow an attribute that represents the same real world concept to have names that may or may not be identical in different relations. In a similar way, we allow attributes that represent different concepts to have the same name in different relations. For example, we could have used the attribute name NAME for both PNAME of PROJECT and DNAME of DEPARTMENT; in this case, we would have two attributes having the same name but representing different real world concepts—project names and department names.

In some *early versions of the relational model* an assumption was made that the same real world concept, when represented by an attribute, would have *identical* attribute names in all relations. This creates problems when the same real world concept is used in different roles (meanings) in the same relation. For example, the concept of social security number appears twice in the EMPLOYEE relation of Figure 6.5, once in the role of employee social security number and the other in the role of supervisor social security number. We gave them distinct attribute names—SSN and SUPERSSN, respectively—because we allow the same concept to have different names.

Integrity Constraints on a Relational Database Schema

Integrity constraints are specified on a database schema and are expected to hold on every database instance of that schema. **Key constraints** specify the *candidate keys* of

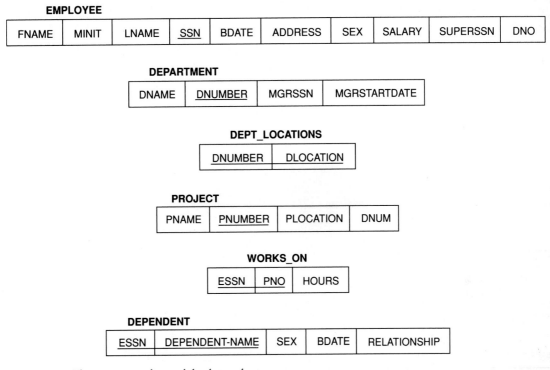

Figure 6.5   The COMPANY relational database schema

each relation schema; candidate key values must be unique for every tuple in any relation instance of that relation schema. In addition to the key constraints, two other types of constraints are considered part of the relational model—entity integrity and referential integrity.

The **entity integrity constraint** states that no primary key value can be null. This is because we use the primary key value to identify individual tuples in a relation; having null values for the primary key implies that we cannot identify some tuples. For example, if two or more tuples had null for their primary keys, we might not be able to distinguish them.

Key constraints and entity integrity constraints are specified on individual relations. The **referential integrity constraint** is a constraint that is specified between two relations and is used to maintain the consistency among tuples of the two relations. Informally, the referential integrity constraint states that a tuple in one relation that refers to another relation must refer to an *existing tuple* in that relation. For example, in Figure 6.6 the attribute DNO of EMPLOYEE gives the department number for which each employee works; hence, its value in every EMPLOYEE tuple must match the DNUMBER value of some tuple in the DEPARTMENT relation.

To define referential integrity more formally, we need first to define the concept of a foreign key. The conditions for a foreign key, given below, specify a referential integrity

EMPLOYEE	FNAME	MINIT	LNAME	SSN	BDATE	ADDRESS	SEX	SALARY	SUPERSSN	DNO
	John	B	Smith	123456789	09-JAN-55	731 Fondren, Houston, TX	M	30000	333445555	5
	Franklin	T	Wong	333445555	08-DEC-45	638 Voss, Houston, TX	M	40000	888665555	5
	Alicia	J	Zelaya	999887777	19-JUL-58	3321 Castle, Spring, TX	F	25000	987654321	4
	Jennifer	S	Wallace	987654321	20-JUN-31	291 Berry, Bellaire, TX	F	43000	888665555	4
	Ramesh	K	Narayan	666884444	15-SEP-52	975 Fire Oak, Humble, TX	M	38000	333445555	5
	Joyce	A	English	453453453	31-JUL-62	5631 Rice, Houston, TX	F	25000	333445555	5
	Ahmad	V	Jabbar	987987987	29-MAR-59	980 Dallas, Houston, TX	M	25000	987654321	4
	James	E	Borg	888665555	10-NOV-27	450 Stone, Houston, TX	M	55000	null	1

DEPT_LOCATIONS	DNUMBER	DLOCATION
	1	Houston
	4	Stafford
	5	Bellaire
	5	Sugarland
	5	Houston

DEPARTMENT	DNAME	DNUMBER	MGRSSN	MGRSTARTDATE
	Research	5	333445555	22-MAY-78
	Administration	4	987654321	01-JAN-85
	Headquarters	1	888665555	19-JUN-71

WORKS_ON	ESSN	PNO	HOURS
	123456789	1	32.5
	123456789	2	7.5
	666884444	3	40.0
	453453453	1	20.0
	453453453	2	20.0
	333445555	2	10.0
	333445555	3	10.0
	333445555	10	10.0
	333445555	20	10.0
	999887777	30	30.0
	999887777	10	10.0
	987987987	10	35.0
	987987987	30	5.0
	987654321	30	20.0
	987654321	20	15.0
	888665555	20	null

PROJECT	PNAME	PNUMBER	PLOCATION	DNUM
	ProductX	1	Bellaire	5
	ProductY	2	Sugarland	5
	ProductZ	3	Houston	5
	Computerization	10	Stafford	4
	Reorganization	20	Houston	1
	Newbenefits	30	Stafford	4

DEPENDENT	ESSN	DEPENDENT_NAME	SEX	BDATE	RELATIONSHIP
	333445555	Alice	F	05-APR-76	DAUGHTER
	333445555	Theodore	M	25-OCT-73	SON
	333445555	Joy	F	03-MAY-48	SPOUSE
	987654321	Abner	M	29-FEB-32	SPOUSE
	123456789	Michael	M	01-JAN-78	SON
	123456789	Alice	F	31-DEC-78	DAUGHTER
	123456789	Elizabeth	F	05-MAY-57	SPOUSE

Figure 6.6 A relational database instance of the COMPANY schema

constraint between the two relation schemas R_1 and R_2. A set of attributes FK in relation schema R_1 is a **foreign key** of R_1 if it satisfies the following two rules:

1. The attributes in FK have the same domain as the primary key attributes PK of another relation schema R_2; the attributes FK are said to **reference** or **refer to** the relation R_2.

2. A value of FK in a tuple t_1 of R_1 either occurs as a value of PK for some tuple t_2 in R_2 or is null. In the former case, we have $t_1[FK] = t_2[PK]$, and we say that the tuple t_1 **references** or **refers to** the tuple t_2.

In a database of many relations, there will usually be many referential integrity constraints. To specify these constraints we must first have a clear understanding of the meaning or role that each set of attributes plays in the various relation schemas of the database. Referential integrity constraints typically arise from the *relationships among the entities* represented by the relation schemas. For example, consider the database shown in Figure 6.6. In the EMPLOYEE relation, the attribute DNO refers to the department for which an employee works; hence, we designate DNO to be a foreign key of EMPLOYEE, referring to the DEPARTMENT relation. This means that a value of DNO in any tuple t_1 of the EMPLOYEE relation must match a value of the primary key of DEPARTMENT—the DNUMBER attribute—in some tuple t_2 of the DEPARTMENT relation or the value of DNO can be null if the employee does not belong to a department. In Figure 6.6 the tuple for employee "John Smith" references the tuple for the "Research" department, indicating that "John Smith" works for this department.

Notice that a foreign key can *refer to its own relation*. For example, the attribute SUPERSSN in EMPLOYEE refers to the supervisor of an employee; this is another employee, represented by a tuple in the EMPLOYEE relation. Hence, SUPERSSN is a foreign key that references the EMPLOYEE relation itself. In Figure 6.6 the tuple for employee "John Smith" references the tuple for employee "Franklin Wong," indicating that "Franklin Wong" is the supervisor of "John Smith."

We can *diagrammatically display referential integrity constraints* by drawing a directed arc from each foreign key to the relation it references. Figure 6.7 shows the schema in Figure 6.5 with the referential integrity constraints displayed in this manner.

All integrity constraints should be specified on the relational database schema if we are interested in maintaining these constraints on all database instances. Hence, in a relational system, the data definition language (DDL) should include provisions for specifying the various types of constraints so that the DBMS can automatically enforce them. Most relational database management systems support key and entity integrity constraints but unfortunately not referential integrity, although some systems are starting to support referential integrity.

The above types of constraints do not include a large class of general constraints, sometimes called *semantic integrity constraints*, that may need to be specified and enforced on a relational database. Examples of such a constraint are "the salary of an employee should not exceed the salary of the employee's supervisor" and "the maximum number of hours an employee can work on all projects per week is 56." Such constraints are not enforced by current commercial relational DBMSs but may be in the future. We will discuss integrity constraints in more detail in Chapter 20.

6.1.6 Update Operations on Relations

There are three basic update operations on relations—insert, delete, and modify. **Insert** is used to insert a new tuple or tuples in a relation, **delete** to delete tuples, and **modify** to change the values of some attributes. Whenever we apply update operations, we must

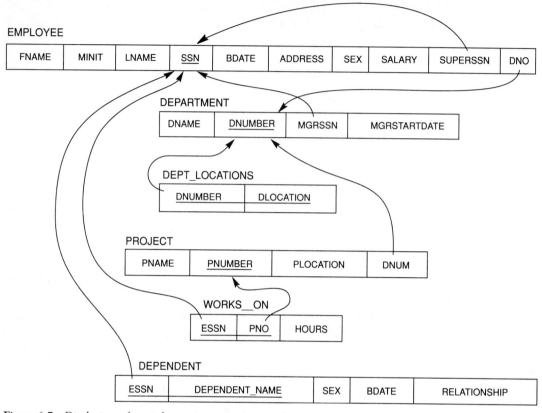

Figure 6.7   Displaying referential integrity constraints on the
COMPANY relational database schema

check that the integrity constraints specified on the relational database schema are not violated. In this section we discuss the types of constraints that may be violated by each update operation and the types of actions that may be taken in case an update causes a violation. We use the database shown in Figure 6.6 for examples and discuss only key constraints, entity integrity constraints, and the referential integrity constraints shown in Figure 6.7. For each type of update we give some example operations and discuss any constraints that each operation may violate.

Examples of the Insert Operation

1. Insert < 'Cecilia', 'F', 'Kolonsky', '677678989', '05-APR-50', '6357 Windy Lane, Katy, TX', F, 28000, null, 4 > into EMPLOYEE.

   —This insertion satisfies all constraints so it is acceptable.

2. Insert < 'Alicia', 'J', 'Zelaya', '999887777', '05-APR-50', '6357 Windy Lane, Katy, TX', F, 28000, '987654321', 4 > into EMPLOYEE.

—This insertion violates the key constraint because another tuple with the same SSN value already exists in the EMPLOYEE relation.

3. Insert < 'Cecilia', 'F', 'Kolonsky', null, '05-APR-50', '6357 Windy Lane, Katy, TX', F, 28000, null, 4 > into EMPLOYEE.

   —This insertion violates the entity integrity constraint (null for the primary key SSN) so it is unacceptable.

4. Insert < 'Cecilia', 'F', 'Kolonsky', '677678989', '05-APR-50', '6357 Windswept, Katy, TX', F, 28000, '987654321', 7 > into EMPLOYEE.

   —This insertion violates the referential integrity constraint specified on DNO because no DEPARTMENT tuple exists with DNUMBER = 7.

If an insertion violates one or more constraints, there are two options to follow. The first option is to *reject the insertion*. In this case, it would be useful if the DBMS could explain to the user why the insertion was rejected. The second option is to attempt to *correct the reason for rejecting the update*. For example, in operation 3 above, the DBMS could ask the user to provide a value for SSN and accept the insertion if a valid SSN value is provided. In operation 4, the DBMS could either ask the user to change the value of DNO to some valid value, or it could ask the user to insert a DEPARTMENT tuple with DNUMBER = 7 and accept the insertion only after such an operation is accepted. Notice that in the latter case the insertion can **cascade** back to the EMPLOYEE relation if the user attempts to insert a tuple for department 7 with a value for MGRSSN that does not exist in the EMPLOYEE relation.

Examples of the Delete Operation

1. Delete the WORKS_ON tuple with ESSN = '999887777' and PNO = 10.

   —This deletion is acceptable.

2. Delete the EMPLOYEE tuple with SSN = '999887777'.

   —This deletion is not acceptable because two tuples in WORKS_ON refer to this tuple. Hence, if the tuple is deleted, referential integrity violations will result.

3. Delete the EMPLOYEE tuple with SSN = '333445555'.

   —This deletion will result in even worse referential integrity violations, because this tuple is referenced by tuples from the EMPLOYEE, DEPARTMENT, WORKS_ON, and DEPENDENT relations.

Of the three types of constraints discussed above—key, entity integrity, and referential integrity—deletion can violate only referential integrity. There are three options if a deletion operation causes a violation. The first option is to *reject the deletion*. The second option is to *attempt to cascade the deletion* by deleting tuples that reference the tuple being deleted. For example, in operation 2, the DBMS could automatically delete the two offending tuples from WORKS_ON with ESSN = '999887777'. A third option is to *modify the referencing attribute values* that cause the violation; each such value is either set to null or changed to reference another valid tuple. Notice that if a referencing attribute that causes a violation is *part of the primary key*, it cannot be set to null because then it would violate entity integrity.

Combinations of the three options are also possible. For example, for operation 3 not to cause a violation, the DBMS may automatically delete all tuples from WORKS_ON and DEPENDENT with ESSN = '333445555'. Tuples in EMPLOYEE with SUPERSSN = '333445555' and the tuple in DEPARTMENT with MGRSSN = '333445555' can either be deleted or have their SUPERSSN and MGRSSN values changed to valid values or to null. Although it may make sense to delete automatically the WORKS_ON and DEPENDENT tuples that refer to an EMPLOYEE tuple, it may not make sense to delete other EMPLOYEE tuples or a DEPARTMENT tuple. In general, when a referential integrity constraint is specified, the DBMS should allow the user to *specify which of the three options* applies in case of a violation of the constraint. Unfortunately, most current commercial relational systems do not provide all these options.

Examples of the Modify Operation

1. Modify the SALARY of the EMPLOYEE tuple with SSN = '999887777' to 28000.
   —Acceptable.
2. Modify the DNO of the EMPLOYEE tuple with SSN = '999887777' to 1.
   —Acceptable.
3. Modify the DNO of the EMPLOYEE tuple with SSN = '999887777' to 7.
   —Unacceptable because it violates referential integrity.
4. Modify the SSN of the EMPLOYEE tuple with SSN = '999887777' to '987654321'.
   —Unacceptable because it violates primary key and referential integrity constraints.

Modifying an attribute that is neither a primary key nor a foreign key usually causes no problems; the DBMS need only check that the new value is of the correct data type and domain. If a primary key value is modified, it is similar to deleting one tuple and inserting another in its place, because we use the primary key to identify tuples. Hence, the issues discussed above under both insertion and deletion come into play. If a foreign key attribute is modified, the DBMS must make sure that the new value refers to an existing tuple in the referenced relation.

6.2 The Relational Algebra

So far, we have been discussing the concepts that the relational model provides for defining the structure of a database. Now we turn our attention to the relational algebra, which is a collection of operations that are used to manipulate entire relations. These operations are used to select tuples from individual relations and to combine related tuples from several relations for the purpose of specifying a query—a retrieval request—on the database. The result of each operation is a new relation, which can be further manipulated by the relational algebra operations.

The relational algebra operations are usually divided into two groups. One group includes set operations from mathematical set theory, which are applicable because each relation is defined to be a *set* of tuples. These operations include UNION, INTERSECTION,

DIFFERENCE, and CARTESIAN PRODUCT. The other group consists of operations developed specifically for relational databases and includes the operations SELECT, PROJECT, and JOIN, among others. We discuss the SELECT and PROJECT operations first, because they are the simplest. Then we discuss set operations. Finally, we discuss the JOIN and other complex operations. We use the relational database shown in Figure 6.6 for our examples.

6.2.1 The SELECT and PROJECT Operations

The SELECT Operation

The SELECT operation is used to select a subset of the tuples in a relation. These tuples must satisfy a **selection condition**. For example, we may wish to select the subset of EMPLOYEE tuples who work in department 4 or those whose salary is greater than 30,000. Each of these two conditions is individually specified using the SELECT operation as follows:

$$\sigma_{DNO=4}(EMPLOYEE)$$
$$\sigma_{SALARY>30000}(EMPLOYEE)$$

In general, the SELECT operation is denoted by

$$\sigma_{<selection\ condition>}(<relation\ name>)$$

where the symbol σ is used to denote the SELECT operator, and the selection condition is a Boolean expression specified on the attributes of the specified relation.

The relation resulting from the SELECT operation has the *same attributes* as the relation specified in <relation name>. The Boolean expression specified in <selection condition> is made up of a number of **clauses** of the form:

<attribute name> <comparison op> <constant value>, or
<attribute name> <comparison op> <attribute name>

where <attribute name> is the name of an attribute of <relation name>, <comparison op> is normally one of the operators $\{=, <, \leq, >, \geq, \neq\}$, and <constant value> is a constant value. Clauses can be arbitrarily connected by the Boolean operators AND, OR, and NOT to form a general selection condition. For example, suppose we want to select the tuples for all employees who either work in department 4 and make over $25,000 per year or work in department 5 and make over $30,000; we can specify the following SELECT:

$$\sigma_{(DNO=4\ AND\ SALARY>25000)\ OR\ (DNO=5\ AND\ SALARY>30000)}(EMPLOYEE)$$

The result is shown in Figure 6.8a.

Notice that the comparison operators in the set $\{=, <, \leq, >, \geq, \neq\}$ apply to attributes whose domains are *ordered values*, such as numeric or date domains. Domains of alphabetic strings of characters are considered ordered alphabetically. Domains of alphanumeric strings of characters are also ordered based on the numeric codes of the characters. If the domain of an attribute is a set of *unordered values*, then only the comparison operators in the set $\{=, \neq\}$ can be applied to that attribute. An example of an unordered domain is the domain Color = {red, blue, green, white, yellow, ...} where no order is specified among the various colors. Some domains allow additional types of comparison

(a)

FNAME	MINIT	LNAME	SSN	BDATE	ADDRESS	SEX	SALARY	SUPERSSN	DNO
Franklin	T	Wong	333445555	08-DEC-45	638 Voss,Houston,TX	M	40000	888665555	5
Jennifer	S	Wallace	987654321	20-JUN-31	291 Berry,Bellaire,TX	F	43000	888665555	4
Ramesh	K	Narayan	666884444	15-SEP-52	975 FireOak,Humble,TX	M	38000	333445555	5

(b)

LNAME	FNAME	SALARY
Smith	John	30000
Wong	Franklin	40000
Zelaya	Alicia	25000
Wallace	Jennifer	43000
Narayan	Ramesh	38000
English	Joyce	25000
Jabbar	Ahmad	25000
Borg	James	55000

(c)

SEX	SALARY
M	30000
M	40000
F	25000
F	43000
M	38000
M	25000
M	55000

Figure 6.8   Illustrating SELECT and PROJECT operations.
(a) $\sigma_{\text{(DNO=4 AND SALARY>25000) OR (DNO=5 AND SALARY>30000)}}$ (EMPLOYEE).
(b) $\pi_{\text{LNAME, FNAME, SALARY}}$(EMPLOYEE).
(c) $\pi_{\text{SEX, SALARY}}$ (EMPLOYEE).

operators; for example, a domain of character strings may allow the comparison operator SUBSTRING-OF.

In general, the result of a SELECT operation can be determined as follows. The <selection condition> is applied independently to each tuple t in the relation R specified by <relation name>. This is done by substituting each occurrence of an attribute A_i in the selection condition by its value in the tuple $t[A_i]$. If the condition evaluates to true, then tuple t is **selected**. All the selected tuples appear in the result of the SELECT operation. The Boolean conditions AND, OR, and NOT have their normal interpretation as follows:

- (cond1 AND cond2) is true if both (cond1) and (cond2) are true; otherwise it is false.

- (cond1 OR cond2) is true if either (cond1) or (cond2) or both are true; otherwise it is false.

- (NOT cond) is true if cond is false; otherwise it is true.

The SELECT operator is unary; that is, it is applied on a single relation. Hence, SELECT cannot be used to select tuples from more than one relation. Also notice that the selection operation is applied to *each tuple individually*; hence, selection conditions cannot apply over more than one tuple. The **degree** of the relation resulting from a SELECT operation is the same as that of the original relation R on which the operation is applied because it has the same attributes as R. The number of tuples in the resulting relation is always *less than or equal to* the number of tuples in the original relation R. The fraction of tuples selected by a selection condition is referred to as the **selectivity** of the condition.

Notice that the SELECT operation is **commutative**; that is,

$$\sigma_{\text{<cond1>}}(\sigma_{\text{<cond2>}}(R)) = \sigma_{\text{<cond2>}}(\sigma_{\text{<cond1>}}(R))$$

Hence, a sequence of SELECTS can be applied in any order. In addition, we can always combine a **cascade** of SELECT operations into a single SELECT operation with a conjunctive (AND) condition; that is,

$$\sigma_{<cond1>}(\sigma_{<cond2>}(...(\sigma_{<condn>}(R))...)) =$$
$$\sigma_{<cond1> \text{ AND } <cond2> \text{ AND } ... \text{ AND } <condn>}(R)$$

The PROJECT Operation

If we think of a relation as a table, then the SELECT operation selects some of the *rows* from the table while discarding other rows. The **PROJECT** operation, on the other hand, selects certain *columns* from the table and discards the other columns. If we are interested in only certain attributes of a relation, we use the PROJECT operation to "project" the relation over these attributes. For example, suppose we want to list each employee's first and last names and salary; then we can use the PROJECT operation as follows:

$$\pi_{LNAME, FNAME, SALARY}(EMPLOYEE)$$

The resulting relation is shown in Figure 6.8b. The general form of the PROJECT operation is

$$\pi_{<attribute \ list>}(<relation \ name>)$$

where π is the symbol used to represent the PROJECT operation and <attribute list> is a list of attributes of the relation specified by <relation name>. The resulting relation has only the attributes specified in <attribute list> and *in the same order as they appear in the list*. Hence, its **degree** is equal to the number of attributes in <attribute list>.

Notice that if the attribute list includes only nonkey attributes of a relation, then it is probable that duplicate tuples will appear in the result. The PROJECT operation implicitly *removes any duplicate tuples*, so that the result of the PROJECT operation is a set of tuples and hence a valid relation. For example, consider the following PROJECT operation:

$$\pi_{SEX, SALARY}(EMPLOYEE)$$

The result is shown in Figure 6.8c. The tuple <F, 25000> appears only once in Figure 6.8c even though this combination of values appears twice in the EMPLOYEE relation. Whenever two or more identical tuples appear when applying a PROJECT operation, only one is kept in the result; this is known as **duplicate elimination** and is necessary to ensure that the result of the PROJECT operation is also a relation—a *set* of tuples.

The number of tuples in a relation resulting from a PROJECT operation will be less than or equal to the number of tuples in the original relation. If the projection list includes a key of the relation, then the resulting relation will have the *same number* of tuples as the original one. Also, notice that

$$\pi_{<list1>}(\pi_{<list2>}(R)) = \pi_{<list1>}(R)$$

as long as <list2> contains the attributes in <list1>; else, the left-hand side is incorrect. Also, commutativity does not hold on PROJECT.

Sequences of Operations

The relations shown in Figure 6.8 do not have any names. In general, we may want to apply several relational algebra operations one after the other. We can either write the operations as a single **relational algebra expression** by nesting the operations or apply one operation at a time and create intermediate result relations. In the latter case, we must name the relations that hold the intermediate results. For example, suppose we want to retrieve the first name, last name, and salary of all employees who work in department number 5; this involves applying a SELECT and a PROJECT operation. We can write a single relational algebra expression as follows:

$$\pi_{\text{FNAME, LNAME, SALARY}}(\sigma_{\text{DNO=5}}(\text{EMPLOYEE}))$$

Figure 6.9a shows the result of this relational algebra expression. Alternatively, we can explicitly show the sequence of operations, giving a name to each intermediate relation, as follows:

$$\text{DEP5\_EMPS} \leftarrow \sigma_{\text{DNO=5}}(\text{EMPLOYEE})$$
$$\text{RESULT} \leftarrow \pi_{\text{FNAME, LNAME, SALARY}}(\text{DEP5\_EMPS})$$

Renaming of Attributes

It is often simpler to break down a complex sequence of operations by specifying intermediate result relations rather than writing a single relational algebra expression. We can also use this technique to **rename the attributes** in the intermediate and result relations. This can be useful when we discuss more complex operations such as UNION and JOIN, as we shall see. We will introduce the notation for renaming here. To rename the

(a)

FNAME	LNAME	SALARY
John	Smith	30000
Franklin	Wong	40000
Ramesh	Narayan	38000
Joyce	English	25000

(b)

TEMP	FNAME	MINIT	LNAME	SSN	BDATE	ADDRESS	SEX	SALARY	SUPERSSN	DNO
	John	B	Smith	123456789	09-JAN-55	731 Fondren,Houston,TX	M	30000	333445555	5
	Franklin	T	Wong	333445555	08-DEC-45	638 Voss,Houston,TX	M	40000	888665555	5
	Ramesh	K	Narayan	666884444	15-SEP-52	975 Fire Oak,Humble,TX	M	38000	333445555	5
	Joyce	A	English	453453453	31-JUL-62	5631 Rice,Houston,TX	F	25000	333445555	5

R	FIRSTNAME	LASTNAME	SALARY
	John	Smith	30000
	Franklin	Wong	40000
	Ramesh	Narayan	38000
	Joyce	English	25000

Figure 6.9 Illustrating relational algebra expressions.
(a) $\pi_{\text{LNAME, FNAME, SALARY}}(\sigma_{\text{DNO=5}}(\text{EMPLOYEE}))$.
(b) The same expression using intermediate relations and renaming of attributes.

attributes in a relation resulting from applying a relational algebra operation, we simply list the new attribute names in parentheses, as in the following example:

$$\text{TEMP} \leftarrow \sigma_{\text{DNO}=5}(\text{EMPLOYEE})$$
$$\text{R(FIRSTNAME,LASTNAME,SALARY)} \leftarrow \pi_{\text{FNAME, LNAME, SALARY}}(\text{TEMP})$$

The above two operations are illustrated in Figure 6.9b. If no renaming is applied, then the names of the attributes in the resulting relation of a SELECT operation are the same as those in the original relation and in the same order. For a PROJECT operation with no renaming, the resulting relation has the same attributes as those in the projection list and in the same order.

6.2.2 Set Theoretic Operations

The next group of relational algebra operations are the standard mathematical operations on sets. They apply to the relational model because a relation is defined to be a set of tuples, and they are used whenever we process the tuples in two relations as sets. For example, suppose we want to retrieve the social security numbers of all employees who either work in department 5 or directly supervise an employee who works in department 5; we can do this using the UNION operation as follows:

$$\text{DEP5\_EMPS} \leftarrow \sigma_{\text{DNO}=5}(\text{EMPLOYEE})$$
$$\text{RESULT1} \leftarrow \pi_{\text{SSN}}(\text{DEP5\_EMPS})$$
$$\text{RESULT2(SSN)} \leftarrow \pi_{\text{SUPERSSN}}(\text{DEP5\_EMPS})$$
$$\text{RESULT} \leftarrow \text{RESULT1} \cup \text{RESULT2}$$

The relation RESULT1 has the social security numbers of all employees who work in department 5, whereas RESULT2 has the social security numbers of all employees who directly supervise an employee who works in department 5. The UNION operation gives us the tuples that are in either RESULT1 or RESULT2 or both. Figure 6.10 illustrates this example.

There are several set theoretic operations that are used to merge the elements of two sets in various ways, including UNION, INTERSECTION, and DIFFERENCE. These operations are binary; that is, they are applied to two sets. When these operations are adapted to relational databases, we must make sure that it is possible to apply the operations to two relations so that the result is also a valid relation. To achieve this, the two relations on which any of the above three operations are applied must have the same **type of tuples**; this condition is called *union compatibility*. Two relations $R(A_1, A_2, ..., A_n)$ and

RESULT1	SSN
	123456789
	333445555
	666884444
	453453453

RESULT2	SSN
	333445555
	888665555

RESULT	SSN
	123456789
	333445555
	666884444
	453453453
	888665555

Figure 6.10 RESULT ← RESULT 1 ∪ RESULT 2

$S(B_1, B_2, ..., B_n)$ are said to be **union compatible** if they have the same degree n, and $dom(A_i) = dom(B_i)$ for $1 \leq i \leq n$. This means that the two relations have the same number of attributes and that each pair of corresponding attributes have the same domain.

We can define the three operations UNION, INTERSECTION, and DIFFERENCE on two union compatible relations R and S as follows:

- UNION—The result of this operation, denoted by $R \cup S$, is a relation that includes all tuples that are either in R or in S or in both R and S. Duplicate tuples are eliminated.

- INTERSECTION—The result of this operation, denoted by $R \cap S$, is a relation that includes all tuples that are in both R and S.

- DIFFERENCE—The result of this operation, denoted by $R - S$, is a relation that includes all tuples that are in R but not in S.

We will adopt the convention that the resulting relation has the same attribute names as the *first* relation R. Figure 6.11 illustrates the three operations. The relations STUDENT and INSTRUCTOR in Figure 6.11a are union compatible and their tuples represent the names of students and instructors, respectively. The result of the UNION operation (Figure 6.11b) shows the names of all students and instructors. Note that duplicate tuples appear only once in the result. The result of the INTERSECTION operation (Figure 6.11c) includes only those who are both students and instructors. Notice that both UNION and INTERSECTION are *commutative operations*; that is,

$$R \cup S = S \cup R, \text{ and } R \cap S = S \cap R.$$

Also, either operation can be applied to *any number of relations*, and both are *associative operations*; that is,

$$R \cup (S \cup T) = (R \cup S) \cup T, \text{ and}$$
$$(R \cap S) \cap T = R \cap (S \cap T).$$

The DIFFERENCE operation is *not commutative*; that is, in general,

$$R - S \neq S - R.$$

Figure 6.11d shows the names of students who are not instructors, and Figure 6.11e shows the names of instructors who are not students.

Next we discuss the CARTESIAN PRODUCT, denoted by **X**, which is also a binary set operation but the relations on which it is applied do *not* have to be union compatible. This operation is used to combine tuples from two relations so that related tuples can be identified.

In general, the result of $R(A_1, A_2, ..., A_n) \text{ X } S(B_1, B_2, ..., B_m)$ is a relation Q with n + m attributes $Q(A_1, A_2, ..., A_n, B_1, B_2, ..., B_m)$ in that order. The resulting relation Q has one tuple for each combination of tuples—one from R and one from S. Hence, if R has n_R tuples and S has n_S tuples, then R X S will have $n_R * n_S$ tuples. As an example to illustrate the use of CARTESIAN PRODUCT, suppose we want to retrieve for each female employee a list of the names of her dependents; we can do this as follows:

FEMALE_EMPS $\leftarrow \sigma_{SEX='F'}(EMPLOYEE)$
EMPNAMES $\leftarrow \pi_{FNAME, LNAME, SSN}(FEMALE\_EMPS)$

(a)

STUDENT	FN	LN
	Susan	Yao
	Ramesh	Shah
	Johnny	Kohler
	Barbara	Jones
	Amy	Ford
	Jimmy	Wang
	Ernest	Gilbert

INSTRUCTOR	FNAME	LNAME
	John	Smith
	Ricardo	Browne
	Susan	Yao
	Francis	Johnson
	Ramesh	Shah

(b)

FN	LN
Susan	Yao
Ramesh	Shah
Johnny	Kohler
Barbara	Jones
Amy	Ford
Jimmy	Wang
Ernest	Gilbert
John	Smith
Ricardo	Browne
Francis	Johnson

(c)

FN	LN
Susan	Yao
Ramesh	Shah

(d)

FN	LN
Johnny	Kohler
Barbara	Jones
Amy	Ford
Jimmy	Wang
Ernest	Gilbert

(e)

FNAME	LNAME
John	Smith
Ricardo	Browne
Francis	Johnson

Figure 6.11   Illustrating the set operations UNION, INTERSECTION, and DIFFERENCE. (a) Two union compatible relations. (b) STUDENT ∪ INSTRUCTOR. (c) STUDENT ∩ INSTRUCTOR. (d) STUDENT − INSTRUCTOR. (e) INSTRUCTOR − STUDENT.

EMP_DEPENDENTS ← EMPNAMES X DEPENDENT
ACTUAL_DEPENDENTS ← $\sigma_{SSN=ESSN}$(EMP_DEPENDENTS)
RESULT ← $\pi_{FNAME, LNAME, DEPENDENT\_NAME}$(ACTUAL_DEPENDENTS)

The resulting relations from the above sequence of operations are shown in Figure 6.12. The EMP_DEPENDENTS relation is the result of applying the CARTESIAN PRODUCT operation to EMPNAMES from Figure 6.12 with DEPENDENT from Figure 6.6. In EMP_DEPENDENTS, every tuple from EMPNAMES is combined with every tuple from DEPENDENT, giving a result that is not very meaningful. We only want to combine a female employee tuple with her dependents, which means the DEPENDENT tuples whose ESSN values match the SSN value of the EMPLOYEE tuple. In ACTUAL_DEPENDENTS, we accomplish this.

The CARTESIAN PRODUCT creates tuples with the combined attributes of two relations. We can then SELECT only related tuples from the two relations by specifying an ap-

FEMALE_EMPS	FNAME	MINIT	LNAME	SSN	BDATE	ADDRESS	SEX	SALARY	SUPERSSN	DNO
	Alicia	J	Zelaya	999887777	19-JUL-58	3321 Castle,Spring,TX	F	25000	987654321	4
	Jennifer	S	Wallace	987654321	20-JUN-31	291 Berry,Bellaire,TX	F	43000	888665555	4
	Joyce	A	English	453453453	31-JUL-62	5631 Rice,Houston,TX	F	25000	333445555	5

EMPNAMES	FNAME	LNAME	SSN
	Alicia	Zelaya	999887777
	Jennifer	Wallace	987654321
	Joyce	English	453453453

EMP_DEPENDENTS	FNAME	LNAME	SSN	ESSN	DEPENDENT_NAME	SEX	BDATE	· · ·
	Alicia	Zelaya	999887777	333445555	Alice	F	05-APR-76	· · ·
	Alicia	Zelaya	999887777	333445555	Theodore	M	25-OCT-73	· · ·
	Alicia	Zelaya	999887777	333445555	Joy	F	03-MAY-48	· · ·
	Alicia	Zelaya	999887777	987654321	Abner	M	29-FEB-32	· · ·
	Alicia	Zelaya	999887777	123456789	Michael	M	01-JAN-78	· · ·
	Alicia	Zelaya	999887777	123456789	Alice	F	31-DEC-78	· · ·
	Alicia	Zelaya	999887777	123456789	Elizabeth	F	05-MAY-57	· · ·
	Jennifer	Wallace	987654321	333445555	Alice	F	05-APR-76	· · ·
	Jennifer	Wallace	987654321	333445555	Theodore	M	25-OCT-73	· · ·
	Jennifer	Wallace	987654321	333445555	Joy	F	03-MAY-48	· · ·
	Jennifer	Wallace	987654321	987654321	Abner	M	29-FEB-32	· · ·
	Jennifer	Wallace	987654321	123456789	Michael	M	01-JAN-78	· · ·
	Jennifer	Wallace	987654321	123456789	Alice	F	31-DEC-78	· · ·
	Jennifer	Wallace	987654321	123456789	Elizabeth	F	05-MAY-57	· · ·
	Joyce	English	453453453	333445555	Alice	F	05-APR-76	· · ·
	Joyce	English	453453453	333445555	Theodore	M	25-OCT-73	· · ·
	Joyce	English	453453453	333445555	Joy	F	03-MAY-48	· · ·
	Joyce	English	453453453	987654321	Abner	M	29-FEB-32	· · ·
	Joyce	English	453453453	123456789	Michael	M	01-JAN-78	· · ·
	Joyce	English	453453453	123456789	Alice	F	31-DEC-78	· · ·
	Joyce	English	453453453	123456789	Elizabeth	F	05-MAY-57	· · ·

ACTUAL_DEPENDENTS	FNAME	LNAME	SSN	ESSN	DEPENDENT_NAME	SEX	BDATE
	Jennifer	Wallace	987654321	987654321	Abner	M	29-FEB-32

RESULT	FNAME	LNAME	DEPENDENT_NAME
	Jennifer	Wallace	Abner

Figure 6.12   Illustrating the CARTESIAN PRODUCT operation

propriate selection condition, as we did in the preceding example. Because this sequence of CARTESIAN PRODUCT followed by SELECT is used quite commonly to identify and select related tuples from two relations, a special operation, called JOIN, was created to specify this sequence as a single operation. We discuss the JOIN operation next. The CARTESIAN PRODUCT is rarely used as a meaningful operation by itself.

6.2.3   The JOIN operation

The JOIN operation, denoted by ⋈, is used to combine *related tuples* from two relations into single tuples. This operation is very important for any relational database with more than a single relation because it allows us to process relationships among relations. To illustrate JOIN, suppose we want to *retrieve the name of the manager of each department*. To get the manager's name, we need to combine each department tuple with the employee tuple whose SSN value matches the MGRSSN value in the department tuple. We do this using the JOIN operation, then project the result over the necessary attributes:

DEPT_MGR ← DEPARTMENT ⋈$_{MGRSSN=SSN}$EMPLOYEE

RESULT ← $\pi_{DNAME, LNAME, FNAME}$(DEPT_MGR)

The first operation is illustrated in Figure 6.13. The example we gave earlier to illustrate the CARTESIAN PRODUCT operation can be specified using the JOIN operation by replacing the two operations

EMP_DEPENDENTS ← EMPNAMES X DEPENDENT

ACTUAL_DEPENDENTS ← $\sigma_{SSN=ESSN}$(EMP_DEPENDENTS)

with

ACTUAL_DEPENDENTS ← EMPNAMES ⋈$_{SSN=ESSN}$DEPENDENT.

The general form of a JOIN operation on two relations $R(A_1, A_2, ..., A_n)$ and $S(B_1, B_2, ..., B_m)$ is

R ⋈$_{<join\ condition>}$ S.

The result of the JOIN is a relation Q with n + m attributes $Q(A_1, A_2, ..., A_n, B_1, B_2, ..., B_m)$ in that order; Q has one tuple for each combination of tuples—one from R and one from S—*whenever the combination satisfies the join condition*. This is the main difference between CARTESIAN PRODUCT and JOIN; in JOIN, only combinations of tuples satisfying the join condition appear in the result, whereas in the CARTESIAN PRODUCT *all* combinations of tuples are included in the result. The join condition is specified on attributes from the two relations R and S and is evaluated for each combination of tuples. Each tuple combination for which the join condition evaluates to true for its attribute values is included in the resulting relation Q as a single tuple.

A join condition is of the form:

<condition> AND <condition> AND ... AND <condition>

where each condition is of the form $A_i \theta B_j$, A_i is an attribute of R, B_j is an attribute of S, A_i and B_j have the same domain, and θ is one of the comparison operators {=, <, ≤, >,

DEPT_MGR	DNAME	DNUMBER	MGRSSN	· · ·	FNAME	MINIT	LNAME	SSN	· · ·
	Research	5	333445555	· · ·	Franklin	T	Wong	333445555	· · ·
	Administration	4	987654321	· · ·	Jennifer	S	Wallace	987654321	· · ·
	Headquarters	1	888665555	· · ·	James	E	Borg	888665555	· · ·

Figure 6.13   Illustrating the JOIN operation

$\geq, \neq$}. A JOIN operation with such a general join condition is called a **THETA JOIN**. Tuples whose join attributes are null *do not* appear in the result.

The most common JOIN involves join conditions with equality comparisons only. Such a JOIN, where the only comparison operator used is =, is called an **EQUIJOIN**. Both examples we had were EQUIJOINs. Notice that in the result of an EQUIJOIN we always have one or more pairs of attributes that have *identical values* in every tuple. For example, in Figure 6.13 the values of the attributes MGRSSN and SSN are identical in every tuple of DEPT_MGR because the equality join condition is specified on these two attributes. Because one of each pair of attributes with identical values is superfluous, a new operation, called **NATURAL JOIN** was created to get rid of the second attribute in an equijoin condition. We denote natural join by *, and it is basically an equijoin followed by removal of the superfluous attributes.[†] An example is

PROJ_DEPT ← PROJECT *$_{\text{DNUM=DNUMBER}}$ DEPARTMENT

The attributes DNUM and DNUMBER are called the **join attributes**. The resulting relation is illustrated in Figure 6.14a. In the PROJ_DEPT relation, each tuple combines a PROJECT tuple with the DEPARTMENT tuple for the department that controls the project. In the resulting relation we keep only the *first join attribute*. Because the comparisons in a join condition of a natural join are always equality comparisons, we can discard the comparison operator and only *list the join attributes* as follows:

PROJ_DEPT ← PROJECT *$_{\text{(DNUM),(DNUMBER)}}$DEPARTMENT

In general, there could be a list of join attributes from each relation, so the general form that we use for NATURAL JOIN is

Q ← R *$_{\text{(<list1>),(<list2>)}}$ S

In this case, <list1> specifies a list of i attributes from R and <list2> specifies a list of i attributes from S. Only the list corresponding to attributes of the first relation R—<list 1>—is kept in the result Q.

If the attributes on which the natural join is specified *have the same names in both relations,* we can leave out the join condition entirely.[††] For example, to apply a natural join on the DNUMBER attribute of DEPARTMENT and DEPT_LOCATIONS, it is sufficient to write

DEPT_LOCS ← DEPARTMENT * DEPT_LOCATIONS

The resulting relation is shown in Figure 6.14b, which combines each department with its locations and has one tuple for each location. It is performed by equating *all* attribute pairs that have the same name in the two relations.

Notice that if no combination of tuples satisfies the join condition, then the result of a JOIN is an empty relation with zero tuples. In general, if R has n_R tuples and S has n_S

[†]A more standard definition of NATURAL JOIN requires that the two join attributes have the same name; we give this definition as a special case later.

[††]The original definition of NATURAL JOIN (Codd 1970) required that the join attributes *always* have the same name. Our more general definition covers both the original NATURAL JOIN and an operation originally called COMPOSITION.

(a)

PROJ_DEPT	PNAME	PNUMBER	PLOCATION	DNUM	DNAME	MGRSSN	MGRSTARTDATE
	ProductX	1	Bellaire	5	Research	333445555	22-MAY-78
	ProductY	2	Sugarland	5	Research	333445555	22-MAY-78
	ProductZ	3	Houston	5	Research	333445555	22-MAY-78
	Computerization	10	Stafford	4	Administration	987654321	01-JAN-85
	Reorganization	20	Houston	1	Headquarters	888665555	19-JUN-71
	Newbenefits	30	Stafford	4	Administration	987654321	01-JAN-85

(b)

DEPT_LOCS	DNAME	DNUMBER	MGRSSN	MGRSTARTDATE	LOCATION
	Headquarters	1	888665555	19-JUN-71	Houston
	Administration	4	987654321	01-JAN-85	Stafford
	Research	5	333445555	22-MAY-78	Bellaire
	Research	5	333445555	22-MAY-78	Sugarland
	Research	5	333445555	22-MAY-78	Houston

Figure 6.14 Illustrating the NATURAL JOIN operation.
(a) PROJ_DEPT ← PROJECT $*_{DNUM=DNUMBER}$DEPARTMENT.
(b) DEPT_LOCS ← DEPARTMENT $*$ DEPT_LOCATIONS.

tuples, the result of a JOIN operation R $\bowtie_{<join\ condition>}$ S will have between zero and n_R*n_S tuples. If there is no <join condition> to satisfy, all combinations of tuples qualify and the JOIN becomes a CARTESIAN PRODUCT.

6.2.4 Complete Set of Relational Algebra Operations

It has been shown that the set of relational algebra operations {σ, π, ∪, −, X} is a **complete** set; that is, any of the other relational algebra operations can be expressed as a *sequence of operations from this set*. For example, the INTERSECTION operation can be expressed using UNION and DIFFERENCE as follows:

$$R \cap S \equiv (R \cup S) - ((R - S) \cup (S - R))$$

Although, strictly speaking, INTERSECTION is not required, it is inconvenient to specify this complex expression every time we wish to specify an intersection. As another example, a JOIN operation can be specified as a CARTESIAN PRODUCT followed by a SELECT operation as we discussed:

$$R \bowtie_{<condition>} S \equiv \sigma_{<condition>} (R \text{ X } S)$$

Similarly, a NATURAL JOIN can be specified as a CARTESIAN PRODUCT followed by SELECT and PROJECT operations. Hence, the various JOIN operations are also *not strictly necessary* for the expressive power of the relational algebra; however, they are very important—as is the INTERSECTION operation—because they are convenient to use and are very commonly applied in database applications. Other operations have been included in the relational algebra for convenience rather than necessity. We discuss one of these—the DIVISION operation—in the next section.

6.2.5   The DIVISION Operation

The DIVISION operation is useful for a special kind of request that occurs frequently in database applications. This request can be illustrated by the query: "Retrieve the names of employees who work on *all* the projects that 'John Smith' works on." To express this query using the DIVISION operation we proceed as follows. First, we retrieve the list of project numbers that 'John Smith' works on in the intermediate relation SMITH_PNOS:

$$\text{SMITH} \leftarrow \sigma_{\text{FNAME='John' AND LNAME='Smith'}}(\text{EMPLOYEE})$$
$$\text{SMITH\_PNOS} \leftarrow \pi_{\text{PNO}}(\text{WORKS\_ON} *_{\text{ESSN=SSN}} \text{SMITH})$$

Next, we create a relation that includes a tuple <PNO, ESSN> whenever the employee whose social security number is ESSN works on the project whose number is PNO in the intermediate relation SSN_PNOS:

$$\text{SSN\_PNOS} \leftarrow \pi_{\text{PNO,ESSN}}(\text{WORKS\_ON})$$

Finally, we apply the DIVISION operation to the two relations, which gives us the desired employees' social security numbers:

$$\text{SSNS(SSN)} \leftarrow \text{SSN\_PNOS} \div \text{SMITH\_PNOS}$$
$$\text{RESULT} \leftarrow \pi_{\text{FNAME,LNAME}}(\text{SSNS} * \text{EMPLOYEE})$$

The above operations are shown in Figure 6.15a. In general, the DIVISION operation is applied to two relations $R(Z) \div S(X)$, where $X \subseteq Z$. Let $Y = Z - X$; that is, Y is the set of attributes of R that are not attributes of S. The result of DIVISION is a relation $T(Y)$ that includes a tuple t if a tuple t_R whose $t_R[Y] = t$ appears in R with $t_R[X] = t_S$ *for every tuple* t_S in S. This means that for a tuple t to appear in the result T of the DIVISION, the values in t must appear in R in combination with *every* tuple in S.

Figure 6.15b illustrates a DIVISION operator where $R = Z = \{A,B\}$, $S = X = \{A\}$, and $T = Y = \{B\}$; that is, X and Y are both single attributes. The resulting relation T has only the single attribute $B = Z - X$. Notice that b_1 and b_4 appear in R in combination with all three tuples in S; that is why they appear in the resulting relation T. All other values of B in R do not appear with all the tuples in S and are not selected—b_2 does not appear with a_2 and b_3 does not appear with a_1.

The DIVISION operator can be expressed as a sequence of π, X, and $-$ operations as follows:

$$\text{T1} \leftarrow \pi_Y(R)$$
$$\text{T2} \leftarrow \pi_Y((S \times \text{T1}) - R)$$
$$\text{T} \leftarrow \text{T1} - \text{T2}$$

6.3   Additional Relational Operations

There are some common database requests that cannot be performed with the standard relational algebra operations described in Section 6.2. Most commercial query languages for relational DBMSs include capabilities to perform these requests. In this section we discuss some types of such requests and define additional operations that can be used to express these requests. These operations can be used to enhance the expressive power of the relational algebra.

(a)

SSN_PNOS	ESSN	PNO
	123456789	1
	123456789	2
	666884444	3
	453453453	1
	453453453	2
	333445555	2
	333445555	3
	333445555	10
	333445555	20
	999887777	30
	999887777	10
	987987987	10
	987987987	30
	987654321	30
	987654321	20
	888665555	20

SMITH_PNOS	PNO
	1
	2

SSNS	SSN
	123456789
	453453453

(b)

R	A	B
	a1	b1
	a2	b1
	a3	b1
	a4	b1
	a1	b2
	a3	b2
	a2	b3
	a3	b3
	a4	b3
	a1	b4
	a2	b4
	a3	b4

S	A
	a1
	a2
	a3

T	B
	b1
	b4

Figure 6.15 Illustrating the DIVISION operation. (a) Dividing SSN_PNOS by SMITH_PNOS. (b) T ← R ÷ S.

6.3.1 Aggregate Functions

The first type of request that cannot be expressed in relational algebra is to specify mathematical **aggregate functions** on collections of values from the database. For example, we may want to retrieve the average or total salary of all employees or the number of employee tuples. Common functions applied to collections of numeric values are SUM, AVERAGE, MAXIMUM, and MINIMUM. The function for counting tuples is usually called COUNT. Each of these functions can be applied to all tuples in a relation.

Another common type of request involves grouping the tuples in a relation by the value of some of their attributes and then applying an aggregate function independently to each group of tuples. An example is grouping employee tuples by DNO, so that each group includes the tuples for employees working in the same department. We can then list each DNO value along with, say, the average salary of employees within the department.

We can define a FUNCTION operation, which can be used to specify these types of requests, as follows:

$$\text{<grouping attributes>} \; \mathcal{F} \; \text{<function list> (<relation name>)}$$

where <grouping attributes> is a list of attributes of the relation specified in <relation name>, and <function list> is a list of (<function> <attribute>) pairs. In each such pair, <function> is one of the allowed functions—such as SUM, AVERAGE, MAXIMUM, MINIMUM, COUNT—and <attribute> is an attribute of the relation specified by <relation name>. The resulting relation has as many attributes as there are in the grouping attributes plus the function list combined. For example, to retrieve each department number, the number of employees in the department, and their average salary, we write:

$$\text{R(DNO, NUMBER\_OF\_EMPLOYEES, AVERAGE\_SAL)} \leftarrow$$
$$_{\text{DNO}}\mathcal{F}_{\text{COUNT SSN, AVERAGE SALARY}}\text{(EMPLOYEE)}$$

The result of this operation is shown in Figure 6.16a.

In the above example, we specified a list of attribute names—between parentheses—for the resulting relation R. If no such list is specified, then the attributes of the resulting relation that correspond to the function list will each be the concatenation of the function name with the attribute name on which the function is applied in the form <function>_<attribute>. For example, the result of the following operation is shown in Figure 6.16b.

$$_{\text{DNO}} \; \mathcal{F} \; _{\text{COUNT SSN, AVERAGE SALARY}}\text{(EMPLOYEE)}$$

If no grouping attributes are specified, the functions are applied to the attribute values of *all the tuples* in the relation, so the resulting relation has a *single tuple only*. For example, the result of the following operation is shown in Figure 6.16c.

$$\mathcal{F} \; _{\text{COUNT SSN, AVERAGE SALARY}}\text{(EMPLOYEE)}$$

It is worth emphasizing that the result of applying an aggregate function is a relation, not a scalar number.

6.3.2 Recursive Closure Operations

Another type of operation that, in general, cannot be specified in the relational algebra is the **recursive closure.** This operation is applied to a **recursive relationship** between tuples of the same type, such as the relationship between an employee and supervisor.

(a)

R	DNO	NO_OF_EMPLOYEES	AVERAGE_SAL
	5	4	33250
	4	3	31000
	1	1	55000

(b)

DNO	COUNT_SSN	AVERAGE_SALARY
5	4	33250
4	3	31000
1	1	55000

(c)

COUNT_SSN	AVERAGE_SALARY
8	35125

Figure 6.16 Illustrating the FUNCTION operation.
(a) $R(\text{DNO,NO\_OF\_EMPLOYEES,AVERAGE\_SAL}) \leftarrow {}_{\text{DNO}}\mathcal{F}_{\text{COUNT SSN,AVERAGE SALARY}}(\text{EMPLOYEE})$.
(b) ${}_{\text{DNO}}\mathcal{F}_{\text{COUNT SSN,AVERAGE SALARY}}(\text{EMPLOYEE})$.
(c) $\mathcal{F}_{\text{COUNT SSN,AVERAGE SALARY}}(\text{EMPLOYEE})$.

This relationship is described by the foreign key SUPERSSN of the EMPLOYEE relation in Figures 6.6 and 6.7, which relates each employee tuple (in the role of supervisee) to another employee tuple (in the role of supervisor). An example of a recursive operation is to retrieve all supervisees of an employee e at all levels, that is, all employees e' directly supervised by e, all employees e" directly supervised by each employee e', all employees e''' directly supervised by each employee e", and so on. Although it is straightforward in the relational algebra to specify all employees supervised by e *at a specific level*, it is difficult to specify all supervisees at all levels. For example, to specify the SSNs of all employees e' directly supervised—*at level one*—by the employee e whose name is 'James Borg' (see Figure 6.6), we can apply the following operations:

$$\text{BORG\_SSN} \leftarrow \pi_{\text{SSN}}(\sigma_{\text{FNAME='James' AND LNAME='Borg'}}(\text{EMPLOYEE}))$$
$$\text{SUPERVISION(SSN1, SSN2)} \leftarrow \pi_{\text{SSN, SUPERSSN}}(\text{EMPLOYEE})$$
$$\text{RESULT1(SSN)} \leftarrow \pi_{\text{SSN1}}(\text{SUPERVISION} \bowtie_{\text{SSN2=SSN}} \text{BORG\_SSN})$$

To retrieve all employees supervised by Borg at level two, that is, all employees e" supervised by some employee e' who is directly supervised by Borg, we can apply another JOIN to the result of the first query as follows:

$$\text{RESULT2(SSN)} \leftarrow \pi_{\text{SSN1}}(\text{SUPERVISION} \bowtie_{\text{SSN2=SSN}} \text{RESULT1})$$

To get both sets of employees supervised at levels one and two by 'James Borg' we can apply the UNION operation to the two results as follows:

$$\text{RESULT3} \leftarrow (\text{RESULT1} \cup \text{RESULT2})$$

The results of these queries are illustrated in Figure 6.17. Although it is possible to retrieve employees at each level and then take their UNION, we cannot, in general, specify a query such as "retrieve the supervisees of 'James Borg' at all levels" if we do not know the *maximum number of levels*, because we would need a looping mechanism.

6.3.3 OUTER JOIN and OUTER UNION Operations

Finally, we discuss some extensions of the JOIN and UNION operations. The JOIN operations described above only match tuples that satisfy the join condition. For example, for a NATURAL JOIN operation R * S, only tuples from R that have matching tuples in S—and vice versa—appear in the result. Hence, tuples without a "related tuple" are eliminated from the result. A set of operations, called OUTER JOINs, was proposed to be used when we want to keep all tuples in R or S or both in the result—whether or not they have matching tuples in the other relation.

For example, suppose we want a list of all employee names and also the name of the departments they manage *if they happen to manage a department;* we can apply an operation **LEFT OUTER JOIN,** denoted by $⋈$, to retrieve the result as follows:

TEMP ← (EMPLOYEE $⋈_{SSN=MGRSSN}$ DEPARTMENT)
RESULT ← $\pi_{FNAME, MINIT, LNAME, DNAME}$(TEMP)

(Borg's SSN is 888665555)

	(SSN)	(SUPERSSN)
SUPERVISION	SSN1	SSN2
	123456789	333445555
	333445555	888665555
	999887777	987654321
	987654321	888665555
	666884444	333445555
	453453453	333445555
	987987987	987654321
	888665555	null

RESULT 1	SSN
	333445555
	987654321

(supervised by Borg)

RESULT 2	SSN
	123456789
	999887777
	666884444
	453453453
	987987987

(supervised by Borg's subordinates)

RESULT	SSN
	123456789
	999887777
	666884444
	453453453
	987987987
	333445555
	987654321

(RESULT1 ∪ RESULT2)

Figure 6.17 Illustrating two-level recursion

RESULT	FNAME	MINIT	LNAME	DNAME
	John	B	Smith	null
	Franklin	T	Wong	Research
	Alicia	J	Zelaya	null
	Jennifer	S	Wallace	Administration
	Ramesh	K	Narayan	null
	Joyce	A	English	null
	Ahmad	V	Jabbar	null
	James	E	Borg	Headquarters

Figure 6.18   Illustrating the LEFT OUTER JOIN operation

The LEFT OUTER JOIN operation keeps every tuple in the *first* or left relation R in R ⋈ S; if no matching tuple is found in S, then the attributes of S in the result are filled or "padded" with null values. The result of the above operations is shown in Figure 6.18.

A similar operation RIGHT OUTER JOIN, denoted by ⋈, keeps every tuple in the *second* or right relation S in the result of R ⋈ S. A third operation FULL OUTER JOIN, denoted ⋈, keeps all tuples in both the left and right relations when no matching tuples are found, padding them with null values as needed.

The **OUTER UNION** operation was developed to take the union of tuples from two relations that are *not union compatible*. This operation will take the UNION of tuples in two relations that are **partially compatible,** meaning that only some of their attributes are union compatible. The attributes that are not union compatible from either relation are kept in the result, and tuples that have no values for these attributes are padded with null values. For example, an OUTER UNION can be applied to two relations whose schemas are STUDENT(Name, SSN, Department, Advisor) and FACULTY(Name, SSN, Department, Rank). The resulting relation schema is R(Name, SSN, Department, Advisor, Rank), and all the tuples from both relations are included in the result. Student tuples will have a null for the Rank attribute, whereas faculty tuples will have a null for the Advisor attribute.

Another capability that exists in most commercial languages but not in the relational algebra is that of specifying operations on values after they are extracted from the database. For example, arithmetic operations such as +, −, * can be applied to numeric values.

6.4   Examples of Queries in the Relational Algebra

In this section we give some additional examples to illustrate the use of the relational algebra operations. All examples refer to the database of Figure 6.6. In general, the same query can be stated in numerous ways using the various relational operations. We will state each query in only one way and leave it to the reader to come up with equivalent formulations.

QUERY 1

Find the name and address of all employees who work for the 'Research' department.

RESEARCH_DEPT ← $\sigma_{DNAME='Research'}$(DEPARTMENT)
RESEARCH_DEPT_EMPS ← (RESEARCH_DEPT $\bowtie_{DNUMBER=DNO}$ EMPLOYEE)
RESULT ← $\pi_{FNAME, LNAME, ADDRESS}$(RESEARCH_DEPT_EMPS)

This query could be specified in other ways; for example, the order of the JOIN and SELECT operations could be reversed or the JOIN could be replaced by a NATURAL JOIN.

QUERY 2

For every project located in 'Stafford', list the project number, the controlling department number, and the department manager's last name, address, and birth date.

STAFFORD_PROJS ← $\sigma_{PLOCATION='Stafford'}$(PROJECT)
CONTR_DEPT ← (STAFFORD_PROJS $\bowtie_{DNUM=DNUMBER}$ DEPARTMENT)
PROJ_DEPT_MGR ← (CONTR_DEPT $\bowtie_{MGRSSN=SSN}$ EMPLOYEE)
RESULT ← $\pi_{PNUMBER, DNUM, LNAME, ADDRESS, BDATE}$ (PROJ_DEPT_MGR)

QUERY 3

Find the names of employees who work on *all* the projects controlled by department number 5.

DEPT5_PROJS(PNO) ← $\pi_{PNUMBER}$($\sigma_{DNUM=5}$(PROJECT))
EMP_PROJ(SSN, PNO) ← $\pi_{ESSN, PNO}$(WORKS_ON)
RESULT_EMP_SSNS ← EMP_PROJ ÷ DEPT5_PROJS
RESULT ← $\pi_{LNAME, FNAME}$(RESULT_EMP_SSNS * EMPLOYEE)

QUERY 4

Make a list of project numbers for projects that involve an employee whose last name is 'Smith' as a worker or as a manager of the department that controls the project.

SMITHS(ESSN) ← π_{SSN}($\sigma_{LNAME='Smith'}$(EMPLOYEE))
SMITH_WORKER_PROJS ← π_{PNO}(WORKS_ON * SMITHS)
MGRS ← $\pi_{LNAME, DNUMBER}$(EMPLOYEE $\bowtie_{SSN=MGRSSN}$ DEPARTMENT)
SMITH_MGRS ← $\sigma_{LNAME='Smith'}$(MGRS)
SMITH_MANAGED_DEPTS(DNUM) ← $\pi_{DNUMBER}$(SMITH_MGRS)
SMITH_MGR_PROJS(PNO) ← $\pi_{PNUMBER}$(SMITH_MANAGED_DEPTS * PROJECT)
RESULT ← (SMITH_WORKER_PROJS ∪ SMITH_MGR_PROJS)

QUERY 5

List the names of all employees with two or more dependents.

Strictly speaking, this query *cannot be done in the relational algebra*. We have to use the FUNCTION operation with the COUNT aggregate function, which is not part of the relational algebra. In the following formulation, we assume that dependents of the *same* employee have *distinct* DEPENDENT_NAME values.

T1(SSN, NO_OF_DEPS) $\leftarrow$ $_{ESSN}\mathcal{F}_{COUNT\ DEPENDENT\_NAME}$(DEPENDENT)

T2 $\leftarrow$ $\sigma_{NO\_OF\_DEPS>2}$(T1)

RESULT $\leftarrow$ $\pi_{LNAME,\ FNAME}$(T2 * EMPLOYEE)

QUERY 6

List the names of employees who have no dependents.

ALL_EMPS $\leftarrow$ π_{SSN}(EMPLOYEE)

EMPS_WITH_DEPS(SSN) $\leftarrow$ π_{ESSN}(DEPENDENT)

EMPS_WITHOUT_DEPS $\leftarrow$ (ALL_EMPS – EMPS_WITH_DEPS)

RESULT $\leftarrow$ $\pi_{LNAME,\ FNAME}$(EMPS_WITHOUT_DEPS * EMPLOYEE)

QUERY 7

List the names of managers who have at least one dependent.

MGRS(SSN) $\leftarrow$ π_{MGRSSN}(DEPARTMENT)

EMPS_WITH_DEPS(SSN) $\leftarrow$ π_{ESSN}(DEPENDENT)

MGRS_WITH_DEPS $\leftarrow$ (MGRS $\cap$ EMPS_WITH_DEPS)

RESULT $\leftarrow$ $\pi_{LNAME,\ FNAME}$(MGRS_WITH_DEPS * EMPLOYEE)

As we mentioned earlier, the same query can, in general, be specified in many different ways. For example, the operations can often be applied in various sequences. In addition, some operations can be used to replace others; for example, the INTERSECTION operation in Query 7 can be replaced by a natural join. As an exercise, the reader should attempt to do each of the above example queries using different operations. In Chapters 7, 8, and 9 we will show how these queries are stated in other relational languages.

6.5 Summary

In this chapter we presented the modeling concepts provided by the relational model of data. We also discussed the relational algebra and additional operations that can be used to manipulate relations. We started by introducing the concepts of domains, tuples, and attributes. We then defined a relation schema as a set of attributes that describe the structure of a relation. A relation, or relation instance, is a set of tuples.

Several characteristics differentiate relations from ordinary tables or files. The first is that tuples in a relation are not ordered. The second concerns ordering of attributes in a relation schema and the corresponding ordering of values within a tuple. We gave an alternative definition of relation that does not require these two orderings, but we continued to use the first definition, which requires attributes and tuple values to be ordered, for convenience. We then discussed values in tuples and introduced null values to represent missing or unknown information. We showed how a relation can be interpreted as a type of assertion or predicate, allowing relations to be used in logic programming.

We then defined a relational database schema and relational database. Several types of constraints can be considered part of the relational model. The concepts of super-key, candidate key, and primary key specify key constraints. The entity integrity constraint prohibits primary key attributes being null. The interrelation constraint of referential integrity is used to maintain consistency of references among tuples from different relations.

The update operations on the relational model are insert, delete, and modify. Each operation may violate certain types of constraints. Whenever an update is applied, the database consistency after the update must be checked to ensure that no constraints are violated.

The relational algebra is a set of operations that are used to manipulate relations. We presented the various operations and illustrated the types of manipulations each is used for. Table 6.1 lists the various relational algebra operations we discussed. The unary relational operators SELECT and PROJECT were discussed first. Then we discussed binary set operations that require relations on which they are applied to be union compatible; these include UNION, INTERSECTION, and DIFFERENCE. The CARTESIAN PRODUCT operation is used to combine tuples from two relations into single larger tuples. We showed how CARTESIAN PRODUCT followed by SELECT can identify related tuples from two relations. The JOIN operations can directly identify and combine related tuples. Join operations include THETA JOIN, EQUIJOIN, and NATURAL JOIN.

We then discussed some types of queries that cannot be stated with the relational algebra operations. We introduced the FUNCTION operation to deal with aggregate types of requests. We discussed recursive queries and how some types of recursive queries can be specified. We then presented the OUTER JOIN and OUTER UNION operations, which extend JOIN and UNION.

Finally, we gave examples to illustrate the use of relational operations to specify queries on a relational database. We will use these queries in subsequent chapters when we discuss various query languages.

Review Questions

6.1. Define the following terms: domain, attribute, n-tuple, relation schema, relation instance, degree of a relation, relational database schema, relational database instance.

6.2. Why are tuples in a relation not ordered?

6.3. Why are duplicate tuples not allowed in a relation?

6.4. What is the difference between a key and a superkey?

6.5. Why do we designate one of the candidate keys of a relation to be primary key?

6.6. Discuss the characteristics of relations that make them different from ordinary tables and files.

6.7. Discuss the various reasons that lead to the occurrence of null values in relations.

6.8. Discuss the entity integrity and referential integrity constraints. Why is each considered important?

Table 6.1   Operations of the Relational Algebra

Operation	Purpose	Notation
SELECT	Select all tuples that satisfy the selection condition from a relation R	$\sigma_{<\text{selection condition}>}(R)$
PROJECT	Produce a new relation with only some of the attributes of R and remove duplicate tuples	$\pi_{<\text{attribute list}>}(R)$
THETA JOIN	Produce all combinations of tuples from R_1 and R_2 that satisfy the join condition	$R_1 \bowtie_{<\text{join condition}>} R_2$
EQUI JOIN	Produce all combinations of tuples from R_1 and R_2 that satisfy a join condition with only equality comparisons	$R_1 \bowtie_{<\text{join condition}>} R_2$, or $R_1 \bowtie_{(<\text{join attributes 1}>),}$ $_{(<\text{join attributes 2}>)} R_2$
NATURAL JOIN	Same as EQUI JOIN except that the join attributes of R_2 are not included in the resulting relation; if the join attributes have the same names, they do not have to be specified at all	$R_1 *_{<\text{join condition}>} R_2$, or $R_1 *_{(<\text{join attributes 1}>),}$ $_{(<\text{join attributes 2}>)} R_2$, or $R_1 * R_2$
UNION	Produces a relation that includes all the tuples in R_1 or R_2 or both R_1 and R_2; R_1 and R_2 must be union compatible	$R_1 \cup R_2$
INTERSECTION	Produces a relation that includes all the tuples in both R_1 and R_2; R_1 and R_2 must be union compatible	$R_1 \cap R_2$
DIFFERENCE	Produces a relation that includes all the tuples in R_1 that are not in R_2; R_1 and R_2 must be union compatible	$R_1 - R_2$
CARTESIAN PRODUCT	Produces a relation that has the attributes of R_1 and R_2 and includes as tuples all possible combinations of tuples from R_1 and R_2	$R_1 \times R_2$
DIVISION	Produce a relation R(X) that includes all tuples t{X} in R_1(Z) that appear in R_1 in combination with every tuple from R_2(Y), where Z = X $\cup$ Y	$R_1(Z) \div R_2(Y)$

6.9. Define foreign key. What is this concept used for?

6.10. Discuss the various update operations on relations and the types of integrity constraints that must be checked for each update operation.

6.11. List the operations of the relational algebra and the purpose of each.

6.12. What is union compatibility? Why do the UNION, INTERSECTION, and DIFFERENCE operations require that the relations on which they are applied be union compatible?

6.13. Discuss some types of queries where renaming of attributes is necessary in order to specify the query unambiguously.

6.14. Discuss the various types of JOIN operations.

6.15. What is the FUNCTION operation? What is it used for?

6.16. How are the OUTER JOIN operations different from the JOIN operations?

6.17. How is the OUTER UNION operation different from UNION?

Exercises

6.18. Show the result of each of the example queries in Section 6.4 if they are applied to the database of Figure 6.6.

6.19. Specify the following queries on the database schema shown in Figure 6.5 using the relational operators discussed in this chapter. Also show the result of each query if applied to the database of Figure 6.6.

    a. Retrieve the names of employees in department 5 who work more than 10 hours per week on the 'ProductX' project.

    b. List the names of employees who have a dependent with the same first name as themselves.

    c. Find the names of employees who are directly supervised by 'Franklin Wong'.

    d. For each project, list the project name and the total hours per week (by all employees) spent on that project.

    e. Retrieve the names of employees who work on every project.

    f. Retrieve the names of employees who do not work on any project.

    g. For each department, retrieve the department name and the average salary of employees working in that department.

    h. Retrieve the average salary of all female employees.

    i. Find the names and addresses of employees who work on at least one project located in Houston but whose department has no location in Houston.

    j. List the last names of department managers who have no dependents.

    k. Generalize Query i above to list the names and addresses of employees who work on a project in one city but whose department has no location in that city.

6.20. Suppose each of the following update operations is applied directly to the database of Figure 6.6. Discuss *all* integrity constraints violated by each operation, if any, and the different ways of enforcing these constraints.

    a. Insert < 'Robert', 'F', 'Scott', '943775543', '21-JUN-42', '2365 Newcastle Rd, Bellaire, TX', M, 58000, '888665555', 1 > into EMPLOYEE.

    b. Insert < 'ProductA', 4, 'Bellaire', 2 > into PROJECT.

   c. Insert < 'Production', 4, '943775543', '01-OCT-88' > into DEPARTMENT.

   d. Insert < '677678989', null, '40.0' > into WORKS_ON.

   e. Insert < '453453453', 'John', M, '12-DEC-60', 'SPOUSE' > into DEPENDENT.

   f. Delete the WORKS_ON tuples with ESSN = '333445555'.

   g. Delete the EMPLOYEE tuple with SSN = '987654321'.

   h. Delete the PROJECT tuple with PNAME = 'ProductX'.

   i. Modify the MGRSSN and MGRSTARTDATE of the DEPARTMENT tuple with DNUM-BER = 5 to '123456789' and '01-OCT-88', respectively.

   j. Modify the SUPERSSN attribute of the EMPLOYEE tuple with SSN = '999887777' to '943775543'.

   k. Modify the HOURS attribute of the WORKS_ON tuple with ESSN = '999887777' and PNO = 10 to '5.0'.

6.21. Consider the AIRLINE relational database schema shown in Figure 6.19, which describes a database for airline flight information. Each FLIGHT is identified by a flight NUMBER, and consists of one or more FLIGHT_LEGs with LEG_NUMBERs 1, 2, 3, etc. Each leg has scheduled arrival and departure times and airports and has many LEG_INSTANCEs—one for each DATE on which the flight travels. FARES are kept for each flight. For each leg instance, SEAT_RESERVATIONs are kept, as are the AIRPLANE used in the leg and the actual arrival and departure times and airports. An AIRPLANE is identified by an AIRPLANE_ID and is of a particular AIRPLANE_TYPE. CAN_LAND relates AIRPLANE_TYPEs to the AIRPORTs in which they can land. An AIRPORT is identified by an AIRPORT_CODE. Specify the following queries in relational algebra:

   a. For each flight, list the flight number, the departure airport for the first leg of the flight, and the arrival airport for the last leg of the flight.

   b. List the flight numbers and weekdays of all flights or flight legs that depart from Houston Intercontinental Airport (airport code 'IAH') and arrive in Los Angeles International Airport (airport code 'LAX').

   c. List the flight number, departure airport code, scheduled departure time, arrival airport code, scheduled arrival time, and weekdays of all flights or flight legs that depart from some airport in the city of Houston and arrive at some airport in the city of Los Angeles.

   d. List all fare information for flight number 'CO197'.

   e. Retrieve the number of available seats for flight number 'CO197' on '09-OCT-89'.

6.22. Consider an update for the AIRLINE database to enter a reservation on a particular flight or flight leg on a given date.

   a. Give the operations for this update.

   b. What types of constraints would you expect to check?

   c. Which of these constraints are key, entity integrity, and referential integrity constraints and which are not?

AIRPORT

AIRPORT_CODE	NAME	CITY	STATE

FLIGHT

NUMBER	AIRLINE	WEEKDAYS

FLIGHT_LEG

FLIGHT_NUMBER	LEG_NUMBER	DEPARTURE_AIRPORT_CODE	SCHEDULED_DEPARTURE_TIME
		ARRIVAL_AIRPORT_CODE	SCHEDULED_ARRIVAL_TIME

LEG_INSTANCE

FLIGHT_NUMBER	LEG_NUMBER	DATE	NUMBER_OF_AVAILABLE_SEATS	AIRPLANE_ID
DEPARTURE_AIRPORT_CODE	DEPARTURE_TIME	ARRIVAL_AIRPORT_CODE	ARRIVAL_TIME	

FARES

FLIGHT_NUMBER	FARE_CODE	AMOUNT	RESTRICTIONS

AIRPLANE_TYPE

TYPE_NAME	MAX_SEATS	COMPANY

CAN_LAND

AIRPLANE_TYPE_NAME	AIRPORT_CODE

AIRPLANE

AIRPLANE_ID	TOTAL_NUMBER_OF_SEATS	AIRPLANE_TYPE

SEAT_RESERVATION

FLIGHT_NUMBER	LEG_NUMBER	DATE	SEAT_NUMBER	CUSTOMER_NAME	CUSTOMER_PHONE

Figure 6.19   The AIRLINE relational database schema

d. Specify all the referential integrity constraints on Figure 6.19.

6.23. Consider the relation

CLASS(Course#, Univ_Section#, InstructorName, Semester, BuildingCode, Room#, TimePeriod, Weekdays, CreditHours).

This represents classes taught in a university with unique Univ_Section#. Give what you think should be various candidate keys and write in your own words the constraints under which each candidate key would be valid.

Selected Bibliography

The relational model was introduced by Codd (1970) in a classic paper. Codd also introduced the relational algebra and laid the theoretical foundations for the relational model in a series of papers (Codd 1971, 1972, 1972a, 1974); he was later given the Turing award, the highest honor of the ACM, for his work on the relational model. In a later paper, Codd (1979) discusses extending the relational model and incorporating NULLs in the relational algebra. The resulting model is known as RM/T. Earlier work by Childs (1968) uses set theory to model databases.

Much research has been conducted on various aspects of the relational model. Todd (1976) describes an experimental DBMS that directly implements the relational algebra operations. Date (1983a) discusses outer joins. Recent research, such as that of Ozsoyoglu and Yuan (1987) and Roth and Korth (1987), has concerned non-first normal form relations. Extensions to incorporate time into the relation model and relational algebra have been reported by Snodgrass and Ahn (1985), Clifford and Tansel (1985), and Navathe and Ahmed (1989), among others. Work on extending relational operations is discussed by Carlis (1986) and Ozsoyoglu et al. (1985). Additional bibliographic notes for other aspects of the relational model and its languages and theory are given in Chapters 7, 8, 9, 13, 14, and 18.

CHAPTER 7

SQL—A Relational Database Language

In Chapter 6 we discussed the relational algebra operations; these operations are very important for understanding the types of requests that may be specified on a relational database. They are also important for query processing and optimization in relational DBMS, as we shall see in Chapter 18. The relational algebra is generally classified as a high-level language because its operations are applied to entire relations. However, there are few commercial DBMS languages based directly on the relational algebra.* This is because a query in the relational algebra is written as a sequence of operations that, when executed, produce the required result. When specifying a relational algebra query, it becomes the responsibility of the user to specify *how*—in what order—to execute the query operations. Most commercial relational DBMSs provide a high-level *declarative* language interface, so the user only specifies *what* the result is, leaving the actual optimization and decisions on how to execute the query to the DBMS.

In this chapter and in Chapter 9 we discuss several languages that have been partially or fully implemented and are available on commercial DBMSs. The best known of these is SQL, whose name is derived from Structured Query Language. We present two other languages, QUEL and QBE, in Chapter 9 after we have discussed in Chapter 8 the relational calculus, which is the formal language on which QUEL and QBE, and to some extent SQL, are based.

Originally, SQL was called SEQUEL (for Structured English QUEry Language) and was designed and implemented at IBM Research as the interface for an experimental relational database system called SYSTEM R. SQL is now the language for IBM's DB2 and SQL/DS commercial relational DBMSs and was the earliest of the high-level database languages, along with QUEL. Variations of SQL have been implemented by most commercial DBMS vendors.

---

*An early experimental DBMS, called ISBL, implemented the relational algebra operations as its query language (Todd 1976).

Even the INGRES DBMS, which is the origin of the QUEL language, now offers SQL as an option. Currently, there is an effort under way by ANSI (the American National Standards Institute) to define a standard version of SQL (ANSI 1986).

SQL is a comprehensive database language; it has statements for data definition, query, and update. Hence, it is both a DDL *and* DML. In addition, it has facilities for defining views on the database, for creating and dropping indexes on the files that represent relations, and for embedding SQL statements into a general-purpose programming language such as PL/I or PASCAL. We will discuss each of these six topics in the following subsections. In our discussion, we will mostly follow the version of SQL used in IBM's DB2 system.

7.1   Data Definition in SQL

SQL uses the terms **table, row,** and **column** for relation, tuple, and attribute, respectively. We will occasionally use these terms although we will continue to use relation, tuple, and attribute as much as possible. The SQL commands for data definition are CREATE TABLE, ALTER TABLE, and DROP TABLE. They are used to specify the attributes of a relation, to add an attribute to a relation, and to delete a relation, respectively. We discuss these next.

7.1.1   The CREATE TABLE Command

This command is used to specify a new relation by giving it a name and specifying each of its attributes. Each attribute is given a name, a data type to specify its domain of values, and some constraints on the attribute. The data types available are usually numeric types and string types. Numeric data types include integer number (INTEGER), real number (FLOAT), and formatted number (DECIMAL(i,j), where i is the total number of decimal digits and j is the number of digits after the decimal point). String data types are of either fixed length (CHAR(n), where n is the number of characters) or varying length (VARCHAR(n), where n is the maximum number of characters).

Because SQL allows NULLs as attribute values, a *constraint* **NOT NULL** may be specified on an attribute if NULL is not permitted for that attribute. In general, we should specify NOT NULL for the primary key attributes of each relation. This constraint is also specified on any other attributes whose values are required to be nonnull. Figure 7.1 shows sample data definition statements in SQL for the relational database schema shown in Figure 6.5.

One important constraint *missing* from the CREATE TABLE command is that of specifying the key attributes for a relation. In the DB2 version of SQL, instead of specifying the key attributes at the conceptual level as part of the CREATE TABLE command, they are specified implicitly at the internal level via the CREATE INDEX command (see Section 7.5), which is used to create an index access structure on one or more attributes. Hence, we *cannot simply specify the constraint that an attribute is a key* unless we also create and maintain an index on that attribute. Some relational DBMSs that implement SQL—for example, the UNIFY DBMS—permit an explicit designation of key attributes at the conceptual level, independent of access structures.

CREATE TABLE EMPLOYEE	(	FNAME	VARCHAR(15)	NOT NULL,
		MINIT	CHAR(1),	
		LNAME	VARCHAR(15)	NOT NULL,
		SSN	CHAR(9)	NOT NULL,
		BDATE	CHAR(9),	
		ADDRESS	VARCHAR(30),	
		SEX	CHAR(1),	
		SALARY	INTEGER,	
		SUPERSSN	CHAR(9),	
		DNO	INTEGER);	

CREATE TABLE DEPARTMENT	(	DNAME	VARCHAR(15)	NOT NULL,
		DNUMBER	INTEGER	NOT NULL,
		MGRSSN	CHAR(9)	
		MGRSTARTDATE	CHAR(9));	

CREATE TABLE DEPT_LOCATIONS	(	DNUMBER	INTEGER	NOT NULL,
		DLOCATION	VARCHAR(15)	NOT NULL);

CREATE TABLE PROJECT	(	PNAME	VARCHAR(15)	NOT NULL,
		PNUMBER	INTEGER	NOT NULL,
		PLOCATION	VARCHAR(15),	
		DNUM	INTEGER	NOT NULL);

CREATE TABLE WORKS_ON	(	ESSN	CHAR(9)	NOT NULL,
		PNO	INTEGER	NOT NULL,
		HOURS	DECIMAL(3,1)	NOT NULL);

CREATE TABLE DEPENDENT	(	ESSN	CHAR(9)	NOT NULL,
		DEPENDENT_NAME	CHAR(15)	NOT NULL,
		SEX	CHAR(1),	
		BDATE	CHAR(9),	
		RELATIONSHIP	VARCHAR(8));	

Figure 7.1 SQL statements to define the COMPANY schema of Figure 6.5

The relations declared through CREATE TABLE statements are called **base tables** (or base relations) in SQL terminology; this means that the relation and its tuples will actually be created and stored as a file by the DBMS. Base relations are distinguished from **virtual relations,** created through the CREATE VIEW statement (see Section 7.4), which may or may not correspond to an actual physical file. In SQL the attributes in a base table are considered to be *ordered in the sequence in which they are specified* in the CREATE TABLE statement. However, rows (tuples) are *not* considered to be ordered.

7.1.2   The DROP TABLE Command

If we decide that a base relation in the database is not needed any longer, we can delete the relation and its definition using the DROP TABLE command. For example, if we no longer wish to keep track of dependents of employees in the database of Figure 6.6, we get rid of the DEPENDENT relation by issuing the command:

DROP TABLE DEPENDENT;

7.1.3   The ALTER TABLE Command

If we decide to add an attribute to one of the base relations in the database, we use the ALTER TABLE command. The new attribute will have NULLs in all the tuples of the relation right after the command is executed; hence, the NOT NULL constraint is *not allowed* for such an attribute. For example, to keep track of jobs of employees in the database of Figure 6.6, we can add an attribute JOB to the EMPLOYEE relation using the command:

ALTER TABLE EMPLOYEE **ADD** JOB VARCHAR(12);

We must still enter a value for the new attribute JOB for each EMPLOYEE tuple. This can be done using the UPDATE command (see Section 7.3).

7.2   Queries in SQL

SQL has one basic statement for retrieving information from a database: the **SELECT statement**. Note that the SELECT statement *has no relationship to* the SELECT operation of the relational algebra, which was discussed in Chapter 6. There are many options and flavors to the SELECT statement in SQL so we will introduce its features gradually. We will use example queries specified on the schema of Figure 6.5 and refer to the sample database instance shown in Figure 6.6 to show the results of some of the example queries.

Before we proceed, we should point out an important distinction between SQL and the formal relational model discussed in Chapter 6; SQL allows a table (relation) to have two or more tuples that are identical in all their attribute values. Hence, in general, an SQL relation is not a *set of tuples* because a set does not allow two identical members; rather it is a **multiset** (sometimes called a bag) of tuples. Some SQL relations are constrained to be sets by using the CREATE UNIQUE INDEX command (see Section 7.5) or by using the DISTINCT option with the SELECT statement (described later in this section). We should be aware of this distinction as we discuss the examples.

7.2.1   Basic SQL Queries

The basic form of the SELECT statement, sometimes called a **mapping** or a **SELECT FROM WHERE block,** is formed of the three clauses SELECT, FROM, and WHERE and has the following form:

```
SELECT    <attribute list>
FROM      <table list>
WHERE     <condition>
```

where

- <attribute list> is a list of attribute names whose values are to be retrieved by the query.
- <table list> is a list of the relation names required to process the query.
- <condition> is a conditional (Boolean) expression that identifies the tuples to be retrieved by the query.

We now illustrate the basic SELECT statement with some example queries. We will label the queries here with the same query numbers given in Chapter 6 and later in Chapters 8 and 9 so that we can cross reference them.

QUERY 0
Retrieve the birthdate and address of the employee whose name is 'John B. Smith'.

Q0: **SELECT** BDATE, ADDRESS
    FROM EMPLOYEE
    WHERE FNAME='John' **AND** MINIT='B' **AND** LNAME='Smith'

This query involves only the EMPLOYEE relation listed in the FROM-clause. The query selects the EMPLOYEE tuples that satisfy the condition of the WHERE-clause, then projects the result on the BDATE and ADDRESS attributes listed in the SELECT-clause. Q0 is similar to the relational algebra expression

$$\pi_{<BDATE,ADDRESS>}(\sigma_{FNAME='John'\ AND\ MINIT='B'\ AND\ LNAME='Smith'}\ (EMPLOYEE))$$

Hence, a simple SQL query with a single relation name in the FROM-clause is similar to a SELECT-PROJECT pair of relational algebra operations. The SELECT-clause of SQL specifies the *projection attributes* and the WHERE-clause specifies the *selection condition*. The only difference is that in the SQL query we may get duplicate tuples in the result of the query because the constraint that a relation is a set is not enforced. Figure 7.2a shows the result of query Q0 on the database of Figure 6.6.

QUERY 1
Retrieve the name and address of all employees who work for the 'Research' department.

Q1: **SELECT** FNAME, LNAME, ADDRESS
    FROM EMPLOYEE, DEPARTMENT
    WHERE DNAME='Research' **AND** DNUMBER=DNO

Query Q1 is similar to a SELECT-PROJECT-JOIN sequence of relational algebra operations. Such queries are often called **select-project-join queries**. In the WHERE-clause of Q1, the condition DNAME = 'Research' is a **selection condition** and corresponds to a SELECT operation in the relational algebra. The condition DNUMBER = DNO is a **join condition,** which corresponds to the condition under which a JOIN is performed in the relational algebra. The result of query Q1 may be displayed as shown in Figure 7.2b. In general, any number of select and join conditions may be specified in a single SQL query. The next example is a select-project-join query with *two* join conditions.

QUERY 2
For every project located in 'Stafford' list the project number, the controlling department number, and the department manager's last name, address, and birthdate.

Q2: **SELECT** PNUMBER, DNUM, LNAME, ADDRESS, BDATE
    FROM PROJECT, DEPARTMENT, EMPLOYEE
    WHERE DNUM=DNUMBER **AND** MGRSSN=SSN **AND**
        PLOCATION='Stafford'

(a)

BDATE	ADDRESS
09-JAN-55	731 Fondren, Houston, TX

(b)

FNAME	LNAME	ADDRESS
John	Smith	731 Fondren, Houston, TX
Franklin	Wong	638 Voss, Houston, TX
Ramesh	Narayan	975 Fire Oak, Humble, TX
Joyce	English	5631 Rice, Houston, TX

(c)

PNUMBER	DNUM	LNAME	BDATE	ADDRESS
10	4	Wallace	20-JUN-31	291 Berry, Bellaire, TX
30	4	Wallace	20-JUN-31	291 Berry, Bellaire, TX

(d)

E.FNAME	E.LNAME	S.FNAME	S.LNAME
John	Smith	Franklin	Wong
Franklin	Wong	James	Borg
Alicia	Zelaya	Jennifer	Wallace
Jennifer	Wallace	James	Borg
Ramesh	Narayan	Franklin	Wong
Joyce	English	Franklin	Wong
Ahmad	Jabbar	Jennifer	Wallace

(e)

SSN
123456789
333445555
999887777
987654321
666884444
453453453
987987987
888665555

(f)

SSN	DNAME
123456789	Research
333445555	Research
999887777	Research
987654321	Research
666884444	Research
453453453	Research
987987987	Research
888665555	Research
123456789	Administration
333445555	Administration
999887777	Administration
987654321	Administration
666884444	Administration
453453453	Administration
987987987	Administration
888665555	Administration
123456789	Headquarters
333445555	Headquarters
999887777	Headquarters
987654321	Headquarters
666884444	Headquarters
453453453	Headquarters
987987987	Headquarters
888665555	Headquarters

(g)

FNAME	MINIT	LNAME	SSN	BDATE	ADDRESS	SEX	SALARY	SUPERSSN	DNO
John	B	Smith	123456789	09-JAN-RR	731 Fondren, Houston, TX	M	30000	333445555	5
Franklin	T	Wong	333445555	08-DEC-45	638 Voss, Houston, TX	M	40000	888665555	5
Ramesh	K	Narayan	666884444	15-SEP-52	975 Fire Oak, Humble, TX	M	38000	333445555	5
Joyce	A	English	453453453	31-JUL-62	5631 Rice, Houston, TX	F	25000	333445555	5

Figure 7.2   Results of queries specified on the database of Figure 6.6.
(a) Result of Q0. (b) Result of Q1. (c) Result of Q2. (d) Result
of Q8. (e) Result of Q9. (f) Result of Q10. (g) Result of Q1C.

The join condition DNUM = DNUMBER relates a project to its controlling department, whereas the join condition MGRSSN = SSN relates the controlling department
to the employee who manages that department. The result of query Q2 is shown in Figure 7.2c.

7.2.2   Dealing with Ambiguous Attribute Names

In SQL we can use the same name for two (or more) attributes as long as the attributes
are in *different relations*. If this is the case, and a query refers to two or more attributes
with the same name, we need to **qualify** the attribute name with the relation name to
prevent ambiguity. This is done by *prefixing* the relation name to the attribute name and
separating the two by a period. To illustrate this, suppose that in Figures 6.5 and 6.6 the

DNO and LNAME attributes of the EMPLOYEE relation were called DNUMBER and NAME and the DNAME attribute of DEPARTMENT was also called NAME; then, to prevent ambiguity, query Q1 would be rephrased as shown in Q1A. We must prefix the attributes NAME and DNUMBER in Q1A to specify which ones we refer to, because the attribute names are used in both relations.

Q1A: **SELECT** FNAME, EMPLOYEE.NAME, ADDRESS
         FROM   EMPLOYEE, DEPARTMENT
         WHERE DEPARTMENT.NAME='Research' **AND**
                DEPARTMENT.DNUMBER=EMPLOYEE.DNUMBER

Ambiguity also arises in the case of queries that refer to the same relation twice, as in the following example. This query did not appear in Chapter 6, and is hence given the number 8 to distinguish it from queries 1 through 7 of Section 6.4.

QUERY 8

For each employee, retrieve the employee's first and last name and the first and last name of his or her immediate supervisor.

Q8: **SELECT** E.FNAME, E.LNAME, S.FNAME, S.LNAME
       FROM   EMPLOYEE E S
       WHERE E.SUPERSSN=S.SSN

In this case, we are allowed to declare alternative relation names E and S, called **aliases,** for the EMPLOYEE relation. Note that in the FROM clause E and S are separated by a *blank space,* not a comma. We can think of E and S as two *different copies* of the EMPLOYEE relation; the first, E, represents employees in the role of supervisees, and the second, S, represents employees in the role of supervisors. We can now join the two copies. Of course, in reality there is *only one* EMPLOYEE relation, and the join condition is meant to join the relation with itself by matching the tuples that satisfy the join condition E.SUPERSSN = S.SSN. Notice that this is an example of a one-level recursive query, as we discussed in Section 6.3.2. As in the relational algebra, we *cannot* specify a general recursive query, with an unknown number of levels, in a single SQL statement.

The result of query Q8 is shown in Figure 7.2d. Whenever one or more aliases are given to a relation, we can use these names to represent different references to that relation. This allows us to have two or more references to the same relation. Notice that, if we want to, we can use this alias naming mechanism in any SQL query, whether or not the same relation needs to be referenced more than once. For example, we could have specified query Q1A as in Q1B below just to shorten the relation names that prefix the attributes.

Q1B: **SELECT** E.FNAME, E.NAME, E.ADDRESS
         FROM   EMPLOYEE E, DEPARTMENT D
         WHERE D.NAME='Research' **AND** D.DNUMBER=E.DNUMBER

7.2.3 *Unspecified* WHERE-*clauses and Use of '*'*

We discuss two more features of SQL here. A *missing* WHERE-*clause* indicates no condition on tuple selection; hence, *all tuples* of the relation specified in the FROM-clause qualify and are selected for the query result. This is equivalent to the condition WHERE TRUE, which means *every row in the table*. If more than one relation is specified in the FROM-clause and there is no WHERE-clause, then the CARTESIAN PRODUCT—*all possible tuple combinations*—of these relations is selected. For example, query Q9 selects all EMPLOYEE SSNs (Figure 7.2e), and query Q10 selects all combinations of an EMPLOYEE SSN and a DEPARTMENT DNAME (Figure 7.2f).

Q9:	**SELECT**	SSN
	FROM	EMPLOYEE

Q10:	**SELECT**	SSN, DNAME
	FROM	EMPLOYEE, DEPARTMENT

It is extremely important not to overlook specifying any selection and join conditions in the WHERE-clause; otherwise, incorrect and very large relations may result. Notice that Q10 is similar to a CARTESIAN PRODUCT operation followed by a PROJECT operation in the relational algebra. If we specify all the attributes of EMPLOYEE and DEPARTMENT in Q10, we get the CARTESIAN PRODUCT. This can be done using the SQL feature we discuss next.

To retrieve all the attribute values of the selected tuples, we do not have to explicitly list the attribute names in SQL; we just specify an *asterisk* (*), which stands for *all the attributes*. For example, query Q1C retrieves all the attribute values of EMPLOYEE tuples who work in DEPARTMENT number 5 (Figure 7.2g), and query Q1D retrieves all the attributes of an EMPLOYEE and the attributes of the DEPARTMENT he works in for every employee working in the 'Research' department. Finally, Q10A specifies the CARTESIAN PRODUCT of the EMPLOYEE and DEPARTMENT relations.

Q1C:	**SELECT**	*
	FROM	EMPLOYEE
	WHERE	DNO=5

Q1D:	**SELECT**	*
	FROM	EMPLOYEE, DEPARTMENT
	WHERE	DNAME='Research' **AND** DNO=DNUMBER

Q10A:	**SELECT**	*
	FROM	EMPLOYEE, DEPARTMENT

7.2.4   *Tables as Sets in* SQL

As we mentioned earlier, in general, SQL does not treat a relation as a set; *duplicate tuples can appear more than once* in a relation or in the result of a query. SQL does not automatically eliminate duplicate tuples in the results of queries for the following reasons:

- Duplicate elimination is an expensive operation. One way to implement it is to sort the tuples first and then eliminate duplicates.

- The user may want to see duplicate tuples in the result of a query, although this may not occur frequently.

- When an aggregate function (see Section 7.2.8) is applied to tuples, in most cases we do not want to eliminate duplicates.

(a) SALARY

    30000
    40000
    25000
    43000
    38000
    25000
    25000
    55000

(b) SALARY

    30000
    40000
    25000
    43000
    38000
    55000

(c) FNAME   LNAME

(d) FNAME   LNAME

    James   Borg

Figure 7.3 Results of some other queries specified on the database shown in Figure 6.6. (a) Result of Q11. (b) Result of Q11A. (c) Result of Q12. (d) Result of Q14.

If we *do want* to eliminate duplicate tuples from the result of an SQL query, we use the key word **DISTINCT** in the SELECT clause, meaning that only distinct tuples should remain in the result. This causes the result of an SQL query to be a relation—a set of tuples—according to the definition of relation given in Chapter 6. For example, query Q11 retrieves the salary of every employee; if several of the employees have the same salary, that salary value will appear as many times in the result of the query, as shown in Figure 7.3a. If we are interested only in distinct salary values, we want each value to appear once, regardless of how many of the employees earn that salary. By using the keyword **DISTINCT** as in Q11A we accomplish this, as shown in Figure 7.3b.

Q11: **SELECT** SALARY
        FROM   EMPLOYEE

Q11A: **SELECT** **DISTINCT** SALARY
        FROM   EMPLOYEE

SQL has directly incorporated some of the set operations of the relational algebra. There is a set union operation (**UNION**), and in some versions of SQL there are also set difference (**MINUS**) and set intersection (**INTERSECT**) operations. The resulting relations of these set operations are sets of tuples; that is, *duplicate tuples are eliminated from the result*. Because the set operations apply only to *union compatible relations*, we must make sure that the two relations on which we apply the operation have the same attributes and the attributes appear in the same order in both relations. The next example illustrates the use of UNION.

QUERY 4

Make a list of all project numbers for projects that involve an employee whose last name is 'Smith' as a worker or as a manager of the department that controls the project.

Q4: **(SELECT** PNUMBER
      FROM   PROJECT, DEPARTMENT, EMPLOYEE

        WHERE   DNUM=DNUMBER **AND** MGRSSN=SSN **AND** LNAME='Smith')
        UNION
        (SELECT PNUMBER
        FROM   PROJECT, WORKS_ON, EMPLOYEE
        WHERE   PNUMBER=PNO **AND** ESSN=SSN **AND** LNAME='Smith')

    The first SELECT query retrieves the projects that involve a 'Smith' as manager of the department that controls the project, and the second retrieves the projects that involve a 'Smith' as a worker on the project. Notice that if several employees have the last name 'Smith', the project names involving any of them would be retrieved. Applying the UNION operation to the two SELECT queries gives the desired result.

7.2.5   Nested Queries and Set Comparisons

Some queries require that existing values in the database be fetched and then used in a comparison condition. Such queries can be conveniently formulated using **nested queries,*** which are complete SELECT queries within the WHERE-clause of another query. That other query is called the **outer query.**** Query 4 is formulated in Q4 without a nested query but can be rephrased to use nested queries as shown in Q4A.

   Q4A: **SELECT** **DISTINCT** PNAME
           FROM   PROJECT
           WHERE   PNUMBER **IN** **(SELECT** PNUMBER
                                 FROM   PROJECT, DEPARTMENT,
                                         EMPLOYEE
                               WHERE   DNUM=DNUMBER **AND**
                                         MGRSSN=SSN
                                       AND LNAME='Smith')
           OR
           PNUMBER **IN** **(SELECT** PNO
                                 FROM   WORKS_ON, EMPLOYEE
                                 WHERE   ESSN=SSN **AND** LNAME='Smith')

    The first nested query selects the project numbers of projects that have a 'Smith' involved as manager, while the second selects the project numbers of projects that have a 'Smith' involved as worker. In the outer query, we select a PROJECT tuple if the PNUMBER value of that tuple is in the result of either nested query. The comparison operator **IN** compares a value v with a set (or multiset) of values V and evaluates to TRUE if v is one of the elements in V.

    In general, we can have several levels of nested queries. We are once again faced with possible ambiguity among attribute names if attributes of the same name exist—one in a relation in the FROM-clause of the *outer query* and the other in a relation in the FROM-clause of the *nested query*. The rule is that a reference to an *unqualified attribute* refers to the relation declared in the **innermost nested query.** For example, in the

---

*Nested queries are sometimes called **embedded queries;** to avoid confusion we will use the term embedded only when we refer to using SQL in conjunction with a general-purpose programming language.
**It is interesting to note that the S in SQL, which stands for structured, describes the structured nesting of SELECT ... FROM ... WHERE ... blocks.

SELECT-clause and WHERE-clause of the first nested query of Q4A, a reference to any unqualified attribute of the PROJECT relation refers to the PROJECT relation specified in the FROM-clause of the nested query. To refer to an attribute of the PROJECT relation specified in the outer query, we can specify and refer to an *alias* for that relation. These rules are similar to scope rules for program variables in a programming language such as PASCAL, which allows nested procedures and functions. To illustrate the potential ambiguity of attribute names in nested queries, consider Query 12 below, whose result is shown in Figure 7.3c.

QUERY 12:
Retrieve the name of each employee who has a dependent with the same first name and same sex as the employee.

```
Q12:   SELECT   E.FNAME, E.LNAME
       FROM     EMPLOYEE E
       WHERE    E.SSN IN  (SELECT  ESSN
                           FROM    DEPENDENT
                           WHERE   ESSN=E.SSN AND
                                   E.FNAME=DEPENDENT_NAME AND
                                   SEX=E.SEX)
```

In the nested query of Q12, we must qualify E.SEX because it refers to the SEX attribute of EMPLOYEE from the outer query, and DEPENDENT also has an attribute called SEX. All unqualified references to SEX in the nested query refer to SEX of DEPENDENT. However, we do not have to qualify FNAME and SSN because the DEPENDENT relation does not have attributes called FNAME and SSN so there is no ambiguity. Notice that we need the SSN = ESSN condition in the WHERE-clause of the nested query; without this condition, we would select employees whose first name and sex match those of *any* dependent, whether or not the dependent is of that particular employee.

Whenever a condition in the WHERE-clause of a nested query references some attribute of a relation declared in the outer query, the two queries are said to be **correlated**. We can understand a correlated query better by considering that *the nested query is evaluated once for each tuple (or combination of tuples) in the outer query*. For example, we can think of Q12 as follows: For *each* EMPLOYEE tuple, evaluate the nested query, which retrieves the ESSN values for all DEPENDENT tuples with the same social security number, sex, and name as the EMPLOYEE tuple; if the SSN value of the EMPLOYEE tuple is *in* the result of the nested query, then select that EMPLOYEE tuple.

In general, a query written with nested SELECT... FROM... WHERE... blocks and using the = or IN comparison operators can *always* be expressed as a single block query. For example, Q12 may be written as in Q12A.

```
Q12A:   SELECT   E.FNAME, E.LNAME
        FROM     EMPLOYEE E, DEPENDENT D
        WHERE    E.SSN=D.ESSN AND E.SEX=D.SEX AND
                 E.FNAME=D.DEPENDENT_NAME
```

The original SQL implementation on SYSTEM R also had a **CONTAINS** comparison operator, which is used to compare two sets. This operator was dropped from the language, possibly because of the difficulty in implementing it efficiently. Most commercial implementations of SQL do *not* have this operator. The CONTAINS operator compares two sets of values and returns TRUE if one set contains all values in the other set. Query 3 illustrates the use of the CONTAINS operator.

QUERY 3

Retrieve the name of each employee who works on *all* the projects controlled by department number 5.

Q3:	**SELECT**	FNAME, LNAME
	FROM	EMPLOYEE
	WHERE	((**SELECT** PNO
		FROM WORKS_ON
		WHERE SSN=ESSN)
		CONTAINS
		(**SELECT** PNUMBER
		FROM PROJECT
		WHERE DNUM=5))

In Q3 the second nested query, which is not correlated with the outer query, retrieves the project numbers of all projects controlled by department 5. For *each* employee tuple, the first nested query, which is correlated, retrieves the project numbers on which the employee works; if these contain all projects controlled by department 5, the employee tuple is selected and the name of that employee is retrieved. Notice that the CONTAINS comparison operator is similar in function to the DIVISION operation of the relational algebra, described in Section 6.2.5.

7.2.6   The EXISTS Function in SQL

Next, we discuss a function, called EXISTS, in SQL that is used to check whether the result of a correlated nested query is empty (contains no tuples) or not. We illustrate the use of EXISTS—and also NOT EXISTS—with some examples. First, we formulate Query 12 in an alternative form that uses EXISTS. This is shown as Q12B below.

Q12B:	**SELECT**	E.FNAME, E.LNAME
	FROM	EMPLOYEE E
	WHERE	**EXISTS** (**SELECT** *
		FROM DEPENDENT
		WHERE E.SSN=ESSN **AND** SEX=E.SEX **AND**
		E.FNAME=DEPENDENT_NAME)

EXISTS and NOT EXISTS are usually used in conjunction with a correlated nested query. In Q12B the nested query references the SSN, FNAME, and SEX attributes of the EMPLOYEE relation from the outer query. We can think of Q12B as follows: For each EMPLOYEE tuple, evaluate the nested query, which retrieves all DEPENDENT tuples with the same social security number, sex, and name as the EMPLOYEE tuple; if at least one tuple EXISTS in the result of the nested query, then select that EMPLOYEE tuple. In general, EXISTS(Q) returns TRUE if there is *at least one tuple* in the result of query Q and returns

FALSE otherwise; NOT EXISTS(Q) returns TRUE if there are *no tuples* in the result of query Q and returns FALSE otherwise. Next, we illustrate the use of NOT EXISTS.

QUERY 6

Retrieve the names of employees who have no dependents.

```
Q6:  SELECT   FNAME, LNAME
     FROM     EMPLOYEE
     WHERE    NOT EXISTS   (SELECT   *
                            FROM     DEPENDENT
                            WHERE    SSN=ESSN)
```

In Q6 the correlated nested query retrieves all DEPENDENT tuples related to an EMPLOYEE tuple. If *none exist*, the EMPLOYEE tuple is selected. We may understand the query better if we think about it in the following way: For *each* EMPLOYEE tuple, the nested query selects all DEPENDENT tuples whose ESSN value matches the EMPLOYEE SSN; if the result of the nested query is empty then no dependents are related to the employee, so we select that EMPLOYEE tuple and retrieve its FNAME and LNAME.

QUERY 7:

List the names of managers who have at least one dependent.

```
Q7:  SELECT   FNAME, LNAME
     FROM     EMPLOYEE
     WHERE    EXISTS   (SELECT   *
                        FROM     DEPENDENT
                        WHERE    SSN=ESSN)

              AND
              EXISTS   (SELECT *
                        FROM     DEPARTMENT
                        WHERE    SSN=MGRSSN)
```

One way to write this query is shown in Q7, where we specify two nested queries; the first selects all DEPENDENT tuples related to an EMPLOYEE, and the second selects all DEPARTMENT tuples managed by the EMPLOYEE. If at least one of the first and at least one of the second exist, we select the EMPLOYEE tuple and retrieve its FNAME and LNAME values. Can you rewrite this query using only a single nested query or no nested queries?

Query 3, which we used to illustrate the CONTAINS comparison operator, can be stated using EXISTS and NOT EXISTS in SQL systems that *do not have the CONTAINS operator*. We show this rephrasing of Query 3 as Q3A below. Notice that we use two-level nesting in Q3A and that this formulation is quite a bit more complex than Q3, which used the CONTAINS comparison operator.

```
Q3A:  SELECT   LNAME, FNAME
      FROM     EMPLOYEE
      WHERE    NOT EXISTS
               (SELECT   *
                FROM   WORKS_ON B
```

WHERE   (B.PNO **IN**   (**SELECT**   PNUMBER
                          FROM   PROJECT
                          WHERE   DNUM=5))
          AND
          NOT EXISTS   (**SELECT**   *
                          FROM   WORKS_ON C
                          WHERE   C.ESSN=SSN
                                         AND C.PNO=B.PNO))

In Q3A the outer nested query selects any WORKS_ON (B) tuples whose PNO is of a project controlled by department 5 *and* there is not a WORKS_ON (C) tuple with the same PNO and the same SSN as that of the EMPLOYEE tuple under consideration in the outer query. If no such tuple exists, we select the EMPLOYEE tuple. The form of Q3A matches the following rephrasing of Query 3: Select each employee such that there does not exist a project controlled by department 5 that the employee does not work on.

Notice that Query 3 is typically stated in the relational algebra using the DIVISION operation discussed in Section 6.2.5. Also, Query 3 is an example of a query that requires a type of quantifier called a **universal quantifier** in the relational calculus (see Section 8.2). Although SQL does not have a universal quantifier, the negated existential quantifier NOT EXISTS can be used to express a universally quantified query, as we discuss in Chapter 8.

7.2.7   *Explicit Sets and* NULLs *in* SQL

We have seen several queries with a nested query in the WHERE-clause. It is also possible to use an **explicit set of values** in the WHERE-clause rather than a nested query. Such a set is enclosed in parentheses in SQL.

QUERY 13
Retrieve the social security numbers of all employees who work on project number 1, 2, or 3.

Q13:   **SELECT**   **DISTINCT** ESSN
          FROM   WORKS_ON
          WHERE   PNO **IN** (1, 2, 3)

SQL allows queries that check if a value is NULL: missing or undefined or not applicable. However, rather than using = or ≠ to compare an attribute to NULL, SQL uses IS or IS NOT. This is because SQL considers each null value distinct from other null values, so equality comparison is not appropriate. It follows that when a join operation is specified, tuples with null values for the join attributes are not included in the result. Query 14 illustrates this, and its result is shown in Figure 7.3d.

QUERY 14
Retrieve the names of all employees who do not have supervisors.

Q14:   **SELECT**   FNAME, LNAME
          FROM   EMPLOYEE
          WHERE   SUPERSSN **IS NULL**

7.2.8   Aggregate Functions and Grouping

In Section 6.3.1 we introduced the concept of an aggregate function as a relational operation. Because grouping and aggregation are required in many database applications, SQL has features that incorporate these concepts.

The first of these features is a number of built-in functions. These are COUNT, SUM, MAX, MIN, and AVG. The COUNT function returns the number of tuples or values specified in a query. The functions SUM, MAX, MIN, and AVG are applied to a set or multiset of numeric values and return, respectively, the sum, maximum value, minimum value, and average of those values. These functions can be used in the SELECT-clause only or in a HAVING-clause that we will introduce below. We illustrate the use of these functions with example queries.

QUERY 15

Find the sum of the salaries of all employees, the maximum salary, the minimum salary, and the average salary.

Q15: **SELECT**   **SUM** (SALARY), **MAX** (SALARY), **MIN** (SALARY),
                AVG (SALARY)
          FROM   EMPLOYEE

Some SQL implementations *may not allow more than one function* in the SELECT-clause; in this case we have to write four queries—one for each of the functions we want to retrieve. If we want to get the above function values for employees of a specific department—say the 'Research' department—we can write Query 16, where the EMPLOYEE tuples are restricted by the WHERE-clause to employees who work for the 'Research' department.

Q16: **SELECT**   **SUM** (SALARY), **MAX** (SALARY), **MIN** (SALARY),
                AVG (SALARY)
          FROM   EMPLOYEE, DEPARTMENT
          WHERE   DNO=DNUMBER **AND** DNAME='Research'

QUERIES 17 AND 18

Retrieve the total number of employees in the company (Q17) and the number of employees in the 'Research' department (Q18).

Q17: **SELECT**   **COUNT** (*)
          FROM   EMPLOYEE

Q18: **SELECT**   **COUNT** (*)
          FROM   EMPLOYEE, DEPARTMENT
          WHERE   DNO=DNUMBER **AND** DNAME='Research'

Here the asterisk (*) refers to the *number of rows* (tuples), so COUNT (*) returns the number of rows in the result of the query. We may also use the COUNT function to count values in a column rather than tuples. For example, to count the number of distinct salary values in the database, we write Q19.

Q19: **SELECT** **COUNT (DISTINCT** SALARY)
FROM EMPLOYEE

Notice that if we write COUNT(SALARY) instead of COUNT(DISTINCT SALARY) in Q19, we get the same result as COUNT(*) because duplicates would not be eliminated. The above examples show how functions are applied to the result of a query. In some cases we may need to use functions to select particular tuples. In such cases we must specify a correlated nested query with the desired function and use that nested query in the WHERE-clause of an outer query. For example, suppose we want to retrieve the names of all employees who have two or more dependents (Query 5); we can write:

Q5: **SELECT** LNAME, FNAME
FROM EMPLOYEE
WHERE **(SELECT** **COUNT** (*)
FROM DEPENDENT
WHERE SSN=ESSN) ≥ 2

The correlated nested query counts the number of dependents that each employee has; if this is greater than or equal to 2, the employee tuple is selected. Again, some implementations of SQL may not permit such a query.

In many cases we want to apply the aggregate functions *to subgroups of tuples in a relation* based on some attribute values. For example, we may want to find the average salary of employees in each department, or the number of employees who work on each project. In these cases we want to group the tuples that have the same value of some attribute(s), called the **grouping attribute**(s), and apply the function to each such group independently. SQL has a GROUP BY-clause for this purpose. The GROUP BY-clause specifies the grouping attributes, which *must also appear in the SELECT-clause,* so that the value of applying each function on the group of tuples appears along with the value of the grouping attribute(s).

QUERY 20

For each department retrieve the department number, the number of employees in the department, and their average salary.

Q20: **SELECT** DNO, **COUNT** (*), AVG (SALARY)
FROM EMPLOYEE
GROUP BY DNO

In Q20 the EMPLOYEE tuples are divided into groups—each group having the same value for the grouping attribute DNO. The COUNT and AVG functions are applied to each such group of tuples separately. Notice that the SELECT-clause includes only the grouping attribute and the functions to be applied on each group of tuples. Figure 7.4a illustrates how grouping works on Q20 and also shows the result of Q20.

QUERY 21

For each project retrieve the project number, project name, and number of employees who work on that project.

(a)

FNAME	MINIT	LNAME	SSN	· · ·	SALARY	SUPERSSN	DNO
John	B	Smith	123456789		30000	333445555	5
Franklin	T	Wong	333445555		40000	888665555	5
Ramesh	K	Narayan	666884444		38000	333445555	5
Joyce	A	English	453453453	· · ·	25000	333445555	5
Alicia	J	Zelaya	999887777		25000	987654321	4
Jennifer	S	Wallace	987654321		43000	888665555	4
Ahmad	V	Jabbar	987987987		25000	987654321	4
James	E	Bong	888665555		55000	null	1

DNO	COUNT (*)	AVG (SALARY)
5	4	33250
4	3	31000
1	1	55000

Result of Q20

Grouping EMPLOYEE tuples by value of DNO

(b)

PNAME	PNUMBER		ESSN	PNO	HOURS
ProductX	1		123456789	1	32.5
ProductX	1		453453453	1	20.0
ProductY	2		123456789	2	7.5
ProductY	2		453453453	2	20.0
ProductY	2		333445555	2	10.0
ProductZ	3		666884444	3	40.0
ProductZ	3		333445555	3	10.0
Computerization	10	· · ·	333445555	10	10.0
Computerization	10		999887777	10	10.0
Computerization	10		987987987	10	35.0
Reorganization	20		333445555	20	10.0
Reorganization	20		987654321	20	15.0
Reorganization	20		888665555	20	null
Newbenefits	30		987987987	30	5.0
Newbenefits	30		987654321	30	20.0
Newbenefits	30		999887777	30	30.0

these groups are not selected by the HAVING condition of Q22

After applying WHERE clause but before applying HAVING

PNAME	PNUMBER		ESSN	PNO	HOURS
ProductY	2		123456789	2	7.5
ProductY	2		453453453	2	20.0
ProductY	2		333445555	2	10.0
Computerization	10	· · ·	333445555	10	10.0
Computerization	10		999887777	10	10.0
Computerization	10		987987987	10	35.0
Reorganization	20		333445555	20	10.0
Reorganization	20		987654321	20	15.0
Reorganization	20		888665555	20	null
Newbenefits	30		987987987	30	5.0
Newbenefits	30		987654321	30	20.0
Newbenefits	30		999887777	30	30.0

PNAME	COUNT (*)
ProductY	3
Computerization	3
Reorganization	3
Newbenefits	3

Result of Q22
(PNUMBER not shown)

After applying the HAVING clause condition

Figure 7.4 Illustrating GROUP BY and HAVING. (a) Illustrating the query Q20. (b) Illustrating the query Q22.

Q21: **SELECT** PNUMBER, PNAME, **COUNT** (*)
          FROM PROJECT, WORKS_ON
          WHERE PNUMBER=PNO
          GROUP BY PNUMBER, PNAME

Q21 shows how we can use a join condition in conjunction with GROUP BY. In this case, the grouping and functions are applied *after* the joining of the two relations. Sometimes we want to retrieve the values of these functions for only those *groups that satisfy certain conditions*. For example, suppose we want to modify Query 21 so that only projects with more than two employees appear in the result. SQL provides a **HAVING-clause,** which can appear only in conjunction with a GROUP BY-clause, for this purpose. HAVING provides a condition on the group of tuples associated with each value of the grouping attributes, and only the groups that satisfy the condition are retrieved in the result of the query. This is illustrated by Query 22.

QUERY 22

For each project *on which more than two employees work* retrieve the project number, project name, and number of employees who work on that project.

Q22:	**SELECT**	PNUMBER, PNAME, **COUNT** (*)
	FROM	PROJECT, WORKS_ON
	WHERE	PNUMBER=PNO
	GROUP BY	PNUMBER, PNAME
	HAVING	**COUNT** (*) > 2

Notice that while selection conditions in the WHERE-clause limit the *tuples* to which functions are applied, the HAVING-clause limits *whole groups*. Figure 7.4b illustrates the use of HAVING and displays the result of Q22.

QUERY 23

For each project retrieve the project number, project name, and number of employees from department 5 who work on that project.

Q23:	**SELECT**	PNUMBER, PNAME, **COUNT** (*)
	FROM	PROJECT, WORKS_ON, EMPLOYEE
	WHERE	PNUMBER=PNO **AND** SSN=ESSN **AND** DNO=5
	GROUP BY	PNUMBER, PNAME

Here we restrict the tuples in each group to those that satisfy the condition specified in the WHERE-clause, namely that they work in department number 5. Notice that we must be extra careful when two different conditions apply—one to the function in the SELECT-clause and another to the function in the HAVING-clause. For example, suppose that we want to count the *total* number of employees with salaries greater than $40,000 who work in each department, but only for those departments where more than five employees work. Here, the condition (SALARY > 40000) applies only to the COUNT function in the SELECT-clause. Suppose we write the following *incorrect* query:

SELECT	DNAME, **COUNT** (*)
FROM	DEPARTMENT, EMPLOYEE
WHERE	DNUMBER=DNO **AND** SALARY>40000
GROUP BY	DNAME
HAVING	**COUNT** (*) > 5

This is incorrect because it will select only departments that have more than five employees *who each earn more than $40,000*. The rule is that the WHERE-clause is executed first to select individual tuples; the HAVING-clause is applied later to select individual groups of tuples. Hence, the tuples are already restricted to employees earning more than $40,000 *before* the function in the HAVING-clause is applied. One way to write the query correctly is to use a nested query* as shown in Q24.

Q24:	**SELECT**	DNAME, **COUNT** (*)
	FROM	DEPARTMENT, EMPLOYEE
	WHERE	DNUMBER=DNO **AND** SALARY>40000 **AND**
		DNO **IN** (**SELECT** DNO
		FROM EMPLOYEE
		GROUP BY DNO
		HAVING **COUNT** (*) > 5)
	GROUP BY	DNAME

7.2.9 Substring Comparisons, Arithmetic Operators, and Ordering

In this section we discuss three more features of SQL that are specific to the DB2 implementation of SQL, although other implementations may have similar features. The first feature allows comparison conditions on only parts of a character string, using the LIKE comparison operator. Partial strings are specified using two reserved characters; '%' (or '*' in some implementations) replaces an arbitrary number of characters, and '_' replaces a single arbitrary character. For example, to retrieve all employees whose address is in Houston, Texas, we can use Q25, which selects all EMPLOYEE tuples whose ADDRESS value includes the substring 'Houston,TX'.

Q25:	**SELECT**	FNAME, LNAME
	FROM	EMPLOYEE
	WHERE	ADDRESS **LIKE** '%Houston,TX%'

Alternatively, to retrieve all employees who were born during the 1950s, we can use Q26. Here, '5' must be the eighth character of the string (according to our format for date), so we use the value '_____5_', with each underscore as a placeholder for an arbitrary character. Notice that the LIKE operator allows us to get around the fact that each value is considered atomic and indivisible.

Q26:	**SELECT**	FNAME, LNAME
	FROM	EMPLOYEE
	WHERE	BDATE **LIKE** '_____5_'

Another feature allows the use of arithmetic in queries. The standard arithmetic operators '+', '−'. '*', and '/' (for addition, subtraction, multiplication, and division, respectively) can be applied to numeric values in a query result. For example, suppose we want to see the effect of giving all employees who work on the 'ProductX' project a 10% raise; we can issue the query shown in Q27 to see what their salaries would become.

Q27:	**SELECT**	FNAME, LNAME, 1.1*SALARY
	FROM	EMPLOYEE, WORKS_ON, PROJECT
	WHERE	SSN=ESSN **AND** PNO=PNUMBER **AND** PNAME='ProductX'

---

*Some SQL implementations may not allow a GROUP BY-clause without a function in the SELECT-clause. Hence, the nested query in this example would not be allowed in such SQL implementations.

Finally, because SQL is a practical language meant for generating listings and reports, it allows the user to order the tuples in the result of a query by the values of one or more attributes using the **ORDER BY** clause. For example, suppose we want to retrieve a list of employees and the projects each works in, but we want the list ordered by the employee's department and within each department ordered alphabetically by name; we can write Q28:

Q28:	**SELECT**	DNAME, LNAME, FNAME, PNAME
	FROM	DEPARTMENT, EMPLOYEE, WORKS_ON, PROJECT
	WHERE	DNUMBER=DNO **AND** SSN=ESSN **AND** PNO=PNUMBER
	ORDER BY	DNAME, LNAME, FNAME

The default order is in ascending order of values. We can specify the keyword **DESC** if we want a descending order of values. The keyword **ASC** can be used to specify ascending order explicitly, even though it is the default. If we want a descending order on DNAME and ascending order on LNAME, FNAME, the ORDER BY clause of Q28 becomes

ORDER BY   DNAME DESC, LNAME ASC, FNAME ASC

7.2.10   Discussion

A query in SQL can consist of up to six clauses, but only the first two, SELECT and FROM, are mandatory. The clauses are specified in the following order, with the clauses between [...] being optional.

SELECT <attribute list>

FROM <table list>

[WHERE <condition>]

[GROUP BY <grouping attribute(s)>]

[HAVING <group condition>]

[ORDER BY <attribute list>]

The SELECT-clause lists the attributes or functions to be retrieved. The FROM-clause specifies all relations needed in the query but not those needed in nested queries. The WHERE-clause specifies the conditions for selection of tuples from these relations. GROUP BY specifies grouping attributes, whereas HAVING specifies a condition on the groups being selected rather than on the individual tuples. The built-in aggregate functions COUNT, SUM, MIN, MAX, and AVG are used in conjunction with grouping. Finally, ORDER BY specifies an order for displaying the result of a query.

A query is evaluated by first applying the WHERE-clause, then GROUP BY and HAVING. If none of the last three clauses (GROUP BY, HAVING, ORDER BY) are specified then we can *think* of a query as being executed as follows: For *each combination of tuples*, one from each of the relations specified in the FROM-clause, evaluate the WHERE-clause; if it evaluates to TRUE, place the values of attributes specified in the SELECT-clause from this tuple combination in the result of the query. Of course, this is not an efficient way to actually implement the query, and each DBMS will have special query optimization routines to decide on an execution plan. We discuss query processing and optimization in Chapter 18.

In general, there are numerous ways to specify the same query in SQL. This flexibility in specifying queries has some advantages but also has some disadvantages. The advantage is that a user can choose the technique he or she is most comfortable with when specifying a query. For example, many queries may be specified with join conditions, or alternatively with some form of nested queries and the IN comparison operator. Some users may be more comfortable with the former approach whereas others may be more comfortable with the latter. From the programmer's and the system's query optimization point of view, it is generally considered better to write a query with as little nesting and implied ordering as possible.

The disadvantage of having numerous ways of specifying the same query is that it may have the effect of confusing the user. The user may not know which technique to use to specify particular types of queries.

Another problem is that it may be more efficient to execute a query specified in one way than the same query specified in an alternative way. Ideally, this should not be the case; the DBMS should process the same query in the same way regardless of how the query is specified. This is quite difficult in practice, as each DBMS will have different methods for processing queries specified in different ways. An additional burden on the user is to figure out which of the alternative specifications is the most efficient. Ideally, the user should worry only about specifying the query correctly. It is the responsibility of the DBMS to execute the query efficiently. However, in practice, it helps if the user is somewhat aware of which types of constructs in a query are more expensive to process than others. For example, a join condition specified on fields on which no indexes exists (see Section 7.5) can be quite expensive when specified on two large relations; hence, the user should create the appropriate indexes *before* specifying such a query.

7.3 Update Statements in SQL

In SQL there are three commands to modify the database; INSERT, DELETE, and UPDATE. We discuss each of these next.

7.3.1 The INSERT Command

In its simplest form, INSERT is used to add a single tuple to a relation. We must specify the relation name and a list of values for the tuple. The values should be listed *in the same order* as the corresponding attributes were specified in the CREATE TABLE command. For example, to add a new tuple to the EMPLOYEE relation shown in Figure 6.5 and specified in the CREATE TABLE EMPLOYEE command in Figure 7.1, we can use U1 below.

> **U1:** **INSERT INTO** EMPLOYEE
> **VALUES** ('Richard','K', 'Marini', '653298653', '30-DEC-52','98 Oak Forest,Katy,TX', 'M', 37000, '987654321', 4)

A second form of the INSERT statement allows specifying explicit attribute names that correspond to the values in the INSERT command. In this case, attributes with NULL values can be *left out*. For example, to enter a tuple for a new EMPLOYEE for whom we only know the FNAME, LNAME, and SSN attributes, we can use U1A. Attributes not specified in U1A are set to NULL, and the values are listed in the same order as *the attributes are listed in the INSERT command itself.*

> **U1A:** **INSERT INTO** EMPLOYEE (FNAME, LNAME, SSN)
> **VALUES** ('Richard', 'Marini', '653298653')

Notice that because the SQL DDL does not specify referential integrity, many SQL implementations *do not enforce referential integrity rules* (see Section 6.1.5). For example, if we issue the command in U2 on the database shown in Figure 6.6, SQL will do the insertion even though no DEPARTMENT tuple exists in the database with DNUMBER = 2. It is the responsibility of the user to check that any such constraints are not violated. However, SQL will reject an INSERT command in which an attribute declared to be NOT NULL does not have a value; for example, U2A would be *rejected* because no SSN value is provided.

> **U2:** **INSERT INTO** EMPLOYEE (FNAME, LNAME, SSN, DNO)
> **VALUES** ('Robert', 'Hatcher', '980760540', 2)

> **U2A:** **INSERT INTO** EMPLOYEE (FNAME, LNAME, DNO) (* rejected update *)
> **VALUES** ('Robert', 'Hatcher', 2)

Finally, a variation of the INSERT command allows us to insert multiple tuples into a relation. This is used mainly in conjunction with creating a relation and loading it with the *result of a query.* For example, suppose we want to create a temporary table that has the name, number of employees, and total salaries for each department; we could write the statements in U3A and U3B. A table DEPTS_INFO is created by U3A and is loaded with the summary information retrieved from the database by the query in U3B. We can now query DEPTS_INFO as any other relation, and when we do not need it any more we can remove it using the DROP TABLE command. Note that the DEPTS_INFO table may not be up to date; that is, if we update either the DEPARTMENT or the EMPLOYEE relations after issuing U3B, the information in DEPTS_INFO *becomes outdated.* We have to create a view (see Section 7.4) to keep such a table up to date.

> **U3A:** **CREATE TABLE** DEPTS_INFO (DEPT_NAME VARCHAR(15),
> NO_OF_EMPS   INTEGER,
> TOTAL_SAL   INTEGER);

> **U3B:** **INSERT INTO** DEPTS_INFO (DEPT_NAME, NO_OF_EMPS,
> TOTAL_SAL)
> **SELECT**   DNAME, COUNT (*), SUM (SALARY)
> **FROM**   DEPARTMENT, EMPLOYEE
> **WHERE**   DNUMBER=DNO
> **GROUP BY** DNAME ;

7.3.2   The DELETE Command

The delete command removes tuples from a relation. It includes a where-clause, similar to that used in an sql query, to select the tuples to be deleted. Tuples are deleted from only one table at a time. Depending on the number of tuples selected by the condition in the where-clause, zero, one, or several tuples can be deleted by a single delete command. A missing where-clause specifies that all tuples in the relation are to be deleted; however, the table remains in the database as an empty table. We must use the drop table command to remove the table completely. The delete commands in U4A to U4D, if each is applied independently to the database of Figure 6.6, will delete zero, one, four, and all tuples, respectively, from the employee relation.

U4A: **DELETE FROM**   EMPLOYEE
             WHERE   LNAME='Brown'

U4B: **DELETE FROM**   EMPLOYEE
             WHERE   SSN='123456789'

U4C: **DELETE FROM**   EMPLOYEE
             WHERE   DNO **IN**   **(SELECT**   DNUMBER
                                         FROM   DEPARTMENT
                                       WHERE   DNAME='Research')

U4D: **DELETE FROM**   EMPLOYEE

7.3.3   *The* UPDATE *Command*

The **UPDATE** command is used to modify attribute values of one or more selected tuples. As in the DELETE command, a WHERE-clause in the UPDATE command selects the tuples to be modified from a single relation. An additional **SET-clause** specifies the attributes to be modified and their new values. For example, to change the location and controlling department number of project number 10 to 'Bellaire' and 5, respectively, we use U5.

U5:   **UPDATE**   PROJECT
        SET   PLOCATION = 'Bellaire', DNUM = 5
        WHERE   PNUMBER=10

It is also possible to modify several tuples with a single UPDATE command. An example is to give all employees in the 'Research' department a 10% raise in salary, shown in U6. In this request, the modified SALARY value depends on the original SALARY value in each tuple, so two references to the SALARY attribute are needed. In U6 the reference to the SALARY attribute on the right refers to the old SALARY value *before modification* and the one on the left to the new SALARY value *after modification*.

U6:   **UPDATE**   EMPLOYEE
        SET   SALARY = SALARY *1.1
        WHERE   DNO **IN**   **(SELECT**   DNUMBER
                                   FROM   DEPARTMENT
                                 WHERE   DNAME='Research')

Notice that each update command applies to a single relation only. If we need to modify multiple relations, we must issue several UPDATE commands. These could be embedded in a general-purpose program, as can other SQL commands, as we discuss in Section 7.6.

7.4 Views in SQL

In this section we introduce the concept of a view in SQL. We then show how views are specified and discuss the problem of updating a view.

7.4.1 Concept of a View in SQL

A **view** in SQL terminology is a single table that is derived from other tables.* These other tables could be base tables or previously defined views. A view does not necessarily exist in physical form; it is considered a **virtual table** in contrast to base tables whose tuples are actually stored in the database. This limits the possible update operations that can be applied to views but does not provide any limitations on querying a view.

We can think of a view as a way of specifying a table that we need to reference frequently, even though it may not exist physically. For example, in Figure 6.5 we may frequently issue queries that retrieve the employee name and project names that the employee works on. Rather than having to specify the join of the EMPLOYEE, WORKS_ON, and PROJECT tables every time we issue that query, we can define a view that is a result of these joins and hence already includes the attributes we wish to retrieve frequently. We can now issue queries on the view, which are specified as single-table retrievals rather than retrievals involving two joins on three tables. We call the tables EMPLOYEE, WORKS_ON, and PROJECT the **defining tables** of the view.

7.4.2 Specification of Views in SQL

The command to specify a view is **CREATE VIEW**. We give the view a (virtual) table name, a list of attribute names, and a query to specify the contents of the view. If none of the view attributes result from applying functions or arithmetic operations, we do not have to specify attribute names for the view as they will be the same as the names of the attributes of the defining tables. The views in V1 and V2 create virtual tables whose schemas are illustrated in Figure 7.5 when applied to the database schema of Figure 6.5.

```
V1:   CREATE VIEW   WORKS_ON1
      AS   SELECT    FNAME, LNAME, PNAME, HOURS
           FROM      EMPLOYEE, PROJECT, WORKS_ON
           WHERE     SSN=ESSN AND PNO=PNUMBER ;

V2:   CREATE VIEW   DEPT_INFO   (DEPT_NAME, NO_OF_EMPS, TOTAL_ SAL)
      AS   SELECT    DNAME, COUNT (*), SUM (SALARY)
           FROM      DEPARTMENT, EMPLOYEE
           WHERE     DNUMBER=DNO
           GROUP BY  DNAME ;
```

In V1 we did not specify any new attribute names for the view WORKS_ON1; in this case WORKS_ON1 inherits the names of the view attributes from the defining tables EMPLOYEE, PROJECT, and WORKS_ON. View V2 explicitly specifies new attribute names for the view DEPT_INFO using a one-to-one correspondence between the attributes specified

---

*This use of the term view is more limited than the user views discussed in Chapters 1 and 2.

WORKS_ON1

FNAME	LNAME	PNAME	HOURS

DEPT_INFO

DEPT_NAME	NO_OF_EMPS	TOTAL_SAL

Figure 7.5   Two views specified on the database schema of
Figure 6.5

in the CREATE VIEW clause and those specified in the SELECT-clause of the query that
defines the view. We can now specify SQL queries on a view—or virtual table—in the
same way we specify queries involving base tables. For example, to retrieve the last name
and first name of all employees who work on 'ProjectX', we can utilize the WORKS_ON1
view and specify the query as in QV1. The same query would require the specification of
two joins if specified on the base relations; the main advantage of a view is to simplify
the specification of certain queries. Views can also be used as a security mechanism (see
Chapter 20).

QV1:   **SELECT**   PNAME, FNAME, LNAME
          FROM   WORKS_ON1
          WHERE   PNAME='ProjectX' ;

A view is *always up to date*; if we modify the tuples in the base tables on which the
view is defined, the view automatically reflects these changes. Hence, the view is not realized at the time of view definition but rather at the time we specify a query on the
view. It is the responsibility of the DBMS and not the user to make sure that the view is up
to date.

If we do not need a view any more, we can use the **DROP VIEW** command to dispose
of it. For example, to get rid of the two views defined in V1 and V2, we can use the SQL
statements in V1A and V2A.

V1A: **DROP VIEW**   WORKS_ON1 ;

V2A: **DROP VIEW**   DEPT_INFO ;

7.4.3   Updating of Views

Updating of views is complicated and can be ambiguous. In general, an update on a view
defined on *a single table* can be mapped to an update on the underlying base table. For a
view involving joins, an update operation may be mapped to update operations on the
underlying base relations *in multiple ways*. The topic of updating views is still an active
research area. To illustrate potential problems with updating a view defined on multiple
tables, consider the WORKS_ON1 view, and suppose we issue the command to update the
PNAME attribute of 'John Smith' from 'ProductX' to 'ProductY'. This view update is
shown in UV1.

UV1:   **UPDATE**   WORKS_ON1
         SET   PNAME = 'ProductY'
         WHERE   LNAME='Smith' **AND** FNAME='John' **AND** PNAME='ProductX'

This query can be mapped into several updates on the base relations to give the desired update on the view. Two possible updates (a) and (b) on the base relations corresponding to UV1 are shown below.

(a):   **UPDATE**   WORKS_ON
         SET   PNO = (**SELECT** PNUMBER **FROM** PROJECT **WHERE**
                   PNAME='ProductY')
         WHERE   ESSN = (**SELECT** SSN **FROM** EMPLOYEE
                         WHERE LNAME='Smith' **AND** FNAME='John') **AND**
                   PNO = (**SELECT** PNUMBER **FROM** PROJECT **WHERE**
                   PNAME='ProductX')

(b):   **UPDATE**   PROJECT
         SET   PNAME = 'ProductY'
         WHERE   PNAME = 'ProductX'

Update (a) relates 'John Smith' to the 'ProductY' PROJECT tuple in place of the 'ProductX' PROJECT tuple and is the most likely desired update. However, (b) would also give the desired update effect on the view, but it accomplishes this by changing the name of the 'ProductX' tuple in the PROJECT relation to 'ProductY'. It is quite unlikely that the user who specified the view update UV1 wants the update to be interpreted as in (b).

Some view updates may not make much sense; for example, modifying the TOTAL_SAL attribute of DEPT_INFO does not make sense because TOTAL_SAL is defined to be the sum of the individual employee salaries. This request is shown as UV2 below. Many possible updates on the underlying base relations can satisfy this view update. Can you guess what such an update might mean and decide how to execute it on the underlying base relations?

UV2:   **MODIFY**   DEPT_INFO
         SET   TOTAL_SAL=100000
         WHERE   DNAME='Research' ;

In general, we cannot guarantee that any view can be updated. A view update is feasible when only *one possible update* on the base relations can accomplish the desired update effect on the view. Whenever an update on the view can be mapped to *more than one update* on the underlying base relations, we must have a certain procedure to choose the desired update. Some researchers have developed methods for choosing the most likely update, while other researchers prefer to have the user choose the desired update mapping during view definition.

In summary, we can make the following observations:

- A view with a single defining table is updatable if the view attributes contain the primary key or some other candidate key of the base relation, because this maps each (virtual) view tuple to a single base tuple.
- Views defined on multiple tables using joins are generally not updatable.
- Views defined using grouping and aggregate functions are not updatable.

7.5 Specifying Indexes in SQL

SQL has statements to create and drop indexes on attributes of base relations. These commands are generally considered to be part of the SQL data definition language (DDL), which we presented in Section 7.1. However, because an index is a physical access path rather than a logical concept, we are presenting the commands to create indexes here in a separate section. As we discussed in Section 7.1.1, specifying a *key constraint*, which should be part of logical data definition, is combined with index specification in the DB2 implementation of SQL but not in all SQL implementations.

Recall from Chapter 5 that an index is a physical access structure that is specified on one or more attributes of a file. In SQL a file corresponds, more or less, to a base relation, so indexes are specified on base relations. The attribute(s) on which an index is created are termed **indexing attributes**. An index makes accessing tuples based on conditions that involve its indexing attributes more efficient. This means that, in general, executing a query will take less time if some attributes involved in the query conditions were indexed than if they were not. This improvement can be dramatic for queries where large relations are involved. In general, if attributes used in selection conditions and in join conditions of a query are indexed, the execution time of the query is greatly improved.

In SQL indexes can be created and dropped dynamically. The **CREATE INDEX** command is used to specify an index. Each index is given a name, which is used to drop the index when we do not need it any more. For example, to create an index on the LNAME attribute of the EMPLOYEE base relation from Figure 6.5, we can issue the command shown in I1.

> **I1:** **CREATE INDEX** LNAME_INDEX
> **ON** EMPLOYEE (LNAME);

In general, the index is arranged in ascending order of the indexing attribute values. If we want the values in descending order, we can add the keyword DESC after the attribute name. The default is ASC for ascending. We can also create an index on a combination of attributes. For example, to create an index on the combination of FNAME, MINIT, and LNAME, we use I2. In I2 we assume we want LNAME in ascending order and FNAME in descending order within the same LNAME value.

> **I2:** **CREATE INDEX** NAMES_INDEX
> **ON** EMPLOYEE (LNAME ASC, FNAME DESC, MINIT);

There are two additional options on indexes in SQL. The first is to specify the **key constraint** on the indexing attribute or combination of attributes. The key word **UNIQUE** following the CREATE command is used to specify a key. For example, to specify an index on the SSN attribute of EMPLOYEE *and at the same time* specify that SSN is a key attribute of the EMPLOYEE base relation, we use I3.

> **I3:** **CREATE UNIQUE INDEX** SSN_INDEX
> **ON** EMPLOYEE (SSN);

Notice that specifying a key is best done before any tuples are inserted in the relation so that the system will enforce the constraint. An attempt to create a unique index on an existing base table will fail if the current tuples in the table do not obey the uniqueness constraint on the indexing attribute. Two NULL values are considered equal for unique indexing purposes; hence, at most one tuple can have a NULL for an attribute on which a UNIQUE INDEX is specified. Of course, the attribute should have the NOT NULL constraint specified in this case.

The reason behind linking the definition of a key constraint with specifying an index is that it is much more efficient to enforce uniqueness of key values on a file if an index is defined on the key attribute. We can check if a duplicate value exists in the index while searching the index. If no index exists, it is necessary in most cases to search the entire file to discover if a duplicate value exists for an attribute.

The second option on index creation is to specify whether an index is a clustering index (see Chapter 5). Join and selection conditions are even more efficient when specified on an attribute with a clustering index. The key word **CLUSTER** is used in this case at the end of the CREATE INDEX command. For example, if we want the EMPLOYEE records indexed and clustered by department number, we create a clustering index on DNO as in I4. A base relation can have *at most one* clustering index but any number of nonclustering indexes.

I4: **CREATE INDEX**   DNO_INDEX
            ON   EMPLOYEE (DNO)
         CLUSTER ;

A *clustering and unique* index in SQL is similar to the *primary index* of Chapter 5. A *clustering but nonunique* index in SQL is similar to the *clustering index* of Chapter 5. Finally, a *nonclustering* index is similar to the *secondary index* of Chapter 5. Each DBMS may have its own type of index implementation technique; for example, multilevel indexes may use B-trees or B^+-trees or some other variations similar to the ones discussed in Chapter 5.

To drop an index, we issue the **DROP INDEX** command. The reason for dropping indexes is that they are expensive to maintain whenever the base relation is updated and they require additional storage. Hence, if we no longer expect to issue queries involving an indexed attribute, we should drop that index. However, *indexes that specify a key constraint should not be dropped* as long as we want the system to continue enforcing that constraint. An example of dropping the DNO index is given below.

I5: **DROP INDEX**   DNO_INDEX;

7.6   Embedded SQL

SQL can also be used in conjunction with a general-purpose programming language such as PASCAL, COBOL, or PL/I. The programming language is called the **host language**. Any SQL statement—data definition, query, update, view definition, or index creation—can be embedded in a host language program. The embedded SQL statement is distinguished from programming language statements by prefixing it with a special character or command so that a **preprocessor** can separate the embedded SQL statements from the host language code. For example, in PL/I the keywords EXEC SQL precede any em-

```
var DNAME: packed array [1..15] of char;
    DNUMBER, RAISE: integer;
    E: record FNAME, LNAME: packed array [1..15] of char;
            MINIT, SEX: char;
            SSN, BDATE, SUPERSSN: packed array [1..9] of char;
            ADDRESS: packed array [1..30] of char;
            SALARY, DNO: integer
    end;
```

Figure 7.6   PASCAL program variables used in E1 and E2

bedded SQL statement. In some implementations SQL statements are passed as parameters in procedure calls.

In general, different systems follow different conventions for embedding SQL statements. To illustrate the concepts of embedded SQL, we will use PASCAL as the host programming language and define our own syntax. We will use a "$" sign to identify SQL statements in the program. Within an embedded SQL command, we may refer to program variables, which are prefixed by a "%" sign.* This allows program variables and database schema objects, such as attributes and relations, to have the same names without any ambiguity.

Suppose we want to write PASCAL programs to process the database of Figure 6.5. We need to declare program variables to match the types of the database attributes that the program will process. These program variables may or may not have names that are identical to their corresponding attributes. We will use the PASCAL program variables declared in Figure 7.6 for all our examples and show PASCAL program segments without variable declarations.

As a first example, we write a repeating program segment (loop) that reads a social security number and prints out some information from the corresponding EMPLOYEE tuple. The PASCAL program code is shown in E1 on page 204, where we assume that appropriate program variables SOC_SEC_NUM and LOOP have been declared elsewhere. The program reads (inputs) a social security number value and then retrieves the EMPLOYEE tuple with that social security number via the embedded SQL command. Embedded SQL retrieval commands need an INTO clause, which specifies the program variables into which attribute values from the database are retrieved. PASCAL program variables in the INTO clause are prefixed with the "%" sign.

In E1 a single tuple is selected by the embedded SQL query; that is why we are able to assign its attribute values directly to program variables. In general, an SQL query can retrieve many tuples. In the latter case the PASCAL program will typically go through the retrieved tuples and process them one at a time. The concept of a cursor is used to allow tuple-at-a-time processing by the PASCAL program.

We can think of a **cursor** as a pointer that points to a *single tuple (row)* from the result of a query. The cursor is declared when the SQL query command is specified in the program. Later in the program, an **OPEN** cursor command fetches the query result from the database and sets the cursor to a position *before the first row* in the result of the query. This becomes the **current row** for the cursor. Subsequently, **FETCH** commands are issued

---

*The ":" sign is used in PL/I.

in the program; each FETCH moves the cursor to the *next row* in the result of the query, making it the current row and copying its attribute values into PASCAL program variables specified in the FETCH command. This is similar to traditional record-at-a-time file processing.

```
E1:   LOOP:= 'Y';
          while LOOP = 'Y' do
              begin
              writeln('input social security number:');
              readln(SOC_SEC_NUM);
              $SELECT FNAME, MINIT, LNAME, ADDRESS, SALARY
              INTO %E.FNAME, %E.MINIT, %E.LNAME, %E.ADDRESS, %E.SALARY
              FROM EMPLOYEE
              WHERE SSN=%SOC_SEC_NUM ;
              writeln( E.FNAME, E.MINIT, E.LNAME, E.ADDRESS, E.SALARY);
              writeln('more social security numbers (Y or N)? ');
              readln(LOOP)
              end;
```

To determine when all the tuples in the result of the query have been processed, an implicit variable, called **SQLCODE,** is used to communicate to the program the status of SQL embedded commands. When an SQL command is executed successfully, a code of 0 (zero) is returned in SQLCODE. Different codes are returned to indicate exceptions and errors. If a FETCH command is issued that results in moving the cursor past the last tuple in the result of the query, a special END_OF_CURSOR code is returned. The programmer uses this to terminate a loop over the tuples in a query result. In general, numerous cursors can be opened at the same time. A **CLOSE** cursor command is issued to indicate that we are done with the result of the query.

An example of using cursors is shown in E2, on page 205, where the EMP cursor is explicitly declared. We assume that appropriate PASCAL program variables have been declared as in Figure 7.6. The program segment in E2 reads (inputs) a department name and then lists the names of employees who work in that department, one at a time. The program reads a raise amount for each employee's salary and updates the employee's salary by that amount.

When a cursor is defined for rows that are to be updated, we must add the clause **FOR UPDATE OF** in the cursor declaration and list the names of any attributes that will be updated by the program. In the UPDATE (or DELETE) command, the condition **WHERE CURRENT OF** cursor specifies that the current tuple is the one to be updated (or deleted).

7.7   Summary

In this chapter we presented the SQL database language. This language or variations of it have been implemented as interfaces to several commercial relational DBMSs, including IBM's DB2 and SQL/DS, ORACLE, INGRES, and UNIFY. The original version of SQL was implemented in the experimental DBMS called SYSTEM R, which was developed at IBM Research. We discussed most features of SQL, even those that may not be available in some implementations. SQL is designed to be a comprehensive language that includes statements for data and index definition, queries, updates, and view definition. We discussed each of these in separate sections of this chapter.

In the final section we presented one approach for embedding SQL in a general-purpose programming language; this approach is similar to the one used in SYSTEM R. We discussed the concept of a CURSOR, which allows a programmer to process the result of a high-level query one tuple at a time.

Table 7.1 shows a summary of the syntax or structure of various SQL statements. This summary is not meant to be comprehensive and describe every possible SQL construct; rather, it is meant to be used for quick reference to the major types of constructs available in SQL. We use BNF notation, where nonterminal symbols are shown in angled brackets <...>, optional parts are shown in square brackets [...], repetitions are shown in braces {...}, and alternatives are shown in parentheses (... | ... | ...).

Appendix B discusses the strengths and weaknesses of SQL as a high-level comprehensive database language.

```
E2:   writeln('enter the department name:'); readln(DNAME);
      $SELECT DNUMBER INTO %DNUMBER
      FROM DEPARTMENT
      WHERE DNAME=%DNAME;
      $DECLARE   EMP CURSOR FOR
                    SELECT SSN, FNAME, MINIT, LNAME, SALARY
                    FROM EMPLOYEE
                    WHERE DNO=%DNUMBER
      FOR UPDATE OF SALARY;
      $OPEN EMP;
      $FETCH EMP INTO %E.SSN, %E.FNAME, %E.MINIT, %E.LNAME,
      %E.SALARY;
      while SQLCODE = 0 do
          begin
          writeln('employee name: ', E.FNAME, E.MINIT, E.LNAME);
          writeln('enter raise amount: '); readln(RAISE);
          $UPDATE EMPLOYEE SET SALARY = SALARY + %RAISE
                          WHERE CURRENT OF EMP;
          $FETCH EMP INTO %E.SSN, %E.FNAME, %E.MINIT, %E.LNAME,
          %E.SALARY;
          end;
      $CLOSE CURSOR EMP;
```

Review Questions

7.1. How do the relations (tables) in SQL differ from the relations defined formally in Chapter 6? Discuss the other differences in terminology.

7.2. Why does SQL allow duplicate tuples in a table or in a query result?

7.3. Why do many SQL implementations permit a key to be defined only in conjunction with an index?

Table 7.1   Summary of SQL Syntax

CREATE TABLE   <table name> (<column name> <column type> [NOT NULL]
                    {, <column name> <column type> [NOT NULL] })

DROP TABLE   <table name>

ALTER TABLE   <table name> ADD <column name> <column type>

SELECT [DISTINCT]   <attribute list>
FROM   <table name> { <alias>} {, <table name> { <alias>} }
[WHERE   <condition>]
[GROUP BY   <grouping attributes> [HAVING <group selection condition>]]
[ORDER BY   <column name> [<order>] {, <column name> [<order>] }]

<attribute list>::= (* I (<column name> I <function>(([DISTINCT]<column name> I *)))
                    {,(<column name> I <function>((([DISTINCT] <column name> I *)) }))
<grouping attributes>::= <column name> { , <column name>}
<order>::= (ASC I DESC)

INSERT INTO   <table name> [(<column name>{, <column name>})]
(VALUES (<constant value> , { <constant value>}) I <select statement>)

DELETE FROM   <table name>
[WHERE   <selection condition>]

UPDATE   <table name>
SET   <column name>=<value expression> { , <column name>=<value expression> }
[WHERE   <selection condition>]

CREATE [UNIQUE] INDEX   <index name>
ON   <table name> (<column name> [<order>] {, <column name> [<order>] })
[CLUSTER]

DROP INDEX   <index name>

CREATE VIEW   <view name> [(<column name> { , <column name> })]
AS   <select statement>

DROP VIEW   <view name>

7.4. How does SQL allow the implementation of the entity integrity constraint described in Chapter 6?

7.5. What is a view in SQL and how is it defined? Discuss the problems that may arise when attempting to update a view.

7.6. What is a cursor? How is it used in embedded SQL?

Exercises

7.7. Consider the database shown in Figure 1.2, whose schema is shown in Figure 2.1. Write appropriate SQL DDL statements to define the database.

7.8. Repeat Exercise 7.7 but use the AIRLINE database schema of Figure 6.19.

7.9. Propose how to extend the data definition language component of SQL so that primary and secondary keys and referential integrity constraints (foreign keys) can be specified independently of indexes.

7.10. Use your extended syntax to modify the DDL statements of Figure 7.1 to specify primary, secondary, and foreign keys on the **COMPANY** database.

7.11. Repeat Exercise 7.10 for the DDL specified in Exercises 7.7 and 7.8.

7.12. How can the key and foreign key constraints be enforced by the DBMS? Is the enforcement technique you suggest difficult to implement? Can the constraint checks be executed in an efficient manner when updates are applied to the database?

7.13. Specify the queries of Exercise 6.19 in SQL. Show the result of each query if applied to the **COMPANY** database of Figure 6.6.

7.14. Specify the following additional queries on the database of Figure 6.5 in SQL. Show the query results if applied to the database of Figure 6.6.

    a. For each department whose average employee salary is more than \$30,000, retrieve the department name and the number of employees working for that department.

    b. Suppose we want the number of *male* employees in each department rather than all employees as in Exercise 7.14a. Can we specify this query in SQL? Why or why not?

7.15. Specify the updates of Exercise 6.20 using the SQL update commands.

7.16. Specify the following queries in SQL on the database schema of Figure 2.1.

    a. Retrieve the names of all senior students majoring in 'COSC' (computer science).

    b. Retrieve the names of all courses taught by Professor King in 1985 and 1986.

    c. For each section taught by Professor King, retrieve the course number, semester, year, and number of students who took the section.

    d. Retrieve the name and transcript of each senior student (Class = 5) majoring in COSC. Transcript includes course name, course number, credit hours, semester, year, and grade for each course completed by the student.

    e. Retrieve the names and major departments of all straight A students (students who have a grade of A in all their courses).

    f. Retrieve the names and major departments of all students who do not have a grade of A in any of their courses.

7.17. Write SQL update statements to do the following on the database schema shown in Figure 2.1.

    a. Insert a new student <'Johnson', 25, 1, 'MATH'> in the database.

b. Change the class of student 'Smith' to 2.

c. Insert a new course <'Knowledge Engineering','COSC4390', 3,'COSC'>.

d. Delete the record for the student whose name is 'Smith' and student number is 17.

7.18. Write PASCAL programs with embedded SQL statements in the style shown in Section 7.6 to do the following tasks on the database schema of Figure 2.1. Define appropriate program variables for each program code.

a. Enter the grades of students in a section. The program should input the section ID and then have a loop that inputs each student's number and grade and inserts this information in the database.

b. Print the transcript of a student. The program should input the student's ID, and print the student's name and a list of <course number, course name, section ID, semester, year, grade> for each section that the student completed.

7.19. Write SQL update statements to create indexes on the database schema shown in Figure 2.1 on the following attributes:

a. A unique clustering index on the StudentNumber attribute of STUDENT.

b. A clustering index on the StudentNumber attribute of GRADE_REPORT.

c. An index on the Major attribute of STUDENT.

7.20. What are the types of queries that would become more efficient for each of the indexes specified in Exercise 7.19?

7.21. Specify the following views in SQL on the COMPANY database schema shown in Figure 6.5.

a. A view that has the department name, manager name, and manager salary for every department.

b. A view that has the employee name, supervisor name, and employee salary for each employee who works in the 'Research' department.

c. A view that has project name, controlling department name, number of employees, and total hours worked per week on the project for each project.

d. A view that has project name, controlling department name, number of employees, and total hours worked per week on the project for each project *with more than one employee working on it.*

7.22. Consider the following view DEPT_SUMMARY, defined on the COMPANY database of Figure 6.6:

```
CREATE VIEW   DEPT_SUMMARY (D, C, TOTAL_S, AVERAGE_S)
AS   SELECT   DNO, COUNT (*), SUM (SALARY), AVG (SALARY)
     FROM     EMPLOYEE
     GROUP BY DNO ;
```

State which of the following queries and updates would be allowed on the view. If a query or update is allowed, show what the corresponding query or update on the base relations would look like and give its result when applied to the database of Figure 6.6.

a. **SELECT**   *

    FROM   DEPT_SUMMARY

b. **SELECT**   D, C

    FROM   DEPT_SUMMARY

    WHERE   TOTAL_S > 100000

c. **SELECT**   D, AVERAGE_S

    FROM   DEPT_SUMMARY

    WHERE   C > (**SELECT** COUNT(*) **FROM** DEPT_SUMMARY **WHERE** D=4)

d. **UPDATE**   DEPT_SUMMARY

    SET   D=3

    WHERE   D=4

e. **DELETE FROM**   DEPT_SUMMARY

    WHERE   C > 4

7.23. Consider the relation schema CONTAINS(Parent_part#, Sub_part#); a tuple <Pi, Pj> in CONTAINS means that part Pi contains part Pj as a direct component. Suppose we choose a part P_k that contains no other parts and we want to find the part numbers of all parts that contain P_k, directly or indirectly at any level; this is a *recursive query* that requires computing the **transitive closure** of CONTAINS. Show that this query cannot be directly specified as a single SQL query. Can you suggest extensions to SQL to allow the specification of such queries?

7.24. Specify the queries and updates of Exercises 6.21 and 6.22, which refer to the AIRLINE database, in SQL.

7.25. Choose some database application that you are familiar with.

    a. Design a relational database schema for your database application.

    b. Declare your relations using the SQL DDL.

    c. Specify a number of queries in SQL that are needed by your database application.

    d. Based on your expected use of the database, choose some attributes that should have indexes specified on them.

    e. Implement your database if you have an SQL system available.

Selected Bibliography

The SQL language, originally named SEQUEL, was a sequel to the language SQUARE (Specifying Queries *as* Relational Expressions), described by Boyce et al. (1975). The syntax of SQUARE was modified into SEQUEL (Chamberlin and Boyce 1974) and then to SEQUEL 2 (Chamberlin et al. 1976), on which SQL is based. The original implementation of SEQUEL was done at IBM Research, San Jose, California.

Reisner (1977) describes a human factors evaluation of SEQUEL in which she found that users have some difficulty with specifying join conditions and grouping correctly.

Date (1984b) contains a critique of the SQL language that points out its strengths and shortcomings. The book by Date and White (1988) describes SQL in the DB2 system. ANSI (1986) outlines the new SQL standard. Various vendor manuals describe the characteristics of SQL as implemented on DB2, SQL/DS, ORACLE, INGRES, UNIFY, and other commercial DBMS products.

The question of view updates is addressed by Dayal and Bernstein (1978) and Keller (1982), among others.

CHAPTER 8

The Relational Calculus—A Formal Query Language

In Chapter 6 we presented the relational data model and discussed the operations of the relational algebra, which are fundamental for manipulating a relational database. Although we described the relational algebra as an integral part of the relational model, it is actually only one type of formal query language for specifying retrievals and forming new relations from a relational database. In this chapter we discuss another formal language for relational databases, the **relational calculus**. Many commercial relational database languages are based on some aspects of relational calculus, including the SQL language discussed in Chapter 7. However, some are more similar to the relational calculus than others; for example, the QUEL and QBE languages presented in Chapter 9 are closer to relational calculus than SQL is.

How is relational calculus different from relational algebra? The main difference is that in relational calculus we write one **declarative** expression to specify a retrieval request, whereas in relational algebra we must write a *sequence of operations*. It is true that these operations can be nested to form a single expression; however, a certain order among the operations is always explicitly specified in a relational algebra expression. This order also specifies a strategy for evaluating the query. Hence, relational algebra is considered **procedural**, even though it has high-level operations that operate on whole relations. In relational calculus there is no description of how to evaluate a query; a calculus expression specifies *what* is to be retrieved rather than *how* to retrieve it. Therefore, the relational calculus is considered to be a declarative or **nonprocedural** language.

There is an important aspect in which the relational algebra and relational calculus are identical. It has been shown that any retrieval that can be specified in the relational algebra can also be specified in the relational calculus and vice versa; in other words, the expressive power of the two languages is *identical*. This led to the definition of the concept of a relationally complete language. A relational query language L is called **relationally complete** if we can express in L any query that can be expressed in the relational calculus. Relational completeness has become an important benchmark for comparing the expressive power of high-level query languages. However, as we saw in Section 6.3, there are some types of frequently required queries in database applications that cannot be expressed in relational algebra or calculus. Most relational query languages are relationally complete but have *more expressive power* than relational algebra or calculus because of additional operations such as aggregate functions, grouping, and ordering.

The relational calculus is a formal language, based on the branch of mathematical logic called predicate calculus. There are two well-known ways in which the predicate calculus can be adapted into a language for relational databases. The first results in a language called the **tuple relational calculus** and the second in a language called the **domain relational calculus**. Both are adaptations of first-order predicate calculus.* In tuple relational calculus, variables range over tuples, whereas in domain relational calculus variables range over domain values of attributes. We discuss these in Sections 8.1 and 8.3, respectively. Section 8.2 discusses how relational calculus quantifiers are handled in the SQL language presented in Chapter 7. All our examples will again refer to the database shown in Figures 6.5 and 6.6.

8.1 Tuple Relational Calculus

We first introduce the notion of tuple variables and range relations in Section 8.1.1. Then we discuss the formal syntax of tuple relational calculus in Section 8.1.2. In Section 8.1.3 we give some example queries in the tuple relational calculus. We then discuss and compare the universal and existential quantifiers in Section 8.1.4. We give additional examples to illustrate the use of universal quantifiers and discuss safe expressions in Section 8.1.5.

8.1.1 Tuple Variables and Range Relations

The tuple relational calculus is based on specifying a number of **tuple variables**. Each tuple variable usually **ranges over** a particular database relation, meaning that the variable may take as its value any individual tuple from that relation. A simple tuple relational calculus query may take the form

{ t | COND(t) }

where t is a tuple variable and COND(t) is a conditional expression involving t. The result of such a query is to retrieve all tuples t that satisfy COND(t). For example, to find

---

*In our presentation, we *do not* assume that the reader is familiar with first-order predicate calculus, which deals with quantified variables and values. To deal with quantified relations or sets of sets, we have to use a higher-order predicate calculus.

all employees whose salary is above $50,000, we can write the following tuple calculus expression:

{ t | EMPLOYEE(t) **and** t.SALARY>50000 }

The condition EMPLOYEE(t) specifies that the range relation of tuple variable t is EMPLOYEE. Each EMPLOYEE tuple t that satisfies the condition t.SALARY>50000 will be retrieved. Notice that t.SALARY references attribute SALARY of tuple variable t; this notation is similar to the way attribute names are qualified with relation names or aliases in SQL. In the notation of Chapter 6, t.SALARY is the same as writing t[SALARY].

The above query would retrieve *all* attribute values for each of the selected EMPLOYEE tuples t. To retrieve only *some* of the attributes, say the first and last names, we write

{ t.FNAME, t.LNAME | EMPLOYEE(t) **and** t.SALARY>50000 }

The latter is similar to the SQL query

```
SELECT    T.FNAME, T.LNAME
FROM      EMPLOYEE T
WHERE     T.SALARY > 50000
```

We can have several tuple variables in a tuple calculus expression. Informally, we need to specify the following in a tuple calculus expression:

1. For each tuple variable t, the relation R that is used as its range. This relation is called the **range relation** of the tuple variable and is specified by a condition of the form R(t).

2. A condition to select particular combinations of tuples; each combination consists of one tuple from each of the range relations. As tuple variables range over their respective range relations, the condition is evaluated for every possible combination of tuples. A particular combination of tuples for which the condition becomes TRUE is called a **selected combination**.

3. A set of attributes of the tuple variables that are to be retrieved, the **requested** attributes. The values of these attributes are retrieved for each selected combination of tuples.

Observe the correspondence of the above items to a simple SQL query; item 1 corresponds to the FROM-clause relation names, item 2 to the WHERE-clause condition, and item 3 to the SELECT-clause attribute list. Before we discuss the formal syntax of tuple relational calculus, consider another query we have seen before.

QUERY 0

Retrieve the birthdate and address of the employee (or employees) whose name is 'John B. Smith'.

Q0 : { t.BDATE, t.ADDRESS | EMPLOYEE(t) **and** t.FNAME='John' **and** t.MINIT='B' **and** t.LNAME='Smith}

In Q0, t is the only tuple variable, which ranges over the tuples in the EMPLOYEE relation. In tuple relational calculus, we first specify the requested attributes t.BDATE and t.ADDRESS for each selected tuple t. Then we specify the condition for selecting a tuple following the bar (|), namely that t be a tuple of the EMPLOYEE relation whose FNAME, MINIT, and LNAME attribute values are 'John', 'B', and 'Smith', respectively.

8.1.2   Formal Specification of Tuple Relational Calculus

A general **expression** of the tuple relational calculus is of the form

$$\{ t_1.A_1, t_2.A_2, ..., t_n.A_n \mid \text{COND}(t_1, t_2, ..., t_n, t_{n+1}, t_{n+2}, ..., t_{n+m}) \}$$

where $t_1, t_2, ..., t_n, t_{n+1}, ..., t_{n+m}$ are tuple variables that are not necessarily distinct, each A_i is an attribute of the relation on which t_i ranges, and COND is a **condition** or formula* of the tuple relational calculus. A formula is made up of predicate calculus **atoms**, which can be one of the following:

1. An atom of the form $R(t_i)$, where R is a relation name and t_i is a tuple variable. This atom identifies the range of the tuple variable t_i as the relation whose name is R.

2. An atom of the form $t_i.A$ **op** $t_j.B$, where **op** is one of the comparison operators in the set $\{ =, \neq, <, \leq, >, \geq \}$, t_i and t_j are tuple variables, A is an attribute of the relation on which t_i ranges, and B is an attribute of the relation on which t_j ranges.

3. An atom of the form $t_i.A$ **op** c or c **op** $t_j.B$, where **op** is one of the comparison operators in the set $\{ =, \neq, <, \leq, >, \geq \}$, t_i and t_j are tuple variables, A is an attribute of the relation on which t_i ranges, B is an attribute of the relation on which t_j ranges, and c is a constant value.

Each of the above atoms evaluates to either TRUE or FALSE for a specific combination of tuples; this is called the **truth value** of an atom. In general, a tuple variable ranges over all possible tuples "in the universe." For atoms of type 1, if the tuple variable is assigned a tuple that is a *member of the specified relation* R, the atom is TRUE; otherwise it is FALSE. In atoms of types 2 and 3, if the tuple variables are assigned to tuples such that the values of the specified attributes of the tuples satisfy the condition, then the atom is TRUE.

A **formula** (condition) can be made up of several atoms connected via the logical operators **and, or,** and **not** and is defined recursively as follows:

1. Every atom is a formula.

2. If F_1 and F_2 are formulas, then so are $(F_1$ **and** $F_2)$, $(F_1$ **or** $F_2)$, **not**(F_1), and **not** (F_2). The truth values of these four formulas are derived from their component formulas F_1 and F_2 as follows:

   a. $(F_1$ **and** $F_2)$ is TRUE if both F_1 and F_2 are TRUE; it is FALSE if either F_1 or F_2 is FALSE.

   b. $(F_1$ **or** $F_2)$ is TRUE if either F_1 or F_2 is TRUE; it is FALSE if both F_1 and F_2 are FALSE.

---

*Also called a **well-formed formula** or **wff** in mathematical logic.

c. **not**(F_1) is TRUE if F_1 is FALSE; it is FALSE if F_1 is TRUE.

d. **not**(F_2) is TRUE if F_2 is FALSE; it is FALSE if F_2 is TRUE.

The truth values for the formulas described in 1 and 2 above are easily understood. In addition, two special symbols called **quantifiers** can appear in formulas; these are the **universal quantifier** ($\forall$) and the **existential quantifier** ($\exists$). Formulas with quantifiers are described in 3 and 4 below; first, we need to define the concepts of free and bound tuple variables in a formula. Informally, a tuple variable t is bound if it is quantified, meaning that it appears in an ($\exists$ t) or ($\forall$ t) clause; otherwise, it is free. Formally, we define a tuple variable in a formula to be **free** or **bound** according to the following rules:

- An occurrence of a tuple variable in a formula F that *is an atom* is free in F.

- An occurrence of a tuple variable t is free or bound in a formula made up of logical connectives—(F_1 **and** F_2), (F_1 **or** F_2), **not**(F_1), and **not**(F_2)—depending on whether it is free or bound in F_1 or F_2 (if it occurs in either). Notice that in a formula of the form F = (F_1 **and** F_2) or F = (F_1 **or** F_2), a tuple variable may be free in F_1 and bound in F_2, or vice versa. In this case, one occurrence of the tuple variable is bound and the other is free in F.

- All *free* occurrences of a tuple variable t in F are **bound** in a formula F' of the form F' = ($\exists$ t)(F) or F' = ($\forall$ t)(F). The tuple variable is bound to the quantifier specified in F'. For example, consider the two formulas:

    F1 : d.DNAME = 'Research'
    F2 : ($\exists$ t) (d.DNUMBER = t.DNO)

The tuple variable d is free in both F1 and F2, whereas t is bound to the $\exists$ quantifier in F2.

We can now give the following rules, 3 and 4, to continue the definition of a formula started earlier:

3. If F is a formula, then so is ($\exists$ t)(F), where t is a tuple variable. The formula ($\exists$ t)(F) is TRUE if the formula F evaluates to TRUE for *some* (at least one) tuple assigned to free occurrences of t in F; otherwise ($\exists$ t)(F) is FALSE.

4. If F is a formula, then so is ($\forall$ t)(F), where t is a tuple variable. The formula ($\forall$ t)(F) is TRUE if the formula F evaluates to TRUE for *every tuple* (in the universe) assigned to free occurrences of t in F; otherwise ($\forall$ t)(F) is FALSE.

The ($\exists$) quantifier is called an existential quantifier because a formula ($\exists$ t)(F) is TRUE if "there exists" some tuple t that makes F TRUE. For the universal quantifier, ($\forall$ t)(F) is TRUE if every possible tuple that can be assigned to free occurrences of t in F is substituted for t and F is TRUE for *every such substitution*. It is called the universal quantifier because every tuple in "the universe of" tuples must make F TRUE.

8.1.3 *Example Queries Using the Existential Quantifier*

We now give examples of queries specified in the tuple relational calculus. We will do many of the same queries shown in Chapter 6 so as to give a flavor of how the same queries are specified in relational algebra and relational calculus. As you will notice, some queries are easier to specify in the relational algebra than in the relational calculus and vice versa.

QUERY 1

Retrieve the name and address of all employees who work for the 'Research' department.

Q1 : { t.FNAME, t.LNAME, t.ADDRESS | EMPLOYEE(t) **and** ($\exists$ d)(DEPARTMENT(d)
   and d.DNAME='Research' **and** d.DNUMBER=t.DNO) }

The *only free tuple variables* in a relational calculus expression should be those that appear to the left of the bar (|). In Q1, t is the only free variable; it is then bound successively to each tuple that *satisfies the conditions* specified in Q1, and the attributes FNAME, LNAME, and ADDRESS are retrieved for each such tuple. The conditions EMPLOYEE(t) and DEPARTMENT(d) specify the range relations for t and d. The condition d.DNAME = 'Research' is a **selection condition** and corresponds to a SELECT operation in the relational algebra, whereas the condition d.DNUMBER = t.DNO is a **join condition** and serves a similar purpose to the JOIN operation.

QUERY 2

For every project located in 'Stafford', retrieve the project number, the controlling department number, and the last name, birthdate, and address of the manager of that department.

Q2 : { p.PNUMBER, p.DNUM, m.LNAME, m.BDATE, m.ADDRESS | PROJECT(p)
   and EMPLOYEE(m) **and** p.PLOCATION='Stafford' **and**
((∃ d)(DEPARTMENT(d) **and** p.DNUM=d.DNUMBER **and** d.MGRSSN=m.SSN))}

In Q2 there are two free tuple variables, p and m. Tuple variable d is bound to the existential quantifier. The query condition is evaluated for every combination of tuples assigned to p and m, and only the combinations that satisfy the condition are selected.

Notice that we can have several tuple variables in a query that range over the same relation. For example, to specify the query Q8—for each employee, retrieve the employee's first and last name and the first and last name of his or her immediate supervisor—all we have to do is specify two tuple variables e and s that both range over the EMPLOYEE relation.

Q8 : { e.FNAME,e.LNAME,s.FNAME,s.LNAME | EMPLOYEE(e) **and** EMPLOYEE(s)
   and e.SUPERSSN=s.SSN }

QUERY 3'

Find the name of each employee who works on *some* project controlled by department number 5. This is a variation of query 3 in which "all" is changed to "some". In this case all we need are two join conditions and two existential quantifiers.

Q3' : { e.LNAME, e.FNAME | EMPLOYEE(e) **and** (($\exists$ x)($\exists$ w)
   (PROJECT(x) **and** WORKS_ON(w) **and** x.DNUM=5 **and** w.ESSN=e.SSN **and**
   x.PNUMBER=w.PNO)) }

QUERY 4

Make a list of all projects that involve an employee whose last name is 'Smith' as a worker or as manager of the controlling department for the project.

Q4 : { p.PNUMBER | PROJECT(p) **and**
    (((∃ e)(∃ w)(EMPLOYEE(e) **and** WORKS_ON(w) **and**
    w.PNO=p.PNUMBER **and** e.LNAME='Smith' **and** e.SSN=w.ESSN))
    or
    ((∃ m)(∃ d)(EMPLOYEE(m) **and** DEPARTMENT(d) **and**
    p.DNUM=d.DNUMBER **and** d.MGRSSN=m.SSN **and** m.LNAME='Smith'))) }

Compare this with the relational algebra version of this query from Chapter 6. The UNION operation in relational algebra can usually be substituted with an **or** connective in relational calculus. In the next section we discuss the relationship between the universal and existential quantifiers and show how one can be transformed into the other.

8.1.4 *Transforming the Universal and Existential Quantifiers*

We now introduce some well-known transformations from mathematical logic that relate the universal and existential quantifiers. It is possible to transform a universal quantifier to an existential quantifier and vice versa and get an equivalent expression. One general transformation to get an equivalent expression can be described informally as follows: Transform one type of quantifier into the other with negation (preceded by **not**); **and** and **or** replace one another; a negated formula becomes unnegated; and an unnegated formula becomes negated. Some special cases of this transformation can be stated as follows, where $\not\exists$ denotes **not**(∃):

(∀ x) (P(x)) ≡ ($\not\exists$ x) (**not**(P(x)))
(∃ x) (P(x)) ≡ **not**(∀ x) (**not**(P(x)))
(∀ x) (P(x) **and** Q(x)) ≡ ($\not\exists$ x) (**not**(P(x)) **or** **not**(Q(x)))
(∀ x) (P(x) **or** Q(x)) ≡ ($\not\exists$ x) (**not**(P(x)) **and** **not**(Q(x)))
(∃ x) (P(x) **or** Q(x)) ≡ **not**(∀ x) (**not**(P(x)) **and** **not**(Q(x)))
(∃ x) (P(x) **and** Q(x)) ≡ **not**(∀ x) (**not**(P(x)) **or** **not**(Q(x)))

Notice also that the following is true, where ⇒ stands for implies:

(∀ x) (P(x)) ⇒ (∃ x) (P(x))
($\not\exists$ x) (P(x)) ⇒ **not**(∀ x) (P(x))

However, the following is *not true*:

not(∀ x) (P(x)) ⇒ ($\not\exists$ x) (P(x))

8.1.5 *Universal Quantifiers and Safe Expressions*

In this section we give examples illustrating the use of the universal quantifier and some of the transformations discussed above. We also briefly discuss the problem of specifying queries with infinite results when using the quantifiers and means of ensuring that this does not happen.

QUERY 3

Find the names of employees who work on *all* projects controlled by department number 5. One way of specifying this query is by using the universal quantifier as shown in Q3.

Q3 : { e.LNAME, e.FNAME | EMPLOYEE(e) **and** (($\forall$ x) (**not**(PROJECT(x)) **or**
((PROJECT(x) **and** (**not**(x.DNUM=5) **or**
(($\exists$ w) (WORKS_ON(w) **and** w.ESSN=e.SSN **and** x.PNUMBER=w.PNO)))))) }

Whenever we use a universal quantifier, it is quite judicious to follow a few rules to ensure that our expression makes sense. We discuss these rules with respect to Q3. We can break up Q3 into its basic components as follows:

Q3 : { e.SSN | EMPLOYEE(e) **and** F' }
F' = ($\forall$ x) (**not**(PROJECT(x)) **or** F_1)
F_1= (($\exists$ x) (PROJECT(x) **and** (**not**(x.DNUM=5) **or** F_2)))
F_2 = ($\exists$ w)(WORKS_ON(w) **and** w.ESSN= e.SSN **and** x.PNUMBER=w.PNO)

The trick is to exclude all tuples in which we are not interested from the universal quantification. We can do this by making the condition TRUE *for all such tuples.* This is necessary because a universally quantified tuple variable, such as x in Q3, must evaluate to TRUE for *every possible tuple* assigned to it. The first tuples to exclude are those that are not in the relation R of interest. Then we exclude the tuples we are not interested in from R itself. Finally, we specify a condition F_2 that must hold on all the remaining tuples in R. In Q3, R is the PROJECT relation. Each tuple e that makes F_2 TRUE *for all remaining PROJECT tuples that have not been excluded* is selected for the query result. Hence, we can explain Q3 as follows:

1. For the formula F' = ($\forall$ x)(F) to be TRUE, we must have the formula F be TRUE *for all tuples in the universe that can be assigned to x.* However, in Q3 we are only interested in F being TRUE for all tuples of the PROJECT relation that are controlled by department 5. Hence, the formula F is of the form (**not**(PROJECT(x)) **or** F_1). The '**not**(PROJECT(x)) **or** ... ' condition is TRUE for all tuples *not in the* PROJECT *relation* and has the effect of eliminating these tuples from consideration in the truth value of F_1. For *every tuple* in the PROJECT relation, F_1 must be TRUE if F is to be TRUE.

2. Using the same line of reasoning, we do not want to consider tuples in the PROJECT relation that are not of interest. Because we want a selected EMPLOYEE tuple to work on all projects controlled by department number 5, we are only interested in PROJECT tuples whose DNUM = 5. We can therefore say

    if (x.DNUM=5) **then** F_2

    which is equivalent to

    (**not**(x.DNUM=5) **or** F_2)

    Formula F_1, hence, is of the form (($\exists$ x) (PROJECT(x) **and** (**not**(x.DNUM=5) **or** F_2))). In the context of Q3, this means that for a tuple x in the PROJECT relation, either its DNUM ≠ 5 or it must satisfy F_2.

3. Finally, F_2 gives the condition that we want to hold for a selected EMPLOYEE tuple: that the employee works on *every PROJECT tuple that has not been excluded yet.* Such EMPLOYEE tuples are selected by the query.

In English, Q3 gives the following condition for selecting an EMPLOYEE tuple e: For every tuple x in the PROJECT relation with x.DNUM = 5, there must exist a tuple w in WORKS_ON such that w.ESSN = e.SSN and w.PNO = x.PNUMBER. This is equivalent to saying that EMPLOYEE e works on every PROJECT x in DEPARTMENT number 5. (Whew!)

Whenever we use universal quantifiers, existential quantifiers, or negation of predicates in a calculus expression, we must make sure that the resulting expression makes sense. A **safe expression** in relational calculus is one that is guaranteed to yield a *finite number of tuples* as its result; otherwise, the expression is called **unsafe**. For example, the expression

$\{ t \mid \textbf{not}(\text{EMPLOYEE}(t)) \}$

is *unsafe* because it yields all tuples in the universe that are *not* EMPLOYEE tuples, which are infinitely many. If we follow the rules for Q3 discussed above, we will get a safe expression when using universal quantifiers. See Ullman (1982) for a formal discussion of safe expressions.

Using the general transformation from universal to existential quantifiers given in Section 8.1.4, we can rephrase the query in Q3 as shown in Q3A below.

Q3A : { e.LNAME, e.FNAME | EMPLOYEE(e) **and** (**not**($\exists$ x) (PROJECT(x)
   and (x.DNUM=5) **and**
(**not**($\exists$ w)(WORKS_ON(w) **and** w.ESSN=e.SSN **and** x.PNUMBER=w.PNO)))) }

We now give some additional examples of queries that use quantifiers.

QUERY 6
Find the names of employees without any dependents.

Q6 : { e.FNAME, e.LNAME | EMPLOYEE(e) **and** (**not**($\exists$ d)(DEPENDENT(d) **and**
   e.SSN=d.ESSN)) }

Using the general transformation rule, Q6 can be rephrased as follows:

Q6A :{ e.FNAME, e.LNAME | EMPLOYEE(e) **and** (($\forall$ d) (**not**(DEPENDENT(d)) **or**
   (($\exists$ d) (DEPENDENT(d) **and** not(e.SSN=d.ESSN))))) }

QUERY 7
List the names of managers who have at least one dependent.

Q7 : { e.FNAME, e.LNAME | EMPLOYEE(e) **and** (($\exists$ d) ($\exists$ p)
   (DEPARTMENT(d) **and** DEPENDENT(p) **and** e.SSN=d.MGRSSN **and**
   p.ESSN=e.SSN)) }

8.2 Quantifiers in SQL

The EXISTS function in SQL is similar to the existential quantifier of the relational calculus. When we write

SELECT ...
FROM ...

```
WHERE   EXISTS   (SELECT    *
                 FROM       R X
                 WHERE      P(X) )
```

in SQL it is equivalent to saying that a tuple variable X ranging over the relation R is existentially quantified. The nested query on which the EXISTS function is applied is normally correlated with the outer query; that is, the condition P(X) includes some attribute from the outer query relations. The WHERE condition of the outer query evaluates to TRUE if the nested query returns a nonempty result that contains one or more tuples.

SQL does not include a universal quantifier. The use of a negated existential quantifier ($\nexists$ x) by writing NOT EXISTS is the way SQL supports universal quantification, as illustrated by Q3 in Chapter 7.

8.3   Domain Relational Calculus

Domain relational calculus, or simply **domain calculus**, is the other type of formal predicate calculus-based language for relational databases. There is one commercial query language, QBE, that is somewhat related to the domain calculus, although QBE was developed prior to the formal specification of domain calculus. We present QBE in Chapter 9.

The domain calculus differs from the tuple calculus in the *type of variables* used in formulas; rather than having variables range over tuples, the variables range over single values from domains of attributes. To form a relation of degree n for a query result, we must have n of these **domain variables**—one for each attribute of the relation. Hence, the number of variables in a domain calculus expression is more than the number for the corresponding tuple calculus expression. An expression of the domain calculus is of the form

$$\{ x_1, x_2, ..., x_n \mid COND(x_1, x_2, ..., x_n, x_{n+1}, x_{n+2}, ..., x_{n+m}) \}$$

where $x_1, x_2, ..., x_n, x_{n+1}, x_{n+2}, ..., x_{n+m}$ are domain variables that range over (not necessarily distinct) domains (of attributes) and COND is a **condition** or **formula** of the domain relational calculus. A formula is made up of **atoms**. The atoms of a formula are slightly different from those for the tuple calculus and can be one of the following:

1. An atom of the form $R(x_1, x_2, ..., x_j)$, where R is the name of a relation of degree j and each x_i, $1 \le i \le j$, is a domain variable. This atom states that a list of values of $<x_1, x_2, ..., x_j>$ must be a tuple in the relation whose name is R, and x_i is the value of the ith attribute value of the tuple. To make a domain calculus expression more concise, we sometimes *drop the commas* in a list of variables; for example, we can write

   $$\{ x_1 x_2 ... x_n \mid R(x_1 x_2 x_3) \text{ and } ... \}$$

   instead of:

   $$\{ x_1, x_2, ..., x_n \mid R(x_1, x_2, x_3) \text{ and } ... \}$$

2. An atom of the form x_i **op** x_j where **op** is one of the comparison operators in the set $\{ =, \ne, <, \le, >, \ge \}$ and x_i and x_j are domain variables.

3. An atom of the form x_i **op** c or c **op** x_j where **op** is one of the comparison operators in the set { =, ≠, <, ≤, >, ≥ }, x_i and x_j are domain variables, and c is a constant value.

As in tuple calculus, atoms evaluate to either TRUE or FALSE for a specific set of values, called the **truth values** of the atoms. In case 1, if the domain variables are assigned values corresponding to a tuple of the specified relation R, then the atom is TRUE. In cases 2 and 3, if the domain variables are assigned values that satisfy the condition, then the atom is TRUE.

In a similar way to the tuple relational calculus, formulas are made up of atoms, variables, and quantifiers, so we will not repeat the specifications for formulas here. We now give some examples of queries specified in the domain calculus. We will use lower-case letters l,m,n,...,x,y,z for domain variables.

QUERY 0
Retrieve the birthdate and address of the employee whose name is 'John B. Smith'.

Q0 : { uv | (∃ q) (∃ r) (∃ s)
  (EMPLOYEE(qrstuvwxyz) **and** q='John' **and** r='B' **and** s='Smith') }

We need ten variables for the EMPLOYEE relation, one to range over the domain of each attribute. Of the ten variables q, r, s, ..., z, only q, r, and s are bound to an existential quantifier and the rest are free. We first specify the requested attributes, BDATE and ADDRESS, by the domain variables u for BDATE and v for ADDRESS. Then we specify the condition for selecting a tuple following the bar (|), namely that the sequence of values assigned to the variables qrstuvwxyz be a tuple of the EMPLOYEE relation and the values for q (FNAME), r (MINIT), and s (LNAME) be 'John', 'B', and 'Smith', respectively. Notice that we existentially quantify *only the variables participating in a condition*.

An alternative notation for writing this query is to assign the constants 'John', 'B', and 'Smith' directly as shown in Q0A, where all variables are free:

Q0A : { uv | EMPLOYEE('John','B','Smith',t,u,v,w,x,y,z) }

QUERY 1
Retrieve the name and address of all employees who work for the 'Research' department.

Q1 : { qsv | (∃ z) (EMPLOYEE(qrstuvwxyz) **and** (∃ l) (∃ m)
  (DEPARTMENT(lmno) **and** l='Research' **and** m=z)) }

A condition relating two domain variables that range over attributes from two relations, such as m = z in Q1, is a **join condition** and serves a similar purpose to the JOIN operation of the relational algebra. On the other hand, a condition that relates a domain variable to a constant, such as l = 'Research' in Q1, is a **selection condition** and corresponds to a SELECT operation in the relational algebra.

QUERY 2
For every project located in 'Stafford', list the project number, the controlling department number, and the last name, birthdate, and address of the manager of that department.

Q2 : { iksuv | (∃ j) (PROJECT(hijk) **and** (∃ t) (EMPLOYEE(qrstuvwxyz) **and**
(∃ m)(∃ n) (DEPARTMENT(lmno) **and** k=m **and** n=t **and** j='Stafford'))) }

QUERY 6

Find the names of employees without dependents.

Q6 : { qs | (∃ t) (EMPLOYEE(qrstuvwxyz) **and** (**not**(∃ l) (DEPENDENT(lmnop) **and**
t=l))) }

We must be careful in queries such as Query 6 to make sure that it is safe. Query 6 can be stated using universal quantifiers instead of the existential quantifiers as shown in Q6A below.

Q6A : { qs | (∃ t) (EMPLOYEE(qrstuvwxyz) **and** ((∀ l) (**not**(DEPENDENT(lmnop)) **or**
not(t=l)))) }

QUERY 7

List the names of managers who have at least one dependent.

Q7 : { sq | (∃ t) (EMPLOYEE(qrstuvwxyz) **and** ((∃ j) (DEPARTMENT(hijk) **and**
((∃ l) (DEPENDENT(lmnop) **and** t=j **and** l=t))))) }

As we mentioned earlier, it can be shown that any query that may be expressed in the relational algebra can be expressed in the domain or tuple relational calculus. In addition, any safe expression in the domain or tuple relational calculus can be expressed in the relational algebra. The specification of the algebra and calculus by Codd (1972) constituted an important theoretical foundation for relational languages and for high-level database languages in general. For a proof of equivalence of relational algebra and relational calculus, see Ullman (1982).

8.4   Summary

The relational calculus is a declarative formal query language for the relational model, which is based on the branch of mathematical logic called predicate calculus. There are two types of relational calculus. The tuple relational calculus uses tuple variables that range over relations, whereas the domain relational calculus uses domain variables.

A query is specified in a single declarative statement, without specifying any order or method for retrieving the result of the query. Hence, the relational calculus is often considered to be a higher-level language than the relational algebra. A relational algebra expression specifies how to retrieve the result of query, whereas a relational calculus expression specifies only what we want to retrieve regardless of how the query may be executed.

We discussed the syntax of relational calculus queries. We also discussed the existential quantifier (∃) and the universal quantifier (∀). We saw that relational calculus variables are bound by these quantifiers. We saw in detail how queries with universal quantification are written and discussed the problem of specifying safe queries whose results are finite. We also discussed rules for transforming universal into existential quantifiers and vice versa. Notice that it is the quantifiers that give expressive power to the relational calculus that make it equivalent to relational algebra.

Notice that the SQL language, described in Chapter 7, also has similarities to the tuple relational calculus. A SELECT-PROJECT-JOIN query in SQL is similar to a tuple relational calculus expression if we consider each relation name in the FROM-clause of the SQL query to be a tuple variable with an implicit existential quantifier. The EXISTS function in SQL is equivalent to the existential quantifier and can be used in its negated form (NOT EXISTS) to specify universal quantification. There is no explicit equivalent of a universal quantifier in SQL. There is no analog to grouping and aggregation functions in the relational calculus.

In the next chapter we discuss two database languages that are related to relational calculus. The language QUEL is very similar to the tuple relational calculus without the universal quantifier, whereas the QBE language has similarities to the domain relational calculus.

Review Questions

8.1. In what sense does relational calculus differ from relational algebra, and in what sense are they similar?

8.2. How does tuple relational calculus differ from domain relational calculus?

8.3. Discuss the meanings of the existential quantifier ($\exists$) and the universal quantifier ($\forall$).

8.4. Define the following terms with respect to the tuple calculus: tuple variable, range relation, atom, formula, expression.

8.5. Define the following terms with respect to the domain calculus: domain variable, range relation, atom, formula, expression.

8.6. What is meant by a safe expression in relational calculus?

8.7. When is a query language called relationally complete?

Exercises

8.8. Specify queries a, b, c, e, f, i, j, and k of Exercise 6.19 in both the tuple relational calculus and the domain relational calculus.

8.9. Specify queries a, b, c, and d of Exercise 6.21 in both the tuple relational calculus and the domain relational calculus.

8.10. Specify queries a, b, c, d, e, and f of Exercise 7.16 in both the tuple relational calculus and the domain relational calculus. Also specify these queries in the relational algebra.

8.11. In a tuple relational calculus query with n tuple variables, what would be the typical minimum number of join conditions? Why? What is the effect of having a smaller number of join conditions?

8.12. Rewrite the domain relational calculus queries that followed Q0 in Section 8.3 in the style of the abbreviated notation of Q0A, where the objective is to minimize the number of domain variables by writing constants in place of variables wherever possible.

8.13. Consider the query: Retrieve the SSNs of employees who work on at least those projects on which the employee with SSN = 123456789 works. This may be stated as (FORALL x) (IF P THEN Q), where:

- x is a tuple variable that ranges over the PROJECT relation.
- P ≡ employee with SSN = 123456789 works on project x.
- Q ≡ employee e works on project x.

Express the query in tuple relational calculus using the rules:

- $(\forall x)(P(x)) \equiv (\not\exists x)(not(P(X)))$.
- (IF P THEN Q) ≡ (not(P) or Q).

8.14. Show how you may specify the following relational algebra operations in both tuple and domain relational calculus.

a. $\sigma_{A=c}(R(A, B, C))$.
b. $\pi_{<A, B>}(R(A, B, C))$.
c. $R(A, B, C) * S(C, D, E)$.
d. $R(A, B, C) \cup S(A, B, C)$.
e. $R(A, B, C) \cap S(A, B, C)$.
f. $R(A, B, C) - S(A, B, C)$.
g. $R(A, B, C) \times S(D, E, F)$.
h. $R(A, B) \div S(A)$.

8.15. Suggest extensions to the relational calculus so that it may express the following types of operations that were discussed in Section 6.3: (a) aggregate functions and grouping, (b) OUTER JOIN operations, and (c) recursive closure queries.

Selected Bibliography

Codd (1971) introduced the language ALPHA, which is based on concepts of tuple relational calculus. ALPHA also includes the notion of aggregate functions, which goes beyond relational calculus. The original formal definition of relational calculus was given by Codd (1972), who also provided an algorithm that transforms any tuple relational calculus expression to relational algebra. Codd defined a language as relationally complete if it is at least as powerful as relational calculus. Ullman (1982) describes a formal proof of the equivalence of relational algebra with the safe expressions of tuple and domain relational calculus.

Ideas of domain relational calculus appeared in the QBE language (Zloof 1975). The concept is formally defined by Lacroix and Pirotte (1977). The ILL language (Lacroix and Pirotte 1977a) is based on domain relational calculus. The QUEL language (Stonebraker et al. 1976) is based on tuple relational calculus with implicit existential quantifiers but no universal quantifier. Additional references on QUEL and QBE appear in the bibliographic notes for Chapter 9.

CHAPTER 9

The QUEL and QBE Languages

In Chapter 8 we studied two formal relational languages—tuple relational calculus and domain relational calculus. In Chapter 7 we studied the SQL database language, which is based to some extent on tuple relational calculus. QUEL is another database language that is based more closely on tuple relational calculus. In QUEL, which we study in Section 9.1, tuple relational calculus is enhanced with functions and grouping facilities.

Another relational language presented in this chapter is QBE (Query By Example). This deserves discussion because of its unique characteristic of exploiting users' intuition and abstraction from examples. QBE is a two-dimensional language in which tables are displayed pictorially and queries are specified by filling in values and variable symbols in the appropriate columns. QBE implements some aspects of domain relational calculus. We present QBE in Section 9.2.

9.1   The QUEL Language

QUEL is a data definition and manipulation language for the popular INGRES relational DBMS. The original version of INGRES, which stands for Interactive Graphics and Retrieval System, was developed as a research project at the University of California at Berkeley in the mid-1970s; this version of INGRES is often called university INGRES. A commercial INGRES DBMS has been marketed by RTI (Relational Technology, Inc.) since 1980. QUEL can be used as an interactive query language or it can be embedded within a host programming language. It includes a range of functionality similar to that provided by SQL. Our presentation here will follow a pattern similar to that used in the presentation of SQL in Chapter 7.

9.1.1   Data and Storage Definition in QUEL

The CREATE Command and QUEL Data Types

The CREATE command is used to specify a **base relation** and its attributes. A **base relation** is a relation whose tuples are physically stored in the database. Several data types are available for attributes. The numeric data types include I1, I2, and I4 for integers of 1, 2, and 4 bytes length, and F4 and F8 for real floating-point numbers of 4 and 8 bytes length. Character string data types include Cn and CHAR(n) for a fixed-length string of n characters and TEXT(n) and VARCHAR(n) for a varying-length string with a maximum length of n characters.* In addition, a DATE data type is available; this provides flexible formats, such as absolute date/time values like '19-OCT-1920 12:00 pm' or relative values like '2 years 4 months' or '1 day 4 hours 30 minutes'. A MONEY data type, which is a 16-digit number with the two rightmost digits representing cents, is also available. Figure 9.1 shows how the EMPLOYEE and DEPARTMENT relations of Figure 6.5 may be declared in QUEL.

The INDEX Command

In QUEL the logical data definition commands are mixed with the specification of storage structures. The INDEX command is used to specify a (first-level only) index on a relation; in fact, an index is treated as an ordered base relation where the only attributes are the indexing attributes, and the DBMS maintains pointers to the corresponding records. In our terminology of Chapter 5, it is a *single-level secondary index*. A multilevel index can be created by specifying a B-TREE over an existing INDEX.

The MODIFY Command and Use of UNIQUE

To specify or change the storage structure on a base relation (or an index), the MODIFY command is used. The available storage structures are ISAM (indexed sequential), HASH, BTREE, HEAP (unordered file), and HEAPSORT (sort the records now but do not maintain the order when new tuples are inserted). The letter C appended before any storage structure name—for example, CHASH or CBTREE—indicates that the files and their access paths will be stored in a compressed form, thus saving some space but slightly increasing retrieval and update time. Each base relation (or index) can have at most one storage structure defined over it. The usual default storage structure for a base relation is the HEAP.

Key attributes are specified by including the key word UNIQUE in a MODIFY command; hence, as in SQL, we cannot specify key attributes independently of a specific storage structure on the relation. To illustrate the use of MODIFY, suppose we want to specify the following: a key and a B-tree on the SSN attribute of EMPLOYEE, an index on the combination of LNAME and FNAME attributes of EMPLOYEE, a key and hash access on the DNAME attribute of DEPARTMENT, and a key and compressed B-tree index on the DNO attribute of DEPARTMENT. The statements in L1 do the above.

---

*Cn was used in university INGRES and has some peculiar behavior when string comparisons are applied. TEXT(n) was introduced in commercial INGRES and gives more predictable results.

L1:	**CREATE** EMPLOYEE	(	FNAME	=	TEXT(15),
			MINIT	=	C1,
			LNAME	=	TEXT(15),
			SSN	=	C9,
			BDATE	=	DATE,
			ADDRESS	=	TEXT(30),
			SEX	=	C1,
			SALARY	=	MONEY,
			SUPERSSN	=	C9,
			DNO	=	I4);
	CREATE DEPARTMENT	(	DNAME	=	TEXT(15),
			DNUMBER	=	I4,
			MGRSSN	=	C9,
			MGRSTARTDATE	=	C9);

Figure 9.1 Declaring the EMPLOYEE and DEPARTMENT
relations of Figure 6.5 in QUEL

L1: **MODIFY** EMPLOYEE **TO BTREE UNIQUE ON** SSN;
INDEX ON EMPLOYEE **IS** NAME_INDEX (LNAME, FNAME);
MODIFY DEPARTMENT **TO HASH UNIQUE ON** DNAME;
INDEX ON DEPARTMENT **IS** DNO_INDEX (DNO);
MODIFY DNO_INDEX **TO CBTREE UNIQUE ON** DNO;

If we decide that a base relation or index is not needed any longer, we can delete it
using the **DESTROY** command. For example, if we no longer want the above two indexes,
we can get rid of them by issuing the command in L2.

L2: **DESTROY** DNO_INDEX, NAME_INDEX ;

The original QUEL does not have commands to add attributes to tables (ALTER in
SQL), nor does it have explicit **NULL** values as in SQL. A missing value is represented by a
blank for string data types and 0 (zero) for numeric data types.

9.1.2 Data Retrieval Queries in QUEL

Basic QUEL Queries

Basic QUEL retrieval queries of the **select-project-join** type are very similar to tuple relational calculus. Two clauses, **RETRIEVE** and **WHERE**, are used; RETRIEVE specifies the attributes to be retrieved—the projection attributes—and WHERE specifies the select and
join conditions. This RETRIEVE…WHERE… construct corresponds to the SELECT…FROM…
WHERE… construct in SQL. The difference is that QUEL does not have a FROM-clause as
SQL does; rather, all attributes in a QUEL query *must be explicitly qualified* either by their
relation name or by a tuple variable declared to range over their relation. Tuple variables
are declared explicitly in the **RANGE** statement of QUEL. We now give some examples of
simple queries in QUEL using the schema of Figure 6.5. We will give the same query numbers used in Chapters 6, 7, and 8.

QUERY 0

Retrieve the birthdate and address of the employee whose name is 'John B. Smith'.

Q0:   RETRIEVE   (EMPLOYEE.BDATE, EMPLOYEE.ADDRESS)
     WHERE   EMPLOYEE.FNAME='John' **AND** EMPLOYEE.MINIT='B' **AND**
                  EMPLOYEE.LNAME='Smith'

Alternatively, we can specify tuple variables in RANGE statements and use the tuple variables in the query. This is particularly convenient if relation names are long. It also becomes necessary if we need multiple references to the same relation in the same query. For the remaining examples, we assume that the RANGE variables in L3 have been declared.

L3:   RANGE OF   E, S **IS** EMPLOYEE,
                  D **IS** DEPARTMENT,
                  P **IS** PROJECT,
                  W **IS** WORKS_ON,
                  DEP **IS** DEPENDENT,
                  DL **IS** DEPT_LOCATIONS

The query in Q0 can be restated as in Q0A using the tuple variables declared in the RANGE statement of L3.

Q0A: RETRIEVE   (E.BDATE, E.ADDRESS)
      WHERE   E.FNAME='John' **AND** E.MINIT='B' **AND** E.LNAME='Smith'

QUERY 1

Retrieve the name and address of all employees who work for the 'Research' department.

Q1:   RETRIEVE   (E.FNAME, E.LNAME, E.ADDRESS)
     WHERE   D.DNAME='Research' **AND** D.DNUMBER=E.DNO

QUERY 2

List the project number, the controlling department number, and the last name, birthdate, and address of the manager of that department for every project located in 'Stafford'.

Q2:   RETRIEVE   (P.PNUMBER, P.DNUM, E.LNAME, E.BDATE, E.ADDRESS)
     WHERE   P.DNUM=D.DNUMBER **AND** D.MGRSSN=E.SSN **AND**
                  P.PLOCATION='Stafford'

For queries such as Q8 below that refer to the same relation more than once, distinct range variables can be declared. For example, in L3 the two range variables E and S are declared to range over EMPLOYEE.

QUERY 8

For each employee, retrieve the employee's first and last name and the first and last name of his or her immediate supervisor.

Q8:   RETRIEVE   (E.FNAME, E.LNAME, S.FNAME, S.LNAME)
     WHERE   E.SUPERSSN=S.SSN

In Q8 the EMPLOYEE relation is joined with itself; range variable E represents employees in the role of supervisees whereas range variable S represents employees in the role of supervisors.

A missing WHERE-clause in QUEL, as in SQL, indicates no condition on tuple selection; hence, all possible combinations of tuples from the relations referenced in the query are selected, and their specified attribute values are projected out. If only a single relation is referenced in the query, then a missing WHERE-clause is similar to the *PROJECT operation* in the relational algebra. If several relations are referenced, a missing WHERE-clause is similar to a CARTESIAN PRODUCT followed by a PROJECT. However, as in SQL, *duplicate tuples are not eliminated* unless explicitly specified.

QUERIES 9 AND 10
Retrieve the SSN values for all EMPLOYEE (Q9) and all combinations of an EMPLOYEE SSN and a DEPARTMENT DNAME (Q10).

Q9: RETRIEVE (E.SSN)

Q10: RETRIEVE (E.SSN, D.DNAME)

To retrieve *all the attributes* of the selected tuples, we use the key word **ALL**; this is similar to the asterisk (∗) notation of SQL. Query Q1D retrieves all attributes of an EMPLOYEE and the DEPARTMENT he or she works in for every employee in the 'Research' department.

Q1D: RETRIEVE (E.ALL, D.ALL)
         WHERE   D.DNAME='Research' **AND** E.DNO=D.DNUMBER

As in SQL, the result of a query in QUEL may have duplicate tuples; hence, a relation is not strictly a set of tuples but a multiset. To eliminate duplicate tuples, the key word **UNIQUE** is specified in the RETRIEVE-clause (similar to DISTINCT in SQL). For example, Query Q11 retrieves all salaries of employees, leaving duplicates, whereas Q11A removes duplicate salaries from the result of the query.

Q11: RETRIEVE (E.SALARY)

Q11A: RETRIEVE UNIQUE (E.SALARY)

Implicit Existential Quantifiers in QUEL

In QUEL any range variable appearing in the WHERE-clause of a QUEL query that does not appear in the RETRIEVE-clause *is implicitly quantified by an existential quantifier*. Hence, fewer quantifiers need to be *explicitly specified* than in the corresponding tuple relational calculus queries.

QUERY 3'
Retrieve the names of employees who work on *some* project that is controlled by department 5.

Q3': RETRIEVE UNIQUE (E.FNAME, E.LNAME)
         WHERE   P.DNUM=5 **AND** P.PNUMBER=W.PNO **AND** W.ESSN=E.SSN

The P and W tuple variables are implicitly quantified by the existential quantifier in Q3'. This is similar to saying "retrieve the first and last name of every employee such that *there exists* some project tuple controlled by department 5 and *there exists* some WORKS_ON tuple showing that the employee works on that project." For queries that involve universal quantifiers or negated existential quantifiers, we must use either the COUNT function or the ANY function. We will defer discussion of such queries until we present QUEL functions in the next subsection.

Functions and Grouping in QUEL

Most of the features of QUEL that we discuss in this and the next subsections provide additional functionality required in database processing that is not provided by the basic relational calculus. The first of these features is a collection of built-in functions. These are **COUNT, SUM, MIN, MAX,** and **AVG** and are similar to the corresponding SQL functions. Additional functions are available in QUEL that *eliminate duplicate tuples before applying the functions* COUNT, SUM, and AVG. The names of these functions are derived by appending a U (for unique) to the end of the corresponding function name, giving **COUNTU, SUMU,** and **AVGU.**

All QUEL functions can be used either in the RETRIEVE-clause or in the WHERE-clause. Whenever a function is used in the RETRIEVE-clause we must give it an *independent attribute name*, which appears as a column header when displaying the query result and whenever we refer to the result of the query.

QUERY 15
Find the sum of the salaries of *all* employees, the maximum salary, the minimum salary, and the average salary.

Q15: **RETRIEVE** (SUMSAL = **SUM** (E.SALARY), MAXSAL = **MAX** (E.SALARY),
                     MINSAL = **MIN** (E.SALARY), AVGSAL = **AVG** (E.SALARY))

Here the resulting relation would have column names SUMSAL, MAXSAL, MINSAL, and AVGSAL. Note that using SUMU and AVGU in place of SUM and AVG would, in general, give a different result.

To apply the above four functions to employees of a specific department—say the 'Research' department—we can write the query as in Q16. Notice how this differs from SQL; in QUEL a WHERE-clause can be included *within each function*, thus allowing different functions to be applied to different tuples in the same query. However, when all the functions are applied to the same tuples, we still must *repeat* the WHERE condition within every function.

Q16: **RETRIEVE**   (SUMSAL = **SUM** (E.SALARY **WHERE** E.DNO=D.DNUMBER
                      AND D.DNAME='Research'),
                      MAXSAL = **MAX** (E.SALARY **WHERE** E.DNO=D.DNUMBER
                      AND D.DNAME='Research'),
                      MINSAL = **MIN** (E.SALARY **WHERE** E.DNO=D.DNUMBER
                      AND D.DNAME='Research'),
                      AVGSAL = **AVG** (E.SALARY **WHERE** E.DNO=D.DNUMBER
                      AND D.DNAME='Research'))

QUERIES 17 AND 18

Retrieve the total number of employees in the company (Q17) and the number of employees in the 'Research' department (Q18).

Q17: RETRIEVE (TOTAL_EMPS = **COUNT** (E.SSN))

Q18: RETRIEVE (RESEARCH_EMPS = **COUNT** (E.SSN **WHERE** E.DNO= D.DNUMBER **AND** D.DNAME='Research'))

In Q17 and Q18 we count the number of values of the key attribute SSN of the EMPLOYEE relation to count the tuples. Currently, QUEL does not allow the use of COUNT(E.ALL), which would correspond roughly to COUNT(*) in SQL.

The above examples show how functions are applied without any grouping of tuples. QUEL provides more powerful facilities for grouping and restriction than those provided by the GROUP BY and HAVING clauses of SQL. The **BY** qualifier in QUEL can be used within each function specification to specify a particular grouping of tuples; hence, different groupings can be used in the same query. Each function can have its own grouping attributes as well as its own WHERE conditions, and grouping can be used in the RETRIEVE-clause *or* in the WHERE-clause. We discuss the use of BY using several examples.

Use of BY in the RETRIEVE-Clause

QUERY 20

For each department, retrieve the department number, the number of employees in the department, and their average salary.

Q20: RETRIEVE (E.DNO, NO_OF_EMPS = **COUNT** (E.SSN **BY** E.DNO), AVG_SAL = **AVG** (E.SALARY **BY** E.DNO))

Q20 groups EMPLOYEE tuples by department number using the BY qualifier by writing "BY E.DNO." Counting the employees by department is written as COUNT(E.SSN BY E.DNO). Similarly, the average salary of employees within each department is specified by AVG (E.SALARY BY E.DNO). Notice that the grouping attribute E.DNO must also appear independently in the RETRIEVE-list for the query to make sense.

QUERY 21

For each project, retrieve the project number, project name, and the number of employees who work on that project.

Q21: RETRIEVE (W.PNO, P.PNAME, NO_OF_EMPS = **COUNT** (W.ESSN **BY** W.PNO, P.PNAME **WHERE** W.PNO=P.PNUMBER))

Q21 illustrates a grouping example where two relations are involved. The relations are joined based on the condition W.PNO = P.PNUMBER, then tuples are grouped by (W.PNO, P.PNAME) and the query result is calculated. The grouping attributes (W.PNO, P.PNAME) must appear in the RETRIEVE list. Q21 illustrates the use of both grouping and a WHERE condition *within the specification of an aggregate function*. This allows several functions to be applied to different sets of tuples within the same query and is somewhat similar to query nesting in SQL. Another example of using BY and WHERE in the RETRIEVE-clause follows.

QUERY 23

For each project, retrieve the project number and the number of employees from department 5 who work on that project.

Q23:   RETRIEVE   (W.PNO, NO_EMPS_IN_D5 =
                    COUNT (W.ESSN BY W.PNO **WHERE** E.DNO=5 **AND**
                    W.ESSN=E.SSN))

Use of BY in the WHERE-Clause

Next we illustrate the use of BY in the WHERE clause. QUEL does not include a HAVING construct as in SQL because grouping can be applied in the same way to either the RETRIEVE-clause or the WHERE-clause or both. Hence, conditions on groups can be stated in a uniform manner.

QUERY 22

For each project on which more than two employees work, retrieve the project number and the number of employees who work on that project.

Q22:   RETRIEVE   (W.PNO, NO_OF_EMPS = **COUNT** (W.ESSN BY W.PNO))
        WHERE   **COUNT** (W.ESSN BY W.PNO) > 2

We should note two features in this example. First, we can use the same grouping function in the RETRIEVE- and the WHERE-clause; in fact, in Q22 we *must* specify the function twice. Second, the result of a function in the WHERE-clause does not require a name, as it would in the RETRIEVE-clause, because its value will not be displayed. The next query illustrates how different WHERE conditions within different aggregate functions can be used in the same query.

QUERY 24

Count the *total* number of employees with salaries greater than $40,000 who work in each department, but *only for those departments where more than five employees work*.

Q24:   RETRIEVE   (E.DNO, NO_OF_EMPS = **COUNT** (E.SSN BY E.DNO
                    WHERE (E.SALARY > 40000)))
                    WHERE COUNT (E.SSN BY E.DNO) >5

As another example, suppose that we want to count the *total* number of employees who work on each project, but only for those projects on which *more than 50 employees with salaries greater than $40,000* work. The query is shown as Q24A below. Here the condition (E.SALARY>40000 AND E.SSN=W.ESSN) applies only to the COUNT function in the WHERE-clause.

Q24A: RETRIEVE   (W.PNO, NO_OF_EMPS = **COUNT** (W.ESSN BY W.PNO))
         WHERE   **COUNT** (W.ESSN BY W.PNO **WHERE** (E.SSN=W.ESSN
                        AND E.SALARY>40000)) > 50

These examples show the power of the BY construct in conjunction with a WHERE condition. In general, this type of query will require a nested query if specified in SQL. It is also possible in QUEL to use functions in the WHERE-clause to select tuples rather than groups. For example, the query "retrieve a list of employee name, department number, and salary for each employee whose salary is higher than the average salary for his or her department" can be specified as in Q24B. This query also requires nesting and is more complex to specify in SQL.

> **Q24B:** **RETRIEVE** (E.LNAME, E.FNAME, E.DNO, E.SALARY)
> **WHERE** E.SALARY > **AVG** (E.SALARY **BY** E.DNO)

Nesting of Aggregate Functions

QUEL also allows for nesting of aggregate functions. For example, if we want to retrieve the average number of employees who work on a project, we must first get the number of employees working on each project and then average all these values. This can be done in a single query in QUEL as in Q24C.

> **Q24C:** **RETRIEVE** (AVG_NO_OF_EMPS_PER_PROJECT = **AVG**(**COUNT** (W.ESSN BY W.PNO)))

This nesting of functions is not possible in SQL. To summarize the grouping and aggregation facilities of QUEL and contrast them with those of SQL, we note that:

- A single query in QUEL can involve functions applied to different tuples by using different WHERE conditions within each function.
- Nesting of aggregate functions is allowed, which is not possible in SQL.
- The same WHERE condition or grouping may have to be repeated within several functions in some queries.

Specifying Explicit Quantifiers in QUEL

Another function in QUEL, **ANY**, is used to specify explicit existential quantification. ANY is applied to a subquery; if the result of the subquery includes at least one tuple, then ANY returns the value 1; otherwise it returns the value 0. Hence, ANY is somewhat similar to the EXISTS function in SQL, except that EXISTS returns TRUE or FALSE (a Boolean constant) rather than a 1 or 0. ANY is usually applied to a nested subquery that uses grouping or a WHERE condition. If a query is stated in relational calculus using the universal quantifier, we can write it in QUEL by transforming the query into an equivalent query with the existential quantifier (see Section 8.1.4) and then stating that query using ANY.

> QUERY 12
> Retrieve the name of each employee who has a dependent with the same first name and same sex as the employee.

> **Q12:** **RETRIEVE** (E.FNAME, E.LNAME)
> **WHERE ANY** (DEP.DEPENDENT_NAME BY E.SSN **WHERE** E.SSN=DEP.ESSN

                    AND E.FNAME=DEP.DEPENDENT_NAME **AND**
                    E.SEX=DEP.SEX) = 1

We can think of Q12 as follows: For each EMPLOYEE tuple, evaluate the nested query, which retrieves all DEPENDENT tuples of that employee (by the condition E.SSN = DEP.ESSN) with the same name and sex as the EMPLOYEE tuple; if at least one tuple is in the result of the embedded query, then select that EMPLOYEE tuple. ANY(Q) returns 1 if there is *at least one tuple* in the result of query Q, and 0 if there are no tuples in the result of query Q.

QUERY 6
Retrieve the names of employees who have no dependents.

Q6: **RETRIEVE**   (E.FNAME, E.LNAME)
          WHERE   **ANY**   (DEP.DEPENDENT_NAME **BY** E.SSN
                                   WHERE E.SSN=DEP.SSN) = 0

In Q6 the nested query retrieves all DEPENDENT_NAMEs related to an EMPLOYEE tuple; if none exists, that EMPLOYEE tuple is selected.

QUERY 3
Find the social security number of employees who work on *all* projects controlled by department number 5.

Q3: **RETRIEVE**   (E.SSN)
          WHERE   **ANY** (P.PNUMBER
                                WHERE   (P.DNUM=5)
                                         AND
                                ANY (W.PNO **BY** E.SSN
                                       WHERE   E.SSN=W.ESSN **AND**
                                       P.PNUMBER=W.PNO) =0) =0

In Q3 the outer nested query selects any P.PNUMBER controlled by department 5 **and** there is not a WORKS_ON tuple with the same PNO and the same SSN as the EMPLOYEE tuple under consideration. If no such project exists, we select the EMPLOYEE tuple. The form of Q3 matches the following rephrasing of the query: Select each employee such that there does not exist a project controlled by department 5 that the employee does not work on.

Additional Features of QUEL

In this section we discuss several additional features of QUEL. First, if we want to form a condition on only part of a character string value, QUEL provides partial string comparisons. Partial strings are specified using two reserved characters; '*' replaces an arbitrary number of characters, and '?' replaces a single arbitrary character. For example, to retrieve all employees whose address is in Houston, Texas, we can use Q25, which selects all EMPLOYEE tuples whose ADDRESS value includes the substring 'Houston,TX'.

Q25: **RETRIEVE** (E.LNAME, E.FNAME)
WHERE E.ADDRESS = '*Houston,TX*'

QUEL allows the use of standard arithmetic operators '+', '–'. '*', and '/' (for addition, subtraction, multiplication, and division, respectively) in a query. Additional functions such as exponentiation, trigonometric functions, and string concatenation are also available. For example, suppose we want to see the effect of giving a 10% raise to all employees who work on the 'ProductX' project; we can issue Q27 to see what their salaries would look like.

Q27: **RETRIEVE** (E.FNAME, E.LNAME, NEW_SALARY = E.SALARY * 1.1)
WHERE E.SSN=W.ESSN **AND** W.PNO=P.PNUMBER **AND** P.PNAME= 'ProductX'

QUEL also allows the retrieval of the result of a query *into a relation*; the INTO keyword is used for this purpose. This relation can then be manipulated further by the user. In addition, a constant value can be specified in a column. For example, to keep the result of Q27 into a relation called PRODUCTX_RAISES that also includes the current salary in each tuple, plus a column called PROJ whose value is 'ProductX' for all tuples, we can use Q27A.

Q27A: **RETRIEVE INTO** PRODUCTX_RAISES (PROJ = 'ProductX', E.FNAME,
E.LNAME, CURRENT_SALARY = E.SALARY,
PROPOSED_ SALARY = E.SALARY * 1.1)
WHERE E.SSN=W.ESSN **AND** W.PNO=P.PNUMBER **AND** P.PNAME= 'ProductX'

QUEL also allows the use of arithmetic operations in conjunction with functions. For example, the query "for each employee count the number of projects that the employee does not work on (from among all projects)" can be stated as shown in Q29.

Q29: **RETRIEVE** (E.SSN, NUMBER_OF_PROJECTS_NOT_WORKING_ON =
(**COUNT** (P.PNUMBER) - **COUNT** (W.PNO BY E.SSN
WHERE W.ESSN=E.SSN)))

Finally, QUEL allows the user to specify one or more values to order the tuples in the result of a query using the **SORT BY** clause. For example, suppose we want to retrieve a list of employees and the projects each works on and we want the list ordered by department and within each department ordered alphabetically by name; we can write Q28.

Q28: **RETRIEVE** (D.DNAME, E.LNAME, E.FNAME, P.PNAME)
WHERE P.PNUMBER=W.PNO **AND** E.DNO=D.DNUMBER **AND**
E.SSN=W.ESSN
SORT BY D.DNAME, E.LNAME, E.FNAME

The SORT BY clause is similar to the ORDER BY clause of SQL.

9.1.3 Update Statements in QUEL

In QUEL there are three statements to modify the database: APPEND, DELETE, and REPLACE. We discuss each of these next.

The APPEND Command

To insert a new tuple in a relation, QUEL provides the APPEND command. In its simplest form, APPEND is used to add a single tuple to a relation. We must specify the relation name and a list of values for the tuple. Each value is preceded by the attribute name it corresponds to. Missing attribute values are set to blank for STRING data types and 0 for numeric data types. For example, to add a new tuple to the EMPLOYEE relation of Figure 6.6, we can use U1.

> U1:   **APPEND TO** EMPLOYEE (FNAME = 'Richard', MINIT = 'K', LNAME = 'Marini',
> SSN ='653298653', BDATE = '30-DEC-52',
> ADDRESS = '98 Oak Forest,Katy,TX',
> SEX = 'M',
> SALARY = 37000, SUPERSSN = '987654321', DNO = 4)

The APPEND command also allows us to insert multiple tuples into a relation by selecting the result of another query. For example, to create a relation that has the name, number of employees, and total salaries for each department, we could write U3A to create a relation DEPTS_INFO, which is then loaded with the summary information retrieved from the database by U3B.

> U3A: **CREATE** DEPTS_INFO   (DEPT_NAME   TEXT(10),
> NO_OF_EMPS   I4,
> TOTAL_SAL   I4);

> U3B: **APPEND TO** DEPTS_INFO (DEPT_NAME = D. DNAME,
> NO_OF_EMPS = **COUNT** (E.SSN BY E.DNO **WHERE**
> D.DNUMBER=E.DNO),
> TOTAL_SAL = **SUM** (E.SALARY **BY** E.DNO **WHERE**
> D.DNUMBER=E.DNO));

Notice that the DEPTS_INFO table may become obsolete if we update either the DE-PARTMENT or the EMPLOYEE relations at a later time. We have to create a view (see Section 9.1.4) to keep such a table up to date automatically.

The DELETE Command

The DELETE command is used to remove tuples from a relation. It includes a WHERE-clause to select the tuples to be deleted. However, tuples can be deleted from only one relation at a time. Depending on the number of tuples selected by the WHERE condition, zero, one, or several tuples are deleted by a DELETE command. The DELETE commands in U4A, U4B, and U4C, when applied independently to the database of Figure 6.6, will delete zero, one, and four tuples, respectively, from the EMPLOYEE relation.

> U4A: **DELETE**   EMPLOYEE
> **WHERE**   E.LNAME='Brown'

> U4B: **DELETE**   EMPLOYEE
> **WHERE**   E.SSN='123456789'

U4C: **DELETE**   EMPLOYEE
        WHERE   E.DNO=D.DNUMBER **AND** D.DNAME='Research'

The REPLACE Command

The REPLACE command is used to modify attribute values. A WHERE-clause selects the tuples to be modified from a single relation. For example, to change the location and controlling department of project 10 to 'Bellaire' and department 5, respectively, we use U5.

U5:   **REPLACE**   PROJECT (PLOCATION = 'Bellaire', DNUM = 5)
        WHERE   P.PNUMBER=10

As another example, suppose we want to give a 10% raise in salary to all employees in the 'Research' department. Here several EMPLOYEE tuples are updated. Two references to the SALARY attribute are given; the one on the right refers to the old SALARY value (before update) and the one on the left to the new SALARY value (after update).

U6:   **REPLACE**   EMPLOYEE (SALARY = E.SALARY *1.1)
        WHERE   E.DNO = D.DNUMBER **AND** D.DNAME='Research'

Notice that each REPLACE command applies to a single relation only. If we need to update multiple relations, we must issue several REPLACE commands. These could be embedded in a program (see Section 9.1.5).

9.1.4 *Specifying Views in* QUEL

A view in QUEL, as in SQL, is a single relation that is derived from other relations. These other relations could be base relations or other views. A view is a virtual relation, in contrast to base relations, whose tuples are actually stored in the database. This limits the possible update operations that can be applied to views (see Section 7.4.3) but does not provide any limitations on querying a view. The command to specify a view in QUEL is DEFINE VIEW. We give the view a (virtual) relation name, a list of attribute names, and a query to specify the view. Two examples of view definition are given in V1 and V2.

V1:   **DEFINE VIEW**   WORKS_ON1 (FNAME = E.FNAME, LNAME = E.LNAME,
                    PNAME = P.PNAME, HOURS = W.HOURS)
        WHERE   E.SSN=W.ESSN **AND** W.PNO=P.PNUMBER ;

V2:   **DEFINE VIEW**   DEPT_INFO   (DEPT_NAME = D.DNAME,
                    NO_OF_EMPS = COUNT (E.SSN **BY** D.DNAME),
                    TOTAL_SAL = SUM (E.SALARY **BY** D.DNAME))
        WHERE   D.DNUMBER=E.DNO ;

We can specify QUEL queries on the views in the same way we specify queries involving base relations. For example, to retrieve the last name and first name of all employees who work on the 'ProductX' project, we can utilize the WORKS_ON1 view and issue QV1. The same query would require two joins if specified directly on the base relations.

```
QV1:   RANGE OF   W1 IS WORKS_ON1;
       RETRIEVE   W1.PNAME, W1.FNAME, W1.LNAME
       WHERE      W1.PNAME='Research' ;
```

We can use the **DESTROY** command to dispose of the view definition. For example, to get rid of the two views defined above, we can use V3.

```
V3:   DESTROY   WORKS_ON1 ;
      DESTROY   DEPT_INFO ;
```

9.1.5   Embedded QUEL

QUEL statements can be embedded in a general-purpose programming language such as PASCAL, C, COBOL, FORTRAN, or BASIC. The embedded version of QUEL is known as EQUEL. All statements in a program that pertain to EQUEL must be flagged with special characters so that they may be extracted by a preprocessor before the program is compiled. We will again use PASCAL as the host programming language in our examples. We identify all EQUEL statements and all program variable declarations referenced within an EQUEL statement by "##". Within an embedded EQUEL command, we may refer only to program variables identified by ##. The result of an EQUEL statement is assigned to such program variables for further processing by the program. For example, consider the following program segment:

```
E0:   ##   var XSSN: packed array [1..9] of char;
      ##       FN, LN: packed array [1..15] of char;

              ...

          read(XSSN);
      ##   RETRIEVE ( FN = E.FNAME, LN = E.LNAME)
      ##       WHERE E.SSN=XSSN ;
      ##   {
          write(FN, LN);
      ##   {
```

In E0 we print the first and last names of an employee after reading the employee's social security number. EQUEL *does not use* the cursor mechanism of embedded SQL. Rather, the program statements right after an EQUEL statement are executed *once for each tuple in the result of an EQUEL query*; this implicit loop—called a **RETRIEVE loop**—is identified by "## {" at its beginning and end. If there is a need to exit the implicit loop before all tuples are processed, the statement ## ENDRETRIEVE can be used to exit the loop. Notice that this implicit loop is used even if the result of the query is a single tuple, as in E0.

Another example, a repeating program segment (loop) that reads a social security number and prints out some information from the corresponding EMPLOYEE record, is shown in E1. In E1 the fields of the program variable EMP—a PASCAL record type—are assigned the result of the EQUEL query. This EQUEL query also retrieves a single record, but we still have to use the implicit loop notation directly following the EQUEL query.

```
E1:    var LOOP: char;
    ##   SOC_SEC_NUM: packed array [1..9] of char;
    ##   EMP: record FN: packed array [1..15] of char;
    ##                 MI: char;
    ##                 LN: packed array [1..15] of char;
    ##                 SS: packed array [1..9] of char;
    ##                 BD: packed array [1..9] of char;
    ##                 ADDR: packed array [1..30] of char;
    ##                 SAL: integer
    ##                 end;

              ...

    ## RANGE OF E IS EMPLOYEE;
    LOOP:= 'Y';
    while LOOP = 'Y' do
        begin
        writeln('input social security number:'); readln(SOC_SEC_NUM);
    ## RETRIEVE ( EMP.FN = E.FNAME, EMP.MI = E.MINIT, EMP.LN = E.LNAME,
    ##              EMP.SS = E.SSN, EMP.BD =
    ##              E.BDATE, EMP.ADDR = E.ADDRESS, EMP.SAL = E.SALARY )
    ##   WHERE E.SSN=SOC_SEC_NUM ;
    ## {
        with EMP do
                writeln( FN, MI, LN, SS, BD, ADDR, SAL);
    ## {
        writeln('more social security numbers (Y or N)? '); readln(LOOP)
        end;
```

Next, we give an example of a query that retrieves multiple records. Suppose we want to print the names of all employees who work in the 'Research' department. This query is shown as E3 below. In E3 the PASCAL statement writeln(FN,LN) is executed once for each tuple in the result of the immediately preceding RETRIEVE query.

```
E3:    ##   var FN, LN: packed array [1..15] of char;
            DN: packed array [1..15] of char;

              ...

    ##   RETRIEVE ( DN = DEPARTMENT.DNUMBER ) WHERE
          DEPARTMENT.DNAME='Research';
    ##   RETRIEVE ( FN = EMPLOYEE.FNAME, LN = EMPLOYEE.LNAME )
          WHERE EMPLOYEE.DNO=DN;
    ## {
            writeln( FN, LN);
    ## {
```

One restriction with EQUEL is that *we cannot specify other database requests* within the implicit loop that follows a query. Hence, it is more difficult to write a program such as E2 of Section 7.6. In E2 we retrieved the employee records of a particular department;

then we went through these tuples one by one, entering a raise amount for each employee and updating that employee tuple. Because the update is a second database command, it *cannot* be specified in EQUEL within the implicit loop that follows the retrieval query. In this sense, embedded SQL is more general because we can have nested database requests. In addition, in embedded SQL multiple cursors can be opened for processing at the same time, whereas in EQUEL an implicit loop must appear *immediately after* the database request.

EQUEL allows parameters of a query such as RANGE variables, relation and attribute names, and even complete conditional expressions to be specified as PASCAL program variables of type character string. For example, consider the program segment E4:

```
E4:   ##   var FN, LN: packed array [1..15] of char;
      ##       COND: packed array [1..50] of char;
      ##       RAISE: integer;

              ...

          writeln('enter employee selection condition:');
          readln(COND);
          writeln('enter raise amount:');
          readln(RAISE);
      ##   REPLACE EMPLOYEE ( SALARY=EMPLOYEE.SALARY+RAISE )
          WHERE COND;
```

In E4 we can enter an arbitrary character string, such as 'E.DNO = 5', as a value for the COND variable during run time. This selects the employee or employees who will get the raise. The embedded update then becomes

```
##   REPLACE E ( SALARY=E.SALARY+RAISE ) WHERE E.DNO=5;
```

We can enter different conditions during different executions of the same program. This gives additional flexibility when writing programs. However, it makes it impossible to compile such an embedded query because it is not completely specified. Hence, embedded QUEL requests are compiled and optimized *at run time* by passing the query to the QUEL processor. If it is desired to compile a QUEL query, say because it appears inside a program loop and will be executed repeatedly, the key word REPEAT can be specified before the embedded query. In this case the only unspecified values in a query must be parameters that will *correspond to constant values in the QUEL query.*

The program segment E5 below updates the salary of each employee in a loop. The REPEAT option is specified so that the QUEL query 'REPLACE EMPLOYEE ...' is not recompiled and reoptimized repeatedly. In E5 the program variables identified by @ are parameters that will have query constants as their values. The embedded query can be optimized and compiled *once*, rather than every time the loop is executed.

```
E5:   ##   var SS: packed array [1..9] of char;
                LOOP: char;
      ##       RAISE: integer;

              ...

          LOOP:='Y';
```

```
        while LOOP='Y' do
            begin
            writeln('enter employee social security number:');
            readln(SS);
            writeln('enter raise amount:');
            readln(RAISE);
##          REPEAT REPLACE EMPLOYEE ( SALARY=EMPLOYEE SALARY+
            @RAISE )
                        WHERE EMPLOYEE.SSN=@SS;
            writeln('more employees (Y or N)?'); readln(LOOP)
            end;
```

9.1.6 Comparison with SQL

The languages SQL and QUEL are currently the two major commercial relational database languages. In this section we briefly compare the two.

- Both QUEL and SQL are based on variations of the tuple relational calculus; however, QUEL is much closer to the tuple relational calculus than is SQL.

- In SQL nesting of SELECT … FROM … WHERE … blocks can be repeated arbitrarily to any number of levels; in QUEL nesting is restricted to one level.

- Both SQL and QUEL use implicit existential quantifiers. Both handle universal quantification in terms of equivalent existential quantification.

- The grouping facility of QUEL—the BY…WHERE… clause—can occur any number of times in the RETRIEVE or WHERE clauses, allowing different groupings in the same query. In SQL only a single grouping per query is permitted via the GROUP BY … HAVING … clause, so nesting of queries is needed to allow different groupings.

- SQL allows some explicit set operations from the relational algebra, such as UNION; these are not available in QUEL but are handled by specifying more complex selection and join conditions.

- QUEL allows the specification of a temporary file to receive the output of a query in a single statement; in SQL we must use a separate CREATE statement to create a table before we can do this.

- The ANY operator returns an integer value of 0 or 1 in QUEL, whereas the EXISTS operator, which is used for similar purposes in SQL, returns a Boolean value of TRUE or FALSE.

- Embedded QUEL uses implicit looping, whereas the concept of cursor and explicit looping are used in embedded SQL. Embedded QUEL allows supplying portions of a query at run time, which is not generally permitted in embedded SQL. There is an exception in dynamic SQL of DB2 (see Section 23.1.6).

9.2 The QBE Language

QBE (Query By Example) is a user-friendly relational query language that was developed at IBM Research. QBE is available as an IBM commercial product as part of the QMF (Query

Management Facility) interface option to DB2. It is different from SQL and QUEL in that the user does not have to specify a structured query explicitly; rather, the query is formulated by filling in **templates** of relations that are displayed on a terminal screen. Figure 9.2 shows how these templates may look for the database of Figure 6.6. The user does not have to remember the names of attributes or relations because they are displayed as part of these templates. In addition, the user does not have to follow any rigid syntax rules for query specification; rather, constants and variables are entered in the columns of the templates to construct an **example** related to the retrieval or update request.

In this section we discuss the various facilities of QBE and show how queries, updates, and views can be specified. QBE is related to the domain relational calculus, as we shall see, and its original specification has been shown to be relationally complete.

9.2.1 *Data Retrieval in* QBE

Retrieval queries are specified by filling in certain columns of the relation templates. When entering constant values into a template, we type them as they are; however, **example values** can also be entered, which are preceded by the "_" (underscore) character. The prefix "P." is used to indicate that the values of a particular column are to be retrieved, where P stands for Print. For example, consider the query Q0: Retrieve the birthdate and address of 'John B. Smith'; this may be specified in QBE as shown in Figure 9.3a.

In Figure 9.3a, we specified an example of the *type of row* in which we are interested. The example values preceded by "_" do not have to match specific values in the database; their values are purely arbitrary; they represent *free domain variables* (see Section 8.3). Actual constant values, such as John, B, and Smith, are used to select tuples from the database with matching values. All columns in which the prefix P. appears have their values retrieved in the query result.

EMPLOYEE	FNAME	MINIT	LNAME	SSN	BDATE	ADDRESS	SEX	SALARY	SUPERSSN	DNO

DEPARTMENT	DNAME	DNUMBER	MGRSSN	MGRSTARTDATE

DEPT_LOCATIONS	DNUMBER	DLOCATION

WORKS_ON	ESSN	PNO	HOURS

PROJECT	PNAME	PNUMBER	PLOCATION	DNUM

DEPENDENT	ESSN	DEPENDENT_NAME	SEX	BDATE	RELATIONSHIP

Figure 9.2 The relational schema of Figure 6.6 as it may be displayed by QBE

(a)

EMPLOYEE	FNAME	MINIT	LNAME	SSN	BDATE	ADDRESS	SEX	SALARY	SUPERSSN	DNO
	John	B	Smith	_123456789	P._9/1/60	P._100 Main, Houston, TX	_M	_25000	_123456789	_3

(b)

EMPLOYEE	FNAME	MINIT	LNAME	SSN	BDATE	ADDRESS	SEX	SALARY	SUPERSSN	DNO
	John	B	Smith		P._9/1/60	P._100 Main, Houston, TX				

(c)

EMPLOYEE	FNAME	MINIT	LNAME	SSN	BDATE	ADDRESS	SEX	SALARY	SUPERSSN	DNO
	John	B	Smith		P._X	P._Y				

(d)

EMPLOYEE	FNAME	MINIT	LNAME	SSN	BDATE	ADDRESS	SEX	SALARY	SUPERSSN	DNO
	John	B	Smith		P.	P.				

Figure 9.3 Four ways of specifying the query Q0 in QBE

As we are interested only in the columns BDATE and ADDRESS, Q0 can be abbreviated as shown in Figure 9.3b. There is no need to specify example values for columns in which we are not interested. Also, because example values are completely arbitrary, we can just specify variable names for them as shown in Figure 9.3c. We can also leave out the example values entirely as shown in Figure 9.3d and just specify a P. under the columns to be retrieved. Clearly, Figure 9.3d is the most succinct way of specifying Q0, and we will use this style in the rest of our examples. Users can be trained to leave out unnecessary example values as they learn QBE.

To see how retrieval queries in QBE are similar to the domain relational calculus, compare Figure 9.3d with the method of specifying Q0 in domain calculus, which is as follows:

Q0 : { uv | EMPLOYEE(qrstuvwxyz) **and** q='John' **and** r='B' **and** s='Smith'}

We can think of each column in a QBE template as an *implicit domain variable*; hence, FNAME corresponds to the domain variable q, MINIT corresponds to r, ..., and DNO corresponds to z. In the QBE query the columns with P. correspond to variables specified to the left of the bar (|) in domain calculus, whereas the columns with constant values correspond to tuple variables with equality selection conditions on them. The condition EMPLOYEE(qrstuvwxyz), and the existential quantifiers are implicit in the QBE query because the template corresponding to the EMPLOYEE relation is used.

In QBE the user interface first allows the user to choose the tables (relations) needed to formulate a query by displaying a list of all relation names. The templates for the chosen relations are then displayed. The user moves to the appropriate columns in the templates and specifies the query. Special keys are used to move to the next or previous column in the current template, to move to the next or previous relation template, and for other common functions. The goal is to minimize the number of keystrokes.

We now give examples to illustrate additional features of QBE. Selection conditions using the equality (=) comparison are specified in QBE by entering a constant value under a column, as shown in Figure 9.3. For example, entering John under FNAME in Q0 specifies the condition (FNAME = 'John'). We must explicitly enter other types of comparison operators, such as > or ≥, before typing a constant value. For example, the query Q0A,

(a)

WORKS_ON	ESSN	PNO	HOURS
	P.	1	>20

(b)

WORKS_ON	ESSN	PNO	HOURS
	P.	_PX	_HX

CONDITIONS

_HX>20 AND (_PX = 1 OR _PX = 2)

(c)

WORKS_ON	ESSN	PNO	HOURS
	P.	1	>20
	P.	2	>20

Figure 9.4 Specifying complex conditions in QBE. (a) The query
QOA. (b) The query QOB with a condition box.
(c) The query QOB without a condition box.

"list the social security numbers of employees who work more than 20 hours per week on project number 1," can be specified as shown in Figure 9.4a.

For more complex conditions the user can ask for a **condition box**, which is created by pressing a particular function key. The user can then type the complex condition.* For example, the query QOB, "list the social security numbers of employees who work more than 20 hours per week on either project 1 or project 2", can be specified as shown in Figure 9.4b.

Some complex conditions can be specified without a condition box, although it may be easier to use the condition box. The rule is that all conditions specified on the same row of a relation template are connected by the **and** logical connective (*all* must be satisfied by a selected tuple), whereas conditions specified on distinct rows are connected by **or** (*at least one* must be satisfied by a selected tuple). Hence, QOB can also be specified as shown in Figure 9.4c by entering two distinct rows in the template. This provides the UNION of the results corresponding to each row.

Now consider the query QOC "list the social security numbers of employees who work on *both* project 1 and project 2"; this cannot be specified as in Figure 9.5a, which lists those who work on *either* project 1 or project 2. The example variable _ES will bind itself to ESSN values in <-, 1, -> tuples *as well as* those in <-, 2, -> tuples. Figure 9.5b shows how to specify QOC correctly, where the condition (_EX = _EY) in the box makes the _EX and _EY variables bind only to identical ESSN values.

In general, once a query is specified, the resulting values are displayed in the template under the appropriate columns. If the result contains more rows than can be displayed on the screen, most QBE implementations will have function keys to allow scrolling up and down the rows. Similarly, if a template or several templates are too wide to appear on the screen, it is possible to scroll sideways to examine all the templates.

---

*Negation with the ¬symbol is *not* allowed in a condition box.

(a)

WORKS_ON	ESSN	PNO	HOURS
	P._ES	1	
	P._ES	2	

(b)

WORKS_ON	ESSN	PNO	HOURS
	P._EX	1	
	P._EY	2	

CONDITIONS

_EX = _EY

Figure 9.5 Specifying EMPLOYEES who work on both projects.
(a) Incorrect specification of an AND condition.
(b) Correct specification.

To specify an ordering among the tuples in a query result, the prefixes AO. (ascending order) and DO. (descending order) may be used. When ordering by more than one attribute, AO(i). and DO(i). are used, where i specifies the order priority. For example, Figure 9.6 shows the query to list projects in descending order by department number (DO(1).); projects controlled by the same department are ordered in ascending order by location (AO(2).); and projects with the same department and location are ordered in ascending order by project number (AO(3).). In QBE any number of prefixes can be cascaded.

A join operation is specified in QBE by using the *same variable** in the columns to be joined. For example, the query Q1, "list the name and address of all employees who work for the 'Research' department," can be specified as shown in Figure 9.7a. Any number of joins can be specified in a single query. When we specify a join, we can also specify a **result table** to display the result of the query, as shown in Figure 9.7a; this is needed if the result includes attributes from two or more relations. If no result table is specified, the system provides the query result in the columns of the various relations, which may make it difficult to interpret and hence meaningless in most cases. Notice that in the example of Figure 9.7a we can do without the result table.

Figure 9.7a also illustrates the feature of QBE for specifying that all attributes of a relation should be retrieved. This is done by placing the P. operator under the relation name in the relation template, as we do with the RESULT relation template. This can be done for any relation template.

PROJECT	PNAME	PNUMBER	PLOCATION	DNUM
	P.	P.AO(3).	P.AO(2).	P.DO(1).

Figure 9.6 Illustrating the ordering operators of QBE

---

*A variable is called an **example element** in QBE manuals.

(a)

EMPLOYEE	FNAME	MINIT	LNAME	SSN	BDATE	ADDRESS	SEX	SALARY	SUPERSSN	DNO
	_FN		_LN			_ADDR				_DX

DEPARTMENT	DNAME	DNUMBER	MGRSSN	MGRSTARTDATE
	Research	_DX		

RESULT			
P.	_FN	_LN	_ADDR

(b)

EMPLOYEE	FNAME	MINIT	LNAME	SSN	BDATE	ADDRESS	SEX	SALARY	SUPERSSN	DNO
	_E1		_E2						_XSSN	
	_S1		_S2	_XSSN						

RESULT				
P.	_E1	_E2	_S1	_S2

(c)

RESULT2		
P.UNQ.	_S1	_S2

Figure 9.7   Illustrating JOIN and result relations in QBE. (a) The query Q1. (b) The query Q8. (c) Illustrating the .UNQ operator that eliminates duplicates.

To join a table with itself, we specify different variables to represent the different references to the table. For example, the query Q8, "for each employee retrieve the employee's first and last name as well as the first and last name of his or her immediate supervisor," can be specified as shown in Figure 9.7b, where the variables starting with E refer to an employee and those starting with S refer to a supervisor.

The prefix UNQ. is a QBE operator that keeps only unique tuples in a query result by eliminating duplicates. For example, to retrieve the names of all supervisors, we can create another result table RESULT2 for query Q8, as shown in Figure 9.7c. RESULT2 keeps only one entry for supervisors who supervise multiple employees by eliminating duplicates.

Next, consider the types of queries that require grouping or aggregate functions. A grouping operator G. can be specified in a column to indicate that tuples should be grouped by value of that column. In addition, common functions can be specified, such as AVG., SUM., CNT. (count), MAX., and MIN. Notice that in QBE the functions AVG., SUM., and CNT. are applied to *distinct values* within a group in the default case. If we want these functions to apply to all values we must use the prefix .ALL in QBE.* This convention is *different* in SQL and QUEL, where the default is to apply a function to all values.

Figure 9.8 illustrates the use of functions and grouping in QBE. Figure 9.8a shows query Q19, which counts the number of *distinct* salary values in the EMPLOYEE relation.

---

*ALL in QBE is unrelated to the universal quantifier. Also, the use of ALL in QUEL is for a different purpose.

(a)

EMPLOYEE	FNAME	MINIT	LNAME	SSN	BDATE	ADDRESS	SEX	SALARY	SUPERSSN	DNO
								P.CNT.		

(b)

EMPLOYEE	FNAME	MINIT	LNAME	SSN	BDATE	ADDRESS	SEX	SALARY	SUPERSSN	DNO
								P.CNT.ALL		

(c)

EMPLOYEE	FNAME	MINIT	LNAME	SSN	BDATE	ADDRESS	SEX	SALARY	SUPERSSN	DNO
				P.CNT.ALL				P.AVG.ALL		P.G.

(d)

PROJECT	PNAME	PNUMBER	PLOCATION	DNUM
	P.	_PX		

WORKS_ON	ESSN	PNO	HOURS
	P.CNT._EX	G._PX	

CONDITIONS

CNT._EX>2

Figure 9.8 Illustrating functions and grouping in QBE. (a) The query Q19. (b) The query Q19A. (c) The query Q20. (d) The query Q22A.

Query Q19A (Figure 9.8b) counts all salary values, which is the same as counting the number of employees. Figure 9.8c shows Q20, which retrieves each department number and the number of employees and average salary within each department; hence, the DNO column is used for grouping as indicated by the G. function in the DNO column. Several of the operators G., P., and ALL. can be specified in a single column.

Figure 9.8d shows query Q22A, which displays each project name and the number of employees working on the project for projects on which more than two employees work. This is the type of query that requires a HAVING clause in SQL because it selects groups with the same PNUMBER based on a function (COUNT ESSN > 2). Notice that the CNT. operator occurring in the ESSN column is *repeated* in the condition box in Figure 9.8d.

QBE has a negation symbol, ¬, which is used in a manner similar to the NOT EXISTS function of SQL. Figure 9.9 shows how it is used with query Q6, which lists the names of employees who have no dependents. The negation symbol ¬ says that we will select values of the _SX variable from the EMPLOYEE relation only if they do not occur in the DEPENDENT relation. The same effect can be produced by placing a ≠ _SX in the ESSN column.

Although the QBE language as originally proposed was shown to support the equivalent of the EXISTS and NOT EXISTS functions of SQL, the QBE implementation in QMF (under the DB2 system) does *not* provide this support. Hence, the QMF version of QBE, which we discuss here, is *not relationally complete*. Queries such as Q3, "find employees who work on *all* projects controlled by department 5," *cannot* be specified.

EMPLOYEE	FNAME	MINIT	LNAME	SSN	BDATE	ADDRESS	SEX	SALARY	SUPERSSN	DNO
	P.		P.	_SX						

DEPENDENT	ESSN	DEPENDENT_NAME	SEX	BDATE	RELATIONSHIP
¬	_SX				

Figure 9.9   Illustrating negation by the query Q6

9.2.2   Update Operations in QBE

There are three QBE operators for modifying the database: I. for insert, D. for delete, and U. for update. The insert and delete operators are specified in the template column under the relation name, whereas the update operator is specified under the columns to be updated.

Insertion of a new tuple is straightforward, as shown in Figure 9.10a, where we insert a new EMPLOYEE tuple. We first specify the I. operator and then enter the tuple values under the appropriate columns. For deletion, we first enter the D. operator and then specify the tuples to be deleted by a condition. The deletion request of Figure 9.10b deletes the employee inserted in 9.10a. One interesting aspect of deletion in QBE is that related tuples from several relations can be deleted in the same request. For example, suppose we want to delete the 'Research' department, as well as all its projects, all the employees who work in it, and the dependents of these employees; we can use the QBE request of Figure 9.10c. By specifying the D. operator in the appropriate templates and specifying the same variables in related templates, we specify all the tuples to be deleted.

To update a tuple, we specify the U. operator under the attribute name followed by the new value of the attribute. We should also select the tuple or tuples to be updated in the usual way. Figure 9.10d shows an update request to increase the salary of 'John Smith' by 10% and also to reassign him to department number 4. As with deletion, it is possible to update related tuples from more than one relation in a single update request.

9.2.3   Other Features of QBE

QBE also has data definition capabilities. The tables of a database can be specified interactively in QBE, and a table definition can also be updated by adding, renaming, or removing a column. Special function keys are used for these various functions. To create an empty template, we press the corresponding function key for that command. We can now give the template a relation name and column names by moving to the appropriate positions and typing the names, one at a time. We can also specify various characteristics for each column, such as whether it is a key of the relation, its data type, and whether an index should be created on that field. A special function key for entering characteristics and another for displaying them are available.

QBE also has facilities for view definition, authorization, storing query definitions for later use, and so on. These follow the same types of interactive specification as the features we discussed above.

QBE does not use the "linear" style of QUEL and SQL; rather, it is a "two-dimensional" language because users specify a query moving around the full area of the screen. Tests on users have shown that QBE is easier to learn than SQL, especially for nonspecialists. In this

(a)

EMPLOYEE	FNAME	MINIT	LNAME	SSN	BDATE	ADDRESS	SEX	SALARY	SUPERSSN	DNO
I.	Richard	K	Marini	653298653	30-DEC-52	98 Oak Forest, Katy, TX	M	37000	987654321	4

(b)

EMPLOYEE	FNAME	MINIT	LNAME	SSN	BDATE	ADDRESS	SEX	SALARY	SUPERSSN	DNO
D.				653298653						

(c)

EMPLOYEE	FNAME	MINIT	LNAME	SSN	BDATE	ADDRESS	SEX	SALARY	SUPERSSN	DNO
D.				_SX						_DX

DEPARTMENT	DNAME	DNUMBER	MGRSSN	MGRSTARTDATE
D.	Research	_DX		

WORKS_ON	ESSN	PNO	HOURS
D.	_SX		
D.		_PX	

PROJECT	PNAME	PNUMBER	PLOCATION	DNUM
D.		_PX		_DX

DEPENDENT	ESSN	DEPENDENT_NAME	SEX	BDATE	RELATIONSHIP
D.	_SX				

(d)

EMPLOYEE	FNAME	MINIT	LNAME	SSN	BDATE	ADDRESS	SEX	SALARY	SUPERSSN	DNO
	John		Smith					U._S*1.1		U.4

Figure 9.10 Modifying the database in QBE. (a) Illustrating insertion. (b) Illustrating deletion. (c) Illustrating deletion of multiple related tuples in QBE. (d) Illustrating update in QBE.

sense, QBE was the first user-friendly relational database language. QBE displays the relation templates, so the user does not have to remember the relation name and attribute names. In QUEL and SQL the user has to remember not only the relation and attribute names but also the query syntax. In QBE there is no rigid syntax because the query is specified by filling in values, variables, and commands in the appropriate columns.

More recently, there have been numerous other user-friendly interfaces for commercial database systems. The use of menus, graphics, and forms is quite common (see Chapter 22). Some DBMSs, such as the PARADOX system, have patterned their user interface after QBE.

9.3 Summary

In this chapter we presented two well-known commercial relational database languages: QUEL and QBE. In Section 9.1 we presented the QUEL database language, which is based on the tuple relational calculus discussed in Section 8.1. This language was implemented originally on the INGRES experimental system and is now available commercially as an RTI (Relational Technology, Inc.) product on various hardware configurations. We discussed most features of QUEL, including statements for data and storage definition, queries, updates, and view definition. We also discussed EQUEL, or embedded QUEL, which is a technique used to embed QUEL in general-purpose programming languages. EQUEL uses implicit loops over query results that contain more than one tuple. This approach is different from embedded SQL, which requires explicit looping using the concept of a CURSOR.

SQL and QUEL are considered the two main commercial relational query languages. There has been a debate for some time as to which is "better." QUEL is much closer to the formal tuple relational calculus, and its grouping structure BY ... WHERE ... is generally considered better than the GROUP BY ... HAVING ... structure of SQL. SQL depends more on nesting of whole queries. However, SQL is on the verge of becoming a standard, and many software vendors have used it as their interface in preference to QUEL.

In Section 9.2 we discussed QBE (Query By Example). It differs from both SQL and QUEL in its style of displaying relation templates and allowing the user to specify queries by entering appropriate "example" values, variables, and functions in the relation template columns. It is related to the domain relational calculus discussed in Section 8.3 and is more user-friendly than SQL and QUEL. QBE is available as part of the QMF product to interface IBM's DB2 system. QBE under QMF is *not* relationally complete because it lacks explicit quantification in the form of $\forall$ or $\nexists$.

Review Questions

9.1. Discuss the rules for specifying grouping attributes and functions in QUEL.

9.2. Discuss the rules for nesting of functions in QUEL.

9.3. Compare the various features of SQL and QUEL, and discuss why you may prefer one over the other for each feature.

9.4. Discuss the rules for nesting of operators in QBE.

9.5. Why must the insert I. and delete D. operators of QBE appear under the relation name in a relation template and not under a column name?

9.6. Why must the update U. operators of QBE appear under a column name in a relation template and not under the relation name?

Exercises

9.7. Write appropriate QUEL data definition statements for some of the database schemas shown in Figure 6.5, Figure 2.1, and Figure 6.19.

9.8. Specify the queries of Exercises 6.19 and 7.14 in QUEL.

9.9. Consider the following query, which is a modification of Q24A: List the SSN of the person who is the youngest in department 5 among employees earning more than $50,000. Can this be done as a single QUEL query? What about SQL? If it cannot be done as a single query, show how it can be done in steps by storing temporary results.

9.10. Specify the updates of Exercise 6.20 using the QUEL update commands.

9.11. Specify the queries of Exercise 7.16 in QUEL.

9.12. Specify the updates of Exercise 7.17 using the QUEL update commands.

9.13. Write PASCAL programs with embedded QUEL (EQUEL) statements in the style shown in Section 9.1 to do the tasks specified in Exercise 7.18.

9.14. Write QUEL statements to create the indexes specified in Exercise 7.19.

9.15. Specify the views of Exercise 7.21 in QUEL.

9.16. Specify the queries and updates of Exercises 6.21 and 6.22 in QUEL.

9.17. Repeat Exercise 7.25, but use QUEL instead of SQL.

9.18. Specify the queries of Exercises 6.19 and 7.14 in QBE.

9.19. Can you specify the query of Exercise 9.9 as a single QBE query?

9.20. Specify the updates of Exercise 6.20 in QBE.

9.21. Specify the queries of Exercise 7.16 in QBE.

9.22. Specify the updates of Exercise 7.17 in QBE.

9.23. Specify the queries and updates of Exercises 6.21 and 6.22 in QBE.

Selected Bibliography

The QUEL language and the INGRES system on which QUEL was implemented are described in Stonebraker et al. (1976). Zook et al. (1977) describes the language for "university INGRES," whereas the commercial version of QUEL is described in RTI (1983). A recent book (Stonebraker 1986) has a compilation of research and survey papers related to the INGRES system.

QBE was originally proposed in Zloof (1975). Thomas and Gould (1975) report the results of experiments comparing the ease of use of QBE to SQL. The commercial QBE functions are described in an IBM manual (1978), and a quick reference card is available (IBM 1978a). Appropriate DB2 reference manuals discuss the QBE implementation for that system.

The Hierarchical Data Model

The hierarchical model of data was developed to model the many types of hierarchical organizations that exist in the real world. Hierarchies in the physical and natural world have been observed and analyzed for centuries. As a result, humans have used hierarchical organization of information to help them better understand the world. There are many examples, such as classification schemes for species in the plant and animal worlds and classification schemes for human languages. Humans also adopted hierarchical structures and naming schemes to deal with the structures they created, such as corporate organization charts, library classification schemes, and governmental hierarchies. The hierarchical data model represents hierarchical organizations in a direct and natural way but has problems when representing situations with nonhierarchical relationships.

There is no original document that describes the hierarchical model as there are for the relational and network models. Rather, several early computer information management systems were developed using hierarchical storage structures. Examples of these systems are System Development Corporation's Time-shared Data Management System (TDMS), Control Data Corporation's Multi-Access Retrieval System (MARS VI), IBM's Information Management System (IMS), and MRI's System-2000 (now sold by SAS Institute).

In this chapter we will present the principles behind the hierarchical model independently of any specific system. Section 10.1 discusses hierarchical schemas and instances. In Section 10.2 the concept of a virtual parent-child relationship is discussed, which is used to overcome the limitations of pure hierarchies. Section 10.3 discusses constraints on the hierarchical model. In Section 10.4 we discuss data definition and data manipulation languages for hierarchical databases. Finally, Section 10.5 contains a summary. Two representative hierarchical systems will be discussed in Part VI of the book, namely IMS and System 2000. In Chapter 12 we compare the hierarchical model with the other data models.

10.1   Hierarchical Database Structures

In this section we discuss the data structuring concepts of the hierarchical model. We first discuss parent-child relationships and how they can be used to form a hierarchical schema in Section 10.1.1. Then we discuss the properties of a hierarchical schema in Section 10.1.2. We discuss hierarchical occurrence trees in Section 10.1.3 and a common method for storing these trees—called the hierarchical sequence—in Section 10.1.4.

10.1.1   Parent-Child Relationships and Hierarchical Schemas

In the hierarchical model there are two main data structuring concepts: records and parent-child relationships. A **record** is a collection of **field values** that provide information on an entity or a relationship instance. Records of the same type are grouped into **record types**. A record type is given a name and its structure is defined by a collection of named **fields** or **data items**. Each field has a certain data type, such as integer, real, or string.

A **parent-child relationship type (PCR type)** is a 1:N relationship between two record types. The record type on the 1-side is called the **parent record type** and the one on the N-side is called the **child record type** of the PCR type. An **occurrence (or instance) of the PCR type** consists of *one record* of the parent record type and *a number of records* (zero or more) of the child record type.

A **hierarchical database schema** consists of a number of hierarchical schemas. Each **hierarchical schema** (or **hierarchy**) consists of a number of record types and PCR types. We will define the properties of a hierarchical schema shortly, but first we show how it is displayed and give an example.

A hierarchical schema is displayed as a **hierarchical diagram**, in which record type names are displayed in rectangular boxes and PCR types are displayed as arcs connecting the parent record type to the child record type. Figure 10.1 shows a simple hierarchical diagram for a hierarchical schema with three record types and two PCR types. The record types are DEPARTMENT, EMPLOYEE, and PROJECT. Field names can be displayed under each record type name as shown in Figure 10.1. In some diagrams, for brevity we display only the record type names.

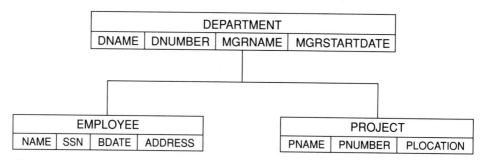

Figure 10.1   A hierarchical schema

We refer to a PCR type in a hierarchical schema by listing the pair (parent record type, child record type) between parentheses. The two PCR types in Figure 10.1 are (DEPARTMENT, EMPLOYEE) and (DEPARTMENT, PROJECT). Notice that PCR types *do not* have a name in the hierarchical model. However, a certain meaning is associated with each PCR type by the database designer. In Figure 10.1 each *occurrence of the* (DEPARTMENT, EMPLOYEE) *PCR type* relates *one* department record to the records of the *many* (zero or more) employees who work in that department. An occurrence of the (DEPARTMENT, PROJECT) PCR type relates a department record to the records of projects controlled by that department. Figure 10.2 shows two PCR occurrences (or instances) for each of these two PCR types.

10.1.2 Properties of a Hierarchical Schema

A hierarchical schema of record types and PCR types must have the following properties:

1. One record type, called the **root** of the hierarchical schema, does not participate as a child record type in any PCR type.

2. Every record type except the root participates as a child record type in *exactly one* PCR type.

3. A record type can participate as parent record type in any number (zero or more) of PCR types.

4. A record type that does not participate as parent record type in any PCR type is called a **leaf** of the hierarchical schema.

5. If a record type participates as parent in more than one PCR type, then *its child record types are ordered*. The order is displayed, by convention, from left to right in a hierarchical diagram.

The definition of a hierarchical schema defines a **tree data structure**. In the terminology of tree data structures, a record type corresponds to a **node** of the tree and a PCR

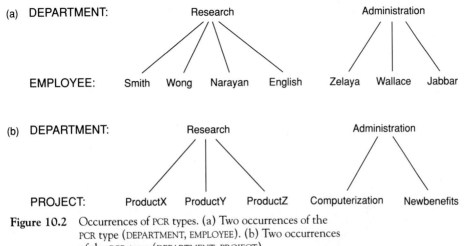

Figure 10.2 Occurrences of PCR types. (a) Two occurrences of the PCR type (DEPARTMENT, EMPLOYEE). (b) Two occurrences of the PCR type (DEPARTMENT, PROJECT).

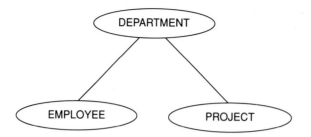

Figure 10.3   Tree representation of the hierarchical schema in
Figure 10.1

type corresponds to an **edge** (or **arc**) of the tree. We will use the terms node and record type, and edge and PCR type, interchangeably. The usual convention of displaying a tree is slightly different from that used in hierarchical diagrams in that each tree edge is shown separately from other edges (Figure 10.3). In hierarchical diagrams the convention is that all edges emanating from the same parent node are joined together (Figure 10.1). We will use this latter hierarchical diagram convention.

The above properties of a hierarchical schema mean that every node except the root has exactly one parent node. However, a node can have several child nodes, and in this case they are ordered from left to right. In Figure 10.1 EMPLOYEE is the first child of DEPARTMENT and PROJECT is the second child. The above properties also limit the types of relationships that can be represented in a hierarchical schema. In particular, M:N relationships between record types *cannot* be directly represented because parent-child relationships are 1:N relationships, and a record type *cannot participate as child* in two or more distinct parent-child relationships. These limitations cause problems when we attempt to describe a database that contains these types of nonhierarchical relationships as a hierarchical schema.

An M:N relationship may be handled in the hierarchical model by allowing *duplication of child record instances.* For example, consider an M:N relationship between EMPLOYEE and PROJECT, where a project can have several employees working on it, and an employee can work on several projects. We can represent the relationship as a (PROJECT, EMPLOYEE) PCR type as shown in Figure 10.4a. In this case a record describing the same employee can be duplicated by appearing once under *each* project that the employee works for. Alternatively, we can represent the relationship as an (EMPLOYEE, PROJECT) PCR type as shown in Figure 10.4b, in which case project records may be duplicated.

EXAMPLE 1:   Consider these instances of the EMPLOYEE:PROJECT relationship:

PROJECT	EMPLOYEES WORKING ON THE PROJECT
A	E1, E3, E5
B	E2, E4, E6
C	E1, E4
D	E2, E3, E4, E5

If the above instances are stored using the hierarchical schema of Figure 10.4a, there will be four occurrences of the (PROJECT, EMPLOYEE) PCR type—one for each pro-

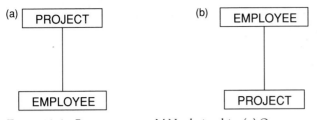

Figure 10.4   Representing an M:N relationship. (a) One
representation of the M:N relationship.
(b) Alternative representation of the M:N
relationship.

ject. However, the employee records for E1, E2, E3, and E5 will appear *twice each* as child
records because each of these employees works on two projects. The employee record for
E4 will appear three times, once under each of projects B, C, and D. Notice that there
may be some data field values in the employee records that are context dependent; that
is, these field values depend on both EMPLOYEE and PROJECT. Such data will be different
in each occurrence of a duplicated employee record because it also depends on the parent project record. An example is a field that gives the number of hours per week that an
employee works on the project. However, the majority of the field values in the employee records, such as employee name, social security number, and salary, would certainly be
duplicated under each project that the employee works for.

To avoid such duplication, a technique is used where several hierarchical schemas
can be specified in the same hierarchical database schema. Relationships like the above
PCR type can now be defined *across* hierarchical schemas, allowing us to circumvent the
problem of duplication discussed above. We discuss this technique in Section 10.2.

10.1.3   Hierarchical Occurrence Trees

Corresponding to a hierarchical schema there will be, in general, many hierarchical occurrences in the database. Each **hierarchical occurrence**, also called an **occurrence tree**,
is a **tree** structure whose root is a single record from the root record type. The occurrence
tree also contains all the children record occurrences of the root record, all children
record occurrences within the PCRs of each of the child records of the root record, and so
on, all the way to records of the leaf record types.

For example, consider the hierarchical diagram shown in Figure 10.5, which represents part of the COMPANY database introduced in Chapter 3 and also used in Chapters 6
to 9. Figure 10.6 shows one hierarchical occurrence tree of this hierarchical schema. In
the occurrence tree, each node is a record occurrence and each arc represents a parent-
child relationship between two records. In both Figures 10.5 and 10.6, we use the characters **D, E, P, T, S,** and **W** to represent **type indicators** for the record types DEPARTMENT,
EMPLOYEE, PROJECT, DEPENDENT, SUPERVISEE, and WORKER, respectively. We shall see the
significance of these type indicators when we discuss hierarchical sequences in the next
section.

We can define occurrence trees more formally using the terminology for tree structures, which we need in our subsequent discussion. In a tree structure, the root is said to

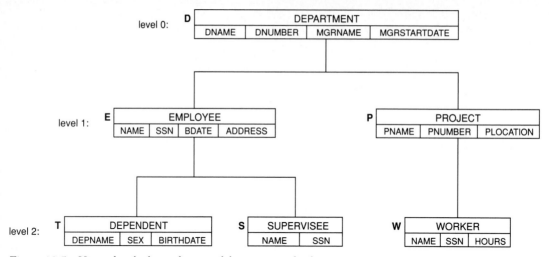

Figure 10.5   Hierarchical schema for part of the COMPANY database

have **level** zero. The level of a nonroot node is one more than the level of its parent node, as shown in Figures 10.5 and 10.6. A **descendent** D of a node N is a node connected to N via one or more arcs such that the level of D is greater than the level of N. A node N and all its descendent nodes form a **subtree** of node N. An **occurrence tree** can now be defined as the subtree of a record whose type is of the root record type.

The root of an occurrence tree is a single record occurrence of the root record type. There can be a varying number of occurrences of each nonroot record type, and each such occurrence must have a parent record in the occurrence tree; that is, each such occurrence must participate in a PCR occurrence. Notice that each nonroot node, together with all its descendent nodes, form a **subtree**, which, taken alone, satisfies the structure

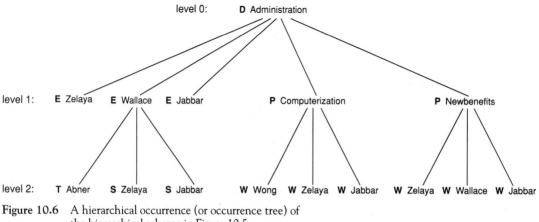

Figure 10.6   A hierarchical occurrence (or occurrence tree) of the hierarchical schema in Figure 10.5

of an occurrence tree for a portion of the hierarchical diagram. Also notice that the level of a record in an occurrence tree is the same as the level of its record type in the hierarchical diagram.

10.1.4 Linearized Form of a Hierarchical Occurrence

A hierarchical occurrence tree can be represented in storage using a variety of data structures. However, a particularly simple storage structure that can be used is the **hierarchical record**, which is a linear ordering of the records in an occurrence tree in the *preorder traversal* of the tree. This order produces a sequence of record occurrences known as the **hierarchical sequence** (or **hierarchical record sequence**) of the occurrence tree, which can be obtained by applying the following recursive procedure to the root of an occurrence tree:

```
procedure Pre_order_traverse ( root record );
    begin
    output ( root record );
    for each child record of root record in left to right order do
            Pre_order_traverse ( child record )
    end;
```

The above procedure, when applied to the occurrence tree in Figure 10.6, gives the hierarchical sequence shown in Figure 10.7. If we use the hierarchical sequence to implement occurrence trees, we need to store a record type indicator with each record because of the different record types and the variable number of child records in each parent-child relationship. The system needs to examine the type of each record as it goes sequentially through the records. Notice that these record type indicators are implementation structures and are not seen by the hierarchical DBMS user.

The hierarchical sequence is often desirable because the child nodes follow their parent node in storage. Hence, given a parent record, all descendent records in its subtree will follow it in the hierarchical sequence and can be retrieved efficiently. Notice, however, that child records are collectively placed after their parent record only if the child records are leaf nodes in the occurrence tree. Otherwise, whole subtrees of each child node are placed after their parent record in left-to-right order.

The hierarchical sequence is also important because some hierarchical query languages, such as that used in IMS, use it as a basis for defining hierarchical database operations. The HDML language we discuss in Section 10.4 is based on the hierarchical sequence.

Next, we define two additional terms that are used by some hierarchical languages. A **hierarchical path** is a sequence of nodes $N_1, N_2, ..., N_i$ where N_1 is the root of a tree and N_j is a child of N_{j-1} for $j = 2, 3, ..., i$. A hierarchical path can be defined either on a hierarchical schema or on an occurrence tree. A hierarchical path is **complete** if N_i is a leaf of the tree. A **broom** is a set of hierarchical paths resulting from the hierarchical path $N_1, N_2, ..., N_i$ along with all the hierarchical paths in the subtree of N_i. For example, (DEPARTMENT, EMPLOYEE, SUPERVISEE) is a complete path in the hierarchical schema of Figure 10.5. In the occurrence tree of Figure 10.6, (Administration, Wallace) is a path, and (Administration, Wallace, {Abner, Zelaya, Jabbar}) is a broom.

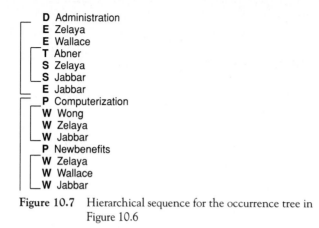

Figure 10.7   Hierarchical sequence for the occurrence tree in Figure 10.6

We can now define a **hierarchical database occurrence** as a sequence of all the occurrence trees that are occurrences of a hierarchical schema. This is similar to the definition of a **forest** of trees in data structures. For example, a hierarchical database occurrence of the hierarchical schema shown in Figure 10.5 would consist of a number of occurrence trees similar to the one shown in Figure 10.6. There would be one occurrence tree for each DEPARTMENT record, and they would be ordered as the first, second, ..., last occurrence tree.

10.2   Virtual Parent-Child Relationships

The hierarchical model has problems when modeling certain types of relationships. These include:

1. M:N relationships.
2. The case where a record type participates as child in more than one PCR type.
3. N-ary relationships with more than two participating record types.

As we saw in Section 10.1.2, case 1 can be represented as a PCR type at the expense of duplicating record occurrences of the child record type. Case 2 can also be represented in a similar fashion, with more duplication of records. Case 3 presents a problem because the PCR is a binary relationship.

Record duplication, in addition to wasting storage space, causes problems with maintaining duplicate copies of the same record consistent. The concept of a virtual (or pointer) record type is used in the IMS system to deal with all the above three cases. The idea is to include more than one hierarchical schema in the hierarchical database schema and to have pointers from nodes of one hierarchical schema to the other to represent the relationships. We do *not* follow IMS terminology but develop the concepts more generally.

A **virtual** (or **pointer**) **record type** VC is a record type with the property that each of its records contains a pointer to a record of another record type VP. VC plays the role of "virtual child" and VC of "virtual parent" in a "virtual parent-child relationship." Each record occurrence c of VC points to exactly one record occurrence p of VP. Rather than duplicating the record p itself in an occurrence tree, we include the virtual record c that points to p. Several virtual records may point to p, but only a single copy of p itself is stored in the database.

Figure 10.8 shows the M:N relationship between EMPLOYEE and PROJECT represented using virtual records. Compare this with Figure 10.4, where the same relationship was represented without virtual records. Figure 10.9 shows the occurrence trees and pointers for the data instances given in Example 1 when the hierarchical schema shown in Figure 10.8a is used. In Figure 10.9 there is only a single copy of each EMPLOYEE record; however, several virtual records may point to the same EMPLOYEE record. Hence, the information stored in an EMPLOYEE record is not duplicated. Information that depends on both parent and child records—such as hours per week that an employee works on a project—is included in the virtual pointer record; such data is popularly known as **intersection data** among hierarchical database users.

Notice that the relationship between EMPLOYEE and EPOINTER in Figure 10.8a is a 1:N relationship and hence qualifies as a PCR type. Such a relationship is called a **virtual parent-child relationship (VPCR) type.** EMPLOYEE is called the **virtual parent** of EPOINTER and, conversely, EPOINTER is called a **virtual child** of EMPLOYEE. Conceptually, PCR types and VPCR types are similar; the main difference between the two is in the way they are implemented. A PCR type is usually implemented using the hierarchical sequence, whereas a VPCR type is usually implemented by having a pointer from a virtual child record to its virtual parent record. This mainly affects the efficiency of certain queries. We shall look at various implementation options when we discuss the IMS system in Chapter 23.

Figure 10.10 shows a hierarchical database schema of the COMPANY database that uses some VPCRs and has no redundancy in its record occurrences. The hierarchical database schema is made up of two hierarchical schemas, one with root DEPARTMENT and the other with root EMPLOYEE. Four VPCRs, all with virtual parent EMPLOYEE, are included to represent the relationships without redundancy. Notice that IMS may not allow this because an implementation constraint in IMS limits a record to be virtual parent of at

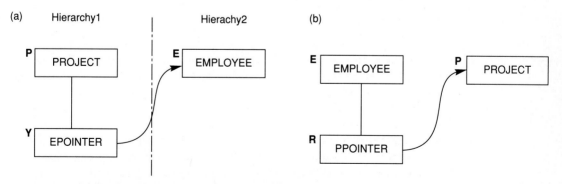

Figure 10.8 Representing an M:N relationship using VPCR types. (a) One representation of the M:N relationship with VPCR types. (b) Alternative representation of the M:N relationship with VPCR types.

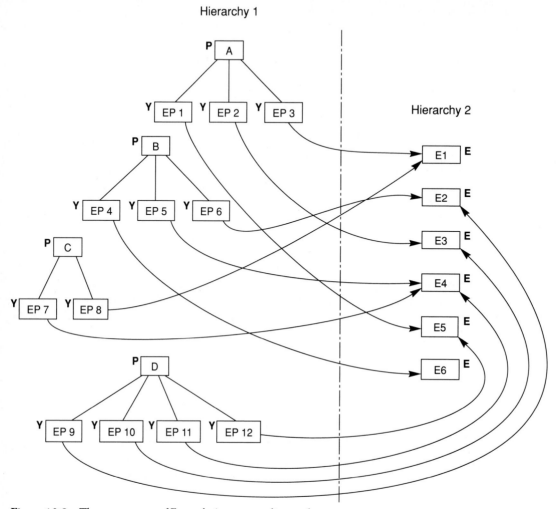

Figure 10.9 The occurrences of Example 1 corresponding to the hierarchical schema in Figure 10.8(a)

most one VPCR; to get around this constraint, one can create dummy children record types of EMPLOYEE in Hierarchy 2 so that each VPCR points to a distinct virtual parent record type.

In general, there will be many feasible methods of designing a database using the hierarchical model. In many cases, performance considerations are the most important factor in choosing one hierarchical database schema over another. Performance depends on the implementation options available on each specific system as well as specific limits set by the DBA at a particular installation—for example, whether certain types of pointers are provided by the system or certain limits on number of levels are imposed by the DBA.

One thing to consider about VPCRs is that they can be implemented in different ways. One option is just to have a pointer in the virtual child to the virtual parent, as we discussed above. A second option is to have, in addition to the child-to-parent pointer, a

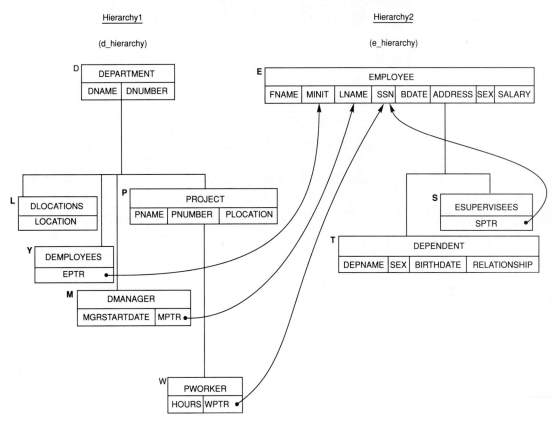

Figure 10.10 A hierarchical schema for the COMPANY database using VPCR types among two hierarchies to eliminate redundant record instances

backward link from the virtual parent to a linked list of virtual child records. The pointer from the virtual parent to the first virtual child record is called a **virtual child pointer**, whereas a pointer from one virtual child to the next is called a **virtual twin pointer**. In this case, the hierarchical model becomes *very similar* to the network model, which we discuss in Chapter 11. This backward link makes it easy to retrieve all the virtual child records of a particular virtual parent record.

10.3 Integrity Constraints in the Hierarchical Model

There are a number of built-in **inherent constraints** in the hierarchical model that exist whenever we specify a hierarchical schema. These include the following constraints:

1. No record occurrences except root records can exist without being related to a parent record occurrence. This has the following implications:

   a. A child record cannot be inserted unless it is linked to a parent record.

    b. A child record may be deleted independently of its parent; however, deletion of a parent record results in all its child and descendent records being deleted automatically.

    c. The above rules do not apply to virtual child records and virtual parent records. The rule here is that a pointer in a virtual child record must point to an existing virtual parent record. Deletion of a virtual parent record should not be allowed while pointers exist to it from virtual child records.

2. If a child record has two or more parent records from the *same* record type, then the child record must be duplicated once under each parent record.

3. A child record having two or more parent records of *different* record types can do so only by having at most one real parent and all the others virtual parents.

In addition, each hierarchical DBMS may have its own additional integrity rules that are particular to its own implementation. For example, in IMS a record type can be the virtual parent in only one VPCR type. This implies that the schema of Figure 10.10 is not allowed by IMS because the EMPLOYEE record is virtual parent in four distinct VPCRs. Another rule in IMS is that a root record type cannot be a virtual child record type in a VPCR type.

Any other constraints that are not implicit in a hierarchical schema must be enforced explicitly by the programmers in the database update programs. For example, if a duplicated record is updated, it is the responsibility of the update program to ensure that all copies are updated in the same way.

10.4 Data Definition and Manipulation in the Hierarchical Model

In this section we give an example of a hierarchical data definition language (**HDDL**) and a hierarchical data manipulation language (**HDML**). These are not the languages of any specific hierarchical DBMS but are used to illustrate the language concepts for a hierarchical database. The HDML we discuss in Section 10.4.2 is based somewhat on the concepts present in the DL/1 language of IMS. We will discuss DL/1 in comparison to HDDL and HDML in Chapter 23.

10.4.1 Defining a Hierarchical Database

The hierarchical data definition language we present here, which we call **HDDL**, is meant to demonstrate how a hierarchical database schema can be defined. Some of the terminology used here is different from that of IMS and other hierarchical DBMSs. To define a hierarchical database schema, we must define the fields of each record type, the data type of each field, and any key constraints on fields. In addition, we must specify a root record type as such, and for every nonroot record type we must specify its (real) parent in a PCR type. Any VPCR types must also be specified.

Figure 10.11 shows the HDDL specification of the database schema shown in Figure 10.10. Most of the statements are self-explanatory. In actual hierarchical DBMSs the

SCHEMA NAME = COMPANY

HIERARCHIES = HIERARCHY1, HIERARCHY2

RECORD
    NAME = EMPLOYEE
    TYPE = ROOT OF HIERARCHY2
    DATA ITEMS =
        FNAME   CHARACTER 15
        MINIT   CHARACTER 1
        LNAME   CHARACTER 15
        SSN   CHARACTER 9
        BDATE   CHARACTER 9
        ADDRESS   CHARACTER 30
        SEX   CHARACTER 1
        SALARY   CHARACTER 10
    KEY = SSN
    ORDER BY LNAME, FNAME

RECORD
    NAME = DEPARTMENT
    TYPE = ROOT OF HIERARCHY1
    DATA ITEMS =
        DNAME   CHARACTER 15
        DNUMBER   INTEGER
    KEY = DNAME
    KEY = DNUMBER
    ORDER BY DNAME

RECORD
    NAME = DLOCATIONS
    PARENT = DEPARTMENT
    CHILD NUMBER = 1
    DATA ITEMS =
        LOCATION   CHARACTER 15

RECORD
    NAME = DMANAGER
    PARENT = DEPARTMENT
    CHILD NUMBER = 3
    DATA ITEMS =
        MGRSTARTDATE CHARACTER 9
        MPTR   POINTER WITH VIRTUAL PARENT = EMPLOYEE

RECORD
    NAME = PROJECT
    PARENT = DEPARTMENT
    CHILD NUMBER = 4
    DATA ITEMS =
        PNAME   CHARACTER 15
        PNUMBER   INTEGER
        PLOCATION   CHARACTER 15
    KEY = PNAME
    KEY = PNUMBER
    ORDER BY PNAME

Figure 10.11   Declarations for the hierarchical schema in
                Figure 10.10   *(continued on next page)*

```
RECORD
    NAME = PWORKER
    PARENT = PROJECT
    CHILD NUMBER = 1
    DATA ITEMS =
        HOURS          CHARACTER 4
        WPTR           POINTER WITH VIRTUAL PARENT = EMPLOYEE

RECORD
    NAME = DEMPLOYEES
    PARENT = DEPARTMENT
    CHILD NUMBER = 2
    DATA ITEMS =
        EPTR           POINTER WITH VIRTUAL PARENT = EMPLOYEE

RECORD
    NAME IS ESUPERVISEES
    PARENT = EMPLOYEE
    CHILD NUMBER = 2
    DATA ITEMS =
        SPTR           POINTER WITH VIRTUAL PARENT = EMPLOYEE

RECORD
    NAME = DEPENDENT
    PARENT = EMPLOYEE
    CHILD NUMBER = 1
    DATA ITEMS =
        DEPNAME                CHARACTER 15
        SEX                    CHARACTER 1
        BIRTHDATE              CHARACTER 9
        RELATIONSHIP           CHARACTER 10
    ORDER BY DESC BIRTHDATE
```

Figure 10.11   *(continued)* Declarations for the hierarchical
                     schema in Figure 10.10

syntax is usually more complicated, and, as we mentioned earlier, the terminology may be different. Notice also that some of the structures, such as EMPLOYEE being a virtual parent of more than one VPCR type, may not be allowed in some hierarchical DBMSs such as IMS.

In Figure 10.11, either each record type is declared to be of type root or a single (real) parent record type is declared for the record type. The data items of the record are then listed along with their data types. We must specify a virtual parent for data items that are of type *pointer*. Data items declared under the KEY clause are constrained to have unique values for each record. Each KEY clause specifies a separate key, and if a single KEY clause lists more than one field then the combination of these field values must be unique in each record.

The CHILD NUMBER clause specifies the left-to-right order of a child record type under its (real) parent record type. In Figure 10.11 these correspond to the left-to-right order shown in Figure 10.10 and are needed to specify the order of the child subtrees of different child record types under a parent record in the hierarchical sequence. For example, under an EMPLOYEE record we first have all subtrees of its DEPENDENT child records

(CHILD NUMBER = 1) followed by all subtrees of its ESUPERVISEES child records (CHILD NUMBER = 2) in the hierarchical sequence.

The ORDER BY clause specifies the order of individual records of the same record type in the hierarchical sequence. For a root record type, this specifies the order of the occurrence trees. For example, EMPLOYEE records are ordered alphabetically by LNAME, FNAME, so the occurrence trees of these records are ordered alphabetically by these fields. For nonroot record types, the ORDER BY clause specifies how the records should be ordered *within each parent record* by specifying a field called a **sequence key**. For example, PROJECT records controlled by a particular DEPARTMENT have their subtrees ordered alphabetically within the same parent DEPARTMENT record by PNAME according to Figure 10.11.

10.4.2 Data Manipulation Language for a Hierarchical Database

We now discuss HDML, which is a record-at-a-time language for manipulating hierarchical databases. The commands of the language must be embedded in a general-purpose programming language, called the **host** language. We use PASCAL as host language in our examples. It is more common to have COBOL or PL/I as the host language, but we use PASCAL to maintain consistency with the rest of this book. Notice that HDML is *not* a language for a particular hierarchical DBMS; rather, we use it to illustrate the concepts of a hierarchical database manipulation language. We discuss how the database communicates information with a user program and the commands for retrieval from and update of the database.

User Work Area (UWA) and Currency Concepts for Using HDML Commands

In a record-at-a-time language, a database retrieval operation retrieves database records into **program variables**. In our examples database records are retrieved into PASCAL program variables. The program can then refer to the program variables to access the field values of the database records. We assume that a PASCAL record type has been declared for each record type in the schema of Figure 10.10. The PASCAL program variables, shown in Figure 10.12, use the *same field names* as those in the database schema of Figure 10.10, whereas *record names* are prefixed with a P_. These program variables exist in what is often called the **user work area**. Notice that it is possible to have these variables declared automatically by referring to the database schema declared in Figure 10.11. Initially, the values of these record variables are undefined. Whenever a data retrieval operation retrieves a database record of a particular type, it is placed in the corresponding UWA program variable.

The HDML we present here is based on the concept of **hierarchical sequence** defined in Section 10.1.4. Following each database command, the last record accessed by the command is called the **current database record**. The DBMS maintains a pointer to the current record. Subsequent database commands proceed *from the current record* and may define a new current record, depending on the type of command. Hence, HDML commands traverse through a hierarchical database retrieving the records required by the query.

```
var P_EMPLOYEE        :   record
                          FNAME: packed array [1..15] of char;
                          MINIT: char;
                          LNAME: packed array [1..15] of char;
                          SSN: packed array [1..9] of char;
                          BDATE: packed array [1..9] of char;
                          ADDRESS: packed array [1..30] of char;
                          SEX: char;
                          SALARY : packed array [1..10] of char
                          end;
    P_DEPARTMENT      :   record
                          DNAME: packed array [1..15] of char;
                          DNUMBER: integer
                          end;
    P_DLOCATIONS      :   record
                          LOCATION: packed array [1..15] of char
                          end;
    P_DMANAGER        :   record
                          MGRSTARTDATE: packed array [1..9] of char;
                          MPTR: database pointer to EMPLOYEE
                          end;
    P_PROJECT         :   record
                          PNAME: packed array [1..15] of char;
                          PNUMBER: integer;
                          PLOCATION: packed array [1..15] of char
                          end;
    P_PWORKER         :   record
                          HOURS: packed array [1..4] of char;
                          WPTR: database pointer to EMPLOYEE
                          end;
    P_DEMPLOYEES      :   record
                          EPTR: database pointer to EMPLOYEE
                          end;
    P_ESUPERVISEE     :   record
                          SPTR: database pointer to EMPLOYEE
                          end;
    P_DEPENDENT       :   record
                          DEPNAME: packed array [1..15] of char;
                          SEX: char;
                          BIRTHDATE: packed array [1..9] of char;
                          RELATIONSHIP: packed array [1..10] of char
                          end;
```

Figure 10.12   PASCAL program variables in the UWA corresponding
to part of the hierarchical schema in Figure 10.10

Originally, the current database record is an "imaginary record" located just before the root record of the first occurrence tree in the database.

If a database has more than one hierarchical schema in it, and these hierarchies are processed together, the IMS system allows the definition of a user view to create a tailor-made hierarchical schema that includes the desired record types connected by VPCR types.* Such a view is treated as a single **hierarchical schema** and has its own **current**

---

*These "view" schemas are called **logical databases** in IMS and will be discussed briefly in Section 23.2.3.

database record. Since we do not intend to go into the details of defining and processing these views, we will assume for convenience that *each hierarchical schema* has its own **current of hierarchy record**. IMS also has provisions for remembering the last record accessed of *each record type*, so we assume that the system keeps track of the **current of record type** for *each record type*—this is a pointer to the last record accessed from the record type. The HDML commands implicitly refer to these **currency indicators**, which are summarized below:

- Current of database.
- Current of hierarchy for each hierarchical schema.
- Current of record type for each record type.

Record-at-a-time programming requires continuous interaction between the user program and the DBMS. **Status information** at the end of each database command must be communicated back to the program. This is accomplished by a variable called **DB_STATUS**, whose value is set by the DBMS software after each database command is executed. We will assume that a value of DB_STATUS = 0 specifies that the last database command was successfully executed.

HDML commands can be categorized as retrieval commands, update commands, and currency retention commands. **Retrieval commands** retrieve one or more database records into the corresponding program variables and may change some currency indicators. **Update commands** are used to insert, delete, and modify database records. **Currency retention commands** are used to mark the current record so that it can be updated or deleted by a subsequent command. The HDML commands are summarized in Table 10.1.

We will now discuss each of these commands and illustrate our discussion with examples using the schema shown in Figure 10.10. We use program segments and *prefix the*

Table 10.1 Summary of HDML Commands

(RETRIEVAL)	
GET	RETRIEVE A RECORD INTO THE CORRESPONDING PROGRAM VARIABLE AND MAKE IT THE CURRENT RECORD. VARIATIONS INCLUDE GET FIRST, GET NEXT, GET NEXT WITHIN PARENT, AND GET PATH.
(RECORD UPDATE)	
INSERT	STORE A NEW RECORD IN THE DATABASE AND MAKE IT THE CURRENT RECORD
DELETE	DELETE THE CURRENT RECORD (AND ITS SUBTREE) FROM THE DATABASE
REPLACE	MODIFY SOME FIELDS OF THE CURRENT RECORD
(CURRENCY RETENTION)	
GET HOLD	RETRIEVE A RECORD AND HOLD IT AS THE CURRENT RECORD SO IT CAN SUBSEQUENTLY BE DELETED OR REPLACED

HDML *commands with a $-sign* to distinguish them from the PASCAL language statements. PASCAL language key words—such as if, then, while, for—are written in lowercase.

The GET Command

The HDML command for retrieving a record is the GET command. There are many variations of GET; the structure of two of these variations is shown below, with optional parts shown between brackets, [...].

- GET FIRST* <record type name> [WHERE <condition>]
- GET NEXT <record type name> [WHERE <condition>]

The simplest is the GET FIRST command, which always starts searching the database from the *beginning of the hierarchical sequence* until it finds the first record occurrence of <record type name> that satisfies <condition>. This record also becomes the current of database, current of hierarchy, and current of record type and is retrieved into the corresponding UWA program variable. For example, to retrieve the "first" EMPLOYEE record in the hierarchical sequence whose name is John Smith, we write EX1.

EX1: $GET FIRST EMPLOYEE WHERE FNAME='John' AND LNAME='Smith';

The DBMS uses the condition following WHERE to search for the first record in order of the hierarchical sequence that satisfies the condition and is of the specified record type. The value of DB_STATUS is set to 0 (zero) if the record is *found successfully*; otherwise, DB_STATUS is set to some other value, 1 say, that indicates *not found*. Other errors or exceptions are indicated by different values for DB_STATUS.

If more than one record in the database satisfies the WHERE condition and we want to retrieve all of them, we must write a looping construct in the host program and use the GET NEXT command. We assume that the GET NEXT starts its search from the *current record of the record type specified in* GET NEXT** and searches forward in the hierarchical sequence to find another record of the specified type satisfying the WHERE condition. For example, to retrieve records of all EMPLOYEEs whose salary is less than $20,000 and print their names, we can write the program segment shown in EX2.

EX2: $GET FIRST EMPLOYEE WHERE SALARY < '20000.00';
       while DB_STATUS = 0 do
           begin
           writeln (P_EMPLOYEE.FNAME, P_EMPLOYEE.LNAME);
           $GET NEXT EMPLOYEE WHERE SALARY < '20000.00'
           end;

In EX2 the while-loop continues until no more EMPLOYEE records in the database satisfy the WHERE-condition; hence, the search goes through to the last record in the database (hierarchical sequence). When no more records are found, DB_STATUS becomes nonzero with a code indicating "end of database reached" and the while-loop terminates. Notice that the WHERE condition in the GET commands is optional. If there is no condi-

---

*This is similar to the GET UNIQUE (GU) command of IMS.

**IMS commands generally proceed forward from the *current of database* rather than from the current of specified record type as we do in HDML commands.

tion, the very next record in the hierarchical sequence of the specified record type is retrieved. For example, to retrieve all EMPLOYEE records in the database, we can use EX3.

```
EX3:   $GET FIRST EMPLOYEE;
       while DB_STATUS = 0 do
            begin
            writeln ( P_EMPLOYEE.FNAME, P_EMPLOYEE.LNAME );
            $GET NEXT EMPLOYEE
            end;
```

The GET PATH and GET NEXT WITHIN PARENT Commands

So far we have considered the retrieval of single records using the GET command. When we have to locate a record deep in the hierarchy, the retrieval may be based on a series of conditions on records along the entire hierarchical path. To accommodate this, we introduce the GET PATH command:

```
GET ( FIRST | NEXT ) PATH <hierarchical path> [ WHERE <condition> ]
```

Here, <hierarchical path> is a list of record types starting from the root along a path in the hierarchical schema, and <condition> is a Boolean expression specifying conditions on the individual record types along the path. Because several record types may be specified, the field names are prefixed by the record type names in <condition>. For example, consider the query: List the lastname and birthdates of all employee-dependent pairs where both have the first name John. This is shown in EX4.

```
EX4:   $GET FIRST PATH EMPLOYEE, DEPENDENT
           WHERE EMPLOYEE.FNAME='John' AND DEPENDENT.DEPNAME='John';
       while DB_STATUS = 0 do
            begin
            writeln (P_EMPLOYEE.LNAME, P_EMPLOYEE.BDATE,
                    P_DEPENDENT.BIRTHDATE);
            $GET NEXT PATH EMPLOYEE, DEPENDENT
                    WHERE EMPLOYEE.FNAME='John' AND
                    DEPENDENT.DEPNAME='John'
            end;
```

We assume that a GET PATH command retrieves *all records along the specified path* into the UWA variables* and the last record along the path becomes the current database record. In addition, all records along the path become the *current records of their respective record types.*

Another common type of query is to find all records of a given type that have *the same parent record.* In this case we need the GET NEXT WITHIN PARENT command, which can be used to loop through the child records of a parent record and has the following format:

```
GET NEXT <child record type name>
     WITHIN [ VIRTUAL ] PARENT [ <parent record type name> ]
     [ WHERE <condition> ]
```

---

*IMS provides the capability of specifying that only *some* of the records along the path are to be retrieved.

This command retrieves the next record of the child record type by searching forward from the *current of the child record type* for the next child record *owned by the current parent record*. If no more child records are found, DB_STATUS is set to a nonzero value to indicate that "there are no more records of the specified child record type that have the same parent as the current parent record." The <parent record type name> is *optional*, and the default is the immediate (real) parent record type of <child record type name>. For example, to retrieve the names of all projects controlled by the 'Research' department, we can write the program segment in EX5:

```
EX5:   $GET FIRST PATH DEPARTMENT, PROJECT
            WHERE DNAME='Research';
            (* the above establishes the 'Research' DEPARTMENT record as
                current parent of type DEPARTMENT, and retrieves the first child
                PROJECT record under that DEPARTMENT record *)
       while DB_STATUS = 0 do
            begin
            writeln ( P_PROJECT.PNAME );
            $GET NEXT PROJECT WITHIN PARENT
            end;
```

In EX5 we can write "WITHIN PARENT DEPARTMENT" rather than just "WITHIN PARENT" in the GET NEXT command with the same effect because DEPARTMENT is the immediate parent record type of PROJECT. However, if we want to retrieve all records owned by a parent that is *not the immediate parent*—for example, all the PWORKER records owned by the same DEPARTMENT record—then we must specify DEPARTMENT as the parent record type in the "WITHIN PARENT" clause.

Notice that there are two main methods for explicitly establishing a parent record as the current record:

- By using GET FIRST or GET NEXT, the record retrieved becomes the current parent record.

- By using a GET PATH command, a hierarchical path of current parent records of the respective record types is established. This can also retrieve the *first child record*, as demonstrated in EX5, so that subsequent GET NEXT WITHIN PARENT commands can be issued.

We can rewrite EX4 without the GET PATH command by using one loop to find EMPLOYEEs with FNAME = 'John' and a nested loop using GET NEXT WITHIN PARENT to find any DEPENDENTs of each such EMPLOYEE with DEPNAME = 'John'. However, the GET PATH command allows us to do this more directly and with a *smaller number of calls* to the DBMS.

Another variation of the GET command would locate the real or virtual parent record of the *current record of a specified child record type*[*]:

```
GET [ VIRTUAL ] PARENT <parent record type name>
OF <child record type name>
```

---

[*]IMS does not have a counterpart for this command without using what IMS calls a **logical database**, which "hides" this operation by thinking of a virtual parent and virtual child as a single record (see Chapter 23).

For example, to retrieve the names and hours per week for each employee who works on 'ProjectX', we can use the GET PARENT command as in EX6.

```
EX6:   $GET FIRST PATH DEPARTMENT, PROJECT, PWORKER
              WHERE PNAME='ProjectX'; (* establish parent record and retrieve first
                                                        child *)
       while DB_STATUS = 0 do
              begin
              $GET VIRTUAL PARENT EMPLOYEE OF PWORKER;
              if DB_STATUS=0 then
                     writeln (P_EMPLOYEE.LNAME, P_EMPLOYEE.FNAME,
                     P_PWORKER.HOURS)
                     else writeln ('error--has no EMPLOYEE
                     virtual parent');
              $GET NEXT PWORKER WITHIN PARENT PROJECT
              end;
```

Notice that we can use a WHERE condition with the GET NEXT WITHIN PARENT command. For example, to retrieve the names of employees who work more than 5 hours per week on 'ProjectX', we can modify the GET NEXT PWORKER WITHIN PARENT command in EX6 to:

```
$GET NEXT PWORKER WITHIN PARENT PROJECT WHERE HOURS > '5.0';
```

We must also modify the GET FIRST PATH command appropriately. Just as we allowed traversing a VPCR from child to parent, as illustrated in EX6, we can also traverse from parent to child using:

```
GET NEXT <virtual child record type name>
       WITHIN PARENT <virtual parent record type name>
```

Calculating Aggregate Functions

Aggregate functions such as COUNT and AVERAGE must be explicitly implemented by the programmer using the facilities of the host programming language. For example, to calculate the number of employees who work in each department and their average salary, we can write EX7.

```
EX7:   $GET FIRST PATH DEPARTMENT, DEMPLOYEES;
       while DB_STATUS = 0 do
              begin
              total_sal:= 0; no_of_emps:= 0; writeln (P_DEPARTMENT.DNAME);
              (* department name *)
              while DB_STATUS = 0 do
                     begin
                     $GET VIRTUAL PARENT EMPLOYEE;
                     total_sal:= total_sal + conv_sal (P_EMPLOYEE.SALARY);
                     no_of_emps:= no_of_emps + 1;
                     $GET NEXT DEMPLOYEES WITHIN PARENT DEPARTMENT
                     end;
```

```
writeln( 'no of emps =', no_of_emps,'avg sal of emps =',
total_sal/no_of_emps);
$GET NEXT PATH DEPARTMENT, DEMPLOYEES
end;
```

We must have program variables declared to accumulate the total salary and number of employees, so we assume that the program variables total_sal:real and no_of_ emps:integer are declared in the program header and that a PASCAL function conv_ sal:real is also declared that converts a salary value from string to real number.

HDML **Commands for Update**

The HDML commands for updating a hierarchical database are shown in Table 10.1. The INSERT command is used to insert a new record. Before inserting a record of a particular record type, we must first place the field values of the new record in the appropriate user work area program variable. For example, suppose we want to insert a new EMPLOYEE record for John F. Smith; we can use the program segment in EX8.

```
EX8:   P_EMPLOYEE.FNAME := 'John';
       P_EMPLOYEE.LNAME := 'Smith';
       P_EMPLOYEE.MINIT := 'F';
       P_EMPLOYEE.SSN := '567342739';
       P_EMPLOYEE.ADDRESS := '40 Walcott Road, Minneapolis, Minnesota
       55433';
       P_EMPLOYEE.BDATE := '10-JAN-55';
       P_EMPLOYEE.SEX := 'M';
       P_EMPLOYEE.SALARY:='30000.00'
       $INSERT EMPLOYEE FROM P_EMPLOYEE;
```

The INSERT command inserts a record into the database. The newly inserted record also becomes the current record for the database, its hierarchical schema, and its record type. If it is a root record, as in EX8, it creates a new hierarchical occurrence tree with the new record as root. The record is inserted in the hierarchical sequence in the order specified by any ORDER BY fields in the schema definition. For example, the new EMPLOYEE record in EX8 is inserted in alphabetic order of its LNAME, FNAME combined value according to the schema definition in Figure 10.11. If no ordering fields are specified in the definition of the root record of a hierarchical schema, a new root record is inserted following the occurrence tree that contained the current database record before the insertion.

To insert a child record, we should make its parent, or one of its sibling records, the current record of the hierarchical schema before issuing the INSERT command. We should also set any virtual parent pointers before inserting the record. To do that, we need a command SET VIRTUAL PARENT, which sets the pointer field in the program variable to the current record of the virtual parent record type.* The record is inserted by finding an appropriate place for it in the hierarchical sequence past the current record. For example, suppose we want to relate the EMPLOYEE record inserted in EX8 as a 40 hour per week worker on the project whose project number is 55; we can use EX9.

---

*The SET VIRTUAL PARENT action is done implicitly in IMS when inserting a logical record that includes the virtual parent in its definition.

```
EX9:    $GET FIRST EMPLOYEE WHERE SSN='567342739'; (* find virtual parent *)
        if DB_STATUS=0 then
                begin
                P_PWORKER.WPTR := SET VIRTUAL PARENT; (* virtual
                parent pointer to current record *)
                P_PWORKER.HOURS := '40.0';
                $GET FIRST PROJECT WHERE PNUMBER=55; (* make (real) parent
                the current record *)
                if DB_STATUS=0 then $INSERT PWORKER FROM P_PWORKER;
                end;
```

To delete a record from the database, we first make it the current record and then issue the **DELETE** command. The **GET HOLD** is used to make the record the current record, where the HOLD key word indicates to the DBMS that the program will delete or update the record just retrieved. For example, to delete all male EMPLOYEEs we can use EX10, which also lists the deleted employee names *before* deleting their records.

```
EX10:   $GET HOLD FIRST EMPLOYEE WHERE SEX='M';
        while DB_STATUS=0 do
                begin
                writeln (P_EMPLOYEE.LNAME, P_EMPLOYEE.FNAME);
                $DELETE EMPLOYEE;
                $GET HOLD NEXT EMPLOYEE WHERE SEX='M';
                end;
```

Notice that deleting a record means that all its descendent records—all records in its subtree—are automatically deleted. However, virtual child records in other hierarchies are not deleted. In fact, before deleting a record, the DBMS should make sure that no virtual child records point to it. Following a successful DELETE command, the current record becomes an "empty position" in the hierarchical sequence corresponding to the record just deleted. Subsequent operations will continue from that position.

To modify field values of a record, we take the following steps:

1. Make the record to be modified the current record and retrieve it into the corresponding UWA program variable using the GET HOLD command.

2. Modify the desired fields in the UWA program variable.

3. Issue the **REPLACE** command.

For example, to give all employees in the 'Research' department a 10% raise, we can use the program shown in EX11.

```
EX11:   $GET FIRST PATH DEPARTMENT, DEMPLOYEES
                WHERE DNAME='Research';
        while DB_STATUS = 0 do
                begin
                $GET HOLD VIRTUAL PARENT EMPLOYEE OF DEMPLOYEES;
                P_EMPLOYEE.SALARY := P_EMPLOYEE.SALARY * 1.1;
                $REPLACE EMPLOYEE FROM P_EMPLOYEE;
                $GET NEXT DEMPLOYEES WITHIN PARENT DEPARTMENT
                end;
```

10.5   Summary

In this chapter we discussed the hierarchical model, which represents data by emphasizing hierarchical relationships. The presentation was general, although some aspects were patterned after the major hierarchical system—IBM's IMS. Departures from IMS were mostly pointed out in the text and in footnotes. The main structures used by the hierarchical model are record types and parent-child relationship (PCR) types. Each PCR type defines a hierarchical 1:N relationship between a parent record type and a child record type. Relationships are strictly hierarchical in that a record type can participate as child in at most one PCR type. This latter restriction makes it difficult to represent a database where numerous relationships exist.

We then saw how hierarchical database schemas can be defined as a number of hierarchical schemas of record types. A hierarchical schema is basically a tree data structure. Corresponding to a hierarchical schema, a number of occurrence trees will exist in the database. The hierarchical sequence of storing database records from an occurrence tree is a preorder traversal of the records in an occurrence tree. The type of each record is stored with the record so that the DBMS can identify the records while searching through records of a hierarchical sequence.

We then discussed the limitations of hierarchical representation when we try to represent M:N relationships, or relationships in which more than two record types participate. It is possible to represent some of these cases by allowing redundant records to exist in the database. The concept of virtual parent-child relationship (VPCR) types is used to permit a record type to have two parents—a real parent and a virtual parent. This VPCR type can also be used to represent M:N relationships without redundancy of database records. We also discussed how more than one hierarchical schema in the hierarchical database schema can be designed for one database and the types of implicit integrity constraints in hierarchies.

We then presented the commands of a hypothetical hierarchical data definition language (HDDL) and of a record-at-a-time hierarchical data manipulation language (HDML). The HDML is based on the hierarchical sequence. We saw how to write programs with embedded HDML commands to retrieve information from a hierarchical database and to update the database.

In general, the hierarchical model works well for database applications that are naturally hierarchical. However, when there are many nonhierarchical relationships, trying to fit those relationships into a hierarchical form is difficult, and the resulting representations are often unsatisfactory.

Although the relational model and relational DBMSs have recently become quite popular, the hierarchical model will be with us for several years to come because there is a big investment in hierarchical DBMSs in the commercial world. In addition, the hierarchical model is quite suitable for situations where the majority of relationships are hierarchical and database access mainly uses these hierarchical relationships.

Review Questions

10.1. Define the following terms: parent-child relationship (PCR) type, root of a hierarchy, leaf of a hierarchy.

10.2. Discuss the main properties of a hierarchy.

10.3. Discuss the problems with using a PCR type to represent an M:N relationship.

10.4. What is an occurrence tree of a hierarchy?

10.5. What is the hierarchical sequence? Why is it necessary to assign a record type field to each record when the hierarchical sequence is used to represent an occurrence tree?

10.6. Define the following terms: hierarchical path, broom, forest of trees, hierarchical database.

10.7. What are virtual parent-child relationship (VPCR) types? How do they enhance the modeling power of the hierarchical model?

10.8. Discuss different techniques that may be used for implementing VPCR types in a hierarchical database.

10.9. Discuss the inherent integrity constraints of the hierarchical model.

10.10. Show how each of the following types of relationships is represented in the hierarchical model: (a) M:N relationships, (b) n-ary relationships with n > 2, (c) 1:1 relationships.

10.11. Why is it necessary to embed the HDML commands in a host programming language such as PASCAL?

10.12. Discuss the following concepts and what each is used for when writing an HDML database program: (a) the user work area (UWA), (b) currency indicators, (c) database status indicator.

10.13. Discuss the different types of GET commands of the HDML and how each affects the currency indicators.

10.14. Discuss how parent records are established as a result of a retrieval command. Why does the GET NEXT WITHIN PARENT command *not* establish a new parent?

10.15. Discuss the update commands of the HDML.

Exercises

10.16. Specify the queries of Exercise 6.19 in HDML embedded in PASCAL on the hierarchical database schema of Figure 10.10. Use the PASCAL program variables declared in Figure 10.12, and declare any additional variables you may need.

10.17. Consider the hierarchical database schema shown in Figure 10.13, which corresponds to the relational schema of Figure 2.1. Write appropriate HDDL statements to define the record types and set types of the schema.

10.18. There is some redundancy in the schema of Figure 10.13; what are the data items that are repeated redundantly? Can you specify a hierarchical database schema for this database without redundancy by using VPCRs?

10.19. Write PASCAL program segments with embedded HDML commands to specify the queries of Exercise 7.16 on the schema of Figure 10.13. Repeat the same queries for your schema of Exercise 10.18.

10.20. Write PASCAL program segments with embedded HDML commands to do the up-

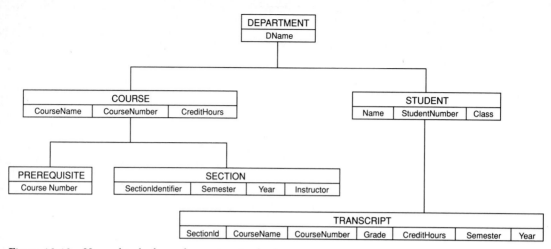

Figure 10.13   Hierarchical schema for a university database

dates and tasks of Exercises 7.17 and 7.18 on the hierarchical database schema of Figure 10.13. Specify any program variables that you need. Repeat the same queries for your schema of Exercise 10.18.

10.21. Choose some database application that you are familiar with or interested in.

a. Design a hierarchical database schema for your database application.

b. Declare your record types, PCR types, and VPCR types using the HDDL.

c. Specify a number of queries and updates that are needed by your database application, and write a PASCAL program segment with embedded HDML commands for each of your queries.

d. Implement your database if you have a hierarchical DBMS system available.

Selected Bibliography

The first hierarchical DBMS, IMS and its DL/1 language, was developed by IBM and North American Aviation (Rockwell International) in the late 1960s. Few early documents exist that describe IMS. McGee (1977) gives an overview of IMS in an issue of *IBM Systems Journal* devoted to IMS. Bjoerner and Lovengren (1982) formalize some aspects of the IMS data model.

The Time-shared Data Management System (TDMS) of System Development Corporation (now Burroughs) (Vorhaus and Mills 1967; Bleier and Vorhaus 1968) and the Remote File Management System (RFMS) developed at the University of Texas at Austin (Everett et al. 1971) are precursors of another major commercial hierarchical system called System 2000, which is now marketed by SAS Inc. We discuss IMS and refer to System 2000 briefly in Chapter 23. Hardgrave (1974, 1980) describes a language, BOLT, for the hierarchical model.

Tsichritzis and Lochovsky (1976) survey hierarchical database management, and general descriptions of the hierarchical model appear in several textbooks, including Ullman (1982) and Korth and Silberschatz (1986). Kroenke and Dolan (1988) discuss DL/1 processing, and Date (1986) presents IMS as an example of a hierarchical system. Kapp and Leben (1978) discuss the DL/1 language in detail from the programmer's viewpoint. Additional bibliography concerning IMS and System 2000 appears in Chapter 23.

CHAPTER **11**

The Network Data Model

In Chapters 6 to 9 we discussed the relational data model and its languages. In Chapter 10 we presented the hierarchical data model. We now discuss the network model, which is the third major data model that has been used as a basis for implementing numerous commercial DBMSs. Historically, the network model structures and language constructs were defined by the CODASYL (Conference on Data Systems Languages) committee, so it is often referred to as the CODASYL network model. More recently, ANSI (American National Standards Institute) made a recommendation for a network definition language (NDL) standard [ANSI 1984].

The original network model and language were presented in the CODASYL Data Base Task Group 1971 report [DBTG 1971]; this is sometimes called the DBTG model. Revised reports in 1978 and 1981 incorporated more recent concepts. In this chapter, rather than concentrate on the details of a particular CODASYL report, we present the general concepts behind network-type databases and use the term network model rather than CODA-SYL model or DBTG model. We present the network model concepts independently of the entity-relationship, relational, or hierarchical data models; comparisons among the various data models are given in Chapter 12.

We will use PASCAL as host language when we present the commands for a network database language, to be consistent with the rest of the book. The original CODASYL/DBTG report used COBOL as host language. The concepts of network database languages can be discussed with numerous host programming languages, but the basic database manipulation commands are the same.

In Section 11.1 we discuss record types and set types, which are the two main data structuring constructs in the network model. In Section 11.2 we present data definition and manipulation languages for network databases. The retrieval and update language in Section 11.2.3 is a record-at-a-time language, similar to the hierarchical model language HDML discussed in Chapter 10. These languages contrast with the high-level relational languages discussed in Chapters 6 to 9, which specify a set of records for retrieval in a single command. Traditionally, the network and hierarchical models are associated with low-level record-at-a-time languages. However, recent research suggests that it is possible

281

to define and use languages similar to the high-level relational languages for network and hierarchical databases. We discuss one such language for the IDMS/R database system in Chapter 23.

11.1   Network Database Structures

There are two basic data structures in the network model—records and sets. We discuss records and record types in Section 11.1.1. In Section 11.1.2 we introduce sets and set types and then discuss constraints on sets in Section 11.1.3. Section 11.1.4 concerns how sets are represented and implemented, and Section 11.1.5 presents special types of sets. We show how 1:1 and M:N relationships are represented in the network model in Section 11.1.6.

11.1.1   Records, Record Types, and Data Items

Data is stored in **records**; each record consists of a group of related data values. We classify records into **record types,** where each record type describes the structure of a group of records that store the same type of information. We give each record type a name and also give a name and format (data type) for each **data item** (or attribute) in the record type. Figure 11.1 shows a record type STUDENT with data items NAME, SSN, ADDRESS, MAJORDEPT, and BIRTHDATE. The **format** (or **data type**) of each data item is also shown in Figure 11.1.

Unlike the relational and hierarchical models, which allow only simple attributes, the network model allows complex data items to be defined. A **vector** is a data item that may have multiple values in a single record.* A **repeating group** allows the inclusion of a set of composite values for a data item in a single record.** For example, if we want to include the transcript of each student within each student record, we can define a TRANSCRIPT repeating group for the student record; TRANSCRIPT is formed of the four data items YEAR, COURSE, SEMESTER, and GRADE, as shown in Figure 11.2. The repeating group is not essential to the modeling capability of the network model, since we can represent the same situation with two record types and a set type (see Section 11.1.2). Repeating groups can be nested several levels deep. Figure 11.3a shows an example of two-level nesting, where we want the transcript values to be grouped by SEMESTER, YEAR. The first level item, TRANSCRIPT, is a repeating group of three data items—SEMESTER, YEAR, and SEMESTER_TRANSCRIPT. The second level item, SEMESTER_TRANSCRIPT, is itself a repeating group of COURSE and GRADE. Figure 11.3b shows a record occurrence of the record type shown in Figure 11.3a.

All the above types of data items are called **actual data items**, because their values are actually stored in the records. **Virtual** (or **derived**) **data items** can be defined in terms of the actual data items. The value of a virtual data item is not actually stored in a record but is derived from the actual data items using some procedure that is defined specifically

---

*This corresponds to a *simple* multivalued attribute in the terminology of Chapter 3.
**This corresponds to a *composite* multivalued attribute in the terminology of Chapter 3.

STUDENT				
NAME	SSN	ADDRESS	MAJORDEPT	BIRTHDATE

data item name	format
NAME	CHARACTER 30
SSN	CHARACTER 9
ADDRESS	CHARACTER 40
MAJORDEPT	CHARACTER 10
BIRTHDATE	CHARACTER 9

Figure 11.1   A record type STUDENT

for this purpose. For example, we can declare a virtual data item AGE for the record type shown in Figure 11.1 and write a procedure to calculate the value of AGE from the value of the actual data item BIRTHDATE in each record.

A typical database application will have numerous record types—from a few to a few hundred. The records from the different types will usually be related in many ways. To represent the possible relationships between records, the network model provides the modeling construct called set type, which we discuss next.

11.1.2   Set Types and Set Instances

A **set type** is a description of a 1:N relationship between two record types. Figure 11.4 shows how we represent a set type diagrammatically as an arrow. This type of diagrammatic representation is called a **Bachman diagram**. Each set type consists of three basic elements:

- A name for the set type.
- An owner record type.
- A member record type.

The set type in Figure 11.4 is called MAJOR_DEPT; DEPARTMENT is the **owner** record type and STUDENT is the **member** record type. This represents the 1:N relationship be-

STUDENT					
		TRANSCRIPT			
NAME	• • •	YEAR	COURSE	SEMESTER	GRADE

Smith	• • •	1984	COSC3320	Fall	A
		1984	COSC3340	Fall	A
		1984	MATH312	Fall	B
		1985	COSC4310	Spring	C
		1985	COSC4330	Spring	B

Figure 11.2   A repeating group TRANSCRIPT

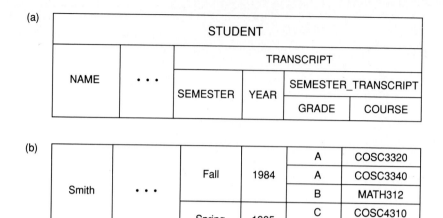

Figure 11.3 Nested Repeating Groups. (a) A nested repeating group TRANSCRIPT of the record type STUDENT. (b) A record occurrence of the record type STUDENT.

tween academic departments and students majoring in those departments. In the database itself, there will be many **set occurrences** (or **set instances**) corresponding to a set type. Each instance relates one record from the owner record type—a DEPARTMENT record in our example—to the set of records from the member record type related to it—the set of STUDENT records for students who major in that department. Hence, each set occurrence is composed of:

- One owner record from the owner record type.
- A number of related member records (zero or more) from the member record type.

A record from the member record type *cannot exist in more than one set occurrence* of a particular set type. This maintains the constraint that a set type represents a 1:N rela-

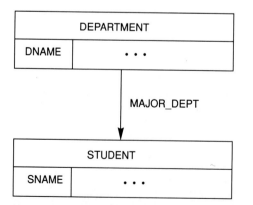

Figure 11.4 The set type MAJOR_DEPT (which is MANUAL OPTIONAL)

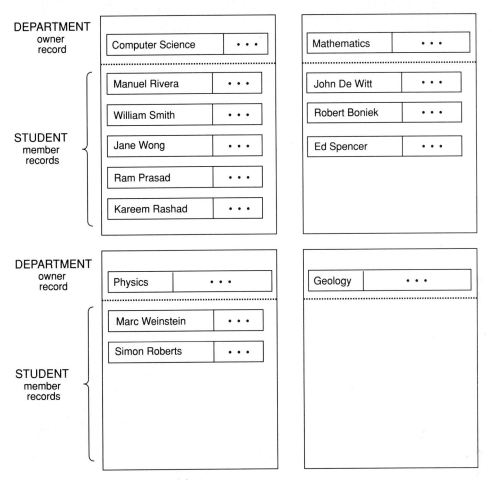

Figure 11.5 Four set instances of the set type MAJOR_DEPT

tionship. In our example a STUDENT record can be related to at most one major DEPART-MENT and hence is a member of at most one occurrence of the MAJOR_DEPT set type.

A set occurrence can be identified either by the *owner record* or by *any of the member records*. Figure 11.5 shows four set occurrences (instances) of the MAJOR_DEPT set type. Notice that each set instance *must* have one owner record but can have any number of member records (**zero** or more). Hence, we usually refer to a set instance by its owner record. The four set instances in Figure 11.5 can be referred to as the 'Computer Science', 'Mathematics', 'Physics,' and 'Geology' sets. Because we are dealing with records, it is customary to use a different representation of a set instance (Figure 11.6) where the records of the set instance are shown linked together by pointers.

In the network model a set instance is *not identical* to the concept of a set in mathematics. There are two principal differences:

- The set instance has one *distinguished element*—the owner record—whereas in a mathematical set there is no such distinction among the elements of the set.

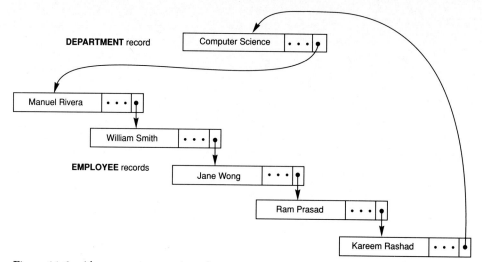

Figure 11.6 Alternate representation of a set instance

• In the network model the member records of a set instance are *ordered*, whereas order of elements is immaterial in a mathematical set. Hence, we can refer to the first, second, i^{th}, and last member records in a set instance. This is important when we discuss the data manipulation language for the network model and makes the representation of a set instance shown in Figure 11.6 appropriate. In Figure 11.6 the record of 'Manuel Rivera' is the first STUDENT (member) record in the 'Computer Science' set, and that of 'Kareem Rashad' is the last member record. The set of the network model is sometimes referred to as an **owner-coupled set** or **co-set** to distinguish it from a mathematical set.

11.1.3   *Constraints on Set Membership*

In the network model there are several constraints that we may specify on set membership. These are usually divided into two main categories, called **insertion options** and **retention options** in CODASYL terminology. These constraints are determined during database design by knowing how a set is required to *behave* when member records are inserted and when owner or member records are deleted. The constraints are specified to the DBMS when we declare the database structure using the data definition language (see Section 11.2.2). Not all combinations of the constraints are possible. We now discuss each type of constraint and then give the allowable combinations.

Insertion Options (Constraints) on Sets

The insertion constraints—or options in CODASYL terminology—on set membership specify what is to happen when we insert a new record in the database that is of a member record type. A record is inserted using the STORE command (see Section 11.2.2). There are two options:

- AUTOMATIC: The new member record is *automatically connected* to an appropriate*
  set occurrence when the record is inserted.

- MANUAL: The new record is not connected to any set occurrence. If desired, the
  programmer can explicitly (manually) connect the record to a set occurrence subsequently by using the CONNECT command.

For example, consider the MAJOR_DEPT set type of Figure 11.4. In this situation
we can have a STUDENT record that is not related to any department through the
MAJOR_DEPT set (if the corresponding student has not declared a major). We should declare the MANUAL insertion option, meaning that when a member STUDENT record is inserted in the database it is not automatically related to a DEPARTMENT record through the
MAJOR_DEPT set (and hence inserted into a set instance of MAJOR_DEPT). The database
user may later insert the record "manually" into a set instance when the corresponding
student declares a major department. This manual insertion is accomplished using an update operation called CONNECT, submitted to the database system, as we shall see in
Section 11.2.3.

The AUTOMATIC option for set insertion is used in situations where we want to insert a member record into a set instance automatically when that record is stored in the
database. We must specify a criterion for *designating the set instance* of which each new
record becomes a member. As an example of such a criterion, consider the set type
shown in Figure 11.7a, which relates each employee to the set of dependents of that employee. We can declare the EMP_DEPENDENTS set type to be AUTOMATIC with the condition that a new DEPENDENT record with a particular EMPSSN value is inserted into the set
instance owned by the EMPLOYEE record with the same SSN value. The DBMS locates the
EMPLOYEE record such that EMPLOYEE.SSN = DEPENDENT.EMPSSN and connects the new
DEPENDENT record automatically to that set instance. Notice that the SSN field should be
declared so that no two EMPLOYEE records have the same SSN; otherwise, more than one
set instance is identified by the above condition. In Section 11.2.2 we will discuss other
criteria for automatically identifying and selecting a set occurrence.

Retention Options (Constraints) on Sets

The retention constraints—or options in CODASYL terminology—specify whether a
record of a member record type can exist in the database on its own or whether it must
always be related to an owner and hence be a member of a set instance at all times.
There are three retention options:

- OPTIONAL: A member record can exist on its own *without being* a member in any
  occurrence of the set. It can be connected and disconnected to set occurrences
  at will using the CONNECT and DISCONNECT commands of the network DML (see
  Section 11.2.3).

- MANDATORY: A member record *cannot* exist on its own; it must *always* be a member in some set occurrence of the set type. It can be reconnected in a single operation from one set occurrence to another using the RECONNECT command of the
  network DML (see Section 11.2.3).

---

*The appropriate set occurrence is determined by a specification that is part of the definition of the set type,
the SET OCCURRENCE SELECTION, which we discuss in Section 11.2.2 when we present the network DDL.

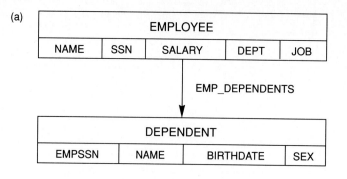

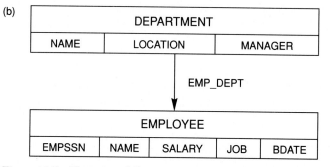

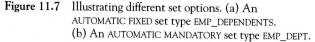

Figure 11.7   Illustrating different set options. (a) An
AUTOMATIC FIXED set type EMP_DEPENDENTS.
(b) An AUTOMATIC MANDATORY set type EMP_DEPT.

- FIXED: As in MANDATORY, a member record *cannot* exist on its own. Moreover, once it is inserted in a set occurrence, it is *fixed*; it *cannot* be reconnected to another set occurrence.

We now illustrate the differences among these options by examples showing when each of these should be used. First, consider the MAJOR_DEPT set type of Figure 11.4. In this situation we may have a STUDENT record that is not related to any department through the MAJOR_DEPT set if the corresponding student has not declared a major, so we declare the set to be OPTIONAL. In Figure 11.7a EMP_DEPENDENTS is an example of a FIXED set type because in this situation we do not expect a dependent to be moved from one employee to another. In addition, every DEPENDENT record must be related to an EMPLOYEE record at all times. In Figure 11.7b we show an example of a MANDATORY set EMP_DEPT that relates an employee to the department the employee works for. We assume that in the situation we are modeling, every employee must be assigned to exactly one department at all times; however, an employee can be reassigned from one department to another.

In general, the MANDATORY and FIXED options are used in situations where a member record should not exist in the database without being related to an owner through some set occurrence. For FIXED, the additional requirement of never moving a member record from one set instance to another is enforced.

Table 11.1 Set Insertion and Retention Options

		Retention Option		
		OPTIONAL	MANDATORY	FIXED
Insertion Option	MANUAL	Application program is in charge of inserting member record into set occurrence. Can CONNECT, DISCONNECT, RECONNECT	Not very useful.	Not very useful.
	AUTOMATIC	DBMS inserts a new member record into a set occurrence automatically. Can CONNECT, DISCONNECT, RECONNECT.	DBMS inserts a new member record into a set occurrence automatically. Can RECONNECT member to a different owner	DBMS inserts a new member record into a set occurrence automatically. *Cannot* RECONNECT member to a different owner

Combinations of Insertion and Retention Options

Not all combinations of insertion and retention options are useful. For example, FIXED and MANDATORY retention options imply that a member record should always be related to an owner, so they should be used with the AUTOMATIC insertion option. In fact, there are only three combinations of these options that normally make sense, and most implementations of the network model allow only these combinations, which are AUTOMATIC-FIXED, AUTOMATIC-MANDATORY, and MANUAL-OPTIONAL.* We can also think of applications where an AUTOMATIC-OPTIONAL set might be useful, namely when the member record is automatically connected to an owner if a particular owner is specified; otherwise, the new member record is not connected to any set instance. These combinations are summarized in Table 11.1.

Set Ordering Options

The member records in a set instance can be ordered in a variety of ways. This is important because of the record-at-a-time nature of the network DML. Order can be based on an ordering field or controlled by the time sequence of insertion of new member records. The available options for ordering can be summarized as follows:

- Sorted by an ordering field: The values of one or more fields from the member record type are used to order the member records within *each set occurrence* in ascending or descending order. The system maintains the order when a new member

---

*The original CODASYL report did not place these restrictions on possible combinations of options.

record is connected to the set instance by automatically inserting the record in its correct position in the order.

- System default: A new member record is inserted in an arbitrary position determined by the system.

- First or last: A new member record becomes the first or last record in the set occurrence *at the time it is inserted*. Hence, this corresponds to having the member records in a set instance stored in chronological (or reverse chronological) order.

- Next or prior: The new member record is inserted after or before the current record of the set occurrence. This will become clearer when we discuss currency indicators in Section 11.2.1.

The desired options for insertion, retention, and ordering are specified when the set type is declared in the data definition language. We will discuss the details of declaring record types and set types in Section 11.2.2 when we discuss the network model data definition language (DDL).

11.1.4   *Representations of Set Instances*

A set instance is commonly represented as a **ring (circular linked list)** linking the owner record and all member records of the set, as shown in Figure 11.6. This is also sometimes called a **circular chain**. The ring representation is symmetric with respect to all records; hence, to distinguish between the owner record and the member records, the DBMS includes a special field, called the **type field**, that has a distinct value (assigned by the DBMS) for each record type. By examining the type field, the system can tell whether the record is the owner of the set instance or is one of the member records. This type field is hidden from the user and used only by the DBMS.

In addition to the type field, a record type is automatically assigned a **pointer field** by the DBMS for *each set type in which it participates as owner or member*. This pointer can be considered to be *labeled* with the set type name to which it corresponds; hence, the system internally maintains the correspondence between these pointer fields and their set types. A pointer is usually called the **NEXT** pointer in a member record and the **FIRST** pointer in an owner record because they point to the next and first member records, respectively. In our example of Figure 11.6, each student record has a NEXT pointer to the next STUDENT record within the set occurrence. The NEXT pointer of the *last member record* in a set occurrence points back to the owner record. If a record of the member record type does not participate in any set instance, then its NEXT pointer will have a special **nil** pointer; this is possible only for OPTIONAL sets. If a set occurrence has an owner but no member records, the FIRST pointer will point right back to the owner record itself or it can be **nil**.

The above representation of sets is one method for implementing set instances. In general, a DBMS can implement sets in a variety of ways. However, the chosen representation must allow the DBMS to do all the following:

- Given an owner record, find all member records of the set occurrence.

- Given an owner record, find the first, i^{th}, or last member record of the set occurrence. If no such record exists, give an indication of that fact.

- Given a member record, find the next (or previous) member record of the set occurrence. If no such record exists, give an indication of that fact.

- Given a member record, find the owner record of the set occurrence.

The circular linked list representation allows the system to do all of the above operations with varying degrees of efficiency. In general, a network database schema will have many record types and set types, so a record type may participate as owner and member in numerous set types. For example, in the network schema shown in Figure 11.10 the EMPLOYEE record type participates as owner in four set types, MANAGES, IS_ A_SUPERVISOR, E_WORKSON, and DEPENDENTS_OF, and participates as member in two set types, WORKS_FOR and SUPERVISEES. In the circular linked list representation, six additional pointer fields are added to the EMPLOYEE record type. However, no confusion arises, because each pointer is labeled and plays the role of FIRST or NEXT pointer for a specific set type.

Other representations of sets allow more efficient implementation of some of the operations on sets mentioned above. We briefly mention five of them here:

- Doubly linked circular list representation: In addition to the NEXT pointer in a member record type, a **PRIOR** pointer points back to the prior member record of the set occurrence. The PRIOR pointer of the first member record can point back to the owner record.

- Owner pointer representation: This can be used in combination with either the linked list or the doubly linked list representation. For each set type an additional **OWNER** pointer is included in the member record type. The OWNER pointer points directly to the owner record of the set.

- Contiguous member records: Rather than linking the member records by pointers, we actually place them in contiguous physical locations, typically following the owner record.

- Pointer arrays: An array of pointers is stored with the owner record. The ith element in the array points to the ith member record of the set instance. This is usually implemented in conjunction with the owner pointer.

- Indexed representation: A small index is kept with the owner record *for each set occurrence*. An index entry contains the value of a key indexing field and a pointer to the actual member record that has this field value. The index may be implemented as a linked list chained by next and prior pointers (the IDMS system allows this option see Section 23.3).

Try to determine which operations can be implemented most efficiently in each representation. Notice that these representations are really implementation issues. Theoretically, the programmer should not be concerned with how sets are implemented but only that they are implemented correctly by the DBMS. However, in practice, the programmer will be interested in the particular implementation of sets in order to write more efficient programs. Most systems will allow the database designer to choose among several options for implementing each set type, and the data definition language will have a MODE statement to specify the chosen representation.

11.1.5   Special Types of Sets

Two special types of sets are allowed in the CODASYL network model: SYSTEM-owned sets and multimember sets. A third type, called a recursive set, was not allowed in the original CODASYL report. We discuss these three special types of sets here.

System-owned (Singular) Sets

A **system-owned** set is a set with no owner record type; instead, the system* is the owner. We can think of the system as a special "virtual" owner record type with only a single record occurrence. System-owned sets serve two main purposes in the network model:

- They provide *entry points* into the database via the records of the specified member record type. Processing can commence by accessing members of that record type, then retrieving related records via other sets.

- They can be used to *order* the records of a given record type using the set ordering specifications. By specifying several system-owned sets on the same record type, its records can be accessed in different orders.

A system-owned set allows the processing of records of a record type using the regular set operations that we will discuss in Section 11.2.3. This type of set is called a **singular** set because there is only one set occurrence of it. The diagrammatic representation of a system-owned set ALL_DEPTS is shown in Figure 11.8a, which allows DEPARTMENT records to be accessed in order of some field, say NAME, with an appropriate set ordering specification.

Multimember Sets

Multimember sets are used in the case where member records of a set may be of *more than one* record type. Consider the case of relating employees to their departments. Suppose we have a single DEPARTMENT record type but employees are grouped into three record types—CLERICAL_EMP, TECHNICAL_EMP, and MANAGERIAL_EMP. A set type DEPT_EMP is used to represent the 1:N relationship that relates a DEPARTMENT record to the records of employees who work in that department. In this case the member records of a set can be of any of the three record types—CLERICAL_EMP, TECHNICAL_EMP, and MANAGERIAL_EMP—so we use a multimember set. This is represented diagrammatically as in Figure 11.8b. The member records of a set occurrence may include records from all three member record types. However, the constraint that each member record appears in at most one set occurrence is still valid to enforce the 1:N nature of the relationship.

Recursive Sets

A set type with the same record type playing the role of both owner and member can be called a **recursive** set. An example of a recursive 1:N relationship that can be represented by a recursive set is the SUPERVISION relationship, which relates a supervisor employee

---

*By system, we mean the DBMS software.

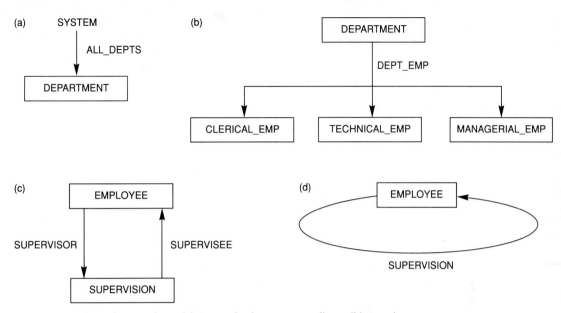

Figure 11.8   Special types of sets. (a) A singular (SYSTEM-owned) set. (b) A multimember set. (c) Representing the recursive set SUPERVISION using a
linking record type. (d) Prohibited recursive set representation.

to the list of employees directly under his or her supervision. In this relationship the
EMPLOYEE record type plays both the roles: that of the owner record type (the supervisor
employee) and that of the member record type (the supervisee employees) in a set type
SUPERVISION.

Recursive sets were prohibited in the original CODASYL model because it is difficult
to process them using the CODASYL data manipulation language (DML). The DML (see
Section 11.2.2) assumes that a record belongs to a single set occurrence of each set type.
With recursive sets the same record can be an owner of one set occurrence and a member
of another set occurrence, both set occurrences being of the same set type. Because of
the above problem, it has become customary to represent a recursive set in the network
model by creating an additional **linking** (or **dummy**) record type. The same technique is
used to represent M:N relationships, as we shall see in the next section. Figure 11.8c
shows the representation of the SUPERVISION relationship using two set types and a
linking record type. In Figure 11.8c the SUPERVISOR set type is really a 1:1 relationship; that is, at most one SUPERVISION member record will exist in each SUPERVISOR set
occurrence. We can think of each SUPERVISION linking record as representing an employee *in the role of supervisor*; that EMPLOYEE's record is the owner record of a SUPERVISION
member record in a set instance of SUPERVISOR. The direct recursive set representation—usually prohibited in the network model—is shown in Figure 11.8d.*

---

*Most network DBMS implementations do not allow the same record type to participate as both owner and
member in the same set type, as in the case of the SUPERVISION set type in Figure 11.8d.

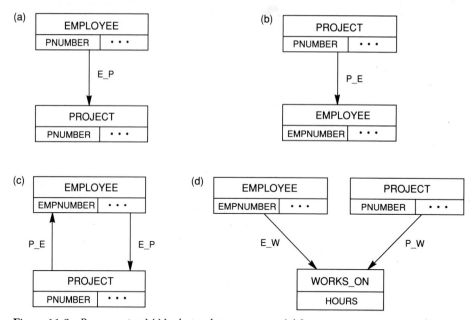

Figure 11.9   Representing M:N relationships using sets. (a) Incorrect representation of an M:N relationship. (b) Incorrect representation of an M:N relationship. (c) Incorrect representation of an M:N relationship. (d) Correct representation of an M:N relationship using a linking (dummy) record type. **Opposite Page** (e) Representing some occurrences of an M:N relationship with "linking occurrences." (f) Some occurrences of the set types E_W and P_W and the linking record type WORKS_ON corresponding to the M:N relationship instances shown in Figure 11.9(e).

11.1.6   Representing 1:1 and M:N Relationships Using Sets

A set type represents a 1:N relationship between two record types. This means that *a record of the member record type can appear in only one set occurrence*. This constraint is automatically enforced by the DBMS in the network model.

To represent a 1:1 relationship between two record types by using a set type, we must restrict each set occurrence to have *a single member record*. The CODASYL model does not provide for automatically enforcing this constraint, so the programmer must check that the constraint is not violated every time a member record is inserted into a set occurrence.

An M:N relationship between two record types cannot be represented by a single set type. For example, consider the WORKS_ON relationship between EMPLOYEEs and PROJECTs. Assume that an employee can be working on several projects simultaneously and that a project will, in general, have several employees working on it. If we try to represent this by a set type, neither the set type in Figure 11.9a nor that in Figure 11.9b will represent the relationship correctly. Figure 11.9a enforces the incorrect constraint that a PROJECT record is related to only one EMPLOYEE record (a single employee works on each project). Figure 11.9b enforces the incorrect constraint that an EMPLOYEE record is related to only one PROJECT record (an employee works on only one project). Using both set types E_P and P_E simultaneously as in Figure 11.9c leads to the same type of problem and is incorrect.

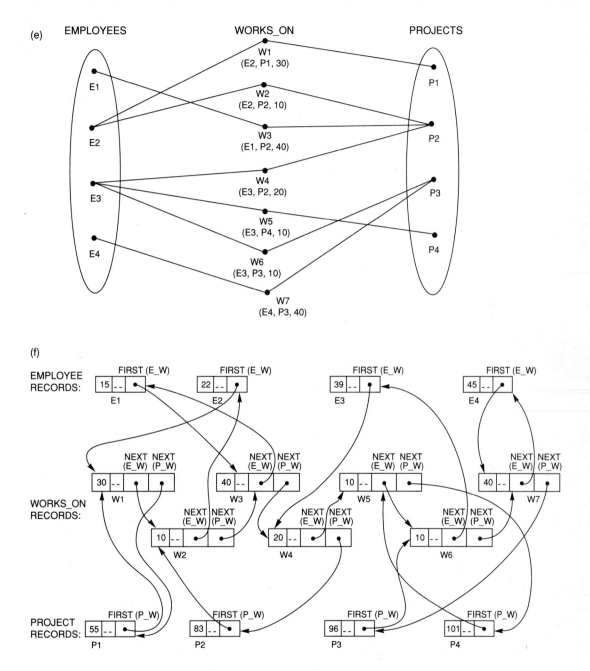

The correct method for representing an M:N relationship in the network model is to use two set types and an additional record type, as shown in Figure 11.9d. This additional record type, WORKS_ON in our example, is called a **linking** (or **dummy**) record type. Each record of the WORKS_ON record type must be owned by one EMPLOYEE record through the E_W set and by one PROJECT record through the P_W set and serves to relate these two owner records. This is illustrated conceptually in Figure 11.9e.

Figure 11.9f is an example of individual record and set occurrences in the linked list representation corresponding to the schema in Figure 11.9d. Each record of the WORKS_ON record type has two NEXT pointers; the one marked NEXT(E_W) points to the next record in an instance of the E_W set, and the one marked NEXT(P_W) points to the next record in an instance of the P_W set. Each WORKS_ON record relates its two owner records. Each WORKS_ON record also contains the number of hours per week that an employee works on a project. The same occurrences in Figure 11.9f are shown in Figure 11.9e by displaying the W records individually without showing the pointers.

To find all projects that a particular employee works on, we start at the EMPLOYEE record and then trace through all WORKS_ON records owned by that EMPLOYEE using the FIRST(E_W) and NEXT(E_W) pointers. At each WORKS_ON record in the set occurrence, we find its owner PROJECT record by following the NEXT(P_W) pointers until we find a record of type PROJECT. For example, for the E2 EMPLOYEE record, we follow the FIRST(E_W) pointer in E2 leading to W1, the NEXT(E_W) pointer in W1 leading to W2, and the NEXT(E_W) pointer in W2 leading back to E2. Hence, W1 and W2 are identified as the member records in the set occurrence of E_W owned by E2. By following the NEXT(P_W) pointer in W1 we reach P1 as its owner, and by following the NEXT(P_W) pointer in W2 (and through W3 and W4) we reach P2 as its owner. Although this may seem complex, it is straightforward once we understand the distinction between NEXT and FIRST pointers for each set. Notice that the existence of direct OWNER pointers for the P_W set in the WORKS_ON records would have simplified the process of identifying the owner PROJECT record of each WORKS_ON record.

In a similar fashion, we can find all EMPLOYEE records related to a particular PROJECT. In this case the existence of owner pointers for the E_W set would simplify processing. All this pointer tracing is done *automatically by the* DBMS; the programmer has DML commands for directly finding the owner or the next member, as we shall discuss in Section 11.2.3.

Notice that we could represent the M:N relationship as in Figure 11.9a (or 11.9b) if we allowed the duplication of PROJECT (or EMPLOYEE) records. In Figure 11.9a a PROJECT record would be duplicated as many times as there were employees working on the project. However, duplicating records creates problems in maintaining consistency among the duplicates whenever the database is updated and is not recommended in general.

11.2   Defining and Manipulating a Network Database

In this section we discuss how to define and manipulate a network database. By manipulating the database, we mean searching for and retrieving records from the database, as well as inserting, deleting, and modifying records and also connecting and disconnecting records from set occurrences. A **data manipulation language** is used for this purpose. The DML associated with the network model consists of record-at-a-time commands that are embedded in a general-purpose programming language called the **host language**.*

---

*Embedded commands of the DML are also called the **data sublanguage**.

In practice, the most commonly used host languages are COBOL* and PL/I. In our examples we will write program segments in PASCAL notation augmented with network DML commands.

We first discuss some basic concepts for record-at-a-time network data manipulation in Section 11.2.1. In Section 11.2.2 we discuss network DDL (data definition language) commands, which are used for declaring the record types, set types, and constraints in a network database schema. In Section 11.2.3 we discuss network DML (data manipulation language) commands and give examples of how they are embedded in a programming language.

11.2.1 Basic Concepts for Network Database Manipulation

To write programs for manipulating a network database, we first need to discuss some basic concepts related to how data manipulation programs are written. A key point is that the database system and the host programming language are two separate software systems that are linked together by a common interface and communicate only through this interface. Because DML commands are record-at-a-time, it is necessary to identify specific records of the database as **current records**. The DBMS itself keeps track of a number of current records and set occurrences by a mechanism known as **currency indicators**. In addition, the host programming language needs local program variables to hold the records of different record types so that their contents can be manipulated by the host program. The set of these local variables in the program is usually referred to as the **user work area (UWA)**. Communication between the DBMS and the host programming language is mainly accomplished through currency indicators and the user work area.

In this section we will discuss these two concepts. Our examples will refer to the network database schema shown in Figure 11.10, which is the network version of the COMPANY schema used in previous chapters. We will assume that recursive sets cannot be directly specified, and hence we represent the SUPERVISION relationship using a linking record type similar to Figure 11.8c.** We will show how this network schema is derived from the corresponding ER schema in Chapter 12.

The User Work Area (UWA)

The UWA is a set of program variables, declared in the host program, to communicate the contents of individual records between the DBMS and the host program. For each record type in the database schema, a corresponding program variable with the same format must be declared in the program. It is customary to use the same record type names and the same field names in the UWA variables as in the database schema. In fact, the UWA variables can be automatically declared in the program by referring to a particular DDL for a database schema. Part of the software that links the DBMS program with the host programming language can scan the data description of the schema, which is stored by the DBMS, and automatically create program variable declarations to correspond to the record types in the schema.

---

*The CODASYL DML in the DBTG report was originally proposed as a data sublanguage for COBOL.
**If recursive sets are allowed, we can represent the relationship by a single set type as shown in Figure 11.8d.

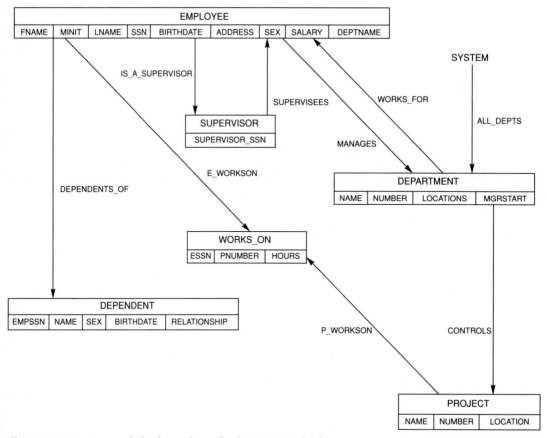

Figure 11.10   A network database schema for the COMPANY database

For the COMPANY schema of Figure 11.10, if an interface between PASCAL and the network DBMS were available, it could create the PASCAL program variables shown in Figure 11.11. A single record of each record type can be copied from or written into the database using the corresponding program variable of the UWA. To read a record from the database, we use the GET command (see Section 11.2.3) to copy a record into the corresponding program variable. Then we can refer to the field values to print or to use for calculations. To write a record into the database, we first assign its field values to the fields of the program variable and then use the STORE command (see Section 11.2.3) to actually store the record in the database.

Currency Indicators

In the network DML, retrievals and updates are handled by moving or **navigating** through the database records, and hence keeping a trace of the search is critical. Currency indicators are a means of keeping track of the most recently accessed records and set occurrences by the DBMS. They play the role of position holders so that we may process new records starting from the ones most recently accessed until we retrieve all the records

```
type LOCATIONRECORD    = ( * this is for the vector field LOCATIONS of DEPARTMENT *)
                         record
                         LOCATION : packed array [1..15] of char ;
                         NEXT : ^LOCATIONRECORD
                         end ;

  var   EMPLOYEE   :     record
                         FNAME : packed array  [1..15] of char ;
                         MINIT : char ;
                         LNAME : packed array [1..15] of char ;
                         SSN : packed array [1..9] of char ;
                         BIRTHDATE : packed array [1..9] of char ;
                         ADDRESS : packed array [1..30] of char ;
                         SEX : char ;
                         SALARY : packed array [1..10] of char ;
                         DEPTNAME : packed array [1..15] of char
                         end ;
        DEPARTMENT :     record
                         NAME : packed array [1..15] of char ;
                         NUMBER : integer ;
                         LOCATIONS : ^LOCATIONRECORD ;
                         MGRSTART : packed array [1..9] of char
                         end ;
        PROJECT    :     record
                         NAME : packed array [1..15] of char ;
                         NUMBER : integer ;
                         LOCATION : packed array [1..15] of char
                         end ;
        WORKS_ON   :     record
                         ESSN : packed array [1..9] of char ;
                         PNUMBER : integer ;
                         HOURS : packed array [1..4] of char
                         end ;
        SUPERVISOR :     record
                         SUPERVISOR_SSN : packed array [1..9] of char
                         end ;
        DEPENDENT  :     record
                         EMPSSN : packed array [1..9] of char ;
                         NAME : packed array [1..15] of char ;
                         SEX : char ;
                         BIRTHDATE : packed array [1..9] of char ;
                         RELATIONSHIP : packed array [1..10] of char
                         end;
```

Figure 11.11   PASCAL program variables for the UWA corresponding to the network schema in Figure 11.10

that contain the information we need. Each currency indicator can be thought of as a record pointer (or record address) that points to a single database record. In a network DBMS several currency indicators are used. These are:

- **Current of record type:** For each record type, the DBMS keeps track of the most recently accessed record of that record type. If no record has been accessed yet from that record type, the current record is undefined.

- **Current of set type:** For each set type in the schema, the DBMS keeps track of the most recently accessed set occurrence from the set type. The set occurrence is specified by a single record from that set, which is either the owner or one of the member records. Hence, the current of set (or current set) points to a record, even though it is used to keep track of a set occurrence. If the program has not accessed any record from that set type, the current of set is undefined.

• **Current of run unit** (CRU): By run unit we mean a database access program that is executing (running) on the computer system. For each run unit, the CRU keeps track of the record most recently accessed by the program; this record can be from *any* record type in the database.

Each time a program executes a DML command, the currency indicators for the record types and set types affected by that command are updated by the DBMS. A clear understanding of how each DML command affects the currency indicators is necessary. Many of the DML commands will both affect and depend on the currency indicators. In Section 11.2.3 we will illustrate how the different DML commands affect currency indicators.

Status Indicators

This is another concept that is needed in order to be able to write data manipulation programs for network databases. There are several **status indicators** that return an indication of success or failure after each DML command is executed. The program can check the values of these status indicators and take appropriate action—either to continue execution or to transfer to an error-handling routine.

We will call the main status variable DB_STATUS and assume that it is implicitly declared in the host program. After each DML command, the value of DB_STATUS indicates whether the command was successful or whether an error or an exception occurred. The most common exception that occurs is the END_OF_SET (**EOS**) exception. This is not an error—it only indicates that no more member records exist in a set occurrence and is frequently used to terminate a program loop that processes every member element of a set instance. A DML command to find the next (or prior) member of a set returns an EOS exception when no next (or prior) member record exists. The program checks for DB_STATUS = EOS to terminate the loop. In Section 11.2.3 we will assume that a DB_STATUS value of 0 (zero) indicates a successfully executed command with no exceptions occurring.

Example to Illustrate Currency Indicators and the UWA

Suppose a program executes database commands that result in the following events on the database instances shown in Figure 11.9f:

• The EMPLOYEE record E3 is accessed.

• By following the FIRST(E_W) pointer in E3, the WORKS_ON record W4 is accessed; by continuing with the NEXT(E_W) pointers in WORKS_ON records, W5 and W6 are accessed.

• The record W6 is retrieved into the corresponding UWA variable.

Figure 11.12 illustrates the effects of the above events on the UWA variables and the DBMS currency indicators when applied to the instances of Figure 11.9f. Figure 11.13 shows how the currency indicators change as the events take place, with an additional

The **FIND ANY** command finds the *first* record in the database of the specified <record type name> such that the field values of the record match the values in the corresponding UWA fields specified in the **USING** clause of the command. In EX1 these fields are FNAME and LNAME, which we call the **search fields** for the FIND command. *Before* issuing the FIND ANY command, the program must assign to the search fields of the UWA variable the values we want the DBMS to use to find a particular record. The DBMS uses a **search criterion** to locate the first database record whose search field(s) values match the search field values in the UWA variable.

In EX1 lines 1 and 2 are equivalent to saying: "Search for the first EMPLOYEE record that satisfies the condition FNAME = 'John' and LNAME = 'Smith' and make it the current record of the run unit (CRU)." The GET statement is equivalent to saying: "Retrieve the CRU record into the corresponding UWA program variable." In general, whenever a FIND command is used, the program should check whether or not it successfully located a record by testing the value of DB_STATUS. A value of 0 means that a record was successfully located, so we write the if ... then statement starting in line 3 before issuing the GET command in line 5 of EX1.

The FIND statement not only sets the CRU but also sets additional currency indicators, namely those for the record type whose name is specified in the command and for any set types in which that record type participates as owner or member. Hence, the above FIND command also sets the currency indicators for the EMPLOYEE record type and for every set type in which the located record participates as owner or member of a set occurrence. However, the GET command always retrieves the CRU, *which may not be the same as the current of record type.** The IDMS/R system combines FIND and GET into a single command, called OBTAIN.

Two variations of EX1 are worth considering. First, if we replace line 5 by just $GET, we retrieve exactly the same result as before. The difference is that including the record type name in the GET command—as in EX1—makes the system check that the CRU is of the specified record type; if not, an error is generated and the CRU is not retrieved into the UWA variable. Hence, if we replace line 5 by, say, $GET DEPARTMENT, an error is generated because the record type specified in the GET command, DEPARTMENT, does not match the record type of the CRU, EMPLOYEE.

If more than one record satisfies our search criterion and we want to retrieve all of them, we must write a looping construct in the host programming language. For example, to retrieve all EMPLOYEE records for employees who work in the Research department and print their names, we can write EX2.

```
EX2:   EMPLOYEE.DEPTNAME := 'Research';
       $FIND ANY EMPLOYEE USING DEPTNAME;
       while DB_STATUS = 0 do
           begin
           $GET EMPLOYEE;
           writeln ( EMPLOYEE.FNAME, ' ', EMPLOYEE.LNAME );
           $FIND DUPLICATE EMPLOYEE USING DEPTNAME
           end;
```

---

*A variation of the network DML has been suggested which uses the GET command to retrieve the *current record of the specified record type*. This makes some programs easier to write. However, most network DBMSs use the GET command to retrieve the CRU, as we discuss here.

This query can be written more efficiently, as we shall see in EX3, but we use it here to illustrate the FIND DUPLICATE command, which is used to locate additional records that satisfy a search criterion.

The **FIND DUPLICATE** command finds the *next* (or duplicate) record, starting from the CRU, that satisfies the search criterion. We cannot use FIND ANY because it always locates the first record satisfying the search criterion. Notice that "first" and "next" records have no special meaning here because we did not specify any order on EMPLOYEE records in the DDL of Figure 11.14b. The system searches for EMPLOYEE records physically in the order in which they are stored. However, once all EMPLOYEE records have been checked in the while-loop for satisfying the search criterion, the system sets DB_STATUS to a "no more records found" exception condition and the loop terminates.

The FIND ANY and FIND DUPLICATE commands are used for searching the records of a particular record type. In the next subsection we discuss the variations of the FIND command that are used to locate records based on set ownership and membership.

DML Commands for Set Processing

For set processing, we have the following variations of FIND:

- FIND (FIRST | NEXT | PRIOR | LAST | ...) <record type name>
    WITHIN <set type name> [USING <field names>]
- FIND OWNER WITHIN <set type name>

In the first of these commands, options other than those shown may be available. In general, once we have established a current set occurrence of a set type, we can use the FIND command to locate various records that participate in the set occurrence. We can locate either the owner record or one of the member records and make that record the CRU. We use the **FIND OWNER** to locate the owner record and one of **FIND FIRST, FIND NEXT, FIND LAST,** or **FIND PRIOR** to locate the first, next, last, or prior member record of the set instance, respectively.

Recall that the current of set indicator can be pointing to either the owner or to any member record of a set occurrence. The FIND OWNER, FIND FIRST, and FIND LAST commands have the same effect regardless of the particular record in the set occurrence that the current of set points to. However, FIND NEXT and FIND PRIOR *do depend* on the current of set. For FIND NEXT, if the current of set is the owner, it locates the first member; if the current of set is any member record except the last member, it locates the next member record; finally, if the current of the set is the last member record in the set, it sets DB_STATUS to the EOS (end-of-set) exception. For FIND PRIOR, corresponding similar actions are taken.

The next example illustrates the use of FIND FIRST and FIND NEXT. The query is to print the names of employees who work in the Research department alphabetically by last name, which is shown in EX3. This is similar to EX2 except for the alphabetic ordering requirement. EX3 retrieves first the 'Research' DEPARTMENT record and then the member EMPLOYEE records owned by that record via the WORKS_FOR set. Recall that in the declaration of the WORKS_FOR set type in Figure 11.14b, we specified that the member records in each set instance of WORKS_FOR are stored by ascending value of LNAME, FNAME, MINIT. By retrieving the EMPLOYEE member records in order, we can print the employee names alphabetically in EX3. Notice how we terminate the loop by checking DB_STATUS. Once the last member record of the set occurrence is located, the subsequent FIND NEXT command sets DB_STATUS to the EOS (end-of-set) exception, so the while-loop terminates.

```
EX3:   DEPARTMENT.NAME := 'Research';
       $FIND ANY DEPARTMENT USING NAME;
       if DB_STATUS = 0 then
            begin
            $FIND FIRST EMPLOYEE WITHIN WORKS_FOR;
            while DB_STATUS = 0 do
                 begin
                 $GET EMPLOYEE;
                 writeln ( EMPLOYEE.LNAME, ' ', EMPLOYEE.FNAME );
                 $FIND NEXT EMPLOYEE WITHIN WORKS_FOR
                 end
       end;
```

The next example illustrates the use of FIND OWNER. The query is to print the project name, project number, and hours per week for each project that employee John Smith works on (assuming there is only one such employee). This is shown in EX4, where we first find the EMPLOYEE record for John Smith. The FIND ANY command makes that record the CRU as well as the current record of the EMPLOYEE record type and the current of set of the E_WORKSON set type. We then loop through each WORKS_ON member record in the current E_WORKSON set, and within each loop we find the PROJECT record that owns the WORKS_ON record via the P_WORKSON set type. The owner record is located using the FIND OWNER command. Notice that we do not have to check DB_STATUS after the FIND OWNER command because P_WORKSON is an AUTOMATIC FIXED set, so every WORKS_ON record must belong to a P_WORKSON set instance.

```
EX4:   EMPLOYEE.FNAME := 'John'; EMPLOYEE.LNAME := 'Smith';
       $FIND ANY EMPLOYEE USING FNAME, LNAME;
       if DB_STATUS = 0 then
            begin
            $FIND FIRST WORKS_ON WITHIN E_WORKSON;
            while DB_STATUS = 0 do
                 begin
                 $GET WORKS_ON;
                 $FIND OWNER WITHIN P_WORKSON;
                 $GET PROJECT;
                 writeln ( PROJECT.NAME, PROJECT.NUMBER,
                          WORKS_ ON.HOURS );
                 $FIND NEXT WORKS_ON WITHIN E_WORKSON
                 end
       end;
```

In EX3 and EX4 we processed all member records of a set instance. We can also selectively process only the member records that satisfy some condition. If the condition is an equality comparison on one (or more) fields, we can append a USING clause to the FIND command. To illustrate this, consider the request to print the names of all employees who work full-time—40 hours per week—on the 'ProductX' project; this example is shown as EX5.

```
EX5:   PROJECT.NAME := 'ProductX';
       $FIND ANY PROJECT USING NAME;
       if DB_STATUS = 0 then
            begin
            WORKS_ON.HOURS:= '40.0';
            $FIND FIRST WORKS_ON WITHIN P_WORKSON USING HOURS;
            while DB_STATUS = 0 do
                 begin
                 $GET WORKS_ON;
                 $FIND OWNER WITHIN E_WORKSON; $GET EMPLOYEE;
                 writeln ( EMPLOYEE.FNAME, EMPLOYEE.LNAME );
                 $FIND NEXT WORKS_ON WITHIN P_WORKSON USING HOURS
                 end
       end;
```

In EX5 the qualification USING HOURS in FIND FIRST and FIND NEXT specifies that only the WORKS_ON records in the current set instance of P_WORKSON whose HOURS field value matches the value in WORKS_ON.HOURS of the UWA, which is set to '40.0' in the program, are found. Notice that the USING clause with FIND NEXT is used to find the *next member record within the same set occurrence*; when we process records of a record type *regardless of the sets they belong to*, we use FIND DUPLICATE rather than FIND NEXT.

If the condition that selects specific member records of a set instance involves comparison operators other than equality, such as less than or greater than, we must retrieve each member record and check whether or not it satisfies the condition in the host program itself. For example, to retrieve the names of all projects on which John Smith works more than '5.0' hours per week, we can modify EX4 into EX6.

```
EX6:   EMPLOYEE.FNAME := 'John'; EMPLOYEE.LNAME := 'Smith';
       $FIND ANY EMPLOYEE USING FNAME, LNAME;
       if DB_STATUS = 0 then
            begin
            $FIND FIRST WORKS_ON WITHIN E_WORKSON;
            while DB_STATUS = 0 do
                 begin
                 $GET WORKS_ON;
                 if convert_to_real(WORKS_ON.HOURS) > 5 then
                      begin
                      $FIND OWNER WITHIN P_WORKSON;
                      $GET PROJECT;
                      writeln ( PROJECT.NAME )
                      end;
                 $FIND NEXT WORKS_ON WITHIN E_WORKSON
                 end
       end;
```

In EX6 we assume that a PASCAL function convert_to_real, which converts the string value of the HOURS field into a real number, has been declared elsewhere.

We can have numerous embedded loops in the same program segment to process several sets, as illustrated by the next example, which also illustrates the use of a SYSTEM-owned set. The query, shown in EX7, is to retrieve the following information: For each department, print the department name and its manager's name; and for each employee who works in that department, print the employee name and the list of project names that the employee works on.

```
EX7:   $FIND FIRST DEPARTMENT WITHIN ALL_DEPTS;
       while DB_STATUS = 0 do
           begin
           $GET DEPARTMENT;
           writeln (DEPARTMENT.NAME); (* department name *)
           (* locate employee who manages the department *)
           $FIND OWNER WITHIN MANAGES;
           if DB_STATUS = 0 then
               begin
               $GET EMPLOYEE; writeln (EMPLOYEE.FNAME,
               EMPLOYEE.LNAME) (* manager name *)
               end;
           (* locate employees working for the department *)
           $FIND FIRST EMPLOYEE WITHIN WORKS_FOR;
           while DB_STATUS = 0 do
               begin
               $GET EMPLOYEE; writeln (EMPLOYEE.LNAME,
               EMPLOYEE.FNAME); (* employee name *)
               (* locate the projects that the employee works on *)
               $FIND FIRST WORKS_ON WITHIN E_WORKSON;
               while DB_STATUS = 0 do
                   begin
                   $FIND OWNER WITHIN P_WORKSON;
                   $GET PROJECT; writeln ( PROJECT.NAME );
                   (* project name *)
                   $FIND NEXT WORKS_ON WITHIN E_WORKSON
                   end;
               $FIND NEXT EMPLOYEE WITHIN WORKS_FOR
               end;
           $FIND NEXT DEPARTMENT WITHIN ALL_DEPTS
           end;
```

Using the Host Programming Language Facilities

Because the network DML is a record-at-a-time language, we need to use the facilities of the host programming language any time a query requires a set of records. We also need to use the host programming language to calculate functions on sets of records, such as

COUNTs or AVERAGEs, which must be explicitly implemented by the programmer. This compares with the easy specification of such functions in high-level languages such as SQL (Chapter 7) and QUEL (Chapter 9).

A final example illustrates how we can calculate functions such as COUNT and AVERAGE. Suppose we want to calculate the number of employees who are supervisors in each department and their average salary; this is shown in EX8. We assume that a PASCAL function convert_to_real, which converts the string value of the SALARY field into a real number, has been declared elsewhere. We must also have program variables total_sal:real and no_of_supervisors:integer declared elsewhere to accumulate the total salary and number of supervisors in each department. In EX8, notice how we test if an employee is a supervisor by determining whether an EMPLOYEE record participates as owner in some instance of the IS_A_SUPERVISOR set.

```
EX8:   $FIND FIRST DEPARTMENT WITHIN ALL_DEPTS;
       while DB_STATUS = 0 do
           begin
           $GET DEPARTMENT;
           write (DEPARTMENT.NAME); (* department name *)
           total_sal:= 0; no_of_supervisors:= 0;
           $FIND FIRST EMPLOYEE WITHIN WORKS_FOR;
           while DB_STATUS = 0 do
               begin
               $GET EMPLOYEE;
               $FIND FIRST SUPERVISOR WITHIN IS_A_SUPERVISOR;
               (* employee is a supervisor if it owns a SUPERVISOR record via
               IS_A_SUPERVISOR *)
               if DB_STATUS = 0 then  (* test if employee is a supervisor *)
                   begin
                   total_sal:= total_sal + convert_to_real (EMPLOYEE.SALARY);
                   no_of_supervisors:= no_of_supervisors + 1
                   end;
               $FIND NEXT EMPLOYEE WITHIN WORKS_FOR;
               end;
           writeln('number of supervisors =', no_of_supervisors);
           writeln('average salary of supervisors =', total_sal/no_of_supervisors);
           writeln( );
           $FIND NEXT DEPARTMENT WITHIN ALL_DEPTS
           end;
```

11.2.5   DML *Commands for Updating the Database*

The DML commands for updating a network database are summarized in Table 11.2. We will first discuss the commands for updating records, namely the STORE, ERASE, and MODIFY commands. These are used to insert a new record, delete a record, and modify some fields of a record, respectively. Following this, we will illustrate the commands that modify set instances, which are the CONNECT, DISCONNECT, and RECONNECT commands.

The STORE Command

The STORE command is used to insert a new record. Before issuing a STORE, we must first set up the UWA variable of the corresponding record type so that its field values contain the field values of the new record. For example, to insert a new EMPLOYEE record for John F. Smith, we can use EX9.

```
EX9:   EMPLOYEE.FNAME := 'John';
       EMPLOYEE.LNAME := 'Smith';
       EMPLOYEE.MINIT := 'F';
       EMPLOYEE.SSN := '567342739';
       EMPLOYEE.ADDRESS := '40 Walcott Road, Minneapolis, Minnesota 55433';
       EMPLOYEE.BIRTHDATE := '10-JAN-55';
       EMPLOYEE.SEX := 'M';
       EMPLOYEE.SALARY := '25000.00';
       EMPLOYEE.DEPTNAME := ' ';
       $STORE EMPLOYEE;
```

The result of the STORE command is to insert the current contents of the UWA record of the specified record type into the database. In addition, if the record type is an AUTOMATIC member of a set type, then the record is automatically inserted into a set instance, which is determined by the SET SELECTION declaration. The newly inserted record also becomes the CRU and the current record for its record type. It also becomes the current of set for any set type that has the record type as owner or member.

Effects of SET SELECTION Options on the STORE Command

In the next few examples we discuss the effect of various AUTOMATIC SET SELECTION options on the STORE command. Recall that in a set type with AUTOMATIC insertion option, a new record of the member record type must be connected to a set instance at the same time it is inserted into the database by a STORE command. We give three examples to illustrate three of the SET SELECTION options: BY STRUCTURAL, BY APPLICATION, and BY VALUE.

First, we illustrate the **BY STRUCTURAL** option. Recall from Section 11.2.2 that this option has the format:

```
SET SELECTION IS STRUCTURAL
<data item> IN <member record type> = <data item> IN <owner record type>
```

in the network DDL. This allows the DBMS to determine *by itself* the set occurrence in which a newly inserted member record is to be connected, and it is illustrated by the declarations for the P_WORKSON and E_WORKSON set types in Figure 11.14b. For example, to relate the EMPLOYEE record with SSN = '567342739', just inserted in EX9, as a 40-hour-per-week worker on the project whose project number is 55, we must create and store a new linking WORKS_ON record with the appropriate ESSN and PNUMBER values, as shown in EX10. The STORE WORKS_ON command in EX10 will automatically connect the newly inserted WORKS_ON record into the E_WORKSON set instance owned by the EMPLOYEE record with SSN = '567342739' and into the P_WORKSON set instance owned by the PRO-

JECT record with NUMBER = 55 by automatically locating these owner records and their set instances. The newly inserted record also becomes the current of set for both these set types. If either of the owner records did not exist in the database, the STORE command would generate an error and the new WORKS_ON record would not be inserted into the database.

```
EX10:   WORKS_ON.ESSN := '567342739';
        WORKS_ON.PNUMBER := 55;
        WORKS_ON.HOURS := '40.0';
        $STORE WORKS_ON;
```

Next, we illustrate the **BY APPLICATION** option. Recall from Section 11.2.2 that this option has the format:

SET SELECTION IS BY APPLICATION

in the network DDL, which specifies that the application program is responsible for selecting the proper set occurrence *before* storing the new member record. This is illustrated by the declaration of the CONTROLS set type in Figure 11.14b. To insert a new PROJECT record for a project that is controlled by the Research department, we must explicitly make the Research DEPARTMENT record the current of set for CONTROLS *before* issuing the STORE PROJECT command, as shown in EX11. The STORE command then automatically connects the new record to the current set instance of CONTROLS owned by the Research DEPARTMENT record.

```
EX11:   PROJECT.NAME := 'XYZ';
        PROJECT.NUMBER := 15;
        PROJECT.LOCATION := 'Minneapolis';
        (* create new PROJECT record in UWA *)
        DEPARTMENT.NAME:= 'Research';
        $FIND ANY DEPARTMENT USING NAME;
        (* set the desired current of set for CONTROLS *)
        $STORE PROJECT;
```

Finally, we illustrate the **BY VALUE** option. Recall from Section 11.2.2 that this option has the format:

SET SELECTION IS BY VALUE OF <data item> IN <owner record type>

in the network DDL, and it is illustrated by the declaration of the IS_A_SUPERVISOR set type in Figure 11.14b. In this case we just set the value of the field specified in the SET SELECTION IS BY VALUE declaration—SSN of EMPLOYEE for the IS_A_SUPERVISOR set—before issuing the STORE command. This should be a key field of the owner record type, and the DBMS uses that value to find the (unique) owner of the new record. For example, to insert a new SUPERVISOR record to correspond to the employee with SSN = '567342739', we use EX12. By providing the value of EMPLOYEE.SSN in the program, the DBMS uses this to select the appropriate owner EMPLOYEE record and automatically connects the new SUPERVISOR record to its set instance.

Notice that we could have declared SET SELECTION BY STRUCTURAL for the IS_A_ SUPERVISOR set type; in fact, this would have been more appropriate in Figure 11.14b.

However, if the SUPERVISOR_SSN field was not included in the SUPERVISOR record type, then the BY STRUCTURAL option cannot be used and BY VALUE would be the most appropriate choice for the IS_A_SUPERVISOR set type. In general, when a UNIQUE field value from the owner record type is duplicated in the member record type, then it is most appropriate to specify SET SELECTION BY STRUCTURAL for automatic sets; otherwise, SET SELECTION must be either BY VALUE OR BY APPLICATION.

> EX12: SUPERVISOR.SUPERVISOR_SSN := '567342739';
> (* create new SUPERVISION record in UWA *)
> EMPLOYEE.SSN := '567342739';
> (* set VALUE of SSN for automatic set selection *)
> $STORE SUPERVISOR;

The ERASE and ERASE ALL Commands

Next, we discuss deletion of records. To delete a record from the database, we first make that record the CRU and then issue the **ERASE** command. For example, to delete the EMPLOYEE record inserted in EX9, we can use EX13.

> EX13: EMPLOYEE.SSN := '567342793';
> $FIND ANY EMPLOYEE USING SSN;
> if DB_STATUS = 0 then $ERASE EMPLOYEE;

One problem to consider with deletion is the effect an ERASE command has on any member records that are *owned by the record being deleted*, which is determined by the set retention option. For example, the effect of the ERASE command in EX13 depends on the set retention for each set type that has EMPLOYEE as an owner. If retention is OPTIONAL, then member records are kept in the database but are disconnected from the owner record before it is deleted. If retention is FIXED, then all member records are deleted along with their owner. Finally, if retention is MANDATORY and some member records are owned by the record to be deleted, then the ERASE command is rejected and an error message is generated. We cannot delete the owner because the member records will then have no owner, which is not permitted for a MANDATORY set. These rules are recursively applied to any additional records owned by other records whose deletion is automatically triggered by an ERASE command. Deletion can thus propagate through the database and can be very damaging if it is not used carefully.

In EX13, when we ERASE the EMPLOYEE record, all WORKS_ON and DEPENDENT records owned by it are automatically deleted because the E_WORKSON and DEPENDENTS_OF sets have a FIXED retention. However, if that EMPLOYEE record owns a SUPERVISOR record via the IS_A_SUPERVISOR set or a DEPARTMENT record via the MANAGES set, then the deletion is rejected by the system because the IS_A_SUPERVISOR and MANAGES sets have MANDATORY retention. We must first explicitly remove those member records from such MANDATORY sets before issuing the ERASE command on their owner record. If the EMPLOYEE record does not own any SUPERVISOR or DEPARTMENT records via IS_A_SUPERVISOR or MANAGES, then the EMPLOYEE record is deleted.

A variation of the ERASE command, **ERASE ALL**, allows the programmer to remove a record and all records owned by it directly or indirectly. This means that *all* member records owned by the record are deleted. In addition, member records owned by any of the deleted records are also deleted down to any number of repetitions. For example, EX14 will delete the Research DEPARTMENT record, as well as all EMPLOYEE records that are owned by that DEPARTMENT via WORKS_FOR and any PROJECT records that are owned by that DEPARTMENT via CONTROLS. In addition, any DEPENDENT, SUPERVISOR, DEPARTMENT, or WORKS_ON records owned by the deleted EMPLOYEE or PROJECT records are also deleted automatically.

```
EX14:   DEPARTMENT.NAME := 'Research';
        $FIND ANY DEPARTMENT USING NAME;
        if DB_STATUS = 0 then $ERASE ALL DEPARTMENT;
```

We can also use a looping program to delete a number of records. For example, suppose we want to delete all employees who work for the Research department, but not the DEPARTMENT record itself; we can use EX15. Notice that the CRU and the current of record type for the record just deleted point to an *"empty" position* where the record that was deleted used to be. Hence, subsequent operations that depend on order will continue from that position onward. For sets, the current of set for any set instance owned by the deleted record becomes undefined, whereas the current of set for any set instance of which the deleted record was a member points to an "empty" position where the record used to be. Hence, FIND NEXT and FIND PRIOR commands on the set instance proceed from the position of the deleted record in the set. That is why the FIND NEXT statement in EX15 works correctly.

```
EX15:   DEPARTMENT.NAME := 'Research';
        $FIND ANY DEPARTMENT USING NAME;
        if DB_STATUS = 0 then
            begin
            $FIND FIRST EMPLOYEE WITHIN WORKS_FOR;
            while DB_STATUS = 0 do
                begin
                $ERASE EMPLOYEE;
                $FIND NEXT EMPLOYEE WITHIN WORKS_FOR
                end
        end;
```

The MODIFY Command

The final command to update records is the MODIFY command, which changes some field values of a record. We should take the following sequence of steps to modify field values of a record:

- Make the record to be modified the CRU.
- Retrieve the record into the corresponding UWA variable.
- Modify the desired fields in the UWA variable.
- Issue the MODIFY command.

For example, to give all employees in the Research department a 10% raise, we can use EX16. We assume the existence of two PASCAL functions convert_to_real and convert_to_string that have been declared elsewhere; the first converts a string value of the SALARY field to a real number, and the second formats a real value to the SALARY field format.

```
EX16:   DEPARTMENT.NAME := 'Research';
        $FIND ANY DEPARTMENT USING NAME;
        if DB_STATUS = 0 then
            begin
            $FIND FIRST EMPLOYEE WITHIN WORKS_FOR;
            while DB_STATUS = 0 do
                begin
                $GET EMPLOYEE;
                EMPLOYEE.SALARY := convert_to_string(convert_to_real
                                        (EMPLOYEE.SALARY)*1.1);
                $MODIFY EMPLOYEE;
                $FIND NEXT EMPLOYEE WITHIN WORKS_FOR
                end
        end;
```

Commands for Updating Set Instances

We now consider the three set update operations, CONNECT, DISCONNECT, and RECONNECT, which are used to insert and remove member records in set instances. The CONNECT command inserts a member record into a set instance. The member record should be the current of run unit and is connected to the set instance that is the current of set for the set type. For example, to connect the EMPLOYEE record with SSN = '567342793' to the WORKS_FOR set owned by the Research DEPARTMENT record, we can use EX17.

```
EX17:   DEPARTMENT.NAME := 'Research';
        $FIND ANY DEPARTMENT USING NAME;
        if DB_STATUS = 0 then
            begin
            EMPLOYEE.SSN := '567342793';
            $FIND ANY EMPLOYEE USING SSN;
            if DB_STATUS = 0 then
                $CONNECT EMPLOYEE TO WORKS_FOR;
        end;
```

In EX17 we first locate the Research DEPARTMENT record so that the current of set of the WORKS_FOR set type becomes the set instance owned by the Research DEPARTMENT record. Then we locate the required EMPLOYEE record so that it becomes the CRU. Finally, we issue a CONNECT command. Notice that the EMPLOYEE record to be connected should *not be a member* of any set instance of WORKS_FOR before the CONNECT command is issued. We must use the RECONNECT command for the latter case. The CONNECT command can be used only with MANUAL sets or with AUTOMATIC OPTIONAL sets. With other AUTOMATIC sets, the system automatically connects a member record to a set instance, governed by the SET SELECTION option specified, as soon as the record is inserted into the database.

The DISCONNECT command is used to remove a member record from a set instance without connecting it to another set instance. Hence, it can be used only with OPTIONAL sets. We make the record to be disconnected the CRU before issuing the DISCONNECT command. For example, to remove the EMPLOYEE record whose SSN = '836483873' from the SUPERVISEES set instance of which it is a member, we use EX18.

EX18:   EMPLOYEE.SSN := '836483873';
         $FIND ANY EMPLOYEE USING SSN;
         if DB_STATUS = 0
             then $DISCONNECT EMPLOYEE FROM SUPERVISEES;

Finally, we discuss the RECONNECT command. This can be used with both OPTIONAL and MANDATORY sets but not with FIXED sets. The RECONNECT command moves a member record from one set instance to another set instance of the same set type. It cannot be used with FIXED sets because a member record cannot be moved from one set instance to another under the FIXED constraint. Before we issue the RECONNECT command, the set instance to which the member record is to be connected should be the current of set for the set type, and the member record to be connected should be the CRU. To do this, we need to use an additional phrase with the FIND command—called the RETAINING CUR-RENCY phrase—which we now discuss.

The RETAINING CURRENCY Phrase

We discuss the RECONNECT command and the **RETAINING CURRENCY** phrase in the context of EX19 below, which removes the current manager of the Research department and assigns the employee whose SSN = '836483873' to become its new manager. Notice that MANAGES is declared to be AUTOMATIC MANDATORY, so another EMPLOYEE record currently owns the Research DEPARTMENT record in the MANAGES set type. Before issuing the RE-CONNECT command, we should make the EMPLOYEE record whose SSN = '836483873' the current of set for the MANAGES set type. We should also make the Research DEPARTMENT record into the CRU, as this is the record to be RECONNECTED to its new manager. However, the Research DEPARTMENT record is already a member of a different MANAGES set instance, so when it is made the CRU it will also become the current of set for the MANAGES set type.

EX19:   EMPLOYEE.SSN := '836483873';
         $FIND ANY EMPLOYEE USING SSN; (* set current of set for MANAGES *)
         if DB_STATUS = 0 then
             begin
             DEPARTMENT.NAME = 'Research';
             $FIND ANY DEPARTMENT USING NAME RETAINING MANAGES
             CURRENCY;
             (* set CRU *without changing* the current of set for MANAGES *)
             if DB_STATUS = 0 then $RECONNECT DEPARTMENT WITHIN
             MANAGES
             end;

To make the record become the CRU *without changing the current of set*, we use the RETAINING CURRENCY phrase appended to the FIND command. In EX19 we use the

RETAINING MANAGES CURRENCY phrase appended to the FIND command. This changes the CRU to the Research DEPARTMENT record but leaves the current of set of MANAGES unchanged; it remains the set instance owned by the EMPLOYEE record whose SSN is 836483873. When we issue the RECONNECT command, the Research DEPARTMENT record—the CRU—is removed from the MANAGES set in which it used to be a member and connected to the MANAGES set owned by the EMPLOYEE record whose SSN = '836483873', which is the current of MANAGES set.

Notice that the record to be moved should be a member of a set instance of the same set type before the RECONNECT command is issued; otherwise, we should use the CONNECT command. A RECONNECT can be substituted by a DISCONNECT and a CONNECT for OPTIONAL sets. However, for MANDATORY sets we must use the RECONNECT command if we want to move a member record from one set instance to another, because it must remain connected to an owner at all times.

11.3 Summary

In this chapter we discussed the network model, which represents data using the building blocks of record types and set types. Each set type defines a 1:N relationship between an owner record type and a member record type. A record type can participate as owner or member in any number of set types. This is the main distinction between set types of the network model and the parent-child relationships of the hierarchical model discussed in Chapter 10. In the hierarchical model, parent-child relationships must obey a strictly hierarchical pattern. The inclusion of virtual parent-child relationships in the hierarchical model makes it closer to the network model. However, because of the restrictions on virtual parent-child relationships in most hierarchical DBMSs, the network model has better modeling capability than the hierarchical model. The modeling capability of the network model may also be considered to be superior to that of the relational model in that it *explicitly* models relationships. The JOIN operations in the relational model actually become visible and materialized as set types in the network model.

We then discussed the types of constraints on set membership that can be specified on a network schema. These are classified into insertion options (MANUAL or AUTOMATIC), retention options (OPTIONAL, MANDATORY, or FIXED), and ordering options.

The circular linked list (or ring) representation of implementing set instances was then discussed. We also discussed other implementation options for set instances that can be used to improve the performance of the circular linked list, such as double linking and owner pointers. Other techniques that can be used to implement sets instead of linked lists, such as contiguous storage or pointer arrays, were also briefly discussed.

We then discussed three special types of sets. SYSTEM-owned or singular sets are used to define entry points to the database. Multimember sets are used for the case when member records can be from more than one record type. Recursive sets are sets that have the same record type participating both as owner and member. Because of implementation difficulties, recursive sets were prohibited in the original CODASYL network model, and it is now customary to represent them by using an additional linking record type and two set types.

M:N relationships, or relationships in which more than two record types participate, can also be represented using a linking record type. In the case of an M:N relationship with two participating record types, two set types and a linking record type are used. In the case of an n-ary relationship in which n record types participate, one linking record type and n set types are needed. One-to-one relationships are not represented explicitly; they can be represented as a set type, but the application programs must make sure that each set instance has at most one member record at all times.

We presented a data definition language (DDL) for the network model. We saw how record types and set types are defined and discussed the various SET SELECTION options that are used with AUTOMATIC sets. These options specify how the DBMS identifies the appropriate set instance of an AUTOMATIC set type to connect a new member record into when the record is stored in the database.

Finally, we presented the commands of a record-at-a-time data manipulation language (DML) for the network model. We saw how to write programs with embedded DML commands to retrieve information from a network database and to update the database. The FIND command is used to "navigate" through the database, setting various currency indicators, whereas the GET command is used to retrieve the CRU into the corresponding UWA program variable. Commands for inserting, deleting, and modifying records and for modifying set instances were also discussed. We will discuss the IDMS commercial network DBMS and its relational upgrade IDMS/R in Chapter 23.

Review Questions

11.1. Discuss the various types of fields (data items) that can be defined for record types in the network model.

11.2. Define the following terms: set type, owner record type, member record type, set instance (set occurrence), AUTOMATIC set type, MANUAL set type, MANDATORY set type, OPTIONAL set type, FIXED set type.

11.3. How are the set instances of a set type identified?

11.4. Discuss the various constraints on set membership and the cases in which each constraint should be used.

11.5. In the circular linked list (ring) representation of set instances, how does the DBMS distinguish between member records and the owner record of a set instance?

11.6. Discuss the various methods of implementing set instances. For each method, discuss which types of set processing FIND commands can be implemented efficiently and which cannot.

11.7. What are SYSTEM-owned (singular) set types used for?

11.8. What are multimember set types used for?

11.9. What are recursive set types? Why are they not allowed in the original CODASYL network model? How can they be implemented using a linking record type?

11.10. Show how each of the following types of relationships is represented in the network model: (a) M:N relationships, (b) n-ary relationships with n > 2, (c) 1:1 relationships.

11.11. Discuss the following concepts and what each is used for when writing a network DML database program: (a) the user work area (UWA), (b) currency indicators, (c) database status indicator.

11.12. Discuss the different types of currency indicators and how each type of navigational FIND command affects each of the currency indicators.

11.13. Describe the various SET SELECTION options for AUTOMATIC set types, and specify the circumstances under which each SET SELECTION option should be chosen.

11.14. State what each of the following clauses in the network DDL specifies: (a) DUPLICATES ARE NOT ALLOWED, (b) ORDER IS, (c) KEY IS, (d) CHECK.

11.15. For what purpose is the RETAINING CURRENCY clause used with the FIND command in the network DDL?

11.16. How does the ERASE ALL command differ from the ERASE command?

11.17. Discuss the CONNECT, DISCONNECT, and RECONNECT commands, and specify the types of set constraints under which each can be used.

Exercises

11.18. Specify the queries of Exercise 6.19 using network DML commands embedded in PASCAL on the network database schema of Figure 11.10. Use the PASCAL program variables declared in Figure 11.11, and declare any additional variables you may need.

11.19. Modify the program segment in EX3 so that it retrieves for *each* department the department name and the names of all employees who work in that department ordered alphabetically.

11.20. Modify the program segment in EX7 so that the following conditions are met, one at a time:

   a. Only departments with greater than 10 employees are listed.

   b. Only employees who work more than 20 total hours are listed.

   c. Only employees with dependents are listed.

11.21. Consider the network database schema shown in Figure 11.15, which corresponds to the relational schema of Figure 2.1. Write appropriate network DDL statements to define the record types and set types of the schema. Choose appropriate set constraints for each set type and justify your choices.

11.22. Write PASCAL program segments with embedded network DML commands to specify the queries of Exercise 7.16 on the schema of Figure 11.15.

11.23. Write PASCAL program segments with embedded network DML commands to do the updates and tasks of Exercises 7.17 and 7.18 on the network database schema of Figure 11.15. Specify any program variables that you need.

11.24. During the processing of the query "find all courses offered by the COSC department, and for each course list its name, its sections, and its prerequisites" on the schema of Figure 11.15, the following steps are performed by the DBMS: (a) Find the DEPARTMENT record for COSC, (b) find a COURSE record for COSC541 as a mem-

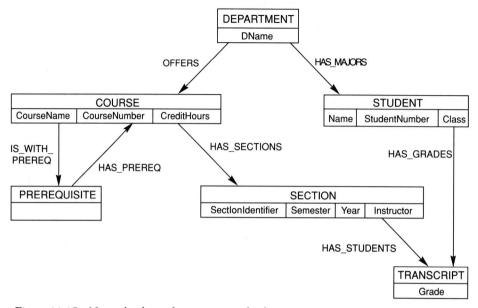

Figure 11.15   Network schema for a university database

ber of OFFERS, (c) find a SECTION record for section S32491 as a member of HAS_SECTIONS, (d) find a PREREQUISITE record occurrence, say P1, as a member of IS_WITH_PREREQ, (e) find a member course record of HAS_PREREQ, say the course MATH143. Show the currency indicators of set types, record types, and the CRU after each of the above events using the notation in Figure 11.13. Assume all currency indicators were nil originally. What happens to the currency of the COURSE record type after step e? Suppose we were to do FIND NEXT COURSE WITHIN OFFERS after step e; what problem will arise and how can we solve it? Hint: Consider using the RETAINING CURRENCY phrase in some of the commands.

11.25. Write procedures in pseudocode (PASCAL style) that may be part of the DBMS software, and outline the action taken by the following DML commands:

  a. Process the STORE <record type> command. This should check for set type definitions in the DBMS catalog to determine which sets the record type participates in as owner or member, and take appropriate action.

  b. Process the ERASE <record type> and ERASE ALL <record type> commands.

11.26. Choose some database application that you are familiar with or interested in.

  a. Design a network database schema for your database application.

  b. Declare your record types and set types using the network DDL.

  c. Specify a number of queries and updates that are needed by your database application, and write a PASCAL program segment with embedded network DML commands for each of your queries.

  d. Implement your database if you have a network DBMS system available.

Selected Bibliography

Early work on the network data model was done by Charles Bachman during the development of the first commercial DBMS, IDS (Bachman and Williams, 1964) at General Electric and later at Honeywell. Bachman also introduced the earliest diagrammatic technique for representing relationships in database schemas, called data structure diagrams (Bachman 1969) or Bachman diagrams. Bachman won the 1973 Turing Award, ACM's highest honor, for his work, and his Turing Award lecture (Bachman, 1973) presents the view of the database as a primary resource and the programmer as a "navigator" through the database. In a 1974 debate between proponents and opponents of the relational approach, he represented the latter (Bachman, 1974).

Other work on the network model was performed by George Dodd (Dodd 1966) at General Motors Research. Dodd (1969) gives an early survey of database management techniques.

The DBTG (Data Base Task Group) of CODASYL (Conference on Data Systems Languages) was set up to propose DBMS standards. The DBTG 1971 report (DBTG 1971) contains schema and subschema DDLs and a DML for use with COBOL. A revised report (CODASYL 1978) was made in 1978, and another draft revision was made in 1981 that has not yet been officially adopted. The X3H2 committee of ANSI (the American National Standards Institute) proposed a standard network language called NDL. It has not been formally approved at the time of writing.

The design of network databases is discussed by Dahl and Bubenko (1982), Whang et al. (1982), Schenk (1974), Gerritsen (1975), and Bubenko et al. (1976). Irani et al. (1979) discuss optimization techniques for designing network schemas from user requirements. Bradley (1978) proposes a high-level query language for the network model.

Many commercial DBMSs based on the network model are discussed in the bibliography of Chapter 23. Network database management is surveyed by Taylor and Frank (1976). Extensive treatments of the network model are offered in the books by Cardenas (1985), Kroenke and Dolan (1988), and Olle (1978).

Comparison of
Data Models

In Chapters 6 to 11 we presented the three main "implementation" data models—relational, network, and hierarchical—that are used extensively in implementing DBMSs. In Chapter 3 we presented the Entity-Relationship (ER) model, which is used extensively in the database design process for conceptual schema design. An important question that arises is how the various models are related to one another. We also need to discuss the advantages and disadvantages of each model and the factors that make one model more suitable than another for a given application. In this chapter we discuss the similarities and differences among the four data models. We show how each logical concept from the ER model can be represented in each of the three popular implementation data models. We also discuss the main types of storage structures, data manipulation languages, and integrity constraints provided by DBMSs based on each of the three models. Finally, we discuss the advantages and disadvantages of each model and of the DBMSs based on these models.

12.1 Comparison of Data Representation Concepts

We first compare how each of the three implementation data models represents the logical data modeling concepts of the ER model. This process is called **mapping** the ER model to each of the other models. Recall that the main concepts of the ER model are entity types (regular, weak), relationship types of different degrees (binary, n-ary), attributes (simple, multivalued, composite), and constraints (keys, relationship cardinality ratios, etc.). Figure 12.1 shows the ER COMPANY schema, which is similar to Figure 3.13. This schema has three regular entity types (EMPLOYEE, DEPARTMENT, PROJECT) and one weak entity type (DEPENDENT). It also has three 1:N relationship types (WORKS_FOR, SUPERVI-

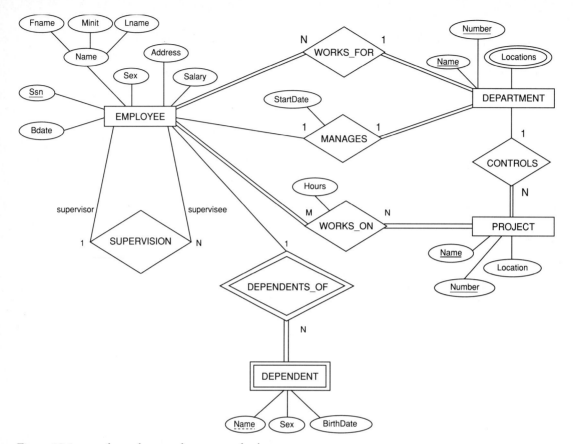

Figure 12.1   ER schema for part of a company database

SION, DEPENDENTS_OF), one 1:1 relationship type (MANAGES), and one M:N relationship type (WORKS_ON). Key attributes are underlined and multivalued attributes, such as the Locations attribute of DEPARTMENT, are shown in double ovals. The situation represented by the ER schema in Figure 12.1 can be summarized in English as follows:

- Each employee works for exactly one department and can work on several projects. An employee may have one direct supervisor, several direct supervisees, and zero or more dependents. An employee may manage at most one department. Employees are described by their SSN, name, address, birthdate, salary, and sex. No two employees have the same SSN value.

- A department is described by its name, number, and locations, and no two departments can have the same name or number. A department is related to exactly one employee who manages the department and to a number of employees who work for the department. A department can also be related to a number of projects that are under its control.

- A project is controlled by exactly one department and has several employees working on the project. A project is described by its name, number, and location. No two projects can have the same name or number.

• Every dependent is related to one employee.

We now show how this schema is typically mapped to each of the three implementation data models. Further discussion of data model mappings will be given in Chapter 15 when we discuss advanced modeling concepts.

12.1.1   *ER-to-Relational Mapping*

The relational schema shown in Figure 12.2 (similar to Figure 6.5) can be derived from the ER schema of Figure 12.1 by the following general mapping procedure. We illustrate each step using examples from the COMPANY schema.

STEP 1:   For each regular entity type E in the ER schema, we create a relation R that includes all the simple attributes of E. For a composite attribute we include only the simple component attributes. We choose one of the key attributes of E as primary key for R. If the chosen key of E is composite, then the set of simple attributes that form it will together form the primary key of R.

In our example we create the relations EMPLOYEE, DEPARTMENT, and PROJECT in Figure 12.2 to correspond to the regular entity types EMPLOYEE, DEPARTMENT, and PROJECT. However, the attributes marked by f.k. (foreign key) or * (relationship attributes) are

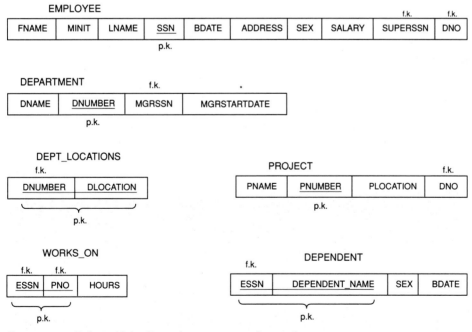

Figure 12.2   Relational database schema corresponding to the ER schema of Figure 12.1

not included yet; they will be added during subsequent steps. We choose SSN, DNUMBER, and PNUMBER as primary keys for the relations EMPLOYEE, DEPARTMENT, and PROJECT, respectively.

STEP 2:   For each weak entity type W in the ER schema with owner entity type E, we create a relation R and include all simple attributes (or simple components of composite attributes) of W as attributes of R. In addition, we include as foreign key attributes of R the primary key attribute(s) of the relation that corresponds to the owner entity type E; this takes care of the identifying relationship type of W. The primary key of R is the combination of the primary key of the owner and the partial key of the weak entity type W.

In our example we create the relation DEPENDENT in this step to correspond to the weak entity type DEPENDENT. We include the primary key of the EMPLOYEE relation— which corresponds to the owner entity type—as an attribute of DEPENDENT; we renamed it to ESSN although this is not necessary. The primary key of the DEPENDENT relation is the combination {ESSN, DEPENDENT_NAME} because DEPENDENT_NAME is the partial key of DEPENDENT.

STEP 3:   For each binary 1:1 relationship type R in the ER schema, we identify the relations S and T that correspond to the entity types participating in R. We choose one of the relations, S say, and include as foreign key in S the primary key of T. It is better to choose an entity type with total participation in R in the role of S. We include all the simple attributes (or simple components of a composite attribute) of the 1:1 relationship type R as attributes of S.

In our example we map the 1:1 relationship type MANAGES from Figure 12.1 by choosing the participating entity type DEPARTMENT to serve in the role of S because its participation in the MANAGES relationship type is total (every department has a manager). We include the primary key of the EMPLOYEE relation as foreign key in the DEPARTMENT relation and rename it MGRSSN. We also include the simple attribute StartDate of the MANAGES relationship type in the DEPARTMENT relation and rename it MGRSTARTDATE.

Notice that an alternative mapping of a 1:1 relationship type is possible by merging the two entity types and the relationship into a single relation. This is particularly appropriate when both participations are total and when the entity types do not participate in any other relationship types.

STEP 4:   For each regular (nonweak) binary 1:N relationship type R, we identify the relation S that represents the participating entity type at the *N-side* of the relationship type. We include as foreign key in S the primary key of the relation T that represents the other entity type participating in R; this is because each entity instance on the N-side is related to at most one entity instance on the 1-side of the relationship type. For example, in the 1:N relationship type WORKS_FOR, each employee is related to one department. We include any simple attributes (or simple components of composite attributes) of the 1:N relationship type as attributes of S.

In our example we now map the 1:N relationship types WORKS_FOR and SUPERVISION from Figure 12.1. For WORKS_FOR we include the primary key of the DEPARTMENT relation as foreign key in the EMPLOYEE relation and call it DNO. For SUPERVISION we include the primary key of the EMPLOYEE relation as foreign key in the EMPLOYEE relation itself (!) and call it SUPERSSN. The CONTROLS relationship is similarly mapped.

STEP 5: For each binary M:N relationship type R, we create a new relation S to represent R. We include as foreign key attributes in S the primary keys of the relations that represent the participating entity types; their combination will form the primary key of S. We also include any simple attributes of the M:N relationship type (or simple components of composite attributes) as attributes of S. Notice that we cannot represent an M:N relationship type by a single foreign key attribute in one of the participating relations—as we did for 1:1 or 1:N relationship types—because of the M:N cardinality ratio.

In our example we map the M:N relationship type WORKS_ON from Figure 12.1 by creating the relation WORKS_ON in Figure 12.2. We include the primary keys of the PROJECT and EMPLOYEE relations as foreign keys in WORKS_ON and rename them PNO and ESSN, respectively. We also include an attribute HOURS in WORKS_ON to represent the Hours attribute of the relationship type. The primary key of the WORKS_ON relation is the combination of the foreign key attributes {ESSN, PNO}.

Notice that we can always map 1:1 or 1:N relationships in a manner similar to M:N relationships. This alternative is particularly useful when few relationship instances exist in order to avoid null values in foreign keys.

STEP 6: For each multivalued attribute A, we create a new relation R that includes an attribute corresponding to A plus the primary key attribute K of the relation that represents the entity type or relationship type that has A as an attribute. The primary key of R is then the combination of A and K. If the multivalued attribute is composite, we include its simple components.

In our example we create a relation DEPT_LOCATIONS. The attribute DLOCATION represents the multivalued attribute Locations of DEPARTMENT, while DNUMBER—as foreign key—represents the primary key of the DEPARTMENT relation. The primary key of DEPT_LOCATIONS is the combination of {DNUMBER, DLOCATION}. A separate tuple will exist in DEPT_LOCATIONS for each location that a department has.

Figure 12.2 shows the relational database schema obtained by the above steps, and Figure 12.9a shows a sample database instance. Notice that we did not discuss the mapping of n-ary relationship types (n > 2) because none exist in Figure 12.1; these can be mapped in a similar way to M:N relationship types by including the following additional step in the mapping procedure.

STEP 7: For each n-ary relationship type R, n > 2, we create a new relation S to represent R. We include as foreign key attributes in S the primary keys of the relations that represent the participating entity types. We also include any simple attributes of the n-ary relationship type (or simple components of composite attributes) as attributes of S. The primary key of S is usually a combination of all the foreign keys that reference the relations representing the participating entity types. However, if the participation constraint (min, max) of one of the entity types E participating in R has max = 1, then the primary key of S can be the single foreign key attribute that references the relation E' corresponding to E; this is because in this case each entity e in E will participate in at

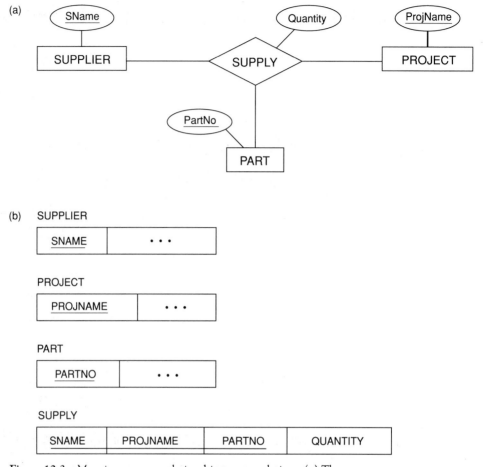

Figure 12.3   Mapping an n-ary relationship type to relations. (a) The n-ary relationship type SUPPLY with n=3. (b) Corresponding relational schema.

most one relationship instance of R and can hence uniquely identify that relationship instance.

For example, consider the relationship type SUPPLY of Figure 3.16a, repeated in Figure 12.3a; this can be mapped to the relation SUPPLY shown in Figure 12.3b whose primary key is the combination of foreign keys {SNAME, PARTNO, PROJNAME}.

The main point to note in a relational schema as compared to an ER schema is that relationship types are not represented explicitly; they are represented by having two attributes A and B, one a primary key and the other a foreign key—over the same domain—included in two relations S and T. Two tuples in S and T are related when they have the same value for A and B. By using the EQUIJOIN (or NATURALJOIN) operation over S.A and T.B, we can combine all pairs of related tuples from S and T and materialize the relationship. When a binary 1:1 or 1:N relationship type is involved, a single join operation is usually needed. For a binary M:N relationship type, two join operations are needed, whereas for n-ary relationship types, n joins will be needed.

For example, to form a relation that includes the employee name, project name, and hours that the employee works on each project, we need to connect each EMPLOYEE tuple to the related PROJECT tuples via the WORKS_ON relation of Figure 12.2. Hence, we must apply the EQUIJOIN operation to the EMPLOYEE and WORKS_ON relations with the join condition SSN = ESSN, then apply another EQUIJOIN operation to the relation resulting from the first equijoin and the PROJECT relation with join condition PNO = PNUMBER. In general, when multiple relationships need to be traversed, numerous join operations must be specified. A relational database user must always be aware of the foreign key attributes to use them correctly in combining related tuples from two or more relations.

Table 12.1 shows the pairs of attributes that are used in EQUIJOIN operations to materialize each relationship type in the COMPANY schema of Figure 12.1. For example, to materialize the 1:N relationship type WORKS_FOR, we apply EQUIJOIN to the relations EMPLOYEE and DEPARTMENT on the attributes DNO of EMPLOYEE and DNUMBER of DEPARTMENT. According to the database in Figure 12.9a, the employees Smith, Wong, Narayan, and English work for department 5 (Research); Zelaya, Wallace, and Jabbar work for department 4 (Administration); and Borg works for department 1 (Headquarters).

Another point to note in the relational schema is that we create a separate relation for *each* multivalued attribute. For a particular entity with a set of values for the multivalued attribute, the key attribute value of the entity is repeated once for each value of the multivalued attribute in a separate tuple. This is because the basic relational model does *not* allow multiple values (or a set of values) for an attribute in a single tuple. For example, because department 5 has three locations, three tuples exist in the DEPT_LOCATIONS

Table 12.1   Join Conditions for Materializing the Relationship Types of the COMPANY ER Schema

ER Relationship	Participating Relations	Join Condition
WORKS_FOR	EMPLOYEE, DEPARTMENT	EMPLOYEE.DNO = DEPARTMENT. DNUMBER
MANAGES	EMPLOYEE, DEPARTMENT	EMPLOYEE.SSN = DEPARTMENT.MGRSSN
SUPERVISION	EMPLOYEE(E), EMPLOYEE(S)	EMPLOYEE(E).SUPERSSN = EMPLOYEE(S).SSN
WORKS_ON	EMPLOYEE, WORKS_ON, PROJECT	EMPLOYEE.SSN = WORKS_ON.ESSN AND PROJECT.PNUMBER = WORKS_ON.PNO
CONTROLS	DEPARTMENT, PROJECT	DEPARTMENT.DNUMBER = PROJECT.DNO
DEPENDENTS_OF	EMPLOYEE, DEPENDENT	EMPLOYEE.SSN = DEPENDENT.ESSN

relation of Figure 12.9a; each tuple specifies one of the locations. Again, an equijoin is needed to relate the values of the multivalued attribute to the values of other attributes of an entity or a relationship instance, but we still get multiple tuples. The relational algebra does not have a NEST or COMPRESS operation that would produce from the DEPT_LOCATIONS relation of Figure 12.9a a set of tuples of the form { <1, Houston>, <4, Stafford>, <5, {Bellaire, Sugarland, Houston}>}. This is a serious drawback of the current normalized or "flat" version of the relational model. The relational languages SQL, QUEL, and QBE also have no features for handling such sets of values within tuples. On this score, the hierarchical and network models have better facilities than the relational model.

In our example we apply EQUIJOIN to DEPT_LOCATIONS and DEPARTMENT on the DNUMBER attribute to get the values of all locations along with other DEPARTMENT attributes. Notice that in the resulting relation the values of the other department attributes will be repeated in separate tuples for every location that a department has.

12.1.2   ER-to-Network Mapping

In a network schema we can explicitly represent a relationship type as a set type if it is 1:N; however, no explicit representation exists if it is 1:1 or M:N. One simple method of representing a 1:1 relationship type is to use a set type but to make each set instance have at most one member record. This ensures the 1:1 constraint because each set instance always has a single owner record and can be enforced by the programs that update the database because the DBMS itself does not enforce it. For M:N relationship types the standard representation is to use two set types and a linking record type as discussed in Chapter 11. The network model allows vector fields and repeating groups, which can be used directly to represent composite and multivalued attributes or even weak entity types, as we shall see.

The network schema shown in Figure 12.4 (similar to Figure 11.10) can be derived from the ER schema of Figure 12.1 by the following general mapping procedure. We illustrate each step using examples from the COMPANY schema.

STEP 1:   For each regular entity type E in the ER schema, we create a record type R in the network schema. All simple (or composite) attributes of E are included as simple (or composite) fields of R. All multivalued attributes of E are included as vector fields or repeating groups of R.

In our example we create the record types EMPLOYEE, DEPARTMENT, and PROJECT and include all their fields shown in Figure 12.4 except the fields marked by an f.k. (foreign key) or a * (relationship attribute). Notice that the LOCATIONS field of the DEPARTMENT record type is a vector field because it represents a multivalued attribute.

STEP 2:   For each weak entity type WE with the owner identifying entity type IE, we can either (a) create a record type W to represent WE, making W the member record type in a set type that relates W to the record type representing IE as owner, or (b) make a repeating group in the record type representing IE to represent the attributes of WE. If we choose the first alternative, we can repeat the key field of the record type representing IE in W.

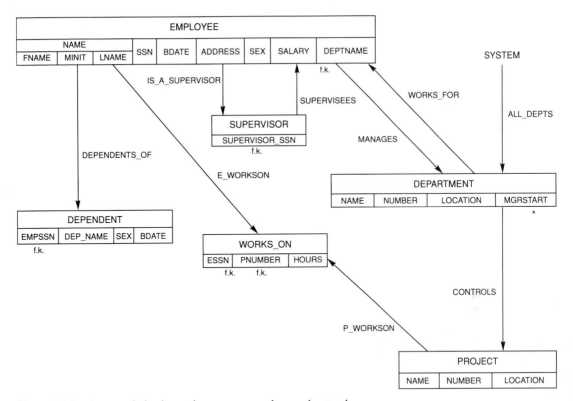

Figure 12.4 A network database schema corresponding to the ER schema of Figure 12.1

In Figure 12.4 we choose the first alternative; a record type DEPENDENT is created and made the member record type of the DEPENDENTS_OF set type, which is owned by EMPLOYEE. We duplicated the SSN key of EMPLOYEE in DEPENDENT and called it EMPSSN. The second alternative of representing DEPENDENTS as a repeating group of EMPLOYEE is shown in Figure 12.5.

STEP 3: For each nonrecursive binary 1:1 or 1:N relationship type R between entity types E1 and E2, we create a set type relating the record types S1 and S2 that represent E1 and E2, respectively. For a 1:1 relationship type we can choose arbitrarily one of S1 and S2 as owner and the other as member; however, it is preferable to choose as member a record type that represents a total participation in the relationship type. Another option for mapping a 1:1 binary relationship type R between E1 and E2 is to create a single record type S that merges E1, E2, and R and includes all their attributes; this is useful if both participations of E1 and E2 in R are total and E1 and E2 do not participate in numerous other relationship types.

For a 1:N relationship type the record type S1 that represents the entity type E1 at the 1-side of the relationship type is chosen as owner, and the record type S2 that repre-

EMPLOYEE							
NAME			SSN	. . .	DEPENDENTS		
FNAME	MINIT	LNAME			DEP_NAME	SEX	BDATE

Figure 12.5   Representing the weak entity type DEPENDENT as a
repeating group

sents the entity type E2 at the N-side of the relationship type is chosen as member. Any attributes of the relationship type R are included as fields in the *member* record type S2.

In general, we can arbitrarily duplicate one (or more) attributes of an owner record type of a set type—whether it represents a 1:1 or a 1:N relationship—in the member record type. If the duplicated attribute is a unique key attribute of the owner, it can be used to declare a structural constraint on the set type or to specify automatic owner selection on set membership as discussed in Chapter 11.

In our example we represent the 1:1 relationship type MANAGES from Figure 12.1 by the set type MANAGES and choose DEPARTMENT as member record type because of its total participation. The StartDate attribute of MANAGES becomes a field MGRSTART of the member record type DEPARTMENT. The two nonrecursive 1:N relationship types from Figure 12.1, WORKS_FOR and CONTROLS, are represented by the two set types WORKS_FOR and CONTROLS in Figure 12.4. For the WORKS_FOR set type we choose to repeat a unique key field NAME of the owner record type DEPARTMENT in the member record type EMPLOYEE and call it DEPTNAME. We choose not to repeat any key field for the CONTROLS set type. In general, a unique field from an owner record type should be repeated in the member record type if a typical GET operation on the member requires the retrieval of the owner field, as this would save an additional GET operation to retrieve the owner. Each GET is usually an additional I/O operation and is hence more expensive than FIND.

STEP 4:   For each binary M:N relationship type R between entity types E1 and E2, we create a linking record type X and make it the member record type in two set types. The set type owners are the record types S1 and S2 that represent E1 and E2. Any attributes of R are made fields of X. We may arbitrarily duplicate the unique (key) fields of the owner record types as fields of X.

In Figure 12.4 we create the linking record type WORKS_ON to represent the M:N relationship type WORKS_ON, and include HOURS as its field. Two set types E_WORKSON and P_WORKSON are created with WORKS_ON as member record type. We choose to duplicate the unique key fields SSN and NUMBER of the owner record types EMPLOYEE and PROJECT in WORKS_ON and call them ESSN and PNUMBER, respectively.

STEP 5:   For each recursive 1:1 or 1:N binary relationship type in which entity type E participates in both roles, create a "dummy" linking record type D and two set types to relate D to the record type X representing E. One or both of the set types will be constrained to have set instances with a single member record—one in the case of a 1:N relationship type and both in the case of a 1:1 relationship type.

In Figure 12.1 we have one recursive 1:N relationship type SUPERVISION. We create the dummy linking record type SUPERVISOR and the two set types IS_A_SUPERVISOR and

SUPERVISEES. The IS_A_SUPERVISOR set type is constrained to have single member records by the database update programs in its set instances. We can think of each dummy SUPERVISOR member record of the IS_A_SUPERVISOR set type as representing its owner EMPLOYEE record *in a supervisory role*. The SUPERVISEES set type is used to relate the "dummy" supervisor record to all EMPLOYEE records that represent the employees that are his or her direct supervisees.

The above steps consider only binary relationship types. Step 6 below shows how n-ary relationship types with n > 2 are mapped by creating a linking record type, similar to the case of an M:N relationship type.

STEP 6: For each n-ary relationship type R, n > 2, we create a linking record type X and make it the member record type in n set types. The owner of each set type is the record type that represents one of the entity types participating in the relationship type R. Any attributes of R are made fields of X. We may arbitrarily duplicate the unique (key) fields of the owner record types as fields of X.

For example, consider the relationship type SUPPLY of Figure 12.3a; this can be mapped to the record type SUPPLY and the three set types shown in Figure 12.6, where we choose not to duplicate any fields of the owners.

Notice that composite and multivalued attributes can be directly represented in the network model. In addition, we can represent weak entity types either as separate record types or as repeating groups within the owner; the latter is useful if the weak entity type does not participate in any additional relationship types. By duplicating a unique (key) field from the owner record type in the member record type, we can specify a structural constraint on set membership or automatic set selection; the DBMS will connect a member record to a set instance only if the same key field value is stored in both owner and member records. This amounts to getting the DBMS to enforce the constraint automatically. Although it is not required to duplicate a matching key field from the owner record type in the member record type, it is recommended to do so whenever possible. The cost is the extra storage space required for the duplicate field in each member record. The

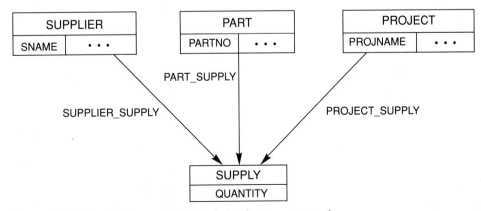

Figure 12.6 Mapping the n-ary (n=3) relationship type SUPPLY of Figure 12.3(a) in the network model

benefits are the automatic constraint enforcement and the availability of the duplicated field in the member record without having to retrieve its owner.

By duplicating the key fields of owner records in member records for all set types in a network schema, we will create record types that are practically identical to the relations of a relational database schema! The only differences will be for recursive relationship types, multivalued attributes, or weak entity types. For recursive 1:1 or 1:N relationship types, we are not required to create a dummy relation in the relational schema, as required in the network model. For weak entity types and multivalued attributes, we are not required to create additional record types in the network schema, as we are required to do in the relational model.

12.1.3   *ER-to-Hierarchical Mapping*

In the hierarchical model only 1:N relationship types can be represented in a particular hierarchy as parent-child relationship (PCR) types. In addition, a record type can have at most one (real) parent record type; hence, M:N relationship types are difficult to represent. The ways to represent M:N relationship types in a hierarchical database include the following:

- Represent the M:N relationship type as though it were a 1:N relationship type. In this case, record instances at the N-side are duplicated because each record may be related to several parents. This representation keeps all record types in a single hierarchy at the cost of duplicating record instances. The application programs that update the database must maintain the consistency of duplicate copies.
- Create more than one hierarchy and have virtual parent-child relationship (VPCR) types (logical pointers) from a record type that appears in one hierarchy to the root record type of another hierarchy. These pointers can be used to represent the M:N relationship type in a manner similar to the network model. Even then, a constraint, adopted from the IMS DBMS model, restricts each record type to having at most one virtual parent.

Because multiple options are available, there is no standard method for mapping an ER schema into a hierarchical schema. We will illustrate the two possibilities discussed above with two hierarchical schemas that can be used to represent the ER schema shown in Figure 12.1.

Figure 12.7a shows a single hierarchy that can be used to represent the ER schema of Figure 12.1. We choose DEPARTMENT as the root record type of the hierarchy. The 1:N relationship types WORKS_FOR and CONTROLS and the 1:1 relationship type MANAGES are represented at the first level of the hierarchy by the record types EMPLOYEE, PROJECT, and DEPT_MANAGER, respectively. However, to limit redundancy, we keep only some of the attributes of an employee who is a manager in the DEPTMANAGER record type. The EMPLOYEE records in a hierarchical tree owned by a particular DEPARTMENT record will represent the employees who work for that department. Similarly, the PROJECT records will represent the projects controlled by that department, and the DEPTMANAGER record will represent the employee who manages the department. An employee who is a manager is represented twice, once as an instance of EMPLOYEE and another as an instance of DEPTMANAGER. The application programs are responsible for maintaining these copies consistent.

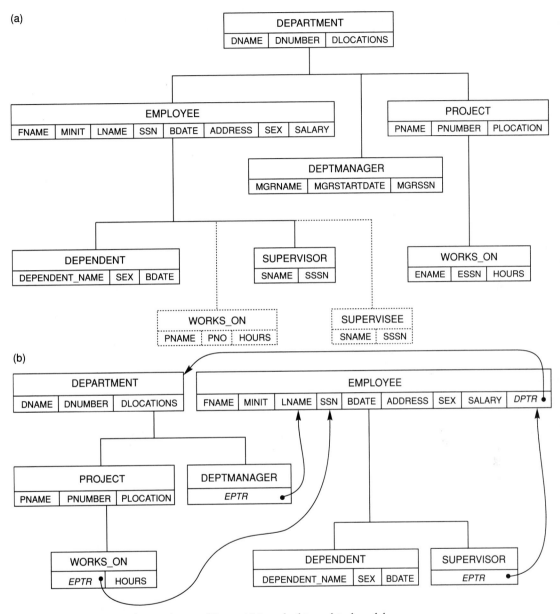

Figure 12.7 Mapping the ER schema of Figure 12.1 to the hierarchical model.
(a) A hierarchical database schema for the COMPANY database
with a single hierarchy. (b) Another hierarchical database
schema for the same database with two hierarchies and four VPCRs.

The 1:N relationship type DEPENDENTS_OF is represented by the record type DEPEN-
DENT as a subordinate of EMPLOYEE. The M:N relationship type WORKS_ON is represented
as a subordinate of PROJECT, but only an employee's ENAME and ESSN are included in
WORKS_ON along with the relationship attribute HOURS. An employee who works on sev-

eral different projects will be represented in as many WORKS_ON record instances. The rest of the information on employees is not replicated in WORKS_ON in order to limit redundancy. Notice that each WORKS_ON record represents one of the employees working on a particular project. Alternatively, we could have represented WORKS_ON as a subordinate record type of EMPLOYEE; in this case, each WORKS_ON record would represent one of the projects that an EMPLOYEE works on, and its fields would be PNAME, PNUMBER, and HOURS as shown by the dotted WORKS_ON box in Figure 12.7a. In the latter case, PROJECT information would be duplicated in multiple WORKS_ON records.

Finally, the SUPERVISION relationship type is represented as a subordinate of EMPLOYEE. We could choose to represent it in either the role of supervisor or that of supervisees. In Figure 12.7a each SUPERVISOR record represents the supervisor of the owner EMPLOYEE record in the hierarchy so the hierarchical relationship represents the supervisor role; each employee will have a single child record SUPERVISOR representing his or her direct supervisor. Alternatively, we could have represented the role of supervisees in the hierarchical relationship, so every EMPLOYEE record that represents a supervisory employee will be related to his or her direct supervisees as child records. This is shown in dotted lines in the box SUPERVISEE in Figure 12.7a. In either case, EMPLOYEE information is replicated in the SUPERVISOR or SUPERVISEE records so we include only a few of the attributes of EMPLOYEE.

There is excessive replication in Figure 12.7a. Information on employees is replicated in the record types EMPLOYEE, DEPTMANAGER, WORKS_ON, and SUPERVISOR because they all represent employees in various roles. We can somewhat limit the replication by representing the ER schema of Figure 12.1 using two or more hierarchies. In Figure 12.7b two hierarchies are used. The first hierarchy has DEPARTMENT as root record type and represents the relationship types CONTROLS, MANAGES, and WORKS_ON. The second hierarchy has EMPLOYEE as root record type and represents the relationship types DEPENDENTS_OF and SUPERVISION. By the use of virtual parent-child relationships and virtual pointers in the WORKS_ON, DEPTMANAGER, and SUPERVISOR record types, we do not replicate any employee information. Each pointer will point to an EMPLOYEE record, but EMPLOYEE information is stored only once as a root record of the second hierarchy. The WORKS_FOR relationship type is represented by a virtual pointer in the EMPLOYEE record with virtual parent DEPARTMENT.*

Finally, consider the mapping of n-ary relationship types, $n > 2$. Figure 12.8 shows two options for mapping the SUPPLY ternary relationship type of Figure 12.3a. Because of the constraint, derived from IMS, that a record type can have at most one virtual parent, we cannot place SUPPLY under PART, say, and include two pointers to two virtual parents PROJECT and SUPPLIER. The option in Figure 12.8a creates *two pointer record types* under SUPPLY with virtual parents PROJECT and SUPPLIER. Another option, shown in Figure 12.8b, is to have SUPPLY as root of a hierarchy and create three pointer record types under it to point to the participating record types as virtual parents.

As we can see, the hierarchical model offers many options for representing the same ER schema. Many additional representations to those discussed above could have been used. The issues of efficient data access and of limiting redundancy versus facilitating re-

---

*Some systems may not allow a root record of a hierarchy, such as EMPLOYEE, to be virtual child in a VPCR, so this pointer to DEPARTMENT would not be allowed in such a system.

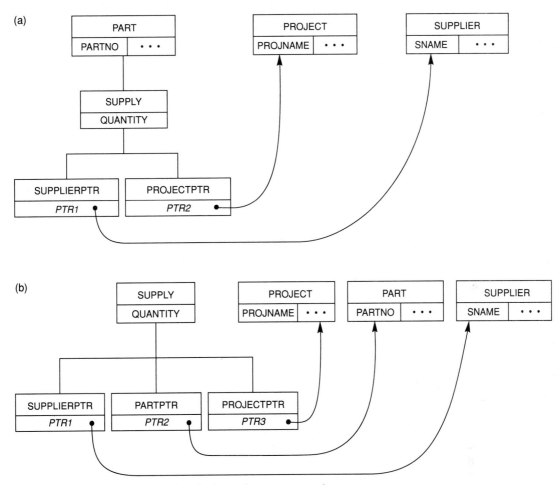

Figure 12.8   Mapping an n-ary (n=3) relationship type SUPPLY from ER to
hierarchical. (a) One option for representing a ternary relationship.
(b) Representing a ternary relationship using three VPCR types.

trieval are important in choosing the particular representation. The hierarchical model is
generally considered inferior in its modeling capability to both the relational model and
the network model for the following reasons:

- M:N relationship types can be represented only by redundant records or by using
  virtual parent-child relationships and pointer records.
- All 1:N relationship types in a hierarchy must be in the same direction.
- A record type in a hierarchy can have at most one (real) owner record type.
- A record type can have at most two parents—one real and one virtual.

In the next section we summarize our discussion by comparing the ways in which
the different models represent the same information.

12.1.4   Comparison of Model Representations

The main difference between representations in the relational and network models is in how relationships are represented. In the relational model connections between two relations are represented by including two attributes with the same domain—one in each of the relations. Individual tuples that have the same value for that attribute are logically related, even though they are not physically connected together. In the network model, 1:N connections between two record types are explicitly represented by the set type construct and the DBMS connects related records together in a set instance by some physical method. As we discussed, if we replicate key attributes from the owner record of a set type in the member record, the record types in the network schema resemble the corresponding relations of the relational schema.

Figures 12.9a and b show an example COMPANY database extension in the relational and network representations. As we can see in Figure 12.9a, tuples in different relations are not explicitly connected together; they are logically related when values of their con-

(a)   EMPLOYEE

FNAME	MINIT	LNAME	SSN	BDATE	ADDRESS	SEX	SALARY	SUPERSSN	DNO
· · ·		Smith	123456789	· · ·				333445555	5
· · ·		Wong	333445555	· · ·				888665555	5
· · ·		Zelaya	999887777	· · ·				987654321	4
· · ·		Wallace	987654321	· · ·				888665555	4
· · ·		Narayan	666884444	· · ·				333445555	5
· · ·		English	453453453	· · ·				333445555	5
· · ·		Jabbar	987987987	· · ·				987654321	4
· · ·		Borg	888665555	· · ·				null	1

DEPARTMENT

DNAME	DNUMBER	MGRSSN	MGRSTARTDATE
Research	5	333445555	10--FEB-83
Administration	4	987654321	30-NOV-79
Headquarters	1	888665555	22-MAY-65

DEPT_LOCATIONS

DNUMBER	DLOCATION
1	Houston
4	Stafford
5	Bellaire
5	Sugarland
5	Houston

WORKS_ON

ESSN	PNO	HOURS
123456789	1	32.5
123456789	2	7.5
666884444	3	40.0
453453453	1	20.0
453453453	2	20.0
333445555	2	10.0
333445555	3	10.0
333445555	10	10.0
333445555	20	10.0
999887777	30	30.0
999887777	10	10.0
987987987	10	35.0
987987987	30	5.0
987654321	30	20.0
987654321	20	15.0
888665555	20	null

PROJECT

PNAME	PNUMBER	PLOCATION	DNO
ProductX	1	· · ·	5
ProductY	2	· · ·	5
ProductZ	3	· · ·	5
Computerization	10	· · ·	4
Reorganization	20	· · ·	1
Newbenefits	30	· · ·	4

DEPENDENT

ESSN	DEPENDENT_NAME	SEX	BDATE
333445555	Alice	· · ·	
333445555	Theodore	· · ·	
333445555	Joy	· · ·	
987654321	Abner	· · ·	
123456789	Michael	· · ·	
123456789	Alice	· · ·	
123456789	Elizabeth	· · ·	

Figure 12.9   Comparing relational and network database instances.
(a) Example relational database extension. (*continued on next page*)

(b)

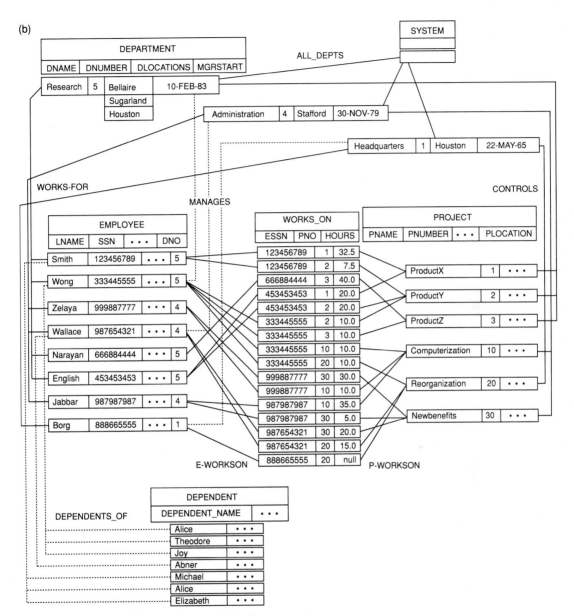

Figure 12.9 (cont.) (b) Example network database extension.

necting attributes match. For example, the tuple representing employee 'Smith' is related to the tuple representing the 'Research' department because the value of DNO in one is the same as the value of DNUMBER in the other. This represents the fact that employee 'Smith' and the 'Research' department are related by the WORKS_FOR relationship type, which is implicitly represented by the foreign key value 5 for DNO in Smith's employee tuple. The relational DBMS user must be aware of this in order to specify the correct EQUI-JOIN operation when needed.

In the network model, records are *physically connected together* when they participate in the same set instance. Hence, a set type physically represents a logical 1:N relationship type. For example, in Figure 12.9b the records for EMPLOYEEs 'Smith', 'Wong', 'Narayan', and 'English' and the record for the DEPARTMENT 'Research' are physically connected together by the DBMS as participants in a set instance of the WORKS_FOR set type. In addition, we can keep the logical connection among the records by duplicating the key field of the owner record in the member records. We can use the field values as a structural constraint or for automatic set selection. If we do not duplicate the owner key in the member record, then the system does not have any means of checking for valid set membership. It is the user's responsibility to link member records to set instances using the CONNECT, DISCONNECT, RECONNECT, or STORE command. The STORE command accomplishes the linking when AUTOMATIC set membership is specified.

Because the network model represents 1:N relationship types explicitly, it is sometimes considered superior to the relational model in modeling capability. However, the relational model is much simpler because only a single modeling concept—the relation—is used, rather than the two modeling concepts in the network model—record types and set types. The simplicity of the relational model and its formal relational algebra operations are considered an advantage over the network model.

The hierarchical model also represents relationships explicitly, but it has serious limitations compared to the network model. Whereas a record type in the network model can be a member in *any number* of set types, it can have only one real parent and one virtual parent in the hierarchical model. This creates problems when modeling M:N and n-ary relationship types. If a schema contains mainly 1:N relationship types in the same direction, it can be modeled naturally as a hierarchy. However, if many relationship types exist, as in the ER schema of Figure 12.1, it is difficult to come up with a good hierarchical representation without duplicating some records or using pointers. Because of this fact, the hierarchical model is generally considered inferior to both the relational and network models as far as modeling capability is concerned.

Table 12.2 contains a comparison of the terminology used by each of the data models. Table 12.3 contains a summary of the discussion on the modeling power of the various data models.

12.2   Comparison of Data Manipulation Languages

We differentiated between two types of database languages: high-level languages that operate on sets of records and low-level languages that operate on a single record at a time. We discussed in detail several formal and commercial relational languages in Chapters 6 to 9 and the hierarchical and network languages in Chapters 10 and 11. Most high-level database languages are associated with the relational model, whereas the network and hierarchical models are associated with record-at-a-time low-level languages. Several high-level query languages have recently been proposed for the ER model, and an ER algebra has been specified, but we did not discuss these languages because they are not available commercially and are not well established yet.

The relational model has several high-level languages. The formal operations of the relational algebra apply to sets of tuples, so they are high-level operations. A query is

Table 12.2 Comparative Terminology of Data Models

Entity-Relationship Model	Relational Model Formal	Informal	Network Model	Hierarchical Model
Entity type schema	Relation schema	Table description	Record type description	Record type description
Entity type	Relation	Table	Record type	Record type (segment in IMS)
Entity instance	Tuple	Row	Record occurrence	Record occurrence
1:N relationship type	—a	—a	Set type	Parent-child relationship (PCR) type
1:N relationship instance	—a	—a	Set occurrence (or set instance)	PCR occurrence (or PCR instance)
Attribute	Attribute	Column	Field or data item	Field or data item
Value set	Domain	Data type	Data type	Data type
Key	Candidate key	Candidate key	—b	—b
—b	Primary key	Primary key	Key or unique field	Sequence key or sequence field
Multivalued attribute	—b	—b	Vector or repeating group	—b
Composite attribute	—b	—b	Repeating group	—b

aNo corresponding concept exists; however, the relationship is established by using foreign keys.
bNo equivalent concept or term.

specified by a *sequence* of relational algebra operations on relations. In relational calculus a single expression—rather than a sequence of operations—specifies a query; we specify *what* we want to retrieve but not *how* to retrieve it. The relational calculus is considered to be at even a higher level than the relational algebra because in the latter we specify a certain order among the high-level operations. This order specifies how the system should retrieve the desired information. The formal basis of the relational calculus is provided by a branch of mathematical logic called predicate calculus. The basic set of relational algebra operations has been shown to have expressive power equivalent to that of the relational calculus.

Commercial languages for the relational model—such as SQL, QUEL, and QBE—are based primarily on the relational calculus. QUEL is based on tuple relational calculus, as, to a lesser degree, is SQL. Both languages introduce some procedurality and order resembling some aspects of relational algebra. They also incorporate facilities for aggregate functions, grouping, sorting, keeping duplicate tuples, and arithmetic, which are outside the realm of basic relational algebra or calculus. QBE is based on domain relational calculus. These are high-level languages that retrieve a set of tuples by a single query. Most relational systems will allow users to enter queries directly in an interactive way or to embed the queries in a programming language.

Table 12.3   Summary of Mapping ER Model Concepts to Relational, Network, or Hierarchical

ER Model Concept	Relational Model	Network Model	Hierarchical Model
Entity type	As a relation	As a record type	As a record type
Weak entity type	As a relation, but include the primary key of the identifying relation	As a record type that is a member in a set type with the identifying record type as owner (or as a repeating group)	As a record type that is a child of the identifying record type
1:1 relationship type	Include primary key of one relation as foreign key of the other relation, or merge into a single relation	Use a set type whose instances are restricted to having one member record, or merge into a single record type	Use a PCR type whose instances are restricted to having a single child record, or merge into a single record type
1:N relationship type	Include the primary key of the "1-side" relation as foreign key in the "N-side" relation	Use a set type	Use a parent-child relationship type
M:N relationship type	Set up a new relation that includes as foreign keys the primary keys of the participating relations	Set up a linking record type and make it a member in set types owned by the participating record types	(a) Use a single hierarchy and duplicate records (b) Use multiple hierarchies and VPCR types
n-ary relationship type	Same as M:N	Same as M:N	(a) Same as M:N (b) Make relationship as parent and participating entity types as children in a single hierarchy.

The network and hierarchical DML commands that we discussed are low level because they search for and retrieve single records. We must use a general-purpose programming language and embed the database commands in the program. In both these languages the concept of current record is crucial in the interpretation of the meaning of DML commands because the effect of a command depends on the current record. The network model DML uses additional currency indicators such as current of set types and current of record types, which also affect the outcome of DML commands. Although these currency concepts facilitate record-at-a-time access, the programmer must be thoroughly familiar with how the different commands affect currency indicators in order to write correct programs. These record-at-a-time commands have their origin in traditional file processing commands.

For the network model, the user must understand the effect of the various variations of the FIND command for record and set access. The effect of the FIND command depends on the current values of the various currency indicators and will also change the values of any affected currency indicators. There is a provision for retaining currency while moving members from one owner to another. For the hierarchical model, the programmer must understand the concept of hierarchical sequence of records. Records are generally accessed in that sequence forward from the current record. Records of different types in the hierarchy must therefore be processed along hierarchical paths from left to right within the tree. Again, exceptions do occur; for example, IMS allows stepping back *within one hierarchical occurrence tree* and then proceeding forward again within that tree.

From the above discussion it is clear that the relational model has a distinct advantage as far as languages are concerned. Both the formal and commercial languages associated with the relational model are quite powerful and are high level. In fact, several network and hierarchical DBMSs, such as IDMS/R and IMS, have implemented high-level query languages that are similar to the relational languages for use with their systems along with the traditional DML commands. Both high-level query language interfaces and traditional embedded DML commands are available in these systems.

12.3   Comparison of Storage Structures

We discussed many of the storage structures used by DBMSs to physically store a database in Chapters 4 and 5. By far the most important current technique is that of indexing. As we saw, a wide variety of options can be used to implement indexes, ranging from B^+-trees to dense indexes. Indexes can be primary (unique) indexes, clustering indexes, or secondary indexes, among other options. Hashing techniques are also important in database systems. For network and hierarchical systems, ring files and hierarchical files are used.

For the relational model, the general technique is to implement each base relation as a separate file. If the user does not specify any storage structure, most relational DBMSs will store the tuples as unordered records in the file. Many relational DBMSs will allow the user to specify dynamically on each file a single primary or clustering index and any number of secondary indexes. The user has the responsibility of choosing the attributes on which the indexes are set up. Some DBMSs allow the specification of a hashing attribute for each file. In general, it is good to specify indexes (or hash keys) on all attributes that will be used frequently in either selection or join conditions. Most relational DBMSs also allow users to drop indexes dynamically.

Some relational DBMSs give the option of mixing records from several base relations together, which is useful when related records from more than one relation are often accessed together. This clustering of records physically places a record from one relation followed by the related records from another relation so that the related records may be retrieved in the most efficient way possible, and it is also used very frequently in hierarchical and network systems.

The network model is usually implemented by using pointers and ring files. This file structure is suitable for implementing sets as discussed in Chapter 11. Most network DBMSs will also present the option of implementing some sets by clustering; that is, the owner record is followed by the member records in physical contiguity for each set instance. This clustering of member records next to their owner record can be done only for a single set type that a record type participates in as member because we can physically cluster the member records based on only one logical 1:N relationship type. The set type that is used most frequently in accessing the records should be chosen for physical clustering. In many cases, indexing or hashing on certain attributes of a record type can also be implemented on the ring file for fast access to individual records of a particular type.

The hierarchical model is usually implemented using hierarchical files, which preserve the hierarchical sequence of the database. In addition, a variety of options including hashing, indexing, and pointers are available, so we can have efficient access to individual records and to related records. Most hierarchical systems provide many such options for "tuning" the performance of a database system.

12.4   Comparison of Integrity Constraints

The ER model has many structural constraints that are not available in the three main implementation data models. We will discuss types of constraints in general and with reference to the ER model in Chapter 20. In this section we concentrate on comparing the relational, hierarchical, and network models with respect to the types of constraints each can represent.

The relational model is generally considered weak on integrity constraints. Two standard constraints are now considered to be part of the model—entity integrity and referential integrity. Commercial DBMSs implement entity integrity via the key constraint and by disallowing null values on a key attribute. Unfortunately, many relational DBMSs combine the specification of a key with that of a physical index. Referential integrity has not been generally available in relational DBMSs. However, some of the newer DBMSs—such as UNIFY—and newer versions of older relational DBMSs are allowing the specification of this constraint. It is expected that referential integrity will be available in most relational DBMSs in the near future.

The hierarchical model has the built-in hierarchical constraint that a record type can have at most one real parent in a hierarchy. Other constraints exist in each individual DBMS; for example, IMS allows only one virtual parent for a record type. There is *no provision* for enforcing consistency among duplicate records; this must be enforced by the application programs that update the database. Key constraints can be specified. The implicit constraint that a child record must be related to a parent record is enforced; also, child records are automatically deleted when their parent or ancestor is deleted.

The network model is the richest among the three implementation models in the types of constraints it specifies and enforces. The set retention option specifies constraints on the behavior of member records in a set with respect to the owner record, such as whether every record must have an owner (MANDATORY or FIXED) or not (OPTIONAL). Automatic set types with SET SELECTION BY STRUCTURAL match the key field of an owner with a field in the member record. The CHECK option can be used to specify a similar constraint for MANUAL nonautomatic set types. Key constraints are specified by the DUPLICATES NOT ALLOWED clause. Hence, many structural constraints on relationship types can be specified to a network DBMS. Unfortunately, not all of these features are implemented on current network DBMSs.

Most DBMSs, whether relational, hierarchical, or network, provide various data types that specify constraints on the values an attribute or field can take. However, they do not provide facilities for specifying and enforcing general semantic constraints, such as "the salary of an employee cannot be higher than the salary of his or her direct supervisor." Such constraints are currently checked and enforced by the programs that update the database.

12.5   Advantages and Disadvantages of the Models and Systems

From the above discussions it is clear that the relational model has a more formal mathematical foundation than the other two—both in the description of its structures and in the languages specified for it. However, it is often criticized because it does not explicitly represent relationships. The network and hierarchical models were developed much earlier than the relational model and both were developed originally as representations of specific commercial systems. Hence, it is understandable that their record-at-a-time languages are close to traditional file system commands. The ER model has been used mainly as a tool for conceptual database design. As we saw in Section 12.1, it is relatively straightforward to map a database schema specified in the ER model into a relational or a network schema, but it is much harder to map it to a hierarchical schema. Many database design tools are based on the ER model and its extensions.

As far as the DBMSs based on the implementation models are concerned, relational DBMSs generally provide greater flexibility. Most relational DBMSs make it easy to expand a schema by adding new relations or by adding new attributes to a relation. In addition, it is usually quite easy to add or drop indexes dynamically as needed. Another advantage of relational DBMSs is that most provide high-level query language interfaces as well as a programming interface, although in many cases the programming interface can access the database only through the high-level language itself, thus limiting the programmer's options. For these reasons, a relational DBMS is more suitable for many small and medium-sized database applications where flexibility and quick system development are important. In cases where the future use of the database is not clear, the flexibility of relational DBMSs provides clear advantages.

However, for large databases that have well-defined applications, relational DBMSs sometimes do not provide the high performance that may be required. This is because access to the database is always through the query language and DBMS system optimizer. Hence, programmers often do not have the capability to access the data in the method they know is the most efficient. Network and hierarchical systems are good for designing and implementing large databases with well-defined queries, transactions, and applications. The database designers and users can spend enough time during system implementation to choose appropriate storage structures and ensure that their applications are programmed in the most efficient way. However, unforeseen future applications may cause very expensive system reorganizations. Table 12.4 summarizes the comparative advantages and disadvantages of the relational, network, and hierarchical models and the current DBMSs based on these models. A plus sign indicates a positive feature and a minus sign indicates a negative one.

Table 12.4   Summary of the Advantages and Disadvantages of the Relational, Network, and Hierarchical Approaches

	Relational	Network	Hierarchical
Modeling/Design			
			– (except for
1. Modeling power (expressiveness)	Neutral	+	hierarchical data)
2. Model simplicity	+	–	–
3. Constraints	Limited	+	Limited
4. Ease of mapping from ER schema	Easy	Easy	Difficult
5. Ease of schema modification	+	–	–
Languages			
1. Type of languages	+ (high-level)	– (low-level)	– (low-level)
2. Query specification	Declarative	Navigational	Navigational
3. Responsibility of application programmer to optimize	Low	High	High
4. Currency	Not applicable	Critical	Critical
5. Allowing programmer to optimize	–	+	+
Performance Experience			
1. Logical data independence	+	–	–
2. Inherent processing efficiency	–	+	+
3. System overhead	Mainly for query optimization	Currency and pointer management	Low
4. Dependency on internal optimization	High	Low	Low

Exercises

12.1. Discuss the basic procedure for mapping an ER database schema to a relational database schema.

12.2. Discuss the basic procedure for mapping an ER database schema to a network database schema. Under what conditions will a network schema closely resemble its relational counterpart?

12.3. Why is it much harder to map an ER database schema to a hierarchical database schema than it is for the other two data models?

12.4. How do the traditional languages of the three data models—relational, network, and hierarchical—compare with one another?

12.5. How do the traditional storage structures used with DBMSs of the three data models—relational, network, and hierarchical—compare with one another?

12.6. How do the integrity constraints of the three data models—relational, network, and hierarchical—compare with one another?

12.7. Discuss the criteria for selecting one type of DBMS over another.

12.8. Design a relational database schema that corresponds to the UNIVERSITY ER schema of Figure 12.10. Specify all the key attributes of relations and any referential integrity constraints. Also specify any constraints that are represented in the ER schema but are not implicit in your relational database schema.

12.9. Design a network database schema that corresponds to the UNIVERSITY ER schema of Figure 12.10. Specify all the unique attributes of record types and any con-

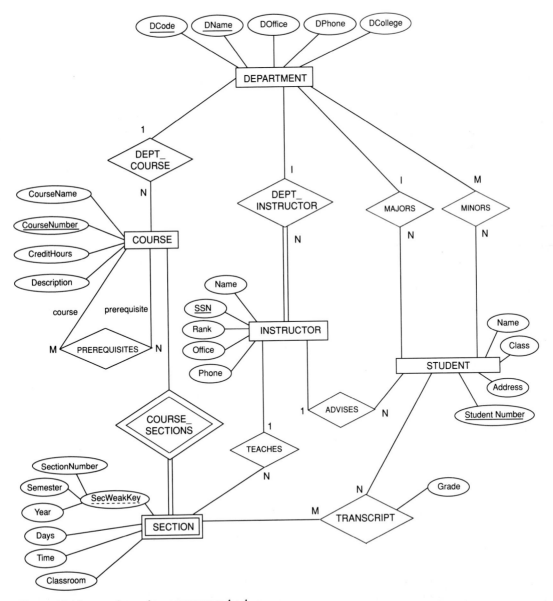

Figure 12.10   ER schema for a UNIVERSITY database

straints on the set types. Also specify any constraints that are represented in the ER schema but are not implicit in your network database schema.

12.10. Design two hierarchical database schemas that correspond to the ER schema of Figure 12.10. One should use only a single hierarchy and *no* VPCR types; the other should use at least two hierarchies and some VRCR types. Specify all the unique attributes of record types, any duplication of data, and any hierarchical constraints. Also specify any constraints that are represented in the ER schema but are not implicit in your hierarchical database schema.

12.11. Repeat Exercises 12.8 to 12.10 but use the AIRLINE ER schema shown in Figure 3.18.

Selected Bibliography

There is not much literature on the direct comparison of data models. However, data model mapping has been studied extensively. Codd's original relational model paper (Codd 1970) shows how the same relational schema can be represented by different hierarchical schemas. Chen's original ER model paper (Chen 1976) discusses basic ER-to-relational and ER-to-network mapping. Various surveys of data models are available. The book by Tsichritzis and Lochovsky (1982) informally discusses data model equivalences. Formal studies on data model equivalence are given by Biller (1979), Borkin (1978), and Jajodia et al. (1983). Elmasri and Wiederhold (1980) discuss how relationships are represented in various data models.

Katz and Wong (1982) discuss operational mapping of well-structured network DML programs into relational queries. Navathe (1980) discusses the structural mapping of network schemas to relational schemas. Larson (1983) discusses how a single DBMS may support both relational and network schemas.

Sakai (1980) studies the mapping of ER to hierarchical schemas using the concept of hierarchical dependency. Iossophidis (1979) discusses the mapping of ER schemas to System-2000 hierarchical schemas. Dumpala and Arora (1983) discuss *reverse* mapping from relational, network, or hierarchical to ER schemas.

Material on DBMS performance can be found in vendor manuals and trade literature as well as DATAPRO and Auerbach reports. Studies on the suitability of the various data models for different types of users and applications are reported in Reisner (1981), Hoffer (1982), and Brosey and Shneiderman (1978). Codd (1982) discusses the advantages of the relational approach.

PART III

DATABASE DESIGN

353

CHAPTER **13**

Functional Dependencies and Normalization for Relational Databases

In Chapters 6 to 9 we presented various aspects of the relational model, including examples of relational databases. Each *relation schema* consists of a number of attributes, and the *relational database schema* consists of a number of relation schemas. So far, we have assumed that attributes are grouped to form a relation schema using the common sense of the database designer or by mapping a schema specified in the Entity-Relationship model into a relational schema as shown in Chapter 12. However, we did not have any formal measure of why one grouping of attributes into a relation schema may be better than another. There was no measure of appropriateness or of the quality of the design except for the intuition of the designer.

In this chapter we discuss some of the theory that has been developed to attempt to choose "good" relation schemas, that is, to measure formally why one set of groupings of attributes into relation schemas may be better than a different set of groupings. The same theory can be used to group fields into record types in other data models, but the theory was developed in the context of the relational model. There are two levels at which we can discuss "goodness" of relation schemas. The first is the **logical level**, which refers to how the users interpret the relation schemas and the meaning of their attributes. Having good relation schemas at this level helps the users to clearly understand the meaning of the data tuples in the relations, and hence to formulate their queries correctly. The second is the manipulation (or storage) level, which refers to how the tuples in a base relation are stored and updated. This level applies only to schemas of base relations—which will be physically stored as files—whereas at the logical level we are interested in schemas of both base relations and views (virtual relations). The relational database design theory developed in this chapter applies mainly to base relations, although some criteria of appropriateness also apply to views as we shall discuss in Section 13.1.

We start in Section 13.1 by informally discussing some criteria for good and bad relation schemas. Then, in Section 13.2 we define the concept of functional dependency, which is the main tool for formally measuring the appropriateness of attribute groupings into relation schemas. Properties of functional dependencies are also studied and analyzed. In section 13.3 we show how functional dependencies can be used to group attributes into relation schemas that are in a normal form. A relation schema is in a normal form when it satisfies a number of desirable features. Normal forms for relational schemas will be defined, leading to progressively better groupings. In Section 13.4 we discuss more general definitions of some normal forms.

Chapter 14 will continue the development of the theory related to the design of good relational schemas. Whereas in this chapter we concentrate on the normal forms for single relation schemas, in Chapter 14 we discuss measures of appropriateness for a whole set of relation schemas that together form a relational database schema. We specify two such properties—the nonadditive (lossless) join property and the dependency preservation property—and discuss algorithms for relational database design that are based on functional dependencies, normal forms, and the aforementioned properties. In Chapter 14 we also define additional types of dependencies and advanced normal forms that further enhance the properties of relation schemas.

13.1   Informal Design Guidelines for Relation Schemas

We will discuss four informal measures of quality for relational schema design in this section. These are:

- Semantics of the attributes.
- Reducing the redundant values in tuples.
- Reducing the null values in tuples.
- Disallowing spurious tuples.

These measures are not always independent of one another, as we shall see in the following subsections.

13.1.1   Semantics of the Relation Attributes

Whenever we group attributes to form a relation schema, we assume that a certain meaning is associated with the attributes. In Chapter 6 we already discussed how each relation can be interpreted as a set of facts or statements. This meaning, or **semantics,** specifies how we can interpret the attribute values stored in a tuple of the relation, in other words, how the attribute values in a tuple are related to one another. In general, the easier it is to explain the semantics of the relation, the better the relation schema design.

To illustrate this, consider a simplified version of the COMPANY relational database schema of Figure 6.5, which is shown in Figure 13.1. Example populated relations of this schema are shown in Figure 13.2. The meaning of the EMPLOYEE relation schema is quite simple—each tuple represents an employee, with values for the employee's

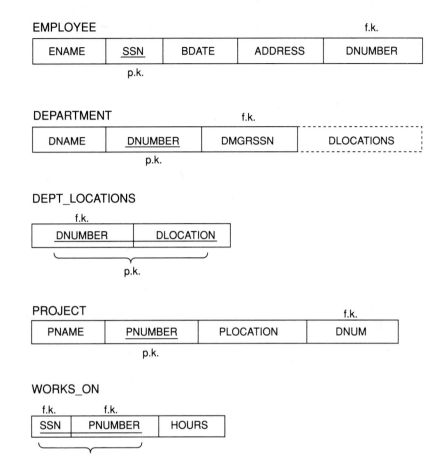

Figure 13.1   Simplified version of the COMPANY relational
database schema

name (ENAME), social security number (SSN), birthdate (BDATE), address (ADDRESS), and
the number of the department that the employee works for (DNUMBER). The DNUMBER
attribute is a foreign key that represents an *implicit relationship* between EMPLOYEE and
DEPARTMENT. The semantics of the DEPARTMENT and PROJECT schemas are also straightforward; each DEPARTMENT tuple represents a department entity and each PROJECT tuple
represents a project entity. The attribute DMGRSSN of DEPARTMENT relates a department
to the employee who is its manager, while DNUM of PROJECT relates a project to its controlling department; both are foreign key attributes. The reader should ignore the attribute DLOCATIONS of DEPARTMENT for the time being as it is used to illustrate normalization concepts in Section 13.3.

The semantics of the other two relation schemas in Figure 13.1 are slightly more
complex. Each tuple in DEPT_LOCATIONS gives a department number (DNUMBER) and
one of the locations of the department (DLOCATION). Each tuple in WORKS_ON gives an
employee social security number (SSN), the project number of *one of* the projects that the
employee works on (PNUMBER), and the number of hours per week that the employee

EMPLOYEE

ENAME	SSN	BDATE	ADDRESS	DNUMBER
Smith,John B.	123456789	09-JAN-55	731 Fondren,Houston,TX	5
Wong,Franklin T.	333445555	08-DEC-45	638 Voss,Houston,TX	5
Zelaya,Alicia J.	999887777	19-JUL-58	3321 Castle,Spring,TX	4
Wallace,Jennifer S.	987654321	20-JUN-31	291 Berry,Bellaire,TX	4
Narayan,Remesh K.	666884444	15-SEP-52	975 Fire Oak,Humble,TX	5
English,Joyce A.	453453453	31-JUL-62	5631 Rice,Houston,TX	5
Jabbar,Ahmad V.	987987987	29-MAR-59	980 Dallas,Houston,TX	4
Borg,James E.	888665555	10-NOV-27	450 Stone,Houston,TX	1

DEPARTMENT

DNAME	DNUMBER	DMGRSSN
Research	5	333445555
Administration	4	987654321
Headquarters	1	888665555

DEPT_LOCATIONS

DNUMBER	DLOCATION
1	Houston
4	Stafford
5	Bellaire
5	Sugarland
5	Houston

WORKS_ON

SSN	PNUMBER	HOURS
123456789	1	32.5
123456789	2	7.5
666884444	3	40.0
453453453	1	20.0
453453453	2	20.0
333445555	2	10.0
333445555	3	10.0
333445555	10	10.0
333445555	20	10.0
999887777	30	30.0
999887777	10	10.0
987987987	10	35.0
987987987	30	5.0
987654321	30	20.0
987654321	20	15.0
888665555	20	null

PROJECT

PNAME	PNUMBER	PLOCATION	DNUM
ProductX	1	Bellaire	5
ProductY	2	Sugarland	5
ProductZ	3	Houston	5
Computerization	10	Stafford	4
Reorganization	20	Houston	1
Newbenefits	30	Stafford	4

Figure 13.2   Example relations for the schema of Figure 13.1

works on that project (HOURS). However, both schemas have a well-defined and unambiguous meaning. The schema DEPT_LOCATIONS represents a multivalued attribute of DEPARTMENT, whereas WORKS_ON represents an M:N relationship between EMPLOYEE and PROJECT. Hence, all the relation schemas in Figure 13.1 may be considered good from the standpoint of having clear semantics. We can hence state the following guideline for a relation schema design:

GUIDELINE 1:   Design a relation schema in such a way that it is easy to explain its meaning. Typically, this means that we should not combine attributes from multiple entity types and relationship types into a single relation. Intuitively, if a relation schema corresponds to one entity type or one relationship type, the meaning tends to be clear. Otherwise, it tends to be a mixture of multiple entities and relationships and hence semantically unclear.

The relation schemas in Figures 13.3a and b also have clear semantics. (The reader should ignore the lines under the relations for now as they are used to illustrate functional dependency notation in Section 13.2.) A tuple in the EMP_DEPT relation schema of Figure 13.3a represents a single employee but includes additional information, namely the name (DNAME) of the department for which the employee works and the social security number (DMGRSSN) of the department manager. For the EMP_PROJ relation of Figure 13.3b, each tuple relates an employee to a project but also includes the employee name (ENAME), project name (PNAME), and project location (PLOCATION). Although there is nothing wrong logically with these two relations, they are considered poor designs because they violate Guideline 1 by *mixing attributes from distinct real-world entities;* EMP_DEPT mixes attributes of employees and departments, and EMP_PROJ mixes attributes of employees and projects. They may be used as views, but they cause problems when used as base relations as we shall discuss in the following section.

13.1.2 Redundant Information in Tuples and Update Anomalies

One goal of schema design is to minimize the storage space that the base relations (files) occupy. Grouping of attributes into relation schemas has a significant effect on storage space. For example, compare the space used by the two base relations EMPLOYEE and DEPARTMENT in Figure 13.2 with the space for an EMP_DEPT base relation in Figure 13.4, which is the result of applying the NATURAL-JOIN operation to EMPLOYEE and DEPARTMENT. In EMP_DEPT the attribute values pertaining to a particular department (DNUMBER, DNAME, DMGRSSN) are repeated for every employee who works for that department. By contrast, the department information appears only once for each department in the DEPARTMENT relation in Figure 13.2, and only the department number (DNUMBER) is repeated in the EMPLOYEE relation for each employee who works in that depart-

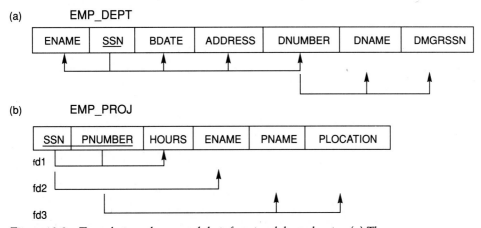

Figure 13.3 Two relation schemas and their functional dependencies. (a) The EMP_DEPT relation schema. (b) The EMP_PROJ relation schema.

EMP_DEPT

ENAME	SSN	BDATE	ADDRESS	DNUMBER	DNAME	DMGRSSN
Smith,John B.	123456789	09-JAN-55	731 Fondren,Houston,TX	5	Research	333445555
Wong,Franklin T.	333445555	08-DEC-45	638 Voss,Houston,TX	5	Research	333445555
Zelaya, Alicia J.	999887777	19-JUL-58	3321 Castle,Spring,TX	4	Administration	987654321
Wallace,Jennifer S.	987654321	19-JUN-31	291 Berry,Bellaire,TX	4	Administration	987654321
Narayan,Ramesh K.	666884444	15-SEP-52	975 FireOak,Humble,TX	5	Research	333445555
English,Joyce A.	453453453	31-JUL-62	5631 Rice,Houston,TX	5	Research	333445555
Jabbar,Ahmad V.	987987987	29-MAR-59	980 Dallas,Houston,TX	4	Administration	987654321
Borg,James E.	888665555	10-NOV-27	450 Stone,Houston,TX	1	Headquarters	888665555

EMP_PROJ

SSN	PNUMBER	HOURS	ENAME	PNAME	PLOCATION
123456789	1	32.5	Smith,John B.	ProductX	Bellaire
123456789	2	7.5	Smith,John B.	ProductY	Sugarland
666884444	3	40.0	Narayan,Ramesh K.	ProductZ	Houston
453453453	1	20.0	English,Joyce A.	ProductX	Bellaire
453453453	2	20.0	English,Joyce A.	ProductY	Sugarland
333445555	2	10.0	Wong,Franklin T.	ProductY	Sugarland
333445555	3	10.0	Wong,Franklin T.	ProductZ	Houston
333445555	10	10.0	Wong,Franklin T.	Computerization	Stafford
333445555	20	10.0	Wong,Franklin T.	Reorganization	Houston
999887777	30	30.0	Zelaya,Alicia J.	Newbenefits	Stafford
999887777	10	10.0	Zelaya,Alicia J.	Computerization	Stafford
987987987	10	35.0	Jabbar,Ahmad V.	Computerization	Stafford
987987987	30	5.0	Jabbar,Ahmad V.	Newbenefits	Stafford
987654321	30	20.0	Wallace,Jennifer S.	Newbenefits	Stafford
987654321	20	15.0	Wallace,Jennifer S.	Reorganization	Houston
888665555	20	null	Borg,James E.	Reorganization	Houston

Figure 13.4 Example relations for the schemas in Figure 13.3 that result from applying NATURAL-JOIN to the relations in Figure 13.2

ment. Similar comments apply to the EMP_PROJ relation (Figure 13.4), which is an augmentation of the WORKS_ON relation by additional attributes from EMPLOYEE and PROJECT.

Another serious problem with using the relations in Figure 13.4 as base relations is the problem of **update anomalies**. These can be classified into insertion anomalies, deletion anomalies, and modification anomalies.* We now discuss these anomalies with regard to the EMP_DEPT relation of Figure 13.4.

Insertion Anomalies

These can be differentiated into two types, illustrated by the following examples using the EMP_DEPT relation:

- To insert a new employee tuple into EMP_DEPT, we must include the attribute values for the department that the employee works for, or nulls if the employee does

---

*These anomalies were identified by Codd (1972a) to justify the need for normalization of relations, as we shall discuss in Section 13.3.

not work for a department as yet. For example, to insert a new tuple for an employee who works in department number 5, we must make sure that we enter the attribute values of department 5 correctly so they are consistent with values for department 5 in other tuples in EMP_DEPT. In the design of Figure 13.2 we do not have to worry about this consistency problem because we enter only the department number in the employee tuple; all other attribute values of department 5 are recorded only once in the database as a single tuple in the DEPARTMENT relation.

- It is difficult to insert a new department that has no employees as yet in the EMP_DEPT relation. The only way to do this is to place null values in the attributes for employee. This causes a problem because SSN is the primary key of EMP_DEPT, and each tuple is supposed to represent an employee entity—not a department entity. Moreover, when the first employee is assigned to that department, we do not need this tuple with null values any more. This problem does not occur in the design of Figure 13.2, because a department is entered in the DEPARTMENT relation whether or not any employees work for it, and whenever an employee is assigned to that department, a corresponding tuple is inserted in EMPLOYEE.

Deletion Anomalies

This problem is related to the second insertion anomaly situation discussed above. If we delete from EMP_DEPT an employee tuple that happens to represent the last employee working for a particular department, the information concerning that department is lost from the database. This problem does not occur in the database of Figure 13.2 because DEPARTMENT tuples are stored separately from EMPLOYEE tuples and only the attribute DNUMBER of EMPLOYEE relates the two.

Modification Anomalies

In EMP_DEPT, if we want to change the value of one of the attributes of a particular department, say the manager of department 5, we must update the tuples of all employees who work in that department; otherwise, the database will become inconsistent. If we overlook the updating of some tuples, the same department will be shown to have two different values for manager in different employee tuples, which should not be the case.

Discussion

Based on the above anomalies, we can state the following guideline:

GUIDELINE 2:   Design the base relation schemas so that no insertion, deletion, or modification anomalies occur in the relations. If any anomalies are present, note them clearly so that the update programs will operate correctly.

The second guideline is consistent with and in a way a restatement of the first guideline. We can also see the need for a more formal approach to help us evaluate whether our design meets these guidelines. Sections 13.2 to 13.4 provide these needed formal concepts. It is important to note that these guidelines may sometimes *have to be violated* in order to *improve the performance* of certain queries. For example, if an important query retrieves information concerning the department of an employee along with employee attributes, the EMP_DEPT schema may be used as a base relation. However, we must make sure that the anomalies in EMP_DEPT are noted and well understood so that whenever the base relation is updated, we do not end up with inconsistencies. In general, it is advisable to use anomaly-free base relations and to specify views that include the JOINs for placing together the attributes frequently referenced in important queries. This reduces the number of JOIN terms specified in the query, making it simpler to write the query correctly, and in many cases* improves the performance. However, we must still make sure that the user understands the meaning of the relation attributes correctly.

13.1.3   Null Values in Tuples

In some schema designs we may group many attributes together into a "fat" relation. If many of the attributes do not apply to all tuples in the relation, we end up with many nulls in the relation. This can be wasteful of space at the storage level and may also lead to problems with understanding the meaning of the attributes and with specifying JOIN operations at the logical level. Another problem with nulls is how we may account for them when aggregate operations such as COUNT or SUM are applied.

Moreover, nulls can have multiple interpretations, such as:

• The attribute *does not apply* to this tuple.
• The attribute value for this tuple is *unknown*.
• The value is *known but absent*, that is, has not been recorded yet.

Having the same representation for all nulls compromises the different meanings. Therefore, we may state another guideline as follows:

GUIDELINE 3:   As far as possible, avoid placing attributes in a base relation whose values may be null. If nulls are unavoidable, make sure that they apply in exceptional cases only and do not apply to a majority of tuples in the relation.

For example, if only 10% of employees have individual offices, there is little justification to include an attribute OFFICE_NUMBER in the EMPLOYEE relation; rather, a relation EMP_OFFICES(ESSN, OFFICE_NUMBER) can be created to include tuples for only the employees with individual offices.

13.1.4   Spurious Tuples

Consider the two relation schemas EMP_LOCS and EMP_PROJ1 in Figure 13.5a, which can be used instead of the EMP_PROJ relation of Figure 13.3b. A tuple in EMP_LOCS means that the employee whose name is ENAME works on *some project* whose location is PLOCATION. A tuple in EMP_PROJ1 means that the employee whose social security number is SSN works HOURS per week on the project whose name, number, and location are PNAME, PNUMBER, and PLOCATION. Figure 13.5b shows relation extensions of EMP_LOCS and

---

*The performance of a query specified on a view that is the JOIN of several base relations depends upon how the DBMS implements the view. Many relational DBMSs materialize a frequently used view so they do not have to perform the JOINs often. The DBMS is still responsible for automatically updating the materialized view when the base relations are updated.

(a)

EMP_LOCS

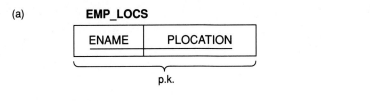

EMP_PROJ1

(b)   **EMP_LOCS**

ENAME	PLOCATION
Smith, John B.	Bellaire
Smith, John B.	Sugarland
Narayan, Ramesh K.	Houston
English, Joyce A.	Bellaire
English, Joyce A.	Sugarland
Wong, Franklin T.	Sugarland
Wong, Franklin T.	Houston
Wong, Franklin T.	Stafford
Zelaya, Alicia J.	Stafford
Jabbar, Ahmad V.	Stafford
Wallace, Jennifer S.	Stafford
Wallace, Jennifer S.	Houston
Borg,James E.	Houston

EMP_PROJ1

SSN	PNUMBER	HOURS	PNAME	PLOCATION
123456789	1	32.5	Product X	Bellaire
123456789	2	7.5	Product Y	Sugarland
666884444	3	40.0	Product Z	Houston
453453453	1	20.0	Product X	Bellaire
453453453	2	20.0	Product Y	Sugarland
333445555	2	10.0	Product Y	Sugarland
333445555	3	10.0	Product Z	Houston
333445555	10	10.0	Computerization	Stafford
333445555	20	10.0	Reorganization	Houston
999887777	30	30.0	Newbenefits	Stafford
999887777	10	10.0	Computerization	Stafford
987987987	10	35.0	Computerization	Stafford
987987987	30	5.0	Newbenefits	Stafford
987654321	30	20.0	Newbenefits	Stafford
987654321	20	15.0	Reorganization	Houston
888665555	20	null	Reorganization	Houston

Figure 13.5 Alternative representation of EMP_PROJ. (a) Representing
EMP_PROJ of Figure 13.3(b) by two relation schemas EMP_LOCS
and EMP_PROJ1. (b) Result of projecting the EMP_PROJ relation
of Figure 13.4 on the attributes of EMP_PROJ1 and EMP_LOCS.

EMP_PROJ1 corresponding to the EMP_PROJ relation extension of Figure 13.4, which are obtained by applying the appropriate PROJECT (π) operations to EMP_PROJ (ignore the dotted lines in Figure 13.5b for now).

Suppose we used EMP_PROJ1 and EMP_LOCS as the base relations instead of EMP_PROJ. This would be a particularly bad schema design, because we cannot recover the information that was originally in EMP_PROJ from EMP_PROJ1 and EMP_LOCS. If we attempt a NATURAL-JOIN operation on EMP_PROJ1 and EMP_LOCS, we get many more tuples than EMP_PROJ had. In Figure 13.6 the result of applying the join to only the tuples *above* the dotted lines in Figure 13.5b are shown to reduce the size of the resulting relation. Additional tuples that were not in EMP_PROJ are called **spurious tuples** because they represent spurious or *wrong* information that is not valid. The spurious tuples are marked by asterisks (*) in Figure 13.6.

Decomposing EMP_PROJ into EMP_LOCS and EMP_PROJ1 is bad because when we JOIN them back using NATURAL-JOIN, we do not get the correct original information. This is because we chose PLOCATION as the attribute that relates EMP_LOCS and EMP_PROJ1, and PLOCATION is neither a primary key nor a foreign key in either EMP_LOCS or EMP_PROJ1. We can now informally state another design guideline:

GUIDELINE 4:   We should design relation schemas so that they can be JOINed with equality conditions on attributes that are either primary keys or foreign keys in a way that guarantees that no spurious tuples are generated.

SSN	PNUMBER	HOURS	PNAME	PLOCATION	ENAME
123456789	1	32.5	ProductX	Bellaire	Smith,John B.
* 123456789	1	32.5	ProductX	Bellaire	English,Joyce A.
123456789	2	7.5	ProductY	Sugarland	Smith,John B.
* 123456789	2	7.5	ProductY	Sugarland	English,Joyce A.
* 123456789	2	7.5	ProductY	Sugarland	Wong,Franklin T.
666884444	3	40.0	ProductZ	Houston	Narayan,Ramesh K.
* 666884444	3	40.0	ProductZ	Houston	Wong,Franklin T.
* 453453453	1	20.0	ProductX	Bellaire	Smith,John B.
453453453	1	20.0	ProductX	Bellaire	English,Joyce A.
* 453453453	2	20.0	ProductY	Sugarland	Smith,John B.
453453453	2	20.0	ProductY	Sugarland	English,Joyce A.
* 453453453	2	20.0	ProductY	Sugarland	Wong,Franklin T.
* 333445555	2	10.0	ProductY	Sugarland	Smith,John B.
* 333445555	2	10.0	ProductY	Sugarland	English,Joyce A.
333445555	2	10.0	ProductY	Sugarland	Wong,Franklin T.
* 333445555	3	10.0	ProductZ	Houston	Narayan,Ramesh K.
333445555	3	10.0	ProductZ	Houston	Wong,Franklin T.
333445555	10	10.0	Computerization	Stafford	Wong,Franklin T.
* 333445555	20	10.0	Reorganization	Houston	Narayan,Ramesh K.
333445555	20	10.0	Reorganization	Houston	Wong,Franklin T.

Figure 13.6   Result of applying the NATURAL JOIN operation to EMP_PROJ1 and EMP_LOCS, with spurious tuples marked by *

This informal guideline obviously needs to be stated more formally. In Chapter 14 we discuss a formal condition, called the nonadditive (or lossless) join property, that guarantees that certain joins do not produce spurious tuples.

13.1.5   Discussion

In Sections 13.1.1 to 13.1.4 we informally discussed the situations that lead to problematic relation schemas and proposed informal guidelines for a good relational design. In the rest of this chapter we will present the formal concepts and theory that may be used to define concepts of "goodness" and "badness" of individual relation schemas more precisely. We will specify several normal forms for relation schemas, the most important of which is called Boyce-Codd normal form or BCNF. *Individual* relation schemas in BCNF are usually good. In Chapter 14 we will give additional criteria to specify that a *set of relation schemas* together forms a good relational database schema. We will also present algorithms that use this theory to design relational database schemas and define additional normal forms beyond BCNF. The normal forms defined in this chapter are based on the concept of a functional dependency, which we describe next, whereas normal forms discussed in Chapter 14 use additional types of data dependencies, such as the multivalued dependencies and join dependencies described in Chapter 14.

13.2   Functional Dependencies

The single most important concept in relational schema design is that of a functional dependency. In this section we formally define the concept, and in Section 13.3 we see how it leads to relation schemas in normal forms.

13.2.1   Definition of Functional Dependency

A functional dependency is a constraint between two sets of attributes from the database. Suppose our relational database schema has n attributes A_1, A_2, ... A_n; let us think of the whole database as being described by a single **universal** relation schema $R = \{ A_1, A_2, ... A_n \}$.* We do not imply that we will actually store the database as a single universal table; we use this concept only in developing the formal theory of data dependencies.**

A **functional dependency**, denoted by $X \rightarrow Y$, between two sets of attributes X and Y that are subsets of R specifies a constraint on the possible tuples that can form a relation instance r of R. The constraint states that for any two tuples t_1 and t_2 in r such that $t_1[X] = t_2[X]$, we must also have $t_1[Y] = t_2[Y]$. This means that the values of the Y component of a tuple in r depend on, or are determined by, the values of the X component,

---

*This concept of a universal relation is important when we discuss the algorithms for relational database design in Chapter 14.

**This assumption means that every attribute in the database should have a *distinct name*. In Chapter 6 we prefixed attribute names by relation names to achieve uniqueness whenever attributes in distinct relations had the same name.

or, alternatively, the values of the X component of a tuple uniquely (or **functionally**) de-termine the values of the Y component. We also say that there is a functional dependency from X to Y or that Y is **functionally dependent** on X. We abbreviate functional dependency by **FD.** The set of attributes X is called the **left-hand side** of the FD, and Y is called the **right-hand side**.

An alternative definition of FD is as follows: In a relation schema R, X functionally determines Y if and only if whenever two tuples of r(R) agree on their X-value, they must necessarily agree on their Y-value. Note that:

- If a constraint on R states that there cannot be more than one tuple with a given X-value in any relation instance r(R)—that is, X is a **candidate key** of R—this implies that X → Y for any subset of attributes Y of R.
- If X → Y in R, this does not say whether or not Y → X in R.

A functional dependency is a property of the meaning or **semantics** of the attributes in a relation schema R. We use our understanding of the semantics of the attributes of R—that is, how they relate to one another—to specify the functional dependencies that should hold on *all* relation instances (extensions) r of R. Whenever the semantics of two sets of attributes in R indicate that a functional dependency should hold, we specify the dependency as a constraint. Relation instances r that satisfy the functional dependency constraints specified on the attributes of R are called **legal extensions** (or **legal relation instances**) of R, because they obey the functional dependency constraints. Hence, the main use of functional dependencies is to further describe a relation schema R by specifying constraints on its attributes that must hold *at all times*.

Consider the relation schema EMP_PROJ in Figure 13.3b; from the semantics of the attributes, we know that the following functional dependencies should hold on the attributes of EMP_PROJ:

(a) SSN → ENAME
(b) PNUMBER → {PNAME, PLOCATION}
(c) {SSN, PNUMBER} → HOURS

These functional dependencies specify (a) that the value of an employee's social security number (SSN) uniquely determines the employee name (ENAME), (b) that the value of a project's number (PNUMBER) uniquely determines the project name (PNAME) and location (PLOCATION), and (c) that a combination of SSN and PNUMBER values uniquely determines the number of hours the employee works on the project per week (HOURS). Alternatively, we can say that ENAME is functionally determined by (or functionally dependent on) SSN or that "given a value of SSN, we know the value of ENAME," and so on.

In Figure 13.3 we also introduce a diagrammatic notation for displaying functional dependencies. Each FD is displayed as a horizontal line. The attributes on the left-hand side of the FD are connected by vertical lines to the horizontal line that represents the FD. The right-hand side attributes of the FD are connected to the horizontal line by arrows pointing toward the attributes as shown in Figures 13.3a and b.

Note that a functional dependency is a *property of the relation schema* (intension) R and not of a particular legal relation instance (extension) r of R. Hence, an FD *cannot* be automatically inferred from a given relation extension r but must be defined explicitly by

TEACH

TEACHER	COURSE	TEXT
Smith	Data Structures	Bartram
Smith	Data Management	Al-Nour
Hall	Compilers	Hoffman
Brown	Data Structures	Augenthaler

Figure 13.7   The TEACH relation

someone who knows the semantics of the attributes of R. For example, in Figure 13.7 a particular relation instance of the TEACH relation schema is shown. Although at first glance we may be tempted to say that TEXT → COURSE, we cannot confirm this unless we know that it is true for all relation instances of TEACH. It is, however, sufficient to demonstrate a single counterexample to disprove a functional dependency. For example, because 'Smith' teaches both 'Data Structures' and 'Data Management', we can conclude that TEACHER does not functionally determine COURSE. We denote this by TEACHER ↛ COURSE. From Figure 13.7 we can also say that COURSE ↛ TEXT. What other functional dependencies can you eliminate by looking at the relation instance of TEACH shown in Figure 13.7?

13.2.2   Inference Rules for Functional Dependencies

We will denote by F the set of functional dependencies that are specified on relation schema R. Typically, the schema designer will specify the functional dependencies that are *semantically obvious*; however, there are usually numerous other functional dependencies that will also hold in *all* legal relation instances that satisfy the dependencies in F. The set of all such functional dependencies is called the **closure** of F and is denoted by F^+. For example, suppose we specify the following set F of obvious functional dependencies on the relation schema of Figure 13.3a:

F = { SSN → {ENAME, BDATE, ADDRESS, DNUMBER} ,
        DNUMBER → {DNAME, DMGRSSN} }

We can **infer** the following additional functional dependencies from F:

SSN → {DNAME, DMGRSSN},
SSN → SSN,
DNUMBER → DNAME

In general, an FD X → Y is **inferred from** a set of dependencies F specified on R if X → Y holds in *every* relation instance r that is a legal extension of R; that is, whenever a relation instance r satisfies all the dependencies in F, X → Y will also hold in r. The closure F^+ of F is the set of all functional dependencies that can be inferred from F. To determine a systematic way to infer dependencies, we must discover a set of **inference rules** that can be used to infer new dependencies from a given set of dependencies. We consider some of these inference rules next. We will use the notation F ⊨ X→Y to denote that the functional dependency X→Y is inferred from the set of functional dependencies F, or alternatively that F infers X→Y.

In the following, we will use an abbreviated notation when discussing functional dependencies. We will concatenate attribute variables and drop the commas for convenience. Hence, the FD $\{X,Y\} \rightarrow Z$ is abbreviated to $XY \rightarrow Z$, and the FD $\{X,Y,Z\} \rightarrow \{U,V\}$ is abbreviated to $XYZ \rightarrow UV$. The following six rules IR1 to IR6 are well-known inference rules for functional dependencies:

(IR1) (Reflexive rule) If $X \supseteq Y$, then $X \rightarrow Y$.

(IR2) (Augmentation rule*) $\{X \rightarrow Y\} \models XZ \rightarrow YZ$.

(IR3) (Transitive rule) $\{X \rightarrow Y, Y \rightarrow Z\} \models X \rightarrow Z$.

(IR4) (Decomposition (or projective) rule) $\{X \rightarrow YZ\} \models X \rightarrow Y$.

(IR5) (Union (or additive) rule) $\{X \rightarrow Y, X \rightarrow Z\} \models X \rightarrow YZ$.

(IR6) (Pseudotransitive rule) $\{X \rightarrow Y, WY \rightarrow Z\} \models WX \rightarrow Z$.

The reflexive rule (IR1) says that a set of attributes always determines itself, which is obvious. The augmentation rule (IR2) says that adding the same set of attributes to both left- and right-hand sides of a dependency results in another valid dependency. By IR3, functional dependencies are transitive. The decomposition rule (IR4) says that we can remove attributes from the right-hand side of a dependency; applying this rule repeatedly can decompose the FD $X \rightarrow \{A_1, A_2, ..., A_n\}$ into the set of dependencies $\{X \rightarrow A_1, X \rightarrow A_2, ..., X \rightarrow A_n\}$. The union rule (IR5) allows us to do the opposite; we can combine a set of dependencies $\{X \rightarrow A_1, X \rightarrow A_2, ..., X \rightarrow A_n\}$ into the single FD $X \rightarrow \{A_1, A_2, ..., A_n\}$.

Each of the above inference rules can be proved from the definition of functional dependency, either by direct proof or **by contradiction**. A proof by contradiction assumes that the rule does not hold and shows that this is not possible. We now prove that the first three rules (IR1 to IR3) are valid. The second proof is by contradiction.

PROOF OF IR1
Suppose that $X \supseteq Y$ and that two tuples t_1 and t_2 exist in some relation instance r of R such that $t_1[X] = t_2[X]$. Then $t_1[Y] = t_2[Y]$ because $X \supseteq Y$; hence, $X \rightarrow Y$ must hold in r.

PROOF OF IR2 (BY CONTRADICTION)
Assume that $X \rightarrow Y$ holds in a relation instance r of R but that $XZ \rightarrow YZ$ does not hold. Then there must exist two tuples t_1 and t_2 in r such that (1) $t_1[X] = t_2[X]$, (2) $t_1[Y] = t_2[Y]$, (3) $t_1[XZ] = t_2[XZ]$, and (4) $t_1[YZ] \neq t_2[YZ]$. This is not possible because from (1) and (3) we deduce (5) $t_1[Z] = t_2[Z]$, and from (2) and (5) we deduce (6) $t_1[YZ] = t_2[YZ]$, contradicting (4).

PROOF OF IR3
Assume that (1) $X \rightarrow Y$ and (2) $Y \rightarrow Z$ both hold in a relation r. Then for any two tuples t_1 and t_2 in r such that $t_1[X] = t_2[X]$, we must have (3) $t_1[Y] = t_2[Y]$ (from assumption (1)), and hence we must also have (4) $t_1[Z] = t_2[Z]$, (from (3) and assumption (2)); hence, $X \rightarrow Z$ must hold in r.

---

*The augmentation rule can also be stated as $\{X \rightarrow Y\} \models XZ \rightarrow Y$; that is, augmenting the left-hand side attributes of an FD produces another valid FD.

Using similar proof arguments, we can prove the inference rules IR4 to IR6 and any additional valid inference rules. However, a simpler way to prove that an inference rule for functional dependencies is valid is to prove it using inference rules that have already been shown to be valid. For example, we can prove IR4 to IR6 using IR1 to IR3 as follows:

PROOF OF IR4

1. $X \rightarrow YZ$ (given).
2. $YZ \rightarrow Y$ (using IR1 and knowing that $YZ \supseteq Y$).
3. $X \rightarrow Y$ (using IR3 on 1 and 2).

PROOF OF IR5

1. $X \rightarrow Y$ (given).
2. $X \rightarrow Z$ (given).
3. $X \rightarrow XY$ (using IR2 on 1 by augmenting with X; note that XX = X).
4. $XY \rightarrow YZ$ (using IR2 on 2 by augmenting with Y).
5. $X \rightarrow YZ$ (using IR3 on 3 and 4).

PROOF OF IR6

1. $X \rightarrow Y$ (given).
2. $WY \rightarrow Z$ (given).
3. $WX \rightarrow WY$ (using IR2 on 1 by augmenting with W).
4. $WX \rightarrow Z$ (using IR3 on 3 and 2).

It has been shown by Armstrong (1974) that inference rules IR1 to IR3 are **sound** and **complete**. By sound, we mean that given a set of functional dependencies F specified on a relation schema R, any dependency that we can infer from F by using IR1 to IR3 will hold in every relation instance r of R that *satisfies the dependencies* in F. By complete, we mean that using IR1 to IR3 repeatedly to infer dependencies until no more dependencies can be inferred will result in the complete set of *all possible dependencies* that can be inferred from F. In other words, the set of dependencies F^+, which we called the closure of F, can be determined from F by using only inference rules IR1 to IR3. Inference rules IR1 to IR3 are known as **Armstrong's inference rules.***

To discover the dependencies in a relation schema R, we can first specify the set of functional dependencies F that can easily be determined from the semantics of the attributes of R. Then we can use Armstrong's inference rules to infer additional functional dependencies that will also hold on R. A systematic way to determine these additional functional dependencies is first to determine each set of attributes X that appears as a left-hand side of some functional dependency in F and then use Armstrong's inference rules to determine the set of all attributes that are dependent on X. Thus, for each set of attributes X, we determine the set X^+ of attributes that are functionally determined by X; X^+ is called the **closure of X under F**. Algorithm 13.1 can be used to calculate X^+.

---

*They are also known as **Armstrong's axioms**, although they are not axioms in the mathematical sense. Strictly speaking, the axioms are the functional dependencies in F since we assume they are correct, while IR1 to IR3 are the inference rules for deducing new functional dependencies.

ALGORITHM 13.1   Determining X^+, the closure of X under F

```
X+ := X;
repeat
      oldX+ := X+;
      for each functional dependency Y→ Z in F do
            if Y ⊆ X+ then X+ := X+ ∪ Z;
until (oldX+ = X+);
```

Algorithm 13.1 starts by setting X^+ to all the attributes in X. By IR1, we know that all these attributes are functionally dependent on X. Using inference rules IR3 and IR4, we add attributes to X^+ using each functional dependency in F. We keep going through all the dependencies in F (the repeat loop) until no more attributes are added to X^+ during a complete cycle through the dependencies in F. For example, consider the relation schema EMP_PROJ in Figure 13.3b; from the semantics of the attributes we specify the following set F of functional dependencies that should hold on EMP_PROJ:

F = { SSN → ENAME, PNUMBER → {PNAME, PLOCATION},
    {SSN, PNUMBER} → HOURS }

Using Algorithm 13.1, we calculate the following closure sets with respect to F:

{ SSN }$^+$ = { SSN, ENAME }
{ PNUMBER }$^+$ = { PNUMBER, PNAME, PLOCATION }
{ SSN, PNUMBER }$^+$ = { SSN, PNUMBER, ENAME, PNAME, PLOCATION,
                     HOURS }

13.2.3   Equivalence of Sets of Functional Dependencies

In this section we discuss the criteria for equivalence between two sets of functional dependencies. First, we give some preliminary definitions that are needed to define equivalence. A set of functional dependencies E is said to be **covered by** a set of functional dependencies F, or, alternatively, F is said to **cover** E, if every FD in E is also in F^+; that is, every dependency in E can be inferred from F. Two sets of functional dependencies E and F are said to be **equivalent** if $E^+ = F^+$. Hence, equivalence means that every FD in E can be inferred from F, and every FD in F can be inferred from E; that is, E is equivalent to F if both E covers F *and* F covers E hold.

We can determine whether F covers E by calculating X^+ with respect to F for each FD X→Y in E, then checking whether this X^+ includes the attributes in Y. If this is the case for *every* FD in E, then F covers E. We determine whether E and F are equivalent by checking that E covers F and F covers E.

13.2.4   Minimal Sets of Functional Dependencies

Another important concept in dependency theory is that of a minimal set of dependencies. A set of functional dependencies F is **minimal** if it satisfies the following three conditions:

1. Every dependency in F has a single attribute for its right-hand side.

2. We cannot remove any dependency from F and still have a set of dependencies that is equivalent to F.

3. We cannot replace any dependency X→A in F with a dependency Y→A, where Y is a proper subset of X, and still have a set of dependencies that is equivalent to F.

We can think of a minimal set of dependencies as a set of dependencies in a standard or canonical form with no redundancies. Conditions 2 and 3 make sure there are no redundancies in the dependencies, and condition 1 ensures that every dependency is in a canonical form with a single attribute on the right-hand side. A **minimal cover** of a set of functional dependencies F is a minimal set of dependencies F_{min} that is equivalent to F. Unfortunately, there can be several minimal covers for a set of functional dependencies. However, we can always find *at least one* minimal cover F_{min} for any set of dependencies F, but there is no simple algorithm to find an F_{min}.

13.3 Normal Forms Based on Primary Keys

In this section we discuss the normalization process and define the first three normal forms for relation schemas. The definitions of second and third normal form presented here are based on the functional dependencies and primary keys of a relation. We will discuss how these normal forms were developed historically and the intuition behind them. More general definitions of these normal forms, which take into account *all candidate keys* of a relation rather than *just the primary key*, are presented in Section 13.4. In Section 13.5 we define Boyce-Codd normal form (BCNF), and in Chapter 14 we define further normal forms that are based on other types of data dependencies.

We first informally discuss what normal forms are and the motivation behind their development in Section 13.3.1 and also recall some of the definitions from Chapter 6 that are needed here. We then present first normal form (1NF) in Section 13.3.2. In Sections 13.3.3 and 13.3.4 we present the definitions of second normal form (2NF) and third normal form (3NF), respectively, that are based on primary keys.

13.3.1 Introduction to Normalization

The normalization process, as first proposed by Codd (1972a), takes a relation schema through a series of tests to "certify" whether or not it belongs to a certain **normal form**. Initially, Codd proposed three normal forms, which he called first, second, and third normal form. A stronger definition of 3NF was proposed later by Boyce and Codd and is known as Boyce-Codd normal form. All these normal forms are based on the functional dependencies among the attributes of a relation. Later, a fourth normal form (4NF) and a fifth normal form (5NF) were proposed, based on the concepts of multivalued dependencies and join dependencies, respectively; these are discussed in Chapter 14.

Normalization of data can be looked on as a process during which unsatisfactory relation schemas are decomposed by breaking up their attributes into smaller relation schemas that possess desirable properties. In fact, one of the objectives of the original normalization process is to ensure that relation schemas have a "good" design by disallowing the update anomalies discussed in Section 13.1.2. Normal forms provide database designers with:

- A formal framework for analyzing relation schemas based on their keys and the functional dependencies among their attributes.

- A series of tests that can be carried out on individual relation schemas so that the relational database can be **normalized** to any degree. When a test fails, the relation violating that test must be decomposed into relations that will individually meet the normalization tests.

It is important to note that normal forms, when considered *in isolation* from other factors, do not guarantee a good database design. It is generally not sufficient to check separately that each relation schema in the database is, say, in BCNF or 3NF. Rather, the process of normalization through decomposition must also ensure additional properties that the relational schemas taken together should possess. Two of these properties are:

- The lossless join or nonadditive join property, which guarantees that the spurious tuple problem discussed in Section13.1.4 does not occur.

- The dependency preservation property, which ensures that all functional dependencies are represented in some of the individual resulting relations.

We will defer the presentation of the formal concepts and techniques that guarantee the above two properties to Chapter 14. In this section we concentrate on an intuitive discussion of the normalization process. Note that the normal forms mentioned in this section are not the only possible ones. Additional normal forms may be defined to meet other desirable criteria based on constraints on relation schemas that were not considered in previously defined normal forms. The normal forms up to BCNF are defined by considering only the functional dependency and key constraints on a relation schema, whereas 4NF considers an additional constraint called a multivalued dependency and 5NF considers an additional constraint called a join dependency. The practical utility of normal forms becomes questionable when the constraints on which they are based are hard to understand or to detect by the database designers and users who must discover these constraints.

Another point worth noting is that the database designers *need not* normalize to the highest possible normal form. Relations may be left in lower normal forms for performance reasons, such as those discussed at the end of Section 13.1.2.

Before proceeding further, we recall from Chapter 6 the definitions of keys of a relation schema. A **superkey** of a relation schema $R = \{A_1, A_2, \ldots, A_n\}$ is a set of attributes $S \subseteq R$ with the property that no two tuples t_1 and t_2 in any relation instance r of R will have $t_1[S] = t_2[S]$. A **key** K is a superkey with the additional property that removal of any attribute from K will result in K not being a superkey any more. The difference between a key and a superkey is that a key has to be "minimal"; that is, if we have a key $K = \{A_1, A_2, \ldots, A_k\}$, then $K - A_i$ is not a key for $1 \leq i \leq k$. For example, in Figure 13.1 {SSN} is a key for EMPLOYEE, whereas {SSN}, {SSN, ENAME}, {SSN, ENAME, BDATE}, etc. are all superkeys.

If a relation schema has more than one "minimal" key, each is called a **candidate key**. One of the candidate keys is *arbitrarily* designated to be the **primary key** of the relation schema, and the others are called secondary keys. Each relation schema must have a primary key. For example, in Figure 13.1 {SSN} is the only candidate key for EMPLOYEE, so it is also the primary key.

An attribute of relation schema R is called a **prime attribute** of R if it is a member of *any key* of R. An attribute is called **nonprime** if it is not a prime attribute; that is, it is not a member of any candidate key of R. For example, in Figure 13.1 both SSN and PNUMBER are prime attributes of WORKS_ON, whereas any other attributes of WORKS_ON are nonprime.

We will now present the first three normal forms—1NF, 2NF, and 3NF—as proposed by Codd (1972a). These were proposed as a sequence to ultimately achieve the desirable state of 3NF relations by progressing through the intermediate states of 1NF and 2NF if needed.

13.3.2   First Normal Form (1NF)

First normal form is now generally considered to be part of the formal definition of a relation; historically, it was defined to disallow multivalued attributes, composite attributes, and their combinations. It states that the domains of attributes must include only *atomic* (simple, indivisible) *values* and that the value of any attribute in a tuple must be a *single value* from the domain of that attribute. Hence, 1NF disallows having a set of values, a tuple of values, or a combination of both as an attribute value for a *single tuple*. In other words, 1NF disallows "relations within relations" or "relations as attributes of tuples." The only attribute values permitted by 1NF are single **atomic** (or **indivisible**) **values** from a domain of such values.

Consider the DEPARTMENT relation schema shown in Figure 13.1 whose primary key is DNUMBER and suppose we extend it by including the DLOCATIONS attribute shown within dotted lines. We assume that each department can have *a number of* locations. The DEPARTMENT schema and an example extension are shown in Figure 13.8. As we can see, this is not in 1NF because DLOCATIONS is not an atomic attribute, as illustrated by the first tuple in Figure 13.8b. There are two ways we can look at the DLOCATIONS attribute:

- The domain of DLOCATIONS contains atomic values, but some tuples can have a set of these values. In this case, DNUMBER ↛ DLOCATIONS.
- The domain of DLOCATIONS contains sets of values and is hence nonatomic. In this case, DNUMBER → DLOCATIONS, because each set is considered a single member of the attribute domain.*

In either case, the DEPARTMENT relation of Figure 13.8 is not in 1NF; in fact, it does not even qualify as a relation according to our definition of relation in Section 6.1. To normalize into 1NF relations, we break up its attributes into the two relations DEPARTMENT and DEPT_LOCATIONS shown in Figure 13.2. The idea is to remove the attribute DLOCATIONS that causes the relation not to be in 1NF and place it in a separate relation DEPT_LOCATIONS along with the primary key DNUMBER of DEPARTMENT. The primary key of this relation is the combination {DNUMBER, DLOCATION} as shown in Figure 13.2. A distinct tuple in DEPT_LOCATIONS exists for *each location* of a department. The DLOCATIONS

---

*In this case we can consider the domain of DLOCATIONS to be the **power set** of the set of single locations; that is, the domain is made up of *all possible subsets* of the set of single locations.

(a)   DEPARTMENT

DNAME	DNUMBER	DMGRSSN	DLOCATIONS

(b)   DEPARTMENT

DNAME	DNUMBER	DMGRSSN	DLOCATIONS
Research	5	333445555	{Bellaire, Sugarland, Houston}
Administration	4	987654321	{Stafford}
Headquarters	1	888665555	{Houston}

(c)   DEPARTMENT

DNAME	DNUMBER	DMGRSSN	DLOCATION
Research	5	333445555	Bellaire
Research	5	333445555	Sugarland
Research	5	333445555	Houston
Administration	4	987654321	Stafford
Headquarters	1	888665555	Houston

Figure 13.8   Illustrating normalization into 1NF. (a) A relation schema that is not in 1NF. (b) Example relation instance. (c) 1NF relation with redundancy.

attribute is removed from the DEPARTMENT relation of Figure 13.8, decomposing the non-1NF relation into the two 1NF relations DEPARTMENT and DEPT_DLOCATIONS of Figure 13.2.

Notice that a second solution to normalize into 1NF is to have a tuple in the original DEPARTMENT relation for each location of a DEPARTMENT, as shown in Figure 13.8c. In this case, the primary key becomes the combination {DNUMBER, DLOCATION}, and redundancy exists in the tuples. The first solution is superior because it does not suffer from this redundancy problem. In fact, if we choose the second solution, it will be decomposed further during subsequent normalization steps into the first solution.

The first normal form also disallows composite attributes that are themselves multivalued. These are called **nested relations** because each tuple can have a relation *within it*. Figure 13.9 shows how an EMP_PROJ relation can be shown if nesting is allowed. Each tuple represents an employee entity, and a relation PROJS(PNUMBER, HOURS) *within each tuple* represents the employee's projects and the hours per week that the employee works on each project. The schema of the EMP_PROJ relation can be represented as follows:

EMP_PROJ(SSN, ENAME, {PROJS(PNUMBER, HOURS)})

The set braces { } identify the attribute PROJS as multivalued, and we list the component attributes that form PROJS between parentheses ( ). It is interesting to note that recent research into the relational model is attemping to allow and formalize nested relations, which were disallowed early on by 1NF. Another notation for nested relations, cur-

(a) **EMP_PROJ**

SSN	ENAME	PROJS	
		PNUMBER	HOURS

(b) **EMP_PROJ**

SSN	ENAME	PNUMBER	HOURS
123456789	Smith,John B.	1	32.5
		2	7.5
666884444	Narayan,Ramesh K.	3	40.0
453453453	English,Joyce A.	1	20.0
		2	20.0
333445555	Wong,Franklin T.	2	10.0
		3	10.0
		10	10.0
		20	10.0
999887777	Zelaya,Alicia J.	30	30.0
		10	10.0
987987987	Jabbar,Ahmad V.	10	35.0
		30	5.0
987654321	Wallace,Jennifer S.	30	20.0
		20	15.0
888665555	Borg,James E.	20	null

(c) **EMP_PROJ1**

SSN	ENAME

EMP_PROJ2

SSN	PNUMBER	HOURS

Figure 13.9 Normalizing nested relations into 1NF. (a) Schema of the
EMP_PROJ relation with a "nested relation" PROJS within EMP_PROJ.
(b) Example extension of the EMP_ PROJ relation with nested
relations within each tuple. (c) Decomposing EMP_PROJ into 1NF
relations by migrating the primary key.

rently popular with database researchers, is to list the schema attributes without giving
names to the nested relations but just including their component attributes as follows:

EMP_PROJ = { SSN, ENAME, {PNUMBER, HOURS} }

Note that SSN is the primary key of the EMP_PROJ relation in Figures 13.9a and b,
while PNUMBER is the **partial** primary key of each nested relation; that is, within each
tuple, the nested relation must have unique values of PNUMBER. To normalize this into
1NF, we remove the nested relation attributes into a new relation and **propagate the pri-**

mary key into it; the primary key of the new relation will combine the partial key with the primary key of the original relation. Hence, decomposition and primary key propagation yield the schemas shown in Figure 13.9c.

This procedure can be applied recursively to a relation that has multiple-level nesting to **unnest** the relation into a set of 1NF relations. This is particularly useful in converting hierarchical schemas into 1NF relations. Also, as we shall see in Chapter 14, restricting relations to 1NF leads to the problems associated with multivalued dependencies and 4NF. Next, we discuss normalization into second normal form.

13.3.3   Second Normal Form (2NF)

The second normal form is based on the concept of a full functional dependency. A functional dependency $X \rightarrow Y$ is a **full functional dependency** if removal of any attribute A from X means that the dependency does not hold any more; that is, for any attribute $A \in X$, $(X - \{A\}) \not\rightarrow Y$. A functional dependency $X \rightarrow Y$ is a **partial dependency** if there is some attribute $A \in X$ that can be removed from X and the dependency will still hold; that is, for some $A \in X$, $(X - \{A\}) \rightarrow Y$. For example, in Figure 13.3b, {SSN, PNUMBER}$\rightarrow$HOURS is a full dependency (neither SSN$\rightarrow$HOURS nor PNUMBER$\rightarrow$HOURS holds). However, the dependency {SSN, PNUMBER}$\rightarrow$ENAME is partial because SSN$\rightarrow$ENAME holds.

A relation schema R is in 2NF if every nonprime* attribute A in R is *fully functionally dependent* on the primary key of R. The EMP_PROJ relation in Figure 13.3b is in 1NF but is not in 2NF. The nonprime attribute ENAME violates the 2NF condition because of fd2, as do the nonprime attributes PNAME and PLOCATION because of fd3. The functional dependencies fd2 and fd3 make ENAME, PNAME, and PLOCATION partially dependent on the primary key {SSN, PNUMBER} of EMP_PROJ, thus violating 2NF.

If a relation is not in 2NF, it can be further normalized into a number of 2NF relations so that the nonprime attributes are associated only with the part of the primary key on which they are fully functionally dependent. The functional dependencies fd1, fd2, and fd3 in Figure 13.3b hence lead to the decomposition of EMP_PROJ into the three relation schemas EP1, EP2, and EP3 shown in Figure 13.10a, each of which satisfies the 2NF constraint. We can see that the relations EP1, EP2, and EP3 are devoid of the update anomalies from which EMP_PROJ of Figure 13.3b suffers.

13.3.4   Third Normal Form (3NF)

The third normal form is based on the concept of a transitive dependency. A functional dependency $X \rightarrow Y$ in a relation schema R is a **transitive dependency** if there is a set of attributes Z that is *not a subset* of any key** of R, and both $X \rightarrow Z$ and $Z \rightarrow Y$ hold. For example, the dependency SSN$\rightarrow$DMGRSSN is a transitive dependency in EMP_DEPT

---

*This is a restricted use of nonprime, which here means that the attribute is not a member of the *primary key* rather than of *any* candidate key as in the general definition of nonprime.

**This is the general definition of transitive dependency. Because we are only concerned with primary keys in this section, we allow transitive dependencies where X is the primary key but Z may be (a subset of) a candidate key.

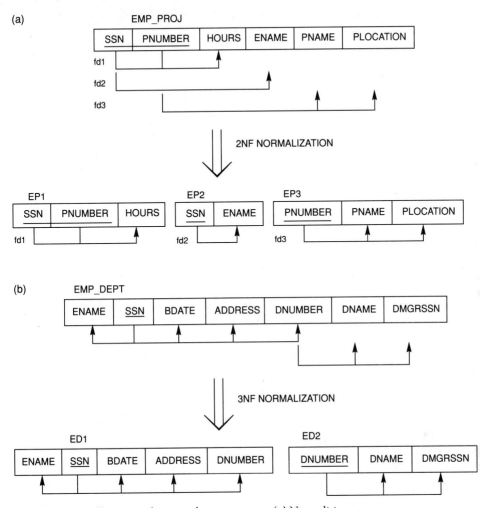

Figure 13.10 Illustrating the normalization process. (a) Normalizing EMP_PROJ into 2NF relations. (b) Normalizing EMP_DEPT into 3NF relations.

of Figure 13.3a. We say that the dependency of DMGRSSN on the key attribute SSN is *transitive via* DNUMBER because both the dependencies SSN→DNUMBER and DNUMBER →DMGRSSN hold, *and* DNUMBER is not a subset of the key of EMP_DEPT. Intuitively, we can see that the dependency of DMGRSSN on DNUMBER is undesirable in EMP_DEPT since DNUMBER is not a key of EMP_DEPT.

According to Codd's original definition, a relation schema R is in **3NF** if it is in 2NF and no nonprime attribute of R is transitively dependent on the primary key. The relation schema EMP_DEPT in Figure 13.3a is in 2NF since no partial dependencies on a key exist. However, EMP_DEPT is not in 3NF because of the transitive dependency of DMGRSSN (and also DNAME) on SSN via DNUMBER. We can normalize EMP_DEPT by decomposing it into the two 3NF relation schemas ED1 and ED2 shown in Figure 13.10b. Intuitively, we see that ED1 and ED2 represent independent entity facts about employees and departments. A NATURAL JOIN operation on ED1 and ED2 will recover the original relation EMP_DEPT without generating spurious tuples.

13.4   General Definitions of Second and Third Normal Forms

In general, we want to design our relation schemas so they have neither partial dependencies nor transitive dependencies, because these types of dependencies cause the update anomalies discussed in Section 13.1.2. According to the definitions of second and third normal forms presented in Section 13.3, the steps for normalization into 3NF relations will disallow partial and transitive dependencies on the primary key. These definitions, however, do not take other candidate keys of a relation, if any, into account.

In this section we give the more general definitions of 2NF and 3NF that take *all* candidate keys of a relation into account. Notice that this does not affect the definition of 1NF since it is independent of keys and functional dependencies. We will use the *general definitions* of prime attributes, partial and full functional dependencies, and transitive dependencies given earlier that consider all candidate keys of a relation, not the definitions that consider only the primary key which were used in the previous definitions of 2NF and 3NF.

13.4.1   General Definition of Second Normal Form (2NF)

A relation schema R is in **second normal form** (2NF) if every nonprime attribute A in R is not partially dependent on *any key* of R.* Consider the relation schema LOTS shown in Figure 13.11a, which describes parcels of land for sale in various counties of a state. Suppose that there are two candidate keys: PROPERTY_ID# and {COUNTY_NAME, LOT#}; that is, LOT#'s are unique only within each county but PROPERTY_ID#'s are unique across counties for the entire state.

Based on the two candidate keys PROPERTY_ID# and {COUNTY_NAME, LOT#}, we know that the functional dependencies fd1 and fd2 of Figure 13.11a hold. We will choose PROPERTY_ID# as the primary key, so it is underlined in Figure 13.11a. Now suppose we are told that the following two additional functional dependencies also hold in LOTS:

> fd3: COUNTY_NAME → TAX_RATE
> fd4: AREA → PRICE

In words, the dependency fd3 says that the tax rate is fixed for a given county (does not vary lot by lot within the same county), while fd4 says that the price of a lot is determined by its area regardless of which county it is in (assume that this is the price of the lot for tax purposes).

---

*This definition can be restated as follows: A relation schema R is in 2NF if every nonprime attribute A in R is fully functionally dependent on *every key* of R.

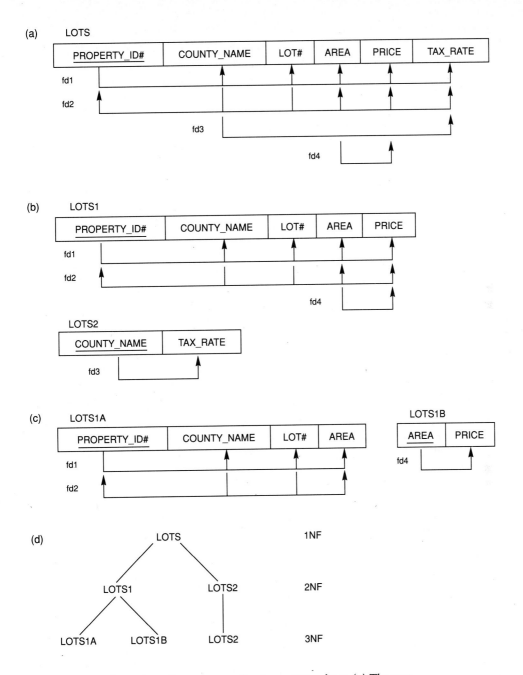

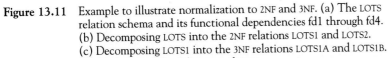

Figure 13.11 Example to illustrate normalization to 2NF and 3NF. (a) The LOTS relation schema and its functional dependencies fd1 through fd4. (b) Decomposing LOTS into the 2NF relations LOTS1 and LOTS2. (c) Decomposing LOTS1 into the 3NF relations LOTS1A and LOTS1B. (d) Summary of normalization of LOTS.

By applying the general definition of 2NF given above, we see that the LOTS relation schema violates 2NF because TAX_RATE is partially dependent (or not fully functionally dependent) on the candidate key {COUNTY_NAME, LOT#} due to fd3. To normalize LOTS into 2NF, we decompose it into the two relations LOTS1 and LOTS2, shown in Figure 13.11b. We construct LOTS1 by removing the attribute TAX_RATE that violates 2NF from LOTS. We place TAX_RATE along with COUNTY_NAME (the left-hand side of fd3 that causes the partial dependency) into another relation LOTS2. Both LOTS1 and LOTS2 are in 2NF. Note that fd4 does not violate 2NF and is carried over to LOTS1.

13.4.2   General Definition of Third Normal Form (3NF)

A relation schema R is in **3NF** if whenever a functional dependency $X \rightarrow A$ holds in R, then either (a) X is a superkey of R or (b) A is a prime attribute of R. According to this definition, LOTS2 (Figure 13.11b) is in 3NF. However, fd4 in LOTS1 violates 3NF because AREA is not a superkey of LOTS1 and PRICE is not a prime attribute. To normalize into 3NF, we decompose LOTS1 into the relation schemas LOTS1A and LOTS1B shown in Figure 13.11c. We construct LOTS1A by removing the attribute PRICE that violates 3NF from LOTS1. We place PRICE along with AREA (the left-hand side of fd4 that causes the transitive dependency) into another relation LOTS1B. Both LOTS1A and LOTS1B are in 3NF.

Two points are worth noting about the above general definition of 3NF:

- This definition can be applied *directly* to test whether a relation schema is in 3NF; it does *not* require us to go through 2NF first. For example, if we apply the 3NF definition to LOTS with the dependencies fd1 through fd4, we find that *both* fd3 and fd4 violate 3NF. We could hence decompose LOTS into LOTS1A, LOTS1B, and LOTS2 directly.

- LOTS1 violates 3NF because PRICE is transitively dependent on each of the candidate keys of LOTS1 via the nonprime attribute AREA.

13.4.3   Interpreting the General Definition of 3NF

A relation schema R violates the general definition of 3NF if a functional dependency $X \rightarrow A$ holds in R that violates *both* conditions (a) and (b) of 3NF. Violating (b) implies that A is a nonprime attribute. Violating (a) implies that X is not a superset of any key of R; hence, X could be nonprime or it could be a proper subset of a key of R. If X is nonprime we will typically have a transitive dependency that violates 3NF, whereas if X is a proper subset of a key of R we will have a partial dependency that violates 3NF (and also 2NF). Hence, we can state a **general alternative definition of 3NF** as follows: A relation schema R is in 3NF if every nonprime attribute of R is:

- Fully functionally dependent on every key of R, and
- Nontransitively dependent on every key of R.

13.5   Boyce-Codd Normal Form (BCNF)

Boyce-Codd normal form is a stricter form of 3NF, meaning that every relation in BCNF is also in 3NF; however, a relation in 3NF is *not necessarily* in BCNF. Intuitively, we can see the need for a stronger normal form than 3NF by going back to the LOTS relation schema of Figure 13.11a with its four functional dependencies fd1 through fd4. Suppose we have thousands of lots in the relation but the lots are from only two counties: Marion County and Liberty County. Suppose also that lot sizes in Marion County are only 0.5, 0.6, 0.7, 0.8, 0.9, and 1.0 acres, whereas lot sizes in Liberty County are restricted to 1.1, 1.2, ..., 1.9, and 2.0 acres. In such a situation we would have the additional functional dependency fd5: AREA $\rightarrow$ COUNTY_NAME. By adding this to the other dependencies, the relation schema LOTS1A still is in 3NF because COUNTY_NAME is a prime attribute.

Intuitively, the area versus county relationship represented by fd5 can be represented by 16 tuples in a separate relation R(AREA, COUNTY_NAME) since there are only 16 possible AREA values. This representation reduces the redundancy of repeating the same information in the thousands of LOTS1A tuples. Hence, we can see a need for a stronger normal form that would disallow LOTS1A and suggest the need for decomposing it. Boyce-Codd normal form serves this need.

This definition of Boyce-Codd differs slightly from that of 3NF. A relation schema R is in **Boyce-Codd normal form** if whenever a functional dependency X→A holds in R, then X is a superkey of R. The only difference between BCNF and 3NF is that condition (b) of 3NF, which allows A to be prime if X is not a superkey, is absent from BCNF. Hence, BCNF is stronger (more restrictive) than 3NF, meaning that any relation schema in BCNF is automatically in 3NF.

In our example, fd5 violates BCNF in LOTS1A because AREA is not a superkey of LOTS1A. Note that fd5 satisfies 3NF in LOTS1A because COUNTY_NAME is a prime attribute (condition (b)), but this condition does not exist in the definition of BCNF. We can decompose LOTS1A into two BCNF relations LOTS1AX and LOTS1AY, shown in Figure 13.12a.

In practice, most relation schemas that are in 3NF are also in BCNF. Only if a dependency X→A exists in a relation schema R with X not a superkey *and* A a prime attribute will R be in 3NF but not in BCNF. The relation schema R shown in Figure 13.12b illustrates the general case of such a relation.

In general, it is best to have relation schemas in BCNF. If that is not possible, 3NF will do. However, 2NF and 1NF are not considered good relation schema designs. These normal forms were developed historically as stepping stones to 3NF and BCNF.

13.6   Summary

In this chapter we discussed in an intuitive fashion several pitfalls in relational database design and then presented some basic formal concepts that are important when designing a relational database. The topics discussed in this chapter are continued in Chapter 14, where we discuss more advanced concepts in relational design theory.

In Section 13.1 we discussed in an informal manner some of the measures that can be used to tell whether a relation schema is "good" or "bad" and provided informal guidelines for a good design. We discussed the problems of update anomalies that occur when redundancies are present in relations. Additional informal measures of good relation schemas were simple and clear attribute semantics and few nulls in the relations corresponding to schemas.

In Section 13.1.4 we discussed the problem of spurious tuples. This problem will be formalized and dealt with in Chapter 14, where we present decomposition algorithms

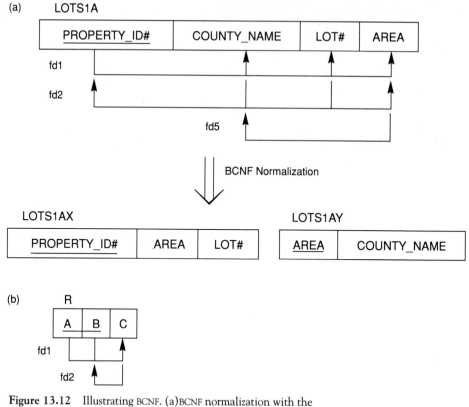

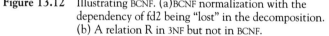

Figure 13.12   Illustrating BCNF. (a)BCNF normalization with the
dependency of fd2 being "lost" in the decomposition.
(b) A relation R in 3NF but not in BCNF.

for relational database design based on functional dependencies. We will discuss the concepts of "lossless join" and "dependency preservation," which are enforced by some of these algorithms. The lossless join property ensures that no spurious tuples will occur. Other topics we discuss in Chapter 14 include multivalued dependencies, join dependencies, and additional normal forms that take these dependencies into account.

In Section 13.2 we presented the concept of functional dependency and discussed some of its properties. Functional dependencies are fundamental constraints that are specified among the attributes of a relation schema. We showed how functional dependencies can be inferred from a set of dependencies and how we can check whether two sets of functional dependencies are equivalent.

In Section 13.3 we used the concept of functional dependency to define normal forms based on primary keys. We provided more general definitions of second normal form (2NF) and third normal form (3NF), which take all candidate keys of a relation into account, in Section 13.4. Finally, we presented Boyce-Codd normal form (BCNF) in Section 13.5 and discussed how it differs from 3NF. We illustrated by examples how these normal forms can be used to decompose an unnormalized relation into a set of relations in 3NF or BCNF.

Review Questions

13.1. Discuss the attribute semantics as an informal measure of goodness for a relation schema.

13.2. Discuss insertion, deletion, and modification anomalies. Why are they considered bad?

13.3. Why are many **null**s in a relation considered bad?

13.4. Discuss the problem of spurious tuples and how we may prevent it.

13.5. Discuss the informal guidelines for relation schema design.

13.6. What is a functional dependency? Who specifies the functional dependencies that hold among the attributes of a relation schema?

13.7. Why can we not deduce a functional dependency from a particular relation instance?

13.8. What is meant by the completeness and soundness of Armstrong's inference rules?

13.9. What is meant by the closure of a set of functional dependencies?

13.10. When are two sets of functional dependencies equivalent? How can we determine their equivalence?

13.11. What is a minimal set of functional dependencies? Does every set of dependencies have a minimal equivalent set?

13.12. Define first, second, and third normal forms when only primary keys are considered. How do the general definitions of 2NF and 3NF that consider all keys of a relation difer from those that consider only primary keys?

13.13. Why is a relation that is in 3NF generally considered good?

13.14. Define Boyce-Codd normal form. How does BCNF differ from 3NF?

13.15. How did the normal forms develop historically?

Exercises

13.16. Suppose we have the following requirements for a university database that is used to keep track of students' transcripts:

a. The university keeps track of each student's name (SNAME), student number (SNUM), social security number (SSSN), current address (SCADDR) and phone (SCPHONE), permanent address (SPADDR) and phone (SPPHONE), birthdate (BDATE), sex (SEX), class (CLASS) (freshman, sophomore, ..., graduate), major department (MAJORDEPTCODE), minor department (MINORDEPTCODE) (if any), and degree program (PROG) (B.A., B.S., ..., Ph.D.). Both SSN and student number have unique values for each student.

b. Each department is described by a name (DEPTNAME), department code (DEPTCODE), office number (DEPTOFFICE), office phone (DEPTPHONE), and college (DEPTCOLLEGE). Both name and code have unique values for each department.

c. Each course has a course name (CNAME), description (CDESC), code number (CNUM), number of semester hours (CREDIT), level (LEVEL), and offering department (CDEPT). The value of code number is unique for each course.

d. Each section has an instructor (INSTRUCTORNAME), semester (SEMESTER), year (YEAR), course (SECCOURSE), and section number (SECNUM). Section number distinguishes different sections of the same course that are taught during the same semester/year; its values are 1, 2, 3, ...; up to the number of sections taught during each semester.

e. A transcript refers to a student (SSSN), a particular section, and a grade (GRADE).

Design a relational database schema for this database application. First show all the functional dependencies that should hold among the attributes. Then design relation schemas for the database that are each in 3NF or BCNF. Specify the key attributes of each relation. Note any unspecified requirements, and make appropriate assumptions to make the specification complete.

13.17. Prove or disprove the following inference rules for functional dependencies. A proof can either be by a proof argument or by using Armstrong's inference rules IR1 to IR3. A disproof should be done by demonstrating a relation instance that satisfies the conditions and functional dependencies in the left-hand side of the inference rule but does not satisfy the conditions or dependencies in the right-hand side.

a. $\{W \rightarrow Y, X \rightarrow Z\} \models \{WX \rightarrow Y\}$.

b. $\{X \rightarrow Y\}$ and $Z \subseteq Y \models \{X \rightarrow Z\}$.

c. $\{X \rightarrow Y, X \rightarrow W, WY \rightarrow Z\} \models \{X \rightarrow Z\}$.

d. $\{XY \rightarrow Z, Y \rightarrow W\} \models \{XW \rightarrow Z\}$.

e. $\{X \rightarrow Z, Y \rightarrow Z\} \models \{X \rightarrow Y\}$.

f. $\{X \rightarrow Y, XY \rightarrow Z\} \models \{X \rightarrow Z\}$.

13.18. Why are the three inference rules IR1 to IR3 (Armstrong's inference rules) important?

13.19. Consider the following two sets of functional dependencies: $F = \{A \rightarrow C, AC \rightarrow D, E \rightarrow AD, E \rightarrow H\}$ and $G = \{A \rightarrow CD, E \rightarrow AH\}$. Check whether they are equivalent.

13.20. Consider the relation schema EMP_DEPT in Figure 13.3a and the following set G of functional dependencies on EMP_DEPT: $G = \{SSN \rightarrow \{ENAME, BDATE, ADDRESS, DNUMBER\}, DNUMBER \rightarrow \{DNAME, DMGRSSN\}\}$. Calculate the closures $\{SSN\}^+$ and $\{DNUMBER\}^+$ with respect to G.

13.21. Is the set of functional dependencies G in Exercise 13.20 minimal? If not, try to find a minimal set of functional dependencies that is equivalent to G. Prove that your set is equivalent to G.

13.22. Why are transitive dependencies and partial dependencies considered bad in a relational schema?

13.23. What update anomalies are there in the EMP_PROJ and EMP_DEPT relations of Figure 13.3 and 13.4?

13.24. In what normal form is the LOTS relation schema in Figure 13.11a with respect to the restrictive interpretations of normal form that take *only the primary key* into account? Would it be in the same normal form if the general definitions of normal form were used?

13.25. Why is BCNF considered better than 3NF?

13.26. Prove that any relation schema with two attributes is in BCNF.

13.27. Why are there spurious tuples in the result of joining the EMP_PROJ1 and EMP_LOCS relations of Figure 13.5 (result shown in Figure 13.6)?

13.28. Consider the relation PATIENT_VISIT shown in Figure 13.13.

    a. Show that both {PATIENT, HOSPITAL} and {PATIENT, DOCTOR} are candidate keys based on the functional dependencies fd1 and fd2, but {HOSPITAL, DOCTOR} is not.

    b. Show that the relation is in 3NF but not in BCNF.

PATIENT_VISIT

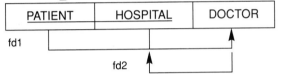

PATIENT_VISIT

PATIENT	HOSPITAL	DOCTOR
Smith	Alachua	Atkinson
Lee	Shands	Smith
Marks	Alachua	Atkinson
Marks	Shands	Shaw
Rao	North Florida	Nefzger

Figure 13.13 The PATIENT_VISIT relation

Selected Bibliography

Functional dependencies were originally introduced by Codd (1970). The original definitions of first, second, and third normal form were also defined by Codd (1972a), where a discussion on update anomalies can be found. Boyce-Codd normal form was defined in Codd (1974). The alternative definition of third normal form is given in Ullman (1982), as is the definition of BCNF that we give here. The textbooks by Ullman (1982) and Maier (1983) contain many of the theorems and proofs concerning functional dependencies. Maier also includes a complex algorithm for finding a minimal set of functional dependencies that is equivalent to a given set.

Armstrong (1974) shows the soundness and completeness of the inference rules IR1 to IR3, and a proof is also given in Ullman (1982). Additional references to relational design theory are given in Chapter 14.

Relational Database Design Algorithms and Further Dependencies

There are two main techniques for relational database schema design. In the first technique we design a conceptual schema in a high-level data model, such as the ER model, and then map the conceptual schema into a set of relations using a mapping procedure such as the one discussed in Section 12.1.1. This can be called a **top down** design. In this technique we can informally apply the normalization principles discussed in Chapter 13, such as avoiding transitive or partial dependencies, *both* during the conceptual schema design and to the relations resulting after the mapping procedure. In the second, more purist approach we can view relational database schema design strictly in terms of functional and other types of dependencies specified on the database attributes. This is sometimes called **relational synthesis**, because relation schemas in 3NF or BCNF are *synthesized* by grouping the appropriate attributes together. Each individual relation schema should represent a logically coherent grouping of attributes and should possess the measures of goodness associated with normalization.

In Chapter 13 we discussed some measures of goodness for individual relation schemas based on their keys and functional dependencies, namely that they are in BCNF or, barring that, in 3NF. During the process of normalization we decompose a relation that is not in a certain normal form into multiple relation schemas that are in the desired normal form. The relational design activity then can be thought of in terms of synthesis and decomposition until a final design is reached. An extreme case of this design process is that of **strict decomposition**. In this approach we start by synthesizing one giant relation schema, called the **universal relation**, which includes all the database attributes. We then repeatedly perform decomposition as long as it is feasible and desirable.

In this chapter we first present several algorithms based on functional dependencies that can be used for relational database design. In Section 14.1 we discuss the concepts of dependency preservation and lossless (or nonadditive) joins, which are used by the design algorithms to achieve desirable decompositions. We show that normal forms are *insufficient on their own* as criteria for a good relational database schema design.

In Section 14.2 we discuss additional types of data dependencies and some of the normal forms they lead to. These data dependencies specify constraints that *cannot be* expressed by functional dependencies. We discuss multivalued dependencies, join dependencies, inclusion dependencies, and template dependencies. We also define fourth normal form (4NF), fifth normal form (5NF), and, briefly, domain-key normal form (DKNF).

14.1   Algorithms for the Design of a Relational Database Schema

In Section 14.1.1 we give examples to show that looking at an *individual* relation to test whether it is in a higher normal form does not, on its own, guarantee a good design; rather, a *set of relations* that together form the relational database schema must possess certain additional properties to ensure a good design. In Section 14.1.2 we discuss one of these properties—the dependency preservation property. In Section 14.1.3 we discuss another of these properties—the lossless or nonadditive join property. We present decomposition algorithms that guarantee these properties, which are formal concepts, as well as guaranteeing that the individual relations are normalized appropriately. Section 14.1.4 discusses problems associated with null values, and Section 14.1.5 summarizes the design algorithms and their properties.

14.1.1   *Relation Decomposition and Insufficiency of Normal Forms*

The relational database design algorithms that we present here start out with a single **universal relation schema** $R = \{A_1, A_2, ..., A_n\}$ that includes *all* the attributes of the database. We implicitly make the universal relation assumption, which states that every attribute name is unique. The set F of functional dependencies that should hold on the attributes of R is specified and made available to the design algorithms. Using the functional dependencies, the algorithms **decompose** the universal relation schema R into a set of relation schemas $D = \{R_1, R_2, ..., R_m\}$ that will become the relational database schema; D is called a **decomposition** of R.

We must make sure that each attribute in R will appear in at least one relation schema R_i in the decomposition so that no attributes are "lost"; formally,

$$\bigcup_{i=1}^{m} R_i = R.$$

This is called the **attribute preservation** condition of a decomposition.

Another goal is to have each individual relation R_i in the decomposition D be in BCNF (or 3NF). However, this condition is not sufficient to guarantee a good database design on its own. We must consider the decomposition as a whole in addition to looking at the properties of individual relations in the decomposition. To illustrate this point, consider the EMP_LOCS relation of Figure 13.5, which is in 3NF and also in BCNF. In fact, any relation schema with only two attributes is automatically in BCNF (Exercise 13.26). Although EMP_LOCS is in BCNF, it still gives rise to spurious tuples when joined with EMP_PROJ$_1$ (which is not in BCNF) (Figure 13.6). Hence, Figure 13.5(a) represents a particularly bad decomposition of EMP_PROJ of Figure 13.3(b) because of its convoluted semantics that PLOCATION gives the location of *one of the projects* on which an employee works. Note that joining EMP_LOCS with PROJECT of Figure 13.2 (which *is* in BCNF) also gives rise to spurious tuples. We need other criteria that, together with the conditions of 3NF or BCNF, prevent such bad designs.

In the next three subsections we discuss such additional conditions that should hold on a decomposition D as a whole.

14.1.2 Decomposition and Dependency Preservation

It is useful that each functional dependency $X \rightarrow Y$ specified in F either appear directly in one of the relation schemas R_i in the decomposition D or alternatively be inferred from the dependencies that appear in some individual R_i relation in D. Informally, this is the dependency preservation condition. We want to preserve the dependencies because each dependency in F represents a constraint on the database. If one of the dependencies is not represented by the dependencies on some individual relation R_i of the decomposition, we will not be able to enforce this constraint by looking only at an individual relation; instead, to enforce the constraint, we will have to join two or more of the relations in the decomposition and then check that the functional dependency holds in the result of the join operation. This is clearly an inefficient procedure that cannot be adopted in a practical system.

Note that it is not necessary that the exact dependencies specified in F appear themselves in individual relations of the decomposition D. It is sufficient that the union of the dependencies that hold on the individual relations in D be equivalent to F. We now define these concepts more formally. First we need a preliminary definition. Given a set of dependencies F on R, the **projection** of F on R_i, denoted by $\pi_F(R_i)$ where R_i is a subset of R, is the set of dependencies $X \rightarrow Y$ in F^+ such that the attributes in $X \cup Y$ are all contained in R_i. Hence, the projection of F on each relation schema R_i in the decomposition D is the set of functional dependencies in F^+, the closure of F, such that all their left- and right-hand side attributes are in R_i.

We say that a decomposition $D = \{R_1, R_2, ..., R_m\}$ of R is **dependency preserving** with respect to F if the union of the projections of F on each R_i in D is equivalent to F; that is,

$$((\pi_F(R_1)) \cup ...\cup (\pi_F(R_m)))^+ = F^+$$

If a decomposition is not dependency preserving, some dependency is **lost** in the decomposition. As we mentioned earlier, to check that a lost dependency holds, we must take the JOIN of several relations in the decomposition to get a relation that includes all left- and right-hand side attributes of the lost dependency and then check that the dependency holds on the result of the JOIN—an option that is not practical.

An example of a decomposition that does not preserve dependencies is shown in Figure 13.12a, where the functional dependency fd2 is lost when LOTS1A is decomposed into {LOTS1AX, LOTS1AY}. However, the decompositions in Figure 13.11 are dependency preserving. The reader should verify both these examples using the formal definition of dependency preservation.

It is always possible to find a dependency-preserving decomposition D with respect to F such that each relation R_i in D is in 3NF. Algorithm 14.1 will create such a decomposition. Note that this algorithm guarantees only the dependency preservation property; it does *not* guarantee the lossless join property that will be discussed in the next section.

> **ALGORITHM 14.1**   Dependency-preserving decomposition into 3NF relation schemas
>
> 1. find a minimal cover G for F ;
> 2. for each left-hand side X of a functional dependency that appears in G
>   create a relation schema {X UNION A_1 UNION A_2 ... UNION A_m} in D,
>   where $X \rightarrow A_1$, $X \rightarrow A_2$, ..., $X \rightarrow A_m$ are the only dependencies in G with
>   X as left-hand side ;
> 3. place any remaining (unplaced) attributes in a single relation schema to ensure
>   the attribute preservation property ;

We will not go through a formal proof, but it can be shown that every relation schema created by Algorithm 14.1 is in 3NF (see Ullman 1982). The proof is based on the fact that G is a minimal cover so that the dependencies in G satisfy the properties of minimality discussed in Section 13.2.4. It is obvious that all the dependencies in G are preserved by the algorithm because each dependency in G appears in one of the relations R_i in the decomposition D. Since G is a minimal cover of F, it is equivalent to F and all the dependencies in F are either preserved directly in the decomposition or are derivable from those in the resulting relations. The only problem is that of finding a minimal cover G of F. We will not discuss this here, as the algorithm to find a minimal cover is rather complex and depends on additional theory that we did not present (see Maier 1983). Algorithm 14.1 is sometimes called the **relational synthesis** algorithm, because each relation schema R_i in the decomposition is "synthesized" from a set of dependencies in G with the same left-hand side. In the next section we discuss another useful property that a decomposition should possess.

14.1.3   Decomposition and Lossless (Nonadditive) Joins

Another property a decomposition D should possess is the lossless join or nonadditive join property, which ensures that no spurious tuples are generated when a NATURAL JOIN operation is applied to the relations in the decomposition. We already illustrated this problem in Section 13.1.4 with the example of Figures 13.5 and 13.6. Because this is a property of a decomposition of relation schemas, the condition of no spurious tuples should hold on *every legal relation instance*, that is, every relation instance that satisfies the functional dependencies specified on the schemas. Hence, the lossless join property is always defined with respect to a specific set F of dependencies.

Formally, a decomposition D = {R_1, R_2, ..., R_m} of R has the **lossless (nonadditive) join** property with respect to the set of dependencies F on R if for *every* relation instance r of R that satisfies F, the following holds (* is the NATURAL JOIN operation):

$$* (\pi_{<R1>}(r), ..., \pi_{<Rm>}(r)) = r$$

The word "lossless" in lossless join refers to loss of information, not loss of tuples. If a decomposition does not have the lossless join property, then we may get additional spurious tuples after the PROJECT and NATURAL JOIN operations are applied; these additional tuples represent erroneous information and hence add wrong information. We prefer the term **nonadditive join** to lossless join because it describes the situation more accurately; if the nonadditive join property holds on a decomposition, then we are guaranteed that no spurious tuples bearing wrong information are added to the result after the PROJECT and NATURAL JOIN operations are applied.

The decomposition of EMP_PROJ into EMP_LOCS and EMP_PROJ1 in Figure 13.5 obviously does not have the lossless join property. In general, we want to be able to check whether a given decomposition D has the lossless join property with respect to a set of functional dependencies F. We can use Algorithm 14.2 to do this checking.

ALGORITHM 14.2   Testing for the lossless join property

1. create a matrix S with one row i for each relation R_i in the decomposition D, and one column j for each attribute A_j in R;
2. set S(i,j):=b_{ij} for all matrix entries;
      (* each b_{ij} is a distinct symbol associated with indices (i,j) *)
3. for each row i representing relation schema R_i
      for each column j representing attribute A_j
          if R_i includes attribute A_j
              then set S(i,j):= a_j;
      (* each a_j is a distinct symbol associated with index (j) *)
4. repeat the following until a loop execution results in no changes to S
      for each functional dependency X→Y in F
          for all rows in S *which have the same symbols* in the columns corresponding to attributes in X
              make the symbols in each column that correspond to an attribute in Y be the same in all these rows as follows: if any of the rows has an "a" symbol for the column, set the other rows to that same "a" symbol in the column—if no "a" symbol exists for the attribute in any of the rows choose one of the "b" symbols that appear in one of the rows for the attribute and set the other rows to that "b" symbol in the column;
5. if a row is made up entirely of "a" symbols, then the decomposition has the lossless join property—otherwise, it does not;

Algorithm 14.2 creates a relation instance r in the matrix S that satisfies all the functional dependencies in F. At the end of the loop of applying functional dependencies, any two rows in S—which represent two tuples in r—that agree in their values for the left-hand side attributes of a functional dependency X→Y in F will also agree in their values for the right-hand side attributes of the dependency. Hence, S satisfies all the functional dependencies in F. It can be shown that if any row in S ends up with all "a" symbols at the end of the algorithm, then the decomposition has the lossless join property with respect to F (see Ullman 1982). If, on the other hand, no row ends up being all "a" symbols, then the relation instance r represented by S at the end of the algorithm will be an example of a relation instance r of R that satisfies the dependencies in F but does not have the lossless join property. This relation serves as a counterexample, so the decomposition D will not have the lossless join property in this case. Note that the "a" and "b" symbols have no special meaning at the end of the algorithm.

Figure 14.1a shows how we apply Algorithm 14.2 to the decomposition of the EMP_PROJ relation schema from Figure 13.3b into the two relation schemas EMP_PROJ1 and EMP_LOCS of Figure 13.5a. The algorithm is not able to change any "b" symbols to "a" symbols; hence, the resulting matrix S does not have a row with all "a" symbols, so the decomposition does not have the lossless join property.

Figure 14.1b shows another decomposition of EMP_PROJ that has the lossless join property, and Figure 14.1c shows how we apply the algorithm to that decomposition. Once a row consists only of "a" symbols, we know that the decomposition has the lossless join property, and so we can stop applying the functional dependencies to the matrix S.

We can now test whether a particular decomposition D obeys the lossless join property with respect to a set of functional dependencies F. The next question is whether there is an algorithm to decompose a relation schema $R = \{A_1, A_2, ..., A_n\}$ into a decomposition $D = \{R_1, R_2, ..., R_m\}$ such that each R_i is in 3NF (or BCNF) *and* the decomposition D has the lossless join property with respect to a set of functional dependencies F on R. The answer is yes; there is an algorithm to create a lossless join decomposition into relation schemas that are in BCNF. Before we give the algorithm, we need to present some properties of lossless join decompositions.

PROPERTY LJ1

A decomposition $D = \{R_1, R_2\}$ of R has the lossless join property with respect to a set of functional dependencies F on R *if and only if* either:

- The FD $((R_1 \cap R_2) \rightarrow (R_1 - R_2))$ is in F^+, or
- The FD $((R_1 \cap R_2) \rightarrow (R_2 - R_1))$ is in F^+.

Note that property LJ1 constitutes an easier test for the lossless join property than does Algorithm 14.2. However, LJ1 is applicable to decompositions into *two relation schemas only*. The reader is encouraged to verify that this property holds on our informal successive normalization examples in Sections 13.3 and 13.4.

PROPERTY LJ2

If a decomposition $D = \{R_1, R_2, ..., R_m\}$ of R has the lossless join property with respect to a set of functional dependencies F on R, and if a decomposition $D_1 = \{Q_1, Q_2, ..., Q_k\}$ of R_i has the lossless join property with respect to the projection of F on R_i, then the decomposition $D_2 = \{R_1, R_2, ..., R_{i-1}, Q_1, Q_2, ..., Q_k, R_{i+1}, ..., R_m\}$ of R has the lossless join property with respect to F.

Property LJ2 says that *if* a decomposition D already has the lossless join property—with respect to F—*and* we further decompose one of the relation schemas R_i in D

(a)   R={SSN, ENAME, PNUMBER, PNAME, PLOCATION, HOURS}   D={R1, R2}
R1=EMP_LOCS={ENAME, PLOCATION}
R2=EMP_PROJ1={SSN, PNUMBER, HOURS, PNAME, PLOCATION}

F={SSN→ENAME;PNUMBER→{PNAME, PLOCATION} ;{SSN,PNUMBER}→HOURS}

	SSN	ENAME	PNUMBER	PNAME	PLOCATION	HOURS
R1	b_{11}	a_2	b_{13}	b_{14}	a_5	b_{16}
R2	a_1	b_{22}	a_3	a_4	a_5	a_6

(no changes to matrix after applying functional dependencies)

(b)

EMP

SSN	ENAME

PROJECT

PNUMBER	PNAME	PLOCATION

WORKS_ON

SSN	PNUMBER	HOURS

(c)   R={SSN, ENAME, PNUMBER, PNAME, PLOCATION, HOURS}   D={R1, R2, R3}
R1=EMP={SSN, ENAME}
R2=PROJ={PNUMBER, PNAME, PLOCATION}
R3=WORKS_ON={SSN, PNUMBER, HOURS}

F={SSN→ENAME;PNUMBER→{PNAME, PLOCATION} ;{SSN,PNUMBER}→HOURS}

	SSN	ENAME	PNUMBER	PNAME	PLOCATION	HOURS
R1	a_1	a_2	b_{13}	b_{14}	b_{15}	b_{16}
R2	b_{21}	b_{22}	a_3	a_4	a_5	b_{26}
R3	a_1	b_{32}	a_3	b_{34}	b_{35}	a_6

(original matrix S at start of algorithm)

	SSN	ENAME	PNUMBER	PNAME	PLOCATION	HOURS
R1	a_1	a_2	b_{13}	b_{14}	b_{15}	b_{16}
R2	b_{21}	b_{22}	a_3	a_4	a_5	b_{26}
R3	a_1	b_{32} a_2	a_3	b_{34} a_4	b_{35} a_5	a_6

(matrix S after applying the first two functional dependencies -
last row is all "a" symbols, so we stop)

Figure 14.1   Illustrating the lossless join testing algorithm. (a) Applying
the algorithm to test for lossless join to the decomposition
of EMP_PROJ into EMP_PROJ1 and EMP_LOCS. (b) Another
decomposition of EMP_PROJ. (c) Applying the algorithm for
testing lossless join to the decomposition of Figure 14.1(b).

into another decomposition D_1 that also has the lossless join property—with respect to $\pi_F(R_i)$—*then* replacing R_i in D by D_1 will result in a decomposition that also has the lossless join property—with respect to F. We implicitly assumed this property in the informal normalization examples of Sections 13.3 and 13.4.

Using the properties LJ1 and LJ2, we can develop Algorithm 14.3 to create a lossless join decomposition D for R with respect to F such that each relation schema R_i in the decomposition D is in BCNF.

ALGORITHM 14.3   Lossless join decomposition into BCNF relations

1. set D <—— { R } ;
2. while there is a relation schema Q in D that is not in BCNF do
   begin
      choose a relation schema Q in D that is not in BCNF ;
      find a functional dependency X→Y in Q that violates BCNF ;
      replace Q in D by two schemas (Q – Y) and (X ∪ Y)
   end;

Each time we go through the loop in Algorithm 14.3, we decompose one relation schema Q that is not in BCNF into two relation schemas. By properties LJ1 and LJ2, the decomposition D will always have the lossless join property. At the end of the algorithm, all relation schemas in D will be in BCNF. The reader can check that the normalization example in Figures 13.11 and 13.12 basically follows this algorithm. The functional dependencies fd3, fd4, and later fd5 violate BCNF, so the LOTS relation is decomposed appropriately into BCNF relations, and the decomposition will satisfy the lossless join property.

If we want our decomposition to have the lossless join property *and* to preserve dependencies, we have to be satisfied with relation schemas in 3NF—rather than BCNF—in our decomposition. A simple modification to Algorithm 14.1, shown as Algorithm 14.4, yields a decomposition D of R that:

- Preserves dependencies.
- Has the lossless join property.
- Is such that each resulting relation schema in the decomposition is in 3NF.

ALGORITHM 14.4   Lossless join and dependency-preserving
decomposition into 3NF relation schemas

1. find a minimal cover G for F ;
      (* F is the set of functional dependencies specified on R *)
2. for each left-hand side X that appears in G
      create a relation schema {X ∪ A_1 ∪ A_1 ...∪ A_m} where
      X→A_1, X→A_2, ..., X→A_m are all the dependencies in G with X as
      left-hand side ;
3. place all remaining (unplaced) attributes in a single relation schema ;
4. if none of the relation schemas contains a key of R, create one more relation
      schema that contains attributes that form a key for R;

It can be shown that the decomposition formed from the set of relation schemas created by the above algorithm is dependency preserving and has the lossless join property. In addition, each relation schema in the decomposition is in 3NF (see Ullman 1982).

It is not always possible to find a decomposition into relation schemas that preserves dependencies and such that each relation schema in the decomposition is in BCNF—rather than 3NF as in Algorithm 14.4. As most 3NF relations are also in BCNF, we can individually check the relation schemas in the decomposition for satisfying BCNF. If some relation schema R_i is in 3NF but not in BCNF, we can choose whether to decompose it further or to leave it as it is in 3NF with some possible update anomalies.

The fact that we cannot always find a decomposition into relation schemas in BCNF that preserves dependencies can be illustrated by the examples in Figure 13.12. The relations LOTS1A (Figure 13.12a) and R (Figure 13.12b) are not in BCNF but are in 3NF. Any attempt to decompose either relation further into BCNF relations will result in loss of the dependency fd2 in LOTS1A or loss of fd2 in R.

It is important to note that the theory of lossless join decompositions is based on the assumption that *no **null** values are allowed for the join attributes*. The next section discusses some of the problems that **null**s may cause in relational decompositions.

14.1.4 Problems with Null Values and Dangling Tuples

We must carefully consider the problems associated with **null**s when designing a relational database schema. There is no fully satisfactory relational design theory as yet that includes **null** values, and research is continuing in this area. One problem occurs when some tuples have **null** values for attributes that will be used to JOIN individual relations in the decomposition. To illustrate this problem, consider the database shown in Figure 14.2a, where two relations EMPLOYEE and DEPARTMENT are shown. The last two employee tuples—Berger and Benitez—represent newly hired employees who have not yet been assigned to a department (assume that this does not violate any integrity constraints). Now suppose that we want to retrieve a list of (ENAME, DNAME) values for all the employees. If we use the * operation on EMPLOYEE and DEPARTMENT (Figure 14.2b), the two aforementioned tuples will *not* appear in the result. The OUTER JOIN operation, discussed in Chapter 6, can deal with this problem. Recall that if we take the OUTER JOIN of EMPLOYEE with DEPARTMENT, then tuples in EMPLOYEE that have **null** for the join attribute will still appear in the result, joined with an "imaginary" tuple in DEPARTMENT with **null**s for all its attribute values. Figure 14.2c shows the result of the OUTER JOIN operation. Unfortunately, not all relational DBMSs provide the OUTER JOIN operation.

In general, whenever a relational database schema is designed where two or more relations are interrelated via foreign keys, particular care must be given for potential null values in foreign keys. This can cause unexpected loss of information in queries that involve joins. Moreover, if nulls occur in other attributes, such as SALARY, their effect on built-in functions such as SUM and AVERAGE should be carefully evaluated.

A related problem is that of **dangling tuples**, which may occur if we carry a decomposition too far. Suppose we decompose the EMPLOYEE relation of Figure 14.2a further into EMPLOYEE_1 and EMPLOYEE_2, shown in Figure 14.3a and 14.3b.[†] If we apply the * operation to EMPLOYEE_1 and EMPLOYEE_2, we get the original EMPLOYEE relation. However, we may use an alternative representation for the case when an employee has

---

[†]This sometimes happens when we apply vertical fragmentation to a relation in the context of a distributed database (see Chapter 21).

(a)

EMPLOYEE

ENAME	SSN	BDATE	ADDRESS	DNUM
Smith, John B.	123456789	09-JAN-55	731 Fondren, Houston, TX	5
Wong, Franklin T.	333445555	08-DEC-45	638 Voss, Houston, TX	5
Zelaya, Alicia J.	999887777	19-JUL-58	3321 Castle, Spring, TX	4
Wallace, Jennifer S.	987654321	20-JUN-31	291 Berry, Bellaire, TX	4
Narayan, Ramesh K.	666884444	15-SEP-52	975 Fire Oak, Humble, TX	5
English, Joyce A.	453453453	31-JUL-62	5631 Rice, Houston, TX	5
Jabbar, Ahmad V.	987987987	29-MAR-59	980 Dallas, Houston, TX	4
Borg, James E.	888665555	10-NOV-27	450 Stone, Houston, TX	1
Berger, Anders C.	999775555	26-APR-55	6530 Braes, Bellaire, TX	**null**
Benitez, Carlos M.	888664444	09-JAN-53	7654 Beech, Houston, TX	**null**

DEPARTMENT

DNAME	DNUM	DMGRSSN
Research	5	333445555
Administration	4	987654321
Headquarters	1	888665555

(b)

ENAME	SSN	BDATE	ADDRESS	DNUM	DNAME	DMGRSSN
Smith, John B.	123456789	09-JAN-55	731 Fondren, Houston, TX	5	Research	333445555
Wong, Franklin T.	333445555	08-DEC-45	638 Voss, Houston, TX	5	Research	333445555
Zelaya, Alicia J.	999887777	19-JUL-58	3321 Castle, Spring, TX	4	Administration	987654321
Wallace, Jennifer S.	987654321	20-JUN-31	291 Berry, Bellaire, TX	4	Administration	987654321
Narayan, Ramesh K.	666884444	15-SEP-52	975 Fire Oak, Humble, TX	5	Research	333445555
English, Joyce A.	453453453	31-JUL-62	5631 Rice, Houston, TX	5	Research	333445555
Jabbar, Ahmad V.	987987987	29-MAR-59	980 Dallas, Houston, TX	4	Administration	987654321
Borg, James E.	888665555	10-NOV-27	450 Stone, Houston, TX	1	Headquarters	888665555

(c)

ENAME	SSN	BDATE	ADDRESS	DNUM	DNAME	DMGRSSN
Smith, John B.	123456789	09-JAN-55	731 Fondren, Houston, TX	5	Research	333445555
Wong, Franklin T.	333445555	08-DEC-45	638 Voss, Houston, TX	5	Research	333445555
Zelaya, Alicia J.	999887777	19-JUL-58	3321 Castle, Spring, TX	4	Administration	987654321
Wallace, Jennifer S.	987654321	20-JUN-31	291 Berry, Bellaire, TX	4	Administration	987654321
Narayan, Ramesh K.	666884444	15-SEP-52	975 Fire Oak, Humble, TX	5	Research	333445555
English, Joyce A.	453453453	31-JUL-62	5631 Rice, Houston, TX	5	Research	333445555
Jabbar, Ahmad V.	987987987	29-MAR-59	980 Dallas, Houston, TX	4	Administration	987654321
Borg, James E.	888665555	10-NOV-27	450 Stone, Houston, TX	1	Headquarters	888665555
Berger, Anders C.	999775555	26-APR-55	6530 Braes, Bellaire, TX	**null**	**null**	**null**
Benitez, Carlos M.	888664444	09-JAN-53	7654 Beech, Houston, TX	**null**	**null**	**null**

Figure 14.2   Illustrating the null value join problem. (a) A database with nulls for some join attributes. (b) Result of applying the NATURAL JOIN operation to the EMPLOYEE and DEPARTMENT relations. (c) Result of applying the OUTER JOIN operation to EMPLOYEE with DEPARTMENT.

not yet been assigned a department. This is shown in Figure 14.3c, where we *do not in-clude a tuple* in EMPLOYEE_3 if the employee has not been assigned a department. This representation contrasts with including a tuple with **null** for DNUM, as in EMPLOYEE_2. Suppose we use EMPLOYEE_3 instead of EMPLOYEE_2. Now if we apply a NATURAL JOIN—or, for that matter, an OUTER JOIN—on EMPLOYEE_1 and EMPLOYEE_3, the tuples for Berger

(a) **EMPLOYEE_1**

ENAME	SSN	BDATE	ADDRESS
Smith, John B.	123456789	09-JAN-55	731 Fondren, Houston, TX
Wong, Franklin T.	333445555	08-DEC-45	638 Voss, Houston, TX
Zelaya, Alicia J.	999887777	19-JUL-58	3321 Castle, Spring, TX
Wallace, Jennifer S.	987654321	20-JUN-31	291 Berry, Bellaire, TX
Narayan, Ramesh K.	666884444	15-SEP-52	975 Fire Oak, Humble, TX
English, Joyce A.	453453453	31-JUL-62	5631 Rice, Houston, TX
Jabbar, Ahmad V.	987987987	29-MAR-59	980 Dallas, Houston, TX
Borg, James E.	888665555	10-NOV-27	450 Stone, Houston, TX
Berger, Anders C.	999775555	26-APR-55	6530 Braes, Bellaire, TX
Benitez, Carlos M.	888664444	09-JAN-53	7654 Beech, Houston, TX

(b) **EMPLOYEE_2**

SSN	DNUM
123456789	5
333445555	5
999887777	4
987654321	4
666884444	5
453453453	5
987987987	4
888665555	1
999775555	null
888664444	null

(c) **EMPLOYEE_3**

SSN	DNUM
123456789	5
333445555	5
999887777	4
987654321	4
666884444	5
453453453	5
987987987	4
888665555	1

Figure 14.3 Illustrating the "dangling tuple" problem. (a) The relation EMPLOYEE_1 that includes all the attributes of the EMPLOYEE relation except for DNUMBER. (b) The relation EMPLOYEE_2 that includes the DNUMBER attribute of EMPLOYEE with null values. (c) The relation EMPLOYEE_3 that does not include the tuples for which DNUMBER has a null value.

and Benitez will disappear. These are called **dangling tuples** because they are represented in only one of the relations that represents employees but not in the other and hence are lost if we apply a join operation.

14.1.5 Discussion

In the preceding subsections we presented several algorithms for relational database design. These algorithms decompose a universal relation schema into a set of relation schemas and are based on the concepts of functional dependencies, normal forms, dependency preservation, and lossless join decomposition. We also discussed the problems with null values and dangling tuples in relational design.

One of the problems with the algorithms discussed here is that the database designer must first specify *all* the functional dependencies among the database attributes. This is *not a simple task* for a large database with hundreds of attributes. Failure to specify one or two important dependencies may result in an undesirable design. Another problem is that these algorithms are not deterministic in general. For example, some of the algorithms require the specification of a minimal cover for the set of functional dependencies, and the result of the algorithm depends on the minimal cover. Because there may be, in general, many minimal covers corresponding to a set of functional dependencies, the algorithm can give different designs for the same set of functional dependencies, each design depending on the particular minimal cover supplied to the algorithm. Some of these designs may not be desirable. Other algorithms produce a decomposition that is dependent on the order in which the functional dependencies are supplied to the algorithm; again, potentially many different designs may arise corresponding to the same set of functional dependencies.

For the above reasons, these algorithms cannot be used blindly. They have not proved to be very popular in practice up to now, and top-down database design using the ER model and other high-level data models is currently used more often. One possibility that has been suggested is to combine the two approaches. For example, we may start with the ER model to produce a conceptual schema and map it to relations. Then we can apply these algorithms to the individual relations obtained from the ER design, specify their functional dependencies, and see whether they need to be decomposed further. Another alternative is to analyze the entity types of the ER design itself and decompose the entity types if needed by applying a similar theory. A discussion of this approach is beyond the scope of this book.

14.2   Other Types of Dependencies and Further Normal Forms

So far we have discussed only functional dependency, which is by far the most important type of dependency in relational database design theory. However, in many cases we have constraints on relations that cannot be specified as functional dependencies. In this section we describe additional types of dependencies that may be used to represent other types of constraints on relations. Some of these dependencies lead to further normal forms.

In Section 14.2.1 we discuss the multivalued dependency and define fourth normal form, which is based on this dependency. Next, in Section 14.2.2, we briefly discuss join dependencies and fifth normal form. Finally, we briefly discuss inclusion dependencies, template dependencies, and domain-key normal form in Sections 14.2.3, 14.2.4, and 14.2.5 respectively.

14.2.1   Multivalued Dependencies and Fourth Normal Form

Multivalued dependencies are a consequence of first normal form, which disallowed an attribute in a tuple from having a set of values or a list of values or a combination of both. If we have two or more multivalued independent attributes in the same relation schema, we get into a problem of having to repeat every value of one of the attributes with every value of the other attribute to keep the relation instances consistent. This constraint is specified by a multivalued dependency.

(a) **EMP**

ENAME	PNAME	DNAME
Smith	X	John
Smith	Y	Anna
Smith	X	Anna
Smith	Y	John

(b) **EMP_PROJECTS**

ENAME	PNAME
Smith	X
Smith	Y

EMP_DEPENDENTS

ENAME	DNAME
Smith	John
Smith	Anna

(c) **SUPPLY**

SNAME	PARTNAME	PROJNAME
Smith	Bolt	ProjX
Smith	Nut	ProjY
Adamsky	Bolt	ProjY
Walton	Nut	ProjZ
Adamsky	Nail	ProjX
Adamsky	Bolt	ProjX
Smith	Bolt	ProjY

(d) **R1**

SNAME	PARTNAME
Smith	Bolt
Smith	Nut
Adamsky	Bolt
Walton	Nut
Adamsky	Nail

R2

SNAME	PROJNAME
Smith	ProjX
Smith	ProjY
Adamsky	ProjY
Walton	ProjZ
Adamsky	ProjX

R3

PARTNAME	PROJNAME
Bolt	ProjX
Nut	ProjY
Bolt	ProjY
Nut	ProjZ
Nail	ProjX

Figure 14.4   Illustrating 4NF and 5NF. (a) The EMP relation with two MVDs ENAME →→ PNAME and ENAME →→ DNAME. (b) Decomposing EMP into two relations in 4NF. (c) The SUPPLY relation with no MVDs that is in 4NF (However, it would not be in 5NF if the JD(R1,R2,R3) holds). (d) Decomposing the SUPPLY relation with the join dependency into three 5NF relations.

For example, consider the relation EMP shown in Figure 14.4a. A tuple in this EMP relation represents the fact that an employee whose name is ENAME works on the project whose name is PNAME and has a dependent whose name is DNAME. However, an employee may work on several projects and may have several dependents, and the employee's projects and dependents are not directly related to one another.* To keep the tuples in the relation consistent, we must keep a tuple to represent every combination of an employee's dependent with an employee's project. We specify this constraint as a multi-

---

*In an ER diagram each would be represented as a multivalued attribute or a weak entity type (see Chapter 3).

valued dependency on the EMP relation. Informally, whenever two *independent* 1:N relationships A:B and A:C are mixed in the same relation by representing all possible combinations, an MVD may arise.

Formal Definition of Multivalued Dependency

Formally, a **multivalued dependency** (MVD) $X \twoheadrightarrow Y$ specified on relation schema R, where X and Y are both subsets of R, specifies the following constraint on any relation instance r of R: If two tuples t_1 and t_2 exist in r such that $t_1[X] = t_2[X]$, then two tuples t_3 and t_4 should also exist* in r with the following properties:

- $t_3[X] = t_4[X] = t_1[X] = t_2[X]$.
- $t_3[Y] = t_1[Y]$, and $t_4[Y] = t_2[Y]$.
- $t_3[R - X - Y] = t_2[R - X - Y]$ and
  $t_4[R - X - Y] = t_1[R - X - Y]$.

Whenever $X \twoheadrightarrow Y$ holds, we say that X **multidetermines** Y. Note that because of the symmetry in the definition, whenever $X \twoheadrightarrow Y$ holds in R, so does $X \twoheadrightarrow (R - X - Y))$. Note also that $(R - X - Y)$ is the same as $R - (X \cup Y) = Z$, say. Hence, $X \twoheadrightarrow Y$ implies $X \twoheadrightarrow Z$, and therefore it is sometimes written as $X \twoheadrightarrow Y/Z$.

The formal definition specifies that, given a particular value of X, the set of values of Y determined by this value of X is completely determined by this value of X alone and *does not depend* on the values of the remaining attributes Z of the relation schema R. Hence, whenever two tuples having distinct values of Y occur with the same value of X, these values of Y must be repeated with every distinct value of Z that occurs with that same value of X. This informally corresponds to Y being a multivalued attribute of the entities represented by tuples in R.

For example, in Figure 14.4a the MVDs ENAME $\twoheadrightarrow$ PNAME and ENAME $\twoheadrightarrow$ DNAME, or ENAME $\twoheadrightarrow$ PNAME/DNAME should hold in the EMP relation. In the tuples shown in Figure 14.4a the employee with ENAME 'Smith' works on projects with PNAME 'X' and 'Y' and has two dependents with DNAME 'John' and 'Anna'. If we stored only the first two tuples in EMP (<'Smith', 'X', 'John'> and <'Smith', 'Y', 'Anna'>), we would incorrectly show associations between project 'X' and 'John' and between project 'Y' and 'Anna' that should not be there because no such meaning is intended in this relation. Hence, we must store the other two tuples (<'Smith', 'X', 'Anna'> and <'Smith', 'Y', 'John'>) to show that {'X', 'Y'} and {'John', 'Anna'} are associated only with 'Smith'; that is, there is no association between PNAME and DNAME in EMP.

An MVD $X \twoheadrightarrow Y$ in R is called a **trivial MVD** if (a) Y is a subset of X or (b) $X \cup Y = R$. For example, the relation EMP_PROJECTS in Figure 14.4b has the trivial MVD ENAME $\twoheadrightarrow$ PNAME. An MVD that satisfies neither (a) nor (b) is called a **nontrivial MVD**. A trivial MVD will hold in *any* relation instance r of R; it is called trivial because it does not specify any constraint on R.

If we have a nontrivial MVD in a relation, as the example in Figure 14.4a shows, we may have to repeat values redundantly in the tuples. In the EMP relation, the values 'X' and 'Y' of PNAME are repeated with each value of DNAME (or, by symmetry, the values

---

*The tuples t_1, t_2, t_3, and t_4 are not necessarily distinct.

'John' and 'Anna' of DNAME are repeated with each value of PNAME). This redundancy is clearly undesirable. However, the EMP schema is in BCNF because *no functional dependencies hold in EMP*. Therefore, we need to define a fourth normal form that is stronger than BCNF, and disallows relation schemas such as EMP. We will present the definition of fourth normal form shortly. However, we first discuss some of the properties of MVDs and how they are related to functional dependencies.

Inference Rules for Functional and Multivalued Dependencies

As with functional dependencies (FDs), we can develop inference rules for MVDs. It is better, though, to develop a unified framework that includes both FDs and MVDs so that both types of constraints are considered together. The following inference rules IR1 to IR8 form a sound and complete set for inferring functional and multivalued dependencies from a given set of dependencies. Assume that all attributes are included in a "universal" relation schema $R = \{A_1, A_2, ..., A_n\}$ and that X, Y, Z, and W are subsets of R.

(IR1) (Reflexive rule for FDs) If $X \supseteq Y$, then $X \rightarrow Y$.

(IR2) (Augmentation rule for FDs) $\{X \rightarrow Y\} \vDash XZ \rightarrow YZ$.

(IR3) (Transitive rule for FDs) $\{X \rightarrow Y, Y \rightarrow Z\} \vDash X \rightarrow Z$.

(IR4) (Complementation rule for MVDs) $\{X \twoheadrightarrow Y\} \vDash \{X \twoheadrightarrow (R - (X \cup Y))\}$.

(IR5) (Augmentation rule for MVDs) If $X \twoheadrightarrow Y$ and $W \supseteq Z$ then $WX \twoheadrightarrow YZ$.

(IR6) (Transitive rule for MVDs) $\{X \twoheadrightarrow Y, Y \twoheadrightarrow Z\} \vDash X \twoheadrightarrow (Z - Y)$.

(IR7) (Replication rule (FD to MVD)) $\{X \rightarrow Y\} \vDash X \twoheadrightarrow Y$.

(IR8) (Coalescence rule for FDs and MVDs) If $X \twoheadrightarrow Y$ and there exists W with the properties that (a) $W \cap Y$ is empty, (b) $W \rightarrow Z$, and (c) $Y \supseteq Z$, then $X \rightarrow Z$.

IR1 to IR3 are Armstrong's inference rules for FDs alone. IR4 to IR6 are inference rules pertaining to MVDs only. IR7 and IR8 relate FDs and MVDs. In particular, rule IR7 says that a functional dependency is a *special case* of a multivalued dependency; that is, every FD is also an MVD. An FD $X \rightarrow Y$ is an MVD $X \twoheadrightarrow Y$ with the additional restriction that at most one value of Y is associated with each value of X.

Given a set F of functional and multivalued dependencies specified on $R = \{A_1, A_2, ..., A_n\}$, we can use the inference rules IR1 to IR8 to infer the (complete) set of all dependencies (functional or multivalued) F^+ that will hold in every relation instance r of R that satisfies F. We again call F^+ the **closure** of F. We now present the definition of 4NF, which is violated when a relation has undesirable multivalued dependencies and hence can be used to identify and decompose such relations.

Fourth Normal Form (4NF)

A relation schema R is in **4NF** with respect to a set of dependencies F if for every *nontrivial* multivalued dependency $X \twoheadrightarrow Y$ in F^+, X is a superkey for R.

The EMP relation of Figure 14.4a is not in 4NF because in the nontrivial MVDs ENAME $\twoheadrightarrow$ PNAME and ENAME $\twoheadrightarrow$ DNAME, ENAME is not a superkey of EMP. We decompose EMP into EMP_PROJECTS and EMP_DEPENDENTS shown in Figure 14.4b. Both EMP_PROJECTS and EMP_DEPENDENTS are in 4NF, because ENAME $\twoheadrightarrow$ PNAME is a trivial MVD in EMP_PROJECTS and ENAME→DNAME is a trivial MVD in EMP_DEPENDENTS. In fact, no nontrivial MVDs hold in either EMP_PROJECTS or EMP_DEPENDENTS. No FDs hold in these relation schemas either.

To illustrate why it is important to keep relations in 4NF, Figure 14.5a shows the EMP relation with an additional employee, 'Brown', who has three dependents ('Jim', 'Joan', and 'Bob') and works on four different projects ('W', 'X', 'Y', and 'Z'). There are 16 tuples in EMP in Figure 14.5a. If we decompose EMP in EMP_PROJECTS and EMP_DEPENDENTS, as shown in Figure 14.5b, we need only store a total of 11 tuples in both relations. Moreover, these tuples are much smaller than the tuples in EMP. In addition, the update anomalies associated with multivalued dependencies are avoided. For example, if Brown starts working on another project, we must insert three tuples in EMP—one for each dependent. If we forget to insert any one of those, the relation becomes inconsistent in that it implies an incorrect relationship between project and dependent. However, only a single tuple need be inserted in the 4NF relation EMP_PROJECTS. Similar problems occur with deletion and modification anomalies if a relation is not in 4NF.

Note that the EMP relation in Figure 14.4a is not in 4NF because it represents two *independent* 1:N relationships—one between employees and the projects they work on and the other between employees and their dependents. We may sometimes have a relationship between three entities that depends on all three participating entities, such as the SUPPLY relation shown in Figure 14.4c (consider only the tuples in Figure 14.4c *above* the dotted line for now). In this case a tuple represents a supplier supplying a specific part *to a particular project*, so there are *no* nontrivial MVDs. The SUPPLY relation is hence already *in* 4NF and should not be decomposed. Note also that relations containing nontrivial MVDs tend to be "all key" relations; that is, their key is all their attributes taken together.

(a) **EMP**

ENAME	PNAME	DNAME
Smith	X	John
Smith	Y	Anna
Smith	X	Anna
Smith	Y	John
Brown	W	Jim
Brown	X	Jim
Brown	Y	Jim
Brown	Z	Jim
Brown	W	Joan
Brown	X	Joan
Brown	Y	Joan
Brown	Z	Joan
Brown	W	Bob
Brown	X	Bob
Brown	Y	Bob
Brown	Z	Bob

(b) **EMP_PROJECTS**

ENAME	PNAME
Smith	X
Smith	Y
Brown	W
Brown	X
Brown	Y
Brown	Z

EMP_DEPENDENTS

ENAME	DNAME
Smith	Anna
Smith	John
Brown	Jim
Brown	Joan
Brown	Bob

Figure 14.5 Illustrating the benefits of 4NF. (a) The EMP relation with some additional tuples. (b) Projecting EMP on EMP_PROJECTS and EMP_DEPENDENTS.

Lossless Join Decomposition into 4NF Relations

Whenever we decompose a relation schema R into $R_1 = (X \cup Y)$ and $R_2 = (R - Y)$ based on an MVD $X \twoheadrightarrow Y$ that holds in R, the decomposition will have the lossless join property. In fact, it can be shown that this is a necessary and sufficient condition for decomposing a schema into two schemas that have the lossless join property, as given by property LJ1' below.

> **PROPERTY LJ1'**
>
> The relation schemas R_1 and R_2 form a lossless join decomposition of R if and only if $(R_1 \cap R_2) \twoheadrightarrow (R_1 - R_2)$ (or, by symmetry, if and only if $(R_1 \cap R_2) \twoheadrightarrow (R_2 - R_1)$).

This is similar to property LJ1 of Section 14.1.3 except that LJ1 dealt with FDs only, whereas LJ1' deals with both FDs and MVDs (recall that an FD is also an MVD). Hence, we can use a slight modification of Algorithm 14.3 to develop Algorithm 14.5, which creates a lossless join decomposition into relation schemas that are in 4NF (rather than BCNF). Note that Algorithm 14.5 does *not* necessarily produce a decomposition that preserves FDs.

> **ALGORITHM 14.5**   Lossless join decomposition into 4NF relations
>
> set D ← { R } ;
> while there is a relation schema Q in D that is not in 4NF do
>   begin
>   choose a relation schema Q in D that is not in 4NF ;
>   find a nontrivial MVD X→→Y in Q that violates 4NF ;
>   replace Q in D by two schemas (Q − Y) and (X ∪ Y)
>   end;

14.2.2   Join Dependencies and Fifth Normal Form

We saw that LJ1 and LJ1' give the condition for a relation schema R to be decomposed into two schemas R_1 and R_2, where the decomposition has the lossless join property. However, there may be some cases where there is no lossless join decomposition into two relation schemas but there is a lossless join decomposition into more than two relation schemas. These cases are handled by join dependency and fifth normal form. It is important to note that these cases occur very rarely and are difficult to detect in practice.

A **join dependency** (JD), denoted by $JD(R_1, R_2, \ldots R_n)$, specified on relation schema R, specifies a constraint on instances r of R. The constraint states that *every legal instance* r of R should have a lossless join decomposition into $R_1, R_2, \ldots, R_n$, that is,

$$* (\pi_{<R1>}(r), \pi_{<R2>}(r), \ldots, \pi_{<Rn>}(r)) = r$$

Note that MVD is a special case of a JD where n = 2. A join dependency $JD(R_1, R_2, \ldots, R_n)$, specified on relation schema R, is a **trivial JD** if one of the relation schemas R_i in $JD(R_1, R_2, \ldots, R_n)$ is equal to R. Such a dependency is called trivial because it has the lossless join property for *any* relation instance r of R and hence does not specify any constraint on R.

We can now specify the fifth normal form, which is also called the project-join normal form. A relation schema R is in **fifth normal form** (5NF) (or **project-join normal**

form (PJNF)) with respect to a set F of functional, multivalued, and join dependencies if for every nontrivial join dependency JD(R_1, R_2, ..., R_n) in F^+ (that is, implied by F) every R_i is a superkey of R.

For an example of a JD, consider once again the SUPPLY relation of Figure 14.4c. Suppose that the following additional constraint always holds: Whenever a supplier s supplies part p, *and* a project j uses part p, *and* the supplier s supplies *at least one* part to project j, *then* supplier s will also be supplying part p to project j. This constraint can be restated in other ways and specifies a join dependency JD(R1, R2, R3) among the three projections R1(SNAME, PARTNAME), R2(SNAME, PROJNAME), and R3(PARTNAME, PROJNAME) of SUPPLY. If this constraint holds, then the tuples below the dotted line in Figure 14.4c must exist in any legal instance of the SUPPLY relation that also contains the tuples above the dotted line. Figure 14.4d shows how the SUPPLY relation *with the join dependency* is decomposed into three relations R1, R2, and R3 that are each in 5NF. Notice that applying NATURAL JOIN to *any two* of these relations produces spurious tuples but applying NATURAL JOIN to *all three together* does not. The reader should verify this on the example relation of Figure 14.4c and its projections in Figure 14.4d. This is because only the JD exists but no MVDs are specified. Also notice that the JD(R1, R2, R3) is specified on all legal relation instances, not just the one shown in Figure 14.4c.

Note that discovering JDs in practical databases with hundreds of attributes is difficult; hence, current practice of database design pays scant attention to them.

14.2.3 Inclusion Dependencies

Inclusion dependencies were defined in order to formalize interrelational constraints. For example, the foreign key (or referential integrity) constraint cannot be specified as a functional or multivalued dependency because it relates attributes across relations; but it can be specified as an inclusion dependency.*

Formally, an **inclusion dependency** R.X < S.Y between a set of attributes X of relation schema R and a set of attributes Y of relation schema S specifies the constraint that, at any point in time where r is a relation instance of R and s is a relation instance of S, we must have:

$$\pi_{<X>}(r) \subseteq \pi_{<Y>}(s)$$

Note that the $\subseteq$ relationship does not necessarily have to be a proper subset. Obviously, the sets of attributes on which the inclusion dependency is specified—X of R and Y of S—must have the same number of attributes. In addition, the domains of corresponding attributes should be compatible. For example, if X = {A_1, A_2, ..., A_n} and Y = {B_1, B_2, ..., B_n}, one possible correspondence is to have DOM(A_i) COMPATIBLE-WITH DOM(B_i) for $1 \leq i \leq n$. In this case we say that A_i **corresponds-to** B_i.

For example, we can specify the following inclusion dependencies on the relational schema in Figure 13.1:

DEPARTMENT.DMGRSSN < EMPLOYEE.SSN
WORKS_ON.SSN < EMPLOYEE.SSN

*Inclusion dependencies can also be used to represent the constraint between two relations that represent a higher-level class/subclass relationship, which we will discuss in Chapter 15.

EMPLOYEE.DNUMBER < DEPARTMENT.DNUMBER
WORKS_ON.PNUMBER < PROJECT.PNUMBER

All the above inclusion dependencies represent **referential integrity constraints**. We can also use the inclusion dependencies to represent **class/subclass relationships**. For example, in the relational schema of Figure 15.12 (see Chapter 15), we can specify the following inclusion dependencies:

EMPLOYEE.SSN < PERSON.SSN
ALUMNUS_DEGREES.SSN < PERSON.SSN
STUDENT.SSN < PERSON.SSN

There are inference rules for inclusion dependencies. Examples of these are the following three:

(IDIR1) R.X < R.X.

(IDIR2) If R.X < S.Y where X = {A1, A2, ..., An} and Y = {B1, B2, ..., Bn} and Ai corresponds-to Bi, then R.Ai < S.Bi for $1 \leq i \leq n$.
(IDIR3) If R.X < S.Y and S.Y < T.Z , then R.X < T.Z .

The above inference rules were shown to be sound and complete for inclusion dependencies. So far, no normal forms have been developed based on inclusion dependencies.

14.2.4 Template Dependencies

No matter how many types of dependencies we come up with, some peculiar constraint may come up that cannot be represented by any of these types of dependencies. The idea behind template dependencies is to specify a template—or example—that defines each constraint or dependency. There are two types of templates—tuple-generating templates and constraint-generating templates. A template consists of a number of **hypothesis tuples** that are meant to show an example of the tuples that may appear in one or more relations. The other part of the template is the **template conclusion**. For tuple-generating templates, the conclusion is a set of tuples that must also exist in the relations if the hypothesis tuples are there. For constraint-generating templates, the template conclusion is a condition that must hold on the hypothesis tuples.

Figure 14.6 shows how we may define functional, multivalued, and inclusion dependencies by templates. Figure 14.7 shows how we may specify a constraint that cannot be specified with any of the dependencies discussed previously as a template dependency. Suppose we want to specify the constraint that "an employee's salary cannot be higher than the salary of his or her direct supervisor" on the relation schema EMPLOYEE in Figure 6.5; we can specify this constraint as a template dependency as shown in Figure 14.7.

14.2.5 Domain-Key Normal Form (DKNF)

We can also always define stricter normal forms that take into account additional types of dependencies and constraints. The idea behind domain-key normal form is to specify, theoretically at least, the "ultimate normal form" that takes into account all possible types of dependencies and constraints. A relation is said to be in DKNF if all constraints

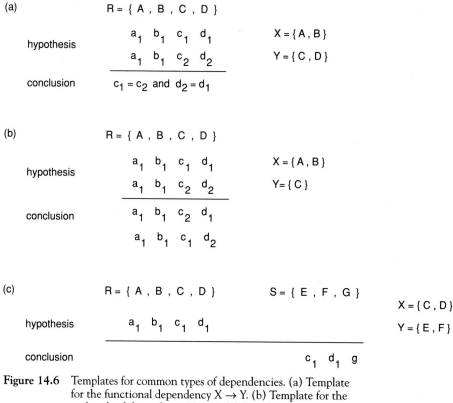

Figure 14.6   Templates for common types of dependencies. (a) Template for the functional dependency $X \rightarrow Y$. (b) Template for the multivalued dependency $X \twoheadrightarrow Y$. (c) Template for the inclusion dependency R.X<S.Y.

and dependencies that should hold on the relation can be enforced simply by enforcing the domain constraints and the key constraints specified on the relation.

For a relation in DKNF, it will be very straightforward to enforce the constraints by simply checking that each attribute value in a tuple is of the appropriate domain and that every key constraint on the relation is enforced. However, it seems quite unlikely that many relatively complex constraints can be included in a DKNF relation; hence, its practical utility is quite limited.

EMPLOYEE = { NAME , SSN , ... , SALARY , SUPERVISORSSN }

	NAME	SSN	...	SALARY	SUPERVISORSSN
hypothesis	a	b		c	d
	d	e		f	g
conclusion				c < f	

Figure 14.7   Template for the constraint that an employee's salary should be less than the supervisor's salary

14.3   Summary

In Section 14.1 we presented the concept of relation decomposition. We then gave algorithms for decomposing a universal relation schema into a set of relation schemas that are in normal forms and that satisfy the lossless join property, the dependency-preserving property, or both properties. All these properties are based on the functional dependencies specified on the attributes of the universal relation.

In Section 14.2 we defined additional types of dependencies and some additional normal forms. Multivalued dependencies led to fourth normal form, and join dependencies led to fifth normal form. We also discussed inclusion dependencies, which are used to specify referential integrity and class/subclass constraints, and template dependencies, which can be used to specify arbitrary types of constraints. Finally, we discussed very briefly the domain-key normal form.

Review Questions

14.1. What is meant by the attribute preservation condition on a decomposition?

14.2. Why are normal forms alone insufficient as a condition for a good schema design?

14.3. What is the dependency preservation property for a decomposition? Why is it important?

14.4. Why can we not guarantee that the relation schemas in a dependency-preserving decomposition be in BCNF?

14.5. What is the lossless join property of a decomposition? Why is it important?

14.6. Discuss the null value and dangling tuple problems.

14.7. What is a multivalued dependency? What type of constraint does it specify? When does it arise?

14.8. Define fourth normal form. Why is it useful?

14.9. Define join dependencies and fifth normal form.

14.10. What types of constraints are inclusion dependencies meant to represent?

14.11. What is the difference between template dependencies and the other types of dependencies we discussed?

Exercises

14.12. Show that the relation schemas produced by Algorithm 14.1 are in 3NF.

14.13. Show that if the matrix S resulting from Algorithm 14.2 does not have a row that is all "a" symbols, then projecting S on the decomposition and joining it back will always produce at least one spurious tuple.

14.14. Show that the relation schemas produced by Algorithm 14.3 are in BCNF.

14.15. Show that the relation schemas produced by Algorithm 14.4 are in 3NF.

14.16. Specify a template dependency for join dependencies.

14.17. Specify all the inclusion dependencies for the relational schema of Figure 6.5.

14.18. Prove that a functional dependency is also a multivalued dependency.

14.19. Consider the example of normalizing the LOTS relation in Section 13.4. Determine whether the decomposition of LOTS into {LOTS1AX, LOTS1AY, LOTS1B, LOTS2} has the lossless join property by applying Algorithm 14.2.

14.20. Show how the MVDs ENAME→→PNAME and ENAME→→DNAME in Figure 14.4a may arise during normalization into 1NF of a relation where the attributes PNAME and DNAME were multivalued (nonsimple).

Selected Bibliography

The theory of dependency preservation and lossless joins is given in the textbook by Ullman (1982), where proofs of some of the algorithms discussed here appear. The lossless join property is analyzed in Aho et al. (1979). The book by Maier (1983) includes a comprehensive discussion of relational dependency theory. The synthesis algorithm for relational design is due to Bernstein (1976). Osborn (1979) discusses a universal relation interface.

Multivalued dependencies are discussed in Zaniolo (1976) and fourth normal form is defined in Fagin (1977). The set of sound and complete rules for functional and multivalued dependencies was given by Beeri et al. (1977). Join dependencies are discussed by Rissanen (1977) and Aho et al. (1979). Inference rules for join dependencies are given by Sciore (1982). Fifth normal form (called project-join normal form) is introduced in Fagin (1979). Inclusion dependencies are discussed by Casanova et al. (1981). Template dependencies are discussed by Sadri and Ullman (1982). Other dependencies are discussed in Nicolas (1978), Furtado (1978), and Mendelzon and Maier (1979). Domain-key normal form is defined by Fagin (1981).

Advanced Data
Modeling Concepts

In Chapter 3 we presented the modeling concepts of the Entity-Relationship (ER) data model, a high-level model that is often used in an early phase of database design. During this phase, which is called **conceptual design**, the data requirements for the database are clearly defined in terms of an ER schema. The ER schema specifies the database structure and many of its constraints independently of any specific DBMS and is then mapped to a schema in a lower-level data model for a specific DBMS, as we discussed in Section 12.1. This mapping phase is known as **logical database design**. Finally, the details of storage structures and access paths for the database are chosen during the **physical database design phase**.

The ER modeling concepts discussed in Chapter 3 are sufficient for representing many database schemas for traditional database applications, which mainly include data processing applications in business and industry. However, since the late 1970s newer applications of database technology are becoming commonplace; these include engineering design (CAD/CAM*) databases, image and graphics databases, cartographic and geological databases, multimedia databases,** and knowledge bases for artificial intelligence applications. These types of databases have more complex requirements than the more traditional applications. To represent these requirements as accurately and explicitly as possible, the need arises for additional "semantic" modeling concepts. A variety of semantic data models have been proposed in the literature. Rather than discuss the many semantic data models proposed, we incorporate their most important concepts into the ER model and call the resulting model the **enhanced-ER** or **EER** model. After presenting the EER model concepts in Section 15.1, we show how these concepts can be mapped to

---

*CAD/CAM is an abbreviation for computer-aided design/computer-aided manufacturing.
**Multimedia databases store data that represent traditional entities, as well as unstructured data such as text, pictures, and voice recordings.

the relational, network, and hierarchical models in Section 15.2; this augments the discussion on mapping the regular ER model concepts that was given in Section 12.1. In Section 15.3 we discuss fundamental abstractions that are used as the basis of many semantic data models. In Section 15.4 we introduce a newer approach, **object-oriented data modeling**, that is gaining in popularity. We also briefly discuss a class of data models called **functional data models** in Section 15.4.

We mainly address conceptual database design in Section 15.1, and in Section 15.2 we discuss logical design concepts that involve mapping the EER model to relational, network, and hierarchical models. Chapter 16 will elaborate on the process of database design and also discuss the information system life cycle. This will enable the reader to place conceptual database design in the proper perspective within the whole database design process.

15.1   Enhanced-ER (EER) Model Concepts

The EER model includes all the modeling concepts of the ER model that were presented in Chapter 3. In addition to these, it includes the concepts of **subclass** and **superclass** and the related concepts of **specialization** and **generalization**. Another concept included in the EER model is that of a **category**. Associated with these concepts is the important mechanism of **attribute inheritance**. In the following subsections we present these concepts. Unfortunately, there is no standard terminology for these concepts, so we use the terminology that is used most commonly. Alternative terminology is given in footnotes. We also describe a diagrammatic technique for displaying these concepts when they arise in an EER schema. We call the resulting schema diagrams **enhanced-ER** or **EER diagrams**.

15.1.1   Subclasses, Superclasses, and Specialization

Subclasses and Superclasses

The first EER model concept we take up is that of a subclass of an entity type. As we discussed in Chapter 3, an entity type is used to represent a set of entities of the same type, such as the set of EMPLOYEE entities in a company database. In many cases an entity type will have numerous additional subgroupings of its entities that are meaningful and need to be represented explicitly because of their significance to the database application. For example, the entities that are members of the EMPLOYEE entity type may be further grouped into SECRETARY, ENGINEER, MANAGER, TECHNICIAN, SALARIED_EMPLOYEE, HOURLY_EMPLOYEE, and so on. The set of entities in each of the latter groupings is a subset of the entities that belong to the EMPLOYEE entity type, meaning that every entity that is a member of one of these subgroupings is also an employee. We call each of these subgroupings a **subclass** of the EMPLOYEE entity type, and EMPLOYEE is called the **superclass** for each of these subclasses.

We call the relationship between a superclass and any one of its subclasses a **super-class/subclass relationship**.* In our previous example, EMPLOYEE/SECRETARY and EMPLOY-EE/TECHNICIAN are two superclass/subclass relationships. Notice that a member entity instance of the subclass represents the *same real-world entity* as some member of the superclass; for example, a SECRETARY entity 'Joan Logano' is also the EMPLOYEE 'Joan Logano'. Hence, the subclass member is the same as the entity in the superclass but in a distinct *specific role*. However, when we implement a superclass/subclass relationship in the database system, we may represent a member of the subclass as a distinct database object, say a distinct record that is related via the key attribute to its superclass entity. In Section 15.2 we discuss various options for representing superclass/subclass relationships in relational, network, and hierarchical databases.

An entity cannot exist in the database merely by being a member of a subclass; it must also be a member of the superclass. An entity that is a member of the superclass can be optionally included as a member of any number of the subclasses. For example, a salaried employee who is also an engineer belongs to the two subclasses ENGINEER and SALARIED_EMPLOYEE of the EMPLOYEE entity type. However, it is not necessary that every entity in a superclass be a member of some subclass.

Attribute Inheritance in Superclass/Subclass Relationships

An important concept associated with subclasses is that of **attribute inheritance**. Because an entity in the subclass represents the same real-world entity from the superclass, it should possess values for its specific attributes *as well as* values of its attributes as a member of the superclass. We say that an entity that is a member of a subclass **inherits** all the attributes of the entity as a member of the superclass. The entity will also inherit all relationship instances for relationship types in which the superclass participates. Note that a subclass, together with all the attributes it inherits from the superclass, is an *entity type* in its own right.

Specialization

Specialization is the process of defining a *set of subclasses* of an entity type; this entity type is called the **superclass** of the specialization. The set of subclasses forming a specialization is defined on the basis of some distinguishing characteristic of the entities in the superclass that expresses a certain kind of distinction among the entities. For example, the set of subclasses {SECRETARY, ENGINEER, TECHNICIAN} is a specialization of the superclass EMPLOYEE entity type that distinguishes among EMPLOYEE entities based on the *job type* of each entity.

Note that we may have several specializations of the same entity type based on different distinguishing characteristics. For example, *another specialization* of the EMPLOYEE entity type may yield the set of subclasses {SALARIED_EMPLOYEE, HOURLY_EMPLOYEE}; this specialization distinguishes among employees based on *method of payment*.

---

*A class/subclass relationship is often called an **IS-A** (or IS-AN) relationship because of the way one refers to the concept. We say "a SECRETARY IS-AN EMPLOYEE," "a TECHNICIAN IS-AN EMPLOYEE," etc.

Enhanced-ER (EER) Diagrams

Figure 15.1 shows how we represent a specialization diagrammatically in an **EER diagram**. The subclasses that define a specialization are attached by lines to a circle, which is connected to the superclass. The subset symbol on each line connecting a subclass to the circle indicates the direction of the superclass/subclass relationship. Any attributes that apply only to entities of a particular subclass—such as TypingSpeed of SECRETARY—are attached to the rectangle representing that subclass. These are called **specific attributes** of the subclass. Similarly, a subclass can participate in **specific relationship types**, such as HOURLY_EMPLOYEE participating in BELONGS_TO in Figure 15.1. We will explain the **d** symbol in the circles of Figure 15.1 and additional EER diagram notation shortly.

Figure 15.2 shows a few entity instances belonging to subclasses of the {SECRETARY, ENGINEER, TECHNICIAN} specialization. Again, note that an entity that is a member of a subclass represents *the same real-world entity* as the entity connected to it in the EMPLOYEE superclass, even though the same entity is shown twice; for example, e_1 is shown in both EMPLOYEE and SECRETARY in Figure 15.2. As we can see, a superclass/subclass relationship such as EMPLOYEE/SECRETARY somewhat resembles a 1:1 relationship *at the instance level* (see Figure 3.11). The main difference is that in a 1:1 relationship two *distinct entities* are related. We can consider an entity in the subclass as being the same entity as in the su-

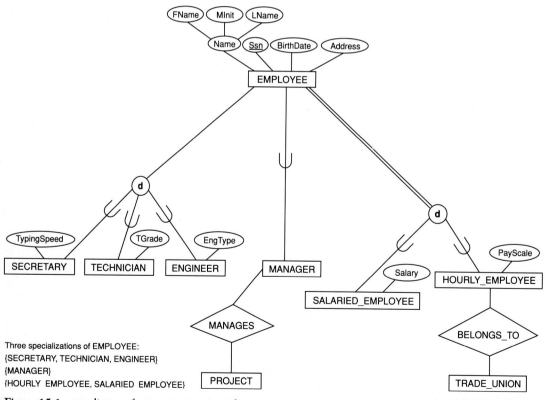

Three specializations of EMPLOYEE:
{SECRETARY, TECHNICIAN, ENGINEER}
{MANAGER}
{HOURLY_EMPLOYEE, SALARIED EMPLOYEE}

Figure 15.1   EER diagram for representing specialization

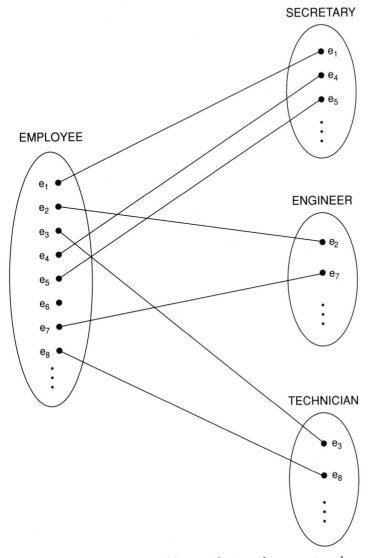

Figure 15.2   Some instances of the specialization of EMPLOYEE into the {SECRETARY, ENGINEER, TECHNICIAN} set of subclasses

perclass but playing a *specialized role*, for example, an EMPLOYEE specialized in the role of SECRETARY or an EMPLOYEE specialized in the role of TECHNICIAN.

Use of Subclasses in Data Modeling

There are two main reasons for including class/subclass relationships in a data model. The first is that certain attributes may apply to only some entities of the (superclass) entity type but not to all the entities. A subclass is defined to group the entities to which these attributes apply. The members of the subclass may still share the majority of their attributes with the other members of the superclass. For example, the SECRETARY subclass may have an attribute TypingSpeed, whereas the ENGINEER subclass may have an attribute EngineerType, but both SECRETARY and ENGINEER share their other attributes as members of the EMPLOYEE entity type.

The second reason for using subclasses is that some relationship types may be participated in only by entities that are members of the subclass. For example, if only HOURLY_ EMPLOYEEs can belong to a trade union, we can represent that fact by creating the subclass HOURLY_EMPLOYEE of EMPLOYEE and relate the subclass to an entity type TRADE_ UNION via the BELONGS_TO relationship type, as illustrated in Figure 15.1.

15.1.2 Generalization

The specialization process discussed above allows us to:

- Define a set of subclasses of an entity type.
- Associate additional specific attributes with each subclass.
- Establish additional specific relationship types between each subclass and other entity types.

We can think of a *reverse process* of abstraction in which we suppress the differences among several entity types, identify their common features, and **generalize** them into a single **superclass** entity type of which the original entity types are special **subclasses**. For example, consider the entity types CAR and TRUCK shown in Figure 15.3a; they can be generalized into the entity type VEHICLE as shown in Figure 15.3b. Both CAR and TRUCK are now subclasses of the **generalized superclass** VEHICLE. We will use the term **generalization** to refer to the process of defining a generalized entity type from the given entity types.

Notice that the generalization process can be viewed as the reverse of the specialization process. Hence, in Figure 15.3 we can view {CAR, TRUCK} as a specialization of VEHICLE, rather than viewing VEHICLE as a generalization of CAR and TRUCK. Similarly, in Figure 15.1 we can view EMPLOYEE as a generalization of SECRETARY, TECHNICIAN, and ENGINEER. A diagrammatic notation to distinguish between generalization and specialization is sometimes used in practice. An arrow pointing to the generalized superclass represents a generalization, whereas arrows pointing to the specialized subclasses represent a specialization. We will not use this notation because the decision as to which process is more appropriate for a particular situation is often subjective. Hence, we advocate *not* drawing any arrows in these situations.

15.1.3 Data Modeling with Specialization and Generalization

So far we have introduced the concepts of subclasses and superclass/subclass relationships, as well as the specialization and generalization processes. In general, a superclass or subclass is a set of entities and hence is also an *entity type*; that is why superclasses and subclasses are shown in rectangles in EER diagrams, which is the same as the notation used for entity types in ER diagrams. We will now discuss in more detail the properties of

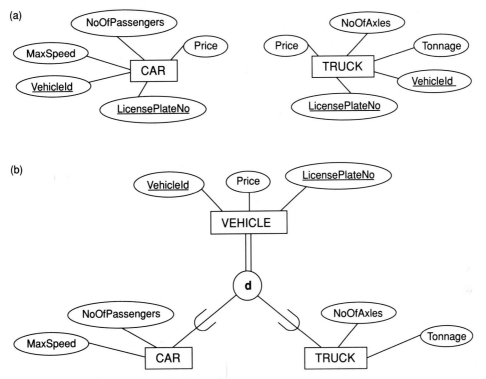

Figure 15.3   Illustrating generalization. (a) Two entity types CAR and TRUCK. (b) Generalizing CAR and TRUCK into VEHICLE.

specializations and generalizations. We first discuss constraints on a single specialization or generalization and then discuss how several specializations or generalizations can be built into hierarchies or lattices.

Constraints on Specialization and Generalization

In the following, we will discuss constraints that apply to a single specialization or a single generalization; however, for brevity, our discussion will refer to specialization only even though it applies to *both specialization and generalization*.

In general, we may have several specializations defined on the same (superclass) entity type, as shown in Figure 15.1. In such a case, entities may belong to subclasses in each of the specializations. Note also that we may have a specialization consisting of a single subclass only, such as the {MANAGER} specialization in Figure 15.1; in such a case we do not use the circle notation.

In some specializations we can determine exactly the entities that will become members of each subclass by placing a condition on the value of some attribute of the superclass. Such subclasses are called **predicate-defined** (or **condition-defined**) **subclasses**. For example, if the EMPLOYEE entity type has an attribute JobType, as shown in Figure 15.4, we can specify the condition of membership in the SECRETARY subclass by

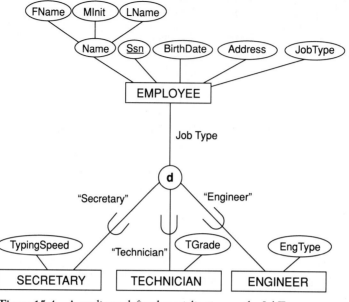

Figure 15.4   A predicate defined specialization on the JobType
attribute of EMPLOYEE

the predicate JobType = 'Secretary', which we call the **defining predicate** of the subclass. This condition is a *constraint* which specifies that members of the SECRETARY subclass must satisfy the predicate and that all entities in the EMPLOYEE entity type whose attribute value for JobType is 'Secretary' must belong to the subclass. We display a predicate-defined subclass by writing the predicate condition next to the line attaching the subclass to its superclass.

If *all subclasses* in a specialization have the membership condition on the *same attribute* of the superclass, the specialization itself is called an **attribute-defined specialization**, and the attribute is called the **defining attribute** of the specialization. We display an attribute-defined specialization as shown in Figure 15.4 by placing the defining attribute name next to the arc from the circle to the superclass.

When we do not have such a condition that determines membership, the subclass is called **user defined**. Membership in such a subclass is determined by the database users when they apply the operation to add an entity to the subclass; hence, membership is *specified individually for each entity by the user*, not by any condition that may be evaluated automatically.

Two other constraints may apply to a specialization. The first is the **disjointness constraint**, which specifies that the subclasses of the specialization must be disjoint. This means that an entity can be a member of *at most one* of the subclasses of the specialization. A specialization that is predicate defined implies the disjointness constraint if the attribute used to define the membership predicate is single valued. Figure 15.4 illustrates this case, where the **d** in the circle stands for disjoint. We also use the **d** notation to specify the constraint that user-defined subclasses of a specialization must be disjoint, as illustrated by the specialization {HOURLY_EMPLOYEE, SALARIED_EMPLOYEE} in Figure 15.1. If the subclasses are not disjoint, their sets of entities may **overlap**; that is, the same entity

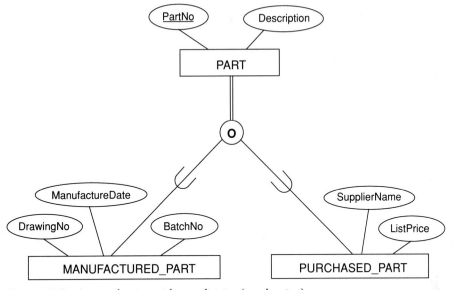

Figure 15.5 A specialization with non-disjoint (overlapping) subclasses

may be a member of more than one subclass of the specialization. This case, which is the default, is displayed by placing an **o** in the circle, as shown in the example of Figure 15.5.

The second constraint on specialization is called the **completeness constraint**, which may be either total or partial. A **total specialization** specifies the constraint that every entity in the superclass must be a member of some subclass in the specialization. For example, if every EMPLOYEE must be either an HOURLY_EMPLOYEE or a SALARIED_EMPLOYEE, then the specialization {HOURLY_EMPLOYEE, SALARIED_EMPLOYEE} of Figure 15.1 is a total specialization of EMPLOYEE; this is shown in EER diagrams by using a double line to connect the superclass to the circle. A single line is used to display a **partial specialization**, which allows an entity not to belong to any of the subclasses. For example, if some EMPLOYEE entities do not belong to any of the subclasses {SECRETARY, ENGINEER, TECHNICIAN} of Figures 15.1 and 15.4, then that specialization is partial. This notation is similar to the total participation of an entity type in a relationship type of the ER model presented in Chapter 3. Note that the disjointness and completeness constraints are *independent*. Hence, we have the following four types of specialization:

- disjoint, total
- disjoint, partial
- overlapping, total
- overlapping, partial

Of course, the correct constraint is determined from the real-world meaning that applies to each specialization. Note that a generalization superclass usually is **total** because the superclass is *derived from* the subclasses and hence contains only the entities that are in the subclasses. Hence, only the latter two options usually apply to generalization.

Insertion and Deletion Rules for Specialization and Generalization

Certain insertion and deletion rules apply to specialization (and generalization) as a consequence of the constraints specified above. Some of these rules are:

- Deleting an entity from a superclass implies that it is automatically deleted from all the subclasses it belongs to.
- Inserting an entity in a superclass implies that the entity is mandatorily inserted in all *predicate-defined* subclasses for which the entity satisfies the defining predicate.
- Inserting an entity in a superclass of a *total specialization* implies that the entity is mandatorily inserted in at least one of the subclasses of the specialization.

The reader is encouraged to make a complete list of rules for insertions and deletions for the various types of specializations.

Specialization Hierarchies, Specialization Lattices, and Shared Subclasses

A subclass may itself have further subclasses specified on it, forming a hierarchy or a lattice of specializations. For example, in Figure 15.6 ENGINEER is a subclass of EMPLOYEE and is also a superclass of ENGINEERING_MANAGER; this represents the real-world constraint that every engineering manager is required to be an engineer. A **specialization hierarchy** has the constraint that every subclass participates (as subclass) in *one* class/subclass relationship, whereas for a **specialization lattice** a subclass can be subclass in *more than one* class/subclass relationship. Hence, Figure 15.6 is a lattice.

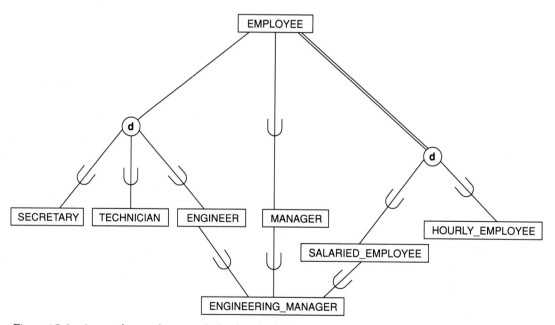

Figure 15.6   A specialization lattice with the shared subclass
ENGINEERING_MANAGER

Figure 15.7 shows another specialization lattice of more than one level. This may be part of a conceptual schema for a university database. Notice that this would have been a hierarchy except for the STUDENT_ASSISTANT subclass, which is a subclass in two distinct class/subclass relationships. All person entities represented in the database are members of the PERSON entity type, which is specialized into the subclasses {EMPLOYEE, ALUMNUS, STUDENT}. This specialization is overlapping; for example, an alumnus may also be an employee. An alumnus may also be a student going for an advanced degree after receiving an undergraduate degree. The subclass STUDENT is superclass for the specialization {GRADUATE_STUDENT, UNDERGRADUATE_STUDENT}, while EMPLOYEE is superclass for the specialization {STUDENT_ASSISTANT, FACULTY, STAFF}. Notice that STUDENT_ASSISTANT is also a subclass of STUDENT. Finally, STUDENT_ASSISTANT is superclass for the specialization into {RESEARCH_ASSISTANT, TEACHING_ASSISTANT}.

In such a specialization lattice or hierarchy, a subclass inherits the attributes not only of its direct superclass but also of all its predecessor superclasses *all the way to the root*. For example, an entity in GRADUATE_STUDENT inherits all the attribute values of that entity as a STUDENT *and* as a PERSON. Note that an entity may exist in several leaf nodes of the hierarchy; for example, a member of GRADUATE_STUDENT may also be a member of RESEARCH_ASSISTANT.

A subclass with *more than one* superclass is called a **shared subclass**. For example, if every ENGINEERING_MANAGER must be an ENGINEER but must also be a SALARIED_EMPLOY-EE and a MANAGER, then ENGINEERING_MANAGER should be a shared subclass of all three superclasses (Figure 15.6). Notice that it is shared subclasses that lead to a lattice; if no shared subclasses existed, we would have a hierarchy rather than a lattice.

Although we used specialization to illustrate our discussion, similar concepts *apply equally* to generalization, as we mentioned at the beginning of this subsection. Hence, we can also speak of **generalization hierarchies** and **generalization lattices**. The next subsection elaborates on the differences between the specialization and generalization processes.

Top-down versus Bottom-up Conceptual Design

In the specialization process we typically start with an entity type and then define subclasses of the entity type by successive specialization; that is, we repeatedly define more specific groupings of the entity type. For example, when designing the specialization hierarchy/lattice in Figure 15.7, we may first specify an entity type PERSON for a university database. Then we discover that three types of persons will be represented in the database: university employees, alumni, and students. We create the specialization {EMPLOYEE, ALUMNUS, STUDENT} for this purpose and choose the overlapping constraint because a person may belong to more than one of the subclasses. We then specialize EMPLOYEE further into {STAFF, FACULTY, STUDENT_ASSISTANT}, and specialize STUDENT into {GRADUATE_STUDENT, UNDERGRADUATE_STUDENT}. Finally, we specialized STUDENT_ASSISTANT into {RESEARCH_ASSISTANT, TEACHING_ASSISTANT}. This successive specialization corresponds to a **top-down conceptual refinement** process during conceptual schema design. So far, we have a hierarchy; we then discover that STUDENT_ASSISTANT is a shared subclass since it is also a subclass of STUDENT, leading to the lattice.

It is possible to arrive at the same hierarchy or lattice from the other direction. In such a case, the process is generalization rather than specialization and corresponds to a

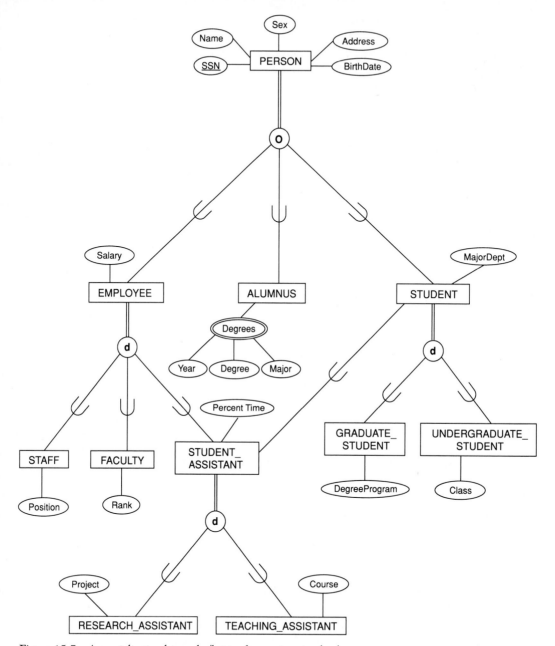

Figure 15.7   A specialization hierarchy/lattice for a university database

bottom-up conceptual synthesis. In structural terms, hierarchies or lattices resulting from either process may be identical; the only difference is the manner or order in which the schema superclasses and subclasses were specified.

In practice, it is likely that neither the generalization process nor the specialization process is followed strictly, but a combination of the two processes is employed. In this case, new classes are continually incorporated into a hierarchy or lattice as they become apparent to users and designers. Notice that the notion of representing data and knowledge using superclass/subclass hierarchies and lattices is quite common in knowledge-based systems and expert systems, which combine database technology with artificial intelligence techniques. For example, frame-based knowledge representation schemes closely resemble class hierarchies.

15.1.4 Categories and Categorization

All of the superclass/subclass relationships we have seen thus far have a *single superclass*. Even a shared subclass such as ENGINEERING_MANAGER in the lattice of Figure 15.6 is the subclass in three *distinct* superclass/subclass relationships, where each of the three relationships has a *single* superclass. In some cases the need arises for modeling a single superclass/subclass relationship with *more than one* superclass, where the superclasses represent different entity types. In this case we call the *subclass* a **category**.*

For example, suppose we have three entity types: PERSON, BANK, and COMPANY. In a database for vehicle registration, an owner of a vehicle can be a person, a bank (holding a lien on a vehicle), or a company. We need to create a class that includes entities of all three types to play the role of vehicle owner. A category OWNER that is a *subclass of the* **union** of the three classes COMPANY, BANK, and PERSON is created for this purpose. We display categories in an EER diagram as shown in Figure 15.8. The superclasses COMPANY, BANK, and PERSON are connected to the circle with the **U** symbol, which stands for the *set union operation*. An arc with the subset symbol connects the circle to the (subclass) OWNER category. If a defining predicate is needed, it is displayed next to the line from the superclass to which the predicate applies. In Figure 15.8 we have two categories: OWNER, which is a subclass of the union of PERSON, BANK, and COMPANY, and REGISTERED_VEHICLE, which is a subclass of the union of CAR and TRUCK.

A category has two or more superclasses that may represent *distinct entity types*, whereas other superclass/subclass relationships always have a single superclass. We can compare a category, such as OWNER in Figure 15.8, with the ENGINEERING_MANAGER shared subclass of Figure 15.6. The latter is a subclass of *each of* the three superclasses ENGINEER, MANAGER, and SALARIED_EMPLOYEE, so an entity that is a member of ENGINEERING_MANAGER must exist in *all three*. This represents the constraint that an engineering manager must be an ENGINEER, a MANAGER, *and* a SALARIED_EMPLOYEE; that is, ENGINEERING_MANAGER is a subset of the *intersection* of the three subclasses. On the other hand, a category is a subset of the *union* of its superclasses. Hence, an entity that is a member of OWNER must exist in *at least one* of the superclasses but does not have to be a member of *all* of them. This represents the constraint that an OWNER may be a COMPANY, a BANK, *or* a PERSON in Figure 15.8. In this example, as in most cases where categories are used, an entity in the category is a member of *exactly one* of the superclasses.

Attribute inheritance works more selectively in case of categories. For example, in Figure 15.8 each OWNER entity will inherit the attributes of either a COMPANY, a PERSON, or a BANK depending on the superclass to which the entity belongs. This can be called **selective inheritance**. On the other hand, a shared subclass such as ENGINEERING_

---

*Our use of the term category is based on the ECR model (Elmasri et al. 1985).

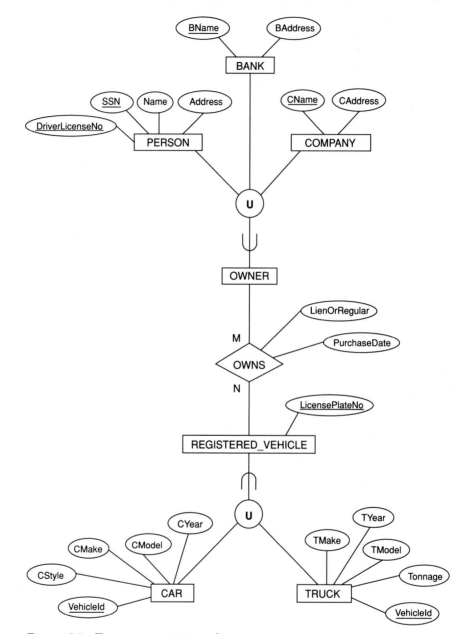

Figure 15.8   Two categories OWNER and REGISTERED_VEHICLE

MANAGER (Figure 15.6) inherits *all* the attributes of its superclasses SALARIED_EMPLOYEE, ENGINEER, and MANAGER.

It is interesting to note the difference between the category REGISTERED_VEHICLE (Figure 15.8) and the generalized superclass VEHICLE (Figure 15.3b). In Figure 15.3b every car and every truck is a VEHICLE, whereas in Figure 15.8 the REGISTERED_VEHICLE category includes some cars and some trucks but not necessarily all of them (for example, some cars or trucks may not be registered). Also, in general, a specialization or generalization such as that in Figure 15.3b, if it were *partial*, would not preclude VEHICLE from containing other types of entities, such as bicycles. However, a category such as REGISTERED_VEHICLE in Figure 15.8 implies that only cars and trucks, but not other types of entities, can be members of REGISTERED_VEHICLE.

A category can be **total** or **partial**. For example, ACCOUNT_HOLDER is a predicate-defined partial category in Figure 15.9a, where c_1 and c_2 are predicate conditions that specify which COMPANY and PERSON entities, respectively, are members of ACCOUNT_HOLDER. However, the category PROPERTY in Figure 15.9b is total because every building and lot must be a member of PROPERTY; this is shown by a double line connecting the category to the circle. Partial categories are indicated by a single line connecting the category to the circle, as in Figures 15.8 and 15.9a.

The superclasses of a category may have different key attributes, as demonstrated by the OWNER category of Figure 15.8, or they may have the same key attribute, as demon-

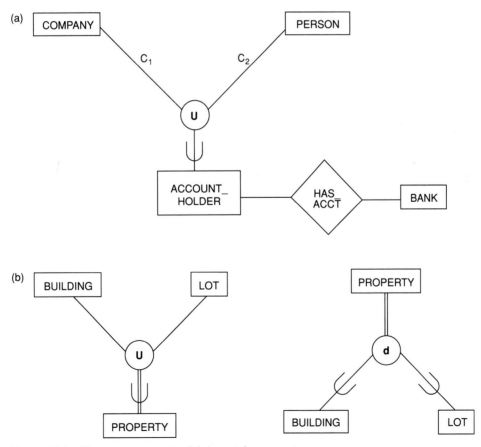

Figure 15.9 Illustrating categories. (a) A partial category ACCOUNT_HOLDER that is a subset of the union of two entity types COMPANY and PERSON. (b) A total category PROPERTY and a similar generalization.

strated by the REGISTERED_VEHICLE category. Notice that in the case where the category is *total* (not partial), it may be alternatively represented as a specialization or a generalization, as illustrated in Figure 15.9b. In this case the choice of which representation to use is subjective. If the two classes represent the same type of entities and share numerous attributes including the same key attributes, generalization is preferred; otherwise, categorization is more appropriate.

15.1.5   Formal Definitions

In the preceding subsections we extended the basic Entity-Relationship model with the concepts of subclasses, class/subclass relationships, specialization, generalization, and categories. We called the resulting model the enhanced-ER or EER model. In this section we summarize these concepts and define them formally in the manner in which we formally defined the concepts of the basic ER model in Chapter 3.

A **class** is a set of entities; this includes any of the EER schema constructs that group together entities such as entity types, subclasses, superclasses, and categories. A **subclass** S is a class whose entities must always be a subset of those entities in another class, called the **superclass** C of the **superclass/subclass** (or IS-A) **relationship**. We denote such a relationship by C/S. For such a superclass/subclass relationship, we must always have

$$S \subseteq C$$

A **specialization** $Z = \{S_1, S_2, ..., S_n\}$ is a set of subclasses that have the same superclass G; that is, G/S_i is a superclass/subclass relationship for $i = 1, ..., n$. G is called a **generalized entity type** (or the **superclass** of the specialization, or a **generalization** of the subclasses $\{S_1, S_2, ..., S_n\}$). Z is said to be **total** if we always have

$$\bigcup_{i=1}^{n} S_i = G$$

otherwise, Z is said to be **partial**. Z is said to be **disjoint** if we always have

$$S_i \cap S_j = \phi \text{ for } i \neq j;$$

otherwise, Z is said to be **overlapping**.

A subclass S of C is said to be **predicate defined** if a predicate p on the attributes of C is used to specify which entities in C are members of S; that is, $S = C[p]$, where $C[p]$ is the set of entities in C that satisfy p. A subclass that is not defined by a predicate is called **user defined**.

A specialization Z (or generalization G) is said to be **attribute defined** if a predicate $A = c_i$, where A is an attribute of G and c_i is a constant value from the domain of A, is used to specify membership in each subclass S_i in Z. Note that if $c_i \neq c_j$ for $i \neq j$, and A is a single-valued attribute, then the specialization will be disjoint.

A **category** T is a class that is a subset of the union of n defining superclasses D_1, $D_2, ..., D_n$, $n > 1$, and is formally specified as follows:

$$T \subseteq (D_1 \cup D_2 ... \cup D_n)$$

A predicate p_i on the attributes of D_i can be used to specify the members of each D_i that are members of T. If a predicate is specified on every D_i, we get

$$T = (D_1[p_1] \cup D_2[p_2] \dots \cup D_n[p_n])$$

Note that we should now extend the definition of **relationship type** given in Chapter 3 by allowing any class—not only entity types—to participate in a relationship. Hence, we should replace the word 'entity type' with 'class' in that definition. The graphical notation of EER is consistent with ER because all classes are represented by rectangles.

15.1.6   Example Database Schema in the EER Model

In this section we give an example of a database schema in the EER model to illustrate the use of the various concepts discussed here and in Chapter 3. Consider a university database that keeps track of students, their majors, transcripts, and registration, as well as the university course offerings. The database also keeps track of the sponsored research projects of faculty and graduate students. This schema is shown in Figure 15.10. Following is a discussion of the requirements that led to this schema.

For each person in the database, it is required to keep information on the person's Name [Name], social security number [Ssn], address [Address], sex [Sex], and birthdate [BDate]. Two subclasses of the PERSON entity type were identified: FACULTY and STUDENT. Specific attributes of FACULTY are rank [Rank] (assistant, associate, adjunct, research, visiting, etc.), office [FOffice], office phone [FPhone], and salary [Salary], and we also relate each faculty member to the academic departments that the faculty member is affiliated with [BELONGS] (a faculty member can be associated with several departments, so the relationship is M:N). A specific attribute of STUDENT is [Class] (freshman = 1, sophomore = 2, ..., graduate student = 5). Each student is also related to his or her major and minor departments, if known ([MAJOR] and [MINOR]), to the course sections he or she is currently attending [REGISTERED], and to the courses completed [TRANSCRIPT]. Each transcript instance includes the grade the student received [Grade] in the course section.

GRAD_STUDENT is a subclass of STUDENT with the defining predicate Class = 5. For each graduate student, we keep a list of previous degrees in a composite, multivalued attribute [Degrees]. We also relate the student to a faculty advisor [ADVISOR] and a thesis committee [COMMITTEE] if one exists.

An academic department has the attributes name [DName], telephone [DPhone], and office number [Office] and is related to the faculty member who is its chairperson [CHAIRS] and to the college to which it belongs [CD]. Each college has attributes college name [CName], office number [COffice], and the name of its dean [Dean].

A course has attributes course number [C#], course name [Cname], and a course description [CDesc]. Several sections of each course are offered, with each section having the attributes section number [Sec#] and the year and quarter in which the section was offered ([Year] and [Qtr]). Section numbers uniquely identify each section. The sections being offered during the current semester are in a subclass CURRENT_SECTION of SECTION, with the defining predicate Qtr = CurrentQtr and Year = CurrentYear. Each section is

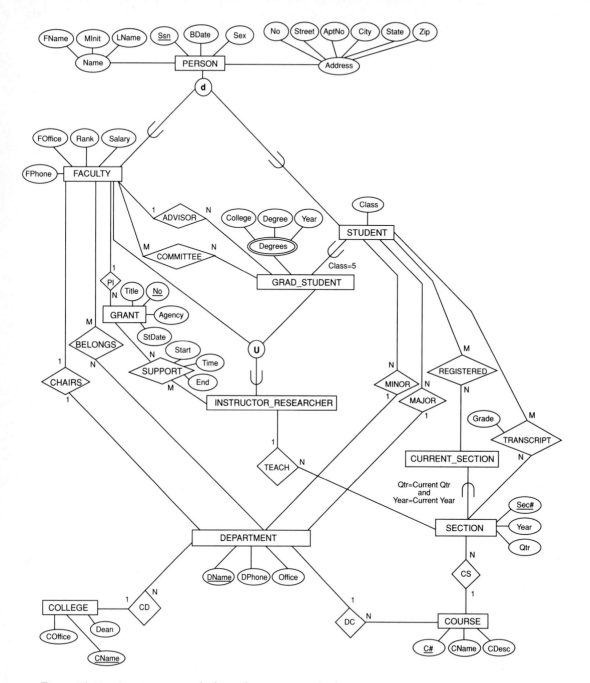

Figure 15.10   An EER conceptual schema for a university database

related to the instructor who taught it or is teaching it (if that instructor is in the database).

The category INSTRUCTOR_RESEARCHER is a subset of the union of FACULTY and GRAD_STUDENT and includes all faculty, as well as graduate students who are supported by teaching or research. Finally, the entity type GRANT keeps track of research grants and contracts awarded to the university. Each grant has attributes grant title [Title], grant number [No], the awarding agency [Agency], and the starting date [StDate]. A grant is related to one principal investigator [PI] and to all researchers it supports [SUPPORT]. Each instance of support has as attributes the starting date of support [Start], the ending date of the support (if known) [End], and the percent of time currently being spent on the project [Time] by the person supported.

15.2 Mapping of EER Model Concepts

In this section we show how the EER model concepts presented in Section 15.1 can be mapped to the relational, network, and hierarchical models. This augments the mapping of ER model concepts to these models, which was presented in Section 12.1. The mapping of ER or EER schemas is typically used during the logical database design phase to create a schema in the data model of the chosen DBMS.

15.2.1 EER-to-Relational Mapping

We now discuss the mapping of EER model concepts to relations by extending the ER-to-relational algorithm that was presented in Section 12.1.1.

Superclass/Subclass Relationships and Specialization (or Generalization)

There are several options for mapping a number of subclasses that together form a specialization (or, alternatively, that are generalized into a superclass), such as the {SECRETARY, TECHNICIAN, ENGINEER} subclasses of EMPLOYEE in Figure 15.4. We can add a further step to our ER-to-relational mapping algorithm from Section 12.1.1, which has seven steps, to handle mapping of specialization. Step 8 below gives the most common options. We then discuss the conditions under which each option should be used. We use Attrs(R) to denote the attributes of relation R and PK(R) to denote the primary key of R.

STEP 8:   Convert each specialization with m subclasses $\{S_1, S_2, ..., S_m\}$ and (generalized) superclass C, where the attributes of C are $\{k, a_1, ..., a_n\}$ and k is the (primary) key, into relation schemas using one of the following options:

> *Option 8A:*   Create a relation L for C with attributes Attrs(L) = $\{k, a_1, ..., a_n\}$ and PK(L) = k. Also create a relation L_i for each subclass S_i, $1 \leq i \leq m$, with the attributes Attrs(L_i) = $\{k\} \cup \{$attributes of $S_i\}$ and PK(L_i) = k.

> *Option 8B:*   Create a relation L_i for each subclass S_i, $1 \leq i \leq m$, with the attributes Attrs(L_i) = $\{$attributes of $S_i\} \cup \{k, a_1, ..., a_n\}$ and PK(L_i) = k.

Option 8C: Create a single relation L with attributes Attrs(L) = {k, a_1, ..., a_n} $\cup$ {attributes of S_1} $\cup$ ... $\cup$ {attributes of S_m} $\cup$ {t} and PK(L) = k. This option is for a specialization whose subclasses are *disjoint*, and t is a **type** attribute that indicates the subclass to which each tuple belongs, if any.

Option 8D: Create a single relation schema L with attributes Attrs(L) = {k, a_1, ..., a_n} $\cup$ {attributes of S_1} $\cup$ ... $\cup$ {attributes of S_m} $\cup$ {t_1, t_2, ..., t_m} and PK(L) = k. This option is for a specialization whose subclasses are *overlapping* (not disjoint), and each t_i, $1 \leq i \leq m$, is a Boolean attribute to indicate whether or not a tuple belongs to subclass S_i. This option has the potential for generating a large number of null values.

Option 8A creates a relation L_i for each subclass S_i; L_i includes the specific attributes of S_i plus the primary key of the superclass C, which is propagated to L_i and becomes its primary key. Another relation L is created for the superclass C and its attributes. An EQUIJOIN operation on the primary key between any L_i and L produces all the specific and inherited attributes of the entities in S_i. This option is illustrated in Figure 15.11a for the EER schema in Figure 15.4. Option 8A works for any constraints on the specialization: disjoint or overlapping, total or partial. Notice that the constraint

$$\pi_{<k>}(L_i) \subseteq \pi_{<k>}(L)$$

must hold for each L_i. This specifies an inclusion dependency $L_i.k < L.k$, as we discussed in Section 14.2.3.

In option 8B the EQUIJOIN operation is *built into* the schema and the relation L is done away with, as illustrated in Figure 15.11b for the EER specialization in Figure 15.3b. This option works well only with both the disjoint and total constraints on the specialization. If the specialization is not total, we lose any entity that does not belong to any of the subclasses S_i. If the specialization is not disjoint, then an entity belonging to more than one of the subclasses will have its inherited attributes from the superclass C stored redundantly in more than one L_i, causing the update anomalies discussed in Chapter 13. With option 8B we do not have any relation that holds all the entities in the superclass C; we need to apply an OUTER UNION operation to the L_i relations to retrieve all the entities in C. The result of the outer union will be similar to the relations under options 8C and 8D except that the type fields will be missing. Also, whenever we search for an arbitrary entity in C, we must search all the m relations L_i. Because of these drawbacks, this option is generally not recommended.

Options 8C and 8D create a single relation to represent the superclass C and all its subclasses. Any entity that does not belong to some of the subclasses will have null values for the specific attributes of these subclasses. These options are hence not recommended if many specific attributes are defined for the subclasses. However, if few specific subclass attributes exist, these mappings are preferable to options 8A and 8B because they do away with the need to specify EQUIJOIN and OUTER UNION operations and hence can result in a more efficient implementation. Option 8C is used for disjoint subclasses by including a single **type** (or **image**) **attribute** t to indicate the subclass to which each tuple belongs; hence, the domain of t could be {1, 2, .., m}. If the specialization is partial, then t can have null values in any tuple that does not belong to any subclass. Notice that if the specialization is predicate defined on a single attribute of C, then that attribute serves the purpose of t and t is not needed; this option is illustrated in Figure 15.11c for

(a) EMPLOYEE

SSN	FName	MInit	LName	BirthDate	Address	JobType

SECRETARY

SSN	TypingSpeed

TECHNICIAN

SSN	TGrade

ENGINEER

SSN	EngType

(b) CAR

VehicleId	LicensePlateNo	Price	MaxSpeed	NoOfPassengers

TRUCK

VehicleId	LicensePlateNo	Price	NoOfAxles	Tonnage

(c) EMPLOYEE

SSN	FName	MInit	LName	BirthDate	Address	JobType	TypingSpeed	TGrade	EngType

(d) PART

PartNo	Description	MFlag	DrawingNo	ManufactureDate	BatchNo	PFlag	SupplierName	LastPrice

Figure 15.11   Illustrating the options for mapping specializations (or generalizations) to relations. (a) Mapping the EER schema of Figure 15.4 to relations using Option A. (b) Mapping the EER schema of Figure 15.3(b) into relations using Option B. (c) Mapping the EER schema of Figure 15.4 using Option C with JobType playing the role of type attribute. (d) Mapping the EER schema of Figure 15.5 using Option D with two boolean type fields MFlag and PFlag.

the EER specialization in Figure 15.4. Option 8D is used for overlapping subclasses by including m *Boolean* type fields, one for *each* subclass. Each type field t_i can have a domain {yes, no}, where a value of yes indicates that the tuple is a member of subclass S_i. This option is illustrated in Figure 15.11d for the EER specialization in Figure 15.5, where MFlag and PFlag are the type fields. Note that it is also possible to create a single type field of m bits instead of the m type fields.

When we have a multilevel specialization (or generalization) hierarchy or lattice, we do not have to follow the same mapping option for all the specializations. We can use one mapping option for part of the hierarchy or lattice and other options for other parts. Figure 15.12 shows one possible mapping into relations for the hierarchy/lattice of Figure 15.7. Here we used option 8A for PERSON/ {EMPLOYEE, ALUMNUS, STUDENT}, option 8C for both EMPLOYEE/ {STAFF, FACULTY, STUDENT_ASSISTANT} and STUDENT/STUDENT_ASSISTANT, and option 8D for both STUDENT_ASSISTANT/ {RESEARCH_ASSISTANT, TEACHING_ASSISTANT} and STUDENT/ {GRADUATE_STUDENT, UNDERGRADUATE_STUDENT}. In Figure 15.12 all attributes whose name ends with 'Flag' are type fields.

Mapping of Shared Subclasses

A shared subclass, such as ENGINEERING_MANAGER of Figure 15.6, is a subclass of several superclasses. These classes must all have the same key attribute; otherwise, the shared

PERSON

SSN	Name	BirthDate	Sex	Address

EMPLOYEE

SSN	Salary	EmployeeType	Position	Rank	PercentTime	RAFlag	TAFlag	Project	Course

ALUMNUS_DEGREES

SSN	Year	Degree	Major

STUDENT

SSN	MajorDept	GradFlag	UndergradFlag	DegreeProgram	Class	StudAssistFlag

Figure 15.12   Mapping the EER specialization hierarchy/lattice shown
in Figure 15.7 using multiple options

subclass would be modeled as a category, which we discuss next. We can apply any of the options discussed in step 8 to a shared subclass although usually option 8A is used. In Figure 15.12 option 8C is used for the shared subclass STUDENT_ASSISTANT. Notice that we could also apply different options to the different superclass/subclass relationships in which a shared subclass participates.

Mapping of Categories

A category is a subclass of the *union* of two or more superclasses, and those classes can have different keys because they can be of different entity types. An example is the OWNER category shown in Figure 15.8, which is a subset of the union of three entity types PERSON, BANK, and COMPANY that have different keys. The other category in Figure 15.8, REGISTERED_VEHICLE, has two superclasses that have the same key attribute.

For mapping a category whose defining superclasses are of different types and hence have different keys, it is customary to specify a new key attribute, called a **surrogate key**, when creating a relation to correspond to the category. This is because the keys of the defining classes are different, so we cannot use any one of them exclusively to identify all entities in the category. We can now create a relation schema OWNER to correspond to the OWNER category, as illustrated in Figure 15.13, and include any attributes of the category in this relation. The primary key of OWNER is the surrogate key OwnerId. We also add the surrogate key attribute OwnerId to each relation corresponding to a superclass of the category to specify the correspondences in values between the surrogate key and the key of each superclass.

For a category whose superclasses have the same key, such as VEHICLE in Figure 15.8, there is no need for a surrogate key attribute because the common key suffices. Mapping the REGISTERED_VEHICLE category, which illustrates this case, is also shown in Figure 15.13.

PERSON

SSN	DriverLicenseNo	Name	Address	OwnerId

BANK

BName	BAddress	OwnerId

COMPANY

CName	CAddress	OwnerId

OWNER

OwnerId

REGISTERED_VEHICLE

VehicleId	LicensePlateNumber

CAR

VehicleId	CStyle	CMake	CModel	CYear

TRUCK

VehicleId	TMake	TModel	Tonnage	TYear

OWNS

OwnerId	VehicleId	PurchaseDate	LienOrRegular

Figure 15.13 Mapping the categories of Figure 15.8 to relations

15.2.2 EER-to-Network Mapping

Recall from Chapter 11 that a network database schema is made up of **record types** and set types. A **set type** is a 1:N relationship between an **owner record type** and a **member record type**. In a network schema diagram, a set type is represented by an arrow pointing from the owner to the member record type. We now discuss the mapping of EER model concepts to record types and set types. This extends the discussion in Section 12.1.2, which presented the mapping of ER model concepts.

Superclass/Subclass Relationships and Specialization (or Generalization)

Options similar to 8A, 8C, and 8D of the relational case (specified in Section 15.2.1) can be used. The main difference is that 1:1 set types are used instead of duplicating the key attribute in option 8A. Although option 8B of not creating a record type for the superclass is possible, it is rarely used because a 1:1 set type can naturally model a superclass/subclass relationship. Recall that a **1:1 set type** is a set type where each set instance has at most one member record. Because this constraint is not part of the network model, the *application programs must enforce it* when a network DBMS is used. We will use the naming convention of starting the names of all such 1:1 set types by IS_A because they represent the fact that each member record represents the same entity as its owner record but in the subclass role. All these set types should be declared MANDATORY to enforce the IS_A subset relationship.

Figure 15.14a shows one possible mapping for the specialization lattice of Figure 15.7. Here we used option 8A for PERSON/ {EMPLOYEE, ALUMNUS, STUDENT}, option 8C for EMPLOYEE/ {STAFF, FACULTY, STUDENT_ASSISTANT} and STUDENT/STUDENT_ASSISTANT, and option 8D for STUDENT_ASSISTANT/ {RESEARCH_ASSISTANT, TEACHING_ASSISTANT} and STUDENT/ {GRADUATE_STUDENT, UNDERGRADUATE_STUDENT}. Note that when we use option 8A, we may *optionally* duplicate a key data item from the owner record type in the

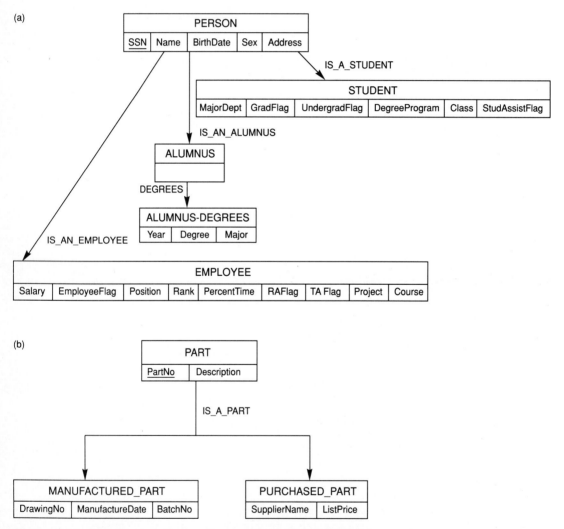

Figure 15.14 Mapping EER concepts to the network model. (a) Mapping the EER schema of Figure 15.7 into a network schema using different options. (b) Using a multi-member MANDATORY set type to map the EER schema of Figure 15.5.

member record type and specify a structural constraint (or AUTOMATIC SET SELECTION) on the set type. In our example of Figure 15.14a, we would have duplicated the SSN data item from PERSON in the member record types EMPLOYEE, ALUMNUS, and STUDENT.

Another option available in the network model is to map a specialization into a multimember MANDATORY set type. This is illustrated in Figure 15.14b, which shows how the EER diagram of Figure 15.5 may be mapped. Note that a multimember set does *not* enforce the disjointness constraint unless it is restricted to be a 1:1 set type by the application programs; hence, it can be used to model both disjoint and overlapping specializations.

Mapping of Shared Subclasses

Option 4A should be used to map a shared subclass, such as ENGINEERING_MANAGER of Figure 15.6. The record type representing a shared subclass would be a member of several 1:1 "IS_A" MANDATORY set types. In Figure 15.14a, option C is used with the shared subclass STUDENT_ASSISTANT.

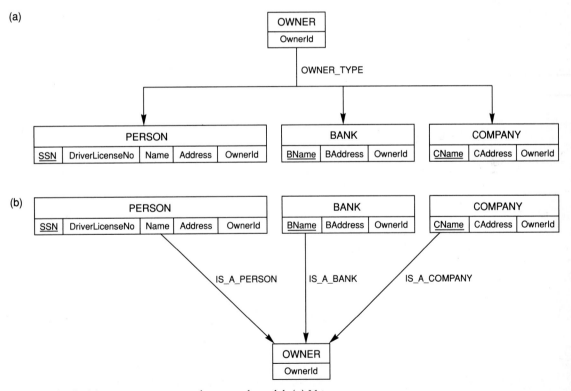

Figure 15.15 Mapping a category to the network model. (a) Using a multi-member set type OWNER_TYPE to represent the OWNER category of Figure 15.8. (b) Using three set types to map the OWNER category.

Mapping of Categories

There are several options for mapping a category. If the defining entity types are *disjoint*—a property that most categories have—we may use a single-owner multimember set type (see Chapter 11) where the owner record type represents the category. We must enforce the additional constraint that every record in the owner record type is connected to *exactly one member* record from one of the member record types. For example, consider the OWNER category shown in Figure 15.8, which is a subset of the union of three disjoint entity types PERSON, BANK, and COMPANY; we can map it into a multimember set as shown in Figure 15.15a. Another option is to make the category a member in several 1:1 OPTIONAL set types, with each defining superclass the owner of one of these set types. This representation is shown in Figure 15.15b for the OWNER category; the additional constraint that every OWNER record must be a member in *one of the set types* must be enforced. The OwnerId Field is optional, and can enforce structural constraints.

15.2.3   EER-to-Hierarchical Mapping

Mapping of Class/Subclass Relationships

A class/subclass relationship can be modeled as a **1:1 parent-child relationship**, which is a parent-child relationship where each parent record has at most one child record. The application programs must enforce this constraint when the hierarchical system is implemented.

Mapping of Shared Subclasses

A shared subclass can be mapped as one 1:1 parent-child relationship and several 1:1 VPCRs, with the shared subclass as the child or virtual child in all of these relationships. However, because of the limitation that a record can have at most one real parent and one virtual parent, this works only for a shared subclass with two superclasses. A more general option is to make the shared subclass parent to each of its superclasses, as shown in Figure 15.16a for the ENGINEERING_MANAGER shared subclass of Figure 15.6. It is also possible to use pointer record types under the subclass with the superclasses as virtual parent record types as shown in Figure 15.16b.

Mapping of Categories

We describe two options for mapping a category. To illustrate these options we use Figure 15.17, which shows a mapping into hierarchies of the schema in Figure 15.8 with the OWNS relationship type as root* record type. In the first option the category is the parent record type and a 1:1 parent-child relationship is defined to each record type that represents a defining class of the category. This is illustrated by the VEHICLE category in Figure 15.17. Note that this works only for a complete category. The second option is to

---

*Each OWNS record will represent a *single relationship instance* and has as children one OWNER and one VEHICLE record that it relates.

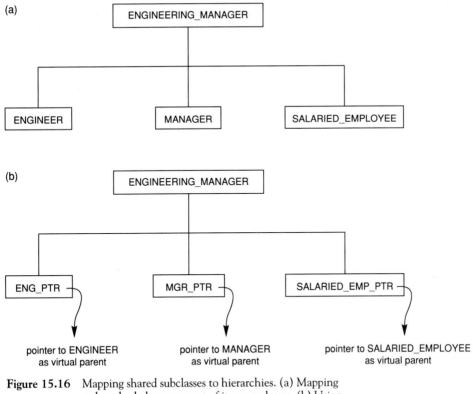

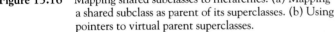

Figure 15.16 Mapping shared subclasses to hierarchies. (a) Mapping a shared subclass as parent of its superclasses. (b) Using pointers to virtual parent superclasses.

create a pointer record type under each record type that corresponds to a defining super-class of the category. A VPCR with the category as virtual parent is created for each such record type, as illustrated by the OWNER category in Figure 15.17.

15.3 Data Abstraction and Knowledge Representation Concepts

In this section we discuss in abstract terms some of the modeling concepts that were de-scribed quite specifically in our presentation of the ER and EER models in Chapter 3 and Section 15.1, respectively. The terminology we use here has been used in the database literature when describing conceptual data modeling and is also used in the artificial in-telligence literature when discussing knowledge representation. **Knowledge representa-tion** (abbreviated as **KR**) is a fundamental area in the field of artificial intelligence. Its goal is to develop concepts to model accurately some "domain of discourse" or "mini-world" of interest in order to store and manipulate knowledge for drawing inferences, making decisions, or just answering questions. The goals are similar to those of semantic

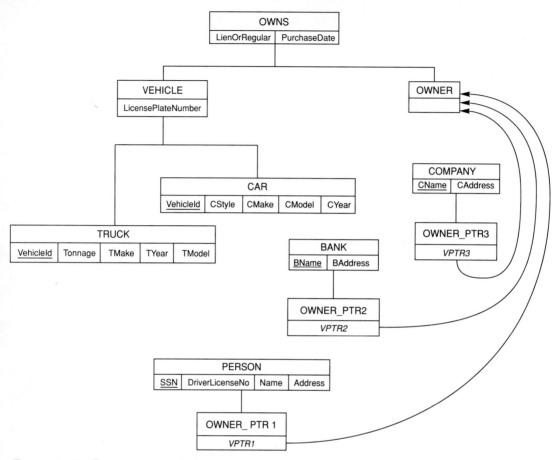

Figure 15.17   Illustrating two methods of mapping categories to the hierarchical model

data models, but there are also some important differences between the two disciplines. We summarize the similarities and differences below.

- Both disciplines use an abstraction process that attempts to identify common properties and important aspects of the objects in the miniworld while attempting to suppress insignificant differences and hide unimportant details of the objects.

- Both disciplines provide concepts, constraints, operations, and languages for the definition of data and the representation of knowledge.

- The scope of KR schemes is generally broader than that of semantic data models. Different forms of knowledge, such as rules (used in inference, deduction, and search), incomplete and default knowledge, and temporal and spatial knowledge, are represented in KR schemes. Semantic data models are being expanded to include some of these concepts.

- KR schemes include **reasoning mechanisms** that are used to deduce additional facts from the facts stored in a database. Hence, whereas most current database systems are limited to answering direct queries, knowledge-based systems using KR schemes can answer queries that involve **inferences** and **deductions** over the stored data.

- Whereas most data models concentrate on the representation of database schemas, or meta-knowledge, KR schemes often mix up the schemas with the instances themselves in order to provide flexibility in representing exceptions. However, this often results in inefficiencies when these KR schemes are implemented, compared to databases, especially when a large amount of data (or facts) needs to be stored.

In this section we discuss five **abstraction concepts** that are used in both semantic data models, such as the EER model, and KR schemes. These are the concepts of classification/instantiation, identification, generalization/specialization, aggregation, and association. The paired concepts classification and instantiation are inverses of one another, and so are generalization and specialization. In addition, the concepts of aggregation and association are related. A discussion of these abstract concepts and their relation to the concrete representations used in the EER model may help to clarify the data abstraction process and to better understand the related process of conceptual schema design.

15.3.1 Classification and Instantiation

The process of **classification** involves classifying similar objects into object classes. We can now describe (in DB) or reason about (in KR) the classes rather than the individual objects themselves. In many cases, groups of objects will share the same types of attributes and constraints, and by classifying objects we simplify the process of discovering their properties. **Instantiation** is the inverse of classification and refers to the generation and specific examination of distinct objects of a class. Hence, an object instance is related to its object class by a relationship that may be called the "IS-AN-INSTANCE-OF" relationship.

In general, objects of a class should have similar structures. However, some of the objects may display properties that make them differ in some aspects from the other objects of the class; these **exception objects** also need to be modeled, and KR schemes generally allow for more varied exceptions than do semantic data models. In addition, certain properties may apply to the class as a whole and not to the individual objects themselves. For example, the class name and the number of objects in the class are **class properties**. The average value of an attribute over all members of a class is another example of a class property.

In the EER model, entities are classified into entity types according to their basic properties and structure. In addition, we can classify entities into subclasses and categories based on additional similarities and differences (exceptions) among them. Objects that are relationship instances are classified into relationship types. Hence, entity types, subclasses, categories, and relationship types are the different types of classes in the EER model. The EER model that we discussed does not provide explicitly for class properties but may be extended to do so.

Knowledge representation models allow multiple classification schemes in which one class is an *instance* of another class (called a **meta-class**). Notice that this *cannot be* directly represented in the EER model, because we have only two levels—classes and instances. The only relationship among classes in the EER model is a superclass/subclass relationship, whereas in some KR schemes an additional class/instance relationship can be represented directly in a class hierarchy. In addition, the instance may itself be another class, allowing multiple-level classification schemes.

15.3.2   Identification

Identification refers to the abstraction process whereby all abstract concepts as well as concrete objects are made uniquely identifiable by means of some **identifier**. For example, a class name uniquely identifies a whole class. An additional mechanism is necessary to tell distinct object instances apart by object identifiers. Moreover, it is necessary to identify multiple manifestations in the database of the same real-world object. For example, we may have a tuple <*Matthew Clarke*, 610618, 376-9821> in a PERSON relation and another tuple <301-54-0836, CS, 3.8> in a STUDENT relation that happens to represent the same real-world entity. There is no way to identify the fact that these two database objects (tuples) represent the same real-world entity unless we make a provision *at design time* for appropriate cross-referencing to supply this identification. Hence, identification is needed at two levels:

- To distinguish among database objects and classes.
- To identify database objects and relate them to their real-world counterparts.

In the EER model, identification of schema constructs is based on giving them unique names. For example, every class in an EER schema, whether it is an entity type, subclass, category, or relationship type, must have a distinct name. In addition, the names of attributes of a given class must also be distinct. Rules for unambiguously identifying attribute name references in a specialization or generalization lattice or hierarchy are also necessary.

At the instance level, the values of key attributes are used to distinguish among entities of a particular entity type. For weak entity types, entities are identified by a combination of their own partial key values and the entities they are related to in the owner entity type(s). Relationship instances are identified by the combination of entities that they relate; this includes one entity from each participating class.

15.3.3   Specialization and Generalization

Specialization is the process of further classifying a class of objects into more specialized subclasses. Generalization is the inverse process of generalizing several classes into a higher-level abstract class that includes the objects in all these classes. Specialization can be called conceptual refinement, whereas generalization can be called conceptual synthesis. As we discussed in Section 15.1, subclasses and categories are used in the EER model to model specialization and generalization. We call the relationship between a subclass and its superclass on which specialization and generalization are based an **IS-A-SUBCLASS-OF** relationship.

15.3.4   Aggregation and Association

Aggregation is an abstraction concept for building composite objects from their component objects. There are two cases where this concept can be related to the EER model.

The first case is where we aggregate attribute values of an object to form the whole object. The second case, which the EER model does not provide for explicitly, involves the possibility of combining objects that are related by a particular relationship instance into a *higher-level aggregate object*. This is sometimes useful when the higher-level aggregate object is to be itself related to another object. In either case, we call this type of relationship between the primitive objects and their aggregate object IS-A-PART-OF or IS-A-COMPONENT-OF.

The abstraction of **association** is used to associate objects from several *independent classes*. Hence, it is somewhat similar to the second use of aggregation. It is represented in the EER model by relationship types. This relationship can be called IS-ASSOCIATED-WITH.

To understand aggregation better, consider the ER schema shown in Figure 15.18a, which stores information concerning interviews by job applicants to various companies. The class COMPANY is an aggregation of the attributes (or component objects) CName (company name) and CAddress (company address), whereas JOB_APPLICANT is an aggregate of Ssn, Name, Phone, and Address. The relationship attributes ContactName and ContactPhone represent the name and phone number of the contact person in the company responsible for the interview. Suppose that some interviews result in job offers while others do not. We would like to treat INTERVIEW as a class to associate it with JOB_OFFER. The schema shown in Figure 15.18b is *incorrect* because it requires each interview relationship instance to have a job offer. The schema shown in Figure 15.18c is not allowed because the ER model does not allow relationships among relationships.

One way to represent this situation is to create a higher-level aggregate class made of COMPANY, JOB_APPLICANT, and INTERVIEW and relate this class to JOB_OFFER as shown in Figure 15.18d. Although the EER model as described here does not have this facility, some semantic data models do allow it and call the resulting object a **composite** or **molecular object**. Other models treat entity types and relationship types uniformly (see Section 15.4).

To represent this situation correctly in the EER model, we need to create a new weak entity type INTERVIEW, as shown in Figure 15.18e, and relate it to JOB_OFFER. Hence, we can always represent these situations correctly in the EER model by creating additional entity types, although it may be conceptually more desirable to allow direct representation of aggregation as in Figure 15.18d or to allow relationships among relationships as in Figure 15.18c.

The main distinction between aggregation and association is that when an association instance is deleted, the participating objects continue to exist. However, if we support the notion of an aggregate object, for example a CAR that is made up of objects ENGINE, CHASSIS, and TIRES, then deleting the aggregate CAR object amounts to deleting its component objects.

15.3.5 Discussion*

In both data modeling and knowledge representation, there has been a tendency to add increasingly powerful constructs to allow a more expressive and accurate representation of the domain of discourse or the miniworld. In the previous subsections we pointed out

---

*This discussion is based on Brachman and Levesque (1984).

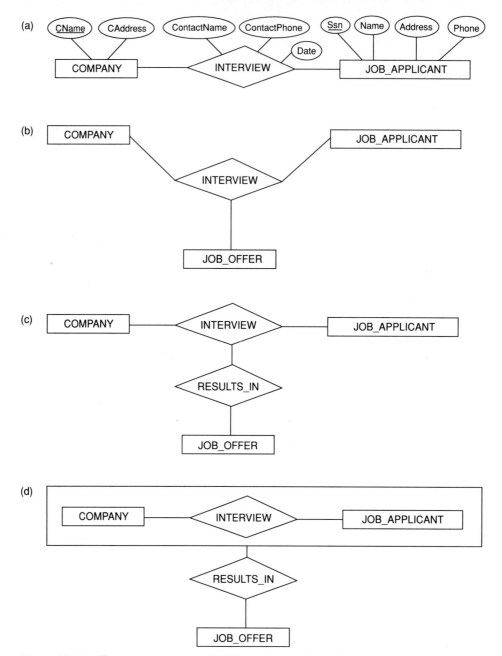

Figure 15.18 Illustrating aggregation. (a) The INTERVIEW relationship
type. (b) Including JOB_OFFER in a ternary relationship type
(incorrect in ER model). (c) Including JOB_OFFER by having
a relationship in which another relationship participates
(not allowed in ER model). (d) Using aggregation and a
composite (molecular) object class to include job offer.
(*continued on next page*)

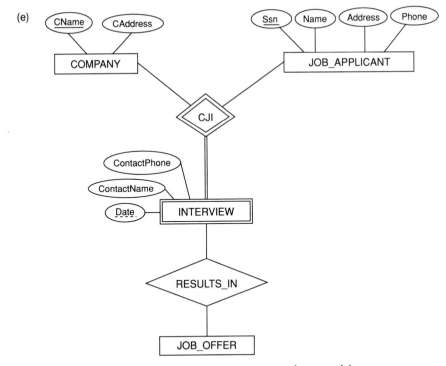

Figure 15.18   (*continued*) (e) Correct representation in the ER model.

the fundamental abstractions that are at the basis of most of these schemes. Some knowledge representation schemes such as KRL (a knowledge representation language) represent knowledge in a procedural form, rather than in declarative form as in most data models. For example, in the EER model many constraints are represented declaratively in the schema. In KRL constraints and inference rules are represented in the form of procedures. This places an additional burden on the system to make sure that the procedures are consistent and that the inferencing processes actually terminate, that is, are tractable. There is a fundamental trade-off that as knowledge representation becomes richer and more general, it becomes less tractable computationally. This trade-off is not as visible in data modeling because there is limited reasoning and inferencing in traditional database applications. However, many emerging database applications do require inferencing, as we shall discuss in Chapter 22.

15.4   Object-oriented and Functional Data Models

As we mentioned at the beginning of this chapter, many data models have been proposed. In Section 15.1 we presented the most important semantic modeling concepts as part of the EER model. In this section we discuss two other types of data models: object-oriented models and functional models.

15.4.1   Object-oriented Data Modeling

In recent years a new trend has been emerging in data modeling and database processing. In this approach a database is considered as a collection of **objects**, where each object represents a physical entity, a concept, an idea, an event, or some aspect of interest to the database application. In the classical **record-oriented** data models—relational, network, and hierarchical—data is viewed as a collection of record types (or relations), each having a collection of records (or tuples) stored in a file. In an **object-oriented system**, real-world objects are represented directly by database objects. **Object identity** is maintained via an object identifier.

For example, consider the real-world object employee; in the relational schema of Figure 6.5, information about an employee is *scattered* over the following relations:

- EMPLOYEE contains most of an employee's attributes.
- DEPARTMENT contains information on an employee's department.
- WORKS_ON contains information on the projects the employee works on.
- DEPENDENT contains information on an employee's dependents.

As more complex types of real-world objects are modeled in emerging database applications, these traditional data models would scatter information on a complex object into more and more relations or record types, leading to the loss of a direct correspondence between a real-world object and its database representation. One goal of object-oriented modeling is to maintain a direct correspondence between real-world and database objects so that objects do not lose their integrity and identity and can easily be identified and operated upon. Because this approach is still being refined, we will mainly point out its salient features rather than present a particular model in detail.

The term **object-oriented** (abbreviated by **O-O**) is used in several disciplines, including programming languages, databases and knowledge bases, artificial intelligence, and computer systems in general. O-O programming languages have their roots in the SIMULA language, which proposed the concept of **class** or **abstract data types** that encapsulate structural properties of objects as well as specify valid operations on types of objects. The SMALLTALK language is the best known O-O language. The main difference between O-O programming languages and databases is that the latter require the existence of **persistent objects** stored permanently in secondary storage, whereas the objects in an O-O programming language last only during program execution.

There has been a large number of proposals for O-O data models and database systems. The following are the essential features of these proposals:

- *Data abstraction and encapsulation:* This refers to the ability to define a set of operations, called **methods** in O-O terminology, that can be applied to the objects of a particular object class (or object type). All access to objects is constrained to be via one of the predefined methods. An object has an **interface** part and an **implementation**; the implementation is *private* and may be changed without affecting the interface. All access to an object is via its interface, which is *public*, that is, can be seen by other objects and by the users of the system. Object classes can be organized into **type hierarchies**, similar to the specialization/generalization hierarchies discussed in Section 15.1.

- *Object identity:* The O-O system maintains an identity for each object that is independent of its attribute values. This is typically represented by an **object identifier**, which is generated by the system and is independent of any key attributes. Hence, any attribute of an object can be updated without destroying its identity.

- *Inheritance:* A subclass inherits both data attributes *and* methods from its superclasses in the type hierarchies. Selective inheritance, where only some attributes and methods are inherited, is also possible.

- *Complex objects:* This is the ability to define new composite objects from previously defined objects in a nested or hierarchical fashion.

In addition to the above features, the implementation of O-O data models typically exhibits the following:

- *Message passing:* Objects communicate and perform all operations, including retrieval of values, computations, and updates, via messages. A **message** consists of an object (or several objects) followed by a method to be applied to these objects.

- *Operator overloading:* This describes a convenient feature of using the same operation name to denote different operations when applied to different types of objects. The meaning of the operation is then "overloaded" and can be resolved only when the object it is applied to is provided. For example, an operation "rotate" is different when applied to a "line" object than when applied to a "square" object. This overloading occurs in O-O systems when methods for distinct object types are given the same name; it is related to the concept of **late binding**, where a message first determines the type of the object it is applied to before it is bound to the appropriate method.

The following are advantages of the O-O approach:

- *Extensibility:* Object types and their methods can be modified as needed. Such changes are **localized** to the relevant object type and hence are much easier than in record-based systems, where many record types may be affected. In addition, new object classes and their methods can be incorporated into the system.

- *Behavioral constraints:* Because of encapsulation, the behavior of each object type is predetermined by a fixed set of methods. Hence, database operations are constrained to be within these behavioral specifications.

- *Flexibility of type definition:* The user is not limited to the modeling concepts of a data model but can define many variations of data types, each with unique properties.

- *Modeling power:* The inheritance of both attributes and methods is a very powerful tool for data modeling. In general, the abstractions of generalization/specialization, identification, and aggregation are well supported in current O-O data models.

The following are disadvantages of the O-O approach:

- *Lack of associations:* The abstraction of association (represented by relationship types in the EER model) is *not* directly supported and is achieved indirectly by allowing interobject references. This is an inherent weakness of the O-O approach and is due to the fact that this approach treats each object as a self-contained unit of information.

- *Behavioral rigidity:* The notion of predetermining and prespecifying all operations by a fixed set of methods is a rigid constraint that is counter to the typically evolving nature of database technology.

- *No high-level query language:* There are no high-level query languages for current O-O data models. The power and elegance of relational algebra or calculus languages do not have counterparts in O-O systems at the time of writing.

15.4.2   Functional Data Models

Functional data models use the concept of a mathematical function as their fundamental modeling construct. Any request for information can be visualized as a function call with certain arguments, and the function returns the required information. There are several proposals for functional data models and query languages, as discussed in the bibliography at the end of this chapter. The DAPLEX model and language are perhaps the best known example.

In the functional data model (FDM), the main modeling primitives are **entities** and **functional relationships** among those entities. There are several standard types of entities at the most basic level; these are STRING, INTEGER, CHARACTER, REAL, etc. and are called **printable entity types**. Abstract entity types that correspond to real-world objects are given the type ENTITY. For example, consider the EER diagram in Figure 15.10; we will show how some of the entity types and relationship types in that schema can be specified in a functional DAPLEX-like notation. The PERSON, STUDENT, COURSE, SECTION, and DEPARTMENT entity types are declared as follows:

```
PERSON( ) → ENTITY
STUDENT( ) → ENTITY
COURSE( ) → ENTITY
SECTION( ) → ENTITY
DEPARTMENT( ) → ENTITY
```

The above statements specify that the functions PERSON, STUDENT, COURSE, SECTION, and DEPARTMENT return abstract entities, and hence these statements serve to define the corresponding entity types. An attribute of an entity type is also specified as a function whose argument (domain) is the entity type and whose result (range) is a printable entity. For example, the following function declarations specify the attributes of PERSON:

```
SSN(PERSON) → STRING
BDATE(PERSON) → STRING
SEX(PERSON) → CHAR
```

Applying the SSN function to an entity of type PERSON returns that PERSON's social security number, which is a printable value of type STRING. To declare composite attributes, such as NAME in Figure 15.10, we have to declare them to be entities and then declare their component attributes as functions as shown below for the NAME attribute:

```
NAME( ) → ENTITY
NAME(PERSON) → NAME
FNAME(NAME) → STRING
MINIT(NAME) → CHAR
LNAME(NAME) → STRING
```

To declare a relationship type, we give it a **role name** in one direction and define it also as a function. For example, the MAJOR and MINOR relationship types of Figure 15.10 that relate students to their major and minor academic departments may be declared as follows:

```
MAJOR(STUDENT) → DEPARTMENT
MINOR(STUDENT) → DEPARTMENT
```

These declarations specify that applying a function MAJOR or MINOR to a STUDENT entity should return as result an entity of type DEPARTMENT. To declare an inverse role name for the same relationship types, we write:

```
MAJORING_IN(DEPARTMENT) → STUDENT (INVERSE OF MAJOR)
MINORING_IN(DEPARTMENT) → STUDENT (INVERSE OF MINOR)
```

The INVERSE OF clause declares that these functions are the inverses of the two previously declared functions and hence specify *the same* relationship types as the other two but in the *reverse direction*. Notice also the double arrows (→»), which specify that applying the MAJOR or MINOR function on a single DEPARTMENT entity can return a *set of entities* of type STUDENT. This specifies that the relationship types are 1:N. This notation can also be used to specify multivalued attributes. To specify an M:N relationship type, we use double arrows in *both directions*, as in the following example:

```
COURSES_COMPLETED(STUDENT) → SECTION
STUDENTS_ATTENDED(SECTION) → STUDENT (INVERSE OF
                                      COURSES_COMPLETED)
```

This declares the TRANSCRIPT relationship of Figure 15.10 in both directions. Some functions may have more than one argument; for example, to declare the GRADE attribute of the above relationship we write:

```
GRADE(STUDENT, SECTION) → CHAR
```

Note that it is not required to declare an inverse for each relationship. For example, the DC and CS relationship types of Figure 15.10, which relate a course to its offering department and a course to its sections that are offered, may be declared in only one direction as follows:

```
OFFERING_DEPARTMENT(COURSE) → DEPARTMENT
SECTIONS_OF(COURSE) → SECTION
```

Figure 15.19a shows a declaration of part of the EER schema of Figure 15.10 in FDM notation, and Figure 15.19b shows a diagrammatic notation for that schema. There is

(a)   ENTITY TYPE DECLARATIONS (INCLUDING THE COMPOSITE ATTRIBUTE NAME):

PERSON( ) → ENTITY	STUDENT( ) → ENTITY
COURSE( ) → ENTITY	SECTION( ) → ENTITY
DEPARTMENT( ) → ENTITY	NAME( ) → ENTITY

ATTRIBUTE DECLARATIONS (INCLUDING THREE DERIVED ATTRIBUTES):

SSN(PERSON) → STRING	BDATE(PERSON) → STRING
SEX(PERSON) → CHAR	NAME(PERSON) → NAME
FNAME(NAME) → STRING	FNAME(PERSON) → FNAME(NAME(PERSON))
MINIT(NAME) → CHAR	MINIT(PERSON) → MINIT(NAME(PERSON))
LNAME(NAME) → STRING	LNAME(PERSON) → LNAME(NAME(PERSON))
CLASS(STUDENT) → STRING	SEC#(SECTION) → INTEGER
YEAR(SECTION) → STRING	QTR(SECTION) → STRING
DNAME(DEPARTMENT) → STRING	DPHONE(DEPARTMENT) → STRING
OFFICE(DEPARTMENT) → STRING	C#(COURSE) → STRING
CNAME(COURSE) → STRING	CDESC(COURSE) → STRING

RELATIONSHIP TYPE DECLARATIONS (INCLUDING INVERSES AND RELATIONSHIP ATTRIBUTES):

MAJOR(STUDENT) → DEPARTMENT
MINOR(STUDENT) → DEPARTMENT
MAJORING_IN(DEPARTMENT) -↠ STUDENT INVERSE OF MAJOR
MINORING_IN(DEPARTMENT) ↠ STUDENT INVERSE OF MINOR
COURSES_COMPLETED(STUDENT) -↠ SECTION
STUDENTS_ATTENDED(SECTION) ↠ STUDENT INVERSE OF COURSES_COMPLETED
GRADE(STUDENT, SECTION) → CHAR
OFFERING_DEPARTMENT(COURSE) → DEPARTMENT
SECTIONS_OF(COURSE) ↠ SECTION

IS-A RELATIONSHIP AND INHERITED ATTRIBUTE DECLARATIONS:

IS_A_PERSON(STUDENT) → PERSON
SSN(STUDENT) → SSN(IS_A_PERSON(STUDENT))
BDATE(STUDENT) → BDATE(IS_A_PERSON(STUDENT))
SEX(STUDENT) → SEX(IS_A_PERSON(STUDENT))
NAME(STUDENT) → NAME(IS_A_PERSON(STUDENT))
FNAME(STUDENT) → FNAME(IS_A_PERSON(STUDENT))
MINIT(STUDENT) → MINIT(IS_A_PERSON(STUDENT))
LNAME(STUDENT) → LNAME(IS_A_PERSON(STUDENT))

Figure 15.19   Illustrating the functional data model. (a) Declaring part of the
EER schema of Figure 15.10 as functions. (*continued on next page*)

also notation for specifying IS-A relationships, derived values, and other advanced modeling concepts in DAPLEX. In Figure 15.19a the function IS_A_STUDENT specifies an IS-A relationship (superclass/subclass relationship in EER terminology) between PERSON and STUDENT.

(b)

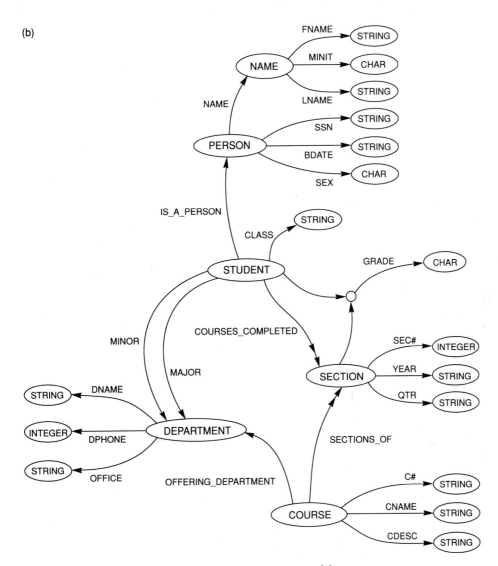

Figure 15.19   *(continued)* (b) Diagrammatic representation of the
FDM schema declared in Figure 15.19(a).

A fundamental concept in FDM is **function composition**. For example, by writing
DNAME(OFFERING_DEPARTMENT(COURSE)), we compose the two functions DNAME and
OFFERING_DEPARTMENT. This can be used to declare **derived functions**; for example,
the functions of FNAME(PERSON) or FNAME(STUDENT) in Figure 15.19a are declared to
be compositions of previously declared functions. This can also be used to specify the inherited attributes explicitly as shown in Figure 15.19a. Notice that we did not show any
derived functions or inverse relationships in the schema diagram of Figure 15.19b, although we could have done so.

Function composition is also the main concept in **functional query languages**. We illustrate this by a simple example. Suppose we want to retrieve the last names of all students majoring in 'Math'; we could write the following query:

```
RETRIEVE LNAME(NAME(IS_A_PERSON(MAJORING_IN(DEPARTMENT))))
WHERE DNAME(DEPARTMENT) = 'Math'
```

Here we use the MAJORING_IN function, which is the inverse of MAJOR. Notice that we could also have used the derived function LNAME(STUDENT) to shorten the above query to:

```
RETRIEVE LNAME(MAJORING_IN(DEPARTMENT))
WHERE DNAME(DEPARTMENT) = 'Math'
```

This is because the inverse function MAJORING_IN(DEPARTMENT) returns STUDENT entities, so we can apply the derived function LNAME(STUDENT) to those entities.

15.5   Summary

In this chapter we first discussed some of the extensions to the ER model that are needed to make it more powerful in its representational capabilities. We called the resulting model the enhanced-ER or EER model. The concept of a subclass and its superclass and the related mechanism of attribute inheritance were presented. We saw how it is sometimes necessary to create additional classes of entities, either because of additional specific attributes or because of specific relationship types. We discussed two main processes for defining superclass/subclass hierarchies and lattices, namely specialization and generalization.

We then showed how to display these new constructs in an EER diagram. We also discussed the various types of constraints that may apply to specialization or generalization. The two main constraints are total/partial and disjoint/overlapping. In addition, a defining predicate for a subclass or a defining attribute for a specialization may be specified. We discussed the differences between user-defined and predicate-defined subclasses and between user-defined and attribute-defined specializations. Finally, we discussed the concept of category, which is a subset of the union of two or more classes, and we gave formal definitions of all the concepts presented.

We then showed in Section 15.2 how EER model concepts can be mapped to relational, network, or hierarchical database structures. These mappings can be used during the logical phase of database design.

In Section 15.3 we discussed the types of abstract data representation concepts. The concepts discussed were classification and instantiation, generalization and specialization, identification, and aggregation and association. We saw how the EER model concepts are related to each of these. We also discussed briefly the discipline of knowledge representation and how it is related to semantic data modeling.

Finally, in Section 15.4, we discussed the concepts of object-oriented and functional data models, which are becoming increasingly popular although they are not well established as yet.

Review Questions

15.1. What is a subclass? When is a subclass needed in data modeling?

15.2. Define the following terms: superclass of a subclass, superclass/subclass relationship, IS-A relationship, specialization, generalization, category, specific attributes.

15.3. Discuss the mechanism of attribute inheritance. Why is it useful?

15.4. Discuss user-defined and predicate-defined subclasses and the differences between the two.

15.5. Discuss user-defined and attribute-defined specializations and the differences between the two.

15.6. Discuss the two main types of constraints on specializations and generalizations.

15.7. What is the difference between a subclass hierarchy and a subclass lattice?

15.8. What is the difference between specialization and generalization? Why do we not display this difference in the schema diagrams?

15.9. How does a category differ from a regular shared subclass? What is a category used for? Illustrate with examples.

15.10. List the various data abstraction concepts and the corresponding modeling concepts in the EER model.

15.11. List the main differences between semantic data modeling and knowledge representation schemes.

15.12. What aggregation feature is missing from the EER model? How can the EER model be further enhanced to support it?

15.13. Discuss the basic trade-off when enhancing knowledge representation and semantic data modeling schemes.

15.14. What is object-oriented modeling? Discuss its features and its advantages and weaknesses.

Exercises

15.15. Design an EER schema for a database application that you are interested in. Specify all constraints that you know should hold on the database. Make sure that the schema has at least five entity types, four relationship types, a weak entity type, a superclass/subclass relationship, a category, and an n-ary (n > 2) relationship type.

15.16. Figure 15.20 shows an example of an EER diagram for a small airport database. The database is used to keep track of airplanes, their owners, and airport employees and pilots for a small private airport. For this database, the requirements were to keep relevant information concerning the airport. From the requirements for this database, the following information was collected. Each airplane has a registration number [Reg$^\#$], is of a particular plane type [OF-TYPE], and is stored in a particular hangar [STORED-IN]. Each plane type has a model number [Model], a ca-

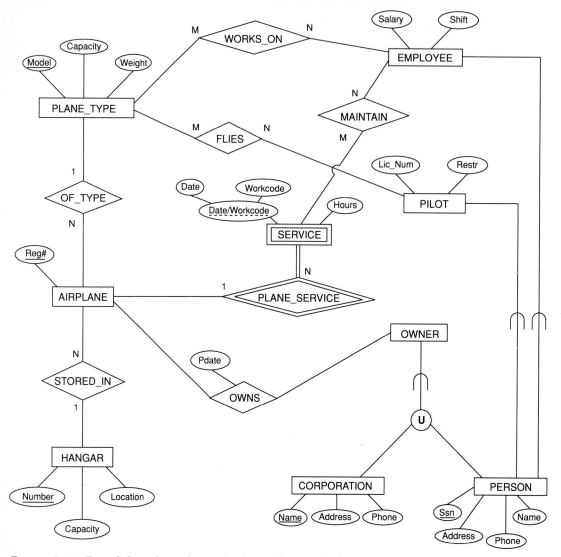

Figure 15.20   Extended-ER schema diagram for the small airport database

pacity [Capacity], and a weight [Weight]. Each hangar has a number [Number], capacity [Capacity], and location [Location]. The database also keeps track of the owners of each plane [OWNS] and the employees who have maintained the plane [MAINTAIN]. Each relationship instance in OWNS relates an airplane to an owner and includes the purchase date [Pdate]. Each relationship instance in [MAINTAIN] relates an employee to a service record [SERVICE]. Each plane undergoes service many times; hence, it is related by [PLANE-SERVICE] to a number of service records. A service record includes as attributes the date of maintenance [Date], the number of hours spent on the work [Hours], and the type of work done [Workcode].

We use a weak entity type [SERVICE] to represent airplane service because the airplane registration number is used in identifying a service record. An owner is either a person or a corporation. Hence, we use a generalization category [OWNER] that is a subset of the union of corporation [CORPORATION] and person [PERSON] entity types. Both pilots [PILOT] and employees [EMPLOYEE] are subclasses of PERSON. Each pilot has specific attributes licence number [Lic-Num] and restrictions [Restr], whereas each employee has specific attributes salary [Salary] and shift worked [Shift]. All person entities in the database will have data kept on their social security number [Ssn], name [Name], address [Address], and telephone number [Phone]. For corporation entities the data kept is name [Name], address [Address], and telephone number [Phone]. The database also keeps track of the types of planes each pilot is authorized to fly [FLIES] and the types of planes each employee can do maintenance work on [WORKS-ON].

a. Map the EER schema of Figure 15.20 into relational, network, and hierarchical schemas.

b. Create a functional data model schema to correspond to the EER schema in Figure 15.20. Use the FDM notation of Figure 15.19b.

15.17. Map the UNIVERSITY EER schema of Figure 15.10 into relational, network, and hierarchical schemas.

15.18. Create a functional data model schema to correspond to the UNIVERSITY EER schema of Figure 15.10. Use the FDM notation of Figure 15.19b.

Selected Bibliography

Many papers have proposed conceptual or semantic data models. We give a representative list below. One group of papers, including Abrial (1974), Senko's DIAM model (1975), the NIAM method (Verheijen and VanBekkum 1982), and Bracchi et al. (1976), presents semantic models that are based on the concept of binary relationships. Another group of early papers discusses methods for extending the relational model to enhance its modeling capabilities. This includes the papers by Schmid and Swenson (1975), Navathe and Schkolnick (1978), Codd's RM/T model (1979), Furtado (1978), and the structural model of Wiederhold and Elmasri (1979).

The ER model was originally proposed by Chen (1976) and is formalized in Ng (1981). Since then, numerous extensions of its modeling capabilities have been proposed, as in Scheuermann et al. (1979), Dos Santos et al. (1979), Teorey et al. (1986), and the Entity-Category-Relationship (ECR) model of Elmasri et al. (1985). Smith and Smith (1977) present the concepts of generalization and aggregation. The semantic data model of Hammer and McLeod (1981) introduced the concepts of class/subclass lattices, as well as other advanced modeling concepts.

Another class of data models called functional data models was originally proposed by Sibley and Kerschberg (1977) and extended by Shipman (1981), who included many advanced modeling concepts as well as the functional query language DAPLEX. Another functional query language is FQL (Buneman and Frankel 1979). The book by Tsichritzis and Lochovsky (1982) discusses and compares data models.

Dittrich (1986) and Zaniolo et al. (1986) survey the basic concepts of object-oriented data models. An early paper on object-oriented databases is Baroody and DeWitt (1981). Su et al. (1988) present an object-oriented data model that is being used in CAD/CAM applications. Fishman et al. (1987) discuss IRIS, an experimental object-oriented DBMS developed at Hewlett-Packard laboratories. Maier et al. (1986) describe the design of another object-oriented system and language called GEMSTONE/OPAL. Andrews and Harris (1987) discuss the Vbase System. Banerjee et al. (1987) discuss data model issues for object-oriented systems.

Although we did not discuss languages for the entity-relationship model and its extensions, there have been several proposals for such languages. Elmasri and Wiederhold (1981) propose the GORDAS query language for the ER model, and it is extended to the ECR model in Elmasri et al. (1985). Another ER query language is proposed by Markowitz and Raz (1983). Senko (1980) presents a query language for his DIAM model. A formal set of operations called the ER algebra was presented by Parent and Spaccapietra (1985). Campbell et al. (1985) present a set of ER operations and show that they are relationally complete. The TAXIS language for specifying transactions in a conceptual manner was proposed in Mylopoulos et al. (1981). User friendly interfaces based on the ER model and other semantic models are presented in Elmasri and Larson (1985), and Czejdo et al. (1987), among many others. Kent (1978, 1979) discusses the shortcomings of traditional data models. Bradley (1978) extends the network model with a high-level language.

A survey of semantic data modeling appears in Hull and King (1987), although their survey is by no means complete. Another survey of conceptual modeling is Pillalamarri et al. (1988). Liskov and Zilles (1975) is an excellent paper discussing abstract data types.

CHAPTER **16**

Overview of the Database Design Process

In this chapter we discuss different phases of the database design process. For small databases that will be used by a single user or a small number of users, database design need not be overly complicated. However, when medium-sized or large databases are designed for use as part of an information system of a large organization, database design becomes complex. This is because many users are expected to use the database, so the system must satisfy the requirements of all these users. Careful design and testing phases are imperative to ensure that all these requirements are satisfactorily met. By medium to large databases we mean those that are used by from about 25 up to hundreds of users, that contain several million bytes of information, and that involve hundreds of queries and application programs. Such databases are widely in use in government, industry, and commercial organizations. Service industries such as banking, utility, insurance, travel, hotel, and communications companies are totally dependent on successful round-the-clock operation of their databases. The systems for these types of applications are often called transaction processing systems because of the large number of transactions that are applied to the database every day. We will concentrate on the database design process for such medium-sized and large databases here. For the remainder of this chapter, *database design* refers to the design process for such an environment. We also discuss how a database fits within the information system of a large organization and the life cycle of a typical information system and its component database system.

In Section 16.1 we discuss why databases have become an important part of information resource management in many organizations. Then we discuss the life cycle of an information system and its component database system in Section 16.2. In Section 16.3

453

we discuss the typical phases of database design for medium-sized or large databases. Section 16.4 is an overview of physical database design. Finally, in Section 16.5 we briefly discuss automated design tools.

16.1   Organizational Context for Using Database Systems

We now discuss briefly how database systems have become a part of the information systems of many organizations. Information systems in the 1960s were dominated by file systems. Organizations have been gradually moving to database systems since the early 1970s. Many organizations have set up departments under a database administrator (DBA) to oversee and control the database life cycle activities (see Section 16.2). Similarly, information resource management (IRM) is recognized by large organizations to be a key to successful management of the business. There are several reasons for this:

- More and more functions in organizations are being computerized, increasing the need to keep large volumes of data available in an up-to-the-minute current state.
- As the complexity of the data and applications grows, complex relationships among the data need to be modeled and maintained.
- There is a tendency toward consolidation of information resources in many organizations.

Database systems satisfy the above three requirements in large measure. Two additional characteristics of database systems are very valuable in the design and management of large databases. These are:

- Data independence, which protects application programs from changes in the underlying logical organization and physical access paths and storage structures.
- External schemas (views), which allow the same data to be used by multiple applications, each application having its own view of the data.

An additional justification for moving to database systems is the low cost of developing new applications when compared to the cost with older file systems. This often justifies the high initial cost of database design and system conversion. The availability of high-level data access languages simplifies writing database applications, while high-level query languages make ad hoc querying of information by higher-level managers feasible.

From the early 1970s to the mid-1980s, the move was toward creating large centralized repositories of data that are managed by a single centralized DBMS. Recently, this trend has been *reversed* because of the following developments:

1. Personal computers and databaselike software products, such as VISICALC, LOTUS 1-2-3, SYMPHONY, PARADOX, and DBASE III and IV, are being heavily utilized by users who previously belonged to the category of casual and occasional database users. Many administrators, engineers, scientists, architects, etc. belong to this category. As a result, the practice of creating **personal databases** is gain-

ing popularity. It is now possible to check out a copy of part of a large database on a mainframe computer, work on it using a personal workstation, and then store it back. Similarly, users can design and create their own databases and then merge them into a larger one.

2. The advent of distributed database management systems (DDBMSs; see Chapter 21) is opening up the option of distributing the database over multiple computer systems for better local control and faster local processing. At the same time, local users can access remote data using the facilities provided by the DDBMS.

3. Many organizations now use **data dictionary systems**, which are mini DBMSs that manage **meta-data** for a database system, that is, data that describes the database structure, constraints, applications, authorizations, etc. These are often used as an *integral tool* for information resource management. A useful data dictionary system should store and manage the following types of information:

   a. Descriptions of the schemas of the database system.

   b. Detailed information on physical database design such as storage structures, access paths, and file and record sizes.

   c. Descriptions of the database users, their responsibilities, and their access rights.

   d. High-level descriptions of the database transactions and applications and the relationships of users to transactions.

   e. The relationship between database transactions and the data items referenced by them. This is useful in determining which transactions are affected when certain data definitions are changed.

   f. Usage statistics such as frequencies of queries and transactions and access counts to different portions of the database.

   This information is available for the database administrators, designers, and authorized users as on-line system documentation. This enables the database administrators to better control the information system and the users to better understand and use the system. In many large organizations a data dictionary system is considered as important as a DBMS.

Recently, great emphasis has also been placed on high-performance **transaction processing systems**, which require around-the-clock nonstop operation and are used in the service industry. These databases are often accessed by hundreds of transactions per minute from remote and local terminals. Transaction performance in terms of the average number of transactions per minute and the average and maximum transaction response time is critical in these applications. A careful physical database design that meets the transaction processing needs is a must in such types of systems.

Some organizations have committed their information resource management to certain DBMS and data dictionary products. Their investment in the design and implementation of very large and complex systems makes it very difficult to change to newer DBMS products, so the organizations become locked in to their current DBMS system. With such large and complex databases, one cannot overemphasize the importance of a careful design that takes into account the need for possible system modifications in the future due to changing requirements. It can be very expensive if a large and complex system cannot evolve and it becomes necessary to move to other DBMS products. It is often extremely costly for an organization to move such a complex database system from one DBMS product to another.

16.2   Life Cycle of an Information System

In a large organization, the database system is typically part of a much larger information system that is used to manage the information resources of the organization. An **information system** includes all resources within the organization that are involved in the collection, management, use, and dissemination of information. In a computerized information system these resources include the data itself, the DBMS software, the computer system hardware and storage media, the persons in the organization who use and manage the data (DBA, end users, parametric users, etc.), the applications software that accesses and updates the data, the application programmers who develop these applications, etc. Hence, the database system is only part of a much larger organizational information system.

In this section we examine a typical life cycle of an information system and how the database system fits into this life cycle. The information system life cycle is often called the **macro life cycle,** whereas the database system life cycle is referred to as the **micro life cycle**.

16.2.1   Information System Life Cycle

The information system (macro) life cycle typically includes the following phases:

1. Feasibility analysis: This is concerned with analyzing potential application areas, performing preliminary cost-benefit studies, and setting up priorities among applications.

2. Requirements collection and analysis: Detailed requirements are collected by interacting with potential users to clearly understand their problems and applications.

3. Design: This phase has two aspects: the design of the database system and the design of the application systems that use and process the database.

4. Implementation: The information system is implemented and becomes a functioning system. The database is loaded and the database transactions are implemented and tested.

5. Validation and acceptance testing: The acceptability of the system in terms of meeting users' requirements and performance criteria is validated. The system is tested against performance criteria and behavior specification.

6. Operation: This may be preceded by conversion of users from an older system as well as user training. The operational phase starts when all system functions are operational and have been validated. As new requirements or applications crop

up, they go through all the previous phases until they are validated and become part of the system. Monitoring of system performance and system maintenance are important activities during the operational phase.

16.2.2   Database Application System Life Cycle

We are concerned with information systems for which a database serves as an integral part. Activities related to the database are referred to as the database application system (micro) life cycle and include the following phases:

1. System definition: The definition of the scope of the database system, its users, and its applications.
2. Design: At the end of this phase a complete logical and physical design of the database system on the chosen DBMS is ready.
3. Implementation: The process of writing the conceptual, external, and internal database definitions, creating empty database files, and implementing the software applications.
4. Loading or data conversion: The database is populated by either loading the data directly or converting existing files into the database system format and then loading them.
5. Application conversion: Any software applications from a previous system are converted to the new system.
6. Testing and validation: The new system is tested and validated.
7. Operation: The database system and its applications are in operation.
8. Monitoring and maintenance: During the operational phase the system is constantly monitored and maintained. Growth and expansion can occur in both data content and software applications. Major modifications and reorganizations may be needed from time to time.

Activities 2, 3, and 4 together are part of the design and implementation phases of the larger information system life cycle discussed in Section 16.2.1. Our emphasis in Section 16.3 will be on activity 2, which covers the database design phase. Most databases in organizations undergo all the above life cycle activities. The conversion steps, 4 and 5, are not applicable when both the database and the applications are new. When moving from an old established system to a new one, activities 4 and 5 tend to be the most time consuming and the effort to accomplish them is often underestimated. In general, there is often feedback among the various steps because of new requirements coming up at every stage.

16.3   The Database Design Process

We now focus on step 2 of the database application system life cycle, which we called database design. The problem of database design can be stated as follows:

Design the logical and physical structure of one or more databases to accommodate the information needs of the users in an organization for a defined set of applications.

The *goals* of database design are multifold: to satisfy the information *content* requirements of the specified users and applications; to provide a natural and easy-to-understand *structuring* of the information; and to support the *processing requirements* and any performance objectives such as response time, processing time, and storage space. These goals are somewhat idealistic in nature; they are very hard to accomplish and measure. The problem is aggravated because the database design process often begins with very informal and poorly defined requirements. By contrast, the result of the design activity is a rigidly defined database schema that cannot easily be modified once the database is implemented.

We can identify six main phases of the database design process:

1. Requirements collection and analysis.
2. Conceptual database design.
3. Choice of a DBMS.
4. Data model mapping (also called logical database design).
5. Physical database design.
6. Database implementation.

The design process typically consists of two parallel activities, as illustrated in Figure 16.1. The first activity involves the design of the **data content and structure** of the database, whereas the second activity concerns the design of **database processing and software applications**. The two activities are closely intertwined. For example, we can identify data items that will be stored in the database by analyzing database applications. In addition, the physical database design phase, during which we choose the storage structures and access paths of database files, depends on the applications that will use these files. On the other hand, we usually specify the design of database applications by referring to the database schema constructs, which are specified during the first activity. As we can see, these two activities strongly influence one another. Traditionally, the two activities were not equally emphasized in most early database design methodologies. In many organizations, database design has been attempted with a primary focus on one or the other of these activities; this may be called **data-driven** or **process-driven** database design. It is now recognized that the two activities should proceed hand in hand.

It is important to note that the six phases mentioned above do not have to proceed strictly in sequence. In many cases we may have to modify the design from an earlier phase during a later phase. These **feedback loops** among phases, and also within phases, are a common occurrence during the database design process. We do not show feedback loops in Figure 16.1 to avoid complicating the diagram.

Phase 1 in Figure 16.1 involves the collection of information concerning the intended use of the database, whereas phase 6 concerns database implementation. Phases 1 and 6 are sometimes considered *not* to be part of database design per se, but part of the more general information system life cycle. The heart of the database design process is phases 2, 4, and 5, which we briefly summarize here:

- *Conceptual database design (phase 2):* The goal of this phase is to produce a conceptual schema for the database that is independent of a specific DBMS. We often use a high-level data model such as the ER or EER model during this phase. In addition

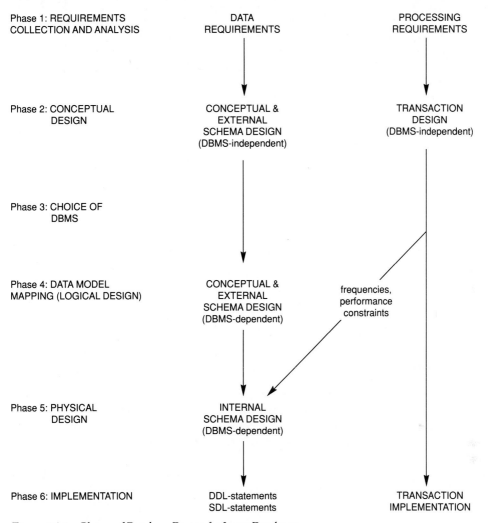

Figure 16.1   Phases of Database Design for Large Databases

to specifying the conceptual schema, we should specify as many of the known database applications or transactions as possible. These applications should also be specified using a notation that is independent of any specific DBMS.

• *Data model mapping (phase 4)*: This is also called **logical database design**. During this phase we **map** (or **transform**) the conceptual schema from the high-level data model used in phase 2 into the data model of the DBMS chosen in phase 3. This phase can start after the choice of an implementation data model rather than waiting for a specific DBMS to be chosen—for example, if we decide to use some relational DBMS but have not yet decided on a particular one. We may call the latter *system-independent* (but *data model-dependent*) logical design. In terms of the three-level DBMS architecture discussed in Chapter 2, the result of this phase is a *conceptual schema* in the chosen data model. In addition, the design of *external schemas* (views) for specific applications is often done during this phase.

- *Physical database design (phase 5)*: During this phase we design the specifications for the stored database in terms of physical storage structures, record placement, and access paths. This corresponds to the design of the *internal schema* in the terminology of the three-level DBMS architecture.

In the following subsections we discuss each of the six phases of database design.

16.3.1   Phase 1: Requirements Collection and Analysis

Before we can effectively design a database, we must know the expectations of the users and the intended uses of the database in as much detail as possible. The process of identifying and analyzing the intended uses is called requirements collection and analysis. To specify the requirements for a database system, we must first identify the other parts of the information system that will interact with the database system. These include new and existing users and applications. The requirements of these users and applications are then collected and analyzed. Typically, the following activities are part of the requirements collection and analysis phase:

- Identification of user groups and application areas: The major application areas and user groups that will use the database are identified. Key individuals within each user group and application area are chosen as the main participants in the subsequent steps of requirements collection and specification.

- Review of existing documentation: Existing documentation concerning the applications is studied and analyzed. Other documentation such as policy manuals, forms, reports, and organization charts is examined and reviewed to determine whether it has any influence on the requirements collection and specification process.

- Analysis of the operating environment and the processing requirements: The current and planned use of the information is studied. This includes analysis of the types of transactions and their frequencies, as well as the flow of information within the system. In addition, the input and output data for the transactions are specified. All the above provide important information about the frequencies and volumes of various database retrieval and update requirements.

- Questionnaires and interviews: Written responses to sets of questions are collected from the potential database users. These questions involve the users' priorities and the importance they place on various applications. In addition, key individuals may be interviewed so that more extensive input can be received from them concerning the worth of information and setting up of priorities.

The above modes of collecting requirements give poorly structured and mostly informal statements of requirements in natural language. These informal requirements are usually transformed into a better structured form by using one of the more formal **requirements specification techniques**. These techniques include HIPO (hierarchical input process output), SADT (structured analysis and design), DFDs (data flow diagrams), Orr-Warnier diagrams, and Nassi-Schneiderman diagrams. All these are diagrammatic methods for organizing and presenting information processing requirements. The diagrams can be in the form of hierarchies, flowcharts, sequential and loop structures, etc., depending on the method. Additional documentation in the form of text, tables, charts, and decision requirements usually accompanies the diagrams. There are complete books that discuss the requirements collection and analysis phase (see bibliographic notes at the end of this chapter). This phase can be quite time consuming but is crucial for the future success of the information system.

Some computer-aided techniques have been proposed to deal with requirements collection and analysis. These techniques include automated tools for requirements analysis to check the consistency and completeness of specifications. The requirements are stored in a single repository, usually called the design database, and can be displayed and updated as the design progresses. An early example is the PROBLEM STATEMENT LANGUAGE and PROBLEM STATEMENT ANALYZER (PSL/PSA) developed by the ISDOS project at the University of Michigan (see bibliographic notes).

16.3.2   Phase 2: Conceptual Database Design

The second phase of database design involves two parallel activities. The first activity, which we call **conceptual schema design,** examines the data requirements of the database resulting from phase 1 and produces a conceptual database schema in a DBMS-independent high-level data model. The second activity, which we call **transaction design,** examines the database applications whose requirements were analyzed in phase 1 and produces high-level specifications for these transactions.

Phase 2a: Conceptual Schema Design

The conceptual schema produced by this phase is usually in a DBMS-independent high-level data model and hence cannot be used directly to implement the database. However, the importance of a DBMS-independent conceptual schema cannot be overestimated for the following reasons:

1. The goal of conceptual schema design is a complete understanding of the database structure, meaning (semantics), interrelationships, and constraints. This is best achieved independently of a specific DBMS because each DBMS typically has idiosyncrasies and restrictions that should not be allowed to influence the conceptual schema design.

2. The conceptual schema is invaluable as a *stable description* of the database contents. The choice of DBMS and later design decisions may change without changing the DBMS-independent conceptual schema.

3. A good understanding of the conceptual schema is crucial for the database users and application designers. Use of a high-level data model, which is usually more expressive and general than the data models of individual DBMSs, is hence quite important.

4. The diagrammatic description of the conceptual schema can serve as an excellent vehicle of communication among database users, designers, and analysts. Because high-level data models usually have concepts that are easier to under-

stand than lower-level DBMS-specific data models, any communication concerning the schema design becomes more exact and more straightforward when using a high-level data model.

It is important to use a high-level data model—often called a semantic or conceptual data model—in this phase of database design. This data model should possess the following characteristics:

1. Expressiveness: The data model should be expressive enough to point out commonly occurring distinctions between different types of data, relationships, and constraints.

2. Simplicity: The model should be simple enough for typical users to understand and use; its concepts should be easily understood by end users.

3. Minimality: The model should have a small number of basic concepts that are distinct and nonoverlapping in meaning.

4. Diagrammatic representation: The model should have a diagrammatic notation for displaying a conceptual schema that is easy to interpret.

5. Formality: A conceptual schema expressed in the data model must represent a formal nonambiguous specification of the data. Hence, the model concepts must be accurately and unambiguously defined.

These requirements are sometimes conflicting. In particular, requirement 1 conflicts with most of the other requirements. Many high-level conceptual models have been proposed for database design (see the selected bibliography for Chapter 15). In the following, we will use the terminology of the enhanced Entity-Relationship (EER) model presented in Chapters 3 and 15 and assume that the EER model is being used in this phase of database design.

APPROACHES TO CONCEPTUAL SCHEMA DESIGN: For conceptual schema design, we must identify the basic components of the schema: the entity types, relationship types, and their attributes. We should also specify which attributes of each entity type are key attributes. Cardinality and participation constraints on relationships, if any, must be specified, together with any weak entity types. Specialization/generalization hierarchies and lattices may also be specified if needed. This design is derived from the requirements collected during phase 1.

There are two approaches to designing the conceptual schema. In the first, which we call the **centralized (or one-shot) schema design approach,** the requirements of the different applications and user groups from phase 1 are merged into a single set of requirements *before starting schema design*. A single schema corresponding to the merged set of requirements is then designed. When many users and applications exist, merging all the requirements can be an arduous and time-consuming task. The assumption behind this approach is that a centralized authority, the DBA, is responsible for deciding how the requirements of different users and applications are merged and for designing the conceptual schema for the whole database. The success of this approach depends on the authority vested in the DBA and the skill of the database designers in the DBA's organization. Once the conceptual schema is designed and finalized, external schemas for the various user groups and applications can be specified by the DBA.

In the second approach, which we call the **view integration approach,** we do not merge the requirements; rather, a schema (or view) is designed for each user group or application based only on its separate requirements. We now have one high-level schema (view) for each such user group or application. A subsequent **view integration** phase is used to merge or integrate these schemas into a **global conceptual schema** for the entire database. The individual views can be reconstructed as external schemas after view integration is complete.

The main difference between the two approaches is in the manner and the stage in which the multiple views or requirements of the many users and applications are reconciled. In the centralized approach, the reconciliation is done manually by the DBA's staff prior to designing any schemas and is applied directly to the requirements collected in phase 1. This approach has traditionally been used in spite of the burden it places on the DBA's staff to reconcile the differences and conflicts among user groups. It assumes that the DBA can come up with a clear definition of the global requirements *before* the conceptual schema design is attempted. Because of the difficulties in accomplishing this task, the view integration approach is now gaining more importance.

In the view integration approach, each user group or application actually designs its own conceptual (EER) schema from its requirements. Then an integration process is applied to these schemas (views) by the DBA to form the global integrated schema. Although view integration can also be done manually, for a large database involving tens of user groups it requires a methodology and the use of automated tools to help in carrying out the integration. The correspondences among the attributes, entity types, and relationship types in various views must be completely specified before the integration can be applied. In addition, problems such as integrating conflicting views and verifying the consistency of the specified inter-schema correspondences must be resolved.

STRATEGIES FOR SCHEMA DESIGN: Given a set of requirements, whether for a single user or for a large user community, we must create a conceptual schema to satisfy these requirements. There are various strategies for designing such a schema. Most of these strategies follow an incremental approach; that is, they start with some schema constructs derived from the requirements and incrementally modify, refine, or build on them. We now discuss some of these strategies:

1. Top-down strategy: Start with a schema containing high-level abstractions and then apply successive top-down refinement. For example, we may start by specifying only a few high-level entity types in the schema. Then, as we specify their attributes, we split them into lower-level entity types and relationship types among these entity types. The process of specialization to refine an entity type into subclasses (see Section 15.1) is another example of a top-down design strategy.

2. Bottom-up strategy: Start with a schema containing basic abstractions and combine or add to these abstractions. For example, we may start with the attributes and group them into entity types and relationship types. We may add new relationship types among entity types as the design progresses. The process of generalization of subclasses into higher-level generalized classes (see Section 15.1) is another example of a bottom-up design strategy.

3. Inside-out strategy: This is a special case of a bottom-up strategy where attention is focused on a central set of concepts that are most evident. Modeling then *spreads outward* by considering new concepts in the vicinity of existing ones. For example, we could specify a few clearly evident entity types in the schema and continue by adding other entity types and relationship types related to each.

4. Mixed strategy: Instead of following any particular strategy throughout the design, the requirements are partitioned using a top-down strategy and part of the schema is designed for each partition using a bottom-up strategy. The various schema parts are then combined.

Figures 16.2 and 16.3 illustrate top-down and bottom-up refinement. An example of a top-down refinement primitive is decomposition of an entity type into several entity types. Figure 16.2a shows a COURSE being refined into COURSE and SEMINAR, and the TEACHES relationship is correspondingly split into TEACHES and OFFERS. Figure 16.2b shows a COURSE_OFFERING entity type being refined into two entity types and a relationship between them. Figure 16.3a shows the bottom-up refinement primitive of generating new relationships among entity types. The bottom-up refinement using generalization is illustrated in Figure 16.3b, where the new concept of VEHICLE_OWNER is "discovered" from the existing entity types FACULTY, STUDENT, and STAFF; this generalization process and diagrammatic notation was discussed in Chapter 15.

SCHEMA (VIEW) INTEGRATION: For large databases with many expected users and applications, it is difficult to try to design the whole database schema at once. In such cases the view integration approach of designing individual schemas and then merging them can be used. Because the individual views can be kept relatively small, design of the schemas is simplified. However, we must have a methodology for integrating the views into a global database schema. Schema integration can be divided into the following subtasks:

1. Identifying correspondences and conflicts among the schemas: Because the schemas are individually designed, it is necessary to specify constructs in the schemas that represent the same real-world concept. These correspondences must be identified before integration can proceed. During this process, several types of conflicts among the schemas may be discovered:

   a. Naming conflicts: These are of two types. A **synonym** occurs when two schemas use different names to describe the same concept; for example, an entity type CUSTOMER in one schema describes the same concept as an entity type CLIENT in another schema. The second type, called a **homonym,** occurs when two schemas use the same name to describe different concepts; for example, an entity type STUDENT represents graduate students in one schema and undergraduate students in another schema.

   b. Type conflicts: The same concept may be represented in two schemas using different modeling constructs. For example, the concept of a DEPARTMENT may be represented as an entity type in one schema and as an attribute in another schema.

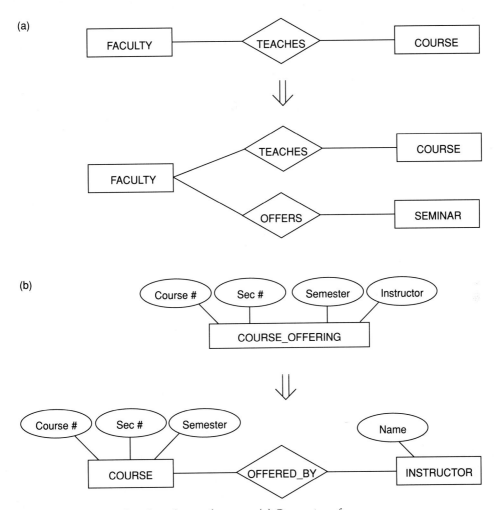

Figure 16.2   Examples of top-down refinement. (a) Generation of a new entity type. (b) Decomposing an entity type into two entity types and a relationship.

c. Domain (value set) conflicts: An attribute may have different domains in two schemas. For example, SSN may be declared as an integer in one schema and as a character string in the other; this is a data type conflict. Similar problems could occur if one schema represented WEIGHT in pounds and the other used kilograms; this is a conflict of the unit of measure used.

d. Conflicts among constraints: Two schemas may represent different constraints on the same concept. For example, the key attribute of an entity type may be a different attribute in each schema. Another example involves different structural constraints on a relationship such as TEACHES; one schema

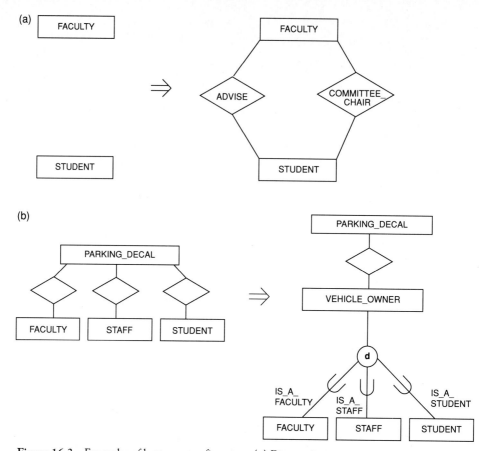

Figure 16.3 Examples of bottom-up refinement. (a) Discovering and adding new relationships. (b) Discovering a new entity type and relating it.

may represent it as 1:N (a course has one instructor) whereas the other schema may represent it as M:N (some courses may have more than one instructor).

2. Modifying views to conform to one another: This process consists of making modifications to some of the schemas so that they conform to other schemas more closely. Some of the conflicts identified in step 1 are resolved during this step.

3. Merging of views: The global schema is created by merging the individual schemas. Corresponding concepts are represented only once in the global schema, and mappings between the views and the global schema are specified as part of the merging process.

4. Restructuring: As a final optional step, the global schema may be analyzed and restructured to remove any redundancies or unnecessary complexity.

Some of these ideas are illustrated by the rather simple example of Figures 16.4 and 16.5. In Figure 16.4 two views are merged to create a bibliographic database. During identification of correspondences between the two views, we discover that RESEARCHER and AUTHOR are synonyms (as far as this database is concerned), and so are CONTRIBUT-ED_BY and WRITTEN_BY. Further, we decide to include a SUBJECT for ARTICLEs in VIEW 1, so we modify VIEW 1 as shown in Figure 16.4 *to conform to* VIEW 2. Figure 16.5 shows the result of merging MODIFIED VIEW 1 with VIEW 2. The relationships BELONGS_TO and WRITTEN_BY are merged, as are the entity types AUTHOR and SUBJECT. We also generalize the entity types ARTICLE and BOOK into the entity type PUBLICATION with their common attribute Title. The attribute Publisher applies only to the entity type BOOK, whereas the attribute Size and the relationship type PUBLISHED_IN apply only to ARTICLE.

Several strategies have been proposed for the process of view integration. These are illustrated in Figure 16.6 and include the following:

1. Binary ladder integration: Two schemas that are quite similar are integrated first. The resulting schema is then integrated with another schema, and this process is repeated until all schemas are integrated. The ordering of schemas for integration can be based on some measure of schema similarity. This strategy is suitable for manual integration because of its step-by-step approach.

2. N-ary integration: All the views are integrated in one procedure after an analysis and specification of their correspondences. This strategy requires computerized tools for large design problems.

3. Balanced binary strategy: Pairs of schemas are integrated first. Then the resulting schemas are paired for further integration, and the procedure is repeated until a final global schema results.

4. Mixed strategy: This is a combination of the above. Initially, the schemas are partitioned into groups based on their similarity, and each group is integrated separately. The intermediate schemas are grouped again and integrated, and so on.

SUMMARY OF PHASE 2A: The result of phase 2a is a conceptual schema in a high-level data model such as the EER model. This schema may be obtained by merging the various user requirements and directly creating the database schema (centralized approach) or by designing a separate schema from the requirements of each user and then integrating those schemas (view integration approach). The data model used in conceptual schema design is DBMS-independent, and the next step is to select a DBMS for implementing the design. We discuss DBMS selection (phase 3) in Section 16.3.3. The purpose of phase 2b, which proceeds in parallel with phase 2a, is to design the characteristics of known database transactions in a DBMS-independent way; these transactions will be used to process and manipulate the database once it is implemented.

Phase 2B: Transaction Design

When a database system is being designed, there are many known applications, or **transactions,** that will run on the database once it is implemented. An important part of database design is to specify the functional characteristics of these transactions early on

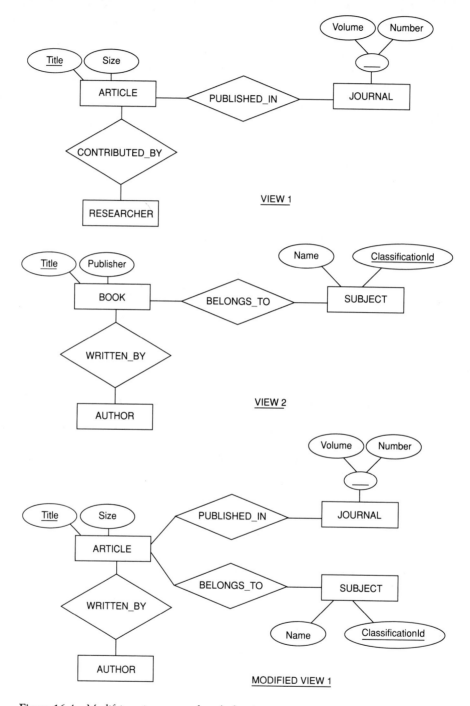

Figure 16.4   Modifying views to conform before integration

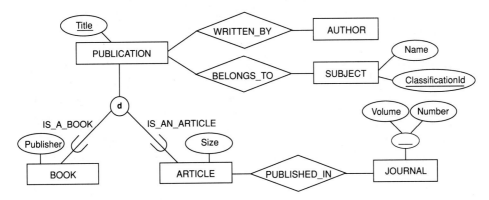

Figure 16.5 Integrated schema after merging views 1 and 2

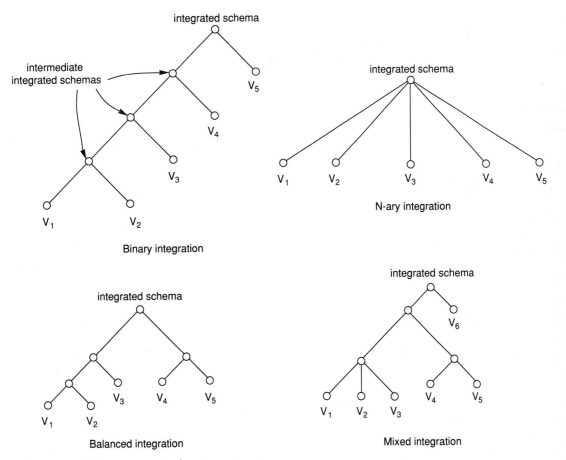

Figure 16.6 Different strategies for view integration

in the design process. This ensures that the database schema includes all the information required by these transactions. In addition, knowing the relative importance of the various transactions and the expected rates of their invocation plays a crucial part in physical database design (phase 5). It is true that only some of the database transactions are known at design time. After the database system is implemented, new transactions are continuously identified and implemented. However, the most important transactions are often known in advance of system implementation and should be specified at an early stage.

One common technique for specifying transactions at a conceptual level is to identify their **input/output** and **functional** behavior. By specifying the input data, output data, and internal functional flow of control, a transaction can be specified in a conceptual and system-independent way. Transactions usually can be grouped into three categories: retrieval transactions, update transactions, and mixed transactions. **Retrieval transactions** are used to retrieve data for display on a screen or for producing a report. **Update transactions** are used to enter new data or modify existing data in the database. **Mixed transactions,** which are the most common, are used for more complex applications that do some retrieval and some update. For example, suppose we are designing an airline reservations database. An example of a retrieval transaction is to list all morning flights on a given date between two cities. An example of an update transaction is to book a seat on a particular flight. A mixed transaction may first display some data, such as a customer reservation on some flight, and then update the database, such as canceling the reservation by deleting it.

Several techniques for requirements specification include notation for specifying **processes,** which in this context are more complex operations that can consist of several transactions. Some of these techniques were mentioned in Section 16.1.1. Other proposals for specifying transactions include TAXIS, GALILEO, and GORDAS (see the bibliography).

Transaction design is just as important as schema design. Unfortunately, many current design methodologies emphasize one over the other. One should go through phases 2a and 2b in parallel, using feedback loops for refinement, until a stable design of schema and transactions is reached.

16.3.3   Phase 3: Choice of a DBMS

The choice of a DBMS is governed by a number of factors. Some factors are technical, others are economic, and still others are concerned with the politics of the organization. The technical factors are concerned with the suitability of the DBMS for the task at hand. Issues to consider here are the type of DBMS (relational, network, hierarchical, other), the storage structures and access paths that the DBMS supports, the types of user interfaces and programmer interfaces available, the types of high-level query languages available, and so on. We discussed these technical factors in Chapter 12 when we compared data models. In this section we concentrate on discussing the economic and organizational factors that affect the choice of DBMS. We first consider the costs of acquiring and operating a DBMS and then look at the benefits of using a DBMS. The following costs must be considered when selecting a DBMS:

1. Software acquisition cost: This is the "up-front" cost of buying the software. The cost of language options, different interfaces such as forms and screens,

recovery/backup options, special access methods, documentation, etc., must be considered. The correct DBMS version for a specific operating system must be selected.

2. Maintenance cost: This is the recurring cost of receiving standard maintenance service from the vendor and for keeping the DBMS version up to date.

3. Hardware acquisition cost: New hardware may be needed, such as additional memory, terminals, disk units, or specialized DBMS storage.

4. Database creation and conversion cost: This is the cost of using the DBMS software either to create the database system from scratch or to convert an existing system to the new DBMS software. In the latter case it is customary to operate the existing system in parallel with the new system until all the applications are fully implemented and tested on the DBMS software. This cost is hard to project and is often underestimated.

5. Personnel cost: Acquisition of DBMS software for the first time by an organization is often accompanied by a reorganization of the data processing department. New positions of database administrator (DBA) and staff are being created in most companies using DBMSs.

6. Training cost: Because DBMSs are often complex systems, the training of personnel to use and program the DBMS is often needed.

7. Operating cost: The cost of continued operation of the database system is typically not worked into an evaluation of alternatives because it is incurred regardless of the DBMS selected.

The benefits of acquiring a DBMS are not so easy to measure and quantify. There are several intangible advantages over traditional file systems, such as ease of use, wider availability of data, and faster access to information. More tangible benefits include reduced application development cost, reduced redundancy of data, and better control and security. Based on a cost-benefit analysis, an organization has to decide when to switch to a DBMS from a file system. This move is generally driven by the following factors:

- Data complexity: As data relationships become more complex, the need for a DBMS is felt more strongly.

- Sharing among applications: The greater the sharing among applications, the more the redundancy among files, and hence the greater the need for a DBMS.

- Dynamically evolving or growing data: If the data changes constantly, it is easier to cope with these changes using a DBMS than a file system.

- Frequency of ad hoc requests for data: File systems are not at all suitable for ad hoc retrieval of data.

- Data volume and need for control: The sheer volume of data and the need to control it sometimes demands a DBMS.

Finally, we discuss some of the economic and organizational factors that affect the choice of one DBMS over another. These include:

1. Structure of the data: If the data to be stored in the database follows a hierarchical structure, a hierarchical-type DBMS should be considered. For data with many interrelationships, a network or relational system may be more appropriate. Rela-

tional technology is gaining in popularity. The type of data model that a DBMS uses is becoming less of an issue because many hierarchical and network DBMSs are now providing relational interfaces.

2. Familiarity of personnel with the system: If the programming staff within the organization is familiar with a particular DBMS, it may be favored to reduce training cost and learning time.

3. Availability of vendor services: The existence of a vendor service facility nearby is desirable to assist in solving any problems with the system. Moving from a non-DBMS to a DBMS environment is generally a major undertaking and requires much vendor assistance at the start.

Before purchasing a DBMS it is necessary to take into account the hardware/software configuration required to run the DBMS and the DBMS portability among different types of hardware. Many commercial DBMSs now have versions that run on many hardware/software configurations. The need of applications for backup, recovery, performance, integrity, and security must also be considered. Many DBMSs are currently being designed as *total solutions* to the information processing and information resource management needs within organizations. Most DBMS vendors are combining their products with the following options or built-in features, which are often categorized as 4GL (fourth generation languages) by commercial vendors:

- Text editors and browsers.
- Report generators and listing utilities.
- Communication software (often called teleprocessing monitors).
- Data entry features such as forms, screens, and menus with automatic editing features.
- Graphical design tools.

These are discussed further in Section 22.1. In some cases it may not be appropriate to use a DBMS at all but may be preferable to develop in-house software for the applications. This may be the case if the applications are very well defined and are *all* known beforehand. In such a case, an in-house custom-designed system may be appropriate to implement the known applications in the most efficient way. However, it is important to note that in most cases new applications that were not foreseen at design time come up *after* system implementation. This is precisely why DBMSs have become very popular: they facilitate the incorporation of new applications without major changes to an implemented system.

16.3.4   Phase 4: Data Model Mapping (Logical Design Phase)

The next phase of database design is to create a conceptual schema and external schemas in the data model of the selected DBMS. This is done by mapping the conceptual and external schemas produced in phase 2a from the high-level data model to the data model of the DBMS. The mapping can proceed in two stages:

1. System-independent mapping: In this step the mapping into the data model of the DBMS does not consider any specific characteristics or special cases that apply

to the DBMS implementation of the data model. We discussed DBMS-independent mapping of an ER schema to a relational, hierarchical, or network schema in Section 12.1 and the mapping of EER model concepts in Section 15.2.

2. Tailoring the schemas to a specific DBMS: Different DBMSs implement a data model using specific modeling features and constraints. We may have to adjust the schemas obtained in step 1 to conform to the specific implementation features of a data model as used in the selected DBMS.

The result of this phase should be DDL statements in the language of the chosen DBMS that specify the conceptual and external level schemas of the database system. However, in many cases the DDL statements include some physical design parameters, so a complete DDL specification must wait until after the physical database design phase is completed.

16.3.5   Phase 5: Physical Database Design

Physical database design is the process of choosing specific storage structures and access paths for the database files to achieve good performance for the various database applications. Each DBMS will offer a variety of options for file organization and access paths. These usually include various types of indexing, clustering of related records on disk blocks, linking related records via pointers, various types of hashing, and so on. Once a specific DBMS is chosen, the physical database design process is restricted to choosing the most appropriate structures for the database files from among the options offered by that DBMS. In this section we give guidelines for physical design decisions in various types of DBMSs.

The following criteria are often used to guide the choice of physical database design options:

1. Response time: This is the elapsed time from submitting a database transaction for execution to receiving a response. A major influence on response time that is under the control of the DBMS is the database access time for data items referenced by the transaction. Response time is also influenced by some factors that are not under DBMS control, such as operating system scheduling or communication delays.

2. Space utilization: This is the amount of storage space used by the database files and their access path structures.

3. Transaction throughput: This is the average number of transactions that can be processed per minute by the database system, and it is a critical parameter of transaction systems such as those used for airline reservations or banking. Transaction throughput must be measured under peak conditions on the system.

Typically, average and worst-case limits on the above parameters are specified as part of the system performance requirements. Analytical or experimental techniques, which can include prototyping and simulation, are used to estimate the average and worst-case values under different physical design decisions to determine whether or not they meet the specified performance requirements.

The performance of file operations depends on the record size and the number of records in the file. Hence, we must estimate these parameters for each file. In addition, we should estimate the update and retrieval patterns for the file cumulatively from all the transactions. Attributes used for selecting records should have primary access paths and secondary indexes constructed for them. Estimates of file growth, either in the record size because of new attributes or in the number of records, should also be taken into account during physical database design.

The result of the physical database design phase is an *initial* determination of storage structures and access paths for the database files. It is almost always necessary to **tune** the physical database design on the basis of its observed performance after the database system is implemented. Most systems include a monitoring utility to collect performance statistics, which are kept in the system catalog or data dictionary for later analysis. These may include statistics on the number of invocations of predefined transactions or queries, input/output activity against files, counts of file pages or index records, and frequency of index usage. As the database system requirements change, it is often necessary to reorganize some files by constructing new indexes or by changing primary access methods. In Section 16.4 we discuss physical design issues related to different types of DBMSs.

16.3.6   Phase 6: Database System Implementation

After the logical and physical designs are completed, we can implement the database system. Language statements in the DDL (data definition language) and SDL (storage definition language) of the selected DBMS are compiled and used to create the database schemas and (empty) database files. The database can now be **loaded** (populated) with the data. If data is to be converted from an earlier computerized system, **conversion routines** may be needed to reformat the data for loading into the new database.

The database transactions must now be implemented by the application programmers. The conceptual specifications of transactions are examined, and corresponding program code with embedded DML (data manipulation language) commands is written and tested. Once the transactions are ready and the data is loaded into the database, the design and implementation phase is over and the operational phase of the database system then begins.

16.4   Physical Database Design Guidelines

In this section we discuss physical database design in more detail. We first discuss the factors that affect physical database design in Section 16.4.1. Then in Sections 16.4.2 to 16.4.4 we discuss general guidelines for physical database design in relational, network, and hierarchical DBMSs.

16.4.1   Factors That Influence Physical Database Design

Physical design is an activity where the goal is not only to come up with the appropriate structuring of data in storage but to do so in a way that guarantees good performance. For a given conceptual schema, there is a large number of physical design alternatives in a given DBMS. It is not possible to make meaningful physical design decisions and performance analyses until we know more about the queries, transactions, and applications that are expected to be run on the database. We must analyze these applications, their expected frequencies of invocation, any time constraints on their execution, and the expected frequency of update operations. We discuss each of these factors next.

Analyzing the Database Queries and Transactions

Before even thinking about a physical database design, we must have a pretty good idea of how we intend to use the database. We should define the queries and transactions that we expect to run on the database in a high-level form. For each *query*, we should specify the following:

1. The files that will be accessed by the query.
2. The fields on which any selection conditions for the query are specified.
3. The fields on which any join conditions for the query are specified.
4. The fields whose values will be retrieved by the query.

The fields listed in 2 and 3 are candidates for definition of additional access structures. For each update transaction or operation, we should specify the following:

1. The files that will be updated.
2. The type of update operation on each file.
3. The fields on which any selection conditions for a delete or modify operation are specified.
4. The fields whose values will be changed by a modify operation.

Again, the fields listed in part 3 above are candidates for access structures. On the other hand, the fields listed in part 4 are candidates for avoiding an access structure because modifying them will require updating the access structures.

Analyzing the Expected Frequency of Invocation of Queries and Transactions

Along with the characteristics of expected queries and transactions, we must consider their expected rates of invocation. This frequency information, along with the field information collected on each query and transaction, is used to compile a cumulative list of expected frequency of use for all queries and transactions. This is expressed as the expected frequency of using each field in each file as a selection field or a join field over all the queries and transactions. Generally, for large volumes of processing, the informal "80-20 rule" applies. This rule states that approximately 80% of the processing is accounted for by only 20% of the queries and transactions. Therefore, in practical situations it is rarely necessary to collect exhaustive statistics and invocation rates on all the queries and transactions. It is sufficient to determine the 20% or so most important ones.

Analyzing the Time Constraints of Queries and Transactions

Some queries and transactions may have stringent performance constraints. For example, a certain transaction may have the constraint that it should terminate within 5 seconds in 95% of the times it is invoked and should never take more than 20 seconds. Such additional performance considerations can be used to place further priorities on the fields that are candidates for access paths. The selection fields used by queries and transactions with time constraints become higher-priority candidates for access structures.

Analyzing the Expected Frequencies of Update Operations

If a file is to be updated very frequently, a minimum number of access paths should be specified for the file because updating the access paths themselves slows down the update operations.

Once we have compiled the above information, we will have a good idea of how we intend to use the database. We will know which fields will be used frequently for selection and join conditions, which files will be updated frequently, and so on. We can now proceed with the physical database design decisions, which consist mainly of deciding on the storage structures and access paths for the database files.

Rarely are all queries and transactions on the database known at the time of physical database design. For example, it is often the case that new applications come up after the database system has been implemented, requiring that new queries and transactions be specified. In such cases it is often necessary to modify some of the physical database design decisions in order to incorporate the new applications into the system. This is called **tuning** the physical design. It may happen that some of the transactions or queries with response time constraints will fail to meet their specified response times. This is another case calling for modifications to the original physical design. In this process the database design is changed to make the transactions that do not satisfy their timing constraints perform more efficiently.

In the following we discuss the general guidelines and heuristics for physical database design for each of the three main types of database systems—relational, hierarchical, and network—that we presented in Part II.

16.4.2 *Physical Database Design Guidelines for Relational Systems*

Most relational systems represent each base relation as a physical database file. The access path options include specifying the type of file for each relation and the attributes on which indexes should be defined. One of the indexes of each file may be a primary or clustering index. In addition, there are several techniques for speeding up frequently used EQUIJOIN operations. We first discuss these techniques and then discuss the choice of file organizations and the selection of indexes.

Techniques for Speeding Up EQUIJOIN Operations

Some relational systems offer an option to store two relations with a 1:N relationship between them as a two-level hierarchical file, sometimes called a **mixed file,** where each record of the 1-side file is stored, followed by the records of the N-side file related to that record. This type of storage structure makes the EQUIJOIN between the two files on this 1:N relationship very efficient. For example, consider the relational database schema in Figure 6.5, and suppose that each relation is implemented as a file. If the EQUIJOIN with condition EMPLOYEE.SSN = WORKS_ON.ESSN is frequently done and must be done as efficiently as possible, we can use a mixed file of the EMPLOYEE and WORKS_ON records. Each EMPLOYEE record will be stored followed by the WORKS_ON records that have the same SSN value.

Another option is to **denormalize** the logical database schema when we design the physical files. This is done to physically place the attributes that are frequently required in a query in the same file records with other attributes involved in the query. We do this by **replicating** (or **duplicating**) the attributes in the file where they are needed. We must compensate for this denormalization by requiring that update transactions maintain the values of replicated attributes consistent with one another. For example, suppose the same frequent query that requires the EQUIJOIN operation discussed above also requires the retrieval of the PNAME attribute of the PROJECT record with PROJECT.PNUMBER = WORKS_ON.PNO. We can then replicate the PNAME attribute in the WORKS_ON records so that the latter join does not need to be executed.

This technique can be carried one step further by physically storing a file that is the result of an EQUIJOIN of two files, although this extreme denormalization should be used only with the utmost care. All types of update anomalies discussed in Chapter 13 will now occur in the file; such anomalies must be dealt with explicitly whenever updates are applied to the file.

Choice of File Organization and Index Selection Guidelines

The most popular option for organizing a separate file in a relational system is to keep the file records unordered and create as many secondary indexes as needed on the file records. The attributes that are used often for selection and join conditions are candidates for secondary indexes.

Another option is to specify an ordering attribute for the file by specifying a primary or clustering index. The attribute that is used most often for join operations should be chosen for ordering the records, since this makes the join operation more efficient (see Chapter 18). If the records are often accessed in order of an attribute, this is another indication that it should be chosen for ordering the file records. Only one of the attributes of each file can be chosen for physically ordering the file records, with a corresponding primary index (if the attribute is a key) or a clustering index (if the attribute is not a key). Most relational systems use the keywords UNIQUE to specify a key and CLUSTER to specify an ordering index.

Choice of Hashing

Some relational systems also offer the option of specifying a hash key attribute rather than an ordering attribute for a relation. If a key attribute is to be used mainly for equality selection and for join, but not for accessing the records in order, we can choose a hash file instead of an ordered file. Another criterion for choosing a hash file is that the size of the file is known and the file is not expected to grow or shrink. If the file changes in size and the relational DBMS offers some dynamic hashing scheme (see Chapter 4), we can still choose hashing for that file.

We can summarize the guidelines for choosing a physical organization for a separate relational file as follows:

1. Choose an attribute that is either used frequently for retrieving the records in order or used most frequently for join operations on the file as an ordering attribute for the file. Create a primary index (if the attribute is a key) or a clustering index (if nonkey) on that attribute if it is also used for selection conditions. This is the *primary access path* to the file records. If no such attribute qualifies, use unordered file records, as this makes record insertion more efficient.

2. For each attribute that is used frequently in selection or join conditions, specify a secondary index on that attribute. Each secondary index serves as a *secondary access path* to the file records.

3. If the file is to be updated very frequently by record insertions and deletions, try to minimize the number of indexes for the file.

4. If an attribute is used frequently for equality selection and join but not for retrieving the records in order of this attribute, a hash file can be used. Static hashing can be used for files whose size does not change much, whereas dynamic hashing is needed for files that are likely to grow rapidly or whose size fluctuates quite frequently. Secondary indexes can also be built on other attributes of the hash file.

Of course, the choice among these options is limited by the storage structures and access paths available on the chosen relational DBMS.

16.4.3   Physical Database Design Guidelines for Network Systems

There are several important physical design options for a network database. The most important among these is to decide on the implementation of each set type. Another important decision, similar to the denormalization issue for relational databases, is to decide whether any fields from an owner record type should be replicated in a member record type for efficiency purposes. In addition, some network DBMSs will allow the definition of hash keys or indexes on a record type. These, together with SYSTEM-owned set types, provide entry points into the database, which are often followed by *navigating from the entry point* by tracing the pointers of sets (**set processing**). Finally, decisions must be made on any ordering fields of record types or of member records within a set type. We discuss these issues below.

Guidelines for Choosing Among Set Implementation Options

There are many options for implementing a set type. We review these different options, which were discussed in Chapter 11, and present guidelines for deciding which option to use:

1. Implementing a set type by physical contiguity: In some network DBMSs the member records can be physically stored following the owner record; this option is called set implementation by **physical contiguity**. This is similar to the mixed file option discussed above for relational databases. If a record type is a member

of several set types, then *only one* of those can be chosen for implementation by physical contiguity. Accessing the member records of a set instance is most efficient in this option, so the set types that are used most often to access *all member records* of an owner are candidates for this implementation option.

2. Implementing a set type by pointer arrays: Another implementation option is to store an array of pointers to the member records with the owner record. If a *single member record*, such as the FIRST, LAST, or ith, is often selected from the owner, this is a good option.

3. Using different options for pointer implementation: Most sets will be implemented by pointers and linked lists. However, there are several types of pointers. We can have a single **next** pointer or both **next** and **prior** pointers in member records of a set. With either of these two options, we can also have an **owner** pointer in each member record, which points directly to the owner record. If the set members are mainly accessed using FIND NEXT, then the next pointer is sufficient. If FIND PRIOR is often used, a prior pointer should be included. Finally, if the owner is often accessed from a member record using FIND OWNER, an owner pointer should be included. This latter option is useful for record types that participate as members in multiple set types, for example, linking record types for M:N relationships, such as the WORKS_ON record type in Figure 12.4. With this option a program can retrieve member records using one set type, say E_WORKSON in Figure 12.4, and then directly find the owner record of each member using the owner pointer of the other set type P_WORKSON.

4. Implementing a set type using indexes: With this method, an index table is created *for each owner record* of a given set type. This table is an index to the member records to make their retrieval much faster.

In a network database the equivalents of most relational EQUIJOIN operations are *prespecified* as set types, as can be seen by comparing the COMPANY database schema in the relational model (Figure 12.2) and in the network model (Figure 12.4). For example, the join condition EMPLOYEE.SSN = WORKS_ON.ESSN on the relational schema in Figure 12.2 is represented by the E_WORKSON set type in Figure 12.4. In the same way, the join condition PROJECT.NUMBER = WORKS_ON.PNUMBER is represented by the P_WORKSON set type. Hence, joins that are executed frequently in the relational model correspond to sets that are traversed frequently in the network model. Such set types are candidates for an efficient implementation option, be it by physical contiguity or by including an owner pointer.

Denormalization for Efficiency or for Structural Constraints

We can replicate some of the fields from an owner record type in the member record type of a set type:

- If a NO DUPLICATES ALLOWED (key) field is replicated, it can be used to specify a structural constraint for a MANUAL set type or AUTOMATIC SET SELECTION for an AUTOMATIC set type. This implies that these replicated fields can have their values accessed from the member record directly *without having to locate and access the owner record,* reducing the access time, especially if there is no owner pointer in the member record.

- Other, nonkey fields may also be replicated in the member for efficiency. However, this replication means that updates to a field in the owner that is replicated in the members must be propagated to all member records by the update program to preserve consistency, thus slowing down some update operations.

This option is similar to denormalization in relational systems. Notice that by specifying a structural constraint with a check option (see Figure 11.14b) on the replicated field or by specifying AUTOMATIC SET SELECTION, the network DBMS will itself ensure that this consistency is maintained, but the DBMS will still have to do additional processing on its own, resulting in slower update operations.

Record Accessing Options

The network model requires **entry points** into the database to commence navigational search for records. These are provided either by means of SYSTEM-owned set types or by specifying an access structure for a particular record type. The default is to do a linear search in an **AREA,** which is a DBTG concept that stands for a logical partition of the database that is assigned to a physically contiguous area on disk. Other LOCATION MODEs for record types in the original DBTG report, which are still followed in many commercial network DBMSs, include the following:

- CALC—The records of the record type are hashed on a specified field of the record type called a CALC KEY. By supplying a value of the CALC KEY, the record is retrieved directly.

- VIA SET—This causes the member records to be stored near the owner; no direct access to the records is available.

- DIRECT—The application program suggests an actual physical page on or near which the record should be stored. The actual storage location (in the form of block address and offset within the block) is returned in a **DBKEY** (database key), which is equivalent to a pointer to the record. The database key concept was suggested in the original DBTG report as an efficiency mechanism but was dropped from later reports.

The direct option is used in unusual circumstances where a program saves a pointer to the record and later uses this pointer to fetch the record directly. Another use of this option is to control the physical location of records. The AREA concept allows the database designer to specify that the records of certain record types be placed *physically near each other* on disk, perhaps on the same cylinder. This makes accessing several of these records, especially when related via sets, much faster. Specification of AREAs is an important physical design decision in systems that support this concept.

Selection of SYSTEM-owned Sets and Record Ordering

SYSTEM-owned sets are defined for processing all the records of a record type in some desired order, typically for use in report generation applications. If an ORDER clause is specified with the SYSTEM-owned set, the records of that record type are ordered by values of the field specified in the ORDER clause. Hence, whenever we intend to access records of a record type in some order we should specify SYSTEM-owned sets on those record types. SYSTEM-owned sets should also be specified if we intend to use records of a record type as "entry points" and then locate records related to them by other sets.

For example, if we frequently make reports that print information on departments and display employee and project information for those departments, we can use a SYSTEM-owned set to access the DEPARTMENT records in Figure 12.4. We can then retrieve the related EMPLOYEE and PROJECT records via the WORKS_FOR, MANAGES, and CONTROLS sets. If we often want the departments accessed in order of department number, we can order the SYSTEM-owned set by the DNO field. If, in addition, we want to access arbitrary DEPARTMENT records, say by value of DNAME, we should also declare a CALC KEY (hash key field) on DNAME of DEPARTMENT.

Record orderings are also important with regular set types. If we want to access the member records of a set instance in order of one of the member record type fields, we should declare the member records to be ORDERed by that field, thus saving the time needed to sort the retrieved records.

16.4.4 Physical Database Design Guidelines for Hierarchical Systems

The main decisions for physical database design for hierarchical systems are closely interrelated with the logical design because of the many options we have for specifying hierarchies for the same high-level database schema. However, there are many additional options, such as choice of hashing or indexing fields for the root record type or choice of "secondary" indexing for nonroot record types and implementation of virtual parent-child relationships. Access to data in a hierarchical database is constrained by the hierarchical structure and typically proceeds by first locating the root record. Within an occurrence tree, the search is conducted either sequentially on the records in the tree or by following certain pointer schemes. The root records may have indexed or hashed access on certain fields to locate the required occurrence tree efficiently. In the following sections we discuss the effect of choosing a suitable logical design for a particular expected use of a hierarchical database and discuss some of the options for implementing virtual parent-child relationships.

A high-level database schema, such as an ER schema, can be mapped into many different hierarchical schemas. The factors we discussed in Section 16.4.1 that affect physical database design will affect the choice of which hierarchical schema to use. We are faced with the following decisions that affect database performance:

1. Choice of root record types of hierarchies: Root record types are entry points to the database, because all the descendent records can be accessed from the root record type in a relatively efficient manner. In addition, access paths such as hashing and indexes can easily be specified on the root record types. Record types that are often used to start a retrieval are good candidates to be chosen as roots of hierarchies.

2. Implementation options for parent-child relationships (PCRs): The most common implementation of a PCR is as a hierarchical file, which uses physical conti-

guity and stores the records as a hierarchical sequence (preorder traversal) as discussed in Chapter 10. However, pointers to facilitate the location of descendent records of a certain record type (called secondary indexes in IMS) may be added. Similarly, pointers to facilitate location of an ancestor record (called physical parent pointers in IMS) may be also added.

3. Choice of pointer records: The pointer record type option minimizes redundancy at the cost of having to define a virtual parent-child relationship (VPCR). Choosing between this option and the option of replicating records in a hierarchy is an important design decision. The former minimizes redundancy, while the latter provides more efficient retrieval at the cost of complicating the update process tremendously.

4. Different options for virtual parent-child relationship implementation: Most VPCRs are implemented by pointers in the child records, which facilitates locating the parent record from the child record. This is similar to the owner pointer in a set type of the network model. To provide access from a virtual parent to its first virtual child, a pointer (called a logical child pointer in IMS) can be used. The child then points to the next virtual child record having the same virtual parent (using a logical twin pointer). This is similar to the next pointers of a set type in network databases. The choice of implementation option depends on the main use of the VPCR.

5. Dummy virtual parent records: Because VPCRs do not have names, it is sometimes desirable to have a record be a virtual parent in *at most one* VPCR. If the logical design chosen has a record type that is a virtual parent in several VPCRs, we can create a dummy record type that is a real child of that record type for each additional VPCR. Each dummy record is now virtual parent in a *single* VPCR.

Hierarchical databases also allow partitioning of a hierarchy into groups of record types for efficiency reasons. This is similar to the AREA concept of DBTG network DBMSs. A group, called a **data set group** in IMS, contains a subtree from the hierarchical schema and is mapped to a contiguous physical storage area. This improves access to records within the subtree by storing them in close proximity. A root of such a group may further be given direct access via a secondary index.

16.5   Automated Design Tools

Most database design is still carried out manually by expert designers, who use their experience and knowledge in the design process. However, there are many aspects of database design that are difficult to carry out by hand and are amenable to automation. For example, it is relatively straightforward to automate much of the data model mapping phase. Detecting conflicts among schemas before integrating them may be quite difficult to do manually. Similarly, quantitatively evaluating different alternatives for physical database design can be very time consuming. Recently, a number of design tools that help with special aspects of database design have begun to appear. These deal with conceptual, mapping, and physical aspects of the design process, as well as with the requirements collection and analysis phase. We will not survey database design tools here, but only mention some of the characteristics that a good design tool should possess. These include:

- An easy-to-use interface: This is critical because it enables the designers to focus on the task at hand and not on understanding the tool. Graphical and natural language interfaces are commonly used. Different interfaces may be tailored to end users or to expert database designers.

- Analytical components: Most tools provide analytical components for tasks that are difficult to perform manually, such as evaluating physical design alternatives or detecting conflicting constraints among views.

- Heuristic components: Aspects of the design that cannot be precisely quantified can be automated by entering heuristic rules in the design tool. These rules are used to evaluate design alternatives heuristically.

- Trade-off analysis: A tool should present the designer with adequate comparative analysis whenever it presents multiple alternatives to choose from.

- Display of design results: Design results, such as schemas, are often displayed in diagrammatic form. Other types of results can be shown as tables, lists, reports, etc. that can be easily interpreted.

- Design verification: This is a highly desirable feature. Its purpose is to verify that the resulting design satisfies the initial requirements.

Currently there is increasing awareness of the value of design tools, and they are becoming a must for large database design problems. The database design process is becoming unthinkable without adequate tool support for large, organization-wide databases. There is also an increasing awareness that schema design and application design should go hand in hand. The emerging CASE (computer-assisted software engineering) tools are attempts to address both these areas. Many tools under development use expert system technology to guide the design process by including design expertise in the form of rules within the expert system. Expert system technology is also useful in the requirements collection and analysis phase, which is typically a laborious and frustrating process. The increased emphasis is on using both data dictionaries and design tools to achieve better designs for complex databases.

16.6 Summary

In this chapter we discussed the different phases of the database design process. We also discussed how databases fit within an information system for information resource management in an organization.

The database design process includes six phases, but the three phases most often associated with database design are conceptual design, logical design (data model mapping), and physical design. We also discussed the initial phase of requirements collection and analysis, which is often considered to be a *predesign phase*. In addition, at some point during the design, choice of a specific DBMS package must be made. We discussed some of the organizational criteria that come into play when selecting a DBMS.

The importance of designing both the schema and the applications (or transactions) was highlighted. This is especially important during the conceptual design phase. We discussed different approaches to conceptual schema design and the difference between centralized schema design and the view integration approach.

In Section 16.4 we discussed the factors that affect physical database design decisions and gave guidelines for choosing among physical design alternatives for relational, network, and hierarchical DBMSs. Finally, we gave a brief discussion on the use of automated design tools.

Review Questions

16.1. What are the six phases of database design? Discuss each phase.

16.2. Which of the above phases are considered the main activities of the database design process itself? Why?

16.3. Why is it important to design the schemas and applications in parallel?

16.4. Why is it important to use an implementation-independent data model during conceptual schema design?

16.5. Discuss the characteristics that a data model for conceptual schema design should possess.

16.6. Compare and contrast the two main approaches for conceptual schema design.

16.7. Discuss the strategies for designing a single conceptual schema from its requirements.

16.8. What are the steps of the view integration approach to conceptual schema design? How would a view integration tool work? Design a sample modular architecture for such a tool.

16.9. What are the different strategies for view integration?

16.10. Discuss the factors that influence the choice of a DBMS package for the information system of an organization.

16.11. What is system-independent data model mapping?

16.12. What are the important factors that influence physical database design?

16.13. Discuss the decisions made during physical database design.

16.14. Discuss the macro and micro life cycles of an information system.

16.15. Discuss the main factors that affect physical database design decisions.

16.16. Discuss the guidelines for physical database design in relational DBMSs.

16.17. Discuss the guidelines for physical database design in network DBMSs.

16.18. Discuss the guidelines for physical database design in hierarchical DBMSs.

Selected Bibliography

There is a vast amount of literature on database design. We first list some of the books that address database design. Wiederhold (1983) is a comprehensive textbook covering all phases of database design with an emphasis on physical design. Two books (Ceri 1983;

Albano et al. 1985) have been published by the DATAID project in Italy, which is a comprehensive project addressing many aspects of database design. Batini et al. (1989), and McFadden and Hoffer (1988) emphasize conceptual and logical database design. Brodie et al. (1984) gives a collection of chapters on conceptual modeling, constraint specification and analysis, and transaction design. Teory and Fry (1982) present a methodology for access path design at the logical level. Yao (1985) is a collection of works ranging from requirements specification techniques to schema restructuring. The book by Atre (1980) discusses database administration and data dictionaries.

We now give references to selected papers that discuss the topics covered in this chapter. Navathe and Kerschberg (1986) discuss all phases of database design and point out the role of data dictionaries. Goldfine and Konig (1988) and ANSI (1989) discuss the role of data dictionaries in database design. Eick and Lockemann (1985) propose a model for requirements collection. Schkolnick (1978) and Carlis and March (1984) present models for the problem of physical database design. March and Severance (1977) discuss record segmentation. Approaches to structured application design are discussed in Gane and Sarson (1979) and De Marco (1979). Whang et al. (1982) present a methodology for physical design of network DBMS.

Schema integration methodologies are compared in Batini et al. (1987). Navathe and Gadgil (1982) propose the mixed strategy to view integration. Detailed work on n-ary view integration can be found in Navathe et al. (1986), Elmasri et al. (1986), and Larson et al. (1989). An integration tool based on Elmasri et al. (1986) is described in Sheth et al. (1988). Motro (1987) discusses integration with respect to preexisting databases. The binary balanced strategy to view integration is discussed in Teorey and Fry (1982). A formal approach to view integration, which uses inclusion dependencies, is given in Casanova and Vidal (1982). Other aspects of integration are discussed in Elmasri and Wiederhold (1979), Elmasri and Navathe (1984), Mannino and Effelsberg (1984), and Navathe et al. (1984a).

All aspects of database administration are reviewed in Weldon (1981). Surveys of data dictionaries are given in Curtice (1981) and Allen et al. (1982). Some well-known commercial database design tools are ERMA, developed by Arthur D. Little Inc. in Cambridge, Massachusetts; Data Designer, developed at Knowledgeware in Atlanta, Georgia; MAST_ER of Infodyne, Inc.; and DDEW of CCA (Computer Corporation of America). Automated design tools are discussed in Bubenko et al. (1971), Albano et al. (1985), and Navathe (1985).

Transaction design is a relatively less researched topic. Mylopoulos et al. (1980) proposed the TAXIS language, and Albano et al. (1987) developed the GALILEO system, both of which are comprehensive systems for specifying transactions. The GORDAS language for the ECR model (Elmasri et al. 1985) contains a transaction specification capability.

SYSTEM IMPLEMENTATION TECHNIQUES

The System Catalog/Data Dictionary

The system catalog, or data dictionary, is at the heart of any general-purpose DBMS. It is a "minidatabase" itself, and its function is to store the *descriptions* of the databases that the DBMS maintains. The catalog stores data that describes each database, which is often called **meta-data**. This includes a description of the conceptual database schema, the internal schema, any external schemas, and any mapping between the schemas at different levels. In addition, information needed by specific DBMS modules, for example, the query optimization module or the security and authorization module, is stored in the catalog.

The term data dictionary is often used to indicate a more general software utility than a catalog. A **catalog** often refers to a utility internal to the DBMS that is closely coupled with the DBMS software; it provides the information stored in it to users and the DBA but is *mainly* accessed by the various software modules of the DBMS itself, such as DDL and DML compilers, query optimizer, transaction processor, report generators, and constraint enforcer. On the other hand, there are many *stand-alone* **data dictionary** software packages that may interact with the software modules of the DBMS but are *mainly* used by the designers, users, and administrators of a computer system for information resource management. In addition to storing data descriptions, such data dictionary systems are used to maintain information on system hardware and software, system documentation, and system users, as well as all sorts of other information relevant to system administration. If a data dictionary is used *only* by designers, users, and administrators and not by the DBMS software, it is called a **passive data dictionary;** otherwise, it is called an **active data dictionary** or **data directory**. Figure 17.1 illustrates the types of active data dictionary interfaces.

Data dictionaries are also used to document the database design process itself by storing information on the results of every design phase and on how the design decisions were reached. This helps in automating the design process by making the design decisions and changes available to all the database designers. This information can be very

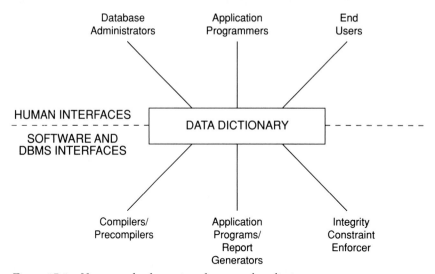

Figure 17.1   Human and software interfaces to a data dictionary

valuable when modifications to the database description are to be made. Also, using the data dictionary during database design means that at the conclusion of the design phase the meta-data is already in the data dictionary.

In this chapter we concentrate on discussing the system catalog rather than on general data dictionary systems. In Section 17.1 we discuss catalogs for relational DBMSs; then we discuss network catalogs in Section 17.2. In Section 17.3 we discuss how a catalog is used by various modules of a DBMS and also describe other types of information that may be stored in a catalog. Because a catalog is itself a minidatabase, we can describe the catalog structure by a schema in some data model. In Sections 17.1 and 17.2, where we discuss catalog structure for the relational and network data models, we give a description of a conceptual schema for each catalog in the EER model to help clarify the conceptual structure of each type of catalog.

17.1   Catalogs for Relational DBMSs

The basic information that must be stored in a catalog of a relational DBMS is a description of the base relations, including the relation names, attribute names, attribute domains (data types), and primary keys. Other conceptual-level information, such as secondary key attributes, foreign keys, and other types of constraints, should also be included. In addition, external-level descriptions of views and internal-level descriptions of storage structures and indexes must be stored in the catalog. Security and authorization information, which specifies the users authorized to access the database relations and views as well as the creators or owners of each relation (see Chapter 20), is also included.

In relational DBMSs it is common practice to store the catalog itself as relations and use the DBMS software for querying, updating, and maintaining the catalog. This allows

REL_AND_ATTR_CATALOG

REL_NAME	ATTR_NAME	ATTR_TYPE	MEMBER_OF_PK	MEMBER_OF_FK	FK_RELATION
EMPLOYEE	FNAME	VSTR15	no	no	
EMPLOYEE	MINIT	CHAR	no	no	
EMPLOYEE	LNAME	VSTR15	no	no	
EMPLOYEE	SSN	STR9	yes	no	
EMPLOYEE	BDATE	STR9	no	no	
EMPLOYEE	ADDRESS	VSTR30	no	no	
EMPLOYEE	SEX	CHAR	no	no	
EMPLOYEE	SALARY	INTEGER	no	no	
EMPLOYEE	SUPERSSN	STR9	no	yes	EMPLOYEE
EMPLOYEE	DNO	INTEGER	no	yes	DEPARTMENT
DEPARTMENT	DNAME	VSTR10	no	no	
DEPARTMENT	DNUMBER	INTEGER	yes	no	
DEPARTMENT	MGRSSN	STR9	no	yes	EMPLOYEE
DEPARTMENT	MGRSTARTDATE	STR10	no	no	
DEPT_LOCATIONS	DNUMBER	INTEGER	yes	yes	DEPARTMENT
DEPT_LOCATIONS	DLOCATION	VSTR15	yes	no	
PROJECT	PNAME	VSTR10	no	no	
PROJECT	PNUMBER	INTEGER	yes	no	
PROJECT	PLOCATION	VSTR15	no	no	
PROJECT	DNO	INTEGER	no	yes	DEPARTMENT
WORKS_ON	ESSN	STR9	yes	yes	EMPLOYEE
WORKS_ON	PNO	INTEGER	yes	yes	PROJECT
WORKS_ON	HOURS	REAL	no	no	
DEPENDENT	ESSN	STR9	yes	yes	EMPLOYEE
DEPENDENT	DEPENDENT_NAME	VSTR15	yes	no	
DEPENDENT	SEX	CHAR	no	no	
DEPENDENT	BDATE	STR9	no	no	

Figure 17.2 Basic catalog for the relational schema of Figure 12.2

DBMS routines as well as users to access the information stored in the catalog whenever they are authorized to do so using the query language of the DBMS and permits generalized access to the catalog.

A catalog structure for a basic relational schema description is shown in Figure 17.2, which shows a catalog relation for storing relation names, attribute names, attribute types, and primary key information. In Figure 17.2 we also show how foreign key constraints can be included in the catalog, even though many relational systems do not represent or enforce this type of constraint. The *description* of the relational database schema shown in Figure 12.2 is shown as the tuples (contents) of the catalog file in Figure 17.2, which we call REL_AND_ATTR_CATALOG. The primary key of REL_AND_ATTR_CATALOG is the combination of attributes {REL_NAME, ATTR_NAME}, because all relation names should be unique and all attribute names within a particular relation schema should also be unique. Another catalog file can store information for each relation, such as tuple size, number of tuples, number of indexes, creator name, etc.

To include information on secondary key attributes of a relation, we can simply extend the above catalog if we assume that an attribute can be a *member of one key only*. In this case we can replace the MEMBER_OF_PK attribute of REL_AND_ATTR_CATALOG with an attribute KEY_NUMBER; the value of KEY_NUMBER is 0 if the attribute is not a member of any key, 1 if it is a member of the primary key, and i > 1 for the ith secondary key, where the secondary keys of a relation are numbered 2, 3, ..., n. However, if an attribute can be a member of *more than one key*, which is the general case, the above representation is not sufficient. One possibility is to store information on key attributes separately in a second catalog relation RELATION_KEYS, with attributes {REL_NAME, KEY_NUMBER, MEMBER_ATTR}

(a)   RELATION_KEYS

REL_NAME	KEY_NUMBER	MEMBER_ATTR

(b)   RELATION_INDEXES

REL_NAME	INDEX_NAME	MEMBER_ATTR	INDEX_TYPE	ATTR_NO	ASC_DESC

(c)   VIEW_QUERIES

VIEW_NAME	QUERY

VIEW_ATTRIBUTES

VIEW_NAME	ATTR_NAME	ATTR_NUM

Figure 17.3 Other possible catalog relations for a relational system. (a) Catalog relation for storing general key information. (b) Catalog relation for storing index information. (c) Catalog relations for storing view information.

that together are the key of RELATION_KEYS. This is shown in Figure 17.3a. The DBMS assigns the value 1 to KEY_NUMBER for the primary key and values 2, 3, ..., n for the secondary keys. Each key will have a tuple in RELATION_KEYS for each attribute that is part of that key, and the value of MEMBER_ATTRIBUTE gives the name of that attribute. This solution allows an attribute to be a member of several keys.

Next, consider information regarding indexes. Again, if an attribute is restricted to being a member of a single index, we can simply add an attribute INDEX_NAME to the REL_AND_ATTR_CATALOG relation to specify that the attribute is part of the set of attributes used to build the named index. In the general case where an attribute can be a member of more than one index we can create another catalog relation as we did for general keys. We can use the RELATION_INDEXES catalog relation shown in Figure 17.3b. The key of RELATION_INDEXES is the combination {INDEX_NAME, MEMBER_ATTR} (assuming index names are unique), which allows an attribute to be a member of several indexes. MEMBER_ATTR is the name of the attribute included in the index. For example, to specify three indexes on the WORKS_ON relation of Figure 12.2—a clustering index on ESSN, a secondary index on PNO, and another secondary index on the combination {ESSN, PNO}—the attributes ESSN and PNO are members of two indexes each. The ATTR_NO and ASC_DESC fields in INDEXES specify the order of each attribute in the index and specify whether the attribute is ordered in ascending or descending order in the index.

Note that some relational systems combine the specification of indexes and keys, as discussed in Chapter 7, even though keys are logical constraints on relations whereas indexes are physical access paths. This makes the system catalog and the DBMS software less complicated.

The definitions of external-level views must also be stored in the catalog of a relational system. A view is specified by a query with a possible renaming of the values appearing in the query result (see Chapter 7). We can use the two catalog relations shown in Figure 17.3c to store view definitions. The first, VIEW_QUERIES, would have two attributes {VIEW_NAME, QUERY} and stores the query (the entire text string) corresponding to the view, and the second, VIEW_ATTRIBUTES, has attributes {VIEW_NAME, ATTR_NAME, ATTR_NUM} to store the names of the attributes of the view. Note that ATTR_NUM is an integer number greater than zero to specify the correspondence of each view attribute to the values in the result of the query. The key of VIEW_QUERIES is VIEW_NAME, and that of VIEW_ATTRIBUTES is the combination {VIEW_NAME, ATTR_NAME}. The catalog will also store authorization information concerning the users who are allowed to use the view.

Most relational systems store their catalog files as DBMS relations. However, because the catalog is accessed very frequently by the DBMS modules, it is important to implement catalog access as efficiently as possible. It has been suggested that it may be more efficient to implement the catalog using a specialized set of data structures and access routines, thus trading generality for efficiency.

Finally, we take a conceptual look at the basic information that is stored in a relational catalog. Figure 17.4 shows a high-level EER schema diagram that may be used to describe part of a relational catalog. This schema can be used to implement a relational catalog using specialized files or any type of DBMS. In Figure 17.4 the RELATION entity type stores the names of relations that appear in a relational schema. Two disjoint subclasses BASE_RELATION and VIEW_RELATION are created for RELATION. The entity type ATTRIBUTE is a weak entity type of RELATION, and its partial key is AttrName. BASE_RELATIONs also have general key and foreign key constraints, as well as indexes,

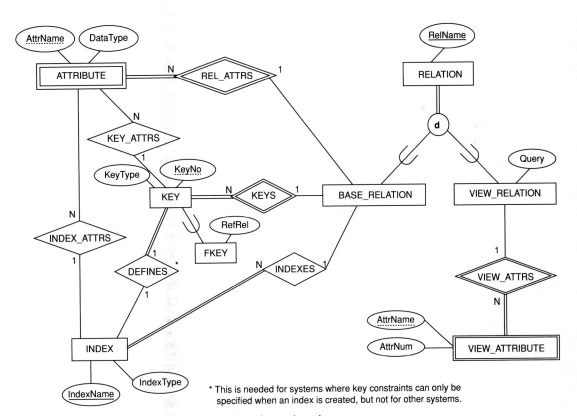

Figure 17.4 Example EER diagram for part of a relational catalog

whereas VIEW_RELATIONs have their defining query as well as the AttrNum to specify correspondence of view attributes to query attributes. Notice that an unspecified constraint in Figure 17.4 is that all attributes related to a KEY or INDEX entity—via the relationships KEY_ATTRS or INDEX_ATTRS—must be related to the same BASE_RELATION entity to which the KEY or INDEX entity is related. KEY_TYPE specifies whether the key is foreign, primary, or secondary. FKEY is a subclass for foreign keys, and includes the name of the referenced relation RefRel.

We discuss additional information that needs to be stored in a catalog in Section 17.3, and we discuss security and authorization in Chapter 20. In Chapter 23 we will describe the actual organization of the catalog of the DB2 relational DBMS.

17.2   Catalogs for Network DBMSs

The basic information that must be stored in a catalog of a network DBMS is a description of the record types and set types. In addition, the information on how each set type is implemented and other physical storage choices must be included in the catalog, and security and authorization information and information concerning external subschemas should also be included.

Figure 17.5 shows an example basic network catalog for describing the record types and set types of a network database schema. The catalog consists of two tables or files,

RECORD_TYPES_CATALOG

RECORD_TYPE_NAME	FIELD_NAME	FIELD_TYPE
EMPLOYEE	FNAME	VSTR15
EMPLOYEE	MINIT	CHAR
EMPLOYEE	LNAME	VSTR15
EMPLOYEE	SSN	STR9
EMPLOYEE	BDATE	STR9
EMPLOYEE	ADDRESS	VSTR30
EMPLOYEE	SEX	CHAR
EMPLOYEE	SALARY	INTEGER
EMPLOYEE	DEPTNAME	VSTR10
DEPARTMENT	NAME	VSTR10
DEPARTMENT	NUMBER	INTEGER
DEPARTMENT	LOCATION	VSTR15
DEPARTMENT	MGRSTART	STR10
PROJECT	NAME	VSTR10
PROJECT	NUMBER	INTEGER
PROJECT	LOCATION	VSTR15
WORKS_ON	ESSN	STR9
WORKS_ON	PNUMBER	INTEGER
WORKS_ON	HOURS	REAL
DEPENDENT	EMPSSN	STR9
DEPENDENT	DEP_NAME	VSTR15
DEPENDENT	SEX	CHAR
DEPENDENT	BDATE	STR9
SUPERVISOR		

(continued on next page)

Figure 17.5   Basic catalog files for storing information on record types and set types

SET_TYPES_CATALOG

SET_TYPE_NAME	OWNER_RECORD_TYPE	MEMBER_RECORD_TYPE
ALL_DEPTS	SYSTEM	DEPARTMENT
WORKS_FOR	DEPARTMENT	EMPLOYEE
MANAGES	EMPLOYEE	DEPARTMENT
CONTROLS	DEPARTMENT	PROJECT
IS_A_SUPERVISOR	EMPLOYEE	SUPERVISOR
SUPERVISEES	SUPERVISOR	EMPLOYEE
E_WORKSON	EMPLOYEE	WORKS_ON
P_WORKSON	PROJECT	WORKS_ON
DEPENDENTS_OF	EMPLOYEE	DEPENDENT

Figure 17.5 *(continued)*

one for describing record types and the other for describing set types, and includes the minimal information necessary for describing a network database schema. The contents of these two files correspond to the network schema of Figure 12.4.

We can easily extend the SET_TYPES_CATALOG by adding information on how each set type is implemented. For example, we could add the flag fields NEXT_POINTER, OWNER_POINTER, PRIOR_POINTER, CONTIGUOUS_MEMBERS, etc., where each flag field has a value of either TRUE or FALSE. This is shown in Figure 17.6a. The set options for each set type must also be stored in the catalog. We can extend the SET_TYPES_CATALOG with the fields RETENTION_OPTION and INSERTION_OPTION, where the values of RETENTION_OPTION

(a) SET_TYPES_CATALOG

SET_TYPE_NAME	• • •	NEXT_POINTER	OWNER_POINTER	PRIOR_POINTER	CONTIGUOUS_MEMBERS

(b) SET_TYPES_CATALOG

SET_TYPE_NAME	• • •	RETENTION_OPTION	INSERTION_OPTION

(c) RECORD_TYPES_CATALOG

RECORD_TYPE_NAME	FIELD_NAME	FIELD_TYPE	VECTOR	REPEATING_GROUP

VECTOR_FIELD_COMPONENTS

RECORD_TYPE_NAME	FIELD_NAME	COMPONENT_FIELD_NAME

UNIQUE-(NO-DUPLICATE)-CONSTRAINTS

RECORD_TYPE_NAME	KEY_NUMBER	FIELD_NAME

Figure 17.6 Some extensions to the basic network catalog. (a) Extending the SET_TYPES_CATALOG to include set implementation information. (b) Including the set type options in the SET_TYPES_CATALOG file. (c) Representing repeating and vector fields and the NO DUPLICATES ALLOWED constraint.

can be one of {MANDATORY, OPTIONAL, FIXED} and the values of INSERTION_OPTION can be one of {AUTOMATIC, MANUAL}, as shown in Figure 17.6b. Any structural constraints on set types and the method for AUTOMATIC SET SELECTION for AUTOMATIC set types must also be specified in the catalog.

We must be able to represent different types of fields, because the network model has options for vector fields and repeating groups. Also, constraints on fields, such as the NO DUPLICATES ALLOWED option specified for key fields, must be recorded in the catalog. Figure 17.6c shows how we may represent the NO DUPLICATES ALLOWED constraint using the technique for representing general keys in a relational catalog. Figure 17.6c also shows how to represent vector or repeating fields in the catalog. The VECTOR and REPEATING_GROUP fields in RECORD_TYPES_CATALOG are flag fields that have values of either TRUE or FALSE. The component fields of a vector (composite) field are stored in the VECTOR_FIELD_COMPONENTS file.

As we did with the relational model, we show a conceptual description of part of a network system catalog as an EER schema in Figure 17.7. This shows the structure of basic information describing record types, set types, and fields. The relationship set MEMBER relates a SET_TYPE entity to its member RECORD_TYPE entity. MULTI_MEMBER set types have additional member record types. SYSTEM_OWNED set types do not have an owner record type, but other set types, which we call REGULAR in Figure 17.7, are related via the

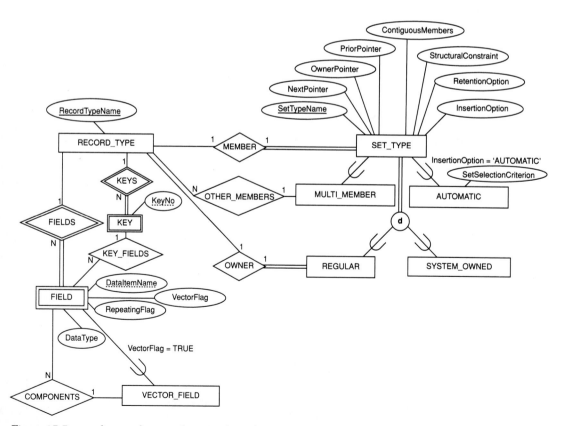

Figure 17.7   EER diagram for part of a network catalog

OWNER relationship set to their owner RECORD_TYPE entity. AUTOMATIC set types are a subclass of SET_TYPE with the membership condition InsertionOption = 'AUTOMATIC', and they have the additional specific attribute SetSelectionCriterion. VECTOR_FIELDs are a subclass of fields that are formed of COMPONENTS.

Note that as in the relational catalog schema of Figure 17.4, an unspecified constraint on Figure 17.7 is that all FIELD entities related to a VECTOR_FIELD entity via COMPONENTS and all FIELD entities related to a KEY entity via KEY_FIELDS must be related to the same RECORD_TYPE entity as the VECTOR_FIELD entity and the KEY entity, respectively.

17.3   Other Catalog Information Accessed by DBMS Software Modules

The DBMS modules use and access a catalog very frequently; that is why it is important to implement access to the catalog as efficiently as possible. In this section we discuss the different ways in which some of the DBMS software modules use and access the catalog. These include the following:

1. DDL (and SDL) compilers: These DBMS modules process and check the specification of a database schema in the data definition language and store that description in the catalog. Schema constructs at all levels—conceptual, internal, and external—are extracted from the DDL (data definition language) and SDL (storage definition language) specifications and entered into the catalog, as is any mapping information among levels, if necessary. Hence, these software modules actually populate the catalog's minidatabase with data, the data being descriptions of database schemas.

2. Query and DML parser and checker: These modules parse queries, DML retrieval statements, and database update statements and check the catalog to determine whether or not all the schema names referenced in these statements are valid. For example, in a relational system a query parser would check that all the relation names specified in the query exist in the catalog and that the attributes specified in the query exist and belong to the appropriate relations. Similarly, in a network system any record types or set types referenced in DML commands are extracted from the catalog, and the DML commands are checked for validity.

3. Query and DML compiler: These compilers need to convert the high-level queries and DML commands into low-level file access commands. The mapping between the conceptual schema and the internal schema file structures is accessed from the catalog during this process. For example, the catalog would include a description of each file and its fields and the correspondences between fields and conceptual-level attributes. Information such as the starting and ending bytes of each field within a record is included in the catalog if it is needed in the low-level file access commands produced by the compiler.

4. Query and DML optimizer: The query optimizer accesses the catalog for implementation information that may be useful to determine the best way to execute a query or DML command (see Chapter 18). For example, the optimizer would access the catalog to check which fields of a relation have hash access structures or

indexes before deciding how to execute a selection or join condition on the relation. Similarly, a set-processing DML command in a network database such as FIND OWNER would check the catalog to determine if an OWNER pointer exists for the member record type or whether it is necessary to trace through NEXT pointers until the owner record is reached.

5. Authorization and security checking: The DBA would have privileged commands to update the authorization and security portion of the catalog (see Chapter 20). All access by a user to a relation or record type would be checked by the DBMS for proper authorization by accessing the catalog.

6. External-to-conceptual mapping of queries and DML commands: Queries and DML commands specified with reference to an external view or schema must be transformed to refer to the conceptual schema before they can be processed by the DBMS. This is accomplished by accessing the catalog description of the view in order to perform the transformation.

Information stored in the catalog is accessed very frequently by practically all the DBMS software modules. The catalog information that we discussed in Sections 17.1 and 17.2 is only the basic information to be included. More sophisticated DBMSs need to store additional information in the catalog. For example, information concerning the number of records of each base relation or record type, the average selectivity of different fields in a base relation, the number of levels in an index, the average number of members in a set instance of a set type, etc. may be used by more sophisticated query optimizers. This information must be automatically updated by the DBMS. In addition, an expanded catalog/data dictionary system may include information that is useful for the database system users, such as design decisions and justifications. As we can see, the catalog is a very important component of any generalized DBMS.

17.4   Summary

In this chapter we discussed the type of information that is included in a DBMS catalog. In Section 17.1 we discussed catalog structure for a relational DBMS and showed how the constructs of the relational model—mainly relations and attributes—can be stored in a catalog. We also discussed how the catalog stores information concerning other relational concepts such as key constraints, indexes, and views and gave a conceptual description—in the form of an EER schema diagram—of the relational model constructs and how they are related to one another.

In Section 17.2 we covered the constructs for network system catalogs and gave a conceptual EER diagram to describe the concepts of the network model. The hierarchical model is discussed in the exercises.

In Section 17.3 we discussed how different DBMS modules access the information stored in a DBMS catalog. We also discussed other types of information that is stored in a catalog.

Review Questions

17.1. What is meant by the term meta-data?

17.2. How are relational DBMS catalogs usually implemented?

17.3. Discuss the types of information included in a relational catalog at the conceptual, internal, and external levels.

17.4. Why do some relational systems combine specification of keys and indexes?

17.5. Discuss the types of information included in a network catalog at the conceptual, internal, and external levels.

17.6. Discuss how some of the different DBMS modules access a catalog and the type of information each accesses.

17.7. Why is it important to have efficient access to a DBMS catalog?

Exercises

17.8. For each of the EER diagrams shown in Figures 17.4 and 17.7, use the mapping algorithms discussed in Chapters 12 and 15 to create an equivalent relational schema. What can each of the relational schemas be used for?

17.9. Write (in English) sample queries against the EER schemas of Figures 17.4 and 17.7 that would retrieve meaningful information about the database schemas from the catalog.

17.10. Using the relational schemas from Exercise 17.8, write the queries you specified in 17.9 in some relational query language (SQL, QUEL, relational algebra).

17.11. Figure 17.8 shows an EER schema diagram to represent the basic information in a catalog for a hierarchical database system. Map this schema to a set of relations, and repeat Exercises 17.9 and 17.10 for this schema.

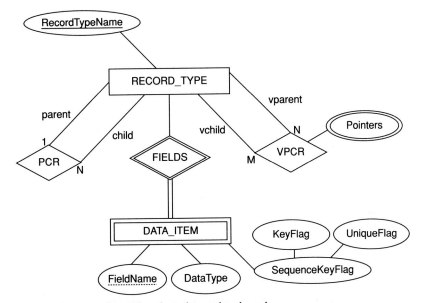

Figure 17.8   ER schema for a basic hierarchical catalog

17.12. Suppose we have a "generalized" DBMS that uses the EER model at the conceptual schema level and relationlike files at the internal level. Draw an EER diagram to represent the basic information for a catalog that represents such an EER database system. First describe the EER concepts as an EER schema (!) and then add mapping information from the conceptual to the internal schema to the catalog.

CHAPTER 18

Query Processing and Optimization

In this chapter we discuss the techniques that are used by a DBMS to process, optimize, and execute high-level queries. A query that is expressed in a high-level query language, such as SQL or QUEL, must first be scanned, parsed, and validated.* The **scanner** identifies the language components (tokens) in the text of a query, while the **parser** checks the syntax of the query to determine whether it is formulated according to the syntax rules (rules of grammar) of the query language. Note that a syntactically correct query must still be validated for being semantically meaningful. An internal representation of a query is then created, usually as a tree or a graph data structure; this is often called a **query tree** or **query graph**. The DBMS must then devise an **execution strategy** for retrieving the result of the query from the internal database files. An execution strategy is a plan for executing the query, accessing the data, and storing the intermediate results. A query typically has many possible execution strategies, and the process of choosing a suitable execution strategy for processing a query is known as **query optimization**.

Figure 18.1 shows the different steps of processing a high-level query. The **query optimizer** module has the task of producing an execution plan and the **code generator** generates the code to execute that plan. The **runtime database processor** has the task of running the query code, whether compiled or interpreted, to produce the query result. If a run time error results, an error message is generated by the runtime database processor.

The term "optimization" is actually a misnomer because in many cases the execution strategy chosen by the DBMS is not the optimal (best) strategy; it is just a **reasonably efficient strategy** for executing the query. Finding the optimal strategy is usually too time consuming except for the simplest of queries and may require information on how the

---

*We will not discuss the parsing and syntax-checking phase of query processing here; this material is discussed in most compiler textbooks.

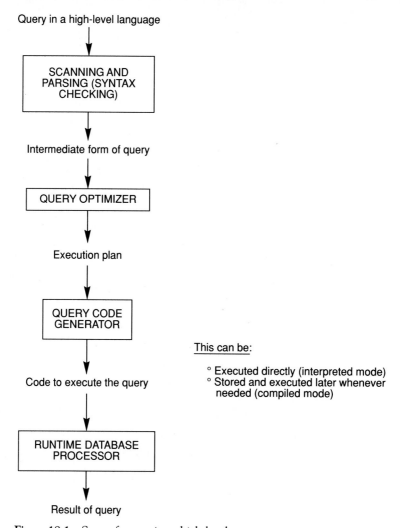

Figure 18.1   Steps of processing a high-level query

files are implemented and even the contents of the files. This information may not be available in the DBMS catalog. Hence, the term "planning of an execution strategy" may be more accurate than "query optimization" for the material discussed in this chapter.

Note that for lower-level navigational database languages, such as the network DML or the hierarchical HDML languages, the programmer must choose the query execution strategy while writing a database program. Hence, in a DBMS that provides only a navigational language, there is *no need or opportunity* for extensive query optimization by the DBMS; rather, the programmer is given the capability to choose the "optimal" execution strategy. On the other hand, a high-level relational query is more declarative in nature—it specifies what the intended result of the query is rather than the details of how the result should be obtained. Hence, query optimization is necessary for high-level relational queries and provides an opportunity for the DBMS to systematically evaluate alternative query execution strategies and to choose an optimal strategy. However, this optimization may itself be expensive and time consuming.

Each DBMS typically has a number of general database access routines, which are written to implement relational operations such as SELECT or JOIN or to implement combinations of these operations. An execution strategy is usually implemented by calling one or more of these access routines. Only strategies that can be implemented by the DBMS access routines and apply to the particular database design can be considered by the query optimization module of a DBMS. We discuss different methods of implementing access routines for processing a query in Section 18.1.

There are two main techniques for query optimization. The first approach is based on **heuristic rules** for ordering the operations in a query execution strategy. The rules typically reorder the operations in a query tree (defined in Section 18.2.1) or determine an order for executing the operations specified by a query graph (defined in Section 18.2.2). The second approach is to **systematically estimate** the cost of different execution strategies and choose the execution plan with the lowest cost estimate. The main cost considered is execution time. The two strategies are usually combined to some extent in a query optimizer. We discuss heuristic optimization methods in Section 18.2 and systematic optimization techniques in Section 18.3.

18.1 Access Routines for Query Processing

A relational DBMS, or a nonrelational DBMS with a high-level relational query language interface, must include **methods,** or **algorithms,** for implementing the types of relational operations that can appear in a query execution strategy. These include the basic relational algebra operations discussed in Chapter 6 and, in many cases, combinations of these operations. In addition, the DBMS must have available methods for processing special operations such as aggregation functions and grouping. For each such operation or combination of operations, one or more **access routines** are written to execute the operation. An access routine may apply to particular storage structures and access paths and in this case can be used only if the files involved in the operation include these access paths. In this section we discuss typical algorithms used by access routines to implement SELECT, JOIN, and other relational operations.

18.1.1 Implementing the SELECT Operation

There are many options for executing a SELECT operation; some options depend on the file having specific access paths and may apply to only some types of selection conditions. Appendix C discusses the performance of the SELECT operation under different types of conditions and various types of access paths. We discuss some of the options for implementing SELECT in this section. We will use the following operations, specified on the relational database of Figure 6.5, to illustrate our discussion.

$$(OP1): \sigma_{SSN=123456789}(EMPLOYEE)$$
$$(OP2): \sigma_{DNUMBER>5}(DEPARTMENT)$$

$$(OP3): \sigma_{DNO=5}(EMPLOYEE)$$
$$(OP4): \sigma_{DNO=5 \text{ AND } SALARY>30000 \text{ AND } SEX=F}(EMPLOYEE)$$
$$(OP5): \sigma_{ESSN=123456789 \text{ AND } PNO=10}(WORKS\_ON)$$

Search Methods for Selection

S1. **Linear search (brute force):** Retrieve *every record* in the file and test whether or not its attribute values satisfy the selection condition.

S2. **Binary search:** If the selection condition involves an equality comparison on a key attribute on which the file is ordered, binary search, which is more efficient than linear search, can be used. An example is OP1 if SSN is the ordering attribute.

S3. **Using a primary index or hash key to retrieve a single record:** If the selection condition involves an equality comparison on a key attribute with a primary index or a hash key—for example, SSN = 123456789 in OP1—we use the primary index or the hash key to retrieve the record.

S4. **Using a primary index to retrieve multiple records:** If the comparison condition is $>$, $\geq$, $<$, $\leq$ on a key field with a primary index—for example, DNUMBER $>$ 5 in OP2—we use the index to find the record satisfying the corresponding equality condition (DNUMBER = 5) and then retrieve all the subsequent records in the (ordered) file. For the condition DNUMBER $<$ 5 we retrieve all the preceding records.

S5. **Using a clustering index to retrieve multiple records:** If the selection condition involves an equality comparison on a nonkey attribute with a clustering index—for example, DNO = 5 in OP3—we use the clustering index to retrieve all the records satisfying the selection condition.

S6. **Using a secondary (B^+-tree) index:** On an equality comparison, this can be used to retrieve a single record if the indexing field has unique values (is a key) or multiple records if the indexing field is not a key. In addition, it can be used to retrieve records on conditions involving $>$, $\geq$, $<$, $\leq$.

Appendix C shows how to estimate the access cost of these selection methods in terms of number of block accesses and access time. Method S1 applies to any file, but all the other methods depend on having the appropriate access path on the attributes involved in the selection condition.

If a condition of a SELECT operation is a **conjunctive condition**—that is, made up of several simple conditions connected with the AND logical connective, such as OP4 above—the DBMS can use the following additional methods to implement the operation:

S7. **Conjunctive selection:** If an attribute involved in any single simple condition in the conjunctive condition has an access path that permits the use of one of the methods S2 to S6, we use that condition to retrieve the records and then check whether or not each retrieved record satisfies the remaining conditions in the conjunctive condition.

S8. **Conjunctive selection using a composite index:** If two or more attributes are involved in equality conditions in the conjunctive condition and a composite index exists on the combined fields—for example, if an index has been created on the composite key (ESSN, PNO) of the WORKS_ON file for OP5—we can use the index directly.

S9. Conjunctive selection by intersection of record pointers*: This method is possible if secondary indexes are available on all the fields involved in equality comparison conditions in the conjunctive condition and the indexes include record pointers (rather than block pointers). Each index can be used to retrieve the record pointers that satisfy the individual condition. The *intersection* of these sets of record pointers gives the record pointers that satisfy the conjunctive condition. The pointers resulting from the intersection can then be used to retrieve those records directly. A variation of this method can also be used if only some of the conditions have secondary indexes, in which case each retrieved record is further tested for whether or not it satisfies the remaining conditions.

Whenever a single condition specifies the selection—such as OP1, OP2, and OP3—we can only check whether or not an access path exists on the attribute involved in that condition. If an access path exists, we may use the method corresponding to that access path; otherwise, we must use the "brute force" linear search approach of method S1. Query optimization for a SELECT operation is needed mostly for conjunctive select conditions whenever *more than one* of the attributes involved in the conditions have an access path. The optimizer must then choose the access path that *retrieves the fewest records* in the most efficient way.

In choosing between multiple simple conditions in a conjunctive select condition, we have to consider the **selectivity** of each condition, which is defined as the ratio of the number of records (tuples) that satisfy the condition to the total number of records (tuples) in the file (relation). This is the probability that a record satisfies the condition if we assume uniform distribution of values. The smaller the selectivity, the fewer tuples are selected by the condition and the higher the desirability of using that condition first to retrieve records. Although exact selectivities of all conditions may not be available, *estimates of selectivities* are often kept in the DBMS catalog and used by the optimizer. For example, the selectivity of an equality condition on a key attribute of relation $r(R)$ is $1/|r(R)|$, where $|r(R)|$ is the number of tuples in relation $r(R)$. The selectivity of an equality condition on an attribute with i *distinct values* is often estimated by $(|r(R)|/i)/|r(R)|$ or $1/i$ by assuming that the records are evenly distributed among the distinct values. Under this assumption, $|r(R)|/i$ records will satisfy an equality condition on this attribute.

Compared to a conjunctive selection condition, a **disjunctive condition,** where simple conditions are connected by the OR logical connective rather than AND, are much harder to process and optimize. For example, consider OP4':

$$(OP4'): \sigma_{\text{DNO=5 OR SALARY>30000 OR SEX=F}}(\text{EMPLOYEE})$$

With such a condition, little optimization can be done because the records satisfying the disjunctive condition are the *union* of the records satisfying the individual condi-

---

*A record pointer uniquely identifies a record and provides the address of the record on disk; hence, it is sometimes called the **record identifier** or **record id.**

tions. Hence, if any *one* of the conditions does not have an access path, we are compelled to use the brute force linear search approach. Only if an access path exists on *every* condition in the disjunctive condition can we optimize the selection by retrieving the records satisfying each condition and then applying the union operation to eliminate duplicate records. Notice that implementing the UNION operation can be expensive (see Section 18.1.4). We could also apply the union to record pointers rather than records if the appropriate access paths to provide record pointers exist for every condition.

A DBMS will have many of the methods discussed above implemented as database access routines. The query optimizer must choose the appropriate routine for executing each SELECT operation in a query tree, unless the SELECT operation is executed within some other access routine that combines the execution of several operations (see Section 18.1.5).

18.1.2   *Implementing the* JOIN *Operation*

The JOIN operation is one of the most time-consuming operations in query processing. Most of the join operations encountered in queries are of the EQUIJOIN and NATURAL JOIN variety, so we consider only these two types here. For the remainder of this chapter, the term **join** refers to an EQUIJOIN (or NATURAL JOIN) unless we specifically state otherwise. There are many possible ways to implement a **two-way join,** which is a join on two files. Joins involving more than two files are called **multiway joins.** The number of possible ways to execute multiway joins grows very rapidly. In the following we discuss some of the techniques for implementing two-way joins. To illustrate our discussion, we refer to the relational schema of Figure 6.5 once more, specifically to the EMPLOYEE, DEPARTMENT, and PROJECT relations. The algorithms we consider are for join operations of the form

$$R \bowtie_{A=B} S$$

where A and B are domain-compatible attributes of R and S, respectively. The methods we discuss can be extended to more general forms of join. We illustrate three of the most common techniques for performing such a join using the following example operations:

$$(\text{OP6}): \text{EMPLOYEE} \bowtie_{\text{DNO=DNUMBER}} \text{DEPARTMENT}$$
$$(\text{OP7}): \text{DEPARTMENT} \bowtie_{\text{MGRSSN=SSN}} \text{EMPLOYEE}$$

Methods for Implementing Joins

J1. **Nested (inner-outer) loop** approach (brute force): For each record t in R(outer loop), retrieve every record s from S (inner loop) and test whether or not the two records satisfy the join condition t[A] = s[B].

J2. Using an **access structure to retrieve the matching record(s):** If an index or hash key exists for one of the two join attributes, say B of S, we can retrieve each record t in R, one at a time, and then use the access structure to retrieve directly all the matching records s from S that satisfy s[B] = t[A].

J3. **Sort-merge join:** If the records of R and S are *physically sorted* (ordered) by value of the join attributes A and B, respectively, we can implement the join in the most efficient way possible. Both files are scanned in order of the join attributes, matching the records that have the same values for A and B. In this method, the records of each file are scanned only once each for matching with the other file, unless both A and B are nonkey attributes, in which case the method needs to be modified slightly. A sketch of the sort-merge join algorithm is given in Figure 18.2a, where we assume the records (tuples) in a file (relation) R are physically ordered on the join attributes. We use R(i) to refer to the ith record in R. A variation of the sort-merge join can be used when secondary indexes exist on both join attributes. The indexes provide the ability to access the records in order of the join attributes but the records themselves are

(a) sort the tuples in R on attribute A; (* assume R has n tuples (records) *)
sort the tuples in S on attribute B; (* assume S has m tuples (records) *)
set i←1, j←1 ;
while (i ≤ n) and (j ≤ m)
do{   if R(i)[A] > S(j)[B]
            then   set j←j+1
        elseif R(i)[A] < S(j)[B]
            then   set i←i+1
            else   { (* R(i)[A]=S(j)[B] , so we output a matched tuple *)
                output the combined tuple <R(i) , S(j)> to T;
                   (* output other tuples that match R(i) , if any *)
                   set l←j+1 ;
                   while (l ≤ m) and (R(i)[A]=S(l)[B])
                   do   {   output the combined tuple <R(i) , S(l)> to T ;
                                set l←l+1
                   }
                   (* output other tuples that match S(j) , if any *)
                   set k←i+1 ;
                   while (k ≤ n) and (R(k)[A]=S(j)[B])
                   do   {   output the combined tuple <R(k) , S(j)> to T ;
                                  set k←k+1
                   }
                   set i←i+1, j←j+1
            }
  }

(b) create a tuple t[<attribute list>] in T' for each tuple t in R;
      (* T' contains the projection result <u>before</u> duplicate elimination *)
    if <attribute list> includes a key of R
      then T ← T'
      else   {   sort the tuples in T';
                set i←1, j←2;
                while i ≤ n
                   do   {   output the tuple T'[i] to T;
                         while T'[i] = T'[j] do j←j+1; (* eliminate duplicates *)
                         i←j ; j←i+1
                   }
        }
    (* T contains the projection result after duplicate elimination *)

Figure 18.2 Implementing the JOIN, PROJECT, UNION, INTERSECTION, and SET DIFFERENCE operations by sorting. (a) Implementing the operation T←R ⋈ $_{A=B}$S, where R has n tuples and S has m tuples. (b) Implementing the operation T←π$_{<attribute list>}$ (R) where R has n tuples. *(continued on next page)*

(c)   sort the tuples in R and S using the same unique sort attributes;
       set i←1, j←1;
       while (i ≤ n) and (j ≤ m)
       do   {   if R(i) > S(j)
                 then   {   output S(j) to T;
                              set j←j+1
                         }
                 elseif R(i) < S(j)
                 then   {   output R(i) to T;
                              set i←i+1
                         }
                 else set j←j+1 (* R(i)=S(j) , so we skip one of the duplicate tuples *)
            }
       if (i ≤ n) then add tuples R(i) to R(n) to T;
       if (j ≤ m) then add tuples S(j) to S(m) to T;

(d)   sort the tuples in R and S using the same unique sort attributes;
       set i←1, j←1;
       while (i ≤ n) and (j ≤ m)
       do   {   if R(i) > S(j)
                 then   set j←j+1
                 elseif R(i) < S(j)
                 then   set i←i+1
                 else   {   output R(i) to T ; (* R(i)=S(j) , so we output the tuple *)
                             set i←i+1, j←j+1
                         }
            }

(e)   sort the tuples in R and S using the same unique sort attributes;
       set i←1, j←1;
       while (i ≤ n) and (j ≤ m)
       do   {   if R(i) > S(j)
                 then   set j←j+1
                 elseif R(i) < S(j)
                 then   {   output R(i) to T; (* R(i) has no matching S(j), so output R(i) *)
                             set i←i+1
                         }
                 else   set i←i+1, j←j+1
            }
       if (i ≤ n) then add tuples R(i) to R(n) to T ;

Figure 18.2   *(continued)* (c) Implementing the operation T←R ∪ S, where R has n tuples and S has m tuples. (d) Implementing the operation T←R ∩ S, where R has n tuples and S has m tuples. (e) Implementing the operation T←R – S, where R has n tuples and S has m tuples.

physically scattered all over the file blocks, so this method may be quite ineffi-cient as every record access may involve accessing a disk block.

J4. **Hash-join:** The records (or record pointers) of both files R and S are hashed to the *same hash file* using the *same hashing function* on the join attributes A of R and B of S as hash keys. A single pass through each file hashes the records (or record pointers) to the hash file buckets. Each bucket is then examined for records from R and S with matching join attribute values to produce the result of the join operation.

In practice, techniques J1 to J3 are implemented by accessing whole blocks of a file rather than individual records. The records in the blocks are then matched. Depending on the available buffer space in memory, the number of blocks that are read in from the file can be adjusted. In the nested-loop approach (J1), it makes a difference which file is chosen for the outer loop and which for the inner loop. To illustrate this, consider OP6 and assume that the DEPARTMENT file consists of r_D = 50 records stored in b_D = 10 disk blocks and the EMPLOYEE file consists of r_E = 5000 records stored in b_E = 2000 disk blocks. Also, assume that n_B = 6 blocks (buffers) in main memory are available for implementing the join method. It is advantageous to read as many blocks as possible at a time into memory from the file whose records are used for the outer loop (n_B – 1 blocks) and one block at a time for the inner-loop file. This reduces the total number of block accesses.

If we use EMPLOYEE as the outer loop, we read each block of the EMPLOYEE file once and the entire DEPARTMENT file (each of its blocks) once for *each time* we read in n_B – 1 blocks of the EMPLOYEE file. We get

Total number of blocks accessed for outer file = b_E

Number of times (n_B – 1) blocks of the outer file are loaded = $\lceil b_E/(n_B - 1) \rceil$

Total number of blocks accessed for inner file = $b_D * \lceil (b_E/(n_B - 1)) \rceil$

Hence, we get the following total number of block accesses:

$b_E + (\lceil (b_E/(n_B - 1)) \rceil * b_D) = 2000 + (\lceil (2000/5) \rceil * 10) = 6000$ block accesses

On the other hand, if we use the DEPARTMENT records in the outer loop, by symmetry we get the following total number of block accesses:

$b_D + (\lceil (b_D/(n_B - 1)) \rceil * b_E) = 10 + (\lceil (10/5) \rceil * 2000) = 4010$ block accesses

As we can see, it is advantageous to use the file *with fewer blocks as the outer-loop file* in method J1 if more than two buffers exist in memory for implementing the join. Hence, the *size* of the files being joined directly affects the performance of the different join techniques.

Another factor that greatly affects the performance of join, particularly method J2, is the percentage of records in a file that will be joined with records in the other file. We call this the **join selection factor** of a file with respect to an equijoin condition with another file. This factor depends not only on the two files to be joined but also on the join fields in case there are multiple equijoin conditions between the two files.

To illustrate this, consider the operation OP7, which joins each DEPARTMENT record with the EMPLOYEE record of the manager of that department. Here, each DEPARTMENT record (50 records in our example) is expected to be joined to a single EMPLOYEE record, but many EMPLOYEE records (4950 of them in our example) will not be joined. Suppose secondary indexes exist on both the attributes SSN of EMPLOYEE and MGRSSN of DEPARTMENT, with the number of index levels x_{SSN} = 4 and x_{MGRSSN} = 2, respectively. We have two options to implement method J2. The first retrieves each EMPLOYEE record and then uses the index on MGRSSN of DEPARTMENT to find a matching DEPARTMENT record. In this case, no matching record will be found for employees who do not manage a department. The number of block accesses for this case is approximately

$b_E + (r_E * (x_{MGRSSN} + 1)) = 2000 + (5000 * 3) = 17,000$ block accesses

The second option first retrieves each DEPARTMENT record and then uses the index on SSN of EMPLOYEE to find a matching EMPLOYEE record. In this case, every DEPARTMENT record will have one matching EMPLOYEE record. The number of block accesses for this case is approximately

$$b_D + (r_D*(x_{SSN}+1)) = 10 + (50*5) = 260 \text{ block accesses}$$

It is clear that the second option is more efficient because the join selection factor of DEPARTMENT with respect to the join condition SSN = MGRSSN is 1, whereas the selection factor of EMPLOYEE with respect to the same join condition is (50/5000). For method J2, the file that has a match for every record (high join selection factor) should be used to retrieve each record (outer loop), while the index is used to retrieve matching records from the file with only a small percentage of its records participating in the join (low join selection factor). In some cases an index may be created specifically for performing the join operation if one does not exist.

Merge-join method J3 is quite efficient. In this case, only a single pass is made through both files. Hence, the number of blocks accessed is equal to the sum of the numbers of blocks in both files. However, both files must be sorted on the join attribute. For this method both OP6 and OP7 would need $b_E + b_D = 2000 + 10 = 2010$ block accesses. However both files are required to be ordered by the join attributes; if one or both are not, they may be sorted specifically for performing the join operation.

Hash-join method J4 is also quite efficient. In this case only a single pass is made through both files, whether or not they are ordered, to produce the hash file entries. If record pointers are used, the hash file can be kept in main memory, but then the records in the two files need to be accessed while combining records to produce the result of the join. If whole records are stored, the hash file must be stored on disk and accessed while combining records to produce the result of the join.

18.1.3   Implementing the PROJECT Operation

A PROJECT operation $\pi_{<attribute\ list>}(R)$ is straightforward to implement if <attribute list> includes a key of relation R, because in this case the result of the operation will have the same number of tuples as R, but with only the values for attributes in <attribute list> in each tuple. If <attribute list> does not include a key of R, then duplicate tuples must be eliminated. This is usually done by sorting the result of the operation and then eliminating duplicate tuples, which appear consecutively after sorting. Figure 18.2b sketches the implementation of the PROJECT operation.

Hashing can also be used to eliminate duplicates; as each record is hashed and inserted into a bucket of the hash file, it is checked against those already in the bucket and if it is a duplicate it is not inserted in the bucket.

18.1.4   Implementing Set Operations

Set operations—UNION, INTERSECTION, SET DIFFERENCE, CARTESIAN PRODUCT—are sometimes expensive to implement. In particular, the Cartesian product operation R X S is quite expensive because the result of the operation includes a record for each combination of records from R and S. In addition, the attributes of the result include all attributes of R and S. If R has n records and j attributes and S has m records and k attributes, the resulting relation will have n * m records and j + k attributes. Hence, it is important to avoid the CARTESIAN PRODUCT operation and to substitute other equivalent operations during query optimization (see Section 18.2).

The other three set operations—UNION, INTERSECTION, and SET DIFFERENCE—apply only to union-compatible relations, which have the same attributes. The customary way to implement these operations is to sort the two relations on the same attributes. After sorting, a single scan through each relation is sufficient to produce the result. For example, we can implement R ∪ S by scanning both sorted files concurrently, and whenever we encounter the same tuple on both relations we keep only one of those in the result. For R ∩ S, we keep in the result only the tuples that appear in both relations. Figures 18.2c to e sketch the implementation of these operations by sorting and scanning. If sorting is done on unique key attributes, the operations are further simplified.

Hashing can also be used to implement UNION, INTERSECTION, and SET DIFFERENCE by hashing both files to the same hash file buckets. For example, to implement R ∪ S, we first hash the records of R to the hash file; then, while hashing the records of S, we do not insert duplicate records. To implement R ∩ S, we first hash the records of R to the hash file. We do not insert records of S in the hash file; rather, while hashing each record of S, if we find an identical record in the bucket, we mark that tuple. Only the marked tuples will appear in the result. To implement R – S, we first hash the records of R to the hash file. We do not insert records of S in the hash file; rather, while hashing each record of S, if we find an identical record in the bucket, we remove that tuple.

18.1.5 Combining Operations in Access Routines

So far, we have assumed that there is a single access routine available in the DBMS for each relational algebra operation. This routine is invoked to execute that operation when needed, creating a new **temporary** file to hold the tuples in the result of the operation. Typically, a query specified in the relational algebra will consist of a sequence of operations. If we always execute a single operation at a time, we must generate as many temporary files as there are operations. Many of these temporary files will be used as input files to subsequent operations. Generating and storing a large temporary file on disk is time consuming. To reduce the number of temporary files, it is common to have access routines for *combinations of operations* that occur frequently and can be implemented efficiently.

For example, rather than implementing a JOIN separately, we can combine it with two SELECT operations on the input files and a final PROJECT operation on the resulting file; all this is implemented by one access routine with two input files and a single output file. Rather than having four temporary files, we apply the access routine directly and get just one result file. In Section 18.2.1 we will discuss how heuristic relational algebra optimization can group together operations for execution by such access routines.

18.2   Heuristic Optimization

In this section we discuss optimization techniques that apply heuristic rules to modify the internal representation of a query—which is usually in the form of a tree or a graph data structure—to improve its expected performance on execution. The parser of a high-level query generates the internal representation, which is then optimized using heuristic rules. Following that, access routines to execute groups of operations based on the access paths available on the files are chosen by the query optimizer.

The main **heuristic rule** is to apply SELECT and PROJECT operations *before* applying the JOIN or other binary operations. This is because the size of the file resulting from a binary operation is a function of the sizes of the input files, in some cases a multiplicative function. The SELECT and PROJECT operations typically reduce the size of a single file and never increase its size. Hence, before applying a join or other binary operation, it is advantageous to reduce the sizes of the input files.

In Section 18.2.1 we introduce the query tree notation, which is used to represent a relational algebra expression. We then show how heuristic optimization rules are applied to convert the tree into an **equivalent** query tree, which represents a relational algebra expression that is more efficient to execute but gives the same result as the original one. Then, in Section 18.2.2, we introduce the query graph notation, which is used to represent a relational calculus expression. We then show how heuristic rules can be applied to the query graph to produce an efficient execution strategy.

18.2.1 Heuristic Optimization of Query Trees (Relational Algebra)

A **query tree** is a tree structure that corresponds to a relational algebra expression by representing the relations as *leaf nodes* of the tree and the relational algebra operations as *internal nodes*. An **execution of the query tree** consists of executing an internal node operation whenever its operands are available and then replacing that internal node by the relation that results from executing the operation. The execution terminates when the root node is executed and replaced by the relation that is the result of the relational algebra expression.

Figure 18.3a shows a query tree for query Q2 of Chapters 6 to 9: For every project located in 'Stafford', retrieve the project number, the controlling department number, and the department manager's lastname, address, and birthdate. This query is specified on the relational schema of Figure 6.5 and corresponds to the relational algebra expression (recall that * stands for NATURAL JOIN):

$$\pi_{\text{PNUMBER,DNUM,LNAME,ADDRESS,BDATE}} (((\sigma_{\text{PLOCATION='Stafford'}}(\text{PROJECT}))$$
$$*_{\text{DNUM=DNUMBER}} (\text{DEPARTMENT})) *_{\text{MGRSSN=SSN}} (\text{EMPLOYEE}))$$

This corresponds to the following SQL query:

Q2: **SELECT** PNUMBER, DNUM, LNAME, BDATE, ADDRESS
      FROM PROJECT, DEPARTMENT, EMPLOYEE
      WHERE DNUM=DNUMBER **AND** MGRSSN=SSN **AND**
              PLOCATION='Stafford'

In Figure 18.3a the three relations PROJECT, DEPARTMENT, and EMPLOYEE are represented by leaf nodes in the tree, while the relational algebra operations of the expression are represented by internal tree nodes. When executing this query tree, the node marked (1) in Figure 18.3a is executed before node (2) because the temporary file corresponding to the result of operation (1) must be available before we can execute operation (2). Similarly, node (2) must be executed before node (3), and so on.

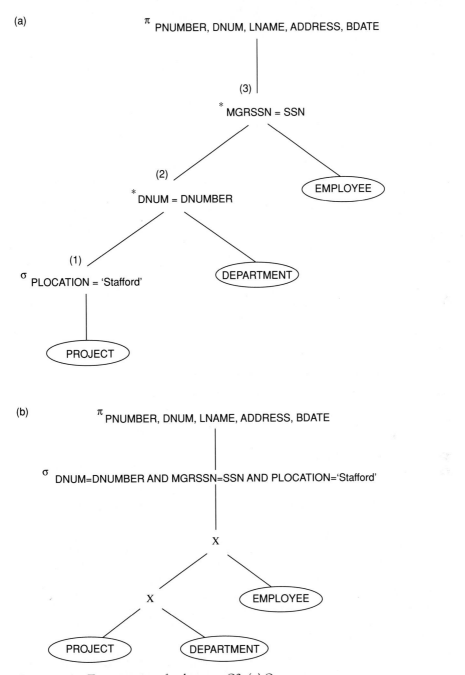

Figure 18.3 Two query trees for the query Q2. (a) Query tree corresponding to the relational algebra expression for Q2. (b) Initial (canonical) query tree for SQL query Q2.

In general, many different relational algebra expressions—and hence query trees—can be equivalent, that is, correspond to the same query. A query may also be stated in various ways in a high-level query language such as SQL (see Chapter 7). The query parser will typically generate a standard **canonical** query tree to correspond to an SQL query, without doing any optimization. For example, for a **select-project-join** query, such as Q2 given above, the query parser can generate the tree shown in Figure 18.3b, which takes the Cartesian product of the relations specified in the FROM-clause and then applies the selection condition of the WHERE-clause followed by the projection on the SELECT-clause attributes.

Such a canonical query tree represents a relational algebra expression that is very inefficient if executed directly because of the Cartesian product operations. For example, if the PROJECT, DEPARTMENT, and EMPLOYEE relations had record sizes of 100, 50, and 150 bytes and contained 100, 20, and 5000 tuples, respectively, the result of the Cartesian product would contain 10 million tuples of record size 300 bytes each. However, the query tree is in a simple standard form. It is now the job of the heuristic query optimizer to transform this **initial query tree** into a **final query tree** that is efficient to execute. The optimizer must include rules for equivalence among relational algebra expressions that can be applied to the initial tree, guided by the heuristic query optimization rules, to produce the final optimized query tree. We first discuss informally how a query tree is transformed using heuristics into an equivalent query tree that represents a more efficient execution strategy. Then we discuss general transformation rules (guidelines) and show how they may be used in an algebraic heuristic optimizer.

Example of Transforming a Query

Consider a query Q: Find the last names of employees born after 1957 who work on a project named "Aquarius," which refers to the database of Figure 6.5. This query can be specified in SQL as follows:

Q: **SELECT**   LNAME
        FROM   EMPLOYEE, WORKS_ON, PROJECT
        WHERE   PNAME='Aquarius' **AND** PNUMBER=PNO **AND** ESSN=SSN **AND**
                  BDATE>'DEC-31-1957'

The initial query tree for Q is shown in Figure 18.4a. Executing this tree directly will first create a very large file containing the Cartesian product of the entire EMPLOYEE, WORKS_ON, and PROJECT files. However, we need only one PROJECT record—for the 'Aquarius' project—and only the EMPLOYEE records for those whose birthdate is after 'DEC-31-1957'. Figure 18.4b shows an improved query tree that first applies the SELECT operations to reduce the number of tuples that appear in the Cartesian product.

A further improvement is achieved by switching the positions of the EMPLOYEE and PROJECT relations in the tree, as shown in Figure 18.4c. This uses the information that PNUMBER is a key attribute of the PROJECT relation, and hence the SELECT operation on the PROJECT relation will retrieve a single record only. We can further improve the query tree by replacing any CARTESIAN PRODUCT operation that is followed by a join condition with a JOIN operation, as shown in Figure 18.4d; this eliminates some Cartesian product operations that typically produce large files. Another improvement is to keep only the attributes needed by subsequent operations in the temporary intermediate rela-

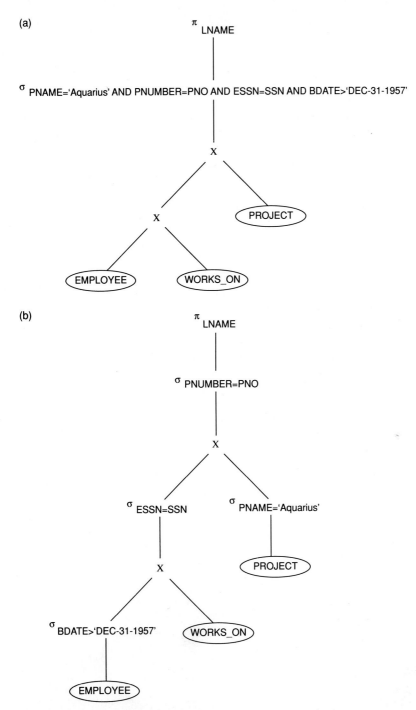

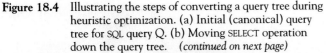

Figure 18.4 Illustrating the steps of converting a query tree during heuristic optimization. (a) Initial (canonical) query tree for SQL query Q. (b) Moving SELECT operation down the query tree. *(continued on next page)*

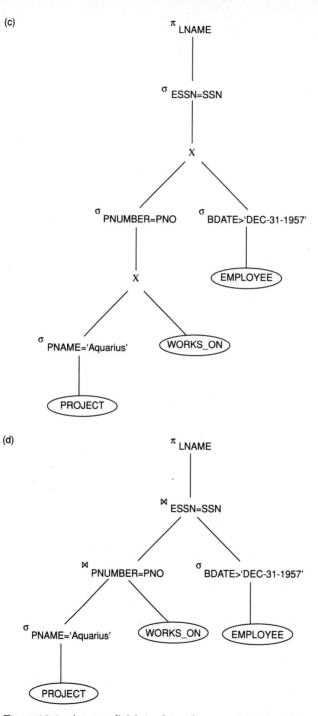

Figure 18.4 *(continued)* (c) Applying the more restrictive SELECT operation first. (d) Replacing CARTESIAN PRODUCT and SELECT with JOIN operations. *(continued on next page)*

(e)

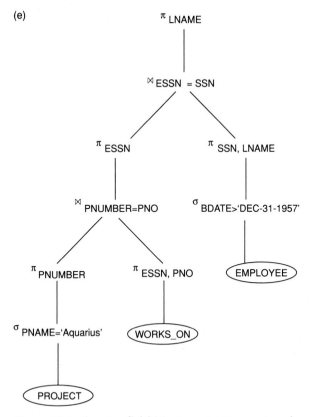

Figure 18.4 *(continued)* (e) Moving PROJECT operations down the query tree.

tions by including PROJECT operations as early as possible in the query tree, as shown in Figure 18.4e. This reduces the attributes (columns) of the intermediate temporary relations, whereas the SELECT operations reduce the number of tuples (records) only.

As we can see from the above example, we can convert a query tree step by step into another query tree that is more efficient to execute. However, we must make sure that the conversion steps always lead to a query tree that is equivalent to the original one. To do this, we must know which transformation rules *preserve this equivalence*. We discuss some of these transformation rules next.

General Transformation Rules for Relational Algebra Operations

There are many rules for transforming relational algebra operations into equivalent ones. Here we are interested in the meaning of the operations and the resulting relations. Hence, if two relations have the same set of attributes in a *different order* but the two relations represent the same information, we will consider that the relations are equivalent. In Section 6.1.2 we gave an alternative definition of relation that makes order of attributes unimportant; we will assume this definition of relation here. We now state some transformation rules without proving them.

1. Cascade of σ: A conjunctive selection condition can be broken up into a cascade (sequence) of individual σ operations.

$$\sigma_{c1 \text{ AND } c2 \text{ AND } ... \text{ AND } cn}(R) \equiv \sigma_{c1} (\sigma_{c2} (...(\sigma_{cn}(R))...))$$

2. Commutativity of σ: The σ operation is commutative.

$$\sigma_{c1} (\sigma_{c2}(R)) \equiv \sigma_{c2} (\sigma_{c1}(R))$$

3. Cascade of π: In a cascade (sequence) of π operations, all but the last one can be ignored.

$$\pi_{List1} (\pi_{List2} (...(\pi_{Listn}(R))...)) = \pi_{List1}(R)$$

4. Commuting σ with π: If the selection condition c involves only the attributes $A1, ..., An$ in the projection list, the two operations can be commuted.

$$\pi_{A1, A2, ..., An} (\sigma_c (R)) \equiv \sigma_c (\pi_{A1, A2, ..., An} (R))$$

5. Commutativity of $\bowtie$ (or X): The $\bowtie$ operation is commutative.

$$R \bowtie_c S \equiv S \bowtie_c R$$

Note that although the order of attributes may not be the same in the relations resulting from the two joins, the "meaning" is the same because order of attributes is not important in the alternative definition of relation that we use here. The X operation is commutative in the same sense as the $\bowtie$ operation.

6. Commuting σ with $\bowtie$ (or X): If all the attributes in the selection condition c involve only the attributes of one of the relations being joined, say R, the two operations can be commuted as follows:

$$\sigma_c (R \bowtie S) \equiv (\sigma_c (R)) \bowtie S$$

Alternatively, if the selection condition c can be written as (c1 and c2), where condition c1 involves only the attributes of R and condition c2 involves only the attributes of S, the operations commute as follows:

$$\sigma_c (R \bowtie S) \equiv (\sigma_{c1} (R)) \bowtie (\sigma_{c2} (S))$$

The same rules apply if the $\bowtie$ is replaced by a X operation. These transformations are very useful during heuristic optimization.

7. Commuting π with $\bowtie$ (or X): Suppose the projection list is $L = \{A1, ..., An, B1, ..., Bm\}$, where $A1, ..., An$ are attributes of R and $B1, ..., Bm$ are attributes of S. If the join condition c involves only attributes in L, the two operations can be commuted as follows:

$$\pi_L (R \bowtie_c S) \equiv (\pi_{A1, ..., An} (R)) \bowtie_c (\pi_{B1, ..., Bm} (S))$$

If the join condition c contains additional attributes not in L, these must be added to the projection list and a final π operation is needed. For example, if attributes $An + 1, ..., An + k$ of R and $Bm + 1, ..., Bm + p$ of S are involved in the join condition but are not in the projection list L, the operations commute as follows:

$$\pi_L (R \bowtie_c S) \equiv$$
$$\pi_L ((\pi_{A1,...,An,An+1,...,An+k} (R)) \bowtie_c (\pi_{B1,...,Bm,Bm+1,...,Bm+p} (S)))$$

For X, there is no condition c so the first transformation rule always applies by replacing $\bowtie_c$ with **X**.

8. Commutativity of set operations: The set operations $\cup$ and $\cap$ are commutative but $-$ is not.

9. Associativity of $\bowtie$, **X**, $\cup$, and $\cap$: These four operations are individually associative; that is, if θ stands for any *one* of these four operations (throughout the expression), we have

$$(R \, \theta \, S) \, \theta \, T \equiv R \, \theta \, (S \, \theta \, T)$$

10. Commuting σ with set operations: The σ operation commutes with $\cup$, $\cap$, and $-$. If θ stands for any *one* of these three operations, we have

$$\sigma_c (R \, \theta \, S) \equiv (\sigma_c (R)) \, \theta \, (\sigma_c (S))$$

11. Commuting π with set operations: The π operation commutes with $\cup$, $\cap$, and $-$. If θ stands for any one of these three operations, we have

$$\pi_L (R \, \theta \, S) \equiv (\pi_L (R)) \, \theta \, (\pi_L (S))$$

12. Other transformations: There are other possible transformations. For example, a selection or join condition c can be converted to an equivalent condition using the rules known as DeMorgan's laws. These are:

$$c \equiv \mathbf{NOT} (c1 \, \mathbf{AND} \, c2) \equiv (\mathbf{NOT} \, c1) \, \mathbf{OR} \, (\mathbf{NOT} \, c2)$$
$$c \equiv \mathbf{NOT} (c1 \, \mathbf{OR} \, c2) \equiv (\mathbf{NOT} \, c1) \, \mathbf{AND} \, (\mathbf{NOT} \, c2)$$

Additional transformations discussed in Chapter 6 are not repeated here. These rules are summarized in Appendix D.

We discuss next how these rules are used in heuristic optimization.

Outline of a Heuristic Algebraic Optimization Algorithm

We can now outline the steps of an algorithm that utilizes some of the above rules to transform an initial query tree into an optimized tree that is more efficient to execute (in most cases). The steps of the algorithm will lead to transformations similar to those discussed in our example of Figure 18.4. The steps of the algorithm are as follows:

1. Using rule 1, break up any SELECT operations with conjunctive conditions into a cascade of SELECT operations. This permits a greater degree of freedom in moving select operations down different branches of the tree.

2. Using rules 2, 4, 6, and 10 concerning commutativity of SELECT with other operations, move each SELECT operation as far down the query tree as is permitted by the attributes involved in the select condition.

3. Using rule 9 concerning associativity of binary operations, rearrange the leaf nodes of the tree so that the leaf node relations with the most restrictive SELECT operations are executed first in the query tree representation. By most restrictive SELECT operations, we mean the ones that produce a relation with the fewest number of tuples or with the smallest absolute size. Either definition can be used since these rules are heuristic. Another possibility is to define most restrictive SELECT as the one with the smallest selectivity; this is more practical because estimated selectivities are often available in the catalog.

4. Combine a CARTESIAN PRODUCT operation with a subsequent SELECT operation whose condition represents a join condition into a JOIN operation.

5. Using rules 3, 4, 7, and 11 concerning cascading of PROJECT and commuting of PROJECT with other operations, break down and move lists of projection attributes down the tree as far as possible by creating new PROJECT operations as needed.

6. As a final step, identify subtrees that represent groups of operations that can be executed by a single access routine for execution by that access routine.

In our example, Figure 18.4b shows the tree of Figure 18.4a after applying steps 1 and 2 of the algorithm, Figure 18.4c shows the tree after applying step 3, Figure 18.4d shows the tree after applying step 4, and Figure 18.4e shows the tree after applying step 5. In step 6 we may group together the operations in the subtree whose root is the operation $\bowtie_{\text{PNUMBER=PNO}}$ if an access routine exists for such a subtree. We may also group the remaining operations into another subtree, where a temporary file replaces the subtree whose root is the operation $\bowtie_{\text{PNUMBER=PNO}}$, because the first grouping means that this subtree is executed first and its result is placed in a temporary file.

Summary of Heuristics for Algebraic Optimization

We now summarize the basic heuristics for algebraic optimization. The main heuristic is to apply first operations that reduce the size of intermediate temporary relations. This includes performing SELECT operations as early as possible to reduce the number of tuples for subsequent operations and performing PROJECT operations as early as possible to reduce the number of attributes in intermediate temporary files. This is done by moving SELECT and PROJECT operations as far down the tree as possible. In addition, SELECT and JOIN operations that are most restrictive—that is, result in relations with the fewest tuples or with the smallest absolute size—should be executed before other similar operations. This is done by reordering the leaf nodes of the tree among one another and adjusting the rest of the tree appropriately.

18.2.2 *Heuristic Optimization of Query Graphs (Relational Calculus)*

The approach we describe now is often called **query decomposition** and was first proposed as a heuristic optimization technique for implementing the QUEL language (Chapter 9) in the INGRES DBMS. QUEL queries are very similar to relational calculus (Chapter 8) and are represented as query graphs. We discuss only select-project-join queries here, although the technique may be extended to more general queries. Recall that a QUEL query may include a number of **tuple variables**—one variable for each relation involved in a certain role in the query.

A **query graph** is a representation of a select-project-join tuple relational calculus expression or QUEL query. Each tuple variable is represented by a **node** in the graph, and **edges** among these nodes represent **join conditions** involving these variables. Constant values appearing in the query are represented by special nodes called **constant nodes**. Constant nodes are connected by edges representing selection conditions to the nodes that represent the tuple variables involved in these conditions.

Figure 18.5 shows a query graph for the following QUEL query, which is specified on the relational schema shown in Figure 6.5 and corresponds to query Q2 of Chapters 6 to 9: For every project located in 'Stafford', retrieve the project number, the controlling department number, and the department manager's lastname, address, and birthdate.

Q2:   **RANGE OF**   P **IS** PROJECT, D **IS** DEPARTMENT, E **IS** EMPLOYEE
          RETRIEVE   (P.PNUMBER, D.DNUMBER, E.LNAME, E.BDATE,
                        E.ADDRESS)
          WHERE   P.DNUM=D.DNUMBER **AND** D.MGRSSN=E.SSN **AND**
                        P.PLOCATION='Stafford'

In Figure 18.5 the tuple variables P, D, and E and the constant value 'Stafford' are represented by nodes in the graph. Constant nodes are displayed in double ovals. The edges are labeled by the corresponding selection or join conditions. Notice that the query graph does *not* specify any *order of execution* on the operations, unlike the query tree, which had implicit order. This makes the query graph a completely neutral representation, specifying *what* the query will retrieve but not *how* to execute the query. The query graph is a **canonical representation** of a select-project-join relational calculus query; each query corresponds to one and only one graph. This is unlike query trees, where many different trees can represent the same query because there are many *equivalent* relational algebra expressions that are different but specify the same query.

Optimizing and Executing a Query Graph by Query Decomposition

We now describe the query decomposition method that heuristically optimizes (derives a "good" execution strategy) and executes a query graph. We illustrate our discussion using the query Q': Find the last names of employees born after 1957 who work on a project

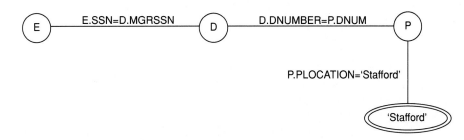

Figure 18.5   Query graph for the query Q2

located in 'Stafford' and controlled by department number 4. This query refers to the database of Figure 6.5 and is specified in QUEL as follows:

Q':	**RANGE OF**	P **IS** PROJECT, W **IS** WORKS_ON, E **IS** EMPLOYEE
	RETRIEVE	(E.LNAME)
	WHERE	P.PLOCATION='Stafford' **AND** P.DNUM=4 **AND**
		P.PNUMBER=W.PNO **AND**
		W.ESSN=E.SSN **AND** E.BDATE>'DEC-31-1957'

Figure 18.6a shows the query graph for Q'. The query decomposition approach uses the heuristic of executing SELECT operations before JOIN or CARTESIAN PRODUCT by identifying **single-variable subqueries** of a query, which involve a single tuple variable and a SELECT condition. These subqueries are executed first, and the projection list of each sub-

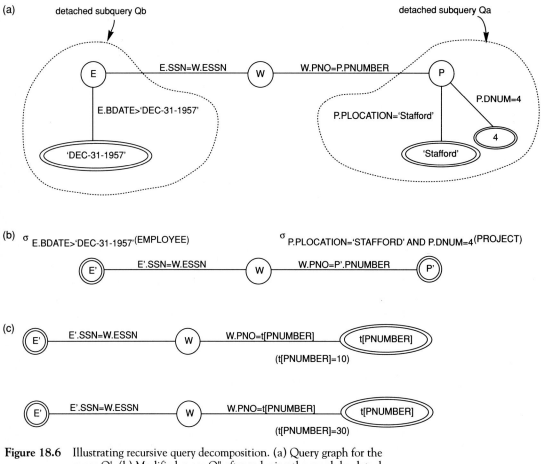

Figure 18.6 Illustrating recursive query decomposition. (a) Query graph for the query Q'. (b) Modified query Q" after reducing the graph by detachment and execution of the single-variable subqueries Qa and Qb. (c) Query graph generated for each tuple t in P' for tuple substitution.
(*continued on next page*)

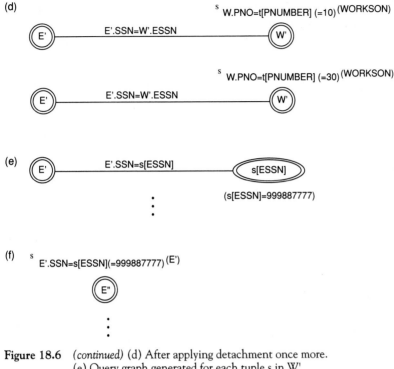

(d)

^{s} W.PNO=t[PNUMBER] (=10) $^{(WORKSON)}$

E' —— E'.SSN=W'.ESSN —— W'

^{s} W.PNO=t[PNUMBER] (=30) $^{(WORKSON)}$

E' —— E'.SSN=W'.ESSN —— W'

(e) E' —— E'.SSN=s[ESSN] —— s[ESSN]

(s[ESSN]=999887777)

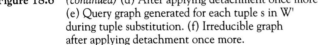

(f) ^{s} E'.SSN=s[ESSN](=999887777) $^{(E')}$

E"

Figure 18.6 *(continued)* (d) After applying detachment once more. (e) Query graph generated for each tuple s in W' during tuple substitution. (f) Irreducible graph after applying detachment once more.

query will include any attributes that are needed in subsequent query processing. A multivariable query is broken into a sequence of single-variable subqueries by detachment and tuple substitution. **Detachment** is the process of identifying and separating a subquery that has a single variable in common with the rest of the query. **Tuple substitution** is the process of substituting a single tuple at a time for one of the variables in the query; that is, the variable is instantiated with *actual corresponding tuples* from the database. This generates for an n-variable query a number of simpler (n − 1)-variable queries—one for each tuple substituted.

Detachment is applied before tuple substitution because it generates two queries from one. Tuple substitution is applied only when detachment is not possible. By using these two operations repeatedly, the query is eventually reduced into a number of irreducible (constant) components, and combining those gives the query result. For query Q', the following single-variable subqueries are detached and executed first:

Qa: **RETRIEVE INTO** P' (P.PNUMBER)
  WHERE P.PLOCATION='Stafford' **AND** P.DNUM=4

Qb: **RETRIEVE INTO** E' (E.LNAME, E.SSN)
  WHERE E.BDATE>'DEC-31-1957'

The graph of Figure 18.6a is now reduced to the graph of Figure 18.6b by removing the constant nodes and including nodes to represent the intermediate relations P' and E' corresponding to the results of the subqueries Qa and Qb. Intermediate relations are represented by **small nodes,** shown as double circles in Figure 18.6b, to indicate that the tuples in these relations have been reduced by applying a select-project query to a relation. When *no more single-variable subqueries can be detached and executed,* and if more than one node remains, the graph represents one or more multivariable queries. Each connected subgraph represents a subquery, and each arc represents a join condition. The Cartesian product operation must be applied to the subqueries corresponding to graph partitions. In our example, the graph in Figure 18.6b has only one partition and represents a modified original query Q'', which is a three-variable query that refers to the WORKS_ON (W) relation and the intermediate relations P' and E' that hold the results of the subqueries:

Q'':   **RETRIEVE**   (E'.LNAME)
           WHERE   P'.PNUMBER=W.PNO **AND** W.ESSN=E'.SSN

The next step is to apply tuple substitution, which specifies an order on the join and Cartesian product operations based on the nested loop method of executing joins (method J1 of Section 18.1.2, but extended for multiway join). However, in the actual implementation, method J2 may be mixed in if appropriate access structures exist on the join attributes. The main optimization decision is to choose which of the relations will be in the outer loop and which in the inner loop. During tuple substitution of this n-variable query, the tuple variable for the outer relation is substituted with one of its tuples at a time during the query evaluation process. For *each tuple* in the outer relation, an $(n - 1)$-variable query with the outer relation variable substituted for by that constant tuple is generated, and we may apply detachment followed by tuple substitution recursively on each of these queries.

The main heuristic for picking a relation for tuple substitution is the number of tuples in the relation. A small relation should be picked first. If the reduced graph has more than one small relation, we should choose the one estimated to have the smallest number of tuples if this can be determined.*

We illustrate tuple substitution for our example of Figure 18.6b. Based on the database extension in Figure 6.6, the relation P' will have two PROJECT tuples with PNUMBER values of 10 and 30, while E' will have three EMPLOYEE tuples with SSN values of 999887777, 453453453, and 987987987. If we choose relation P' for tuple substitution, we can replace the graph of Figure 18.6b by the two graphs shown in Figure 18.6c—one graph for each tuple t in P'. After retrieving the result of each of these graphs, we take their UNION to form the result of the original graph of Figure 18.6b. For each of the graphs shown in Figure 18.6c, the node on which tuple substitution was applied can be broken down into one (or more) constant nodes, and we reapply the decomposition algorithm recursively to each graph. At the end of the algorithm the result of the original query is produced. Figures 18.6d to f illustrate the remainder of the process for our query. The results of each graph produced by tuple substitution are "UNIONed" together.

---

*In practice, the process of choosing the variable for tuple substitution, called **variable selection,** is more involved. Other factors such as the availability of access paths on relations can be used to estimate the costs of choosing different variables.

18.3 Systematic Query Optimization Using Cost Estimates

Another approach to query optimization is not to depend solely on heuristic rules. Rather, the query optimizer, possibly after using some heuristics, will estimate and compare the costs of executing a query using different execution strategies and choose the strategy with the *lowest cost estimate*. For this approach to work well, we must be able to give accurate cost estimates for each execution strategy so that different strategies are compared fairly and realistically. In addition, we must limit the number of execution strategies to be considered; otherwise, too much time will be spent on the cost estimation for the many possible execution strategies. Hence, this approach is more suitable for **compiled queries** where the optimization is done at compile time and the resulting execution strategy code is stored and executed directly at runtime. For **interpreted queries,** where the entire process shown in Figure 18.1 occurs at runtime, a full-scale optimization may slow down the response time. Some DBMSs apply a more elaborate optimization for compiled queries and a partial, less time-consuming optimization for interpreted queries.

We call this approach **systematic query optimization,*** and it is similar to traditional optimization techniques where a solution to a problem is searched for in the solution space while minimizing an objective (cost) function. The cost functions used in query optimization are estimates and not exact cost functions, so the optimization may select a query execution strategy that is not the optimal one. In Section 18.3.1 we discuss the components of query execution cost. In Section 18.3.2 we discuss the type of information needed in cost functions. This information is kept in the DBMS catalog. In Section 18.3.3 we give examples of cost functions for SELECT operation, and in Section 18.3.4 we discuss cost functions for two-way JOIN operations.

18.3.1 Cost Components for Query Execution

The cost of executing a query includes the following components:

1. Access cost to secondary storage: This is the cost of searching for, reading, and writing data blocks that reside on secondary storage, mainly on disk. In addition to accessing the database files themselves, temporary intermediate files that are too large to fit in main memory buffers and hence are stored on disk also need to be accessed. The cost of searching for records in a database file or a temporary file depends on the type of access structures on that file, such as ordering, hashing, and primary or secondary indexes. In addition, factors such as whether the file blocks are allocated contiguously on the same disk cylinder or scattered on the disk affect the access cost (see Appendix C).

2. Storage cost: This is the cost of storing the intermediate temporary files that are generated by an execution strategy for the query (see Appendix C).

3. Computation cost: This is the cost of performing in-memory operations on the data buffers during query execution. Such operations include searching for records, sorting records, merging records for join, and performing computations on field values.

---

*This approach was first used in the optimizer for the SYSTEM R experimental DBMS developed at IBM.

4. Communication costs: The cost of shipping the query and its results from the database site to the site or terminal where the query originated.

For large databases, the main emphasis is on minimizing the access cost to secondary storage. In fact, many cost functions ignore other factors and compare different query execution strategies in terms of the number of block transfers between disk and memory. For smaller databases, where most of the data in the files involved in the query can be completely stored in memory, the emphasis should be on minimizing computation cost. In distributed databases, where many sites are involved (see Chapter 21), communication cost must be minimized also. It is difficult to include all the cost components in a (weighted) cost function because of the difficulty in assigning suitable weights to the cost components. That is why many cost functions consider a single factor only—disk access. In the next section we discuss some of the information that is needed for formulating cost functions.

18.3.2 Catalog Information Used in Cost Functions

To estimate the costs of various execution strategies, we must keep track of any information that is needed for cost functions. This information is stored in the DBMS catalog, where it is accessed by the query optimizer. First, we must know the size of each file. For a file whose records are all of the same type, the **number of records (tuples)** r and the **number of blocks** b, or close estimates of them, are needed. The **blocking factor** bfr for the file may also be needed in some cost functions. For a mixed file containing records of more than one type, we need the total number of blocks and the number of records of each record type that are stored in the file. For simplicity, we will not discuss mixed files further; their cost functions are more complex than the ones we discuss here.

For each nonmixed file we must also keep track of the primary access method and the primary access attributes. The file records may be unordered, ordered by an attribute with or without a primary or clustering index, or hashed on a key attribute. We must also keep track of all secondary indexes and indexing attributes. The **number of levels** x of each multilevel index (primary, secondary, or clustering) is needed for cost functions that estimate number of block accesses during query execution. In some cost functions the **number of first-level index blocks** b_{I1} is needed.

Another important parameter is the **number of distinct values** d of an indexing attribute. The value d may be provided for any nonkey attribute, whether or not the attribute is used for indexing. This allows estimation of the **selection cardinality** s of an attribute, which is the *average* number of records that will satisfy an equality selection condition on that attribute. For a key attribute, s = 1. For a nonkey attribute, by making an assumption that the d distinct values are uniformly distributed among the records, we get

$$s = (r / d)$$

Information such as the number of index levels is easy to maintain because it does not change very often. However, other information may change frequently; for example, the number of records r in a file changes every time a record is inserted or deleted. The query optimizer will need reasonably close but not necessarily completely up-to-the-minute values of these parameters for use in estimating the cost of various execution strategies. In the next two sections we see how some of these parameters are used in cost functions for a systematic query optimizer.

18.3.3 Examples of Cost Functions for SELECT

We now give cost functions for selection algorithms S1 to S8 discussed in Section 18.1.1 in terms of number of block transfers between memory and disk. These cost functions are estimates that ignore computation time, storage cost, etc., as discussed in Section 18.3.1. The cost for method Si is referred to as C_{Si} block accesses.

S1. Linear search (brute force) approach: We search all the file blocks to retrieve all records satisfying the selection condition, so we get $C_{S1a} = b$. For an equality condition on a key, we will search only half the file blocks on the average before finding the record, so we get $C_{S1b} = (b/2)$.

S2. Binary search: We access approximately $C_{S2} = \log_2 b + \lceil (s/bfr) \rceil - 1$ file blocks. Notice that this typically reduces to $\log_2 b$ if the equality condition is on a unique (key) attribute because $s = 1$ in this case.

S3. Using a primary index (S3a) or hash key (S3b) to retrieve a single record: For a primary index, we retrieve one more block than the number of index levels, so $C_{S3a} = x + 1$. For hashing, we get approximately $C_{S3b} = 1$.

S4. Using an ordering index to retrieve multiple records: If the comparison condition is $>$, $\geq$, $<$, or $\leq$ on a key field with an ordering index, we can assume very roughly that half the file records will satisfy the condition. This gives a cost function $C_{S4} = x + (b/2)$. This is a very rough estimate, and although it may be correct on the average, it may be quite inaccurate in individual cases.

S5. Using a clustering index to retrieve multiple records: Given an equality condition, we can assume that s records will satisfy the condition, where s is the selection cardinality of the indexing attribute. This means that $\lceil (s/bfr) \rceil$ file blocks will be accessed, giving $C_{S5} = x + \lceil (s/bfr) \rceil$.

S6. Using a secondary (B$^+$-tree) index: On an *equality* comparison, we can again assume that s records will satisfy the condition, where s is the selection cardinality of the indexing attribute. However, because the index is nonclustering, each of the records may reside on a different block so we get a cost estimate $C_{S6a} = x + s$. This reduces to $x + 1$ for a key indexing attribute. If the comparison condition is $>$, $\geq$, $<$, or $\leq$ and we assume (very roughly) that half the file records satisfy the condition, then we can estimate that half the first-level index blocks are accessed, plus half the file records via the index. The cost estimate for this case, very approximately, is $C_{S6b} = x + (b_{I1}/2) + (r/2)$.

S7. Conjunctive selection: We either use S1 or use of one of the methods S2 to S6 discussed above. In the latter case we use one condition to retrieve the records and then check whether or not each retrieved record satisfies the remaining conditions in the conjunction in memory.

S8. Conjunctive selection using a composite index: Same as S3a, S5, or S6a, depending on the type of index.

Example of Using the Cost Functions

Suppose that the EMPLOYEE file of Figure 6.5 has r_E = 10,000 records stored in b_E = 2000 disk blocks with blocking factor bfr_E = 5 records/block and has the following access paths:

1. A clustering index on SALARY with levels x_{SALARY} = 3 and selection cardinality s_{SALARY} = 20.

2. A secondary index on the key attribute SSN with x_{SSN} = 4 (s_{SSN} = 1).

3. A secondary index on the nonkey attribute DNO with x_{DNO} = 2 and first-level index blocks b_{I1DNO} = 4. There are d_{DNO} = 125 distinct values for DNO, so the selection cardinality of DNO is s_{DNO} = (r_E/d_{DNO}) = 80.

4. A secondary index on SEX with x_{SEX} = 1. There are d_{SEX} = 2 values for the sex attribute, so the selection cardinality is s_{SEX} = (r_E/d_{SEX}) = 5000.

We illustrate the use of cost functions with the following examples:

$$\text{(OP1): } \sigma_{SSN=123456789}(\text{EMPLOYEE})$$
$$\text{(OP2): } \sigma_{DNO>5}(\text{EMPLOYEE})$$
$$\text{(OP3): } \sigma_{DNO=5}(\text{EMPLOYEE})$$
$$\text{(OP4): } \sigma_{DNO=5 \text{ AND } SALARY>30000 \text{ AND } SEX=F}(\text{EMPLOYEE})$$

The cost of the brute force (linear search) option S1 will be estimated as C_{S1a} = b_E = 2000 (for a selection on a nonkey attribute) or C_{S1b} = ($b_E/2$) = 1000 (average cost for a selection on a key attribute). For OP1 we can use either method S1 or S6a; the cost estimate for S6a will be C_{S6a} = x_{SSN} + 1 = 4 + 1 = 5, and it is chosen over method S1, whose average cost is C_{S1b} = 1000. For OP2 we can use either method S1 with estimated cost C_{S1a} = 2000 or method S6b with estimated cost C_{S6b} = x_{DNO} + ($b_{I1DNO}/2$) + ($r_E/2$) = 2 + (4/2) + (10,000/2) = 5004, so we choose the brute force approach for OP2. For OP3 we can use either method S1 with estimated cost C_{S1a} = 2000 or method S6a with estimated cost C_{S6a} = x_{DNO} + s_{DNO} = 2 + 80 = 82, so we choose method S6a.

Finally, consider OP4, which has a conjunctive selection condition. We need to estimate the cost of using any one of the three components of the selection condition to retrieve the records, plus the brute force approach. The latter gives cost estimate C_{S1a} = 2000. Using the condition (DNO = 5) first gives the cost estimate C_{S6a} = 82. Using the condition (SALARY>30,000) first gives a cost estimate C_{S4} = x_{SALARY} + ($b_E/2$) = 3 + (2000/2) = 1003. Using the condition (SEX = F) first gives a cost estimate C_{S6a} = x_{SEX} + s_{SEX} = 1 + 5000 = 5001. The optimizer would then choose method S6a on the secondary index on DNO because it has the lowest cost estimate. The condition (DNO = 5) is used to retrieve the records, and the remaining part of the conjunctive condition (SALARY > 30,000 AND SEX = F) would be checked for each selected record in memory.

18.3.4   Examples of Cost Functions for JOIN

To develop reasonably accurate cost functions for join operations, we need to have an estimate for the size (number of tuples) of the file resulting *after* the join operation. This is usually kept as a ratio of the size (number of tuples) of the join file to the size of the

Cartesian product file if both are applied to the same input files and is called the **join selectivity** js. If we denote the number of tuples of a relation R by $|R|$, we have

$$js = |(R \bowtie_c S)| \; / \; |(R \times S)| = |(R \bowtie_c S)| \; / \; (\, |R| * |S| \,)$$

If there is no join condition c, then js = 1 and the join is the same as the Cartesian product. If no tuples from the relations satisfy the join condition, then js = 0. In general, $0 \le js \le 1$. For a join where the condition c is an equality comparison R.A = S.B, we get the following two special cases:

1. If A is a key of R, then $|(R \bowtie_c S)| \le |S|$, so $js \le (1/|R|)$.
2. If B is a key of S, then $|(R \bowtie_c S)| \le |R|$, so $js \le (1/|S|)$.

An estimate of the join selectivity for commonly occurring join conditions will give the query optimizer the capability to estimate the size of the resulting file after the join operation, given the sizes of the two input files, by using the formula $|(R \bowtie_c S)|$ = js $* |R| * |S|$. We can now give some sample *approximate* cost functions for estimating the cost of some of the join algorithms given in Section 18.1.2. The join operations are of the form

$$R \bowtie_{A=B} S$$

where A and B are domain-compatible attributes of R and S, respectively. Assume that R has b_R blocks and S has b_S blocks.

J1. Nested loop approach: Suppose we use R for the outer loop; then we get the following cost function to estimate the number of block accesses for this method assuming *two memory buffers*. We assume the blocking factor for the resulting file is bfr_{RS} and the join selectivity is known:

$$C_{J1} = b_R + (b_R * b_S) + ((js * |R| * |S|)/bfr_{RS})$$

The last part of the formula is the cost of writing the resulting file to disk. This cost formula can be modified to take into account different numbers of memory buffers as discussed in Section 18.1.2.

J2. Using an access structure to retrieve the matching record(s): If an index exists for the join attribute B of S with index levels x_B, we can retrieve each record in R and then use the index to retrieve all the matching records t from S that satisfy t[B] = s[A]. The cost depends on the type of index. For a secondary index where s_B is the selection cardinality* for the join attribute B of S, we get

$$C_{J2a} = b_R + (|R| * (x_B + s_B)) + ((js * |R| * |S|)/bfr_{RS})$$

For a clustering index where s_B is the selection cardinality of B, we get

$$C_{J2b} = b_R + (|R| * (x_B + (s_B/bfr_B))) + ((js * |R| * |S|)/bfr_{RS})$$

---

*Note that selection cardinality was defined as the average number of records satisfying an equality condition on an attribute, which is the average number of records that have the same value for the attribute and hence will be joined to a single record in the other file.

For a primary index, we get

$$C_{J2c} = b_R + (|R|*(x_B + 1)) + ((js*|R|*|S|)/bfr_{RS})$$

If a hash key exists for one of the two join attributes, say B of S, we get

$$C_{J2d} = b_R + (|R|*h) + ((js*|R|*|S|)/bfr_{RS})$$

where $h \geq 1$ is the average number of block accesses to retrieve a record given its hash key value.

J3. Sort-merge join: If the files are already sorted on the join attributes, the cost function for this method is

$$C_{J3a} = b_R + b_S + ((js*|R|*|S|)/bfr_{RS})$$

If we must sort the files, the cost of sorting must be added. We can approximate the sorting cost by $k*b*\log_2 b$ for a file of b blocks, where k is a constant factor. Hence, we get the following cost function:

$$C_{J3b} = k*((b_R*\log_2 b_R) + (b_S*\log_2 b_S)) + b_R + b_S + ((js*|R|*|S|)/bfr_{RS})$$

Example of Using the Cost Functions

Suppose we have the EMPLOYEE file described in the example of the previous section and assume that the DEPARTMENT file of Figure 6.5 consists of $r_D = 125$ records stored in $b_D = 13$ disk blocks. Consider the join operations:

$$\text{(OP6): EMPLOYEE} \bowtie_{DNO=DNUMBER} \text{DEPARTMENT}$$
$$\text{(OP7): DEPARTMENT} \bowtie_{MGRSSN=SSN} \text{EMPLOYEE}$$

Suppose we have a primary index on DNUMBER of DEPARTMENT with $x_{DNUMBER} = 1$ level and a secondary index on MGRSSN of DEPARTMENT with selection cardinality $s_{MGRSSN} = 1$ and levels $x_{MGRSSN} = 2$. Assume that the join selectivity for OP6 is $js_{OP6} = (1/|DEPARTMENT|) = 1/125$ because DNUMBER is a key of DEPARTMENT. Also assume that the blocking factor for the resulting join file $bfr_{ED} = 4$ records per block. We can estimate the costs for the JOIN operation OP6 using the applicable methods J1 and J2 as follows:

1. Using method J1 with EMPLOYEE as outer loop:

$$C_{J1} = b_E + (b_E*b_D) + ((js_{OP6}*r_E*r_D)/bfr_{ED}) =$$
$$2000 + (2000*13) + (((1/125)*10{,}000*125)/4) = 30{,}500$$

2. Using method J1 with DEPARTMENT as outer loop:

$$C_{J1} = b_D + (b_E*b_D) + ((js_{OP6}*r_E*r_D)/bfr_{ED}) =$$
$$13 + (13*2000) + (((1/125)*10{,}000*125)/4) = 28{,}513$$

3. Using method J2 with EMPLOYEE as outer loop:

$$C_{J2c} = b_E + (r_E*(x_{DNUMBER} + 1)) + ((js_{OP6}*r_E*r_D)/bfr_{ED}) =$$
$$2000 + (10{,}000*2) + (((1/125)*10{,}000*125)/4) = 24{,}500$$

4. Using method J2 with DEPARTMENT as outer loop:

$$C_{J2a} = b_D + (r_D*(x_{DNO}*s_{DNO})) + ((js_{OP6}*r_E*r_D)/bfr_{ED}) =$$
$$13 + (125*(2*80)) + (((1/125)*10,000*125)/4) = 22,513$$

Case 4 has the lowest cost estimate and will be chosen. Notice that if 14 memory buffers (or more) were available for executing the join instead of just 2, 13 of them could be used to hold the entire DEPARTMENT relation in memory and the cost for case 2 could be drastically reduced, making it just $b_E + b_D + ((js_{OP6}*r_E*r_D)/bfr_{ED})$ or 4513, as discussed in Section 18.1.2. As an exercise, the reader should perform a similar analysis for OP7.

18.3.5 Cost Functions for Combination Access Routines

So far, we have discussed cost functions for access routines for a single operation of type SELECT or EQUIJOIN. As we mentioned in Section 18.1.5, it is often more efficient to implement combinations of several groups of operations in order to reduce the number of temporary files. A common combination is to have a single access routine to perform SELECT operations on one or two files that will be joined by the access routine just before performing the JOIN operation and following that with a final PROJECT operation. The cost functions for such routines would combine the SELECT cost functions with the JOIN cost functions. The effect of the final PROJECT operation is mainly to reduce the record size of the result file, hence reducing the blocking factor and the overall cost. We will leave it as an exercise to develop cost functions for these combination access routines and for the other types of operations discussed in Section 18.1.

18.4 Semantic Query Optimization

A different approach to query optimization, called **semantic query optimization,** has recently been suggested. This technique may be used in combination with the techniques discussed above and uses constraints specified on the database schema in order to modify one query into another query that is more efficient to execute. We will not discuss this approach in detail but only illustrate it with an example. Consider the SQL query:

```
SELECT   E.LNAME, M.LNAME
FROM     EMPLOYEE E M
WHERE    E.SUPERSSN=M.SSN AND E.SALARY>M.SALARY
```

This query retrieves the names of employees who earn more than their supervisors. Suppose we had a constraint on the database schema that stated that no employee can earn more than his or her direct supervisor. If the semantic query optimizer checks for the existence of this constraint, it need not execute the query at all because it knows that the result of the query will be empty. Techniques known as **theorem proving** can be used for this. This may save considerable time if the checking of constraints can be done efficiently. However, searching through many constraints to find ones that are applicable to a given query and that may semantically optimize it can also be quite time consuming. With the advent of knowledge-based and expert systems, it is possible that semantic query optimization techniques may be incorporated into the DBMSs of the future.

18.5   Summary

In this chapter we gave an overview of the techniques used by DBMSs in processing and optimizing high-level queries. In Section 18.1 we discussed how various relational algebra operations may be executed by a DBMS. We saw that some operations, particularly SELECT and JOIN, may have many execution options. We also discussed how access routines to the database can implement combinations of operations.

In Section 18.2 we discussed heuristic approaches to query optimization, which use heuristic rules to improve the efficiency of query execution. In Section 18.2.1 we showed how a query tree that represents a relational algebra expression can be heuristically optimized by reorganizing the tree nodes. We also gave equivalence-preserving transformation rules that may be applied to a query tree. A summary of these transformations is given in Appendix D. In Section 18.2.2 we discussed the query graph notation, which represents a relational calculus expression, and showed how it may be optimized and executed by a technique called query decomposition. This technique breaks up a query into simpler ones and includes heuristics to order the execution of query operations.

In Section 18.3 we discussed the systematic or cost estimation approach to query optimization. We showed how cost functions are developed for some access routines and how these cost functions are used to estimate the cost of different execution strategies. Finally, we mentioned the technique of semantic query optimization in Section 18.4.

Review Questions

18.1. What is meant by the term "access routine"? Why is it important to implement several relational operations in a single access routine?

18.2. Discuss the different algorithms for implementing each of the following relational operators and the circumstances under which each algorithm can be used: SELECT, JOIN, PROJECT, UNION, INTERSECT, MINUS, XPROD.

18.3. What is meant by the term "heuristic optimization"? Discuss the main heuristics that are applied during query optimization.

18.4. How does a query tree represent a relational algebra expression? What is meant by an execution of a query tree? Discuss the rules for transformation of query trees and when each rule should be applied during optimization.

18.5. How do query graphs represent relational calculus expressions? Discuss the query decomposition approach to optimizing and executing a query graph.

18.6. What is meant by systematic query optimization?

18.7. Discuss the cost components for a cost function that is used to estimate query execution cost. Which cost components are used most often as the basis for cost functions?

18.8. Discuss the different types of parameters that are used in cost functions. Where is this information kept?

18.9. List the cost functions for the SELECT and JOIN methods discussed in Section 18.1.

18.10. What is meant by semantic query optimization? How does it differ from other query optimization techniques?

Exercises

18.11. Consider SQL queries Q1, Q8, Q1B, Q4 and Q27 from Chapter 7.

   a. Draw at least two query trees that can represent *each* of these queries. Under what circumstances would you use each of your query trees?

   b. Draw the initial query tree for each of these queries; then show how the query tree is optimized by the algorithm outlined in Section 18.2.1.

   c. Compare for each query your own query trees of part a and the initial and final query trees of part b.

18.12. Draw the query graph for each of the QUEL queries Q0, Q1, Q3' Q8, Q1D, and Q27 from Chapter 9; then show how the query graph is optimized and executed by the query decomposition algorithm of Section 18.2.2.

18.13. Develop cost functions for the PROJECT, UNION, INTERSECTION, SET DIFFERENCE, and CARTESIAN PRODUCT algorithms discussed in Sections 18.1.3 and 18.1.4.

18.14. Develop cost functions for the combination access routine that consists of two SELECTs, a JOIN, and a final PROJECT. This routine is described in Section 18.3.5.

18.15. Calculate the cost functions for different options of executing the JOIN operation OP7 in Section 18.3.4.

Selected Bibliography

An early reference to query optimization is Rothnie (1975), which describes optimization of two-variable queries in the DAMAS experimental DBMS. Palermo (1974) shows how relational calculus expressions can be converted to relational algebra then optimized. A detailed algorithm for relational algebra optimization is given by Smith and Chang (1975). Hall (1976) discusses relational algebra transformations in the PRTV experimental DBMS. The textbook by Ullman (1982) also discusses query tree and relational algebra optimization.

The decomposition algorithm for QUEL, used in the experimental INGRES DBMS, was presented by Wong and Youssefi (1976), and Youssefi and Wong (1979) discusses its performance. Ullman (1982) gives a recursive algorithm based on query decomposition. Whang (1985) discusses query optimization in OBE (Office-By-Example), which is a system based on QBE.

Systematic optimization using cost functions was used in the SYSTEM R experimental DBMS and is discussed in Astrahan et al. (1976). Selinger et al. (1979) discusses the optimization of multiway joins in SYSTEM R. Join algorithms are discussed in Gotlieb (1975), Blasgen and Eswaran (1976), and Whang et al. (1982). Kim (1982) dicusses transformations of nested SQL queries into canonical representations. Optimization of aggregate functions is discussed in Klug (1982). DeWitt et al. (1984) discuss query optimization in main memory databases.

Yao (1979) gives a comparative analysis of many known query processing algorithms. A survey paper by Jarke and Koch (1984) gives a taxonomy of query optimization and includes a bibliography of work in this area. Kim et al. (1985) discuss advanced topics in query optimization. Semantic query optimization is discussed in King (1981) and Malley and Zdonick (1986). Aho et al. (1979a) discuss a technique of optimization for relational calculus queries with only equality comparisons, ANDs, and existential quantifiers based on tableaus, which are tables where columns represent attributes and rows represent conditions. Ullman (1982) discusses tableaus. Sagiv and Yannakakis (1980) extend tableaus to handle UNION and SET DIFFERENCE.

Beck et al. (1989) discuss a technique called classification, which can be used to optimize queries on a semantic data model. Recently, there is increasing interest in parallel algorithms for executing queries, such as the work by Mikkilineni and Su (1988).

Transactions, Recovery, and Concurrency Control

In this chapter we present the concept of an atomic transaction; this is used to represent a logical unit of database processing. We discuss concurrency control techniques, which are used to ensure that multiple transactions submitted by various users do not interfere with one another in a way that produces incorrect results. We also present the techniques for recovery from transaction failures. In Section 19.1 we informally discuss why concurrency control and recovery are necessary in a database system. In Section 19.2 we formally introduce the concept of an atomic transaction and discuss additional concepts related to transaction processing in database systems. Section 19.3 presents the concept of serializability of concurrent transaction executions, which can be used to define correct execution sequences of concurrent transactions. In Section 19.4 we discuss concurrency control techniques based on locking, and in Section 19.5 we discuss other concurrency control techniques. Section 19.6 discusses recovery techniques.

19.1 Introduction to Concurrency and Recovery

In this section we informally introduce the concepts of concurrent execution of transactions and recovery from transaction failures. In Section 19.1.1 we compare single-user and multiuser database systems and show how concurrent execution of transactions can take place in multiuser systems. Section 19.1.2 shows by informal examples why concurrency control techniques are needed in multiuser systems. Finally, in Section 19.1.3 we discuss why techniques are needed to recover from failure by presenting the different ways in which transactions can fail while executing.

19.1.1   Single-User versus Multi-User Systems

One criterion for classifying a database system is by the number of users who can use the system *concurrently*; that is, at the same time. A DBMS is **single-user** if at most one user at a time can use the system and is **multiuser** if many users can use the system concurrently. Single-user DBMSs are mostly restricted to microcomputer systems; most other DBMSs are multiuser. For example, an airline reservations system is used by hundreds of travel agents and reservation clerks concurrently. Systems in banks, insurance agencies, stock exchanges, etc. are also used by many users who submit many transactions concurrently to the system.

Multiple users can use computer systems simultaneously because of the concept of **multiprogramming,** which allows the computer to process multiple programs (or transactions) at the same time. If only a single central processing unit (CPU) exists, it can actually be processing at most one program at a time. However, multiprogramming operating systems execute some commands from one program, then suspend that program and execute some commands from the next program, and so on. A program is resumed at the point where it was suspended when it gets its turn to use the CPU again. Hence, concurrent execution of the programs is actually **interleaved,** as illustrated in Figure 19.1 (same as Figure 4.3), which shows two programs A and B executing concurrently in an interleaved fashion. Interleaving also keeps the CPU busy when an executing program requires an input or output (I/O) operation, such as reading a block from disk. The CPU is switched to execute another program rather than remaining idle during I/O time.

If the computer system has multiple hardware processors (CPUs), then **simultaneous** processing of multiple programs is possible, leading to simultaneous rather than interleaved concurrency as illustrated by programs C and D in Figure 19.1. One CPU executes program C at the same time that another CPU is executing program D. Most of the theory concerning concurrency control in databases is developed in terms of interleaved concurrency, although it may be adapted to simultaneous concurrency. Hence, for the remainder of this chapter we assume the *interleaved model of concurrent execution.*

In a multiuser DBMS, the stored data items are the primary resources that may be accessed concurrently by user programs, which are constantly retrieving and modifying the database. The *execution of a program* that accesses or changes the contents of the

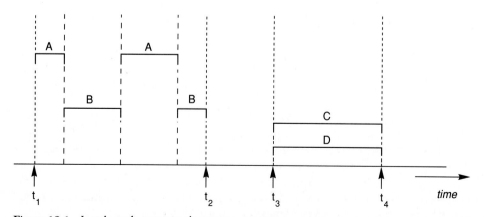

Figure 19.1   Interleaved versus simultaneous concurrency

database is called a **transaction**. The transactions submitted by the various users may execute concurrently and may access and update the same database records. If this concurrent execution is uncontrolled, it may lead to problems such as an *inconsistent database*. In the next section we motivate the need for concurrency control by discussing *informally* three of the problems that may occur when concurrent transactions execute in an uncontrolled manner.

19.1.2 Why Concurrency Control Is Needed

Several problems can occur when concurrent transactions execute in an uncontrolled manner. We illustrate some of these problems using a simple airline reservation database in which a record is stored for each airline flight. Each record includes the number of reserved seats on that flight as a *named data item*, among other information. Figure 19.2a shows a transaction T_1 that *cancels* N reservations from one flight whose number of reserved seats is stored in the database item named X and *reserves* the same number of seats on another flight whose number of reserved seats is stored in the database item named Y. Figure 19.2b shows a simpler transaction T_2 that just *reserves* M seats on the first flight referenced in transaction T_1, whose number of reserved seats is stored in database item X. To simplify our example, we do not show additional portions of the transactions such as checking whether a flight has enough seats available before reserving additional seats.

Note that when a database program is written, it will have the flight numbers, their dates, and the number of seats to be booked as parameters; hence, the same program can be used to execute many transactions, each with different flights and numbers of seats to be booked. For concurrency control purposes, a transaction is a *particular execution* of a program on a specific date, flight, and number of seats. In Figures 19.2a and b, the transactions T_1 and T_2 are *specific executions* of the programs that refer to the specific flights whose numbers of seats are stored in data items X and Y in the database. We now discuss the types of problems we may encounter with these two transactions.

The Lost Update Problem

This occurs when two transactions that access the same database items have their operations interleaved in a way that makes the value of some database item incorrect. Suppose that transactions T_1 and T_2 are submitted at approximately the same time, and their operations are interleaved as shown in Figure 19.3a; the final value of item X will be incorrect because T_2 reads the value of X *before* T_1 changes it in the database, and hence

```
(a)  read_item (X);          (b)  read_item (X);
     X:=X-N;                       X:=X+M;
     write_item (X);               write_item (X);
     read_item (Y);
     Y:=Y+N;
     write_item (Y);
```

Figure 19.2   Two sample transactions. (a) Transaction T_1.
(b) Transaction T_2.

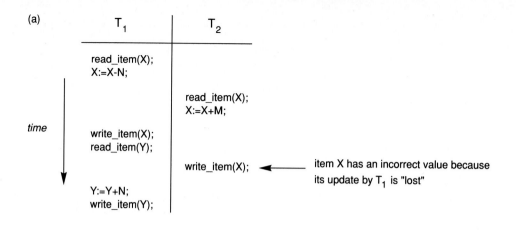

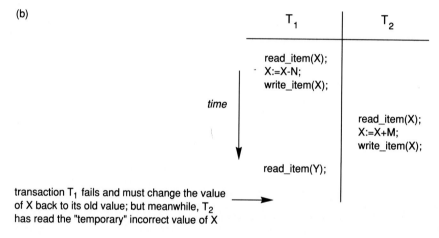

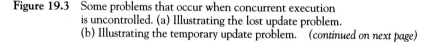

Figure 19.3   Some problems that occur when concurrent execution
is uncontrolled. (a) Illustrating the lost update problem.
(b) Illustrating the temporary update problem.   *(continued on next page)*

the updated value resulting from T_1 is lost. For example, if X = 80 at the start (originally
there were 80 reservations on the flight), N = 5 (T_1 cancels 5 seats on the flight corresponding to X and reserves them on that corresponding to Y), and M = 4 (T_2 reserves 4
seats on X), the final result should be X = 79 but in Figure 19.3a it is X = 84 because the
update that canceled 5 seats was *lost*.

The Temporary Update Problem

This occurs when one transaction updates a database item and then the transaction fails
for some reason (see Section 19.1.3). The updated item is accessed by another transaction before it is changed back to its original value. Figure 19.3b shows an example
where T_1 updates item X and then fails before completion, so the system must change X

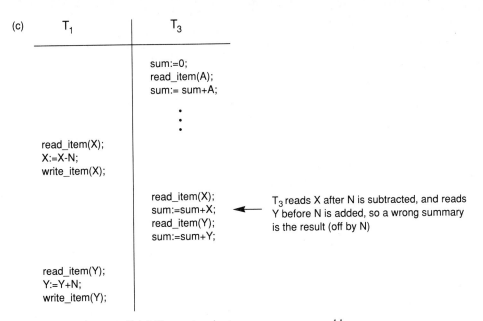

(c)

T_1	T_3

	sum:=0;
	read_item(A);
	sum:= sum+A;

	⋮

read_item(X);
X:=X-N;
write_item(X);	

	read_item(X); ← T_3 reads X after N is subtracted, and reads sum:=sum+X; Y before N is added, so a wrong summary read_item(Y); is the result (off by N) sum:=sum+Y;

read_item(Y);
Y:=Y+N;
write_item(Y);	

Figure 19.3 *(continued)* (c) Illustrating the incorrect summary problem.

back to its original value. Before it does so, transaction T_2 reads the "temporary" value of X, which will not be recorded permanently in the database because of the failure of T_1.

The Incorrect Summary Problem

Another problem occurs if one transaction is calculating an aggregate summary function on a number of records while other transactions are updating some of these records. The aggregate function may calculate some values before they are updated and others after they are updated. For example, suppose a transaction T_3 is calculating the total number of reservations on all the flights; meanwhile, transaction T_1 is executing. If the interleaving of operations shown in Figure 19.3c occurs, the result of T_3 will be off by an amount N because T_3 reads the value of X *after* N seats are subtracted from it and reads the value of Y *before* those N seats are added to it.

In Sections 19.3 to 19.5 we will discuss the concurrency control concepts and techniques that are used so that these types of problems do not occur when transactions execute concurrently and access the same data items.

19.1.3 *Why Recovery Is Needed*

Whenever a transaction is submitted to a DBMS for execution, the system is responsible for making sure that either (a) all the operations in the transaction are completed successfully and their effect is recorded permanently in the database or (b) the transaction has no effect whatsoever on the database or on any other transactions. What the DBMS must not permit to happen is that some operations of a transaction T are applied to the database while other operations of T are not. This may happen if a transaction **fails** after executing some of its operations but before executing all of them.

Types of Failures

There are several possible reasons for a transaction to fail in the middle of execution. Some of these reasons are:

1. A computer failure (system crash): A hardware or software error occurs in the computer system during transaction execution. If the hardware crashes, the contents of the computer internal memory may be lost.

2. A transaction or system error: Some operation in the transaction may cause it to fail, such as integer overflow or division by zero. Transaction failure may also occur because of erroneous parameter values or because of a logical programming error. In addition, the user may interrupt the transaction during its execution on purpose—for example, by issuing a control-C in a VAX/VMS or UNIX environment.

3. Local errors or exception conditions detected by the transaction: During transaction execution, certain conditions may occur that necessitate cancellation of the transaction. For example, data for the transaction may not be found. A condition, such as insufficient account balance in a banking database, may cause a transaction, such as fund withdrawal from that account, to be canceled. This may be done by a programmed ABORT in the transaction itself.

4. Concurrency control enforcement: The concurrency control method may decide to abort the transaction, to be restarted later, because it violates serializability or because several transactions are in a state of deadlock (see Sections 19.3 and 19.4).

5. Disk failure: Some disk blocks may lose their data because of a read or write malfunction or because of a disk read/write head crash. This may happen during a read or a write operation of the transaction.

6. Physical problems and catastrophes: This is an endless list that includes power or air conditioning failure, fire, theft, sabotage, overwriting disks or tapes by mistake, mounting of a wrong tape by the operator, etc.

Failures 1, 2, 3, and 4 are more common than 5 or 6. Whenever a failure of type 1 through 4 occurs, it is necessary that the system keep sufficient information to recover from the failure. Disk failure or other catastrophic failures of type 5 or 6 do not happen frequently; if they do occur, it is a major task to recover from these types of failure. We discuss concepts and techniques for recovery from failure in Section 19.6.

The concept of an atomic transaction is fundamental to many techniques for concurrency control and recovery from failures. In the next section we present the transaction concept and discuss why it is important.

19.2   Transaction and System Concepts for Recovery and Concurrency Control

As mentioned earlier, the *execution of a program* that includes database access operations is called a **database transaction** or simply **transaction**. If the database operations in a transaction do not update any data in the database but only retrieve data, the transaction is called a **read-only transaction**. In this chapter we are mainly interested in transactions that do some updates to the database, so the word transaction refers to a program execution that *updates the database* unless we explicitly state otherwise.

19.2.1 Read and Write Operations of a Transaction

We deal with transactions at the level of data items and disk blocks for the purpose of discussing concurrency control and recovery techniques. At this level, the database access operations that a transaction can include are:

- **read_item(X)**: Reads a database item named X into a program variable. To simplify our notation, we assume *the program variable is also named* X.
- **write_item(X)**: Writes the value of program variable X into the database item named X.

As we discussed in Chapter 4, the basic unit of data transfer from the disk to the computer main memory is one block. In general, a data item will be the field of some record in the database, although it may be a larger unit such as a record or even a whole block. Executing a read_item(X) command includes the following steps:

1. Find the address of the disk block that contains item X.
2. Copy that disk block into a buffer in main memory (if that disk block is not already in some main memory buffer).
3. Copy item X from the buffer to the program variable named X.

Executing a write_item(X) command includes the following steps:

1. Find the address of the disk block that contains item X.
2. Copy that disk block into a buffer in main memory (if that disk block is not already in some main memory buffer).
3. Copy item X from the program variable named X into its correct location in the buffer.
4. Store the updated block in the buffer back to disk (either immediately or at some later point in time).

Step 4 is the one that actually updates the database on disk. In some cases the buffer is not directly stored to disk in case additional changes are to be made to the buffer. Usually, the decision of when to store back a modified disk block that is in a main memory buffer is handled by the recovery manager or the operating system.

A transaction will include read_item and write_item operations to access the database. Figure 19.2 showed examples of two very simple transactions. Concurrency control and recovery mechanisms are mainly concerned with the database access commands in a transaction. In the next section we discuss the typical states that a transaction goes through from the time it is submitted for execution.

19.2.2 Transaction States and Additional Operations

A transaction is an atomic unit of work that is either completed in entirety or not done at all. For recovery purposes, the system needs to keep track of when the transaction starts, terminates, and commits (see below). Hence, the recovery manager keeps track of the following operations:

- BEGIN_TRANSACTION: This marks the beginning of transaction execution.

- READ or WRITE: These specify read or write operations on the database items that are executed as part of a transaction.

- END_TRANSACTION: This specifies that READ and WRITE transaction operations have ended and marks the end limit of transaction execution. However, at this point it may be necessary to check whether the changes of the transaction can be permanently applied to the database (committed) or whether the transaction has to be aborted because it violates concurrency control or for some other reason. We will discuss various techniques that require this checking throughout this chapter.

- COMMIT_TRANSACTION: This signals a *successful end* of the transaction so that any changes (updates) executed by the transaction can be safely **committed** to the database and will not be undone.

In addition to the above operations, some recovery techniques require additional operations that include the following:

- ROLLBACK (or ABORT): This signals that the transaction has *ended unsuccessfully*, so that any changes or effects that the transaction may have applied to the database must be *undone*.

- UNDO: Similar to rollback except that it applies to a single operation rather than to a whole transaction.

- REDO: This specifies that certain *transaction operations* must be *redone* to ensure that all the operations of a committed transaction have been applied successfully to the database.

Figure 19.4 shows a state transition diagram that describes how a transaction moves through its execution states. A transaction goes into an **active** state immediately after it starts execution, where it can issue READ and WRITE operations. When the transaction ends, it moves to the **partially committed** state. At this point, some concurrency control

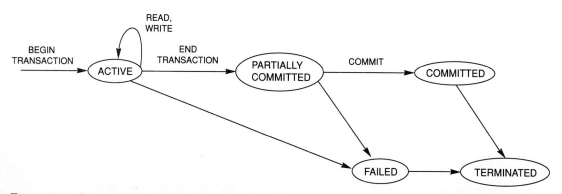

Figure 19.4   State transition diagram for transaction execution

techniques require that certain *checks* be made to ensure that the transaction did not interfere with other executing transactions. In addition, some recovery protocols need to ensure that a system failure will not result in an inability to record the changes of the transaction permanently (usually by recording changes in a system log, discussed in the next subsection). Once both checks are successful, the transaction is said to reach its commit point and enters the **committed state**. Commit points are discussed in more detail in Section 19.2.4. Once a transaction enters the committed state, it has concluded its execution successfully.

However, a transaction can go to the **failed** state if one of the checks fails or if it is aborted during its active state. The transaction may have to be rolled back to undo the effect of its WRITE operations on the database. The **terminated** state corresponds to the transaction leaving the system. Notice that failed or aborted transactions may be *restarted* later, either automatically or after being resubmitted, as brand new transactions.

19.2.3 The System Log

To be able to recover from transaction failures, the system maintains a **log** (sometimes called a **journal**). The log keeps track of all transaction operations that affect the values of database items. This information may be needed to recover from transaction failures. The log is kept on disk so that it is not affected by any type of failure except for disk or catastrophic failure. In addition, the log is periodically backed up to archival storage (tape) to guard against such catastrophic failures. We now list the types of entries that are written to the log. In these entries, T refers to a unique **transaction-id** that is generated automatically by the system and used to identify each transaction.

1. [start_transaction,T]: This log entry records that transaction T starts execution.
2. [write_item,T,X,old_value,new_value]: This log entry records that transaction T changes the value of database item X from old_value to new_value.
3. [read_item,T,X]: This log entry records that transaction T reads the value of database item X.
4. [commit,T]: This log entry records that transaction T has completed all accesses to the database successfully, and its effect can be committed (recorded permanently) to the database.

As we shall see in Section 19.6, some protocols for recovery do not require that READ operations—item 3 above—be written to the log, whereas other protocols require these entries for recovery. In the former case, the overhead of recording operations in the log is reduced because fewer operations—only WRITEs—are recorded in the log. In addition, some protocols require simpler WRITE entries that do not include new_value.

Notice that we assume that transactions cannot be nested. We are also assuming that *all* permanent changes to the database occur within transactions, so that the notion of recovery from a transaction failure amounts to either undoing or redoing the *recoverable* transaction operations individually, transaction by transaction, from the log. If the system crashes, we can recover to a consistent database state by examining the log and using one of the techniques described in Section 19.6. Because the log contains a record of every WRITE operation that changes the value of some database item, it is possible to **undo** the effect of these WRITE operations of a transaction T by tracing backward through the log and resetting all items changed by a WRITE operation of T to their old_values. We can also **redo** the effect of the WRITE operations of a transaction T by tracing forward through the log and setting all items changed by a WRITE operation of T to their new_values. Redoing the operations of a transaction may be needed if all its updates are recorded in the log but a failure occurs before we can be sure that all the new_values have been written permanently in the actual database.

19.2.4   Commit Points and Checkpoints

Commit Point of a Transaction

A transaction T reaches its **commit point** when all its operations that access the database have been executed successfully *and* the effect of all the transaction operations on the database has been recorded in the log. Beyond the commit point, the transaction is said to be **committed,** and its effect is assumed to be *permanently recorded* in the database. The transaction then writes an entry [commit,T] into the log. If a system failure occurs, we search back in the log for all transactions T that have written a [start_transaction,T] entry into the log but have not written their [commit,T] entry yet; these transactions may have to be *rolled back* to undo their effect on the database during the recovery process. Transactions that have written their commit entry in the log must also have recorded all their WRITE operations in the log—otherwise they would not be committed, so their effect on the database can be *redone* from the log entries.

Notice that the log file must be kept on disk. However, as discussed in Chapter 4, updating a disk file involves the following:

1. Copying the appropriate block of the file from disk to a buffer in main memory.
2. Updating the buffer in main memory.
3. Copying the buffer back from main memory disk.

It is common to keep one block of the log file in main memory until it is filled with log entries and then write it back to disk only once rather than writing it to disk every time a log entry is added. This saves the overhead of multiple disk writes of the same file block. At the time of a system crash, only the log entries that have been *written back to disk* are considered in the recovery process because the contents of main memory may be lost. Hence, *before* a transaction reaches its commit point, any portion of the log that has not been written to the disk yet must now be written to the disk. This process is called **force writing** the log file before committing a transaction.

Checkpoints in the System Log

Another type of entry in the log is called a **checkpoint.*** A [checkpoint] record is written into the log periodically at that point when the system writes out to the database on disk the effect of all WRITE operations of committed transactions. Hence, all transactions

---

*The term "checkpoint" has been used to describe more restrictive situations in some systems, such as DB2. It has also been used in the literature to describe different concepts.

that have their [commit,T] entries in the log before a [checkpoint] entry will not require their WRITE operations to be *redone* in case of a system crash.

The recovery manager of a DBMS must decide at what intervals to take a checkpoint. The interval may be measured in time—say every m minutes—or in terms of the number t of committed transactions since the last checkpoint, where the values of m or t are system parameters. Taking a checkpoint may consist of the following actions by the recovery manager:

1. Suspend execution of transactions temporarily.
2. Force write all updated database blocks in main memory buffers to disk.
3. Write a [checkpoint] record to the log and force write the log to disk.
4. Resume executing transactions.

A checkpoint record in the log may also include additional information, such as a list of active transaction ids, and the locations (addresses) of the first and most recent (last) records in the log for each active transaction. This can facilitate undoing of transaction operations, which is needed when a transaction is rolled back in some recovery methods.

19.2.5   Desirable Properties of Transactions

There are several properties that atomic transactions should possess. These properties need to be enforced by the concurrency control and recovery methods of the DBMS, although some methods do not enforce all the properties. The following are desirable properties of transactions:

1. **Atomicity**: A transaction is an atomic unit of processing; it is either performed in its entirety or not performed at all.
2. **Consistency preservation**: A correct execution of the transaction must take the database from one consistent state to another.
3. **Durability or permanency**: Once a transaction changes the database and the changes are committed, these changes must never be lost because of subsequent failure.
4. **Isolation**: A transaction should not make its updates visible to other transactions until it is committed; this property, when enforced strictly, solves the temporary update problem discussed in Section 19.1.2 and makes cascading rollbacks of transactions unnecessary (see Section 19.6). In general, various *levels of isolation* are permitted by different methods of concurrency control and recovery, as we shall see.
5. **Serializability**: This is a criterion that most concurrency control methods enforce. Informally, if the effect of running transactions in an interleaved fashion is equivalent to running them serially in some order they are considered serializable. We discuss serializability in detail in Section 19.3.

The atomicity property requires that we execute a transaction to completion. It is the responsibility of the recovery method to ensure atomicity. If a transaction fails to complete for some reason, such as a system crash in the midst of transaction execution, the recovery method must undo any effects of the transaction on the database.

The consistency preservation property is generally considered to be the responsibility of the programmers who write the database programs. Recall that a **database state** is a collection of all the stored data items (values) in the database at a given point in time. A **consistent state** of the database satisfies the constraints specified in the schema as well as any other constraints that should hold on the database. A database program should be written in a way that guarantees that if the database is in a consistent state before executing the transaction, it will be in a consistent state after the *complete* execution of the transaction if *no interference with other transactions* occurs. It is the responsibility of the programmer and the semantic integrity subsystem of the DBMS (see Chapter 20) to ensure the consistency preservation property.

The durability property is the responsibility of the recovery method, while serializability is the responsibility of the concurrency control method. Isolation is enforced by some recovery methods, but other recovery methods do not enforce it at the expense of more complex recovery techniques involving cascading rollback, as we shall discuss in Section 19.6.

19.2.6   Schedules of Transactions

Suppose that two users—airline reservation clerks—submit to the DBMS transactions T_1 and T_2 of Figure 19.2 at approximately the same time. If no interleaving is permitted, there are only two possibilities of ordering the operations of the two transactions for execution:

1. Execute all the operations of transaction T_1 (in sequence) followed by all the operations of transaction T_2 (in sequence).

2. Execute all the operations of transaction T_2 (in sequence) followed by all the operations of transaction T_1 (in sequence).

These are shown in Figures 19.5a and b, respectively. If interleaving of operations is allowed, there will be many possible orders in which the system can execute the individual operations of the transactions. Two possible sequences are shown in Figure 19.5c. Each such ordering is called a *schedule* of executing the transactions T_1 and T_2.

In general, a **schedule** S of n transactions is a sequential ordering of the operations of the n transactions subject to the constraint that, for each transaction T that participates in S, if operation i is performed before operation j in T, then operation i will be performed before operation j in S. The constraint simply states that a schedule maintains the order of operations within the individual transactions. However, the ordering of operations among the different transactions can be interleaved arbitrarily, each ordering leading to a different schedule.

An important aspect of concurrency control, called **serializability theory,** attempts to determine which schedules are "correct" and which are not and to develop techniques that allow only correct schedules. The next section defines serializability of schedules, presents some of this theory, and shows how it may be used in practice.

19.3 Serializability of Schedules and Its Uses

In Section 19.3.1 we define a serializable schedule as a schedule that is equivalent to some serial schedule. We then discuss in Section 19.3.2 different ways in which equivalence of schedules can be defined. In Section 19.3.3 we show how a schedule can be tested for serializability. Section 19.3.4 discusses the uses of serializability in concurrency control methods.

19.3.1 Serial, Nonserial, and Serializable Schedules

Figure 19.5 shows several possible schedules for transactions T_1 and T_2 of Figure 19.2. Schedules A and B in Figures 19.5a and b are called serial schedules because the operations of each transaction are executed consecutively without any interleaved operations from the other transaction. In a serial schedule, the entire transactions are performed in

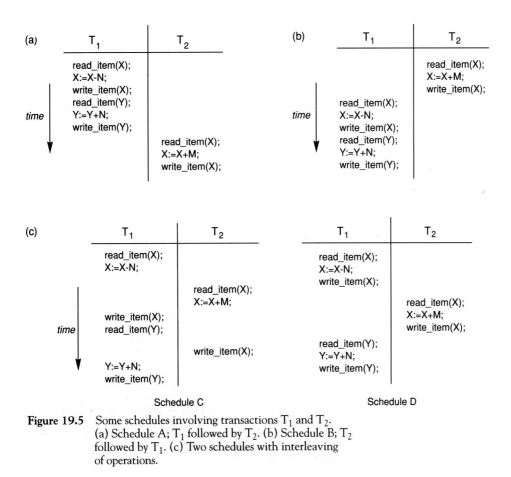

Figure 19.5 Some schedules involving transactions T_1 and T_2.
(a) Schedule A; T_1 followed by T_2. (b) Schedule B; T_2 followed by T_1. (c) Two schedules with interleaving of operations.

serial order: T_1 then T_2 in Figure 19.5a and T_2 then T_1 in Figure 19.5b. Schedules C and D in Figure 19.5c are called nonserial because each sequence interleaves operations from the two transactions; in other words, the transactions are not performed in their entirety without interleaving.

Formally, a schedule S is **serial** if, for every transaction T participating in the schedule, all the operations of T are executed consecutively in the schedule; otherwise, the schedule is called **nonserial**. One reasonable assumption we can make, if we consider the transactions to be *independent*, is that *every serial schedule is considered correct*. This is so because we assume that every transaction is correct if executed on its own (by the consistency preservation property of Section 19.2.5) and that transactions do not depend on one another. Hence, it does not matter which transaction is executed first. As long as every transaction is executed from beginning to end without any interference from the operations of other transactions, we get a correct end result on the database. The problem with serial schedules is that they limit concurrency or interleaving of operations. In a serial schedule, if a transaction waits for an I/O operation to complete, we cannot switch the CPU processor to another transaction, thus wasting valuable CPU processing time and making serial schedules generally unacceptable.

To illustrate our discussion, consider the schedules in Figure 19.5 and assume that the initial values of database items are $X = 90$, $Y = 90$ and that $N = 3$ and $M = 2$. After executing transactions T_1 and T_2, we would expect the database values to be $X = 89$ and $Y = 93$ according to the meaning of the transactions. Sure enough, executing either of the serial schedules A or B gives the correct results. Now consider the nonserial schedules C and D. Schedule C (same as Figure 19.3a) gives the results $X = 92$ and $Y = 93$, in which the X value is erroneous, whereas schedule D gives the correct results.

Schedule C gives an erroneous result because of the lost update problem discussed in Section 19.1.2; transaction T_2 reads the value of X *before* it is changed by transaction T_1, so that only the effect of T_2 on X is reflected in the database. The effect of T_1 on X is *lost*, overwritten by T_2, leading to the incorrect result for item X. However, some nonserial schedules give the correct expected result, such as schedule D. We would like to determine which of the nonserial schedules *always* give a correct result and which may give erroneous results. The concept used to characterize schedules in this manner is that of serializability of a schedule.

A schedule S of n transactions is **serializable** if it is *equivalent to some serial schedule* of the same n transactions. We will define the concept of equivalence of transactions shortly. Note that there are (n)! possible serial schedules of n transactions and many more possible nonserial schedules. We can form two disjoint groups of the nonserial schedules: those that are equivalent to one (or more) of the serial schedules, and hence are serializable, and those that are not equivalent to *any* serial schedule and hence are not serializable.

Saying that a nonserial schedule S is serializable is equivalent to saying that it is correct, because it is equivalent to a serial schedule, which is considered correct. The remaining question is: When are two schedules considered "equivalent"? We discuss this in the following section.

19.3.2   Equivalence of Schedules

There are several ways to define equivalence of schedules. Simple definitions of schedule equivalence make the theory of serializability somewhat straightforward, but the assumptions made by these definitions are often unrealistic. Other definitions of schedule equivalence are more realistic but make serializability theory more complex. We will discuss several of the equivalence definitions and see how each affects serializability.

Result Equivalence and Commutative Equivalence

The simplest, but least satisfactory, definition of schedule equivalence is by comparing the effects of the schedules on the database. Two schedules are called **result equivalent** if they produce the same final state of the database. However, two different schedules may accidentally produce the same final state. For example, in Figure 19.6a, schedules S_1 and S_2 will produce the same final database state if they execute on a database with an initial value of $X = 100$, but for other initial values of X the schedules are *not* result equivalent. In addition, these two schedules execute different transactions, so they definitely should not be considered equivalent. Hence, result equivalence is not used to define equivalence of schedules.

A second definition of equivalence makes some *assumptions* on the types of update operations that a transaction may include. For example, we may assume that all operations on database items are commutative. The commutative property states that if one operation changes the value of item X to $f_1(X)$, and another operation sets the value of X to $f_2(X)$, then $f_1(f_2(X)) = f_2(f_1(X))$. This implies that the order of operations is not important as long as exactly the same set of operations is applied to each item in both

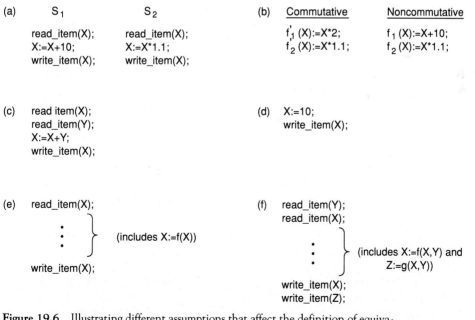

Figure 19.6 Illustrating different assumptions that affect the definition of equivalence of schedules. (a) Two schedules that are equivalent for the initial value of $X = 100$. (b) Commutative and non-commutative operations. (c) New value dependent on several database items. (d) New value independent of database items. (e) New value depends on old value of item only (constrained write assumption). (f) Unconstrained write assumption.

schedules. However, commutativity of operations usually does not hold, so this assumption will disallow many types of operations. In Figure 19.6b, operations f_1 and f_2 are not commutative, whereas f_1' and f_2' are.

Order Equivalence, the Constrained Write Assumption, and the Unconstrained Write Assumption

The safest and most general approach to defining schedule equivalence is not to make any assumption on the types of operations included in the transactions. For two schedules to be equivalent, each data item affected by the schedules should have the operations applied to that item in both schedules be *in the same order*. In order not to examine the exact operations within a transaction, the assumption is that a transaction updates an item based on its old value, which is read by the transaction. Hence, we need only be concerned with the read_item(X) and write_item(X) operations in a transaction. This is called the **constrained write** (or **read before write**) assumption.

This constrained write assumption is reasonable for many types of database transactions, but not all. For example, the new value of an item X may depend not only on its old value but also on the values of other database items, as illustrated in Figure 19.6c. Another possibility is that the new value of X may be independent of any database value, as shown in Figure 19.6d. The **unconstrained write** assumption allows the latter two possibilities. As we shall see in Section 19.3.3, the assumption we choose affects the method of determining whether a schedule is serializable. A simple algorithm exists for testing the serializability of a schedule under the constrained write assumption, but it is harder to determine serializability under the unconstrained write assumption.

Using the constrained write assumption, we assume that the new value of an item is dependent only on its old value. Hence, we can assume that between read_item(X) and write_item(X) in every transaction, some computational operations are applied to calculate the new value of X based on its original value. We can summarize these computational operations by a function $f(X)$ applied to X between the read_item(X) and write_item(X) operations of each transaction, as shown in Figure 19.6e. On the other hand, if we use the unconstrained write assumption, we can specify two sets of items for each transaction:

1. The **read set** is the set of all items read by the transaction.
2. The **write set** is the set of all items written by the transaction.

In the case of unconstrained writes, we can assume that the new value of each database item in the write set is dependent on the values of some of the items in the read set, as illustrated in Figure 19.6f. The definition of equivalence of schedules, given earlier, is the same under both the constrained and unconstrained write assumptions. However, the distinction between assumptions makes an important difference when we discuss testing for serializability of schedules in Section 19.3.3.

Equivalence of Schedules for Defining Serializable Schedules

For serializability purposes, we define two schedules as equivalent only if they both include the participation of exactly the same transactions. In addition, the final effect of the two schedules on the database must be the same *regardless of the starting database state*. More formally, two schedules S_1 and S_2 in which exactly the same transactions T_1, T_2, ..., T_n participate are **equivalent** if:

1. For each read_item(X) operation executed by transaction T_i in S_1, if the value of X read by this operation was last written by a write_item(X) operation executed by transaction T_j in S_1, then the same read_item(X) operation of T_i in S_2 must read the value of X written by the same write_item(X) operation of T_j in S_2.

2. For each item X on which a write_item(X) operation is applied in the schedules, if the final write_item(X) in schedule S_1 is executed by transaction T_i, then the final write_item(X) in schedule S_2 must be the same write_item(X) operation executed by T_i.

The above definition of equivalence of schedules says that every read operation in S_2 must read the same value as the corresponding read operation in S_1. In addition, the last value written into the database for every item should be the same for both schedules. According to this definition, schedule D of Figure 19.5c is equivalent to the serial schedule A of Figure 19.5a. In both these schedules, the read_item(X) of T_2 reads the value of X written by T_1, while the other read_item operations read the database values from the initial database state. In addition, T_1 is the last transaction to write item Y and T_2 the last transaction to write X in both schedules. Because A is a serial schedule, and schedule D is equivalent to A, D is a *serializable schedule*.

Schedule C of Figure 19.5c is not equivalent to either of the two possible serial schedules A and B. It is not equivalent to A because the read_item(X) operation in T_2 reads the value written by T_1 in schedule A but reads the original value of X in schedule C, thus violating rule 1 for equivalence. Schedule C is also not equivalent to B because it violates both rules 1 and 2 for equivalence. Hence, schedule C is *not serializable*. In the next section we give algorithms to determine whether a schedule is serializable or not under the constrained write assumption.

19.3.3 Testing for Serializability of a Schedule

As we mentioned earlier, there is a simple algorithm to determine the serializability of a schedule under the constrained write assumption. The algorithm is more complicated for the unconstrained write assumption. It is important to point out that most concurrency control methods *do not* actually test for serializability. Rather, protocols, or rules, are developed that guarantee a schedule to be serializable if they hold on *all* the individual transactions that participate in the schedule. We discuss the algorithms for testing serializability of schedules here to gain a better understanding of these protocols, which are discussed in Sections 19.4 and 19.5.

Testing Serializability Under Constrained Write

Algorithm 19.1 will test a schedule for serializability under the constrained write assumption. The algorithm looks at only the read_item and write_item operations in the schedule. To test whether a schedule S is serializable, a **precedence graph** is constructed for the

ALGORITHM 19.1   Testing serializability of a schedule S under
the constrained write assumption

(1)   for each transaction T_i participating in schedule S
create a node labeled T_i in the precedence graph;
(2)   for each case in S where T_j executes a read_item(X) that reads the value
of item X written by a write_item (X) command executed by T_i
create an edge $(T_i \rightarrow T_j)$ in the precedence graph;
(3)   for each case in S where T_j executes write_item(X) after T_i executes a
read_item(X)
create an edge $(T_i \rightarrow T_j)$ in the precedence graph;
(4)   the schedule S is serializable if and only if the precedence graph has no
cycles;

schedule. A precedence graph is a **directed graph** $G = (N,E)$ that consists of a set of nodes $N = \{T_1, T_2, ..., T_n\}$ and a set of directed edges $E = \{e_1, e_2, ..., e_m\}$. There is one node in the graph for each transaction T_i in the schedule. Each edge e_i in the graph is of the form $(T_j \rightarrow T_k)$, $1 \le j \le n$, $1 \le k \le n$, where T_j is called the **starting node** of e_i and T_k is called the **ending node** of e_i.

The precedence graph is constructed as shown in Algorithm 19.1. If there is a cycle in the precedence graph, schedule S is not serializable; if there is no cycle, then S is serializable. A **cycle** in a directed graph is a *sequence* of edges $C = ((T_j \rightarrow T_k), (T_k \rightarrow T_p),..., (T_i \rightarrow T_j))$ with the property that the starting node of each edge—except the first edge—is the same as the ending node of the previous edge, and the starting node of the first edge is the same as the ending node of the last edge. Hence, the sequence starts and ends at the same node.

In the precedence graph, an edge from T_i to T_j means that transaction T_i must come before transaction T_j in any serial schedule that is equivalent to S according to the definition of schedule equivalence given earlier. If there is no cycle in the precedence graph, we can create an **equivalent serial schedule** S' that is equivalent to S by ordering the transactions that participate in S as follows: Whenever an edge exists in the precedence graph from T_i to T_j, T_i must appear before T_j in the equivalent serial schedule S'. The latter process is known as topological sorting. Note that the edges $(T_i \rightarrow T_j)$ in a precedence graph can optionally be labeled by the name(s) of the data item(s) that led to creating the edge.

In general, there can be several serial schedules equivalent to S if the precedence graph has no cycle. On the other hand, if the precedence graph has a cycle, it is easy to show that we cannot create any equivalent serial schedule, so schedule S is not serializable. Figures 19.7a to d show the precedence graphs created for schedules A to D, respectively, of Figure 19.5. The precedence graph for schedule C has a cycle, so it is not serializable. The graph for schedule D has no cycle, so it is serializable, and the equivalent serial schedule is T_1 followed by T_2. The graphs for schedules A and B have no cycles, as expected, because the schedules are *serial* and hence serializable.

Another example, in which three transactions participate, is shown in Figure 19.8. Figure 19.8a shows the read_item and write_item operations in each transaction. Two schedules E and F for these transactions are shown in Figures 19.8b and c, respectively. We show the precedence graphs for schedules E and F in Figures 19.8d and e. Schedule E is not serializable, because the corresponding precedence graph has cycles. Schedule F is serializable, and the serial schedule equivalent to F is shown in Figure 19.8e. Although

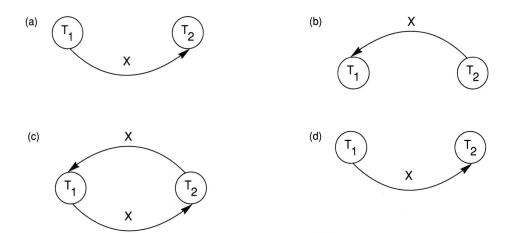

Figure 19.7 Constructing the precedence graphs for schedules A to D to test
for serializability under constrained write. (a) Precedence graph for
schedule A of Figure 19.5. (b) Precedence graph for schedule B of
Figure 19.5. (c) Precedence graph for schedule C of Figure 19.5
(not serializable). (d) Precedence graph for schedule D of Figure 19.5
(serializable, equivalent to schedule A).

only one equivalent serial schedule exists for schedule F, in general there may be more
than one equivalent serial schedule for a serializable schedule. Figure 19.8f shows a
precedence graph that represents a schedule which has two equivalent serial schedules.

Algorithm 19.1 gives a simple method for testing serializability under the constrained write assumption. Unfortunately, under the more general and more realistic assumption of unconstrained write, the algorithm to test for serializability is more complex.
The problem was shown to be NP-complete, meaning that it is highly improbable that an
efficient algorithm can be found for this problem. The textbook by Ullman (1982) presents an algorithm for testing serializability under the unconstrained write assumption.

19.3.4 Uses of Serializability

As we discussed above, saying that a schedule S is serializable, that is, S is equivalent to
a serial schedule, is tantamount to saying that S is correct. Note that a schedule being
serializable is distinct from being *serial*. A serial schedule represents inefficient processing
because no interleaving of operations from different transactions is permitted. This can
lead to low CPU utilization while a transaction waits for disk I/O, thus slowing down processing considerably. A serializable schedule gives us the benefits of concurrent execution without giving up any correctness.

In practice, it is quite difficult to test for the serializability of a schedule. The interleaving of operations from concurrent transactions is typically determined by the operating system scheduler. Factors such as system load, time of transaction submission, and
priorities of transactions contribute to the ordering of operations in a schedule by the operating system. Hence, it is practically impossible to determine how the operations of a
schedule will be interleaved beforehand to ensure serializability.

(a)

transaction T₁	transaction T₂	transaction T₃
read_item (X); write_item (X); read_item (Y); write_item (Y);	read_item (Z); read_item (Y); write_item (Y); read_item (X); write_item (X);	read_item (Y); read_item (Z); write_item (Y); write_item (Z);

(b)

transaction T₁	transaction T₂	transaction T₃
	read_item (Z); read_item (Y); write_item (Y);	
		read_item (Y); read_item (Z);
read_item (X); write_item (X);		
time		write_item (Y); write_item (Z);
	read_item (X);	
read_item (Y); write_item (Y);		
	write_item (X);	

(c)

transaction T₁	transaction T₂	transaction T₃
		read_item (Y); read_item (Z);
read_item (X); write_item (X);		
time		write_item (Y); write_item (Z);
	read_item (Z);	
read_item (Y); write_item (Y);		
	read_item (Y); write_item (Y); read_item (X); write_item (X);	

Figure 19.8   Another example of serializability testing.
(a) The READ and WRITE operations of three transactions.
(b) Schedule E of the transactions T_1, T_2, and T_3.
(c) Schedule F of the transactions T_1, T_2, and T_3.
(continued on next page)

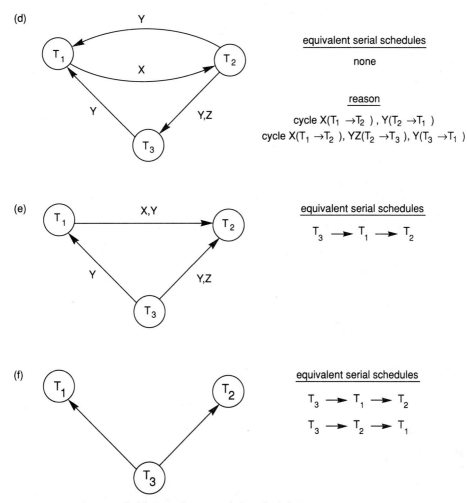

(d)

Y

T_1 T_2

X

Y   Y,Z

T_3

equivalent serial schedules

reason

cycle X($T_1 \rightarrow T_2$) , Y($T_2 \rightarrow T_1$)
cycle X($T_1 \rightarrow T_2$), YZ($T_2 \rightarrow T_3$), Y($T_3 \rightarrow T_1$)

(e)   X,Y

T_1 T_2

Y   Y,Z

T_3

equivalent serial schedules

$T_3 \longrightarrow T_1 \longrightarrow T_2$

(f)

T_1 T_2

T_3

equivalent serial schedules

$T_3 \longrightarrow T_1 \longrightarrow T_2$

$T_3 \longrightarrow T_2 \longrightarrow T_1$

Figure 19.8   *(continued)* (d) Precedence graph for schedule E.
(e) Precedence graph for schedule F. (f) A precedence
graph with two equivalent serial schedules.

   If transactions are executed at will and then the resulting schedule is tested for serializability, we must cancel the effect of the schedule if it turns out not to be serializable.
This is a serious problem that makes this approach impractical. Another problem is that
when transactions are submitted continuously to the system, it is difficult to determine
when a schedule begins and when it ends. This compounds the problem and makes it
even harder to test for serializability in a practical system.
   Hence, the approach taken in most practical systems is to determine methods that
ensure serializability without having to test for serializability of the schedules themselves
after they are executed. One such method uses the theory of serializability to determine
protocols or sets of rules that, if followed by *every* individual transaction, will ensure serializability of *all schedules in which the transactions participate*. Now, we can check that

every transaction follows these protocols when we write every individual database program. Hence, in this approach we never have to concern ourselves with the schedules themselves. These protocols mainly use the techniques of **locking** of data items to prevent multiple transactions from accessing the items concurrently and are described in Section 19.4.

Other methods for concurrency control use transaction **timestamps**. A timestamp is a unique identifier for each transaction generated by the system, and transactions can be ordered according to their timestamps to ensure serializability. Again, we do not have to concern ourselves with testing of serializability of the schedules in this approach, but we have to check that transaction order is maintained on every item accessed in the schedule. Timestamps are also sometimes used in a concurrency control scheme that keeps multiple versions of items. We discuss timestamp-based approaches to concurrency control in Sections 19.5.1 through 19.5.4.

Another factor that affects concurrency control is the **granularity** of the items, that is, what portion of the database an item represents. An item can be as small as a single value or as large as the database itself. Of course, in the latter case, very little concurrency is allowed. We discuss granularity of items in Section 19.5.5.

19.4   Locking Techniques for Concurrency Control

One of the main techniques used to control concurrent execution of transactions is based on the concept of locking of data items. A **lock** is a variable associated with a data item in the database and describes the status of that item with respect to possible operations that can be applied to the item. Generally, there is one lock for each data item in the database. We use locks as a means of synchronizing the access by concurrent transactions to the database items. In Section 19.4.1 we discuss the nature and types of locks. Then we present protocols that use locking to guarantee serializability of transaction schedules in Section 19.4.2. Finally, in Section 19.4.3 we discuss two problems associated with the use of locks, namely deadlock and livelock, and show how these problems are handled.

19.4.1   Types of Locks

Several types of locks can be used in concurrency control. We will first present binary locks, which are simple but somewhat restrictive in their use. Then we will discuss other types of locks, such as shared locks and exclusive locks, which provide more general locking capabilities.

Binary Locks

A **binary lock** can have two **states** (or **values**): locked and unlocked, or 1 and 0 for simplicity. A distinct lock is associated with *each* database item X. If the value of the lock on X is 1, item X *cannot be accessed* by a database operation that requests the item. If the value of the lock on X is 0, the item can be accessed when requested. We refer to the *value* of the lock associated with item X by LOCK(X).

```
lock_item (X):
   B: if LOCK (X)=0  (* item is unlocked *)
      then LOCK (X)← 1  (* lock the item *)
      else begin
         wait  (until lock (X)=0  and
            the lock manager wakes up the transaction);
         go to B
         end;


unlock_item (X):
   LOCK (X)←0  (* unlock the item *)
   if any transactions are waiting
      then wakeup one of the waiting transactions;
```

Figure 19.9 Lock and unlock operations for binary locks

Two operations, lock_item and unlock_item, must be included in the transactions when binary locking is used. A transaction requests access to an item X by issuing a **lock_item(X)** operation. If LOCK(X) = 1, the transaction is forced to wait; otherwise, the transaction sets LOCK(X) := 1 (locks the item) and is allowed access. When the transaction is through using the item, it issues an **unlock_item(X)** operation, which sets LOCK(X) := 0 (unlocks the item), so X may be accessed by other transactions. Hence, a binary lock enforces *mutual exclusion* on the data item. A description of the lock_item(X) and unlock_item(X) operations is shown in Figure 19.9.

Note that the lock_item and unlock_item operations must be implemented as indivisible units; that is, no interleaving should be allowed once a lock or unlock operation is started until the operation terminates or the transaction waits. In Figure 19.9, the wait command within the lock_item(X) operation is usually implemented by putting the transaction on a waiting queue for the item X until X is unlocked and the transaction is granted access to it. Other transactions that also want to access X are placed on the same queue. Hence, the wait command is considered to be outside the lock_item operation. The DBMS will have a **lock manager** subsystem to keep track of and control access to locks.

When the binary locking scheme is used, every transaction must obey the following rules:

1. A transaction T must issue the operation lock_item(X) before any read_item(X) or write_item(X) operations in T.

2. A transaction T must issue the operation unlock_item(X) after all read_item(X) and write_item(X) operations are completed in T.

3. A transaction T will not issue a lock_item(X) operation if it already holds the lock on item X.

4. A transaction T will not issue an unlock_item(X) operation unless it already holds the lock on item X.

Between the lock_item(X) and unlock_item(X) operations in transaction T, T is said to **hold the lock** on item X. At most one transaction can hold the lock on a particular item. If all transactions follow rules 1 to 4, no two transactions can access the same item concurrently. The transactions can still proceed concurrently if they access different items in the database. Notice that it is quite simple to implement a binary lock; all that is needed is a binary-valued variable, LOCK, associated with each data item X in the database. In its simplest form, each lock can be a record with two fields: <data item name, LOCK>.

Shared and Exclusive Locks

The binary locking scheme described above is too restrictive in general, because at most one transaction can hold a lock on a given item. We should allow several transactions to access the same item X if they all access X for *reading purposes only*. However, if a transaction is to write an item X it must have exclusive access to X.

To allow concurrent access to the same item by several transactions that read the item, we use a different type of lock called a **multiple-mode lock**. In this scheme there are three locking operations: read_lock(X), write_lock(X), and unlock(X). A lock associated with an item X, LOCK(X), now has three possible states: "read locked," "write locked," or "unlocked." A read-locked item is also called **share locked,** because other transactions are allowed to read the item, whereas a write-locked item is called **exclusive locked** because a single transaction exclusively holds the lock on the item.

One simple, though not completely general, method for implementing the above three operations on a multiple-mode lock is to keep track of the number of transactions that hold a shared lock on an item. Each lock can be a record with three fields: <data item name, LOCK, no_of_reads>. The value of LOCK is one of read locked, write locked, or unlocked, suitably coded. The three operations read_lock(X), write_lock(X), and unlock(X) are described in Figure 19.10. Again, each of the three operations should be considered indivisible; no interleaving should be allowed once one of the operations is started until either the operation terminates or the transaction is placed on a waiting queue for the item.

When we use the multiple-mode locking scheme, every transaction must obey the following rules:

1. A transaction T must issue the operation read_lock(X) or write_lock(X) before any read_item(X) operation in T.

2. A transaction T must issue the operation write_lock(X) before any write_item(X) operation in T.

3. A transaction T must issue the operation unlock(X) after all read_item(X) and write_item(X) operations are completed in T.

4. A transaction T will not issue a read_lock(X) operation if it already holds a read (shared) lock or a write (exclusive) lock on item X. This rule may be relaxed, as we discuss below.

5. A transaction T will not issue a write_lock(X) operation if it already holds a read (shared) lock or write (exclusive) lock on item X. This rule may be relaxed, as we discuss below.

6. A transaction T will not issue an unlock(X) operation unless it already holds a read (shared) lock or a write (exclusive) lock on item X.

```
read_lock (X):
    B: if LOCK (X)="unlocked"
        then begin LOCK (X)← "read-locked";
                    no_of_reads(X)← 1
            end
        else if LOCK(X)="read-locked"
                then no_of_reads(X)← no_of _reads(X) + 1
                else begin wait (until LOCK (X)="unlocked" and
                            the lock manager wakes up the transaction);
                        go to B
                    end;


write_lock (X):
    B: if LOCK (X)="unlocked"
        then LOCK (X)← "write-locked"
        else begin
            wait (until LOCK(X)="unlocked" and
                the lock manager wakes up the transaction);
            go to B
            end;


unlock_item (X):
    if LOCK (X)="write-locked"
        then begin LOCK (X)← "unlocked"
            wakeup one of the waiting transactions,if any
            end
        else if LOCK(X)="read-locked"
                then begin
                    no_of_reads(X)← no_of_reads(X) -1;
                    if no_of_reads(X)=0
                        then begin LOCK (X)="unlocked";
                                wakeup one of the waiting transactions, if any
                                end
                    end;
```

Figure 19.10   Locking and unlocking operations for two-mode
(read-write or shared-exclusive) locks

Sometimes it is desirable to relax conditions 4 and 5 above. For example, it is possible for a transaction T to issue a read_lock(X) and then later on to **upgrade** the lock by
a write_lock(X) operation. If T is the only transaction with a read lock on X at the time
it issues the write_lock operation, we can upgrade the lock. It is also possible for a transaction T to issue a write_lock(X) and then later on to **downgrade** the lock by a
read_lock(X) operation. If we allow upgrading and downgrading of locks, we must include transaction identifiers in the record structure for each lock to store the information
on which transactions hold locks on the item and change the descriptions of the
read_lock(X) and write_lock(X) operations in Figure 19.10 appropriately. We leave this
as an exercise for the reader.

Using binary locks or multiple-mode locks in transactions, as described above,
does not guarantee serializability of schedules in which the transactions participate. Fig-

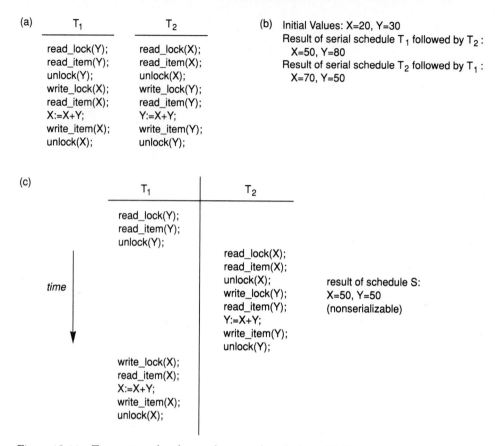

Figure 19.11   Transactions that do not obey two-phase locking. (a) Two
transactions T_1 and T_2. (b) Results of possible serial schedules
of T_1 and T_2. (c) A non-serializable schedule S that uses locks.

ure 19.11 shows an example where the above locking rules are followed but a nonserializable schedule may still result. This is because in Figure 19.11a the items Y in T_1 and X in T_2 were *unlocked too early.* This allows a schedule such as the one shown in Figure 19.11c to occur, which is not a serializable schedule and hence gives incorrect results. To guarantee serializability, we must follow *an additional protocol* concerning the positioning of locking and unlocking operations in every transaction. The best known protocol, two-phase locking, is described in the next section.

19.4.2   *Guaranteeing Serializability by Two-Phase Locking*

A transaction is said to follow the **two-phase locking protocol*** if *all* locking operations (read_lock, write_lock) precede the *first* unlock operation in the transaction. Such a transaction can be divided into two phases: an **expanding (or growing) phase,** during

---

*This is unrelated to the two-phase commit protocol for recovery in distributed databases (see Section 19.6.5 and Chapter 21).

which new locks on items can be acquired but none can be released, followed by a **shrinking phase,** during which existing locks can be released but no new locks can be acquired.

If upgrading of locks is allowed, the above definition is unchanged. However, if downgrading of locks is also allowed, the definition must be changed slightly, because *all downgrading must be done in the shrinking phase*. Hence, a read_lock(X) operation that downgrades an already held write lock on X can appear only in the shrinking phase of the transaction.

Transactions T_1 and T_2 of Figure 19.11a do not follow the two-phase locking protocol. This is because the write_lock(X) operation follows the unlock(Y) operation in T_1, and similarly the write_lock(Y) operation follows the unlock(X) operation in T_2. If we enforce two-phase locking, the transaction can be rewritten as T_1' and T_2', as shown in Figure 19.12. Now, the schedule shown in Figure 19.11c is not permitted for T_1' and T_2' under the rules of locking described in Section 19.4.1.

It can be proved that, if *every* transaction in a schedule follows the two-phase locking protocol, then the schedule is guaranteed to be serializable; this is why this protocol is so important. In this case it is unnecessary to test for serializability of schedules any more. The locking mechanism, by enforcing locking rules, will also enforce serializability when all transactions follow the two-phase locking protocol. The programmers must make sure that every individual transaction follows the two-phase locking protocol. This is comparatively easy, since we can check each transaction individually when the database programs are written.

Note that we have been tacitly assuming that the transaction support provided by the DBMS includes the operations read_lock, write_lock, and unlock. Moreover, we assume that the DBMS supports lockable items by implementing the lock information in some form. Most DBMSs will have a software module, the **lock manager,** to process locking and unlocking commands appropriately.

Two-phase locking may limit the amount of concurrency that can occur in a schedule. This is because a transaction T may not be able to release an item X after it is done with using X if T must lock an additional item Y later on; or conversely, T must lock the additional item Y before it needs it so that it can release X. Hence, X must remain locked by T until all items that the transaction needs have been locked; only then can X

T_1'	X and Y values for initial X=20, Y=30	T_2'	X and Y values for initial X=20, Y=30
read_lock (Y); read_item (Y); write_lock (X); unlock (Y);	Y =30	read_lock (X); read_item (X); write_lock (Y); unlock (X);	X =20
read_item (X); X:=X+Y;	X =20	read_item (Y); Y:=X+Y;	Y =30
write_item (X); unlock (X);	X =50	write_item (Y); unlock (Y);	Y =50

Figure 19.12 Transactions T_1' and T_2' that are the same as T_1 and T_2 of Figure 19.11 but which follow the two-phase locking protocol

be released by T. Meanwhile, another transaction wanting to access X may be forced to wait even though T is done with using X; conversely, if Y is locked earlier than it is needed, another transaction wanting to access Y is forced to wait even though T is not using Y yet. This is the price for guaranteeing serializability of all schedules without having to check the schedules themselves. The benefit is the guaranteed correctness of the resulting permanent values in the database.

Although two-phase locking guarantees serializability, the use of locks can cause two additional problems: deadlock and livelock. These problems are inherent in any scheme that uses locking. We discuss these problems and their solutions in the next section.

19.4.3 Dealing with Deadlock and Livelock

Deadlock occurs when each of two transactions is waiting for the other to release an item. A simple example is shown in Figure 19.13a, where the two transactions T_1' and T_2' are deadlocked in a partial schedule; T_1' is waiting for T_2' to release item X, while T_2' is waiting for T_1' to release item Y. Meanwhile, neither can proceed to unlock the item that the other is waiting for. At this point, other transactions can access neither item X nor item Y. Deadlock is also possible with more than two transactions involved, as we shall see.

One solution to prevent deadlock is to use a **deadlock prevention protocol**. One deadlock prevention protocol requires that every transaction lock all the items it needs in advance; if any of the items cannot be obtained, then none of the items are locked. Rather, the transaction waits and then tries again to lock all the items it needs. This solution obviously further limits concurrency. A second protocol, which also limits concurrency, is to order all the items in the database and make sure that a transaction that needs several items will lock them according to that order. This requires that the programmer be aware of the chosen order of the items, which is not very practical in the database context.

A second approach to dealing with deadlock is **deadlock detection**. Rather than make sure that deadlock will never occur, we execute our transactions without deadlock control and periodically check if the system is in a state of deadlock. This solution is attractive if we know there will be little interference among the transactions; that is, different transactions will rarely access the same items at the same time. This can happen if the transactions are short and each transaction locks only a few items. It can also hap-

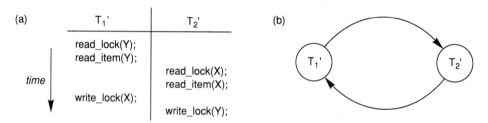

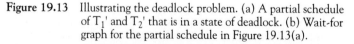

Figure 19.13   Illustrating the deadlock problem. (a) A partial schedule of T_1' and T_2' that is in a state of deadlock. (b) Wait-for graph for the partial schedule in Figure 19.13(a).

pen if the transaction load is light. If, on the other hand, transactions are long and each transaction uses many items, or the transaction load is quite heavy, it is possible to have frequent deadlocks. In the latter case, it is advantageous to use a deadlock prevention scheme.

A simple way to detect a state of deadlock is to construct a **wait-for graph**. One node is created in the wait-for graph for each transaction that is currently executing in the schedule. Whenever a transaction T_i is waiting to lock an item X that is currently locked by transaction T_j, we draw a directed edge $(T_i \rightarrow T_j)$. We have a state of deadlock if and only if the wait-for graph has a cycle. One problem with this approach is determining *when* the system should check for deadlock. Criteria such as the number of currently executing transactions or the period of time several transactions have been waiting to lock items may be used to determine that it is time for the system to check for deadlock. Figure 19.13b shows the wait-for graph for the partial schedule shown in Figure 19.13a. If we discover that the system is in a state of deadlock, some of the transactions causing the deadlock must be aborted, and any effect they may have had on the database must be undone or rolled back (see Section 19.6).

Another problem that may occur when we use locking is **livelock**. A transaction is in a state of livelock if it cannot proceed for an indefinite period of time while other transactions in the system continue normally. This may occur if the waiting scheme for locked items is unfair, giving priority to some transactions over others. The standard solution for livelock is to have a fair waiting scheme. One such scheme uses a **first-come-first-serve** queue; transactions are enabled to lock an item in the order in which they originally requested to lock the item. Another scheme allows some transactions to have priority over others but increases the priority of a transaction the longer it waits, until it eventually gets the highest priority and proceeds.

19.5   Other Concurrency Control Techniques and Issues

The use of locks, combined with the two-phase locking protocol, allows us to guarantee serializability of schedules. The order of transactions in the equivalent serial schedule is based on the order in which executing transactions lock the items they require. If a transaction needs an item that is already locked, it may be forced to wait until the item is released. A different approach that guarantees serializability is that of using transaction timestamps to order transaction execution for an equivalent serial schedule. In Section 19.5.1 we define timestamps. Then we discuss how serializability is enforced by ordering transactions based on their timestamps in Section 19.5.2 and by keeping multiple versions of the data items that are updated in Section 19.5.3. We also discuss a technique called optimistic concurrency control in Section 19.5.4. We address the issue of granularity of data items and how it affects concurrency control in Section 19.5.5.

19.5.1   Timestamps

A **timestamp** is a unique identifier created by the DBMS to identify a transaction. Typically, timestamp values are assigned in the order in which the transactions are submitted to the system, so a timestamp can be thought of as the *transaction start time*. We will refer to the timestamp of transaction T as **TS(T)**. Concurrency control techniques based on timestamps do not use locks; hence, deadlocks *cannot* occur.

Timestamps can be generated in several ways. One possibility is to have a counter that is incremented each time its value is assigned to a transaction. The transaction timestamps will be numbered 1,2,3, ... in this scheme. A computer counter has a finite maximum value, so the system must periodically reset the counter to zero when no transactions are executing for some short period of time. Another way to implement timestamps is to use the current value of the system clock.

19.5.2   Concurrency Control Based on Timestamp Ordering

One method of concurrency control that uses timestamps is to order the transactions based on their timestamps. A schedule in which the transactions participate is then serializable, and the equivalent serial schedule has the transactions in order of their timestamp values. This technique is called **timestamp ordering**. Note how this differs from two-phase locking. In two-phase locking, a schedule is serializable by being equivalent to *some* serial schedule allowed by the locking protocols, whereas in timestamp ordering, the schedule is equivalent to the *particular* serial order that corresponds to the order of the transaction timestamps.

To allow as much concurrency as possible, we let the transaction operations execute freely. We must ensure that, for each item accessed by more than one transaction in the schedule, the order in which the item is accessed does not violate the serializability of the schedule. To do this, we associate with each database item X two timestamp (**TS**) values:

1. **read_TS(X)**: The **read timestamp** of item X; this is the largest timestamp among all the timestamps of transactions that have successfully read item X.

2. **write_TS(X)**: The **write timestamp** of item X; this is the largest of all the timestamps of transactions that have successfully written item X.

Whenever some transaction T tries to issue a read_item(X) or a write_item(X) operation, we compare the timestamp of T with the read timestamp and the write timestamp of X to ensure that the timestamp order of execution of the transactions is not violated. If the timestamp order is violated by the operation, then transaction T will violate the equivalent serial schedule. In this case T must be aborted, and any effect it may have had on the database must be undone. Then T is resubmitted to the system as a new transaction with a *new* timestamp. Note that if T is aborted and rolled back, any transaction T_1 that may have used a value written by T must also be rolled back. Similarly, any transaction T_2 that may have used a value written by T_1 must also be rolled back, and so on. The latter effect is known as **cascading rollback** and is one of the problems associated with timestamp ordering. We will discuss transaction rollback, including cascading rollbacks, in Section 19.6.

The concurrency control algorithm must check if the timestamp ordering of transactions is violated in the following two cases:

1. Transaction T issues a write_item(X) operation:

   a. If read_TS(X) > TS(T), then abort and roll back T and reject the operation. This is because some transaction with a timestamp greater than TS(T)—and hence *after* T in the timestamp ordering—has already read the value of item X before T had a chance to write X, thus violating the timestamp ordering.

b. If write_TS(X) > TS(T), then do not execute the write operation but continue processing. This is because some transaction with timestamp greater than TS(T)—and hence after X in the timestamp ordering—has already written the value of X. Hence, we must ignore the write_item(X) operation of T because it is already outdated so the previous valid update would not be lost. Note that any conflict arising from this situation would be detected by case a.

c. If neither the condition in a nor the condition in b occurs, then execute the write_item(X) operation of T and set write_TS(X) to TS(T).

2. Transaction T issues a read_item(X) operation:

a. If write_TS(X) > TS(T), then abort and roll back T and reject the operation. This is because some transaction with timestamp greater than TS(T)—and hence *after* T in the timestamp ordering—has already written the value of item X before T had a chance to read X, thus violating the timestamp ordering.

b. If write_TS(X) ≤ TS(T), then execute the read_item(X) operation of T and set read_TS(X) to the larger of TS(T) and the current read_TS(X).

The timestamp ordering protocol, like the two-phase locking protocol, guarantees serializability of schedules. However, some schedules are possible under each protocol that are not allowed under the other. Hence, neither protocol allows *all possible* serializable schedules. As mentioned earlier, deadlock does not occur with timestamp ordering. However, livelock may occur if a transaction is continuously aborted and restarted. The latter problem is known as the **cyclic restart** problem.

19.5.3 Multiversion Concurrency Control Techniques

Other protocols for concurrency control, which may also use the concept of timestamps, keep the old values of a data item when the item is updated. These are known as **multiversion concurrency control** techniques, because several versions (values) of an item are maintained. When a transaction requires access to an item, the timestamp of the transaction is compared to the timestamps of the different versions of the item. An appropriate version is chosen to maintain the serializability of the currently executing schedule, if possible.

There are *several* proposed multiversion concurrency control schemes. We discuss one of these as an example. In this multiversion technique, several versions X_1, X_2, ..., X_k of each data item X are kept by the system. For each version, the value of version X_i and the following two timestamps are kept:

1. read_TS(X_i): The **read timestamp** of X_i; this is the largest of all the timestamps of transactions that have successfully read *version* X_i.

2. write_TS(X_i): The **write timestamp** of X_i; this is the timestamp of the transaction that wrote the value of version X_i.

In this scheme, whenever a transaction T is allowed to execute a write_item(X) operation, a new version X_{k+1} of item X is created, with both the write_TS(X_{k+1}) and the read_TS(X_{k+1}) set to TS(T). Correspondingly, when a transaction T is allowed to read the value of version X_i, the value of read_TS(X_i) is set to the larger of read_TS(X_i) and TS(T).

To ensure serializability, we use the following two rules to control the reading and writing of data items:

1. If transaction T issues a write_item(X) operation, and version i of X has the highest write_TS(X_i) of all versions of X that is also *less than or equal to* TS(T), and TS(T) < read_TS(X_i), then abort and roll back transaction T; otherwise, create a new version X_j of X with read_TS(X_j) = write_TS(X_j) = TS(T).

2. If transaction T issues a read_item(X) operation, find the version i of X that has the highest write_TS(X_i) of all versions of X that is also *less than or equal to* TS(T); then return the value of X_i to transaction T.

In case 1 transaction T may be aborted and rolled back. This happens if T is attempting to write a version of X that should have been read by another transaction with timestamp equal to read_TS(X_i); however, the other transaction already read a different version of X, written by the transaction with timestamp equal to write_TS(X_i). If this conflict occurs, T is rolled back; otherwise, a new version of X, written by transaction T, is created. Note that if T is rolled back, it is possible that cascading rollback can occur.

19.5.4   Optimistic Concurrency Control Techniques

In all the concurrency control techniques we discussed so far, a certain degree of checking is done *before* a database operation can be executed. For example, in locking, a check is done to determine whether the item being accessed is locked. In timestamp ordering, the transaction timestamp is checked against the read and write timestamps of the item. This checking represents overhead during transaction execution, with the effect of slowing down the transactions.

In **optimistic concurrency control** techniques, *no checking* is done while the transaction is executing. In order to allow this, updates in the transaction are *not* applied directly to the database items until the transaction reaches its end. During transaction execution, all updates are applied to *local copies* of the data items that are kept for the transaction. At the end of transaction execution, a **validation phase** checks whether any of the transaction updates violate serializability. Certain information needed by the validation phase must be kept with the local copies of data items. If serializability is not violated, the transaction is committed and the database is updated from the local copies; otherwise, the transaction is aborted and restarted at a later time.

There are three phases of an optimistic concurrency control protocol:

1. The **read phase:** A transaction can read values of data items from the database. However, updates are applied only to local copies of the data items kept in the transaction workspace.

2. The **validation phase:** Checking is performed to ensure that serializability will not be violated if the transaction updates are applied to the database.

3. The **write phase:** If the validation phase is successful, the transaction updates are applied to the database; otherwise, the updates are discarded and the transaction is restarted.

The idea behind optimistic concurrency control is to do all the checks at once; hence, transaction execution proceeds with a minimum of overhead until the validation phase is reached. If there is little interference among the transactions, most transactions will be validated successfully. However, if there is much interference, then many transactions will execute to completion only to have their results discarded and to be restarted later. Under these circumstances, optimistic techniques will not work well. The techniques are called "optimistic" because they assume that little interference will occur and hence there is no need to do checking during transaction execution.

Optimistic techniques are generally used in conjunction with timestamps. We will describe one example of an optimistic protocol that uses transaction timestamps and also requires that the write_sets and read_sets of the transactions be kept. In addition, start and end times for some of the three phases need to be kept for each transaction. The **write_set** of a transaction is the set of items written by the transaction, whereas the **read_set** is the set of items read by the transaction. In its validation phase for transaction T_i, the protocol checks that T_i does not interfere with any committed transactions or with any other transactions currently in their validation phase. The validation phase for T_i checks that for each such transaction T_j that is committed or is in its validation phase, *one* of the following conditions holds:

1. Transaction T_j completes its write phase before T_i starts its read phase.
2. T_i starts its write phase after T_j completes its write phase, and the read_set of T_i has no items in common with the write_set of T_j.
3. Both the read_set and the write_set of T_i have no items in common with the write_set of T_j, and T_j completes its read phase before T_i completes its read phase.

If any one of the above three conditions holds, there is no interference and T_i is validated successfully. If none of the above three conditions hold, the validation of transaction T_i fails and it is aborted and restarted later because it is possible that interference had occurred.

19.5.5 Granularity of Data Items

All concurrency control techniques assumed that the database was formed of a number of items. A database item could be chosen to be one of the following:

- A database record.
- A field value of a database record.
- A disk block.
- A whole file.
- The whole database.

Several trade-offs must be considered in choosing the data item size. We shall discuss data item size in the context of locking, although similar arguments can be made for other concurrency control techniques.

First note that the larger the data item size, the lower is the degree of concurrency permitted. For example, if the data item size is a disk block, then a transaction T that needs to lock a record A must lock the whole disk block X that contains A. This is because a lock is associated with the whole data item X. Now if another transaction S wants to lock a different record B that happens to reside in the same block X, it is forced to wait until the first transaction releases the lock on block X. If the data item size was a single record, transaction S could proceed as it would by locking a different data item (record A) than that locked by T (record B).

On the other hand, the smaller the item size, the more items will exist in the database. Because every item is associated with a lock, the system will have a larger number of locks to be handled by the lock manager. More lock and unlock operations will be issued, causing a higher overhead. In addition, more storage space is required for the locks, which are themselves records. For timestamps, storage is required for the read_TS and write_TS for each data item, and the overhead of handling a large number of items is similar to that in the case of locking.

The size of data items is often called the **data item granularity**. Fine granularity refers to small item sizes, whereas coarse granularity refers to large item sizes. Given the above trade-offs, the obvious question to ask is: What is the best item size? The answer is that *it depends on the types of transactions*. If a typical transaction accesses a small number of records, it is advantageous to have the data item granularity be one record. On the other hand, if a transaction typically accesses many records of the same file, it may be better to have block or file granularity so that the transaction will consider all those records as one (or a few) data items.

Most concurrency control techniques will have a uniform data item size. However, some techniques have been proposed that have variable item sizes. In these techniques, depending on the types of transactions that are currently executing on the system, the data item size may be changed to the granularity that best suits these transactions.

19.6   Recovery Concepts and Techniques

In this section we discuss some of the techniques that are used to recover from transaction failures. We already discussed the different causes of failure, such as system crashes and transaction errors, in Section 19.1.3. We also presented many of the concepts that are used by the recovery processes, such as the system log, checkpoints, and commit points, in Section 19.2.

We first give an informal outline of typical recovery processes in Section 19.6.1. We then discuss the process of rolling back (undoing) the effect of a transaction in Section 19.6.2. In Section 19.6.3 we present recovery techniques based on deferred update, and in Section 19.6.4 we present techniques based on immediate update. Other recovery protocols, such as shadow paging, are discussed in Section 19.6.5. Finally, techniques for recovery from catastrophic failure are discussed in Section 19.6.6.

The techniques we discuss here are *not* descriptions of recovery as implemented in a specific system. Our emphasis is on describing conceptually several different approaches to recovery. For descriptions of recovery features in specific systems, the reader should consult the bibliographic notes and the user manuals for those systems.

It is important to note that recovery techniques are often intertwined with the concurrency control mechanisms. Certain recovery techniques are best used with specific concurrency control methods. We will attempt to discuss recovery concepts independently of concurrency control mechanisms but will discuss the circumstances under which a particular recovery mechanism is best used with a certain concurrency control protocol.

19.6.1 Recovery Outline

Recovery from transaction failures usually means that the database is *restored* to some state from the past so that a correct state—close to the time of failure—can be *reconstructed* from that past state. To do this, the system must keep information about changes to data items during transaction execution outside the database. This information is typically kept in the **system log,** as discussed in Section 19.2.3. A typical strategy for recovery may be summarized informally as follows:

1. If there is extensive damage to a wide portion of the database due to catastrophic failure, such as a disk crash, the recovery method restores a past copy of the database that was *dumped* to archival storage (typically tape) and reconstructs a more current state by reapplying or *redoing* committed transaction operations from the log up to the time of failure.

2. When the database is not physically damaged but has become inconsistent due to noncatastrophic failures of types 1 through 4 of Section 19.1.3, the strategy is to reverse the changes that caused the inconsistency by *undoing* some operations. It may also be necessary to *redo* some legitimate changes that could have been lost during this reversal process or for some other reason in order to restore a consistent state of the database. In this case we do not need a complete archival copy of the database. Rather, the entries kept in the system log are consulted during recovery.

We can distinguish two main techniques for recovery from noncatastrophic transaction failures. The **deferred update** techniques do not actually update the database until *after* a transaction reaches its commit point; then the updates are recorded in the database. If a transaction fails before reaching its commit point, it will not have changed the database in any way. It may be necessary to redo the effect of the operations of a committed transaction from the log because their effect may not yet have been recorded in the database.

In the **immediate update** techniques, the database may be updated by some operations of a transaction *before* the transaction reaches its commit point. However, these operations are typically recorded in the log *on disk* by force writing before they are applied to the database so that recovery is possible. If a transaction fails after recording some changes in the database but before reaching its commit point, the effect of its operations on the database must be undone; that is, the transaction must be rolled back.

19.6.2 Transaction Rollback

If a transaction fails for whatever reason after updating the database, it may be necessary to **roll back** the transaction. Any data item values that have been changed by the transaction must be returned to their previous values. The log entries are used to recover the old values of data items that must be rolled back.

If a transaction T is rolled back, then any transaction S that read the value of some data item X written by T must also be rolled back. Similarly, once S is rolled back, any transaction R that read the value of some data item Y written by S must also be rolled back, and so on. This phenomenon is called **cascading rollback**. Cascading rollback, as we can imagine, can be quite time consuming. That is why some recovery mechanisms based on deferred update are designed such that cascading rollback *is never required*. Other recovery mechanisms may require cascading rollback.

Figure 19.14 shows an example where cascading rollback is required. The read and write operations of three individual transactions are shown in Figure 19.14a. In Figure 19.14b we show the system log at the point of a system crash for a particular execution schedule of these transactions. For the purpose of this example, we show [commit, T_1] and [commit, T_2] entries in the log after T_1 and T_2 conclude their operations. However,

	T_1	T_2	T_3
(a)	read_item(A)	read_item(B)	read_item(C)
	read_item(D)	write_item(B)	write_item(B)
	write_item(D)	read_item(D)	read_item(A)
		write_item(D)	write_item(A)

		A	B	C	D
		30	15	40	20
(b)	[start-transaction,T_3]				
	[read_item,T_3,C]				
*	[write_item,T_3,B,15,12]		12		
	[start-transaction,T_2]				
	[read_item,T_2,B]				
**	[write_item,T_2,B,12,18]		18		
	[start-transaction,T_1]				
	[read_item,T_1,A]				
	[read_item,T_1,D]				
	[write_item,T_1,D,20,25]				25
	[commit,T_1]				
	[read_item,T_2,D]				
**	[write_item,T_2,D,25,26]				26
	[commit,T_2]				
	[read_item,T_3,A]				

←system crash

* T_3 is rolled back because it did not reach its commit point
** T_2 is rolled back because it reads the value of item B written by T_3
The rest of the [write,...] entries in the log are redone

Figure 19.14   Illustrating cascading rollback. (a) The read and write operations of three transactions. (b) System log at point of crash.   *(continued on next page)*

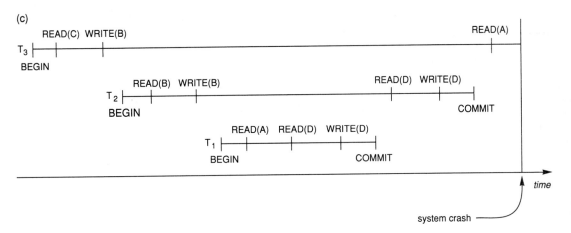

Figure 19.14 *(continued)* (c) Operations before the crash.

T_2 has *not reached its commit point*, technically speaking, because it has read a value for item B from the uncommitted transaction T_3 and hence may have to be rolled back.

The values of data items A, B, C, and D, which are used by the transactions, are shown to the right of the system log entries. We assume that the original item values, shown in the first line, are A = 30, B = 15, C = 40, and D = 20. At the point of system failure, transaction T_3 has not reached its conclusion and must be rolled back. The WRITE operations of T_3, marked by a single * in Figure 19.14b, are the T_3 operations that are undone during transaction rollback. Figure 19.14c graphically shows the operations of the different transactions along the time axis.

We must now check for cascading rollback. From Figure 19.14c we see that transaction T_2 reads the value of item B that was written by transaction T_3; this can also be determined by examining the log. Because T_3 is rolled back, T_2 must now also be rolled back. As we mentioned earlier, a committed transaction *generally cannot be rolled back* by the recovery procedure, but we assume this is possible for the purpose of our example. The WRITE operations of T_2, marked by ** in the log, are the ones that are undone. Even though T_2 placed its [commit, T_2] entry in the log before the system crash, it must be rolled back because the value of item B that it read becomes invalid after T_3 is rolled back. Note that only write_item operations need to be undone during transaction rollback; read_item operations are recorded in the log only to determine if cascading rollback of additional transactions is necessary.

Note that if a transaction is allowed to read only values written by transactions *that have already reached their commit point*, then cascading rollback is never needed. This rule would not allow the operation [read_item, T_2, B] to occur until after T_3 commits, so the sequence of operations in Figures 19.14b and c would not be allowed. This limits concurrency.

Some recovery methods, when used in conjunction with certain concurrency control protocols, never require transaction rollback. An example is a *deferred update* method of recovery used with the two-phase locking protocol for concurrency control; we discuss this in Section 19.6.3. If rollback of transactions is never required by the recovery method, we can keep *more limited information* in the system log. It is not necessary to keep the old values of data items written by an operation; only the new values are kept to redo the transaction operations if need be. There is also no need to record any read_item operations in the log because these are needed only for determining cascading rollback. Hence, when transaction rollback is never required by the recovery mechanism, only the following types of log entries are needed:

- [start_transaction,T],
- [write_item,T,X,new_value], and
- [commit,T].

19.6.3   Recovery Techniques Based on Deferred Update

The idea behind deferred update techniques is to defer or postpone any actual updates to the database itself until the transaction completes its execution successfully and reaches its commit point. During transaction execution, the updates are recorded only in the log and in the transaction workspace. After the transaction reaches its commit point and the log is force written to disk, the updates are recorded in the database itself. If a transaction fails before reaching its commit point, there is no need to undo any operations because the transaction has not affected the database in any way.

We can state a typical deferred update protocol as follows:

1. A transaction cannot change the database until it reaches its commit point.
2. A transaction does not reach its commit point until all its update operations are recorded in the log *and* the log is force written to disk.

In other words, a transaction does not record its changes in the database itself until it reaches its commit point and has all these changes recorded permanently in the log.

Usually, the method of recovery from failure is closely related to the concurrency control method in multiuser systems. First we discuss recovery in single-user systems, where no concurrency control is needed, so we can understand the recovery process independently of any concurrency control method. Then we discuss how concurrency control affects the recovery process.

Recovery Using Deferred Update in a Single-User Environment

In such an environment, the recovery algorithm can be rather simple. The algorithm RDU_S (recovery using deferred update in a single-user environment) uses a REDO procedure, given below, for redoing certain write_item operations and works as follows:

PROCEDURE RDU_S
Start from the last entry in the log and read backward through the log entries to the beginning of the log. Make two lists of transactions: the committed transactions, which have written a [commit,T] entry in the log, and the uncommitted transactions, which have written a [start_transaction,T] but have not written a [commit,T] entry (at most one transaction will fall in this category because the system is

single-user). Apply the REDO operation to all the write_item operations of the committed transactions from the log *in the order in which they were written to the log.*
The REDO procedure is defined as follows:

PROCEDURE REDO(WRITE_OP)
Redoing a write_item operation WRITE_OP consists of examining its log entry [write_item,T,X,new_value] and setting the value of item X in the database to new_value.

The REDO operation is required to be **idempotent;** that is, executing it over and over is equivalent to executing it just once. In fact, the whole recovery process should be idempotent. This is so because if the system were to fail during the recovery process, the next recovery attempt might REDO certain write_item operations that had already been redone during the first recovery process. The result of recovery from a crash *during recovery* should be the same as that of recovering *with no crash during recovery!*
Note that the transaction in the uncommitted list will have had no effect on the database because of the deferred update protocol and is ignored completely by the recovery process. By ignoring the uncommitted transaction, it is *implicitly rolled back* because none of its operations were reflected in the database. However, the transaction must now be resubmitted to the system either automatically by the recovery process or by the user.
Figure 19.15 shows an example of recovery in a single-user environment, where the first failure occurs during execution of transaction T_2 as shown in Figure 19.15b. The recovery process will redo the [write_item,T_1,D,20] entry in the log by resetting the value of item D to 20 (its new value). The [write,T_2, ...] entries in the log are ignored by the recovery process because no entry [commit,T_2] is in the log. If a second failure occurs

(a)

T_1	T_2
read_item(A)	read_item(B)
read_item(D)	write_item(B)
write_item(D)	read_item(D)
	write_item(D)

(b)   [start-transaction,T_1]
       [write_item,T_1,D,20]
       [commit,T_1]
       [start-transaction,T_2]
       [write_item,T_2,B,10]
       [write_item,T_2,D,25] ← system crash

The [write-item, ...] operations of T_1 are redone
T_2 log entries are ignored by the recovery process

Figure 19.15   Recovery using deferred update in a single-user environment. (a) The read and write operations of two transactions. (b) System log at point of crash.

during recovery from the first failure, the same recovery process is repeated from start to finish with identical results.

If the log file is long, as it usually is, the above process of redoing the operations of *all* committed transactions can be quite time consuming, and much of it is really unnecessary. We would expect that much of the redoing of operations of committed transactions is not really needed because most committed transactions will already have recorded their changes in the database. We should really redo only write_item operations of committed transactions *that have not yet been recorded* in the database. The concept of checkpoints, discussed in Section 19.2.4, is used to reduce this problem. When checkpoints are included in the log, all committed transactions *before* the most recent [checkpoint] entry in the log are known to have recorded their updates permanently. Hence, the recovery process is applied only to transactions T whose [commit, T] entry is written in the log *after* the most recent [checkpoint] entry in the log.

Deferred Update with Concurrent Execution in a Multiuser Environment

For multiuser systems with concurrency control, the recovery process may be more complex, depending on the protocols used for concurrency control. In many cases, the concurrency control and recovery processes are integrated into a single method that handles both tasks. We can say that, in general, the greater the degree of concurrency we wish to achieve, the more difficult the task of recovery becomes.

Consider a system where concurrency control uses two-phase locking and prevents deadlock by preassigning all locks to items needed by a transaction before the transaction starts execution. To combine the deferred update method for recovery with this concurrency control technique, we can keep all the locks on items in effect *until the transaction reaches its commit point*. After that, the locks can be released. Assuming that [checkpoint] entries are included in the log, a possible recovery algorithm for this case, which we call RDU_M (recovery using deferred update in a multiuser environment), is given below. This procedure uses the REDO procedure defined earlier.

> **PROCEDURE RDU_M (WITH CHECKPOINTS)**
> Starting from the last entry in the log, go backward to the most recent [checkpoint] entry in the log. Make two lists of transactions: the committed transactions T, which have written a [commit,T] entry in the log *after* the last [checkpoint] entry and whose write_item operations will be redone, and the uncommitted transactions T', which have their [start_transaction,T'] in the log but have not written a [commit,T'] entry into the log. REDO all the WRITE operations of the committed transactions from the log *in the order in which they were written into the log*. The transactions that did not commit are effectively canceled and must be resubmitted.

Figure 19.16 shows a possible schedule of executing transactions. When the checkpoint was taken at time t_1, transaction T_1 had committed whereas transactions T_3 and T_4 had not. Before the system crash at time t_2, T_3 and T_2 were committed but not T_4 and T_5. According to the RDU_M method, there is no need to redo the write_item operations of transaction T_1—or any transactions committed before the last checkpoint time t_1. However, write_item operations of T_2 and T_3 must be redone because both trans-

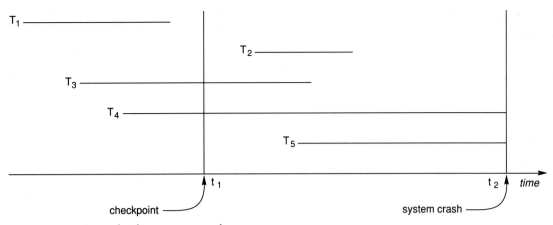

Figure 19.16 Example of recovery in a multi-user environment

actions reached their commit points after the last checkpoint. Recall that the log is force written before committing a transaction. Transactions T_4 and T_5 are ignored—they are effectively canceled or rolled back because none of their write_item operations were recorded in the database under the deferred update protocol. We will refer to Figure 19.16 later to illustrate other recovery protocols.

A drawback of the method described above is that it limits the concurrent execution of transactions because *all items remain locked until the transaction reaches its commit point*. The main benefit of the method is that transaction operations never need to be undone because:

1. A transaction does not record its changes in the database until it reaches its commit point, that is, until it completes its execution successfully. Hence, a transaction is never rolled back because of failure during transaction execution.

2. A transaction will never read the value of an item that is written by an uncommitted transaction because items remain locked until a transaction reaches its commit point. Hence, no cascading rollback will occur.

Figure 19.17 shows an example of recovery for a multiuser system that utilizes the recovery and concurrency control method described above.

Transaction Actions That Do Not Affect the Database

A transaction will, in general, have actions that do not affect the database, such as generating and printing messages or reports from information retrieved from the database. If a transaction fails before completion, we may not want the user to get these reports, since the transaction failed to complete. Hence, such reports should be generated only *after the transaction reaches its commit point*. A common method of dealing with such actions is to issue the commands that generate the reports but keep them as batch jobs. The batch jobs are executed only after the transaction reaches its commit point. If the transaction does not reach its commit point because of a failure, the batch jobs are canceled.

	T_1	T_2	T_3	T_4
(a)	read_item(A)	read_item(B)	read_item(A)	read_item(B)
	read_item(D)	write_item(B)	write_item(A)	write_item(B)
	write_item(D)	read_item(D)	read_item(C)	read_item(A)
		write_item(D)	write_item(C)	write_item(A)

(b)   [start_transaction,T_1]
      [write_item,T_1,D,20]
      [commit,T_1]
      [checkpoint]
      [start_transaction,T_4]
      [write_item,T_4,B,15]
      [write_item,T_4,A,20]
      [commit,T_4]
      [start_transaction,T_2]
      [write_item,T_2,B,12]
      [start_transaction,T_3]
      [write_item,T_3,A,30]
      [write_item,T_2,D,25] ←system crash

T_2 and T_3 are ignored because they did not reach their commit points
T_4 is redone because its commit point is after the last system checkpoint

Figure 19.17   Recovery using deferred update with concurrent
transactions. (a) The read and write operations
of four transactions. (b) System log at point
of crash.

19.6.4   Recovery Techniques Based on Immediate Update

In these techniques, when a transaction issues an update command, the database can be
updated "immediately" without having to wait for the transaction to reach its commit
point. However, in many of these techniques an update operation must still be recorded
in the log (on disk) *before* it is applied to the database so that we can recover in case of
failure. This is sometimes known as a **write-ahead log protocol**.

When immediate update is allowed, provisions must be made for *undoing* the effect
of update operations on the database because a transaction can fail after it has applied
some updates to the database itself. Hence, recovery schemes based on immediate update must include the capability to roll back a transaction by undoing the effect of its
write_item operations.

In one write-ahead log protocol* the log records are divided into two types—those
needed for REDO (write_item entries containing new values only, generated at a commit

---

*This was proposed for the experimental DBMS SYSTEM R, developed at IBM Research.

point) and those needed for UNDO (write_item entries containing old and new values and read_item entries). This protocol states that:

- A transaction cannot update the physical database until all UNDO-type log records for that transaction—up to this point in time—have been force written to disk.
- A transaction is not allowed to complete the processing of commit until all the REDO-type and UNDO-type log records for that transaction have been force written to disk.

Recovery Based on Immediate Update in a Single-User Environment

We first consider a single-user system so we can examine the recovery process separately from concurrency control. If a failure occurs in a single-user system, the executing transaction at the time of failure may have recorded some changes in the database. The effect of all such operations must be undone as part of the recovery process. Hence, the recovery algorithm needs an UNDO procedure, described below, to undo the effect of certain write_item operations that have been applied to the database by examining their system log entry. The recovery algorithm RIU_S (recovery using immediate update in a single-user environment) also uses the REDO procedure defined earlier.

PROCEDURE RIU_S

1. Start from the last entry in the log and read backward. Make two lists of transactions: the committed transactions, which have written a [commit,T] entry in the log, and the uncommitted transactions, which have written a [start_transaction,T] but have not written a [commit,T] entry in the log (at most one transaction will fall in this category because the system is single-user).
2. Undo all the write_item operations of the *uncommitted* transaction from the log using the UNDO procedure described below.
3. Redo all the write_item operations of the *committed* transactions from the log in the order in which they were written in the log using the REDO procedure.

The UNDO procedure is defined as follows:

PROCEDURE UNDO(WRITE_OP)

Undoing a write_item operation WRITE_OP consists of examining its log entry [write_item,T,X,old_value,new_value] and setting the value of item X in the database to old_value. Undoing a number of write_item operations from one or more transactions from the log must proceed in the *reverse order* from the order in which the operations were written in the log.

Checkpoints can be utilized in the same way as discussed earlier for the deferred update technique. Rather than *redoing* all write_item operations of *committed* transactions from the log, we redo only transactions whose [commit,T] entry is *after* the most recent [checkpoint] entry in the log. However, *all* write_item operations of *uncommitted* transactions must be *undone*; checkpointing has no effect on the undoing part of the recovery procedure.

Immediate Update with Concurrent Execution

When concurrent execution is permitted, the recovery process will again depend on the protocols used for concurrency control. The concurrency control and recovery processes are usually integrated into a single method that handles both tasks. When we deal with immediate update and with concurrent transactions, we are faced with the possibility of cascading rollback of transactions. This happens if a transaction T whose operations are undone has updated a database item X and the value of X has subsequently been read by another transaction T' before being changed back to its previous value. The procedure RIU_M (recovery using immediate updates for a multiuser environment) gives an outline of a recovery technique for concurrent transactions with immediate update. Assume that the log may include checkpoints as discussed above.

> **PROCEDURE RIU_M**
>
> 1. Start from the last entry in the log and read backward.. Make two lists of transactions: the committed transactions, which have written a [commit,T] entry in the log after the last [checkpoint] entry, and the uncommitted transactions, which have a [start_transaction, T] but have not written a [commit,T] entry into the log.
> 2. Make a list of transactions that have read some value written by a write_item operation of an uncommitted transaction for cascading rollback. Apply this step recursively to any transactions that must be rolled back to make a list of all the transactions that must be rolled back.
> 3. Undo all the write_item operations of the *uncommitted* transactions and the transactions to be *rolled back* using the UNDO procedure. The operations should be undone in the reverse of the order in which they were written into the log.
> 4. Redo all the write_item operations of the *committed* transactions from the log in the order in which they were written into the log.

Step 2 is the most complex one in this procedure. Before we undo any operations, we must determine all the transactions to be rolled back so that all the operations are undone together, in one sweep, in the reverse of the order in which they were written in the log.

19.6.5   Other Recovery Techniques

In this section we briefly review a technique called **shadow paging,** which is a recovery technique that does not strictly require a log, although a log is sometimes kept with it. Then we briefly discuss recovery techniques for when a transaction involves access to **multiple databases,** possibly stored under different types of DBMSs.

Shadow Paging

This recovery scheme does not require the use of a log in a single-user environment. In a multiuser environment, it may require a log if a log is needed for the concurrency control method.* Shadow paging considers the database to be made up of a number of fixed-size disk pages (or disk blocks), say n, for recovery purposes. A **page table** (or **directory**) with n entries is constructed, where the ith page table entry points to the ith database page on disk. The page table is kept in main memory if it is not too large and all references—reads or writes—to database pages on disk go through the page table. When a transaction begins executing, the **current page table**—whose entries point to the most recent or current database pages on disk—is copied into a **shadow page table**. The shadow page table is then saved on disk while the current page table is used by the transaction.

During transaction execution, the shadow page table is *never* modified. When a write_item operation is performed, a new copy of the modified database page is created but the old copy of that page is *not overwritten*. Instead, the new page is written elsewhere—on some previously unused disk block. The current page table entry is modified to point to the new disk block, whereas the shadow page table is not modified and continues to point to the old unmodified disk block.

To recover from a failure during transaction execution, it is sufficient to free the modified database pages and to discard the current page table. The state of the database before transaction execution is available through the shadow page table, and that state is recovered by reinstating the shadow page table to become the current page table once more. The database thus is returned to the state prior to the transaction that was executing when the crash occurred, and any modified pages are discarded. Committing a transaction corresponds to discarding the previous shadow page table.

The advantage of shadow paging is that it makes undoing the effect of the executing transaction very simple. In addition, there is no need to redo any transaction operations. In a multiuser environment with concurrent transactions, logs and checkpoints must be incorporated into the shadow paging technique. One disadvantage of shadow paging is that the updated database pages change location on disk. This makes it difficult to keep related database pages close together on disk without complex storage management strategies. Furthermore, if the page table (directory) is large, the overhead of writing shadow page tables to disk as transactions commit is significant.

Recovery in Multidatabase Transactions

So far, we have implicitly assumed that a transaction accesses a single database. In some cases a single transaction, called a **multidatabase transaction**, may require access to multiple databases. These databases may even be stored on different types of DBMSs; for example, some DBMSs may be relational whereas others are hierarchical or network DBMSs. In such a case, each DBMS involved in the multidatabase transaction will have its own recovery technique and transaction manager separate from the other DBMSs. This situation is somewhat similar to the case of a distributed database management system (see Chapter 21) where parts of the database reside at different sites that are connected by a communication network.

To maintain the atomicity of a multidatabase transaction, it is necessary to have a two-level recovery mechanism. A **global recovery manager,** or **coordinator,** is needed in

---

*For example, the experimental DBMS SYSTEM R uses shadow paging along with checkpointing and logging.

addition to the local recovery managers. The coordinator usually follows a protocol called the **two-phase commit protocol,** whose two phases can be stated as follows:

Phase 1: When all participating databases signal the coordinator that the part of the multidatabase transaction involving each has concluded, the coordinator sends a message "prepare for commit" to each participant to get ready for committing the transaction. Each participating database receiving that message will force write all log records to disk and then send a "ready to commit" or "OK" signal to the coordinator. If the force writing to disk fails or the local transaction cannot commit for some reason, the participating database sends a "cannot commit" or "not OK" signal to the coordinator. If the coordinator does not receive a reply from a database within a certain time interval, it assumes a "not OK" response.

Phase 2: If all participating databases reply "OK," the coordinator sends a "commit" signal for the transaction to the participating databases. Because all the local effects of the transaction have been recorded in the logs of the participating databases, recovery from failure is now possible. Each participating database completes transaction commit by writing a [commit] entry for the transaction in the log and permanently updating the database if needed. If one or more of the participating databases have a "not OK" response to the coordinator, the coordinator sends a message to "roll back" the local effect of the transaction to each participating database. This is done by undoing the transaction operations using the log.

The net effect of the two-phase commit protocol is that either all participating databases commit the effect of the transaction or none of them do. In case any of the participants—or the coordinator—fail, it is always possible to recover to a state where either the transaction is committed or it is rolled back. A failure during or before phase 1 will usually require the transaction to be rolled back, whereas a failure during phase 2 means the transaction can recover and commit.

19.6.6   Database Backup and Recovery from Catastrophic Failures

So far, all the techniques we have discussed apply to noncatastrophic failures. A key assumption we made was that the system log is maintained on the disk and is not lost as a result of the failure. The recovery techniques we discussed use the entries in the system log to recover from the failure by bringing the database back to a consistent state. As we discussed, write_item operations of *committed transactions* may have to be **redone,** whereas write_item operations of *uncommitted transactions* may have to be **undone**.

The recovery manager of a DBMS must also be equipped to handle more catastrophic failures such as disk crashes. The main technique used to handle such crashes is that of **database backup.** The whole database and the log are periodically copied onto a cheap storage medium such as magnetic tapes. In case of a catastrophic system failure, the latest backup copy can be reloaded from the tape to the disk and the system restarted. However, transactions executed since the last backup copy was made may be lost.

In order not to lose all the effects of transactions that have been executed since the last backup, it is customary to back up the system log by periodically copying it to magnetic tape. The system log is usually substantially smaller than the database itself and hence can be backed up more frequently. When the system log is backed up, the users do not lose all their transactions since the last database backup. All committed transactions that have been recorded in the portion of the system log that has been backed up can have their effect on the database reconstructed. A new system log is started after each database backup operation. Hence, to recover from disk failure, the database is first re-created on disk from its latest backup copy on tape. Following that, the effects of all the committed transactions whose operations have been entered in the backed up copy of the system log are reconstructed.

19.7   Summary

In this chapter we discussed DBMS techniques for controlling concurrent access to a database and for recovery from failures and crashes. In Section 19.1 we compared single-user to multiuser systems and then presented examples of how uncontrolled execution of concurrent transactions in a multiuser system can lead to incorrect results and database values. We also discussed the various types of failures that may occur during transaction execution.

In Section 19.2 we discussed the concept of a database transaction and the desirable properties of atomicity, consistency preservation, durability, isolation, and serializability. We also discussed several concepts that are used in recovery and concurrency control methods. The system log keeps track of database accesses and uses this information to recover from failures. A transaction either succeeds and reaches its commit point or fails and has to be rolled back. A committed transaction has its changes permanently recorded in the database. Checkpoints are used to indicate that all committed transactions up to the checkpoint have recorded their updates permanently in the database.

We defined a schedule as an execution sequence of the operations of several transactions with possible interleaving. In Section 19.3 we defined equivalence of schedules and saw that a serializable schedule is equivalent to some serial schedule. A serializable schedule is considered correct. We then presented algorithms for testing the serializability of a schedule. Finally, we discussed why it is impractical to test for serializability in a real system but that it can be used to define and verify concurrency control protocols.

In Section 19.4 we discussed the concept of locking. Both binary locks and exclusive/shared locks were discussed. The two-phase locking protocol, which guarantees serializability without the need for testing individual schedules, was presented. We discussed the deadlock and livelock problems associated with locking and solutions to these problems. In Section 19.5 we discussed timestamps, which are unique, system-generated transaction identifiers. We discussed other concurrency control techniques, including timestamp ordering, multiversion techniques, and optimistic techniques. Finally, we discussed how granularity of data items affects concurrency control.

In Section 19.6 we discussed the techniques for recovery from transaction failures. The main goal of recovery is to ensure the atomicity property of a transaction. If a transaction fails before completing its execution, the recovery mechanism has to make sure the transaction has no lasting effects on the database. We first gave an informal outline for a recovery process and then discussed the problem of cascading rollback.

We then discussed two different approaches to recovery: deferred update and immediate update. Deferred update techniques postpone any actual updating of the database until a transaction reaches its commit point. The transaction force writes the log to disk before recording the updates in the database. This approach, when used with certain concurrency control methods, may never require transaction rollback, and recovery simply consists of redoing the operations of transactions committed after the last checkpoint from the log. Immediate update techniques may apply changes to the database before the transaction reaches a successful conclusion. In some protocols, any changes applied to the database must first be recorded in the log and force written to disk so that these operations can be undone if necessary. When using immediate update, it is sometimes necessary to check for cascading rollback, which can be time consuming and expensive.

We discussed the shadow paging technique for recovery, which keeps track of old database pages using a shadow page table. This technique does not require a log in single-user systems but still needs the log for recovery in multiuser systems. We also discussed the two-phase commit protocol, which is used for recovery from failures involving multidatabase transactions. Finally, we discussed recovery from catastrophic failures, which is typically done by backing up the database and the log to tape. The log can be backed up more frequently and used to redo operation from the last database backup.

Review Questions

19.1. What is meant by concurrent execution of database transactions in a multiuser system? Discuss why concurrency control is needed by giving informal examples.

19.2. Discuss the different types of transaction failures. What is meant by catastrophic failure?

19.3. Discuss the actions taken by the read_item and write_item operations on a database.

19.4. Draw a state diagram and discuss the typical states that a transaction goes through during execution.

19.5. What is the system log used for? What are the typical kinds of entries in a system log? What are checkpoints and why are they important? What are transaction commit points and why are they important?

19.6. Discuss the atomicity, durability, and consistency preservation properties of a database transaction.

19.7. What is a schedule? What is a serial schedule? What is a serializable schedule? Why is a serial schedule considered correct? Why is a serializable schedule considered correct?

19.8. Discuss the different measures of transaction equivalence. What is the difference between the constrained write and the unconstrained write assumptions? Which is more realistic?

19.9. What are binary locks? How can their operations be implemented? How do binary locks sometimes limit concurrency unnecessarily?

19.10. What are multiple-mode (shared/exclusive) locks? How can their operations be implemented? How do they improve concurrency over binary locks?

19.11. Discuss the rules that must be followed by transactions in a scheme that uses binary locks and in a scheme that uses shared/exclusive locks.

19.12. What is the two-phase locking protocol? How does it guarantee serializability?

19.13. Discuss the problems of deadlock and livelock and the different approaches to dealing with these problems.

19.14. What is a timestamp? How does the system generate timestamps?

19.15. Discuss the timestamp ordering protocol for concurrency control.

19.16. Discuss a multiversion technique for concurrency control.

19.17. How do optimistic concurrency control techniques differ from other concurrency control techniques? Discuss the typical phases of an optimistic concurrency control method.

19.18. How does the granularity of data items affect the performance of concurrency control? What are the factors that affect selection of granularity size for data items?

19.19. What is meant by transaction rollback? Why is it necessary to check for cascading rollback? Which recovery techniques do not require rollback?

19.20. Discuss the UNDO and REDO operations and the recovery techniques that use each.

19.21. Discuss the deferred update technique of recovery. What is the main advantage of this technique? Under what circumstances does it not require transaction rollback in a multiuser environment?

19.22. How does recovery handle transaction operations that do not affect the database, such as printing of reports by the transaction?

19.23. Discuss the immediate update recovery technique in both single-user and multiuser environments. What are the advantages and disadvantages of immediate update?

19.24. Describe the shadow paging recovery technique. Under what circumstances does it not require a log?

19.25. Describe the two-phase commit protocol for multidatabase transactions.

19.26. Discuss how recovery from catastrophic failures is handled.

Exercises

19.27. Change transaction T_2 in Figure 19.2b to read:

```
read_item(x);
X:= X+M;
if X > 90 then exit
        else write_item(X);
```

Discuss the final result of the different schedules in Figure 19.3 where M = 2 and N = 2 with respect to the following questions: Does adding the above condition change the final outcome? Does the outcome obey the implied consistency rule (that the capacity of X is 90)?

19.28. Repeat the above by adding a check in T_1 so that Y does not exceed 90.

19.29. List all possible schedules for transactions T_1 and T_2 from Figure 19.2, and determine which are serializable (correct) and which are not.

19.30. How many *serial* schedules exist for the three transactions in Figure 19.8a?

19.31. List all possible schedules for the three transactions in Figure 19.8a, and determine which of those schedules are serializable and which are not. For each serializable schedule, list all equivalent serial schedules.

19.32. Modify the transactions in Figure 19.8a so that they obey the two-phase locking protocol, and then list all the possible schedules for the modified transactions. First use binary locks, then use shared/exclusive locks. Are there any serializable schedules from Exercise 19.31 that do not appear among these schedules? What can you deduce from your finding?

19.33. Prove that Algorithm 19.1 correctly determines the serializability of a schedule under the constrained write assumption. Hint: Show that if a cycle exists in the graph, then no equivalent serial schedule exists, and if no cycle exists, then there is at least one equivalent serial schedule.

19.34. Prove that the two-phase locking protocol guarantees serializability of schedules under the constrained write assumption. Hint: Show by Algorithm 19.1 that if a precedence graph has a cycle, then at least one of the transactions participating in the schedule does not obey the two-phase locking protocol.

19.35. Modify the data structures for multiple-mode locks, and the algorithms for read_lock(X), write_lock(X), and unlock(X) given in Figure 19.10, so that upgrading and downgrading of locks are possible. Hint: The lock needs to keep track of the transaction id(s) that hold the lock, if any.

19.36. Apply the timestamp ordering algorithm to the schedules of Figure 19.8b and c, and determine whether the algorithm will allow the execution of the schedules.

19.37. Repeat Exercise 19.36, but use the multiversion method discussed in Section 19.5.3.

19.38. Suppose the system crashes before the [read_item, T_3,A] entry is written to the log in Figure 19.14b; will that make any difference in the recovery process?

19.39. Suppose the system crashes before the [write_item,T_2,D,25,26] entry is written to the log in Figure 19.14b; will that make any difference in the recovery process?

19.40. Figure 19.18 shows the log corresponding to a particular schedule at the point of a system crash for the four transactions T_1, T_2, T_3, and T_4 of Figure 19.17. Suppose we use the *immediate update protocol* with checkpointing described in Section 19.6.4. Describe the recovery process from the system crash. Specify which transactions are rolled back, which operations in the log are redone and which (if any) are undone, and whether any cascading rollback takes place.

19.41. Suppose we use the deferred update protocol for the example in Figure 19.18. Show how the log would be different in the case of deferred update by removing the unnecessary log entries; then describe the recovery process using your modified log. Assume that two-phase locking is used so that only redo operations are applied, and specify which operations in the log are redone and which are ignored.

[start_transaction,T_1]

[read_item,T_1,A]

[read_item,T_1,D]

[write_item,T_1,D,20]

[commit,T_1]

[checkpoint]

[start_transaction,T_2]

[read_item,T_2,B]

[write_item,T_2,B,12]

[start_transaction,T_4]

[read_item,T_4,B]

[write_item,T_4,B,15]

[start_transaction,T_3]

[write_item,T_3,A,30]

[read_item,T_4,A]

[write_item,T_4,A,20]

[commit,T_4]

[read_item,T_2,D]

[write_item,T_2,D,25] ← system crash

Figure 19.18   Example schedule and corresponding log

Selected Bibliography

The concept of atomic transaction is discussed in Gray (1981). The two-phase locking protocol is presented in Eswaran et al. (1976). Testing of seriability is discussed in Papadimitriou (1979). The books by Bernstein et al. (1988) and Papadimitriou (1986) are devoted to concurrency control and recovery. Locking is discussed in Gray et al. (1975), Lien and Weinberger (1978), Kedem and Silbershatz (1980), and Korth (1983). Timestamp-based concurrency control techniques are discussed in Bernstein and Goodman (1980) and Reed (1983). Optimistic concurrency control is discussed in Kung and Robinson (1981) and Bassiouni (1988). Papadimitriou and Kanellakis (1979) discuss multiversion techniques. Locking granularities are analyzed in Ries and Stonebraker (1977). Bhargava and Reidl (1988) present an approach for dynamically choosing among various concurrency control and recovery methods.

Verhofstad (1978) presents a tutorial and survey of recovery techniques in database systems. Gray (1978) discusses recovery along with other system aspects of implementing operating systems for databases. The shadow paging technique is discussed Lorie (1977), and Gray et al. (1981) discuss the recovery mechanism in SYSTEM R. Lockeman and Knutsen (1968), Davies (1972), and Bjork (1973) are early papers that discuss recovery. Chandy et al. (1975) discusses transaction rollback. Lilien and Bhargava (1985) discuss the concept of integrity block and its use to improve the efficiency of recovery. Nested transaction concepts are given in Moss (1982) and Haerder and Rothermel (1987). Several textbooks discuss recovery in database systems, including Wiederhold (1983), Date (1983), Korth and Silberschatz (1986), and Ullman (1982).

CHAPTER 20

Security and Integrity Constraints

In this chapter we briefly discuss two important issues that must be addressed when implementing a database system. The first, **database security and protection,** includes the techniques used for protecting the database; persons who are not authorized to access a part of or the whole database must not be allowed to do so. The second, **database semantic integrity,** includes the techniques used to keep the database in a consistent state with respect to the constraints specified on the database. In order to prevent an inconsistent database state, when an update is applied to the database, the semantic integrity checking part of the system should determine if the update will cause a constraint violation.

Notice that the term integrity is sometimes used to cover both semantic integrity and transaction integrity. The latter includes the concurrency control and recovery techniques discussed in Chapter 19. In this chapter we will use the term **integrity** to refer to *semantic integrity constraints only*.

Although the concepts of security and integrity are quite distinct, there are some similarities between the two. Both concepts can be stated in terms of **constraints** as follows:

- Security is specified in terms of **authorization constraints,** whereas integrity is specified in terms of **integrity constraints**.

- Both types of constraints are stored in the DBMS catalog so that they can be enforced by the appropriate constraint enforcement software modules.

- The DBMS is responsible for monitoring user interaction with the database to ensure that both security and integrity constraints are not violated.

We first give an overview of security techniques in Section 20.1 and then discuss techniques for enforcing integrity constraints in Section 20.2.

20.1   Database Security and Protection

Database security is a very broad problem that addresses many issues. These include the following:

- Legal and ethical issues regarding the right to access certain information. Some information may be deemed to be private and cannot be accessed legally by unauthorized persons. In the U.S., several states and the federal government have privacy-of-information laws.

- Policy issues at the governmental, institutional, or corporate level as to what kind of information should be made publicly available. This involves information such as credit ratings and personal medical records.

- System-related issues such as the levels at which various security functions should be handled (for example, physical hardware level, operating system level, DBMS level). We mainly discuss security at the DBMS level here.

In a multiuser database system, the DBMS must provide techniques to enable certain users to access selected portions of a database without having access to the rest of the database. This is particularly important when a large integrated database is to be used by many different users within the same organization. Each group of users usually has a set of applications that access only a subset of the database. Sensitive information such as employee salaries should be kept confidential from most of the database system users. A DBMS typically includes a **database authorization subsystem** to provide for ensuring the security of portions of a database against unauthorized access. A system of granting and revoking privileges to different classes of users is a customary technique for controlling database authorization. We discuss authorization techniques, which provide different access authority to different database users, in Section 20.1.3.

Another security problem common to all computer systems is that of preventing unauthorized persons from accessing the system itself. Certain persons may want to gain access to the system illegally—either to obtain information or to maliciously change a portion of the database. The security mechanism of a DBMS must include provisions for protecting access to the database system as a whole. This function is called **access control** and is handled by creating user accounts and passwords to control the login process by the DBMS. We discuss access control techniques in Section 20.1.2.

A third security problem associated with databases is that of controlling the access to a statistical database. A **statistical database** is used to provide statistical information or summaries of values based on various criteria. For example, a database for population statistics may be used to provide statistics based on age groups, income levels, size of household, education levels, etc. Statistical database users such as government statisticians or market research firms are allowed to access the database to retrieve statistical information about a population but not to access the detailed confidential information on specific individuals. Security for statistical databases must ensure that information on individuals cannot be accessed. It is sometimes possible to deduce certain facts concerning individuals from queries that involve only summary statistics on groups; this also must not be permitted. This problem is called **statistical database security** and is discussed briefly in Section 20.1.4.

Another security technique that may be applied to databases is **data encryption**. This technique is commonly used to protect from unauthorized access sensitive data that is being transmitted via satellite or some other type of communication network. Encryption can also be used to further protect sensitive portions of a database. The data is **encoded** using some coding algorithm. An unauthorized user who accesses encoded data will have difficulty in deciphering it, but authorized users are provided with decoding or decrypting algorithms (or keys) to decipher the data. Encrypting techniques that are very difficult to decode without a key have been developed for military applications. We will not discuss encryption algorithms here.

A complete discussion of security in computer systems and databases is outside the scope of this textbook. We give only a brief overview of database security techniques here. The interested reader can refer to one of the textbooks in the bibliography at the end of this chapter for a more comprehensive discussion. In the next section we discuss the role of the database administrator (DBA) in database security. We then discuss the techniques used by the DBMS to provide the DBA with tools to enforce security by specifying access rights and authorizations to various users.

20.1.1   Database Security and the DBA

As we discussed in Chapter 1, the DBA is the central authority for managing a database system. The DBA's responsibilities include granting privileges to users who need to use the system. The DBA has a **privileged account** in the DBMS, sometimes called a **system account,** which provides powerful capabilities that are not provided to regular database accounts and users. These include the granting and revoking of privileges to individual accounts, users, or user groups and include the following types of actions:

1. Account creation: This action creates a new account and password for a user or a group of users to enable them to access the DBMS.
2. Privilege granting: This action permits the DBA to grant certain privileges to certain accounts.
3. Privilege revocation: This action permits the DBA to revoke (cancel) certain privileges that have been given to certain accounts.

The DBA is responsible for the overall security of the database system. Action 1 above is used to control access to the DBMS as a whole, as we discuss in Section 20.1.2, whereas actions 2 and 3 are used to control database authorizations, as we discuss in Section 20.1.3.

20.1.2   Access Protection, User Accounts, and Database Audits

Whenever a person or a group of persons need to access a database system, they must first apply for a user account. The DBA will then create a new **account number** and **password** for the user if there is a legitimate need for that person to access the database. The user must now **log in** to the DBMS by entering the account number and password whenever database access is needed. The DBMS checks that the account number and password are valid, and if they are, the user is permitted to use the DBMS and access the database. Application programs can also be considered as users and can be required to supply passwords.

It is straightforward to keep track of database users and their accounts and passwords by creating a table or file with the two fields Account_Number and Password. This table can easily be maintained by the DBMS. Whenever a new account is created, a new record is inserted into the table. Canceling an account means that the corresponding record must be deleted from the table.

The database system must also keep track of all operations on the database that are applied by a certain user throughout each **login session,** which consists of the sequence of database interactions that a user performs from the time of logging in to the time of logging off. When a user logs in, the DBMS can record the user's account number and associate it with the terminal from which the user logged in. All operations applied from that terminal are attributed to the user account until the user logs off. It is particularly important to keep track of update operations that are applied to the database so that if the database is tampered with, the DBA can find out which user did the tampering.

To keep a record of all updates applied to the database and the particular user who applied each update, we can modify the system log discussed in Section 19.2. Recall that the **system log** includes an entry for each operation applied to the database that may be required for recovery from a transaction failure or system crash. We can expand the log entries so that they also include the account number of the user and the on-line terminal id that applied each operation recorded in the log. If any tampering with the database is suspected, a **database audit** is performed, which consists of examining all accesses and operations applied to the database during a certain time period by reviewing the log. When an illegal or unauthorized operation is found, the DBA can determine the account number used to perform this operation. Database audits are particularly important for sensitive databases that are updated by many transactions and users, such as a banking database that is updated by many bank tellers. A database log that is used mainly for security purposes is sometimes called an **audit trail**.

The DBA must also be able to provide different privileges to different accounts. Some accounts may be authorized to use only certain files from the database or even only certain fields. In addition, even though two different accounts may be given access to the same file, one account may be allowed to update the file whereas the other account is allowed only to read it. In the next section we discuss the types of privileges that can be given to individual accounts and how these privileges are controlled.

20.1.3 Privileges and Authorization Mechanisms

The typical method of enforcing authorizations in a database system is based on granting and revoking of privileges. Let us consider privileges in the context of a relational DBMS. In particular, we will discuss a system of privileges that is somewhat similar to the one originally developed for the SQL language (see Chapter 7). Many current relational DBMSs use some variation of this technique. In Chapter 23 we discuss further details of the authorization mechanism in the DB2 relational DBMS. The main idea is to include additional statements in the query language that allow the DBA and selected users to grant and revoke privileges.

In the following we use the terms "user" and "account" interchangeably. The DBMS must provide selective access to each relation in the database from only specific accounts. Operations may also be controlled; having an account does not necessarily entitle the account holder to all the functionality provided by the DBMS. As we can see, there are two levels for assigning privileges to use the database system:

1. The account level: At this level, the DBA specifies the particular privileges that each account holds independently of the relations in the database.

2. The relation level: At this level, we can control the privileges to access each individual relation or view in the database.

The privileges at the **account level** apply to the capabilities provided to the account itself and can include the CREATE privilege to create a base relation, the CREATE VIEW privilege, the ALTER privilege to add or remove attributes from relations, the DROP privilege to delete relations or views, the MODIFY privilege to insert, delete, or update tuples, and the SELECT privilege to retrieve information from the database using a SELECT query. Note that these account privileges apply to the account in general. If a certain account does not have the CREATE privilege, no relations can be created from that account. If the account does not have MODIFY privilege, no relation can be updated from the account, and so on.

The second level of privileges applies to the individual relations, whether they are base relations or virtual (view) relations. In the following, the term relation refers to either a base relation or a view unless we explicitly specify one or the other. We can consider privileges at the account level as granting a general functionality (type of command) for the account. Privileges at the relation level then specify the individual relations on which each type of command can be applied. A certain privilege on an individual relation cannot be granted to an account unless it has the corresponding account privilege. For example, a certain account cannot update the DEPARTMENT relation unless it is granted the MODIFY privilege as a whole. Many relational DBMSs do not distinguish between the two levels of granting privileges, and they provide privileges at the *relation level only*. Although this is quite general, it makes it difficult to create accounts with limited privileges.

To control the granting and revoking of relation privileges, each relation R in a database is assigned an **owner account**, which is typically the account that was used when the relation was created in the first place. The owner of a relation is given all privileges on that relation. This means that all relations that were created from an account can be accessed by that account using all access privileges granted to the account. The owner account holder can now pass on these privileges on any of the owned relations to other users by **granting** privileges to their accounts. In SQL the following types of privileges can be granted on each individual relation R:

- SELECT (retrieval) privilege on R: Gives the account retrieval privilege. In SQL the account can use the SELECT statement to retrieve tuples from R.

- MODIFY privileges on R: This gives the account the capability to modify tuples of R. In SQL this privilege is further divided into UPDATE, DELETE, and INSERT privileges to apply the corresponding SQL command to R. In addition, the UPDATE privilege can specify that only certain attributes of R can be updated by the account.

- ALTER privilege on R: This gives the account the capability to change the definition of R by adding or removing attributes. In SQL it gives the account the capability to use the ALTER command on R.

Note that to create a view, the account must have SELECT privilege on *all relations* involved in the view definition.

Specifying Authorization Using Views

The mechanism of **views** is an important authorization mechanism in its own right. For example, if the owner A of a relation R wants another account B to be able to retrieve only some fields of R, then A can create a view V of R that includes only those attributes and then grant SELECT on V to B. The same applies to limiting B to retrieving only certain tuples of R; a view V' can be created by defining the view using a query that selects only those tuples from R that A wants to allow B to access. We illustrate this discussion with the example given at the end of this section.

Revoking of Privileges

In some cases we may want to grant some privilege to a user for a temporary period. For example, the owner of a relation may want to grant SELECT privilege to a user for a specific task and then revoke that privilege once the task is accomplished. Hence, we must have a mechanism for **revoking** privileges that have been granted. In SQL a REVOKE command is included for the purpose of canceling privileges. We will see how the REVOKE command is used in our example below.

Propagation of Privileges and the GRANT Option

Whenever the owner A of a relation R grants a privilege on R to another account B, the privilege can be given to B with or without the **GRANT OPTION**. If the GRANT OPTION is given, this means that B can now also grant that privilege on R to other accounts. Suppose B is given the GRANT OPTION by A and then grants the privilege on R to a third account C, also with GRANT OPTION. In this way, privileges on R can **propagate** to other accounts without the knowledge of the owner of R. If the owner account A now revokes the privilege granted to B, all the privileges that B propagated based on that privilege should automatically be revoked by the system. Hence, a DBMS that allows propagation of privileges must keep track of how all the privileges were granted so that revoking of privileges can be done correctly.

Techniques to limit the propagation of privileges have been developed, although they have not yet been implemented in most DBMSs. Limiting **horizontal propagation** to an integer number i means that an account B given the GRANT OPTION can grant the privilege to at most i other accounts. **Vertical propagation** is more complicated; it limits the depth of the granting of privileges. Granting a privilege with vertical propagation of zero is equivalent to granting the privilege with *no GRANT OPTION*. If account A grants a privilege to account B with vertical propagation set to an integer number j > 0, this means that the account B has the GRANT OPTION on that privilege, but B can grant the privilege to other accounts only with a vertical propagation *less than j*. In effect, vertical propagation limits the sequence of grant options that can be given from one account to the next based on a single original grant of the privilege. We will illustrate this in the following example.

EMPLOYEE

NAME	SSN	BDATE	ADDRESS	SEX	SALARY	DNO

DEPARTMENT

DNUMBER	DNAME	MGRSSN

Figure 20.1 The two relations EMPLOYEE and DEPARTMENT

An Example

In this example we use the SQL authorization commands as much as possible in the way they are provided in the DB2 system (see also Section 23.1.6). When we illustrate a particular concept that is not available in SQL or DB2, we explicitly say so. Suppose the DBA creates four accounts A1, A2, A3, and A4 and wants only A1 to be able to create base relations; then the DBA must issue the following GRANT command in SQL:

GRANT CREATETAB **TO** A1;

The CREATETAB (create table) privilege gives account A1 the capability to create new database tables (base relations) and is hence an *account privilege*. Now suppose A1 creates the two base relations EMPLOYEE and DEPARTMENT shown in Figure 20.1; then A1 is the owner of these two relations and hence has all the *relation privileges* on each of them. Next, suppose that account A1 wants to grant to account A2 the privilege to insert and delete tuples in both of these relations. However, A1 does not want A2 to be able to propagate these privileges to additional accounts. Then A1 can issue the following command:

GRANT INSERT, DELETE **ON** EMPLOYEE, DEPARTMENT **TO** A2;

Note that the owner account A1 of a relation automatically has the GRANT OPTION, allowing it to grant privileges on the relation to other accounts. However, account A2 cannot grant the INSERT and DELETE privileges on the EMPLOYEE and DEPARTMENT tables because A2 was not given the GRANT OPTION in the above command. Next, suppose A1 wants to allow account A3 to retrieve information from either of the two tables and also to be able to propagate the SELECT privilege to other accounts. Then A1 can issue the command:

GRANT SELECT **ON** EMPLOYEE, DEPARTMENT **TO** A3
WITH GRANT OPTION;

The clause "WITH GRANT OPTION" means that A3 can now propagate the privilege to other accounts using GRANT. For example, A3 can grant the SELECT privilege on the EMPLOYEE relation to A4 by issuing the command:

GRANT SELECT **ON** EMPLOYEE **TO** A4;

Note that A4 cannot propagate the SELECT privilege to other accounts because the GRANT OPTION was not given to A4 along with the privilege. Now suppose that A1 decides to revoke the SELECT privilege on the EMPLOYEE relation from A3; then A1 can issue the command:

REVOKE SELECT **ON** EMPLOYEE **FROM** A3;

The DBMS must now automatically revoke the SELECT privilege on EMPLOYEE from A4 also, because A3 granted that privilege to A4 and A3 does not have the privilege any more. Next, suppose that A1 wants to give back to A3 a limited capability to SELECT from the EMPLOYEE relation. The limitation is to retrieve only the NAME, BDATE, and ADDRESS attributes and only the tuples with DNO = 5. Then A1 can create the following view:

CREATE VIEW A3EMPLOYEE **AS**
SELECT NAME, BDATE, ADDRESS
FROM EMPLOYEE
WHERE DNO=5;

After the view is created, A1 can grant SELECT on the view A3EMPLOYEE to A3 as follows:

GRANT SELECT **ON** A3EMPLOYEE **TO** A3 **WITH** GRANT OPTION;

Finally, suppose A1 wants to allow A2 to update only the SALARY attribute of EMPLOYEE; then A1 can issue the following command:

GRANT UPDATE **ON** EMPLOYEE (SALARY) **TO** A2;

The UPDATE privilege can specify particular attributes that may be updated in a relation. Other privileges (SELECT, INSERT, DELETE) are not attribute specific, as this specificity can easily be controlled by creating the appropriate views that include only the desired attributes. However, because updating of views is not always possible, the UPDATE privilege is given the option to specify specific attributes of a base relation that may be updated.

Note that it is possible for a user to receive a certain privilege from two or more sources. For example, A4 may receive a certain UPDATE R privilege from *both* A2 and A3. In such a case, even though A2 may revoke this privilege from A4, A4 continues to have the privilege by virtue of having been granted it from A3. If A3 later revokes the privilege from A4, A4 totally loses the privilege.

We now briefly illustrate the horizontal and vertical propagation limits, which are not available in DB2 or other relational systems at the time of writing. Suppose A1 grants SELECT to A2 on the EMPLOYEE relation with horizontal propagation = 1 and vertical propagation = 2. Then A2 can grant SELECT to at most one account because of the horizontal propagation limitation that is set to 1. In addition, A2 cannot grant the privilege to another account except with vertical propagation = 0 (no GRANT OPTION) or 1 because of the vertical propagation limitation that was set to 2 when A2 was given the privilege. This means that A2 must reduce the vertical propagation by at least 1 when passing the privilege to others. As we can see, horizontal and vertical propagation techniques are designed to limit the propagation of privileges.

PERSON

NAME	SSN	INCOME	ADDRESS	CITY	STATE	ZIP	SEX	LAST_DEGREE

Figure 20.2   The PERSON relation

20.1.4   Statistical Database Security

Statistical databases are used mainly for the production of statistics on various populations. The database may contain confidential data on many individuals, which should be protected from user access. However, users are allowed to retrieve statistical information on the populations, such as averages, counts, sums, and standard deviations. The techniques developed to protect the privacy of individual information in statistical databases are outside the scope of this book. We will only illustrate the problem very briefly here with a simple example. The interested reader can refer to the bibliography for texts that provide a complete discussion of statistical databases and their security. We illustrate the problem with the relation shown in Figure 20.2, which shows a PERSON relation with the attributes NAME, SSN, INCOME, ADDRESS, CITY, STATE, ZIP, SEX, and LAST_DEGREE.

A **population** is a set of tuples of a file that satisfy some selection condition. Hence, each selection condition on the PERSON relation will specify a specific population of PERSON tuples. For example, the condition SEX = 'M' specifies the male population, the condition (SEX = 'F' AND (LAST_DEGREE = 'M.S.' OR LAST_DEGREE = 'PH.D.')) specifies the female population that has an M.S. or PH.D. degree as the highest degree, and the condition CITY = 'Houston' specifies the population that lives in Houston.

Statistical queries involve applying statistical functions to a population of tuples. For example, we may want to retrieve the number of individuals in a population or the average income. However, statistical users are not allowed to retrieve individual data, such as the income of a specific person. **Statistical database security** techniques must prohibit the retrieval of individual data. This can easily be controlled by prohibiting queries that retrieve attribute values and allowing only queries that involve statistical aggregate functions such as COUNT, SUM, MIN, MAX, AVERAGE, and STANDARD DEVIATION. Such queries are sometimes called **statistical queries**.

In some cases it is possible to **deduce** the values of individual tuples from a sequence of statistical queries. This is particularly true when the conditions result in a population with a small number of tuples. To illustrate this, suppose we use the following two statistical queries:

Q1:   **SELECT** COUNT(*) **FROM** PERSON
      WHERE <condition>

Q2:   **SELECT** AVERAGE(INCOME) **FROM** PERSON
      WHERE <condition>

Now suppose we are interested in finding the SALARY of 'Jane Smith', and we know that she has a PH.D. degree and she lives in the city of Bellaire, Texas. We issue the statistical query Q1 with the following condition:

(LAST_DEGREE='PH.D.' AND SEX='F' AND CITY='Bellaire' AND STATE='Texas')

If we get a result of 1 for this query, we can now issue Q2 with the same condition and find the INCOME of 'Jane Smith'. Even if the result of Q1 on the above condition is not 1 but is a small number, say 2 or 3, we can issue statistical queries using the functions MAX, MIN, and AVERAGE and know the possible range of values for the INCOME of 'Jane Smith'.

The possibility of deducing individual information from statistical queries is reduced if no statistical queries are permitted whenever the number of tuples in the population specified by the selection condition is below some threshold. Another technique for prohibiting retrieval of individual information is to prohibit sequences of queries that refer repeatedly to the same population of tuples. Also, it is possible to introduce deliberately slight inaccuracies or "noise" into the results of statistical queries to make it difficult to deduce individual information from the results. The interested reader is referred to the bibliography for a discussion of these techniques.

20.2   Specifying and Enforcing Database Integrity Constraints

When we design a schema for a particular database application, one of the important activities is to identify the **integrity constraints** that must hold on the database. We first discuss the types of integrity constraints that are encountered frequently in database applications in Section 20.2.1. Then in Section 20.2.2 we discuss the techniques that are used by DBMSs to specify these constraints. In Section 20.2.3 we compare the various data models in terms of the types of constraints each model represents naturally. Finally, in Section 20.2.4 we discuss the techniques that DBMSs use to enforce these integrity constraints.

20.2.1   Types of Integrity Constraints

We usually implement a database to store information about some *part of the real world,* which we called the **miniworld** in Chapter 1. In any miniworld situation, there are always many rules, called **integrity constraints,** that govern this situation. We want to specify most of these integrity constraints to the DBMS and, if possible, have the DBMS be responsible for enforcing them.

Implicit, Explicit, and Inherent Constraints of a Data Model

In any data model, there are some types of integrity constraints that can be specified and represented in the database schemas of that model. These are called the **implicit constraints** of the data model, and are specified using the DDL. Each data model includes a different set of implicit constraints that can be directly represented in its schemas. In general, high-level data models represent more types of constraints implicitly than lower-level data models. However, no data model is capable of representing all types of constraints that may occur in a miniworld; hence, it is usually necessary to specify additional **explicit constraints** on each particular database schema that represents a particular miniworld application. A third type of constraints is the **inherent constraints** of the data model itself, which do not have to be specified in a schema but are assumed to hold by the definition of the model constructs.

We discussed the constraints of each data model when we presented the various data models in Parts I through III of the book. Examples of implicit and inherent constraints of the various data models include the following:

- ER model: Constraints such as key attributes and structural constraints on relationship types are implicitly specified in an ER schema. An inherent constraint in the ER model is that every relationship instance of an n-ary relationship type R relates *exactly one entity from each entity type participating in R in a specific role.*

- Relational model: Keys and entity integrity and referential integrity constraints are generally considered to be implicit in the relational model, although some relational systems do not implicitly represent referential integrity constraints. An inherent constraint in the *formal* relational model is that an attribute value is indivisible (atomic).

- Hierarchical model: Hierarchical rules, such as the rule that a root record cannot have a parent or the rule that every nonroot record has exactly one real parent, are inherent constraints of the hierarchical model.

- Network model: Key (UNIQUE) constraints on fields and rules that govern set types (INSERTION and RETENTION options) are implicitly specified in a network schema. Inherent constraints include the rule that a record instance cannot be a member of more than one set instance of a particular set type.

- EER model: Constraints on specializations/generalizations, such as disjointness or totality, are implicitly specified in an EER schema. An inherent constraint in the EER model is that every entity instance in a subclass must also exist in its superclass.

In general, every data model is basically a set of concepts and rules or assertions that specify the structure and the implicit constraints of a database describing a miniworld. A given implementation of a data model in a *particular* DBMS will usually support only some of the inherent and implicit constraints of the data model automatically. At the time of writing, support and enforcement of integrity constraints is a weak point of many existing relational DBMSs.

State and Transition Constraints of a Database Application

We can classify the following types of constraints that occur frequently in database applications:

1. Database **state constraints**: These are constraints on the **state** of the database. Recall that a database state or instance refers to all the data in the database at a particular point in time. A database state is **consistent** if it satisfies all state constraints. Examples of state constraints are:

   a. Value set (domain) constraints on the possible values that an attribute can take.

   b. Attribute key (uniqueness) constraints, which specify whether an attribute—or set of attributes—is a unique (key) attribute of an entity type. No two entity instances of the entity type should have the same value for a key attribute.

    c. Attribute structural constraints, which specify whether an attribute is single valued or multivalued and whether or not **null** is allowed for the attribute.

    d. Relationship structural constraints, which specify the cardinality ratios and total/partial constraints of entity sets that participate in a relationship set. These include referential integrity constraints.

    e. Superclass/subclass constraints, which specify disjointness or totality of specializations/generalizations.

    f. General semantic integrity constraints, that is, state constraints that do not fall in any of the above categories.

State constraints apply to a particular state of the database and should hold on every state where the database is *not in transition*, that is, not in the process of being updated. Hence they are sometimes called **static constraints**. State constraints should be checked whenever the database state is changed by an update transaction. A transaction should include sufficient checks to guarantee that whenever the database is in a consistent state before transaction execution, it should also be in a consistent state after transaction execution. As we discussed in Chapter 19, a transaction is an atomic update unit. The concurrency control and recovery methods should guarantee that either all the transaction operations are executed or none are.

  2. Database **transition constraints:** A transition constraint is a constraint on the transition from one state to another, not on an individual state. An example is that the Salary attribute of an employee can only be increased; this means that any update to the Salary attribute is accepted only if the new value of Salary is greater than the old value. Note that the constraint is neither on the state of the database before the update nor on the state after the update; it is specified on the transition between states and involves values of attributes both *before* and *after* the transaction. In general, transition constraints occur less frequently than state constraints and are sometimes called **dynamic constraints**. Because of their nature, they are more difficult to enforce and are mainly specified as *explicit constraints*.

Figure 20.3 summarizes the different classifications of constraints. The following example illustrates the various types of constraints in the ER model.

Example

We illustrate the different types of constraints discussed above using the ER schema shown in Figure 3.13. First, domain constraints are specified by associating every simple attribute with a value set. For example, the value set of the Ssn attribute of EMPLOYEE could be specified as the data type character string of length 9, and for the Bdate attribute the value set could be specified as a valid date between JAN-01-1900 and DEC-31-1975. The DBMS can check any new values of attributes to make sure they satisfy the domain constraints.

Next, for each entity set we specify the key attributes. In our example, Ssn is a key of EMPLOYEE, Number is a key of DEPARTMENT, Name is a key of DEPARTMENT, etc. All keys are underlined in Figure 3.13. If a set of attributes forms a key, we create a compos-

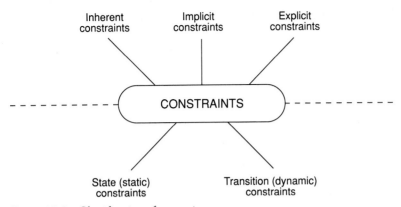

Figure 20.3   Classification of constraints

ite attribute that includes the set and make it a key. To represent the constraint that no two employees should have identical names, we specify that the composite attribute Name—composed of FName, MInit, LName—be a key. The DBMS should check that any new entity inserted in the database has a value for each key attribute that is distinct from all other values of the key attribute for entities currently in the database.

Structural constraints on relationships specify constraints on the participation of entities in relationship instances. For example, the constraints "every employee works for exactly one department" and "every department has exactly one manager and an employee can manage at most one department" can be represented diagrammatically as structural constraints on the WORKS_FOR and MANAGES relationships in Figure 3.13 (or alternatively as in Figure 3.14). The data definition language (DDL) used to specify a database schema should provide constructs for the specification of *all* implicit constraints of the data model including structural constraints.

Finally, we could have general state constraints—sometimes called **semantic constraints**—that do not fall in any of the above categories. An example is the constraint "the salary of an employee must not be greater than the salary of the manager of the department that the employee works for." Another example could be that "the total number of hours that each employee works on all his projects should not exceed 45 hours per week (including overtime)." These constraints and other explicit constraints cannot be specified directly in the schema using the DDL and must be specified using one of the techniques discussed in the next section.

20.2.2   Specifying Explicit Integrity Constraints

Inherent constraints *do not need to be specified* in the DDL when defining a database schema; they are inherent properties of the data model constructs themselves. Implicit constraints that are supported by a DBMS are *specified in the DDL* during schema definition. The DBMS is then responsible for automatically enforcing these constraints. In this section we discuss the various approaches for specifying explicit constraints, which are beyond the scope of the DDL in most current DBMSs.

Specifying Explicit Constraints Procedurally in the Transactions

One method of specifying explicit constraints is to include checking statements in the update transactions. This is called the **procedural specification of constraints** (or the **coded constraints** technique). The constraints are coded into appropriate transactions by the programmer. For example, consider the general constraint that "the salary of an employee must not be greater than the salary of the manager of the department that the employee works for," specified on the ER schema of Figure 3.13. To enforce this constraint, it must be checked in *every update transaction* that may violate the constraint. This includes any transaction that modifies the salary of an employee, any transaction that inserts a new employee or relates an employee to a department, any transaction that assigns a new manager to a department, etc. In every such transaction, part of the code of the transaction must explicitly check that the constraint will not be violated. If the constraint is violated, the transaction must be aborted without making any changes to the database. This ensures that the transaction behaves not only as an atomic unit for concurrency and recovery purposes but also as an atomic unit for semantic integrity control.

The above technique for handling explicit constraints is used by many existing DBMSs. It is also used in object-oriented modeling, where explicit constraints can be encoded as part of the methods or operations that are **encapsulated** with the objects (see Section 15.4.1). This approach is completely general because the checks are typically programmed in a general-purpose programming language. This technique also allows the programmer to code the checks in an efficient way. However, it is not very flexible and places an extra burden on the programmer, who must know all the constraints that a transaction may violate and must include checks to ensure that none of the constraints will be violated. A misunderstanding, omission, or error by the programmer may leave the database in an inconsistent state.

Another drawback of specifying constraints procedurally is that constraints can change with time as the rules in a miniworld situation change. If a constraint changes, it is the responsibility of the DBA to instruct appropriate programmers to recode all the transactions affected by the change. This again leaves the possibility of overlooking some transactions and hence leaving errors in constraint representation. If one transaction is changed and another is not, then the two transactions will check for different constraints, causing possible inconsistencies in the database.

Specifying Explicit Constraints Declaratively as Assertions

A second, more formal technique has been suggested for representing explicit constraints. In this approach a **constraint specification language,** usually based on some variation of the relational calculus, is used to specify or declare all the explicit constraints that hold on a schema. In this **declarative approach** there is a clean separation between the **constraint base,** in which the constraints are stored in a suitably encoded form, and the **integrity control subsystem** of the DBMS, which accesses the constraint base to apply the constraints appropriately to the affected transactions.

When using this technique, constraints are often called **integrity assertions,** or simply **assertions,** and the specification language is called an **assertion specification language.** The term assertion is used in place of explicit constraint, and the assertions are specified as declarative statements. This approach has been suggested for use with relational DBMSs. The SQL language includes the ASSERT statement for assertion specification, although this statement is *not* implemented in many current relational DBMSs.

The integrity control subsystem will compile the assertions, which are then stored in the DBMS catalog, where the integrity control subsystem can refer to them and *automatically* enforce them. Update transactions can now be written *without any constraint-checking statements*. This approach is very appealing from the standpoint of the users and programmers because of its flexibility. Update transactions are now very easy to write because no checking for constraint violations is necessary. A constraint can be changed independently of the transactions without having to recode any transactions; we only have to cancel the old assertion and specify its replacement in the assertion specification language. The new assertion is compiled and replaces the canceled assertion in the DBMS catalog. Unfortunately, this technique has proved very difficult to implement so far, because the integrity control subsystems have proved to be complex and inefficient. Research on making this approach more efficient is continuing.

We now give an example to show how an assertion may be declared in SQL. Consider the relational schema in Figure 20.1. We can specify the constraint "The salary of an employee must not be greater than the salary of the manager of the department that the employee works for" in SQL using the ASSERT* statement as follows:

ASSERT SALARY_CONSTRAINT **ON** EMPLOYEE E M, DEPARTMENT:
E.SALARY<M.SALARY **AND** E.DNO=DNUMBER **AND** MGRSSN=M.SSN ;

The keyword **ASSERT** indicates that a constraint is being defined and is followed by the name of the constraint, SALARY_CONSTRAINT, which can be used to refer to the constraint or drop it later. Following the **ON** keyword are the relations affected by the constraint. Finally, the assertion condition is specified. A constraint condition is similar to the condition of a WHERE-clause in SQL. Whenever some tuples in the database cause the condition of an ASSERT statement to evaluate to FALSE, the constraint is **violated**. The constraint is **satisfied** by a database state if *no combination of tuples* in that database state violates the constraint.

Triggers

In many cases it is convenient to specify the type of action to be taken in case of a constraint violation. Rather than having only the option of aborting the transaction that causes a violation, other options should be available. For example, it may be useful to specify a constraint that, if violated, should cause some user to be informed. A manager may want to be informed if an employee's travel expenses exceed a certain limit by receiving a message whenever this occurs. The action that the DBMS must take in this case is to send an appropriate message to that user, and the constraint is used to **monitor** the database. Other actions may be specified, such as executing a specific procedure or triggering other updates. In the procedural approach, all such actions can be specified by encoding them in the appropriate transactions. For the declarative approach, a mechanism called a trigger has been proposed to implement such actions.

---

*Most relational DBMSs do not implement the **ASSERT** statement at all or implement it in a restricted form that may not allow this constraint to be specified.

A **trigger** specifies a **condition** and an **action** to be taken in case that condition occurs. The condition is usually specified as an assertion that invokes or "triggers" the action when it becomes TRUE. It is also possible to define conditions for triggers within
transactions. For example, we may define a trigger procedure that is invoked when a particular transaction reaches its commit point to check whether the transaction should
be committed or aborted, and if the transaction should be aborted, the trigger can undo
the effect of the transaction on the database. A DEFINE TRIGGER statement was proposed
in SQL to specify triggers, although not all SQL implementations include it.

To illustrate how a trigger may be specified in SQL, suppose we wish to specify a trigger to notify the department manager if any employee in the manager's department has a
higher salary than the manager. We can define the following trigger*:

```
DEFINE TRIGGER SALARY_CONSTRAINT
ON EMPLOYEE E M, DEPARTMENT:
E.SALARY>M.SALARY AND E.DNO=DNUMBER AND MGRSSN=M.SSN
ACTION_PROCEDURE INFORM_MANAGER (MGRSSN) ;
```

The above trigger specifies that the procedure INFORM_MANAGER should be executed
whenever the trigger condition occurs. Note the difference between ASSERT and
TRIGGER: an ASSERT statement should prohibit an update that violates the assertion condition (makes it FALSE), whereas a trigger allows the update to take place but executes
the action procedure when the trigger condition occurs (becomes TRUE). Hence, the
ASSERT condition specified earlier and the TRIGGER condition given above are *inverses* of
each other ("less than" is replaced by "greater than").

Note that triggers combine the declarative and procedural approaches. The trigger
condition is declarative, while its action is procedural. In general, it may be useful to
specify triggers not only on explicit constraints but also on implicit constraints. For example, in the network model the action to delete member records if the owner is deleted
can be specified on a MANDATORY set if the DELETE ALL command is used (see Chapter 11). Note that it is necessary to check for cycles of triggers; otherwise infinite loops
may occur.

20.2.3 Integrity Constraints in Various Data Models

We now briefly compare the various data models with respect to how each represents
constraints and the types of implicit constraints associated with each. A more complete
discussion is included in the individual chapters that describe each of the data models.

Relational Model

The implicit constraints available in the relational model include value set (domain)
constraints and key constraints on attributes. Referential integrity is also sometimes considered to be an implicit constraint in the relational model, although it is usually not
represented in a relational schema or in the DDLs of popular relational languages such
as SQL and QUEL. To make referential integrity an implicit constraint, it is necessary to

---

*Our syntax here is different from that proposed for SQL.

include some statements in the data definition language to allow the specification of referential integrity constraints in a database schema. Note that referential integrity is a structural constraint on relationships between tuples. Also, if a relational DBMS allows the ASSERT statement or some similar construct, referential integrity can be expressed as explicit constraints by appropriate ASSERT statements.

In the relational model, all other types of constraints are explicit and are either specified as assertions or coded in the update transactions.

Network Model

In the network model, value set (data type) and key (unique) constraints are implicit, as are some structural constraints on 1:N relationships. The latter are specified as options when a set type is declared. Recall that a set type is basically a 1:N relationship between two record types. The INSERTION and RETENTION options on a set type are structural constraints on the 1:N relationship. For example, a MANDATORY set type specifies that every member record must be related to an owner record (total membership), whereas an optional set type allows a member record to exist without being related to an owner (partial membership). Structural constraints on sets specify the owner record to which a member record can be connected by a condition on the attributes of the owner and member record types.

In addition, structural constraints on attributes are available, since composite (vector) and multivalued (repeating group) attributes are allowed. All other types of constraints are encoded in the update programs and hence are specified as explicit constraints in the network model.

Notice that AUTOMATIC set types are an implicit form of a trigger. Here, the *condition* is that a member record is inserted in the database. The *action* to be taken is that an owner record is found for that member record—using the SET SELECTION procedure—and the member record is connected to that owner record. Another example of an implicit network model trigger is the DELETE ALL command, which deletes the specified record but also triggers the deletion of all member records owned by that record.

Hierarchical Model

The basic inherent hierarchical constraint is that every record in a hierarchy must have an owner except for root records. This is again a structural constraint on a 1:N relationship. Value set and key constraints are implicitly specified. Other inherent constraints involve VPCRs, such as the constraint that a pointer must reference an existing virtual parent record. Most other constraints are encoded in the update programs as explicit constraints.

Entity-Relationship Model

The ER model described in Chapter 3 includes as implicit constraints the value set constraints, key constraints, attribute structural constraints, and a full array of relationship structural constraints. The enhanced-ER (EER) model of Chapter 15 has additional implicit constraints that govern superclass/subclass relationships and specializations/generalizations. Other general constraints that do not fall into the above types must be specified in some constraint specification language or coded procedurally. Several constraint specification languages have been proposed for the ER model, but a discussion is outside the scope of this textbook. The interested reader is referred to the bibliography at the end of the chapter.

20.2.4   Enforcing the Integrity Constraints

Implicit constraints are specifed to the DBMS through the data definition language during the process of creating the database schema. The DDL compiler stores these constraints in the DBMS catalog. The DBMS software can now automatically enforce appropriate implicit constraints each time and update occurs by referring to the catalog.

   If the DBMS uses an assertion specification language, then explicit constraints that are specified in the language are maintained in a way similar to the implicit constraints, except that the algorithms to enforce general constraints specified as assertions are more complex than those for enforcing a small set of well-defined constraint types. Otherwise, explicit constraints are coded in the transactions and it is the responsibility of the database programmers and DBA to see that they are coded correctly.

20.3   Summary

In this chapter we discussed two different topics of concern in implementing DBMSs: enforcing security and enforcing integrity constraints. Security enforcement deals with controlling access to the database system as a whole and controlling authorization to access specific portions of a database. The former is usually done by assigning accounts with passwords to users. The latter can be controlled using a system of granting and revoking of privileges to individual accounts for accessing specific parts of the database. We also very briefly discussed the problem of controlling access to statistical databases to protect the privacy of individual information while providing statistical access to populations of records.

   In Section 20.2 we turned our attention to the problem of specifying and enforcing integrity constraints. We distinguished between inherent constraints of a data model that are properties of the model constructs, implicit constraints that are specified in a database schema by the DDL, and explicit constraints that have to be specified separately. We also distinguished between state constraints and transition constraints and presented the two main techniques for specifying explicit constraints: procedural specification by encoding checks for the constraints in the update transactions and declarative specification by specifying assertions and using an integrity control subsystem in the DBMS. We also discussed the trigger mechanism, which can be used either for monitoring database conditions or for integrity enforcement. Finally, we listed some implicit constraints that can be represented in ER, relational, network, and hierarchical data models.

Review Questions

20.1. Discuss what is meant by each of the following terms: database authorization, access control, data encryption, privileged (system) account, database audit, audit trail.

20.2. Discuss the types of privileges at the account level and those at the relation level.

20.3. Which account is designated as the owner of a relation? What privileges does the owner of a relation have?

20.4. How is the view mechanism used as an authorization mechanism?

20.5. What is meant by granting a privilege?

20.6. What is meant by revoking a privilege?

20.7. Discuss the system of propagation of privileges with horizontal and vertical propagation limits.

20.8. List the types of privileges available in SQL.

20.9. What is a statistical database? Discuss the problem of statistical database security.

20.10. What is the difference between inherent constraints, implicit constraints, and explicit constraints?

20.11. What is the difference between state constraints and transition constraints? Discuss the different types of state constraints.

20.12. Compare the procedural and declarative techniques for specifying and enforcing explicit constraints. How are assertions specified in SQL?

20.13. What is a trigger? How is a trigger specified in SQL? In what sense is a trigger a mixture of procedural and declarative specifications?

20.14. Compare the types of implicit constraints that can be represented in the schemas of each of the following data models: ER model, relational model, network model, hierarchical model, EER model.

20.15. How are implicit constraints enforced? Discuss the different approaches to enforcing explicit constraints.

20.16. How are constraints specified in object-oriented data models?

Exercises

20.17. Consider the relational database schema of Figure 6.5. Suppose that all the relations were created by and hence are owned by the DBA. The DBA wants to grant the following privileges to user accounts A, B, C, D, and E:

    a. Account A can retrieve or modify any relation except DEPENDENT and can grant any of these privileges to other users.

    b. Account B can retrieve all the attributes of EMPLOYEE and DEPARTMENT except for SALARY, MGRSSN, and MGRSTARTDATE.

    c. Account C can retrieve or modify WORKS_ON but can only retrieve the FNAME, MINIT, LNAME, SSN attributes of EMPLOYEE and the PNAME, PNUMBER attributes of PROJECT.

    d. Account D can retrieve any attribute of EMPLOYEE or DEPENDENT and can modify DEPENDENT.

    e. Account E can retrieve any attribute of EMPLOYEE but only for EMPLOYEE tuples that have DNO = 3.

    Write SQL statements to grant these privileges. Use views where appropriate.

20.18. Suppose that privilege a of Exercise 20.17 is to be given with GRANT OPTION but only so that account A can grant it to at most five accounts, and each of these accounts can propagate the privilege to other accounts but *without* grant privilege. What would the horizontal and vertical propagation limits be in this case?

20.19. Consider the ER diagram of Figure 3.14 and the corresponding relational database schemas of Figures 6.5 and 6.7.

   a. Make a list of all the implicit constraints that are specified in the ER schema of Figure 3.14. List these constraints as statements in English.

   b. Which of the implicit constraints in part a are not implicit in the relational database schema of Figure 6.5? Try to specify as many as possible of the missing constraints in the form of explicit SQL assertions. Which additional constraints are implicit in the relational schema of Figure 6.7 that are not implicit in Figure 6.5?

   c. Which of the implicit constraints in part a are not implicit in the network database schema of Figure 11.10?

   d. Which of the implicit constraints in part a are not implicit in the hierarchical database schema of Figure 10.10?

   e. Compare the missing implicit constraints in the relational, network, and hierarchical schemas in your solutions of parts b, c, and d. Which of the models has the fewest missing constraints?

20.20. Specify a trigger on the relational database schema of Figure 6.5 that will inform a department manager (by executing a procedure INFORM_DMGR(DNUM)) whenever one of the projects controlled by the department he or she manages has more than 10 employees or fewer than 3 employees.

Selected Bibliography

Authorization based on granting and revoking of privileges was proposed for the SYSTEM R experimental DBMS and is presented in Griffiths and Wade (1976). Stonebraker and Wong (1974) discuss access control by query modification, which was proposed for use in the INGRES relational DBMS. Several books discuss security in databases and computer systems in general, including the books by Leiss (1982a) and Fernandez et al. (1981). Denning and Denning (1979) is a tutorial paper on data security.

Many papers discuss different techniques for the design and protection of statistical databases. These include Chin (1978), Chin and Ozsoyoglu (1981), Leiss (1982), and Denning (1980). Ghosh (1984) discusses the use of statistical databases for quality control. There are also many papers discussing cryptography and data encryption, including Diffie and Hellman (1979), Rivest et al. (1978), and Akl (1983).

The importance of specifying and maintaining integrity constraints has been recognized for a long time. Early papers discussing integrity constraints in the relational model include Hammer and McLeod (1975), Stonebraker (1975), Eswaran and Chamberlin (1975), Chen (1976) and Schmidt and Swenson (1975). Wiederhold and Elmasri (1979) and Codd (1979) extend the relational model by categorizing relations based on their constraints. They also discuss insertion and deletion of tuples based on these constraints, as does Chen (1976). Elmasri and Wiederhold (1980) compare several models with regard to the constraints they represent on relationships. Most semantic data models (see the bibliography for Chapter 15) discuss integrity constraints, and each model has its own extended set of implicit constraints.

Integrity assertions and triggers were proposed for use in the SYSTEM R relational DBMS and are discussed in Eswaran et al. (1976) and Astrahan et al. (1976). Chamberlin et al. (1976) proposed the ASSERT and TRIGGER statements as features of SQL, but they have not been fully implemented to date. Research into efficient enforcement of integrity assertions is reported in Hammer and Sarin (1978), Bernstein et al. (1980), Badal and Popek (1979), and Hsu and Imielinsky (1985). The book by Tsichritzis and Lochovsky (1982) includes a discussion on integrity constraints.

CURRENT TRENDS IN DATABASE SYSTEMS

CHAPTER 21
Distributed Databases

CHAPTER 22
Emerging Database Technologies and Applications

Distributed Databases

So far, we have implicitly assumed that the data and the DBMS software that constitute a database system reside on a single hardware machine, with associated secondary storage devices such as disks for on-line database storage and tapes for backup. Such a system is called a **centralized database system** because all system components reside at a single computer or **site**. It is true that a centralized database can be accessed remotely via terminals connected to the site; however, the data and DBMS software principally reside at a single site. In recent years there has been a rapid trend toward the **distribution** of computer systems over multiple sites that are connected together via a **communication network**. In this chapter we discuss the development of **distributed database systems** (DDBSs) and the techniques used in their implementation. The software used to implement such a system is called a **distributed database management system (DDBMS)**.

In Section 21.1 we discuss the general concepts of distributed databases, including the reasons for data and system distribution, architectural issues, and the techniques for dividing up and allocating a database over several sites. Then we present the problems with implementing DDBSs and some of the proposed solutions to these problems. We first discuss distributed query processing in Section 21.2 and then distributed concurrency control and recovery techniques in Section 21.3.

21.1 Distributed DBMS Concepts and Architecture

We first give an overview of the factors that have led to the development of DDBSs in Section 21.1.1. Then in Section 21.1.2 we present, in general terms, the architecture of a DDBS. In Section 21.1.3 we discuss the techniques for dividing up and distributing a database over the various sites. These techniques are referred to as **distributed database design**. We also discuss the use of data replication in a DDBS. In Section 21.1.4 we categorize different types of DDBSs.

21.1.1 Reasons for Distribution and DDBMS Functions

A **distributed database** is a collection of data that belongs logically to the same system but is physically spread over the sites of a computer network. Several factors have led to the development of DDBSs. Below we list some of the potential advantages of DDBSs:

- Distributed nature of some database applications: Many database applications are *naturally distributed* over different locations. For example, a company may have locations at different cities, or a bank may have multiple branches. It is natural for databases used in such applications to be distributed over these locations. A company may keep a database at each of its locations to store the data pertaining to that location. Many **local users** access only the data at this location, but other **global users**—such as company headquarters—may require access to data stored at several of these locations. Notice that the data at each local site typically describe a "miniworld" at that site. The sources of data and the majority of users and applications for the local database will physically reside at that site. On the other hand, global users may only occasionally access such local data.

- Increased reliability and availability: These are two of the most common potential advantages cited for distributed databases. **Reliability** is broadly defined as the probability that a system is up at a particular moment in time, whereas **availability** is the probability that the system is continuously available during a time interval. When the data and DBMS software are distributed over several sites, one site may fail while other sites continue in operation. Only the data and software that exist at the failed site cannot be accessed; other data and software can still be used. This improves both reliability and availability. Further improvement is achieved by judiciously *replicating* data and software at more than one site. In a centralized system, failure of that single site makes the whole system unavailable to all users.

- Allowing data sharing while maintaining some measure of local control: In some types of DDBSs (see Section 21.1.4) it is possible to control the data and software locally at each site. However, certain data can be accessed by other remote sites through the DDBMS software. This allows *controlled* sharing of data throughout the distributed system.

- Improved performance: By distributing a large database over multiple sites, smaller databases will exist at each site. Local queries and transactions accessing data at a single site will potentially demonstrate better performance because of having to process smaller local databases. In addition, each site will have a smaller number of transactions executing than if all transactions were submitted to a single centralized database. For transactions that involve access to more than one site, processing at the different sites may proceed in parallel, which can reduce the transaction execution and response time.

Distribution leads to increased complexity in the system design and implementation. To satisfactorily achieve the potential advantages listed above, the DDBMS software must be able to provide *additional functions* to those of a centralized DBMS. Some of these are:

- To access remote sites and transmit queries and data among the various sites via a communication network.

- To keep track of the data distribution and replication in the DDBMS catalog.
- To devise execution strategies for queries and transactions that access data from more than one site.
- To decide on which copy of a replicated data item to access.
- To maintain the consistency of copies of a replicated data item.
- To recover from individual site crashes and from new types of failures such as failure of a communication link.

These functions themselves increase the complexity of a DDBMS over a centralized DBMS. Before we can realize the full potential advantages of distribution, we must find satisfactory solutions to these issues. Including all this additional functionality is hard to deal with, and finding optimal solutions is a step beyond that. Additional complexities appear when we consider the design of a distributed database. In addition to the database design issues discussed in Part III of the book, we must now decide on how to distribute the data over sites and what data, if any, to replicate.

21.1.2   Architecture of a DDBS

At the physical **hardware** level, the main factors that distinguish a DDBS from a centralized system are the following:

- There are multiple computers, called **sites** or **nodes**.
- These sites must be connected by some type of **communication network** to transmit data and commands among sites, as shown in Figure 21.1.

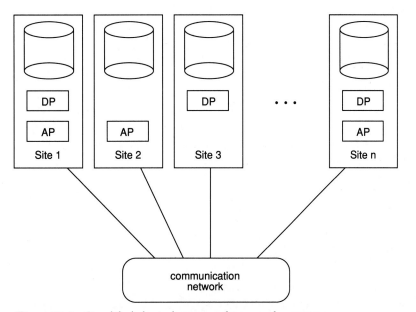

Figure 21.1   Simplified physical system architecture for a DDBS

The sites may all be located in physical proximity—say, within the same building or typically within a 1-mile radius—and connected via a **local area network,** or they may be geographically distributed over large distances and connected via a **long-haul network**. Local area networks typically use cables, whereas long-haul networks use telephone lines or satellites. It is also possible to use a combination of the two types of networks.

Networks may have different **topologies** that define the direct communication paths among sites. For example, it is possible that a direct link exists between sites 1 and 2 and sites 2 and 3 but not between sites 1 and 3; in such a case, communication between sites 1 and 3 must pass through site 2. The type and topology of the network used may have a significant effect on performance and hence on the strategies for distributed query processing and distributed database design. However, for high-level architectural issues, it does not matter which type of network is used; it only matters that each site is able to communicate, directly or indirectly, with every other site. For the remainder of this section we assume that some type of communication network exists among sites regardless of the topology.

Application Processors and Data Processors

To manage the complexity of a DDBMS, it is customary to divide its software into three main *modules:*

- The **data processor (DP)** software is responsible for local data management at a site, much like centralized DBMS software.

- The **application processor (AP)** software is responsible for most of the distribution functions; it accesses data distribution information from the DDBMS catalog and is responsible for processing all requests that require access to more than one site.

- The **communications software** (sometimes in conjunction with a **distributed operating system**) provides the communication primitives that are used by the AP to transmit commands and data among the various sites as needed. This is not strictly part of the DDBMS but provides primitives and services needed by the AP to perform its functions.

The AP is responsible for generating a distributed execution plan for a multisite query or transaction and for supervising distributed execution by sending commands to DPs and other APs. These commands include local queries and transactions to be executed by a DP as well as commands to transmit data to other APs or DPs. Hence, AP software should be included at any site where multisite queries are submitted. We discuss distributed query processing in Section 21.2. Another function controlled by the AP is that of ensuring consistency of replicated copies of a data item by employing distributed (or global) concurrency control techniques. The AP must also ensure the atomicity of global transactions by performing global recovery when certain sites fail. We discuss distributed recovery and concurrency control in Section 21.3.

In a DDBS it is possible that some sites contain both AP and DP software, whereas other sites contain only one or the other, as illustrated in Figure 21.1. A site that is used mainly for the DP function is often called a **back-end machine,** and a site that is used primarily for the AP function is called a **front-end machine**. A back end can include specialized database search hardware to execute local queries and transactions with high speed and is also responsible for local concurrency control and recovery. A front end can be a diskless workstation, but it may also be a powerful minicomputer to which numerous user terminals are connected and may be responsible for maintaining the distributed catalog and coordinating distributed execution, global concurrency control, and global recovery. Figure 21.2 shows a logical view of a DDBS, where APs and DPs are shown without specifying the site on which each resides.

Distribution Transparency

An important function of the AP is to *hide* the details of data distribution from the user; that is, the user should write global queries and transactions as though the database were centralized, without having to specify the sites at which the data referenced in the query or transaction resides. This property is called **distribution transparency**. Some DDBMSs do not provide distribution transparency, requiring that users be aware of the details of data distribution. In this case, users must specify the sites at which the data referenced in global queries and transactions reside. In the latter situation, a user will typically *append the site name* to any references to a relation, file, or record type. In the former situation, the user is presented with a schema that does not include any distribution information, and the DDBMS itself keeps track of the sites at which data is located in the **DDBMS catalog**. Using this information, an AP can break down a query into a number of subqueries that can be executed at the various sites and plan how results of subqueries are to be transmitted to other sites for further processing and for producing the result. DDBMSs that provide distribution transparency make it simpler for users to specify queries and transactions but require more complex software. DDBMSs that do not provide distribution transparency make it the responsibility of the user to specify the site of each relation or file, leading to simpler software.

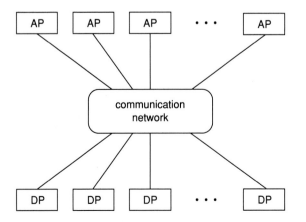

Figure 21.2   Simplified logical system architecture for a DDBS

21.1.3   Data Fragmentation, Replication, and Allocation Techniques for Distributed Database Design

In this section we discuss the techniques that are used to break up the database into logical units, called **fragments,** that may be assigned for storage at the various sites. We also discuss the use of **data replication** so that certain data may be stored in more than one site, as well as the process of **allocating** fragments—or replicas of fragments—for storage at the various sites. These techniques are used during the process of **distributed database design**. The information concerning data fragmentation, allocation, and replication is stored in a **global system catalog** that is accessed by an AP as needed by the various functions of the AP.

Data Fragmentation

In a DDBS, decisions must be made regarding which site is used to store which portions of the database. For now, we will assume that there is *no replication*; that is, each file—or portion of a file—is to be stored at only one site. We discuss replication and its effects later in this section. We will also use the terminology of *relational databases* because it is used most often in discussing distributed databases. Similar concepts apply to other data models. Hence, we assume that we start with a relational database schema and must decide on how to distribute the relations over the various sites. To illustrate our discussion, we use the relational database schema in Figure 6.5.

Before we decide on how to distribute the data, we must determine the *logical units* of the database that are to be distributed. The simplest logical units are the relations themselves; that is, each *whole* relation will be stored at a particular site. In our example, we must decide on a site to store each of the relations EMPLOYEE, DEPARTMENT, PROJECT, WORKS_ON, and DEPENDENT of Figure 6.5. However, in many cases a relation can be divided into smaller logical units for distribution. For example, consider the company database shown in Figure 6.6, and assume there are three computer sites—one for each department in the company. Of course, in an actual situation, there will be many more tuples in the relations. We may want to store the database information concerning each department at the computer site for that department. To do this, we need to partition each relation using a technique called **horizontal fragmentation**.

Horizontal Fragmentation

A **horizontal fragment** of a relation is a subset of the tuples in that relation. The tuples that belong to the horizontal fragment are specified by a condition on one or more attributes of the relation. Often, only a single attribute is involved. For example, we may define three horizontal fragments on the EMPLOYEE relation of Figure 6.6 with the following conditions: (DNO = 5), (DNO = 4), and (DNO = 1); each fragment contains the EMPLOYEE tuples working for a particular department. Similarly, we may define three horizontal fragments for the PROJECT relation of Figure 6.6 with the conditions (DNUM = 5), (DNUM = 4), and (DNUM = 1); each fragment contains the PROJECT tuples controlled by a particular department. As we can see, horizontal fragmentation divides a relation "horizontally" by grouping rows or creating subsets of tuples, where each subset has a certain logical meaning. These fragments can then be assigned to different sites in the distributed system.

Vertical Fragmentation

Another type of fragmentation is called **vertical fragmentation**. A **vertical fragment** of a relation keeps only certain attributes in the relation that are related together in some way. For example, we may want to fragment the EMPLOYEE relation into two vertical fragments where the first fragment includes personal information—NAME, BDATE, ADDRESS, and SEX—and the second includes work-related information—SSN, SALARY, SUPERSSN, DNO. This vertical fragmentation is not quite proper because if the two fragments are stored separately we cannot put the original employee tuples back together as there is *no common attribute* between the two fragments. To be able to do this, it is necessary to include the *primary key attribute* in any vertical fragment so that the full relation can be reconstructed from the vertical fragments. Hence, we must add the SSN attribute to the personal information fragment. Vertical fragmentation divides a relation "vertically" by clustering columns.

Notice that each horizontal fragment on a relation R can be specified by a $\sigma_{Ci}(R)$ operation in the relational algebra. A set of horizontal fragments whose conditions C1, C2, ..., Cn include all the tuples in R—that is, every tuple in R satisfies (C1 OR C2 OR ... OR Cn)—is called a **complete horizontal fragmentation** of R. In many cases a complete horizontal fragmentation is also **disjoint**—that is, no tuple in R satisfies (Ci AND Cj) for any $i \neq j$. Our two examples of horizontal fragmentation for the EMPLOYEE and PROJECT relations given above were both complete and disjoint. In order to reconstruct the relation R from a *complete* horizontal fragmentation, we need to apply the UNION operation to the fragments.

A vertical fragment on a relation R can be specified by a $\pi_{Li}(R)$ operation in the relational algebra. A set of vertical fragments whose projection lists L1, L2, ..., Ln include all the attributes in R but share only the primary key attribute of R is called a **complete vertical fragmentation** of R. In this case the projection lists satisfy the following two conditions:

- L1 $\cup$ L2 $\cup$ ... $\cup$ Ln = ATTRS(R), and
- Li $\cap$ Lj = PK(R) for any $i \neq j$, where ATTRS(R) is the set of attributes of R and PK(R) is the primary key of R.

To reconstruct the relation R from a *complete* vertical fragmentation, we apply the OUTER UNION operation to the fragments. Note that we could also apply the NATURAL JOIN operation and get the same result for a complete vertical fragmentation. The two vertical fragments of the EMPLOYEE relation with projection lists L1 = {SSN, NAME, BDATE, ADDRESS, SEX} and L2 = {SSN, SALARY, SUPERSSN, DNO} constitute a complete vertical fragmentation of EMPLOYEE.

Two horizontal fragments that are neither complete nor disjoint are those defined on the EMPLOYEE relation of Figure 6.5 by the conditions (SALARY > 50000) and (DNO = 4); they may not include all EMPLOYEE tuples, and they may also include common tuples. Two vertical fragments that are not complete are those defined by the attribute lists L1 = {SSN, NAME, ADDRESS} and L2 = {SSN, NAME, SALARY}, as they violate both conditions of a complete vertical fragmentation.

Mixed Fragmentation

We can intermix the two types of fragmentation, yielding a **mixed fragmentation**. For example, we may combine the horizontal and vertical fragmentations of the EMPLOYEE relation given earlier into a mixed fragmentation that includes six fragments. In this case the original relation can be reconstructed by applying UNION *and* OUTER UNION (or NATURAL JOIN) operations in the appropriate order. In general, a **fragment** of a relation R can be specified by a SELECT-PROJECT combination of operations $\pi_L(\sigma_C(R))$. If C = TRUE and L ≠ ATTRS(R) we get a vertical fragment, whereas if C ≠ TRUE and L = ATTRS(R) we get a horizontal fragment. Finally, if C ≠ TRUE and L ≠ ATTRS(R) we get a mixed fragment. Notice that a relation can itself be considered a fragment with C = TRUE and L = ATTRS(R). In the following, the term *fragment* will now be used to refer to a relation or to any of the above types of fragments.

A **fragmentation schema** of a database is a definition of a set of fragments that includes *all* attributes and tuples in the database and satisfies the condition that the whole database can be reconstructed from the fragments by applying some sequence of OUTER UNION (or NATURAL JOIN) and UNION operations. It is also sometimes useful—although not necessary—to have all the fragments be disjoint except for the repetition of primary keys among vertical (or mixed) fragments. In the latter case, all replication and distribution of fragments is clearly specified at a subsequent stage, separately from fragmentation.

An **allocation schema** describes the allocation of fragments to sites of the DDBS; hence, it is a mapping that specifies for each fragment the site(s) at which it is stored. If a fragment is stored at more than one site, it is said to be **replicated**. We discuss data replication and allocation next.

Data Replication and Allocation

Replication is useful in improving the availability of data. The most extreme case is replication of the *whole database* at every site in the distributed system, thus creating a **fully replicated** distributed database. This can improve availability remarkably because the system can continue to operate as long as at least one site is up. It also improves performance of retrieval for global queries because the result of such a query can be obtained locally from any one site; hence, a retrieval query can be processed at the local site where it is submitted if that site includes a DP. The disadvantage of full replication is that it can slow down update operations drastically because a single logical update must be performed on every copy of the database to keep the copies consistent. This is especially true if there are many copies of the database. Full replication makes the concurrency control and recovery techniques more expensive than if there was no replication, as we shall see in Section 21.3.

The other extreme from full replication is to have **no replication**; that is, each fragment is stored at exactly one site. In this case all fragments *must* be disjoint, except for the repetition of primary keys among vertical (or mixed) fragments. This is also called **nonredundant allocation**.

Between these two extremes, we have a wide spectrum of **partial replication** of the data; that is, some fragments of the database may be replicated whereas others are not. The number of copies of each fragment can range from one up to the number of sites in the distributed system. Furthermore, the fragments need not be disjoint. A description of the replication of fragments is sometimes called a **replication schema**.

Each fragment—or each copy of a fragment—must be assigned to a particular site in the distributed system. This process is called **data distribution** (or **data allocation**). The choice of sites and the degree of replication depend on performance and availability goals of the system and on the types and frequencies of transactions submitted at each site. For example, if high availability is required and if transactions can be submitted at any site and most transactions are retrieval only, a fully replicated database is a good choice. However, if certain transactions that access particular parts of the database are mostly submitted at a particular site, then the corresponding set of fragments can be allocated at that site only. Data that is accessed at multiple sites can be replicated at those sites. If many updates are performed, it may be useful to limit replication. Finding an optimal or even a good solution to distributed data allocation is a complex optimization problem.

Example of Fragmentation, Allocation, and Replication

We now consider an example of fragmenting and distributing the company database of Figures 6.5 and 6.6. Suppose that the company has three computer sites—one for each current department. Sites 2 and 3 are for departments 5 and 4, respectively. At each of these sites, we expect frequent access to the EMPLOYEE and PROJECT information for the employees *who work in that department* and the projects *controlled by that department*. Further, we assume that these sites mainly access the NAME, SSN, SALARY, and SUPERSSN attributes of EMPLOYEE. Site 1 is used by company headquarters and accesses all employee and project information regularly, in addition to keeping track of DEPENDENT information for insurance purposes.

According to these requirements, the whole database of Figure 6.6 can be stored at site 1. To determine the fragments to be replicated at sites 2 and 3, we can first horizontally fragment the EMPLOYEE, PROJECT, DEPARTMENT, and DEPT_LOCATIONS relations by department number—called DNO, DNUM, and DNUMBER, respectively, in Figure 6.5. We can then vertically fragment the resulting EMPLOYEE fragments to include only the attributes {NAME, SSN, SALARY, SUPERSSN, DNO} in the resulting mixed fragmentation. Figure 21.3 shows the mixed fragments EMPD5 and EMPD4, which include the EMPLOYEE tuples satisfying the conditions DNO = 5 and DNO = 4, respectively. The horizontal fragments of PROJECT, DEPARTMENT, and DEPT_LOCATIONS are similarly fragmented by department number. All these fragments—stored at sites 2 and 3—are replicated because they are also stored at the headquarters site 1.

We must now fragment the WORKS_ON relation and decide which fragments of WORKS_ON to store at sites 2 and 3. We are confronted with the problem that there is no attribute of WORKS_ON that directly indicates the department to which each tuple belongs. In fact, each tuple in WORKS_ON relates an employee e to a project p. We could fragment WORKS_ON based on the department d in which e works *or* based on the department d' that controls p. Fragmentation becomes easy if we have a constraint that states

(a)

EMPD5	FNAME	MINIT	LNAME	SSN	SALARY	SUPERSSN	DNO
	John	B	Smith	123456789	30000	333445555	5
	Franklin	T	Wong	333445555	40000	888665555	5
	Ramesh	K	Narayan	666884444	38000	333445555	5
	Joyce	A	English	453453453	25000	333445555	5

DEP5	DNAME	DNUMBER	MGRSSN	MGRSTARTDATE
	Research	5	333445555	22- MAY-78

DEP5_LOCS	DNUMBER	LOCATION
	5	Bellaire
	5	Sugarland
	5	Houston

WORKS_ON5	ESSN	PNO	HOURS
	123456789	1	32.5
	123456789	2	7.5
	666884444	3	40.0
	453453453	1	20.0
	453453453	2	20.0
	333445555	2	10.0
	333445555	3	10.0
	333445555	10	10.0
	333445555	20	10.0

PROJS5	PNAME	PNUMBER	PLOCATION	DNUM
	Product X	1	Bellaire	5
	Product Y	2	Sugarland	5
	Product Z	3	Houston	5

(b)

EMPD4	FNAME	MINIT	LNAME	SSN	SALARY	SUPERSSN	DNO
	Alicia	J	Zelaya	999887777	25000	987654321	4
	Jennifer	S	Wallace	987654321	43000	888665555	4
	Ahmad	V	Jabbar	987987987	25000	987654321	4

DEP4	DNAME	DNUMBER	MGRSSN	MGRSTARTDATE
	Administration	4	987654321	01-JAN-85

DEP4_LOCS	DNUMBER	LOCATION
	4	Stafford

WORKS_ON4	ESSN	PNO	HOURS
	333445555	10	10.0
	999887777	30	30.0
	999887777	10	10.0
	987987987	10	35.0
	987987987	30	5.0
	987654321	30	20.0
	987654321	20	15.0

PROJS4	PNAME	PNUMBER	PLOCATION	DNUM
	Computerization	10	Stafford	4
	Newbenefits	30	Stafford	4

Figure 21.3   Example to illustrate the allocation of fragments to sites. (a) Relation fragments at site 2. (b) Relation fragments at site 3.

that d = d' for all WORKS_ON tuples; that is, employees can work only on projects controlled by the department they work for. However, there is no such constraint in our database of Figure 6.6. For example, the WORKS_ON tuple <333445555, 10, 10.0> relates an employee who works for department 5 with a project controlled by department 4. In this case we could fragment WORKS_ON based on *both* the department in which the employee works *and* the department that controls the project, as shown in Figure 21.4.

(a)

G1	ESSN	PNO	HOURS
	123456789	1	32.5
	123456789	2	7.5
	666884444	3	40.0
	453453453	1	20.0
	453453453	2	20.0
	333445555	2	10.0
	333445555	3	10.0

C1=C AND (PNO IN (SELECT PNUMBER
FROM PROJECT
WHERE DNUM=5))

G2	ESSN	PNO	HOURS
	333445555	10	10.0

C2=C AND (PNO IN (SELECT PNUMBER
FROM PROJECT
WHERE DNUM=4))

G3	ESSN	PNO	HOURS
	333445555	20	10.0

C3=C AND (PNO IN (SELECT PNUMBER
FROM PROJECT
WHERE DNUM=1))

(b)

G4	ESSN	PNO	HOURS

C4=C AND (PNO IN (SELECT PNUMBER
FROM PROJECT
WHERE DNUM=5))

G5	ESSN	PNO	HOURS
	999887777	30	30.0
	999887777	10	10.0
	987987987	10	35.0
	987987987	30	5.0
	987654321	30	20.0

C5=C AND (PNO IN (SELECT PNUMBER
FROM PROJECT
WHERE DNUM=4))

G6	ESSN	PNO	HOURS
	987654321	20	15.0

C6=C AND (PNO IN (SELECT PNUMBER
FROM PROJECT
WHERE DNUM=1))

(c)

G7	ESSN	PNO	HOURS

C7=C AND (PNO IN (SELECT PNUMBER
FROM PROJECT
WHERE DNUM=5))

G8	ESSN	PNO	HOURS

C8=C AND (PNO IN (SELECT PNUMBER
FROM PROJECT
WHERE DNUM=4))

G9	ESSN	PNO	HOURS
	888665555	20	**null**

C9=C AND (PNO IN (SELECT PNUMBER
FROM PROJECT
WHERE DNUM=1))

Figure 21.4 Complete and disjoint fragments of the WORKS_ON relation. (a) Fragments of WORKS_ON for employees working in department 5 (C=ESSN IN (SELECT SSN FROM EMPLOYEE WHERE DNO=5)). (b) Fragments of WORKS_ON for employees working in department 4 (C=ESSN IN (SELECT SSN FROM EMPLOYEE WHERE DNO=4)). (c) Fragments of WORKS_ON for employees working in department 1 (C=ESSN IN (SELECT SSN FROM EMPLOYEE WHERE DNO=1)).

In Figure 21.4 the union of fragments G1, G2, and G3 gives all WORKS_ON tuples for employees who work *for department 5*. Similarly, the union of fragments G4, G5, and G6 gives all WORKS_ON tuples for employees who *work for department 4*. On the other hand, the union of fragments G1, G4, and G7 gives all WORKS_ON tuples for projects *controlled by department 5*. The condition for each of the fragments G1 through G9 is shown in Figure 21.4. The relations that represent M:N relationships, such as WORKS_ON, often have several possible logical fragmentations. In our distribution of Figure 21.3, we choose to include all fragments that can be joined to either an EMPLOYEE tuple or a PROJECT tuple at sites 2 and 3. Hence, we place the union of fragments G1, G2, G3, G4, and G7 at site 2 and the union of fragments G4, G5, G6, G2, and G8 at site 3. Notice that fragments G2 and G4 are replicated at both sites. This allocation strategy permits the join between the local EMPLOYEE or PROJECT fragments at site 2 or site 3 and the local WORKS_ON fragment to be performed completely locally. This clearly demonstrates how complex the problem of database fragmentation and allocation is for large databases. The bibliographic notes give references to some of the work done in this area.

21.1.4   Types of Distributed Database Systems

The term distributed database management system can be applied to describe a variety of systems that differ from one another in many respects. The main thing that all such systems share is the fact that data and software are distributed over multiple sites connected by some form of communication network. In this section we discuss various types of DDBMSs and the criteria and factors that make some of these systems different.

The first factor that we consider is the **degree of homogeneity** of the DDBMS software. If all DPs (or individual local DBMSs) use identical software and also all APs use the same software, the DDBMS is called **homogeneous;** otherwise, it is called **heterogeneous**. Another factor that is related to the degree of homogeneity is the **degree of local autonomy**. If all access to the DDBMS must go through an AP, then the system has **no local autonomy**. On the other hand, if *direct access* by local transactions to a DP is permitted, the system has some degree of local autonomy.

At one extreme of this autonomy spectrum, we have a DDBMS that "looks like" a centralized DBMS to the user. A single conceptual schema exists, and all access to the system goes through an AP, and no local autonomy exists. At the other extreme of this spectrum, we encounter a type of DDBMS called a **federated DDBMS** (or a **multidatabase system**). In such a system, each DP is an independent and autonomous centralized DBMS that has its own local users, local transactions, and DBA and hence a very high degree of *local autonomy*. Each DP can authorize access to particular portions of its database by specifying an **export schema,** which specifies the part of the database that may be accessed by a certain class of nonlocal users. An AP in such a system is essentially an additional interface to several DPs (local DBMSs) that allows a multidatabase (or global) user to access data stored in several of these *autonomous databases*. Notice that a federated system is a hybrid between distributed and centralized systems; it is a centralized system for the local autonomous users and a distributed system for the global users.

In a heterogeneous multidatabase system, one DP may be a relational DBMS, another a network DBMS, a third a hierarchical DBMS; in such a case it is necessary to have a canonical system language and include language translators in the AP (or in each DP) to translate subqueries from the canonical language to the language of each DP.

A third aspect that may be used to categorize distributed databases is the **degree of distribution transparency** or alternatively the **degree of schema integration**. If the user sees a single integrated schema without any information concerning fragmentation, replication, or distribution, the DDBMS is said to have a *high degree of distribution transparency* (or schema integration). On the other hand, if the user sees all fragmentation, allocation, and replication, the DDBMS has *no distribution transparency* and no schema integration. In the latter case the user must refer to specific fragment copies at specific sites by appending the site name before a relation or fragment name.

This is part of the complex problem of **naming** in distributed systems. In the case of a DDBMS that does not provide distribution transparency, it is up to the user to *unambiguously specify* the name of a particular relation or fragment copy. This is more severe in a multidatabase system, because each DP (local DBMS) presumably was developed independently, so conflicting names may have been used at different DPs. However, in the case of a DBMS that provides an integrated schema, naming becomes an internal system problem because the user is provided with a single unambiguous schema. The DDBMS must store *all correspondences* among the integrated schema objects and the objects distributed across the various DPs in the **distribution catalog**.

21.2 Query Processing and Optimization in Distributed Databases

In this section we discuss briefly how a DDBMS processes and optimizes a query. We first discuss the communication costs in processing a distributed query and then discuss a special operation, called a semijoin, that is used in optimizing some types of queries in a DDBMS.

21.2.1 Data Transfer Costs of Distributed Query Processing

We discussed the issues involved in processing and optimizing a query in a centralized DBMS in Chapter 18. In a distributed system there are several additional factors that must be taken into account, which further complicate query processing. The first and most important additional factor to consider is the cost of transferring data over the network. This data includes intermediate files that are transferred to other sites for further processing, as well as the final result files that may need to be transferred to the site where the query result is needed. Although these costs may not be very high if the sites are connected via a high-performance local area network, they become quite significant in other types of networks. Hence, many DDBMS query optimization algorithms consider the goal of reducing the *amount of data transfer* as the main optimization criterion in choosing a distributed query execution strategy.

   We illustrate this with two simple example queries. Suppose the EMPLOYEE and DEPARTMENT relations of Figure 6.5 are distributed as shown in Figure 21.5. We will assume in this example that neither relation is fragmented. According to Figure 21.5, the size of the EMPLOYEE relation is $100*10,000 = 10^6$ bytes, and the size of the DEPARTMENT relation is $35*100 = 3500$ bytes. Consider the query Q: "For each employee, retrieve the employee name and the name of the department for which the employee works." This can be stated as follows in the relational algebra:

$$Q: \pi_{FNAME,LNAME,DNAME}(EMPLOYEE \bowtie_{DNO=DNUMBER} DEPARTMENT)$$

   The result of this query will include 10,000 records, assuming that every employee is related to a department. Suppose that each record in the query result is *40 bytes long*. The query is submitted at a distinct site 3, which is called the **result site** because the query result is needed there. Neither the EMPLOYEE nor the DEPARTMENT relations reside at site 3. There are three simple strategies for executing this distributed query:

1. Transfer both the EMPLOYEE and DEPARTMENT relations to the result site and perform the query at site 3. In this case we need to transfer a total of 1,000,000 + 3500 = 1,003,500 bytes.

SITE 1:

EMPLOYEE

FNAME	MINIT	LNAME	SSN	BDATE	ADDRESS	SEX	SALARY	SUPERSSN	DNO

10,000 records
each record is 100 bytes long
SSN field is 9 bytes long   FNAME field is 15 bytes long
DNO field is 4 bytes long   LNAME field is 15 bytes long

SITE 2:

DEPARTMENT

DNAME	DNUMBER	MGRSSN	MGRSTARTDATE

100 records
each record is 35 bytes long
DNUMBER field is 4 bytes long   DNAME field is 10 bytes long
MGRSSN field is 9 bytes long

Figure 21.5   Example to illustrate volume of data transferred

2. Transfer the EMPLOYEE relation to site 2, execute the query at site 2, and send the result to site 3. The size of the query result is 40*10,000 = 400,000 bytes, so we transfer 400,000 + 1,000,000 = 1,400,000 bytes.

3. Transfer the DEPARTMENT relation to site 1, execute the query at site 1, and send the result to site 3. In this case we transfer 400,000 + 3500 = 403,500 bytes.

If minimizing the amount of data transfer is the optimization criterion, we would choose strategy 3. Consider another query Q': "For each department, retrieve the department name and the name of the department manager." This can be stated as follows in the relational algebra:

$$Q: \pi_{DNAME,FNAME,LNAME}(DEPARTMENT \bowtie_{MGRSSN=SSN} EMPLOYEE)$$

Again, suppose the query is submitted at site 3. The same three strategies for executing query Q apply to Q', except that the result of Q' will include only 100 records, assuming each department has a manager:

1. Transfer both the EMPLOYEE and DEPARTMENT relations to the result site and perform the query at site 3. In this case we need to transfer a total of 1,000,000 + 3500 = 1,003,500 bytes.

2. Transfer the EMPLOYEE relation to site 2, execute the query at site 2, and send the result to site 3. The size of the query result is 40*100 = 4000 bytes, so we transfer 4000 + 1,000,000 = 1,004,000 bytes.

3. Transfer the DEPARTMENT relation to site 1, execute the query at site 1, and send the result to site 3. In this case we transfer 4000 + 3500 = 7500 bytes.

Again, we would choose strategy 3 and in this case by an overwhelming margin over strategies 1 and 2. The above three strategies are the most obvious ones for the case where the result site (site 3) is different from all the sites that contain files involved in the query (sites 1 and 2). However, suppose that the result site was site 2; then we have two simple strategies:

4. Transfer the EMPLOYEE relation to site 2, execute the query, and present the result to the user at site 2. Here, we transfer the same number of bytes—1,000,000—for both Q and Q'.

5. Transfer the DEPARTMENT relation to site 1, execute the query at site 1, and send the result back to site 2. In this case we transfer 400,000 + 3500 = 403,500 bytes for Q and 4000 + 3500 = 7500 bytes for Q'.

A more complex strategy, which sometimes works better than these simple strategies, uses an operation called **semijoin**. We introduce this operation and discuss distributed execution using semijoins next.

21.2.2 Distributed Query Processing Using Semijoin

The idea behind distributed query processing using the semijoin operation is to reduce the number of tuples in a relation before transferring it to another site. Intuitively, the idea is to send the joining column of one relation R to the site where the other relation S is located. This column is then joined with S, and the join attributes and the attributes required in the result are projected out and shipped back to the original site and joined with R. Hence, only the joining column of R is transferred in one direction, and a subset of S with no extraneous tuples is transferred in the other direction. If only a small fraction of the tuples in S participate in the join, this could be quite an efficient solution to minimizing data transfer.

To illustrate this, consider the following strategy for executing Q or Q':

1. Project the join attributes of DEPARTMENT at site 2 and then transfer those attributes to site 1. For Q, we transfer $F = \pi_{DNUMBER}(DEPARTMENT)$, whose size is $4*100 = 400$ bytes, whereas for Q' we transfer $F' = \pi_{MGRSSN}(DEPARTMENT)$, whose size is $9*100 = 900$ bytes.

2. Join the transferred file with the EMPLOYEE relation at site 1, and transfer the required attributes from the resulting file to site 2. For Q, we transfer $R = \pi_{<DNO, FNAME, LNAME>} (F \bowtie_{DNUMBER=DNO} EMPLOYEE)$, whose size is $34*10,000 = 340,000$ bytes, whereas for Q' we transfer $R' = \pi_{<MGRSSN, FNAME, LNAME>} (F' \bowtie_{MGRSSN=SSN} EMPLOYEE)$, whose size is $39*100 = 3900$ bytes.

3. Execute the query by joining the transferred file R or R' with DEPARTMENT, and present the result to the user at site 2.

Using this strategy, we transfer 340,400 bytes for Q but only 4800 bytes for Q'. The reason is that we limited the EMPLOYEE tuples transmitted to site 2 in step 2 to only those tuples that will *actually be joined* with a DEPARTMENT tuple in step 3. For query Q, this turned out to include all EMPLOYEE tuples so little improvement was achieved. However, for Q' only 100 out of the 10,000 EMPLOYEE tuples.

The semijoin operation was devised to formalize this strategy. A **semijoin** operation $R \bowtie_{A=B} S$, where A and B are domain-compatible attributes of R and S, respectively, produces the same result as the relational algebra expression $\pi_{<R>}(R \bowtie_{A=B} S)$. In a distributed environment where R and S reside at different sites, the semijoin is typically implemented by first transferring $F = \pi_{<B>}(S)$ to the site where R resides and then joining F with R, thus leading to the strategy discussed above.

Notice that the semijoin operation is not commutative; that is,

$$R \ltimes S \neq S \ltimes R$$

21.2.3 Query and Update Decomposition

In a DDBMS with *no distribution transparency*, the user phrases a query directly in terms of specific fragments. For example, consider another query Q: "Retrieve the names and hours per week for each employee who works on some project controlled by department 5," which is specified on the distributed database where the relations at sites 2 and 3 are shown in Figure 21.3, and those at site 1 are shown in Figure 6.6 as in our earlier example. A user who submits such a query must specify whether it references the PROJS5 and WORKS_ON5 relations at site 2 or the PROJECT and WORKS_ON relations at site 1. It is also the responsibility of the user to maintain consistency of replicated data items when updating a DDBMS with *no replication transparency*.

On the other hand, a DDBMS that supports *full distribution, fragmentation, and replication transparency* will allow the user to specify a query or update request on the schema of Figure 6.5 just as though the DBMS were centralized. For updates, the DDBMS is responsible for maintaining *consistency among replicated items* by using one of the distributed concurrency control algorithms discussed in Section 21.3. For queries, a **query decomposition** module must break up or decompose a query into **subqueries** that can be executed at the individual sites. In addition, a strategy for combining the results of the subqueries to form the query result must be generated. Whenever the DDBMS determines that an item referenced in the query is replicated, it must choose or **materialize** a particular replica that is referenced during query execution.

To determine which replicas include the data items referenced in a query, the DDBMS refers to the fragmentation, replication, and distribution information stored in the DDBMS catalog. For vertical fragmentation, the attribute list for each fragment is kept in the catalog. For horizontal fragmentation, a condition, sometimes called a **guard**, is kept for each fragment. This is basically a selection condition that specifies which tuples exist in the fragment, and it is called a guard because *only tuples that satisfy this condition* are permitted to be stored in the fragment. For mixed fragments, both the attribute list and the guard condition are kept in the catalog.

In our earlier example, the guard conditions for fragments at site 1 (Figure 6.6) are TRUE, and the attribute lists are all * (all attributes of a relation are in the attribute list for each fragment), because all tuples and all attributes of each relation are stored at site 1. For the fragments shown in Figure 21.3, we have the guard conditions and attribute lists shown in Figure 21.6. When the DDBMS decomposes an update request, it can determine which fragments must be updated by examining their guard conditions. For example, a user request to insert a new EMPLOYEE tuple <'Alex', 'B', 'Coleman', '345671239', '22-APR-64', '3306 Sandstone, Houston, TX', M, 33000, '987654321', 4> would be decomposed by the DDBMS into two update requests: the first inserts the above tuple in the EMPLOYEE fragment at site 1, and the second inserts the tuple <'Alex', 'B', 'Coleman', '345671239', 33000, '987654321', 4> in the EMPD4 fragment at site 3.

EMPD5
  attribute list: FNAME,MINIT,LNAME,SSN,SALARY,SUPERSSN, DNO
guard condition: DNO=5

DEP5
  attribute list: * (all attributes DNAME,DNUMBER,MGRSSN,MGRSTARTDATE)
guard condition: DNUMBER=5

DEP5_LOCS
  attribute list: * (all attributes DNUMBER,LOCATION)
guard condition: DNUMBER=5

PROJS5
  attribute list: * (all attributes PNAME,PNUMBER,PLOCATION,DNUM)
guard condition: DNUM=5

WORKS_ON5
  attribute list: * (all attributes ESSN,PNO,HOURS)
guard condition: ESSN IN (π_{SSN}(EMPD5))
              OR PNO IN ($\pi_{PNUMBER}$(PROJS5))

EMPD4
  attribute list: FNAME,MINIT,LNAME,SSN,SALARY,SUPERSSN, DNO
guard condition: DNO=4

DEP4
  attribute list: * (all attributes DNAME,DNUMBER,MGRSSN,MGRSTARTDATE)
guard condition: DNUMBER=4

DEP4_LOCS
  attribute list: * (all attributes DNUMBER,LOCATION)
guard condition: DNUMBER=4

PROJS4
  attribute list: * (all attributes PNAME,PNUMBER,PLOCATION,DNUM)
guard condition: DNUM=4

WORKS_ON4
  attribute list: * (all attributes ESSN,PNO,HOURS)
guard condition: ESSN IN (π_{SSN}(EMPD4))
              OR PNO IN ($\pi_{PNUMBER}$(PROJS4))

Figure 21.6 Illustrating guard conditions and attribute lists for fragments. (a) Guards and attribute lists for relation
fragments at site 2. (b) Guards and attribute lists for
relation fragments at site 3.

For query decomposition, the DDBMS can determine which fragments may contain
the required tuples by comparing the query condition with the guard conditions. For example, consider the query Q: "Retrieve the names and hours per week for each employee
who works on some project controlled by department 5"; this can be specified in SQL on
the schema of Figure 6.5 as follows:

Q: **SELECT** FNAME, LNAME, HOURS
       FROM   EMPLOYEE, PROJECT, WORKS_ON
       WHERE   DNUM=5 **AND** PNUMBER=PNO **AND** ESSN=SSN

Suppose the query is submitted at site 2, which is where the query result will be
needed. The DDBMS can determine from the guard condition on PROJS5 and WORKS_ON5

that all tuples satisfying the conditions (DNUM = 5 AND PNUMBER = PNO) reside at site 2. Hence, it may decompose the query into the following relational algebra subqueries:

$$T1 \leftarrow \pi_{ESSN} (PROJS5 \bowtie_{PNUMBER=PNO} \text{WORKS\_ON5})$$
$$T2 \leftarrow \pi_{ESSN, FNAME, LNAME} (T1 \bowtie_{ESSN=SSN} \text{EMPLOYEE})$$
$$RESULT \leftarrow \pi_{FNAME, LNAME, HOURS} (T2 * \text{WORKS\_ON5})$$

This decomposition can be used to execute the query using a semijoin strategy. The DDBMS knows from the guard conditions that PROJS5 contains exactly those tuples satisfying (DNUM = 5) and that WORKS_ON5 contains all tuples to be joined with PROJS5; hence, subquery T1 can be executed at site 2 and the projected column ESSN is sent to site 1. Subquery T2 can then be executed at site 1 and the result sent back to site 2, where the final query result is calculated and displayed to the user. An alternative strategy would be to send the query Q itself to site 1, which includes all the database tuples, where it would be executed locally and the result would be sent back to site 2. The query optimizer would estimate the costs of both strategies and choose the one with the lower cost estimate.

21.3   Concurrency Control and Recovery in Distributed Databases

For concurrency control and recovery purposes, numerous problems arise in a distributed DBMS environment that are not encountered in the centralized DBMS environment. Some of these problems are the following:

- Dealing with **multiple copies** of the data items: The concurrency control method is responsible for maintaining consistency among these copies. The recovery method is responsible for making a copy consistent with other copies if the site on which the copy is stored fails and recovers later.

- Failure of individual sites: The DDBMS should continue to operate with its running sites if possible when one or more individual sites fail. When a site recovers, its local database must be brought up to date with the rest of the sites before it rejoins the system.

- Failure of communication links: The system must deal with failure of one or more of the communication links that connect the sites. An extreme case of this problem is that **network partitioning** may occur. This breaks up the sites into two or more partitions where the sites within each partition can communicate only with one another and not with sites in other partitions.

- Distributed commit: Problems arise with committing a transaction that is accessing databases stored on multiple sites if some sites fail during the commit process. The **two-phase commit protocol** (see Section 19.6.5) is often used to deal with this problem.

- Distributed deadlock: Deadlock may occur among several sites, so techniques for dealing with deadlocks must be extended to take this into account.

Distributed concurrency control and recovery techniques must deal with these and other problems. In the following subsections, we give an overview of some of the techniques that were suggested to deal with recovery and concurrency control in DDBMSs. In Section 21.3.1 we present distributed concurrency control techniques that are based on selecting certain sites to coordinate the concurrency control process for replicated data items. Section 21.3.2 discusses techniques based on the concept of voting among sites that store replicas of the data item. Section 21.3.3 briefly discusses distributed recovery techniques.

21.3.1 Distributed Concurrency Control Based on a Distinguished Copy of a Data Item

To deal with replicated data items in a distributed database, a number of concurrency control methods have been proposed that extend the concurrency control techniques for centralized databases. We will discuss these techniques in the context of extending centralized *locking*, although they could be used to extend other centralized concurrency control techniques, such as timestamp ordering, to the distributed case. The idea is to designate *a particular copy* of each data item as a **distinguished copy**. The locks for this data item are kept *with the distinguished copy*, and all locking and unlocking requests are sent to the site that contains that copy.

In the following subsections we discuss a number of different methods that are based on this idea but that differ in the method of choosing the distinguished copies. We first discuss the **primary site** technique, where all distinguished copies are kept at the same site. A modification of this approach is the primary site with a **backup site**. Another approach is the **primary copy** method, where the distinguished copies of the various data items can be stored in different sites. A site that includes a distinguished copy of a data item basically acts as the **coordinator site** for concurrency control on that item. We will discuss techniques for choosing a new coordinator if a coordinator site fails during processing.

Primary Site Technique

In this method a single **primary site** is designated to be the coordinator *for all database items*. Hence, all locks are kept at that site, and all requests for locking or unlocking for any data item are sent to that site. The primary site will respond to all requests for locks, either granting the lock request or indicating that the lock request cannot be granted. This method is hence an extension of the centralized locking approach. For example, if all transactions follow the two-phase locking protocol, then serializability will be guaranteed. The advantage of this approach is that it is a simple extension of the centralized approach and hence is not overly complex. However, there are certain inherent disadvantages. One disadvantage is that all locking requests are sent to a single site, possibly overloading that site and causing a system bottleneck. Another disadvantage is that failure of the primary site will paralyze the system, since all locking information was kept at that site. This can limit system reliability and availability.

Notice that although all locks are accessed at the primary site, the items themselves can be accessed at any site at which they reside. For example, once a transaction obtains a read_lock on a data item from the primary site, it can access any copy of that data item. However, once a transaction obtains a write_lock and updates a data item, the DDBMS is responsible for updating *all copies* of the data item before releasing the lock.

Primary Site with Backup Site

This approach addresses the second disadvantage of the primary site method by designating a second site to be a **backup site**. All locking information is maintained at both the primary and backup sites. In the case of failure of the primary site, the backup site can take over as primary site, and a new backup site is chosen. This simplifies the process of recovery from failure of the primary site, since the backup site takes over and processing can resume after a new backup site is chosen and the lock status information is copied to that site. However, it slows down the process of acquiring locks because all lock requests and granting of locks must be recorded at *both the primary and backup sites* before a response is sent to the requesting transaction. The problem of the primary and backup sites being overloaded with requests and slowing down the system remains.

Primary Copy Technique

This method attempts to distribute the load of lock coordination among various sites by having the distinguished copies of different data items *stored at different sites*. Failure of one site will affect any transactions that are accessing locks on items whose primary copies reside at that site, but other transactions are not affected. This method can also use backup sites to enhance reliability and availability.

Choosing a New Coordinator Site in Case of Failure

Whenever a coordinator site fails in any of the above techniques, the sites that are still running must choose a new coordinator. In the case of the primary site approach with *no* backup site, all executing transactions must be aborted and restarted, and the recovery process is quite tedious. Part of the recovery process is to choose a new primary site and create a lock manager process and all lock information at that site. For methods that use backup sites, transaction processing is suspended while the backup site is designated as the new primary site and a new backup site is chosen and is sent copies of all the locking information from the new primary site.

If a backup site X is going to become the new primary site, X can choose the new backup site from among the running sites. However, if no backup site existed, or if both primary and backup sites are down, a process called **election** can be used to choose the new coordinator site. In this process, any site Y that attempts to communicate with the coordinator site repeatedly and fails can assume that the coordinator is down and can start the election process by sending a message to all running sites proposing that Y be the new coordinator. As soon as Y receives a majority of yes votes, Y can declare that it is the new coordinator. The election algorithm itself is quite complex, but this is the main idea behind the election method. The algorithm resolves any attempt by two or more sites to become coordinator at the same time. The references in the bibliography at the end of this chapter discuss the process in detail.

21.3.2   Distributed Concurrency Control Based on Voting

The concurrency control methods for replicated items discussed above all use the idea of a distinguished copy that maintains the locks for that item. In the **voting method** there is no distinguished copy; rather, a lock request would be sent to all sites that include a copy of the data item. Each copy maintains its own lock and can grant or deny it. If a transaction that requests a lock is granted that lock by *a majority* of the copies, it holds the lock and informs *all copies* that it has been granted the lock. If a transaction does not receive a majority of votes granting it a lock within a certain *time-out period*, it cancels its request and informs all sites of the cancellation.

The voting method is considered a truly distributed concurrency control method, since the responsibility of decision resides with all the sites involved. Simulation studies have shown that voting has higher message traffic among sites than the distinguished copy methods. If the algorithm takes into account possible site failures during the voting process, it becomes quite complex.

21.3.3   Distributed Recovery

The recovery process in distributed databases is quite involved. We will give only a very brief idea of some of the issues here. In some cases it is quite difficult even to determine when a site is down without exchanging numerous messages with other sites. For example, suppose that site X sends a message to site Y and expects a response from Y but does not receive it. There are several possible explanations:

- The message was not delivered to Y because of communication failure.
- Site Y is down and could not respond.
- Site Y is running and sent a response but the response was not delivered.

Without additional information or the sending of additional messages, it is difficult to determine what actually happened.

Another problem with distributed recovery is distributed commit. When a transaction is updating data at several sites, it cannot commit until it is sure that the effect of the transaction on *every* site cannot be lost. This means that every site must have recorded the local effects of the transactions permanently in the local site log on disk. The two-phase commit protocol, discussed in Section 19.6.5, is often used to ensure the correctness of distributed commit.

21.4   Summary

In this chapter we gave an introduction to distributed databases. This is a very broad topic, and we discussed only some of the basic techniques used with distributed databases. We first discussed the reasons for distribution and the potential advantages of using distributed databases over centralized systems. We then described the architecture of a DDBMS and distinguished three main software components of a DDBMS: the application processors (APs), data processors (DPs), and communication software. We defined the concepts of data fragmentation, replication, and distribution and distinguished be-tween horizontal and vertical partitions of relations. We discussed the use of data replica-tion to improve system reliability and availability. We also defined the concept of distribution transparency and the related concepts of fragmentation transparency and replication transparency. In Section 21.1.4 we categorized DDBMSs using criteria such as degree of homogeneity of software modules and degree of local autonomy.

In Section 21.2 we illustrated some of the techniques used in distributed query pro-cessing. The cost of communication among sites is considered a major factor in distrib-uted query optimization. We compared different techniques for executing joins and presented the semijoin technique, which is often an efficient technique for joining rela-tions that reside on different sites.

In Section 21.3 we briefly discussed the concurrency control and recovery tech-niques used in DDBMSs. We showed some of the additional problems that have to be dealt with in a distributed environment that do not appear in a centralized environment.

Review Questions

21.1. What are the main reasons for and potential advantages of distributed databases?

21.2. What additional functions does a DDBMS have over a centralized DBMS?

21.3. What are the main software modules of a DDBMS? Discuss the main functions of each of these modules.

21.4. What is a fragment of a relation? What are the main types of fragments? Why is fragmentation a useful concept in distributed database design?

21.5. Why is data replication useful in DDBMSs? What are the typical units of data that are replicated?

21.6. What is meant by data allocation in distributed database design? What are the typical units of data that are distributed over sites?

21.7. How is a horizontal partitioning of a relation specified? How can a relation be put back together from a complete horizontal partitioning?

21.8. How is a vertical partitioning of a relation specified? How can a relation be put back together from a complete vertical partitioning?

21.9. Discuss what is meant by the following terms: degree of homogeneity of a DDBMS, degree of local autonomy of a DDBMS, federated DBMS, distribution transparency, fragmentation transparency, replication transparency.

21.10. Discuss the naming problem in distributed databases.

21.11. Discuss the different techniques for executing an equijoin of two files located at different sites. What are the main factors that affect the cost of data transfer?

21.12. Discuss the semijoin method for executing an equijoin of two files located at dif-ferent sites. Under what conditions is an equijoin strategy efficient?

21.13. Discuss the factors that affect query decomposition. How are guard conditions and attribute lists of fragments used during the query decomposition process?

21.14. How is the decomposition of an update request different from the decomposition of a query? How are guard conditions and attribute lists of fragments used during the decomposition of an update request?

21.15. Discuss the factors that do not appear in centralized systems that affect concurrency control and recovery in distributed systems.

21.16. Compare the primary site method with the primary copy method for distributed concurrency control. How does the use of backup sites affect each?

21.17. When are voting and elections used in distributed databases?

Exercises

21.18. Consider the data distribution of the COMPANY database, where the fragments at sites 2 and 3 are shown in Figure 21.3 and the fragments at site 1 are shown in Figure 6.6. For each of the following queries, show at least two strategies of decomposing and executing the query. Under what conditions would each of your strategies work well?

    a. For each employee in department 5, retrieve the employee name and the names of the employee's dependents.

    b. Print the names of all employees who work in department 5 but who work on some project *not* controlled by department 5.

Selected Bibliography

The textbook by Ceri and Pelagatti (1984a) is devoted to distributed databases, as is the forthcoming textbook by Ozsu and Valduriez. Fragmentation is discussed in Ceri and Pelagatti (1984a). Federated database systems are discussed in McLeod and Heimbigner (1985). Principles of computer communication networks are discussed in the textbook by Tanenbaum (1981).

    Distributed query processing, optimization, and decomposition are discussed in the papers by Hevner and Yao (1979), Apers et al. (1983), Ceri and Pelagatti (1984), and Kerschberg et al. (1982). Bernstein and Goodman (1981) discuss the theory behind semijoin processing. Wong (1983) discusses the use of relationships in relation fragmentation. Concurrency control and recovery schemes are discussed and compared in Garcia-Molina (1978), Ries (1979), and Bernstein and Goodman (1981a). Elections in distributed systems are discussed in Garcia-Molina (1982).

    A concurrency control technique for replicated data that is based on voting is presented by Thomas (1979). Gifford (1979) proposes the use of weighted voting, and Paris (1986) describes a method called voting with witnesses. Jajodia and Mutchler (1987) discuss dynamic voting. A technique called available copy is proposed by Bernstein and Goodman (1984) and one that uses the idea of a group is presented in ElAbbadi and Toueg (1988). Schlageter (1981), Bassiouni (1988), and Ceri and Owicki (1983) discuss optimistic methods for DDB concurrency control. Garcia-Molina (1983) and Kumar and

Stonebraker (1987) discuss a technique that uses the semantics of the transactions. Distributed concurrency control techniques based on locking and distinguished copies are presented by Menasce et al. (1980) and Minoura and Wiederhold (1982). Obermark (1982) presents algorithms for distributed deadlock detection. Lamport (1978) discusses problems with generating unique timestamps in a distributed system.

A survey of recovery techniques in distributed systems is given by Kohler (1981). Skeen (1981) discusses non-blocking commit protocols, and Reed (1983) discusses atomic actions on distributed data. A recent book edited by Bhargava (1987) presents various approaches and techniques for distributed recovery and concurrency control.

Techniques for schema integration in federated databases are presented by Elmasri et al. (1986) and Motro (1987). Onuegbe et al. (1983) discuss the translation and local optimization problem. Elmagarmid and Helal (1988) and Gamal-Eldin et al. (1988) discuss the update problem in heterogeneous DDBSs.

Techniques for distributed data allocation are proposed in Morgan and Levin (1977), Ramamoorthy and Wah (1979), Chu and Hurley (1982), and Kamel and King (1985), among others. Distributed database design involving horizontal and vertical fragmentation, allocation, and replication is addressed in Ceri et al. (1983), Navathe et al. (1984), Ceri et al. (1982), Wilson and Navathe (1986), and Elmasri et al. (1987).

A number of experimental distributed DBMSs have been implemented. These include distributed INGRES (Epstein et al. 1978), DDTS (Devor and Weeldreyer 1980), SDD-1 (Rothnie et al. 1980), System R* (Lindsay et al. 1984), SIRIUS-DELTA (Ferrier and Stangret 1982), and MULTIBASE (Smith et al. 1981). The OMNIBASE system (Rusinkiewicz et al. 1988) is a federated DDBMS. Many commercial DBMS vendors have announced distributed systems, although some DDBMSs have somewhat limited capabilities. It is expected that full-fledged commercial DDBMSs will be available in the near future.

Emerging Database Technologies and Applications

So far in this book we have been discussing the various techniques of modeling data, designing databases, and implementing them on computers. The term **database technology** is used to refer collectively to the *proven techniques* used on a *wide scale* in industry and government as well as by individual personal database users to perform the above functions on a *day-to-day* basis. The bulk of what we have discussed is already a part of current database technology. In every discipline of human endeavor, technology always lags behind ongoing research by several years. Database technology is no exception. Therefore, the research work under way today that has the potential of becoming a viable technology will not be available for general consumption for another 5 to 10 years. In this textbook it is not possible for us to include details of a number of such ongoing promising research efforts. We intend, however, to give the reader a broad perspective on the current state of the art in databases and database systems research in this chapter. We will attempt to bring out the major issues and point out the difficult problems rather than discuss the proposed solutions in detail. References to pertinent literature are given whenever appropriate. A few additional references appear in the bibliography.

This chapter is organized as follows: Section 22.1 is an overview of the progression of database technology, roughly over the last 25 years. Section 22.2 discusses the emerging nonconventional areas of applications that are making use of this technology and will continue to place further demands on it. Section 22.3 is devoted to a specific discussion of a particularly important topic—knowledge base management. We end the chapter with Section 22.4, where we outline some emerging technologies and give pointers to research needed in the near future.

Table 22.1 Database Technology Trends

	1960s to Mid-1970s	1970s to Mid-1980s	Late 1980s	Future
Data Model	Network Hierarchical	Relational	Semantic Object-oriented Logic	Merging data models, knowledge representation, and programming languages
Database Hardware	Mainframes	Mainframes Minis PCs	Faster PCs Workstations Database machines Back ends	Parallel processing Optical memories
User Interface	None Forms	Query languages	Graphics Menus Query-by-forms	Natural languages Speech input
Program Interface	Procedural	Embedded query languages	4GL Logic programming	Integrated database and programming languages
Presentation and Display	Reports	Report generators	Business graphics Image output	Generalized display managers
Processing	Processing data	Information and transaction processing	Transaction processing Knowledge processing	Distributed knowledge processing

One **disclaimer:** This chapter is *not* a complete summary of ongoing research. Omissions of some research areas should not be considered as implying any bias. The vast field of database management research, where every year at least 200 to 300 papers are published through refereed conferences and journals, is difficult to condense in this small chapter.

22.1   Progression of Database Technology*

Table 22.1 summarizes the progression of database technology for the last 25 or so years. The table is divided into three columns to correspond roughly to the three identifiable periods. The last column stands for expected future developments. We discuss this table row by row.

---

*The authors would like to acknowledge the influence of a presentation by Dr. Prem Uppaluru from Bell Communications Research on this section.

22.1.1   Data Models

The network and hierarchical models came about in the 1960s. Since its introduction in 1970 there has been rapidly increasing interest in the relational model because of its desirable properties including its formal basis, homogeneity, and well-defined set of algebraic operations, as well as calculus-based languages. Shortcomings of the relational model in terms of its semantic expressive power led to interest in semantic models. This has grown since the late 1970s, particularly with the advent of the Entity-Relationship model (Chen 1976), Semantic Hierarchy Model (Smith and Smith 1977), and Semantic Data Model (Hammer and McLeod 1981). In his rm/t model, Codd (1979) suggested that there is a need to add more expressive power to the relational data model by providing it with certain abstractions from the above models. The interest in semantic models continues in the 1980s. With the expanding horizons of database applications (Section 22.2), the need for the abstractions that we discussed in Section 15.3 is being felt even more intensely.

Logic is being proposed as an underlying data model for relational and other representation schemas. The relational calculus (see Chapter 8) is based on a branch of logic called first-order predicate calculus, and hence use of logic already exists to characterize relational queries. The relationship between logic and relational databases is well brought out in Gallaire et al. (1984). Logic provides a formalism that can be used in query languages, integrity modeling, query evaluation, treatment of null values, dealing with incomplete information, etc. Logic also leads to a formal understanding of deduction in databases.

Another visible trend is toward the **object-oriented data models**. We considered their basic characteristics and advantages in Section 15.4.1. The future is likely to see further proliferation of object-oriented DBMSs (we discuss one recent product called Vbase in Section 23.4), further use of logic for deductive databases, and a merging of knowledge representation, programming languages, and data models (Brodie et al. 1984; Albano et al. 1985).

22.1.2   Database Hardware

Over the last 25 years there has been quite a revolution in growth of storage capacities of computers, microminiaturization of the circuitry, and increased processing speeds. The cost of components has fallen steadily and dramatically. The amount of data that could be processed in a certain amount of time has been growing. Moreover, larger databases are becoming feasible on smaller equipment. Sizable databases could only be handled by mainframes and minis until only a few years ago. With the advent of powerful hardware, it is now possible to implement major DBMS products on workstations and personal computers. Relational DBMSs like ORACLE, RIM, and UNIFY and object-oriented DBMSs like Vbase are available on these. The functionality of low-end database products such as Lotus 1-2-3, the Dbase series, Informix, or Paradox is also continuously expanding with more powerful hardware that affords windowing and graphics capabilities as well as higher speeds.

Even though storage costs have declined and main storage capacities of systems have grown considerably, the overall performance of database systems is still a great concern. Also, the advances in software, which incorporate sophisticated data modeling, have been very gradual (as we shall see in Section 22.2) compared to those in processors and I/O architecture. This is due to the mismatch between access speeds of secondary storage devices and those of central processing units leading to inevitable delays in processing large volumes of data stored on disk. Compared to the advances in speeds of processors (attributed to new logic technologies as well as availability of parallel processing), the rate of increase of speeds of secondary storage devices (mainly disks) has been slow.

To deal with these problems, several alternative suggestions have been made for special hardware geared for the data management functions. These alternatives, generically known as **database machines** or computers, include back-end processors, intelligent (logic per track) devices, multiprocessor systems, associative memory systems, and special-purpose processors. The Intelligent Database Machine (IDM) introduced by Britton-Lee in 1982 is the first commercial database machine. Teradata's DBC/1012 is a recent entry; it is the only multiprocessor database computer available commercially that has a very flexible reconfigurable architecture. Research on alternative architectures and simulation of their performance are ongoing activities. Su (1988) provides an excellent survey of research efforts in database computers. However, typically, most of them have remained as designs on paper or small prototype implementations because of lack of resources to build actual full-scale hardware or even prototypes.

Because of the demands of high-volume transaction processing and of ever-increasing processor speeds (especially in supercomputers), much attention will be given to database machines and to parallel processing architectures. However, from the experience of the last 10 years it is hard to predict what, if any, will emerge in the way of economically viable and commercially feasible solutions.

From the standpoint of new storage hardware, optical storage devices, which are presently write-once and read-forever types, are being modified into read-write devices and will soon be economically affordable. They have very high capacities (in the range of 10^{12} bytes) and open up the possibility of storing vast amounts of information by recording updated information without erasing old information. A read-write optical disk has already been introduced in the market. The NEXT computer will contain 256 Mbyte magneto-optical storage. Even with the moderate-cost write-once optical disks available today, with a physical write rate of one page per second, a disk used for a normal workload can last 1 year (Gait 1988). This opens up a number of exciting new prospects for historical data storage and retrieval (see temporal applications in Section 22.2.4).

22.1.3   User Interfaces

In Chapter 1 we pointed out the large spectrum of people who are typical users of DBMSs. When DBMSs were introduced in the late 1960s, end users had *no* direct access to databases. Their interactions were limited to verbally communicating their requirements to programmers. Filling forms was one of the first interactive modes of data entry suitable for a large population of users. Most interaction still occurred with batch programs in procedural languages.

Query languages became popular in the 1970s. We discussed the query languages SQL (Chapter 7) and QBE and QUEL (Chapter 9) for the relational data model. It is quite remarkable that for all practical purposes such a major DBMS product as IMS (see Section 23.2 for details) does *not* have a query language. The network data model has also survived without much query language support except for specialized high-level user commands that customers and vendors may have developed on their own. The availability of graphics workstations has tremendously increased the potential for creating non-syntactic interfaces to DBMSs, where a user is not burdened with having to use a specific syntax. Interfaces making extensive use of windowing capabilities, pull-down menus, and icons are likely to grow and become more sophisticated.

Most DBMSs are aiming to add facilities called **Query by Forms**. They allow users to invoke "parameterized" queries where run time parameters are supplied and a predefined query is recompiled or reinterpreted and executed. Other user facilities include *icon-based* interfaces, where a user touches icons or images on the screen to formulate a query, and mouse-based interfaces, where a *mouse* or *touch-sensitive* screen permits cursor movement while specifying a query.

Natural language interfaces have been explored for some time. Codd's (1978) Rendezvous System used a lexicon and converted natural language queries into relational calculus with a predefined set of phrase transformation rules. It engaged in a long-winded clarification dialogue with the user. Harris's (1978) INTELLECT system, now available commercially, searches a database to discover the user's intended meaning after using grammar rules of English syntax. Today's natural language systems suffer from the fact that they represent a heavy overhead, require a database-specific lexicon to be built, and allow ambiguities in query specification. As a result the user may not be aware of how the system actually interpreted a query and the system has no way of predicting exactly what the user may want. Icon- and mouse-based interfaces are equally easy at times and much more economical.

The technology of *speech recognition and understanding* is still not sophisticated enough to allow speech input to be viable in a major way in the near future. That approach, however, has a phenomenal potential for opening the doors of databases to people of all ages and all levels of sophistication and making database-based computer-aided instruction available to the masses.

22.1.4 Program Interfaces

Even today, the bulk of programming in the commercial world, which may account for 70 to 80% (a rough guess!) of actual database processing, is done in conventional programming languages—mostly in COBOL and PL/1. These languages, plus FORTRAN, Assembler, and ALGOL, have been the mainstay of database applications. The C language has recently entered the scene and is gaining ground rapidly.

The 1970s saw the emergence of query languages that were embedded in programming languages for large-scale application program development. We saw examples of *embedding* SQL (Chapter 7) and QUEL (Chapter 9).

A departure from the above is now occurring in two areas. First, the **Fourth-Generation Languages** (4GLs, a term coined commercially without a precise definition) are becoming increasingly popular. They allow the user to give a high-level specification of an application in the 4GL language. The system (or a tool) then *automatically generates* the application code. For example, INGRES provides an Application by Forms interface, where the application designer develops an application by using forms displayed on the screen rather than writing a program for it. 4GLs are, however, not the ultimate panacea for data management and for most report generation that they are made out to be. Their built-in database support is minimal.

Second, it is now possible to interface a conventional or a deductive DBMS* to a logic programming language, for example, PROLOG. Such an integration is accomplished easily when the DBMS query language is based on predicate calculus. This leads to an *integrated programming system* where the inferencing and recursion of the logic programming language are coupled with the efficient manipulation of facts in the DBMS. We will elaborate on this further in Section 22.3.

22.1.5   Presentation and Display

The original output devices on computer systems were line printers and card punchers. Most output was presented either as line-by-line reports or as calculated values punched into cards and subjected to further processing. The language RPG (Report Generation Language) was the beginning of a trend to make report generation a specialized activity that could be specified in terms of high-level report generation commands.

Today, report generators are a standard feature with most DBMSs. Examples are INGRES's report writer, IDMS's CULPRIT package, and UNIFY's lst and rpt processors. Special report definition languages are provided in which users specify formatting, spacing, pagination, levels of totals, headers, justification, etc.

With interactive access to databases for a variety of users, report generation became possible by invoking the report generator or specifying reports via forms (for example, INGRES's Report by Forms). With the advent of PCs, users are expecting to have a great deal of information packed graphically on the screen. Most DBMS packages are supplying **business graphics** output in a variety of forms, including x-y plots (scatter plots) using linear regression, bar charts, pie charts, and line plots (containing piecewise linear approximations of curves that appear as a set of connected lines). With color graphics, aesthetically pleasing as well as impressive displays are becoming commonplace. These types of displays require the query output to be postprocessed by a display manager.

By integrating image technology with database processing and by storing digitized voice as data, some of today's experimental systems are able to produce image and voice output. Digitized image storage is becoming quite common. Specialized hardware for speech synthesis may become commercially available in the next few years.

22.1.6   Nature of Processing

Database technology was originally introduced as a response to the problems of file processing with its associated disadvantages (see Section 1.3). The main applications are in business data processing—inventory management, payroll, general ledger billing, order processing, sales reporting, and so on.

During the late 1970s, the technology started to be applied in a variety of domains from different disciplines. High-level applications that summarized data into information

---

*We do not intend to define deductive databases formally here. Suffice it to say that a conventional database becomes deductive by the addition of a theory with certain axioms and deductive laws. See Gallaire et al. (1984).

for tactical and strategic planning were generated. Reliable and secure, DBMSs became a resource of centralized information with which a large number of geographically separated applications/users could interact. This has been made possible by advances in **data communications technology** including broadband and satellite communication networks. The major users of DBMS technology today use it for **transaction processing**.

Airlines, major hotel chains, insurance companies, banks, retail chain stores, automobile and appliance dealerships, etc. operate today by using reliable rapid transaction processing and on-line real-time updates. Today it is possible to book a seat in a theatre on Broadway from a remote town in Oregon. These applications will continue to place higher and higher demands on this technology of on-line transaction processing.

Other applications categorized as **knowledge processing** are around the corner. They involve rules and inferencing mechanisms for deriving view information that is not explicitly stored in the database. More user-friendly interfaces for naive users will make information available to a wider population and with less drudgery. We will expand on **knowledge base management** in Section 22.3. The combination of distributed processing and knowledge bases is likely to lead to distributed knowledge processing in the future.

22.2   Emerging Database Applications

The applications of database technology are expanding continually. Since data is at the heart of any information system, as computing becomes more widely available each discipline will come up with its unique set of applications. It is not our objective to go through such lists of applications in detail. We wish to identify major categories of applications that are recognized today as presenting a good potential as well as a great challenge to database technology. Special modeling characteristics of each application area will be highlighted.

22.2.1   Engineering Design and Manufacturing

The difficult goal of computer-integrated design and manufacturing requires the effective management of the design and manufacturing information. This topic spans subareas denoted by several acronyms: CAD—computer-aided design, CAM—computer-aided manufacturing, CAE—computer-aided engineering, and CIM—computer-integrated manufacturing. An integrated approach to managing manufacturing information requires compatible representation and manipulation of information in different phases of the product life cycle. This includes business applications such as sales forecasting, order processing, product planning, production control, inventory control, and cost accounting; design and engineering of the product together with planning for materials requirements; manufacturing-related applications including manufacturing resource planning and control; and applications of group technology for parts classification, robotics, and manufacturing process control (including NC—numerical control programming) (Bray 1988).

The standard advantages of database technology help to integrate the above areas (see Sections 1.6 and 1.7). A great deal of research is being directed to both the design and manufacturing problems, and a major emphasis today is on developing DBMSs particularly suited to computer-aided design applications. Figure 22.1 shows the variety of data that is relevant and how a number of applications may be supported in the design environment once this data is captured.

Engineering design is an exploratory and iterative process. The engineering design activity for complex systems such as airplanes or automobiles is conducted by project teams, and the design of a component or a subsystem continuously evolves under a set of design guidelines, resource limitations, and design constraints. Intermittently, designs are cross-checked against other independently evolving designs and, finally, "permanent" designs or versions are stored.

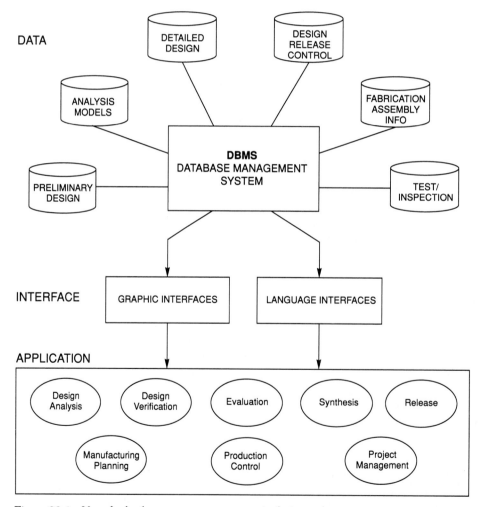

Figure 22.1 Use of a database management system in design and applications

Role of Database Management in CAD

Two current areas of investigation are the design of VLSI (very large scale integration) electronic systems and the design of mechanical structures and systems. A basic challenge in mechanical design is **geometric modeling,** which refers to representing the physical shape of mechanical parts. Shape of parts provides a common thread through the design, analysis, and manufacturing cycle for parts. Different CAD systems employ different geometric modeling techniques, including wire frame modeling, surface modeling, and solid modeling. It is a traumatic experience for the user to transport data among different CAD systems or from a CAD system to a CAM system. The National Bureau of Standards is defining a common neutral interface or format of data called Initial Graphics Exchange Specification (IGES 1983) to facilitate such interchange of data. Unless such a standard database representation is used, database technology cannot be harnessed effectively.

Structural engineering deals with problems ranging from the design of trusses in buildings to the design of complex launch pad assemblies for spacecraft. Whether buildings, mechanical assemblies, bridges, or spaceships are involved, structures are constrained by geometries and require the selection of an optimal set of members to meet weight constraints and design limits and provide reliability under different loadings. Databases can play an important role in storing information centrally for use with analytical tools (e.g., finite-element analysis), graphics (typically three-dimensional graphics on CAD systems), simulations, and optimal design algorithms. In chemical engineering databases are used for plant design and process control. The reasons for using a centralized database system for design data are:

- Part of a design can be synthesized, analyzed, coordinated, and documented while individual project teams work on different parts of the design.

- Constraints related to identical standards, designs, and specifications and other physical properties, design style, and topological relationships can be verified and enforced automatically.

Engineering design data is difficult to capture and represent by using conventional data models (Chapters 6–11) and DBMSs for the following reasons:

- Engineering design data contains a nonhomogeneous collection of design objects. Classical data models deal with homogeneous collections.

- Classical DBMSs are good for formatted data (scalars), short strings, and fixed-length records. Digitized designs are long strings; they have variable-length records or textual information; they often contain vectors and matrices of values.

- Temporal and spatial (see Section 22.2.4) relationships are important in designs for layout, placement, and assembly operations.

- Design data is characterized by a large number of types, each with a small number of instances. Conventional databases have just the opposite situation.

- Schemas *evolve constantly* in design databases because designs go through a long period of evolution.

- Transactions in design databases are of long duration; a designer may "check out" a design object and work on it for several weeks before restoring it (in its modified form) to the database. Similarly, updates are far-reaching because of topological relationships, functional relationships, tolerances, etc. One change is likely to affect a large number of design objects.

- It is necessary to keep old versions and create new versions of the same object. A design log must be maintained for tracing the evolution of a design and possibly backtracking through it.

- Making a design permanent, releasing it to production, archiving it, etc. are specialized functions in a design database.

- Design data must not be duplicated at lower levels of design; since design elements (e.g., gates in electrical circuits or nuts and bolts in mechanical design) are used in a highly repetitive way, redundancy control is required to suppress certain common attributes. For example, when identical bolts are used at two places, the positional coordinates are stored but other attributes are not repeated. In such cases, a library of design objects can be maintained.

Because of these demands, new data modeling approaches are being proposed to manage VLSI designs as well as mechanical designs. Object-oriented models (see Section 15.4.1) are favored because they possess the following characteristics:

- *Common model*—the designer's miniworld can be mapped into the database objects by a one-to-one mapping.

- *Uniform interface*—all objects are treated uniformly by accessing them through methods (or user-defined operations).

- *Support of complex objects*—object-oriented models for engineering designs must allow creation of arbitrarily complex objects involving hierarchies and lattices (Batory and Buchmann 1984).

- *Information hiding and support of abstractions*—the abstraction mechanism can provide the essential external features of objects for design while hiding internal representation or implementation details. Generalization and aggregation are easily supported.

- *Modularity, flexibility, extensibility, and tailorability*—object-oriented databases support schema evolution more easily than conventional models; new objects or new operations can easily be added and old ones modified or deleted.

Notable efforts in the above direction include a project at the University of Southern California (Afsarmanesh et al. 1985), the ORION system (Kim et al. 1987) at the Microelectronics and Computer Technology Corporation, and an effort at the University of California, Berkeley (Katz 1985). A project at the Database Systems Research and Development Center at the University of Florida is attempting to develop a semantic model-based integrated environment (Su et al. 1988) for design and manufacturing on top of an object-oriented DBMS.

Extensions of the relational and network models to accommodate CAD data have been reported but have not been very successful (Wiederhold et al. 1982; Stonebraker et al. 1983). The standard implementation issues discussed in Part IV are further aggravated in design databases. Long transactions and concurrency control of such transactions still remain as research issues.

22.2.2   *Office Systems and Decision Support Systems*

Automation of office work is one of the fastest growing areas of application of information systems (Ellis and Nutt 1980). The growing interest and activity in **office information systems (OISs)** is evident from the fact that a new journal called ACM *Transactions on Office Information Systems* was launched in 1983 by the Association for Computing Machinery. Database technology is having a major impact on office work because much of it falls in the category of *programmable work*, where the events are predictable and the responses are known. Computers and in particular database systems can have a major influence on this type of work. The other extreme is *emergent creative work*, according to the taxonomy of Ciborra et al. (1984), where the events are unpredictable and the responses are unknown. The office work of top management, international money traders, etc. falls into this category and requires the assistance of decision support systems. We will first briefly point out the differences between information systems and OISs; then we briefly review a data-based model of an OIS and finally make a few comments on decision support systems.

Office Information Systems versus Conventional Database Applications*

Like CAD applications, OIS applications place a higher demand on a DBMS while centralizing the information in a given office environment. This is due to the following characteristics of OIS applications:

- Semantic richness—Office data tends to be semantically rich and requires support for unstructured messages, letters, text, annotations, chain of forwarding addresses, oral communications, etc. There are *stereotypical information groupings* in an office, such as business letters or quarterly progress reports with standardized formats.

- Time factor—The time factor and timing constraint must be modeled to capture the following types of information: the total travel time of a document along a path, duration of activities, calendars and schedules, allowable response time to reply to a message, automatic generation of reminders, etc.

- Lack of structure—Office activities tend to be much more unstructured than other information systems. Instructions to perform work are incomplete and irregular; constant communication and dialogue are necessary.

- High interconnectivity—Compared to a manufacturing workcell that uses machine tools, an office typically represents a much more complex group of elements, each performing a variety of functions and interconnected in multiple directions to elements of different types. It is therefore difficult to model the work flow in an office accurately, and automation and productivity improvements are difficult to achieve using a well-defined office design methodology.

- Office constraints and evolution—Because an office is a group of humans, it is subject to constant evolution in which the authorities and job responsibilities of individuals change. It is therefore difficult to model all constraints definitively.

---

*This section is largely derived from Bracchi and Pernici (1984, 1987).

- Interactive interface—OISs are highly interactive. It should be possible for even the lowest-level worker in an office to communicate to an OIS. User groups are diverse and span the whole spectrum from naive to sophisticated. This makes interface design challenging.

- Filtering of information—Most offices have a built-in hierarchy. It is necessary to filter and summarize information in a pyramid style within the system. Low-level transactions must be summarized before being passed up to the next level of management. Aggregation of data elements should be performed automatically at different prespecified and user-controlled intervals.

- Priorities, scheduling, reminders—All of these are important characteristics of different elements of work; a variety of interrupts are generated and must be handled in the office constantly.

It is evident that office automation is not an easy task. A database at the heart of an OIS must be capable of meeting all of the above requirements. Because of these factors, we see "islands of mechanization" in offices today rather than a totally automated office. Many conceptual modeling and design methodologies for OISs have been proposed; examples are OFFIS (Konsynski et al. 1982), OAM (Sirbu et al. 1981), and MOBILE-Burotique (Dumas et al. 1982).

Data-based Model of an Office Information System

Data-based models group data into forms that resemble paper forms in an office. The Office-By-Example project at IBM Research (Zloof 1982) developed a language called Office By Example (OBE) that is an extension of the QBE language described in Chapter 9. OBE models a variety of objects using the basic relational table paradigm: forms, reports, documents, address lists, message lists, menus, etc. The system allows data types such as image, text, and time. The functions specified on these objects include word processing, querying, and automatic triggering of activities (for example, send letter when payment is more than n days overdue, where n is a run time parameter or is obtained from some table). Authorization, message communication and forwarding, and document manipulation are examples of other functions handled through the same interface. The main point of data-based office models is to represent the office from the viewpoint of objects manipulated by office workers. The object-oriented approach again seems promising here. A major activity in offices is document processing, storage, and retrieval. The current work in multimedia databases (see Section 22.4.1) should be of great benefit to OISs.

Decision Support Systems (DSSs)

Office systems or business data processing systems in general offer decision support to upper-level office workers in several ways:

- Analysis of office data—Data must be presented to the user at the right level of detail using the right display after performing proper filtering.

- Controlling the state of the system—An OIS must have features to determine its own state and to evaluate it. Any discrepancies or exceptional conditions requiring attention should be brought to the attention of the right individuals.

- Support of analytical decision-making tools—Besides ad hoc decisions, managers are called on to make long-term strategic and business planning decisions. Alternative choices must be considered and analyzed. A DSS must have the knowledge of alternatives as well as the models to perform optimization or perform "intelligent" choices.

- Support for organizational design and office system design changes—The DSS should have some features that allow organizational restructuring or information flow modification without disrupting normal operations.

DSSs are being designed today with a DBMS as their central component. In general, a DSS allows the user to perform control and monitoring functions; it must also allow the user to enforce policy decisions (constraints) and actions (procedures). Though a variety of systems have been proposed, the literature is too vast to summarize here.

22.2.3   Statistical and Scientific Database Management*

The use of computers to manage scientific and statistical information is not new. However, database technology was rather late in reaching statisticians and scientists. There are two broad types (Wong 1984) of scientific and statistical databases (SSDBs): micro and macro. **Micro SSDBs** contain records of individual entities or events such as raw census data. **Macro SSDBs** contain summary information derived from the former by performing statistical operations such as cross-tabulations or regression analysis. Examples are statistics on causes of death and summaries of seismic activity by region. Most DBMSs offered today can handle one of the two kinds of data but not both; conventional data models and DBMSs are not well suited for handling macro SSDBs.

Workshops on SSDB management were initiated at Lawrence Berkeley Laboratory in 1981 and continued annually since then. In these workshops many specialized data modeling approaches, techniques, and languages have been proposed for SSDBs. Data compression techniques have also been advocated for sparse matrix types of data. Inferencing and security control techniques have also been proposed. Furthermore, SSDBs have been proposed for statistical sampling and testing in manufacturing together with real-time control of test sequences for quality control (Ghosh 1984, 1986).

In the following points, we highlight the problems posed by SSDBs vis-à-vis conventional DBMSs:

1. *Data definition:* Micro SSDBs tend to have hundreds of attributes per record. They exhibit large variability among field sizes. Schema changes (adding or dropping fields) without reloading a database must be supported. While data is collected over a long period of time, schemas may undergo changes. A variety of data types including time series, vectors, and matrices is needed. For macro SSDBs to model the semantics adequately, a construct supporting cross-products of attributes is necessary (Su 1985).

2. *Data manipulation:* Micro SSDBs need statistical operations such as cross-tabulation or sampling. Macro SSDBs need a variety of aggregations by suppressing one or more summary attributes, for example, income by age group versus income by age group by sex.

---

*This section is largely derived from Wong (1984).

3. *User interfaces:* Adequate support to remember names of hundreds of fields and their abbreviations is an absolute necessity for statistical users. Any interface must include some form of browsing. Users' exploratory investigation and incremental query building must be supported. Users should be able to view record internal structure with some semantically meaningful groupings. *Meta-data browsing* support is essential for users to determine which database or what portion of a database they should be looking at.

4. *Physical modeling:* Since micro SSDBs tend to be sparse, compression, transposed files, and index encoding must be utilized for efficient storage. Operators must act against compressed data.

5. *Data dictionary:* Large SSDBs require extensive data dictionaries with names, aliases, codes, data derivation procedures, data sources, data quality measures, and usage information.

6. *System facilities:* Most SSDBs are static retrieval-only systems. The locking at low levels of granularity is an overkill for most SSDBs. Statisticians would prefer an elaborate logging of searches so that backtracking is facilitated. We referred to statistical inference in Section 20.1. Statistical inference control is a very difficult problem that is still being researched. Since users typically work with subsets of data, there is a proliferation of private subset copies.

This list amply points out the limitations of conventional DBMSs. A few special DBMSs have been on the market (e.g., SIR) that address several of the above issues.

22.2.4   Spatial and Temporal Database Management

In this subsection we cover two important types of data that have started receiving the attention of database modeling researchers only recently. In Section 22.2.1, while discussing CAD/CAM applications, we alluded to geometric modeling. Whether in the context of CAD/CAM, in architectural and civil engineering design, or in cartography and geological surveys, it is important to model the space dimension. Today's data models are lacking in this area. The spatial semantics is captured by three common representations:

- Solid representation—the space is divided up into pieces of various sizes. The spatial characteristics of an entity are then represented by the set of these pieces associated with that entity.

- Boundary representation (or wire frame models)—the spatial characteristics are represented by line segments or boundaries.

- Abstract representation—relationships with spatial semantics are used, such as ABOVE, NEAR, IS-NEXT-TO, BEHIND, to associate entities.

The PROBE project at Computer Corporation of America (Dayal et al. 87) provided support for spatial data in the functional data model DAPLEX (Shipman 1981). While it is clear that many applications would benefit from such facilities, different application domains have varying requirements. For example, in VLSI applications space is two-dimensional and discrete; basic objects to be stored are points, line segments, rectangles, and polygons. In solid modeling for most manufacturing applications, space is three-dimensional and continuous and the basic objects are parametrically defined curves and surfaces. The operations relevant to each application area are also different.

Temporal Data Management

Temporal information is a special one-dimensional case of spatial information. Temporal aspects built into databases must include three types of support for time: time points, time intervals, and abstract relationships involving time (before, after, during, simultaneously, concurrently, etc.). There is also a **history** aspect of databases, which is very important for applications such as project management, patient histories in hospitals, maintenance histories of equipment, and administrative and operational control in office systems.

One limitation of current databases is that information becomes effective at the same moment as it is recorded in the database. There are no provisions for making a distinction between the *registration time* when certain data is entered and the *logical time* period during which the specific data values are valid. In fact, sometimes a *transaction time* must be recorded for an event. Many database updates in real applications are either *retroactive* (they became effective at some previous point in time) or *proactive* (they will become effective at some time in the future). Another limitation is that current systems maintain no history of changes. Each update potentially destroys old facts. The database thus represents only the current state of some domain rather than a history of that domain. To deal with the above requirements, data models are needed that explicitly incorporate time, separating time-varying information from time-invariant information and representing them separately. One proposed model is the Temporal Relational Model (TRM) of Navathe and Ahmed (1988). In this model, attributes are divided into time-varying and non-time-varying ones and so are relations. In time-varying relations two timestamp attributes are appended representing start time and end time of the logical time over which the tuple is valid. This approach is called *tuple time stamping*. Figure 22.2 shows a time-varying EMPLOYEE relation in TRM.

For this model, a time normalization is proposed to avoid temporal anomalies; the SQL query language is extended into Temporal SQL (TSQL) with a variety of features like the WHEN clause, temporal ordering, time-slice, aggregate functions, grouping, and a

EmpNo	Salary	Position	T_S	T_E
33	20K	Typist	12	24
33	25K	Secretary	25	35
45	27K	Jr. Engineer	28	37
45	30K	Sr. Engineer	38	42

Notes: T_S : Time-Start
T_E : Time-End

Figure 22.2 A time varying relation in the Temporal Relational Model

moving-time window. Another school of thinking proposes *attribute time stamping,* which appends a new attribute value with a timestamp at each update time (Ben-Zvi 1982, Clifford and Tansel 1985). This results in unnormalized relations with a much more complicated algebra and query language; furthermore, relationships involving non-time-varying keys *cannot* be represented in this approach.

With the advent of optical write-once disks that can store 10^{13} bytes of data, appending updates to history data will become viable. Further work in the implementation aspects and commercial feasibility of these models is necessary. Implementation of these data models will also place demands on operating systems for time management, recording, and synchronization of multiuser time frames.

22.3   Databases, Knowledge Bases, and Expert Systems

22.3.1   *Data versus Knowledge*

In Section 15.3 we contrasted *knowledge representation* (KR) and semantic data modeling. The main distinction is that the scope of KR is broader: KR schemes include some reasoning mechanisms for inferencing or deducing information from stored data; they provide flexible representations for modeling types as well as instances in a single framework. We also saw that both schemes essentially support the same five fundamental abstraction types.

Today there is growing interest in moving from databases to **knowledge bases** (KBs). Knowledge is information at a higher level of abstraction. For example, "Mr. Jones is 45 years old" may be considered to be a fact in a database. "Mr. Jones is middle aged" is not such a precise fact; it is a broader, higher form of knowledge. Similarly, while "Mr. Jones had an accident on January 17, 1988 in New York at the ramp leading in from I-495 to I-278" is a fact, "Mr. Jones is a reckless driver" is knowledge. "All middle-aged men are reckless" is another higher-level element of knowledge, which may represent a poor inference because it is not generally correct.

It is thus very hard to define and quantify knowledge. Knowledge is typically generated by experts in some domain of expertise. Thus knowledge is used to define, control, and interpret the data in a database.

As we stated in Section 15.3, knowledge comes in various forms (Wiederhold 1984):

- Structural knowledge—knowledge about dependencies and constraints among the data (for example, "insertion into benefit plan x is subject to preregistration in benefit plan y").

- General procedural knowledge—certain knowledge that can be described only by a procedure or a method (for example, a procedure to determine the "credit-worthiness" of a customer).

- Application-specific knowledge—knowledge determined by the rules and regulations applicable in a specific domain (for example, computation of the cheapest fare between two cities on an airline).

- Enterprise-directing knowledge—a higher form of knowledge that allows an enterprise to make decisions. For example, on a companywide basis this knowledge includes the cost of relocating and retraining employees as well as some measure of the benefit in the form of morale and loyalty of keeping employees on the job for more than n years.

Intensional knowledge is defined as the knowledge beyond the factual content of the database. Such knowledge can be fully specified *before* the database is established. Database systems exist to manage the data and meta-data, which is **extensional knowledge** or knowledge embedded in facts and instances. Knowledge systems use not only the extensional knowledge but also the intensional knowledge, possibly in the form of rules in a rule base. **Derived knowledge** is a form in which extensional knowledge and intensional knowledge are mixed. A database may store relations called father (Father_name, Child_name), mother (Mother_name, Child_name), and person (Person_name, Sex). From these three basic relations, it would be possible to define a variety of family relationships from cousins to uncles to grandfathers, which is the job of a rule base. In Figure 22.3 we show a general schematic where the DBMS and KBMS are juxtaposed.

Most KB systems today store the intensional knowledge in the form of rules. Other representations include logical assertions, semantic networks, and frames. We refer to the inferencing and control strategy of a KB as *strategic knowledge*.

22.3.2   Expert Database Systems

Expert systems (ESs) are systems that use a body of knowledge pertaining to some specific application domain and use an inferencing mechanism (called the *inference engine*) to

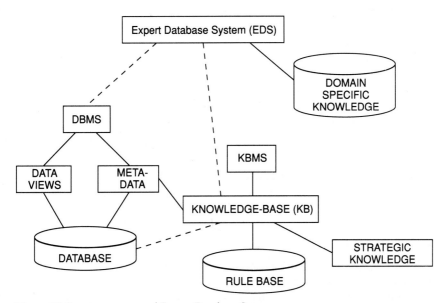

Figure 22.3   DBMS, KBMS and Expert Database Systems

find solutions to complex problems. An ES requires data specific to a problem and *heuristics*, or rules and guidelines, that govern the problem-solving process. An expert system has been defined as "a computer program that embodies the expertise—the principles and procedures—of *one or more experts in some domain* and applies this knowledge to make useful inferences for the user of the system" (Hayes-Roth et al. 1983).

Let us see how a KB and a knowledge base management system (KBMS) differ from an ES. The ES, while running its inference engine, constantly needs information to solve the problem and come to conclusions. The KB provides the information the ES requires. So the ES is actually a piece of software that sits atop the KB. The inferencing capability of the KBMS is different from that of the ES. The inferencing within a KBMS is for purposes of understanding the meta-relations and deriving new data, whereas inferencing in the ES is for the process of arriving at a solution by applying the heuristic principles that pertain to the domain. When an ES relies on a DBMS to supply facts or actually embodies the functionality of a DBMS, it is sometimes called an **Expert Database System (EDS),** although this nomenclature is far from being universally accepted. In Figure 23.3 we show this relationship between an EDS, a DBMS, and a KBMS. Notice that the KBMS may have its own general form of knowledge, shown as strategic knowledge in this figure. On the other hand, an ES or an EDS has a specific set of knowledge related to the application domain. The popularity of the expert database concept is demonstrated by the attendance at a conference series started in 1984, called the International Conference on Expert Database Systems (EDS 1984, 1986, 1988).

Let us now consider the different approaches to realizing expert database systems and knowledge base management systems. For the type of knowledge they deal with, they have many similarities: both must reason about facts; both must process general forms of queries that ask questions not just about the explicit facts but also about the implied and derived facts. The difference between an ES and a KBMS is basically only in the type of knowledge processed. The former has a narrow domain; the latter can be more general in purpose. A KB in a KBMS is typically more structured in organization and functionality than in an ES.

Approaches to Achieving EDSs*

THE HOMOGENEOUS APPROACH   This integrates data manipulation functions and deductive functions into a single system called a *deductive database system*. The facts and deductive rules are both represented uniformly in a single programming system. This approach is best exemplified by PROLOG, which is becoming increasingly popular in the database community. A deductive database in PROLOG is defined as in Figure 22.4 (adapted from Missikoff and Wiederhold 1986).

While the facts in this database are only about mother and father, using the deductive rules we can answer the following types of queries:

	IN PROLOG
Is Mary a parent of Linda?	? parent (Linda, Mary).
Who is the grandmother of Linda?	? grandmother (Linda, X).
Who are Barbara's parents?	? parent (Barbara,Y).**

---

*This discussion is influenced by Missikoff and Wiederhold (1986).

**Standard PROLOG will return only one value for Y. To get additional values, further user input may be required.

Rules (Knowledge)

```
grandfather (C,F) :- parent (C,Z), father (Z,F)
grandmother (C,M) :- parent (C,Z), mother (Z,M)
parent (C,P) :- mother (C,P)
parent (C,P) :- father (C,P)
child (P,C) :- parent (C,P)
```

Facts (Data)

```
father (art,bob)
father (bob,charles)
father (barbara, charles)

mother (linda, mary)
mother (lenny, mary)
mother (mary, nancy)
mother (barbara, nancy)
```

Figure 22.4   A deductive database (in PROLOG)

PROLOG offers the additional advantage that PROLOG predicates can also be interpreted as relations. Hence, a set of facts such as that shown in Figure 22.4 may reside in a relational database. The integration of PROLOG for deductive reasoning with a relational database for large-scale data handling is being pursued at two levels:

1. Enhancing PROLOG for better data management. This approach preserves the desirable features of PROLOG as a programming language. It requires building better I/O, data structure management, and access method support within PROLOG. The algorithms supplied by PROLOG, its memory management, etc. have to be changed. All data is still managed within main memory. This has been implemented by some researchers (Sammut and Sammut 1983).

2. Providing for an efficient interface between PROLOG and secondary storage databases. This provides DBMS functionality to PROLOG. Examples are MU-PROLOG (Naish and Thom 1982) and concurrent PROLOG (Dahl 1984).

THE HETEROGENEOUS APPROACH—EXPERT SYSTEMS PLUS DBMS   This approach considers a cooperation between two distinct systems, the ES and the DBMS, one for knowledge management and the other for database management. The critical issue is the design of the interface, which leads to two alternatives:

1. Loose coupling: This approach maintains the separate identity of the two systems. The interaction consists of the ES formulating a query and the DBMS compiling and optimizing the query, retrieving the data, and passing it to the ES. The critical issue is an efficient technique of formulating the queries to minimize the traffic of data and the number of DBMS calls. Several studies have been made using PROLOG and a relational DBMS.

A shortcoming of this approach is that the separation of the deductive phase and the data retrieval phase is not clear-cut; hence some batching of data requests is necessary. The ES buffer sizes place limitations on how much data can be retrieved; furthermore, consistency is a problem because data used by the ES can be simultaneously updated within the DBMS.

2. Tight coupling: In this approach the DBMS and the ES act as an integrated system. The logic programming language, say PROLOG, becomes the added logic programming interface of the DBMS, while from the user's standpoint the programming language is enriched with the full data handling power of the DBMS. In PROLOG the user does *not* explicitly control data manipulation. This approach avoids the shortcomings listed above but is known to suffer from serious performance problems. EDUCE (Bocca 1986, 1986a) is one of the first systems in this category. The decision of when and how to access data during rule processing still remains a crucial one.

3. Alternatively, an EDS can be regarded as an enhanced DBMS to which deductive capabilities have been added and which acts as a general-purpose ES with alternative choice for control strategies. This view is taken by Missikoff and Wiederhold (1984).

Currently, there is no consensus on which of the several alternatives listed above would be optimal. The Japanese Fifth Generation Project has adopted the loose coupling approach (Ohsuga 1982) and the authors personally favor this approach (Whang and Navathe 1987). A great deal of activity is under way to address issues related to different forms of coupling and performance issues; in particular, recursive query processing strategies (Lu et al. 1987).

22.4   Emerging Technologies and Needed Research

So far we have covered a wide range of issues. In this last section we point out briefly the emerging relevant technologies that are represented by ongoing research projects and end with some pointers to needed research areas.

22.4.1   *Emerging Relevant Database Technologies*

Several new technologies are emerging in the context of database management. We simply outline them here.

Multimedia Database Technology

Recent advances in computer systems have proliferated the types of information stored in computer systems. **Multimedia information** is information in the form of images (vector or raster, still or moving) and audio information containing digitized speech or music. Storage of images on optical video disks allows about 50,000 image frames on one disk with an access time of 1 or 2 seconds per frame. Speech requires a large volume of storage; data encoding rates vary from 2.4K bits per second for predictive coding to 64K bits per second for pulse code modulation. At these rates, 1 minute of speech takes from 18K to 480K of storage.

There are a number of multimedia applications:

- Multimedia document management with image, audio, and text information packaged as documents. Christodoulakis et al. (1984) have developed a system in which they call these multimedia messages. A query like "find all images that are about Toronto" requires that "Toronto" be manually entered to describe the image. A system may involve image understanding software to determine who or what is in the image. A hypertext system allows a user to retrieve text objects nonsequentially. Hypertext is based on concepts that originated as far back as 1945 (Bush 1945), and the first experimental system was designed in 1968 (Engelbart and English 1968). Now there are commercially available implementations of Hypertext. Hypertext systems can be considered as a type of OIS that supports unstructured office data from multiple media and certain OIS functions mentioned earlier.

- CAD output containing drawings, pictures, and functional specifications of some design objects. An example is the SID system at the University of Tokyo (Kunii and Harada 1980).

- Image databases with images and text about the images stored together. This includes a wide range of applications. A major application is generation of maps of different kinds. The DIMAP system at the University of Illinois, Chicago, combines a relational DBMS with an image manipulation system (Chang et al. 1979). Chang and Fu (1981) have developed a Picture-query-by-example interface to the image database system inspired by the QBE language discussed in Chapter 9. Digital images are also produced by medical equipment including computed tomography (CT) scanners and nuclear magnetic resonance (NMR) scanners. They can be classified and used in medical diagnosis (Dwyer et al. 1982).

Multimedia database technology is likely to play a significant role with advances in image processing and understanding and further developments in the coding, storage, organization, indexing, and retrieval of images, text, and speech.

Distributed and Federated Database Technology

We discussed distributed database management in Chapter 21. As we saw, the technical issues of distributed transaction and query processing, concurrency control, recovery, etc. are harder to resolve than with centralized databases. Although research has been ongoing in this area for at least 15 years, few commercially viable major products have been introduced (exceptions include systems like TANDEM's ENCOMPASS).

It appears that the federated DBMS alternative (see Section 21.1) may become more popular than the homogeneous distributed form of processing. It is a good compromise that provides a large degree of local autonomy coupled with shared access.

The technology of hierarchical arrangement of DBMSs going from PCs to minis to mainframes is also slowly developing. With the open-ended architecture among vendors announced recently, data interchange will be highly facilitated among different DBMSs on different types of hardware and software using different data models.

Extensible DBMSs

As we saw in Section 22.2, there is a need to build new DBMSs to meet the challenges of the new applications. DBMSs are complex pieces of software with complicated algorithms and relationships among components. This will become clear from the examples of commercial DBMSs in the next chapter. Because it takes a long time to develop a DBMS, a new modular approach has been proposed that builds DBMSs out of "DBMS parts" or building blocks.

Such an **extensible database management system** would assemble prewritten modules (algorithms) into new "tailor-made DBMSs". This approach has the following obvious advantages:

- New DBMS development will be rapid and economical.

- Technological or algorithmic improvements can be quickly incorporated into the reusable modules and, as a result, the system will always remain up to date.

- Proposed new techniques and algorithms can be evaluated without making significant modifications to the system.

This approach is pursued by the GENESIS project at the University of Texas (Batory et al. 1986) and EXODUS at the University of Wisconsin (Graefe and Dewitt 1987, Carey et al. 1986, 1986a, 1988). It contrasts with another approach proposed to deal with new applications: that of building DBMSs with extensible functionality by providing a wide set of features. This **full-functionality approach** is exemplified by the PROBE (Dayal et al. 1987) and STARBURST (Schwarz et al. 1986) projects. At present, both of these approaches are too experimental to predict their viability.

Semantic Database Technology

This is another recent development in which databases are based on some conceptual or semantic data model and implemented directly. The first commercial product in this area is SIM of UNISYS. Previously, the entity-relationship model was implemented directly in the ZIM system by XANTHE Corporation. This trend will enable users to do the conceptual design of their database in a conceptual data model and implement it directly. It avoids the overhead of mapping to a conventional model at design time. However, performance issues remain a major stumbling block. The entire range of object-oriented DBMSs (see Section 23.4) would fall into this category too.

24.4.2   Needed Future Research and Development

For completeness, we list below the areas that need further research in the immediate future:

User Interfaces

Despite the current advances in user interfaces stated in Section 22.1, a few areas remain to be explored:

1. Customized languages—Casual and occasional users need languages that are easy to use and fit well with their problem domains. An account executive in an in-

vestment firm deals with a different set of terms and processing requirements than a production supervisor in a manufacturing company. If both are using the same system, each should be given a customized interface. Currently, these are not impossible to provide, but involve a heavy programming effort. Future systems should make it easier to generate a customized set of language constructs for each set of users.

2. Alternative paradigms for accessing databases—The system called Spatial Data Management System (SDMS) of Computer Corporation of America (Herot 1980) is a good example of getting away from the records- and files-oriented approach to data management. SDMS simulates an environment in which data is organized in a three-dimensional space such as an office. It bases the search of data on the principle that people are good at locating information by knowing where it is placed and by knowing some physical appearance attributes of the medium or container in which it is recorded. Such a system allows a natural "spatial exploration" through the database, encourages browsing, and uses icons as dictionary information (meta-data). This system is able to store and display illustrations and pictures from videodisks and other media.

In the future we might see more developments along these lines that would also incorporate other forms of information, including movies and animations and, going a step further, even smells and tastes!

3. Natural language interface in multiple languages—With faster means of communication, it is already becoming necessary to make the same database under the same DBMS available to Americans, Italians, Japanese, etc. at the same time. Today's natural language interfaces are inefficient and inadequate. Future interfaces will demand multilingual support. There are related problems of displaying information in different scripts, allowing editing of text involving multiple languages (for example, English and Arabic, where the latter is read from right to left), storing aliases in different languages, and so on.

Database Integration

In the context of federated database management systems (FDBMSs), it will become feasible to integrate geographically dispersed data stored in different DBMSs and under different models into a single conceptual schema of a database.

By **database integration** we refer to three subproblems: integrating schemas of local databases into a global schema, mapping actual data from the local schemas to the global schema, and mapping queries against the global schema into queries against local schemas. The problem of global schema design is currently in the research realm (see, for example, Elmasri et al. (1986); Mannino and Effelsberg (1984)). A few systems such as MULTIBASE (Smith et al. 1981), DDTS (Devor and Weeldryer 1980), and OMNIBASE (Rusinkiewicz et al. 1988) actually dealt with the internal system problems of mapping data and queries back and forth between the global and constituent databases. The schema integration tools project jointly undertaken by Honeywell Research and the University of Florida developed design tools suitable for integrating diverse databases (Sheth et al. 1988).

Interface with Software Engineering Technology

The primary goal of software engineering is to develop ways to make the software development process easier, more effective, and more efficient. A prime end product of the software engineering activity is application software. With DBMSs becoming so commonplace, the application software development should be considered in the context of DBMSs. Merging of the concepts from both of these disciplines should occur in the following areas:

1. Design databases: A large design activity such as developing a large software system is like large design projects in other areas, such as building a skyscraper, a power station, or a manufacturing facility. A large system design can be hierarchically decomposed into designs of smaller and smaller components. Each component evolves, design specifications change, and new design alternatives appear. A proper way to consolidate and track the design information is to create a database for it.

2. Application generation from high-level specification: This area is of great interest in commercial application development. Several commercial application generators are on the market. The main incentive is that it reduces the effort and cost of application development. This goal is shared by DBMSs. Hence, in the future we are likely to see application generators closely coupled with underlying DBMSs.

3. Software tools: This is an important area of future development. The tools have two purposes: to reduce the drudgery of certain tasks for humans and to improve the performance of certain machines. Various types of tools are needed with DBMSs. Tools of the first type include requirements specification and analysis tools, conceptual design tools, tools for view integration, tools for schema mapping among models, tools for physical design and optimization, and partitioning and allocation tools. Tools of the second type include performance monitoring, tuning, reorganizing, and restructuring tools. The past few years have seen tremendous activity in tool development. However, there exist few tools that provide good interfaces and that can interface easily with other tools. Of course, there are a few exceptions. We expect vigorous activity in tool development in the next few years.

4. Prototyping: This is a popular topic among software engineering enthusiasts, but it has received little attention in the database area. Prototyping of databases and applications can go a long way toward validating the design of schemas, refining the structures, and evaluating the relative frequencies of queries (transactions). We are likely to see substantial development in this area. Increasing availability of personal computers and workstations makes the role of prototyping even more significant.

Interface with Artificial Intelligence Technology

In Section 22.3 we discussed the integration of an important discipline of artificial intelligence (AI) called expert systems with database management systems. We also discussed knowledge base and database management. This is certainly a promising direction for the future. However, issues related to performance, incomplete information, fuzzy information, etc. need further research. Logic and databases constitute a very active research area. Application of the logic formalism to database problems will throw some light on the difficult problems outlined above, and more homogeneous solutions (Section 22.3) will be developed by combining logic programming with database management.

Database Machines and Architecture

Research on database machines has focused primarily on the efficient retrieval and storage of large quantities of data. In artificial intelligence, architectures have been designed to support directly processing based on some knowledge representation scheme (e.g., LISP machines); these machines do not consider issues related to the efficient retrieval and manipulation of large quantities of data. One future direction of research on database machines would be to design a computer that integrates the problem-solving components with the data management functions. Another is to develop hardware for database management functions, such as security and integrity control, concurrency control, and transaction management, that are currently implemented by software, and constitute a major performance overhead. Research into parallel architectures for knowledge-based systems will also be needed.

Interface with Programming Language Technology

Research on query languages—query language design, query modification, optimization, and compilation—is ongoing in relation to hard application areas of CAD, office systems, and statistical, spatial, and temporal database management. Further work is needed on proving the equivalence of models and languages and formalizing their semantics.

We conclude this chapter with Figure 22.5, which shows that in future information modeling and processing applications in the diverse areas to which databases will be applied, database technology must work hand in hand with the related technologies of software engineering, artificial intelligence, programming languages, and distributed systems. Users will engage in problem-solving activities with the database as a focus and these other technologies to support various facets of the problem-solving process.

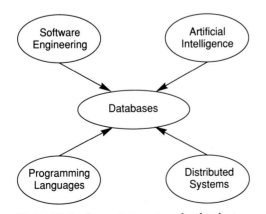

Figure 22.5 Future integration of technologies

Selected Bibliography

Much of the relevant bibliography for this chapter has been already referenced in the various sections. Below, we give a few additional references. The book edited by Gallaire and Minker (1978) contains an early collection of papers on databases and logic. Brachman and Levesque (1984) elaborate on the distinction between databases and knowledge bases. Lafue and Smith (1984) present a knowledge based system for semantic integrity management. The series of conference proceedings on Expert Database Systems (EDS 1984, 1986, 1988) provide papers related to databases, logic, expert and knowledge-based systems, and techniques concerning the integration of database and artificial intelligence technologies.

Many research projects concern the integration of logic and databases. The NAIL! system at Stanford University is discussed in Morris et al. (1986) and Ullman (1985). Chang and Walker (1984) describe PROSQL, a PROLOG interface to SQL/DS. The POSTGRES system is discussed in Stonebraker and Rowe (1986) and Stonebraker et al. (1987). Implementation of deductive and inferential databases is described by Kifer and Lozinskii (1986) and Lozinskii (1986). Various techniques for evaluating recursive queries are discussed by Ceri and Tanka (1987), Ioannidis and Wong (1988), Lu et al. (1988), Sacca and Zaniolo (1987), and Vielle (1988).

Another topic of current research, which we have not discussed, concerns the incorporation of incomplete and imprecise (fuzzy) information in databases. Some papers that discuss incomplete information include Lipski (1979), Vassiliou (1980), Imielinski and Lipski (1981), and Liu and Sunderraman (1988). Techniques for dealing with fuzzy information are discussed in Zadeh (1983) and Zvieli (1986).

An early survey paper on backend database machines is Maryanski (1980). Techniques for implementing main-memory databases are discussed by DeWitt et al. (1984). Applications of multi-media databases are discussed in Christodoulakis and Faloutsos (1986).

Dittrich (1986) is a survey of the object-oriented approach. Maier et al. (1986) describe the GEMSTONE/OPAL object-oriented system. The Darmstadt Database Kernel System is described in Paul et al. (1987). Navathe and Pillalamarri (1988) discuss how to make the ER model, discussed in Chapters 3 and 15, into an object-oriented model.

Many projects address databases for engineering design. Haskin and Lorie (1982) and Lorie and Plouffe (1983) discuss complex design objects in databases. Eastman (1987) discusses the facilities needed for engineering databases. Kemper et al. (1987) describe an object-oriented DBMS for engineering applications. Geometric modeling and spatial data processing are discussed by Kemper and Wallrath (1987) and Orenstein (1986). The R-tree data structure for indexing spatial data is presented in Guttman (1984). Schema evolution is discussed by Banerjee et al. (1987a), and CAD databases for VLSI are discussed in Du and Ghanta (1987).

Recently, there is growing interest in real-time databases, such as the work by Abbott and Garcia-Molina (1988). A temporal data model and query language for relational databases is described in Gadia (1988). Tsichritzis (1982) discusses forms management.

COMMERCIAL DATABASE SYSTEMS

CHAPTER 23
Examples of Relational (DB2), Hierarchical (IMS),
Network (IDMS), and other DBMSs (VBASE)

CHAPTER 23

Examples of Relational, Hierarchical, Network, and Other Systems

In this chapter we review representative commercial DBMS products corresponding to the major data models we addressed in this book. These include the relational, hierarchical, and network data models. In addition, we take a brief look at an object-oriented DBMS product. For each DBMS we adopt the following organization:

- Introduction to the system.
- Basic modular architecture and features.
- Data definition and system catalog details, if any.
- Data manipulation, including various language interfaces.
- Storage of databases in the system.
- Internal features and development tools, if any.
- Evaluation of the system.

Under each data model we primarily discuss one DBMS in detail and sometimes mention some other products. The systems covered are DB2 for relational, IMS for hierarchical, IDMS for network, and Vbase for object-oriented systems.

23.1   A Relational System—DB2

In this section we review a popular DBMS product of IBM called DB2.

663

23.1.1   Introduction

After the introduction of the relational model by Codd in 1970, there was a flurry of activity to experiment with relational ideas. One of the first relational DBMSs was the Peterlee Relational Test Vehicle at the IBM United Kingdom Scientific Center around 1975. A major research and development effort was also initiated at IBM's San Jose (now called Almaden) Research Center in the 1970s. It led to the announcement of two commercial relational DBMS products by IBM in the 1980s: the SQL/DS for DOS/VSE (disk operating system/virtual storage extended) and VM/CMS (virtual machine/conversational monitoring system) environments; and DB2 for the MVS operating system. Another major relational DBMS is INGRES, developed at the University of California, Berkeley in the early 1970s and commercialized by Relational Technology, Inc. in the late 1970s. ORACLE by Oracle, Inc. and UNIFY by UNIFY, Inc. are two other popular relational DBMSs introduced for minis and mainframes in the early 1980s.

We introduced the relational data model and relational algebra in Chapter 6. We have already discussed the query languages SQL (Chapter 7) and QBE (Chapter 9), which are available under SQL/DS and DB2, and the language QUEL, available under INGRES. In this chapter we take an in-depth look at DB2.

Besides the relational DBMSs mentioned above, a large number of other products have appeared in the last few years. They include RBASE 5000, RIM, RDB, INFORMIX, and PARADOX. The word "relational" is also used somewhat inappropriately by several vendors to refer to their products as a marketing gimmick. In order to qualify as a relational DBMS, a system must have at least the following properties*:

1. It must store data as relations where each column is independently identified by its column name and the ordering of rows is immaterial.

2. The operations available to the user as well as those used internally by the system should be true relational operations; that is, they should be able to generate new relations from old relations.

3. The system must support at least one variant of the join operation.

Although we could add to this list, we propose these criteria as a very minimal set for testing whether a system is relational. It is easy to see that many so-called relational DBMSs do not satisfy the above criteria.

We will now describe DB2, which is one of the more widely used mainframe relational systems today.

23.1.2   Basic Architecture of DB2

The name DB2 is an abbreviation for Database 2. It is a relational DBMS product of IBM for the MVS operating system. Figure 23.1 shows the relationships among various components of DB2. DB2 allows concurrent access to databases by IMS/VS-DC (Information Management System/Virtual Storage-Data Communications—we discuss IMS in Section 23.2), CICS (Customer Information Control System), and TSO (Time Sharing Option)

---

*Codd (1985) specified 12 rules for determining whether a DBMS is relational. We have listed the rules in the appendix to this chapter.

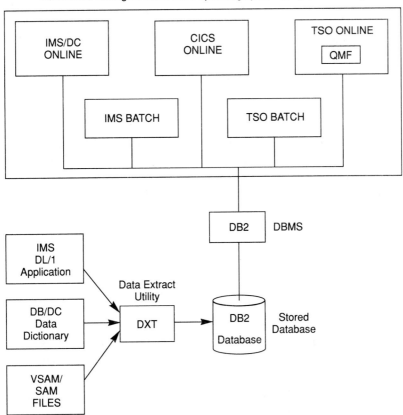

Transaction Managers under MVS operating system (only one needed)

Figure 23.1   An overview of the organization of DB2 System with
a partial view of supporting features.

users, both interactive and batch. The DB2 databases can be accessed by application programs written in COBOL, PL/1, FORTRAN, or IBM assembly language.

Figure 23.1 conveys the following information:

1. A DB2 application consisting of programs written in the above languages runs
   under the control of *exactly one* of the three subsystems—IMS, CICS, or TSO. The
   IMS, CICS, and TSO DB2 applications run distinctly. In fact, they are described in
   separate sets of manuals.

2. The same DB2 databases may be shared by IMS, CICS, and TSO applications. CSP
   (Cross Systems Product) allows an application developed under TSO to run under
   CICS and vice versa.

3. A given application of IMS, CICS, or TSO written to access DB2 databases is regarded as a DB2 interactive application.

4. Besides DB2 databases, IMS databases are also accessible from a DB2 application
   under the IMS or CICS environment but not under the TSO environment. The

same TSO application may be executed either as batch or on line by directing the I/O in the program to files or using terminals for I/O.

As shown in Figure 23.1, two other facilities called QMF and DXT play an important role in the use of DB2.

QMF (QUERY MANAGEMENT FACILITY): The QMF is a separate product from DB2 that acts as a query language and report writer. It simply runs as an on-line TSO application. It supports ad hoc querying in either SQL or QBE and displays the results of SQL or QBE queries as formatted reports. It can access both DB2 and SQL/DS databases. The output of QMF can be directed to other utilities to draw bar charts (with the Interactive Chart Utility) and other graphical data displays (with the Graphical Data Display Manager). Users interactively build forms to control the display of query results.

DXT (DATA EXTRACT): Data Extract is a utility program that extracts data from IMS databases or VSAM (Virtual Storage Access Method) or SAM (Sequential Access Method) files and converts it into a sequential file. DXT can specify extraction requests interactively or as batch jobs. This sequential file is in a format suitable for direct loading into a DB2 database. DXT is an independent IBM product.

RELATIONSHIP BETWEEN SQL/DS AND DB2: SQL/DS is a DB2-like relational DBMS that belongs to the "DB2 family." The data definition and manipulation facilities of the two systems are essentially the same, with only minor syntactic differences. Both systems use SQL as an interactive query language as well as a database programming language by embedding it in a host language (see Section 7.6). The QMF and DXT facilities may be used for both DB2 and SQL/DS. However, the physical storage of data in SQL/DS and DB2 is different. For example, concepts like DB2 tablespaces have no analog in SQL/DS. DB2 also supports specialized techniques for handling large databases and heavy workloads that are unique to the MVS operating system. Whereas DB2 provides an interactive SQL facility for end users via DB2I, SQL/DS is able to provide some end-user facilities via its ISQL (interactive SQL) component.

Organization of Data and Processes in DB2

Let us first see how DB2 databases are perceived by users and application programs. All data is viewed as relations or "tables," a legitimate DB2 term. Tables are of two types: *base tables*, which physically exist as stored data, and *views*, which are virtual tables without a separate physical identity in storage. The concept of views was introduced in Chapter 6 and their creation and processing using SQL were discussed in Section 7.4. Views work essentially the same way for DB2. A base table consists of one or more VSAM files.

APPLICATION PROCESSING: Figure 23.2 shows the preparation of a DB2 application in embedded SQL in a simplified manner. It indicates the sequence of processes through which a user application must pass in order to access a DB2 database. The major components of the SQL application flow are the precompiler, bind, run time supervisor,* and stored data manager. Briefly, they perform the following functions:

---

*The terms run time supervisor and stored data manager are not in DB2 manuals. They are adapted from Date (1986).

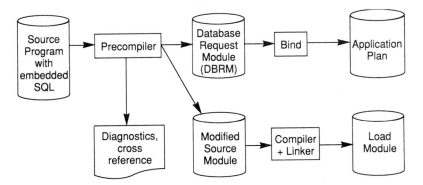

Figure 23.2   Application Preparation

- **Precompiler:** As discussed in Chapters 1 and 7, the job of the precompiler is to process embedded SQL statements in a host language program. The precompiler generates two kinds of output: the original source program, with the embedded SQL replaced by CALLs, and database request modules (DBRMs), which are collections of SQL statements in a parse tree form.

- **Bind:** This component accommodates both types of SQL requests: those arising in application programs to be executed over and over again and ad hoc queries that execute only once. For the first category, after performing a detailed analysis and query optimization as discussed in Chapter 18, one or more related DBRMs are compiled *only once* into an application plan. The cost of this binding is thus amortized across the repeated executions of the program and is found to be well justified. The bind process also permits an application to construct and submit a (dynamic) SQL statement for immediate execution. Bind parses all SQL statements. Whereas manipulative statements of SQL are bound to produce executable code, the definition, authorization, and control statements in SQL are parsed by bind and left in a form that is interpreted at run time.

- **Run time supervisor:** This refers to the services of DB2 that control the application execution at run time. The execution of an SQL call within an actual application program goes through the processing steps shown in Figure 23.3. When the load module of the application program is executing and comes to a CALL inserted by the precompiler, control goes to the run time supervisor via the appropriate language interface module of DB2. The run time supervisor retrieves the application plan, uses the control information in it, and requests that the stored data manager actually access the database.

- **Stored data manager:** This is the system component that manages the physical database. It includes what DB2 calls the Data Manager, as well as the Buffer Manager, Log Manager, etc. Together they perform all the necessary functions of dealing with the stored database—search, retrieve, update—as required by the application plan. This component appropriately updates the indexes. To get the best performance out of buffer pools, it employs sophisticated buffering techniques such as read-ahead buffering and look-aside buffering. The stored data manager is able to provide hashed and linked access to the system tables in the system cata-

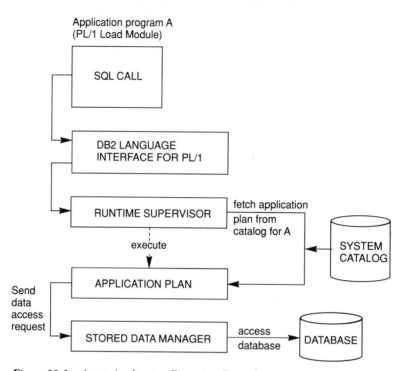

Figure 23.3   A PL/1 Application Execution Example in DB2

log. The data manager accesses data or indexes by supplying page identifiers to the buffer manager. The page size is 4096 bytes and corresponds to the page size of the operating system.

INTERACTIVE PROCESSING: DB2 also allows on-line users to access the database by using the DB2I (DB2 interactive) facility, which is an on-line application running under DB2. For an on-line user to establish communication with this on-line application, the services of a data communication (DC) manager must be used. In the case of a DB2 user wishing to gain such access, the (DC) manager function is performed by either the TSO component of MVS, the data communication facility DC of IMS, or the CICS—see Figure 23.1. DB2I accepts SQL statements from a terminal and passes them to DB2 for execution. Even during interactive execution, SQL is compiled and an application plan is generated for it; the results are passed back from the execution to the terminal. This plan is discarded after execution.

Other Related Functions for Compilation and Execution of SQL

Several functions are required during the compilation and execution of SQL queries or applications. We quickly review the more important ones below:

- Optimization: This function deals with the choice of an optimum access plan to implement an SQL retrieval or update request.

- Recompilation of application plans: Whenever an index is created or dropped using CREATE INDEX or DROP INDEX the corresponding application plan is marked "invalid" in the catalog by the run time supervisor. At a subsequent invocation of an invalid plan, the bind is invoked to recompile it using the then current set of indexes. This whole process of *automatic binding* is transparent to the user.

- Authorization checking: Bind also checks whether the user who invoked bind is allowed to perform the operations involved in the DBRM(s) to be bound. DB2 uses an authorization identifier of the requester to determine whether access privileges are allowed. IMS and CICS supply authorization identifiers and control their usage. TSO defaults to the user identifier. Each connecting environment tells DB2 its connection type through the IDENTIFY facility. To prevent unauthorized IDENTIFY requests, an installation can control who can connect to DB2 and what connection type they are permitted to use.

23.1.3   Data Definition in DB2

We covered the data definition facilities of SQL in Section 7.1. The definition facilities allow the creation, deletion, and alteration (when appropriate) of base tables, views, and indexes. The statements include:

FOR TABLES	FOR VIEWS	FOR INDEXES
CREATE TABLE	CREATE VIEW	CREATE INDEX
ALTER TABLE		ALTER INDEX
DROP TABLE	DROP VIEW	DROP INDEX

There is no ALTER VIEW statement. ALTER INDEX does exist but deals with the physical parameters of an index. In Chapter 7 (Figure 7.1) we showed a complete definition of a relational database in terms of CREATE TABLE statements, which applies to DB2. No ordering of tuples is explicitly imposed on base tables during creation. The ordering of columns is implicit by virtue of the order of the column names in the CREATE TABLE statement. However, this order is rarely significant during manipulation.

DB2 supports the following data types: INTEGER (31 bits and sign), SMALLINT (15 bits and sign, small integer), DECIMAL (t, d) with t the total number of digits and d the number of decimal positions, FLOAT (64 bits with a hexadecimal 15-digit fraction and a multiplier in the range 16^{-65} to 16^{64}), CHAR (up to a 255-byte string), VARCHAR (a variable character string whose length may be up to the page size).

DB2 supports the concept of null values. Any column can contain a null value unless the definition of that column in CREATE TABLE explicitly specifies **NOT NULL**. A column in which null values are allowed is physically represented in the stored database by two columns: the data column itself and a hidden indicator column 1 byte wide where a value of X'FF' means that the corresponding data value is to be ignored, i.e., is a null; an X'00' indicates that the corresponding value is a true (nonnull) value.

The System Catalog

In DB2 the tables called catalog are accessible via SQL for the database administrator or other authorized users, but the directory tables cannot be accessed via SQL; they are strictly for the system's use. The DB2 system catalog contains a variety of information including the definitions of base tables, views, indexes, applications, users, access privileges, and application plans, along the lines of what we discussed in Chapter 17. These descriptions are referred to by the system in order to perform certain tasks; for example, during query optimization the bind component accesses the catalog to obtain index information.

DB2 takes a uniform approach to storing the data and the catalog—both are stored as tables. Instead of giving an exhaustive description of the catalog, we will highlight its contents by referring only to a few important tables.

1. SYSTABLES: This has one entry for every base table in the system. The information for each table contains, among other things, its name, the name of the creator, and the total number of columns in the table.

2. SYSCOLUMNS: This contains one entry for every column (attribute) defined in the system. For every column name, the name of the table to which it belongs, its type, and other information are stored. The same column name may appear in multiple tables.

3. SYSINDEXES: This contains for each index the name of the index, the name of the indexed table, the name of the user who created the index, etc.

QUERYING CATALOG INFORMATION: Because the catalog is organized in terms of the tables, it can be queried using SQL just like any other table. For example, consider the query

```
SELECT   NAME
FROM     SYSTABLES
WHERE    COLCOUNT>5
```

This SQL query accesses the catalog to list the names of tables containing more than five columns.

The name of the creator for the catalog tables is SYSIBM. Hence, the complete name of a table like SYSTABLES is referenced as SYSIBM.SYSTABLES. The system automatically creates catalog entries for the catalog tables. Authorized users have access to the catalog for querying. Thus, those having SELECT privilege on system catalogs, if they are not familiar with the structure of the database, can query the catalog to find out more about it.

For example, the query

```
SELECT   TBNAME
FROM     SYSIBM.SYSCOLUMNS
WHERE    NAME='DNUMBER'
```

lists the names of tables DEPARTMENT and DEPT_LOCATIONS (see Figure 6.5) that contain the column DNUMBER. The availability to the user of the same SQL interface to access meta-data and not just data is an important facility of DB2.

UPDATING CATALOG INFORMATION: Whereas querying the catalog is informative as far as users are concerned, updating the catalog can be really devastating. For example, a routine SQL update request like

```
DELETE
FROM     SYSIBM.SYSTABLES
WHERE    CREATOR=NAVATHE
```

would remove all the tables created by NAVATHE in the catalog. As a result, the definitions of these tables do not exist any longer even though the tables still exist. The tables have essentially become inaccessible! To guard against such situations, UPDATE, DELETE, and INSERT operations are *not* permitted against the tables in the catalog. The corresponding functionality is offered by ALTER TABLE, DROP TABLE, and CREATE TABLE, respectively, which are the data definition statements in SQL. The SQL COMMENT statement serves the useful purpose of storing textual information about a table or a column in the catalog.

For example, referring back to the database definition in Figure 7.1, the statement "COMMENT ON COLUMN DEPENDENT.ESSN IS 'If dependent has both parents as employees, the dependent is represented twice.'" is stored in the appropriate REMARKS columns of the entry in the SYSCOLUMNS table.

23.1.4   Data Manipulation in DB2

SQL is the primary data manipulation language of DB2. In Chapter 7, we discussed a version of SQL that closely corresponds to its implementation in DB2. For quick reference, we list the types of retrievals and updates that are supported by DB2 SQL (the numbers refer to example queries in Chapter 7; additional explanations are given when necessary):

1. Simple retrievals from tables: (Q0).

2. Listing entire width of the table on rows meeting a prespecified condition: (Q1C).

3. Retrievals with elimination of duplicate rows: (Q11A).

4. Retrievals with computed values from columns: (Q15).

5. Ordering of the result of a query: (Q28).

6. Retrievals with conditions involving sets and ranges. These are effected with various types of constructors:

   a. Using IN: (Q13).
   b. Using BETWEEN (this is not discussed in Chapter 7): DB2 allows a construction with BETWEEN or NOT BETWEEN; e.g., "WHERE SALARY BETWEEN 50,000 AND 100,000" is permitted.
   c. Using LIKE: (Q25, Q26).
   d. Using NULL in comparisons: (Q14).

7. Multitable retrievals involving JOINS: (Q1, Q2, Q8, etc.).

8. Nested queries: The nesting can be achieved by passing the results of the inner subquery to the outer query using IN (see Q12, Q4A). In general, queries can be nested to any level. As demonstrated in Q4A, the inner and outer subqueries may refer to the same table.

9. Use of EXISTS: Existential quantification (Chapter 8) is supported by connecting two subqueries using EXISTS (Q7). Since there is no direct support for universal quantification, it is achieved by means of NOT EXISTS (Q3A) (see Section 8.2).

10. Use of built-in functions: The functions currently provided in DB2 SQL are COUNT, SUM, AVG, MAX, and MIN. EXISTS is also considered a built-in function, although instead of returning a numeric or string value it returns a truth value.

11. Grouping (Q20, Q21) and conditions on groups (Q22).

12. UNION: It is possible to take a union of the results of subqueries. The results must be union compatible (see Chapter 6 for definition). The facility to include strings in the SELECT statement comes in handy in conjunction with UNION in DB2. For example, to list people who worked more than 40 hours and those who worked on project P5:

> **SELECT** ESSN, 'worked more than 40 hours'
> **FROM** WORKS_ON
> **WHERE** HOURS>40
> **UNION**　　**SELECT** ESSN, 'worked on project P5'
> 　　　　　　**FROM** WORKS_ON
> 　　　　　　**WHERE** PNO = P5

The results may look like:

> 1000 worked more than 40 hours.
>
> 1002 worked more than 40 hours.
>
> 1003 worked more than 40 hours.
>
> 1002 worked on project P5.
>
> 1007 worked on project P5.

Note that, if there were no string constraints in the SELECT clause, the duplicate entity (1002) would have been eliminated.

13. CONTAINS, INTERSECTION, and MINUS: DB2 SQL does *not* support these operators. They must be handled using EXISTS and NOT EXISTS. Also, OUTER UNION is *not* supported in DB2.

14. Insertion: U1, U1A, U3B.

15. Deletion: Accomplished by using DELETE (U4A to U4D). To delete the definition of the table completely, a DROP TABLE must be used.

16. Modification: Accomplished using UPDATE (U5, U6).

EVALUATION OF SQL FACILITIES IN DB2:   In the foregoing discussion we listed the available features of the SQL language in DB2. The retrieval and updating operations apply to both base tables and views. In summary, the retrieval operations are quite extensive. The FORALL quantifier is not supported and must be handled using NOT EXISTS. Similarly, only set UNION is supported; other set operations must be supported by creating intermediate tables combined with the EXISTS built-in function.

Updating facilities in DB2 SQL have two shortcomings:

1. When an INSERT, DELETE, or UPDATE involves a subquery, the nested subquery cannot refer to the table that is the target of the operation. For example, to up-

date the value of hours in all rows to the average of hours, the following type of construction would be desirable. However, it is *not* permissible in DB2.

```
UPDATE   WORKS_ON
SET      HOURS=X
WHERE    X =  (  SELECT AVG(HOURS)
                 FROM   WORKS_ON )
```

(A construction that eliminates X by eliminating the WHERE clause and nests SELECT within UPDATE would be even better.) In actuality, the result is accomplished by first obtaining the average and then using that average to set up another query.

2. The second drawback, which is quite severe, is the absence of referential integrity constraints in DB2 (see Section 6.1.5). Because the DDL facility of SQL does not allow one to specify referential integrity constraints, the corresponding checks on insertion and deletion of tuples from relations involving these constraints are not carried out automatically by the system. Because the relationships between the foreign key values and the corresponding primary key values are not maintained, keeping the data consistent across relations becomes an application responsibility. This situation is likely to be corrected in the next version of DB2.*

View Processing

As discussed in Section 7.4, a view may be defined in DB2 by CREATE VIEW AS followed by an SQL query. The following points apply to view definition in DB2:

- A view definition may involve one or more tables; it may use joins as well as built-in functions.
- If column names are not specified in the view definition, they may be assigned automatically except when built-in functions, arithmetic expressions, or constraints are used.
- The SQL query used in view definition may not use UNION or ORDER BY.
- Views may be defined on top of existing views.
- When a view is defined using the clause WITH CHECK OPTION, an INSERT or UPDATE against such a view undergoes a check to see that the view-defining predicate is indeed satisfied. For example, in the following, the view-defining predicate is Balance > 500:

```
CREATE VIEW   CREDIT_WORTHY
AS  SELECT    CUST#, Name, Phone#
    FROM      CUST
    WHERE     BALANCE>500
WITH CHECK OPTION
```

---

*At the time of writing, referential integrity is not available in DB2.

RETRIEVALS FROM VIEWS: Views are treated like any base tables for specifying retrieval queries. Problems can occur when an attribute of the views is a result of a built-in function applied to an underlying base table. For example, consider the following view definition:

```
CREATE VIEW   DEPT_SUMMARY (D#, TOTSALARY)
AS            SELECT DNO, SUM(SALARY)
              FROM EMPLOYEE
GROUP BY   DNO
```

Now let us consider two queries:

• The query

```
SELECT   D#
FROM     DEPT_SUMMARY
WHERE    TOTSALARY > 100000
```

is *not* valid because after converting the WHERE clause it looks like WHERE SUM(SALARY) > 100,000, and a built-in function is *not* allowed in a WHERE clause. The correct conversion (can you write what it should be?) contains a HAVING clause, but DB2 cannot come up with such a converted query.

• The query

```
SELECT   SUM(TOTSALARY)
FROM     DEPT_SUMMARY
```

is *also invalid* because SUM(TOTSALARY) is equivalent to SUM(SUM(SALARY)), and DB2 does not allow a nested built-in function.

UPDATING OF VIEWS: We discussed view update problems in Section 7.4.3. DB2 has no facility to investigate what a user wants to do when he or she specifies a view update. In addition, there is no facility to analyze and determine whether a certain update provides a unique set of updates on the base relations. Therefore, it takes a rather restricted approach by allowing updates on only single-relation views. Furthermore, *even for single-relation views*, the following restrictions apply:

• A view is not updatable if (a) its definition involves a built-in function, (b) its definition involves DISTINCT in the SELECT clause, or (c) its definition includes a subquery and the FROM clause in that subquery refers to the base table on which the view is defined or (d) there is a GROUP BY in the view definition.

• If a field of the view is derived from an arithmetic expression or a constant, INSERT or UPDATE are *not* allowed; however, DELETE is allowed (since a corresponding row may be deleted from the base table).

Use of Embedded SQL

Embedded SQL has been covered in detail in Section 7.6. Here we give a few details regarding the use of embedded SQL in DB2. As we discussed, SQL can be embedded in PL/1, COBOL, FORTRAN, and assembly language programs.

- Any base tables or views used by the program should be declared by means of a DECLARE statement. This makes the program easy to follow, as well as helping the precompiler perform syntax checks.

- Embedded SQL statements must be preceded by EXEC SQL (we used '$' in Section 7.6) and are entered at a place where any host language *executable* statement can go.

- Embedded SQL may involve data definition facilities, such as CREATE TABLE and DECLARE CURSOR, that are purely declarative.

- SQL statements may reference host language variables preceded by colons (we used '%' in Section 7.6).

- Host variables that receive values from SQL must have data types compatible with the SQL field definitions. Compatibility is defined very loosely; e.g., character strings of varying length or numeric data of binary or decimal nature are considered compatible. DB2 performs appropriate conversions.

- SQL Communication Area (SQLCA) serves as the common feedback area between the application program and DB2. A status indicator SQLCODE contains a numeric value showing the result of a query (e.g., zero indicates successful completion, +100 indicates that the query executed but the result is null).

- No cursor is required for an SQL retrieval query that returns a single tuple or for UPDATE, DELETE, INSERT statements (except when the CURRENT OF a record is required—see Section 7.6).

- A special utility program called DCLGEN (declarations generator) may be used to construct DECLARE TABLE statements automatically in PL/1 from the CREATE TABLE definitions in SQL. PL/1 or COBOL structures to correspond to the table definitions are also automatically generated.

- The WHENEVER statement placed out of line allows the SQLCODE to be checked for a specific condition. Examples are:

WHENEVER   NOTFOUND PERFORM X;
WHENEVER   SQLERROR GO TO Y;

In the above, NOTFOUND and SQLERROR are system key words corresponding to SQLCODE = 100 and SQLCODE other than 0 or 100, respectively.

23.1.5   *Storage of Data in* DB2

A database in DB2 is a collection of logically related objects. These objects are the various physically stored tables and indexes. DB2 uses a special terminology to describe the partitioned areas of storage. **Tablespace** refers to the part of secondary storage where tables are stored and **indexspace** refers to the part where indexes are stored. Figure 23.4 shows a schematic of the DB2 storage structure. The total collection of data in a system consisting of user databases DBX and DBY and the system catalog database are shown.

A **page** is the basic unit of data transfer between secondary and primary storage. A dynamically extendible collection of pages is called a **space**. Each space belongs to a **storage group,** which is a collection of direct access storage areas from the same device

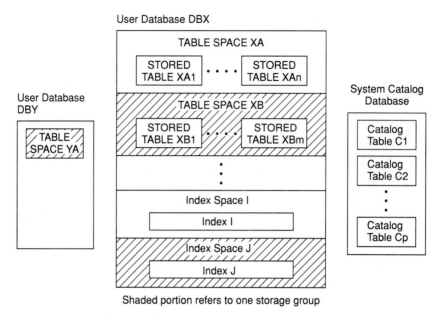

Figure 23.4   A schematic of DB2 storage structure

type. There is no 1:1 correspondence between a database and a storage group. In Figure 23.4 the same storage group contains an indexspace and tablespace from database DBX and a tablespace from database DBY. A **database** is a unit of **start/stop** that the console operator enables or disables via a START or STOP command. Tables can be moved from one database to another without any effect on the users or user programs.

Storage groups are managed using VSAM files (entry-sequenced data sets). Within a page, DB2 manages the reorganization without using VSAM at all. Views do not occupy corresponding storage. They can be defined over multiple tables from different databases. DB2 allows the DBA and the system administrator to specify the details of the storage structure using different statements. For each object described (e.g., table, tablespace, index, indexspace, database, storage group), the three statements used uniformly are CREATE, ALTER, and DROP. Users are *not* required to know about the internal storage organization in order to use the system. Although a tablespace is required to store a table, the system assigns a *default* tablespace when the creator of a table fails to specify one. A database is a logical entity whose physical components can be freely moved and manipulated without affecting the integrity of the database. CREATE TABLESPACE gives the database to which the tablespace belongs. In the remainder of this section we will elaborate further on the storage structure objects described above.

Tablespaces and Stored Tables

A tablespace for a given table is specified in the CREATE TABLE statement for that table. The page size in a tablespace is either 4096 or 32,768 bytes. A tablespace can grow in size by adding more storage from a storage group, with an upper limit of 64 billion bytes. A tablespace is the unit of storage subjected to reorganization or recovery by a console command. Since it would be very inefficient to manage a large tablespace in this way, DB2 allows tablespaces to be partitioned.

A nonpartitioned tablespace is called a **simple tablespace**. In most cases a simple tablespace holds one table. Multiple tables, say EMPLOYEE and DEPARTMENT, may be stored in the same tablespace to improve performance if there is a high probability that they will be accessed together. The index, if any, for a table goes into an indexspace. A table with a clustering index (see Chapter 5) is loaded initially into the tablespace in order by the key, using a load utility. Intermittent gaps are left to hold inserted records. Without a clustering index, records may be loaded in any order. Insertions go to the end of the file.

A **partitioned tablespace** contains one table partitioned into (grouped by) value ranges of some partitioning field(s). A clustering index is *required* on those fields and cannot be changed. Thus, the EMPLOYEE table may be partitioned using a clustering index on DNO. The advantage of partitioned tablespaces is that each partition is treated as a separate storage object for recovery and reorganization and may be associated with a different storage group.

Each row in a table is a **stored record**. It is a string of bytes comprising a prefix containing system control information and up to n stored fields, where n is the number of columns in the base table. Null fields at the end of a varying-length record are *not* stored. Internally, each record has a unique **record id (RID)** within a database; it consists of the page number and the byte offset from the start of the page of a slot that, in turn, contains the record's starting position within the page.

Each **stored field** comprises:

- A prefix field containing the length of data if it is varying (including the null indicator).
- A null indicator prefix that indicates whether the field contains a null value.
- An encoded data value.

DB2 has adopted a strategy of storing all data types in such a way that they are regarded as byte strings and the "compare logical" instruction always yields a correct result (even for data type INTEGER). The interpretation of byte strings is not the concern of the stored data manager. Varying fields occupy only the actual space required. Data compression or encryption is left open to a user-provided procedure, which may be interposed each time a stored record is read or stored. Records *within a page* can be reorganized without changing their RIDs.

Indexspaces and Indexes

An indexspace corresponds to the storage occupied by an index. It is automatically created. Indexpages are 4096 bytes long, but they can be locked a quarter page at a time. An indexspace that contains a clustering index for a partitioned tablespace is itself considered partitioned.

Indexes are B^+-trees (see Chapter 5) where each node is a page. The leaf pages are chained together to provide sequential access to the records (in the tablespace). A table may have one clustered and any number of nonclustered indexes. The leaf pages of a nonclustered index access the records of the tablespace in an order different from their physical ordering. Hence, for efficient sequential processing of a table, it is essential to have a clustered index.

23.1.6   Internal Features of DB2

In this section we summarize the features of DB2 related to security, authorization, and transaction processing.

Security and Authorization

In Chapter 20 we presented an overview of the security and authorization mechanisms. Most of the discussion there is pertinent to DB2. We discuss below a few details about the availability of these mechanisms in DB2. Generally speaking, security of data is addressed at two levels in DB2:

1. The view mechanism can be used to hide sensitive data from unauthorized users.
2. The authorization subsystem, which gives specific privileges to certain users, allows them to grant those privileges to other users selectively and dynamically and to revoke them at will.

The DB2 GRANT and REVOKE commands and the GRANT OPTION feature are discussed in Section 20.1. Specific considerations with respect to these commands that apply in DB2 are given below. The DBA or an appropriate administrator is entrusted with the decision of granting specific privileges to users and revoking the privileges. This policy decision may be conveyed to DB2 in the form of CREATE VIEW or the GRANT and REVOKE statements. This information resides in the system catalog. The system's responsibility is to enforce these decisions at run time when retrieval or update operations are attempted; this function is performed by the bind component (see Figure 23.2).

USER IDENTIFICATION: Legitimate users are known to DB2 in terms of an authorization ID (identifier) assigned by system administrators. It is the user's responsibility to use that ID when signing onto the system. Users of DB2 sign first on either CICS, IMS, or TSO; that subsystem passes on the ID to DB2. Hence, the responsibility for checking the user ID falls to one of these subsystems. The keyword USER refers to a system variable whose value is an authorization ID. If a certain user is using a view (for retrieval or update), the variable USER contains the ID of the user who is *using* the view and *not* the one who created it. Thus,

```
CREATE    VIEW OWN_TABLES
AS        SELECT  *
          FROM    SYSIBM.SYSTABLES
          WHERE   CREATOR=USER
```

is a view definition that selects the tables created by the presently logged in user. SYSIBM.SYSTABLES and CREATOR are keywords in DB2. If a user with ID sbn134 is logged on and executes the query

```
SELECT    *
FROM      OWN_TABLES
```

the USER in the view is bound to sbn134 and the result of the query is to retrieve from SYSTABLES the entries that were created by sbn134.

VIEWS AS A SECURITY MECHANISM: It is possible to use views for security purposes by blocking out unwanted data from unauthorized users. By choosing appropriate conditions in the WHERE clause as well as including only the columns in the SELECT clause that a user may be permitted to see, certain data can be kept hidden from a user. Views defined over system catalog information, such as the view illustrated above, permit a user to see only selected parts of the catalog. By applying aggregation functions such as AVG and SUM, a user may be shown a statistical summary of the base table and not individual values.

In DB2, when a record is INSERTED or UPDATED through a view, the requirement that the new or updated row in the table must obey the view-defining condition(s) or predicates is *not* enforced. This can potentially lead to a situation where the new or updated record disappears immediately from the user's view but appears in the underlying base table. To prevent such insertions or deletions, the CHECK OPTION should be used in the view definition.

GRANT AND REVOKE MECHANISMS: GRANT and REVOKE statements in SQL determine specific operations granted to or revoked from a user. The general discussion of Section 20.1 holds here. Privileges GRANTed to users may be classified in the following broad categories:

- Table and view privileges—apply to base tables and views.
- Database privileges—apply to operations with a database (e.g., creating a table).
- Application plan privileges—refer to execution of application plans.
- Storage privileges—deal with the use of certain storage objects, namely table-spaces, storage groups, and buffer pools.
- System privileges—apply to system operations such as creating a new database.

There are certain "bundled" privileges, a term that refers to a tailor-made assortment of privileges. They are:

- SYSADM (system administrator) privilege is the highest-order privilege and includes all possible privileges in the system.
- DBADM (database administrator) privilege on a specific database allows the holder to execute any operation on that database.
- DBACTRL (database control) privilege on a specific database is similar to DBADM except that only control operations and no data manipulation operations (e.g., in SQL) are allowed.
- DBMAINT (database maintenance) privilege on a specific database allows the holder to execute read-only maintenance operations (e.g., backup) on the database. It is a subset of the DBACTRL privilege.
- SYSOPR (system operator) privilege allows the holder to perform only console operator functions with no access to the database.

There is one authorization ID that has the SYSADM privilege, and it represents the system administration function. Other IDs may hold the SYSADM privilege, but that privilege may be revoked. PUBLIC is a system keyword and includes all authorizations IDs.

A few final notes on the way these features are implemented in DB2:

- A major performance benefit results from the fact that many authorization checks can be applied at the time of bind (compile time) instead of delaying them until execution time.

- DB2 works with various accompanying systems; together with them, it provides system security. The individual control mechanisms of MVS, VSAM, IMS, and CICS offer additional protection.

- The entire array of authorization and security mechanisms is optional. They may be disabled, permitting any users to have all types of access privileges.

Transaction Processing

We discussed the concept of transactions and the problems of recovery and concurrency control related to transaction processing in Chapter 19. Here we will describe only the features specific to DB2 and SQL.

First, let us use the embedded SQL example E2 from Section 7.6 and modify it to demonstrate how an actual transaction is written in DB2. We use PL/1 here, since DB2 does not accept PASCAL. The transaction is to give a raise R to an employee with social security number S.

```
TRANS1: PROC OPTIONS (MAIN);
EXEC SQL WHENEVER SQLERROR GO TO ERROR_PROC;
DCL S FIXED DECIMAL (9.0);
DCL R FIXED DECIMAL (7.2);
GET LIST (S, R);
EXEC SQL UPDATE EMPLOYEE
SET SALARY = SALARY + :R
WHERE SSN = :S;
EXEC SQL WHENEVER NOTFOUND GO TO PRINT_MSG;
COMMIT;
GO TO EXIT;
PRINT_MSG: PUT LIST ('EMPLOYEE', S, 'NOT IN DATABASE'); GO TO EXIT;
ERROR_PROC: ROLLBACK;
EXIT: RETURN;
END TRANS1;
```

In the above example, the transaction may fail if there is no employee with social security number S (NOTFOUND) or if SQLCODE returns a negative value (SQLERROR).

We may also insert checks into the program, such as making sure that the salary is not null, failure of which may cause the transaction to fail. The COMMIT operation signals a successful end of transaction; it instructs the transaction manager to commit the change to the database—i.e., to make it permanent, leaving the database in a consistent state. The ROLLBACK, on the other hand, signals an unsuccessful end of transaction. It instructs the transaction manager *not* to make any permanent change to the database but to leave it in the state it was in before this transaction execution began.

Note that a typical transaction may involve a number of retrievals and updates; however, there is *only one* COMMIT operation in the program, so either *all* changes are applied or *none* is applied. The ROLLBACK operation uses the log entries and appropriately restores an updated item to its previous value.

Every DB2 operation is executed in the context of some transaction. This includes those entered interactively through DB2I. An application consists of a series of transactions. Transactions *cannot* be nested inside one another.

COMMIT AND ROLLBACK IN DB2:   The DB2 DBMS is *subordinate* to the transaction manager (IMS, CICS, or TSO) under which it is running. It acts as one of the resource managers providing a service to the transaction manager. Hence, the following points must be noted:

- COMMIT and ROLLBACK are not database operations. They are instructions to the transaction manager, which is not part of the DBMS.

- If a transaction updates an IMS database and a DB2 database, either all of the updates (both to IMS and to DB2) should be committed or all should be rolled back.

- A "synchronization point" (abbreviated syncpoint) defines a point at which the database is in a consistent state. The beginning of a transaction, COMMIT, and ROLLBACK each establishes a syncpoint. Nothing else establishes a syncpoint.

- The COMMIT operation signals a successful end of transaction, establishes a syncpoint, commits all updates to the database made since the previous syncpoint, closes all open cursors, and releases all locks (with some exceptions).

- The ROLLBACK operation signals an unsuccessful end of transaction, establishes a syncpoint, closes all open cursors, and releases all locks (with some exceptions).

EXPLICIT LOCKING FACILITIES: DB2 supports a number of different lock types. The DB2 user is mainly concerned with the exclusive (X) and shared (S) locks. We discussed different kinds of locks and their uses in Section 19.4.1. Besides the internal locking mechanism, DB2 provides some explicit locking facilities. A transaction can issue the following statement:

LOCK TABLE <table-name> IN <mode-type> MODE;

The mode-type can be EXCLUSIVE or SHARE. The table-name must be a base table. An exclusive lock allows the transaction to lock the table entirely; the lock is released when the program (not the transaction) terminates. However, a shared lock allows other transactions to concurrently acquire a shared lock on the same table or part of the table. Until all shared locks are released, no exclusive lock may be acquired on the table or part of it.

This facility is provided to improve the efficiency of transactions that need to process a single large table (e.g., produce a listing of 10,000 employees from the employee table) by dispensing with the locking overhead of issuing and releasing individual record-level locks.

SUMMARY OF TRANSACTION PROCESSING AND CONCURRENCY CONTROL: DB2 uses the concept of transactions for all data manipulation, including those initiated from DB2I. Syncpoints are the border points between transactions when the database is in a consistent state. The COMMIT and ROLLBACK facilities discussed above apply to the TSO environment only. IMS and CICS environments use equivalent operations. Concurrency control is based on a locking protocol in DB2. Every record accessed by a transaction is locked with an S (shared) lock; if the transaction updates the record, the S lock is upgraded to an X (exclusive) lock.

Although this solves the basic concurrency problems, the possibility of deadlock remains. A negative SQLCODE value returned after an SQL operation that requests a lock signifies a deadlock. To break a deadlock, the transaction manager chooses one of the deadlocked transactions as a *victim*, rolls it back automatically, or requests that it roll itself back. This transaction will release all locks and will enable some other transaction to proceed.

Dynamic SQL

The dynamic SQL facility is designed exclusively for supporting on-line applications. In some applications where there is a great deal of variability, instead of writing a specific SQL query for every possible condition, it is much more convenient to construct parts of the SQL query dynamically (at run time) and then to bind and execute them dynamically. This process occurs when SQL statements are interactively entered through DB2I or QMF. However, we will consider how *embedded* SQL statements are constructed dynamically. Without getting into the details of the syntax, we will outline this facility.

A character string is defined in the host language with some initial content:

DCL QSTRING CHAR (256) VARYING INITIAL
'DELETE FROM EMPLOYEE WHERE CONDITION'.

An SQL variable (SQLVARBL below) is declared to hold the SQL query at run time:

EXEC SQL **DECLARE** SQLVARBL STATEMENT;

The QSTRING will be appropriately modified by changing, say, the WHERE part of the query from the terminal. The following PREPARE statement would cause the QSTRING to be precompiled, bound, converted into object code, and stored in SQLVARBL:

EXEC SQL **PREPARE** SQLVARBL FROM :QSTRING;

Finally, the EXECUTE statement actually executes this compiled code:

EXEC SQL **EXECUTE** SQLVARBL;

Note that PREPARE accepts all the different SQL statements except an EXEC SQL. Statements to be prepared may not contain references to host variables. However, they may contain parameters that are denoted by question marks. The parameter values are supplied at run time via program variables. For example, suppose the WHERE condition in QSTRING in the above example was replaced by "SALARY >? AND SALARY <?"; then EXEC SQL EXECUTE SQLVARBL USING :LOW_LIMIT, :UPPER_LIMIT would substitute the value of *program variables* LOW_LIMIT and HIGH_LIMIT in place of the two question marks, respectively.

This discussion pertains to SQL statements that do not return any data to the program. When data values have to be retrieved via a SELECT statement that is generated dynamically, the program typically does not know about such variables in advance. Hence, that information is supplied dynamically using another dynamic SQL statement called DESCRIBE. The description of expected results is returned in an area called SQL Descriptor Area (SQLDA). Storage is allocated for such variables using the host programming language. Finally, the result is retrieved a row at a time using cursor operations. Updating of the results using the CURRENT option is also supported.

23.2 A Hierarchical System—IMS

23.2.1 Introduction

In this section we survey a major hierarchical system, Information Management System, or IMS. Although IMS essentially implements the hypothetical hierarchical data model described in Chapter 10, there are many features peculiar to this complex system. We highlight the architecture and special types of view processing and storage structures in IMS and compare DL/1, IMS's data language, with the HDML of Chapter 10.

IMS is one of the earliest DBMSs and it ranks as the dominant system in the commercial market for support of large-scale accounting and inventory systems. IBM manuals refer to the full product as IMS/VS (Virtual Storage) and, typically, the full product is installed under the MVS operating system. IMS DB/DC is the term used for installations that utilize the product's own subsystems to support the physical database (DB) and to provide data communications (DC).

However, other important versions exist, in terms of the numbers of installations, which support only the IMS data language (DL/1). Such DL/1-only configurations can be implemented under MVS, but a more common form is seen with installations that use the DOS/VSE operating system. These systems issue their calls to VSAM files and use IBM's Customer Information Control System (CICS) for data communications. The trade-off is a sacrifice of support features for the sake of simplicity and improved through put.

The original IMS/360 Version 1 product was introduced by IBM in 1968 following a joint development project with North American Rockwell. A number of major revisions to IMS have followed. Along with enhancements to the basic functionality, these have incorporated or accommodated major technological advances as they came along: modern communications networking, direct record access (augmented "fast path"), and secondary indexes among others. IMS development now embodies several thousand man-years of effort, much of that driven by the needs of an articulate user community.

IMS has no built-in query language, which can be seen as a major shortcoming. Partial responses to this situation appeared early-on with IBM's IQF (interactive query facility) and other add-on products sold by vendors or developed by users. One common and high-flexibility solution, today, is to down-load information from the typically enormous IMS database to a separate relational system. Then, with relevant summary data moved to a microcomputer or the mainframe's SQL/DS, individual corporate entities can carry out their own information system functions.

A number of versions of IMS have been marketed to work with various IBM operating systems including OS/MFT, OS/MVT, OS/VS1, OS/VS2, and MVS. The system comes with a variety of options, not all of which will be covered. IMS runs under different versions on the IBM 370 and 30XX family of computers. The data definition and manipulation language of IMS is Data Language One, or DL/1. Application programs written in COBOL, PL/1, FORTRAN, and BAL (Basic Assembly Language) interface with DL/1.

System 2000 (S2K) is another popular hierarchical system that follows a different version of the hierarchical data model. It operates on a wide range of systems including IBM 360/370, 43XX, and 30XX models, UNIVAC 1100 series, CDC 6000 series, and CYBER 70 and 170 series. System S2K can be configured with options such as a nonprocedural query language for nonprogrammers, a procedural language interface to COBOL, PL/1, and FORTRAN, a sequential file processing capability, and a teleprocessing monitor. In the rest of this section, we describe various aspects of IMS.

23.2.2   Basic Architecture of IMS

Figure 23.5 shows the internal organization of IMS in terms of various layers of definitions and mappings. IMS uses its own terminology, which is sometimes confusing or misleading.

A stored hierarchy in IMS is called a **physical data base (PDB)**. For a given installation, the data in the database will comprise several physical databases. Each physical database has a data definition or a schema written in DL/1. IMS calls this definition a DBD,

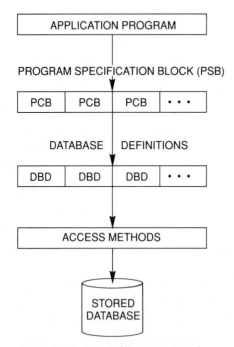

Figure 23.5   Internal Organization of IMS

for *data base description*. The compiled form of a DBD is stored internally; it includes information on how the database definition is mapped into storage and what access methods are applicable.

IMS provides a view facility that is fairly complex. A view can be defined by choosing part of a physical database or by choosing parts of a number of physical databases and interlinking them into a new hierarchy. We shall refer to these as type 1 and type 2 views, respectively. (Note that the type nomenclature is our own.)

A type 1 view is a subhierarchy and is defined by means of a **Program Communication Block** or PCB. A type 2 view must be defined in DL/1 in terms of a *logical DBD*. The resulting structure is called a **logical database (LDB)**. Physical and logical databases are discussed in Section 23.2.3.

A user application program needs to access data from several isolated physical databases or from type 1 or type 2 views. In high-volume on-line transaction systems, re-entrant data access modules are used. All the data descriptions needed by an application are packaged in a **Program Specification Block** or PSB. A PSB contains different chunks of description, corresponding to type 1 or type 2 view definitions. These chunks are stored as Program Communication Blocks. *Each application must have a distinct PSB, even though it may be identical to another PSB.* The application program in COBOL, PL/1, FORTRAN, or BAL invokes DL/1 via a call to get IMS to service a retrieval or update operation. The IMS system in turn communicates with the user via the PCB, which is (defined in the application program as) an area addressable via a pointer passed to the program. Current status information is posted to the PCB. The data manipulation language of IMS is also DL/1; it will be compared in Section 23.2.4 to the HDML of Chapter 10. IMS mainly supports five access methods, HSAM, HISAM, HDAM, HIDAM, and MSDB, which in turn use the built-in access methods of the operating system to manage various files. We shall review them briefly in Section 23.2.4.

Figure 23.6 shows how two applications called SALES and GENERAL LEDGER may actually share underlying physical databases in IMS via DBDs, PCBs, and PSBs.

23.2.3 *Logical Organization of Data in* IMS

The data model concepts we introduced in Chapter 10 are sufficient to describe IMS databases with some minor differences of nomenclature. Primarily, records are called as segments, and relationships are distinguished into physical and logical (instead of real and virtual). The terminology of Chapter 10 is cross-referenced with that of IMS and System 2000 in Table 23.1.

Physical Databases

An IMS physical database (PDB) refers to the hierarchy that is actually stored. It is defined in the form of a physical DBD using the DL/1 language. Figure 23.7 shows the definition of a physical database that corresponds to the hierarchy shown in Figure 10.5. It contains six segment types, each of which can have an arbitrary number of occurrences in the database. For the schema of Figure 10.10 we would need to use two physical database definitions. The definition of the virtual parent-child relationships shown in Figure 10.10 is included in both of these physical DBDs and is quite complicated.

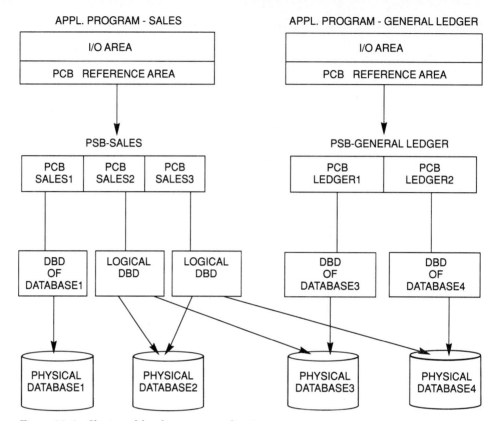

Figure 23.6   Sharing of data by two IMS applications

We make the following important points about the database definition:

- The database description is written in terms of the macros DBD, SEGM, FIELD, DBD-GEN, FINISH, and END. The SEGM macro defines a segment and the FIELD macro defines a field. Other macro names are self-explanatory.

- Each macro uses certain key words. The hierarchical logical structure of the database is defined by virtue of the "PARENT =" specifications of the segments.

- The order of occurrence of the SEGM statements is the means of ordering of segments within the logical schema. This top-to-bottom left-to-right ordering is significant. Changing this ordering yields a *different* physical database.

- A sequence field (optionally) designates a field within a segment type by which its occurrences may be ordered. The specific value of a sequence field is called the key of that segment occurrence.

- Sequence fields may be unique, which is the default, or nonunique. To designate a nonunique sequence field, one uses M (for multiple) in the FIELD definition as: FIELD NAME = (PARTNAME, SEQ.M), ...

- A unique sequence field is required for the root segment if the database is stored

Table 23.1 Hierarchical Model Terminology

Chapter 10 Term	IMS Term	System 2000 Term
1. Record type	Segment type	Repeating group record
2. Record occurrence	Segment occurrence	Record occurrence
3. Field or data Item	Field	Data item
4. Sequence field as key	Sequence field	Key
5. Parent-child relationship type	Physical parent-child relationship type	Hierarchical schema relationship
6. Virtual parent-child relationship type	Logical parent-child relationship type	Not provided except at run time
7. Hierarchical database schema	Physical or logical database definition (done in DBD)	Schema tree
8. Root of hierarchy	Root segment	Root record
9. Occurrence tree of a hierarchy	Physical database record	Data tree
10. Hierarchical record sequence	Hierarchical sequence	No special term
11. Pointer record type	Pointer segment type	No similar concept

using HISAM and HIDAM (see Section 23.2.5) because this provides an index key for the primary index.

- Combinations of two or more fields are recognized as new fields. This allows a combination of fields to be treated as a composite key. For example, STATENAME, CITYNAME may together be given a new field name, say SCNAME, which can be defined as a sequence field.

A number of concepts introduced in Chapter 10 apply directly to the physical databases. They are quickly reviewed below in the context of IMS. An occurrence tree is called a **physical database record**. It contains all the data in the *occurrence tree*. The linearized form of an occurrence tree within a physical database record is produced by a *preorder traversal* of the segment occurrences (see Section 10.1.4). The sequence of segments from any segment up to the root by going through a series of successive parent segments is called its **hierarchical path**. A concatenation of keys (including segment type codes) along this path leading up to a segment is called the **hierarchical sequence key** of that segment. The hierarchical sequence key of a DEPENDENT occurrence in a physical database record for the database of Figure 10.5 may be

1 | '000005' | 2 | '369278157' | 4 | 'JOHN...'.

Here 1, 2, and 4 are respectively the segment type codes of DEPARTMENT, EMPLOYEE, and DEPENDENT, assigned automatically by IMS, and '000005', '369278157', and 'JOHN...' are sequence keys along the hierarchical path up to that segment occurrence for JOHN.

```
 1 DBD   NAME = COMPANY
 2 SEGM NAME = DEPARTMENT, BYTES = 28
 3 FIELD NAME = DNAME, BYTES = 10, START = 1
 4 FIELD NAME = (DNUMBER, SEQ), BYTES = 6, START = 11
 5 FIELD NAME = MGRNAME, BYTES = 3, START = 17
 6 FIELD NAME = MGRSTARTDATE, BYTES = 9, START = 20

 7 SEGM  NAME = EMPLOYEE, PARENT = DEPARTMENT, BYTES = 79
 8 FIELD NAME = NAME, BYTES = 31, START = 1
 9 FIELD  NAME = (SSN, SEQ), BYTES = 9, START = 32
10 FIELD NAME = BDATE, BYTES = 9, START = 41
11 FIELD NAME = ADDRESS, BYTES = 30, START = 50

12 SEGM NAME = DEPENDENT, PARENT = EMPLOYEE, BYTES = 25
13 FIELD NAME = (DEP_NAME, SEQ), BYTES = 15, START = 1
14 FIELD NAME = SEX, BYTES = 1, START = 16
15 FIELD NAME = BIRTHDATE, BYTES = 9, START = 17

16 SEGM NAME =  SUPERVISEE, PARENT = EMPLOYEE, BYTES = 24
17 FIELD NAME = NAME, BYTES = 15, START = 1
18 FIELD NAME = SSN, BYTES = 9, START = 16

19 SEGM NAME =  PROJECT, PARENT = DEPARTMENT, BYTES = 16
20 FIELD NAME = PNAME, BYTES = 10, START = 1
21 FIELD NAME = (PNUMBER, SEQ), BYTES = 6, START = 11

22 SEGM NAME = WORKER, PARENT = PROJECT, BYTES = 26
23 FIELD NAME = NAME, BYTES = 15, START = 1
24 FIELD NAME = (SSN, SEQ), BYTES = 9, START = 16
25 FIELD NAME = HOURS, BYTES = 2, START = 25
26 DBDGEN
27 FINISH
28 END
```

Figure 23.7   Physical database definition for hierarchy for Figure 10.5

The physical database records in an IMS database occur in sequence by the key of its root segment. Within a physical database record, the segments occur in ascending order of their hierarchical sequence key.

Type 1 Views in IMS—Subsets of Physical Databases

IMS allows two kinds of views, or "logical databases"* (an IMS term) to be constructed from physical databases. For easy reference we call them type 1 and type 2 logical databases, or type 1 and type 2 views, which is our own nomenclature. Incidentally, addition-

---

*IMS uses the term logical database loosely with two meanings corresponding to the two types of views. A logical database or LDB is, however, defined only for the virtual hierarchy or type 2 view.

al confusion arises in IMS because only type 2 views are actually defined with a logical database definition; type 1 views are defined using a PCB.

A type 1 logical database schema defines a *subhierarchy* of a physical database schema by observing these rules:

1. The root segment type must be part of the view.
2. Nonroot segment types may be omitted.
3. If a segment type is omitted, all its children segment types must be omitted.
4. From the segments that are included any field type may be omitted.

For example, a large number of type 1 views can be defined for the database of Figure 10.5. Two valid type 1 views are shown in Figure 23.8a. They are meaningful for two different applications. The one deals with dependents and the other deals with workers who work on projects.

Two other subhierarchies are also shown in Figure 23.8b. In the first, the EMPLOYEE segment is omitted but its child segment is included. This violates rule 3 above. In the second subhierarchy, the root segment DEPARTMENT is omitted, which violates rule 1. Hence both of these subhierarchies are invalid views in IMS. Every type 1 hierarchy is defined by means of a PCB. The PCB for the DEPENDENT_VIEW in Figure 23.8a is shown in Figure 23.9.

As shown, the PCB includes the important PCB, SENSEG, and SENFLD macro statements. The KEYLEN parameter in PCB (statement 1) specifies the total maximum length of the concatenated (hierarchical sequence) key (excluding segment type codes) needed by the subhierarchy.

A SENSEG (sensitive segment) statement includes a segment in its entirety in the subhierarchy and declares a processing option—PROCOPT—for it. The allowable options are G (get), I (insert), D (delete), and R (replace) or a combination such as GIR.

A processing option of K (key sensitivity) is assigned to a segment when one wishes to exclude access to it but is forced to include it in the view because of rule 3 above. IMS *automatically suppresses the delivery of such data* to the application program. Observe its use in statement 4 in Figure 23.9. As a result, a user cannot see the EMPLOYEE data but is allowed to retrieve department and dependents as well as to insert data on new de-

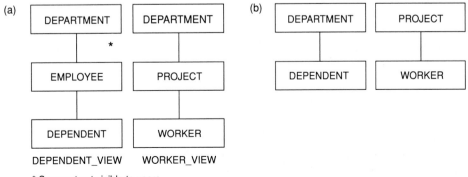

* Segment not visible to users

Figure 23.8   Type1 views in IMS on the database in Figure 10.5.
(a) Two Valid Views. (b) Two Invalid Views.

```
1 PCB            DBNAME=COMPANY, KEYLEN=30
2 SENSEG         NAME=DEPARTMENT, PROCOPT=G
3 SENFLD         NAME=DNAME, START=1
4 SENSEG         NAME=EMPLOYEE, PARENT=DEPARTMENT, PROCOPT=K
5 SENSEG         NAME=DEPENDENT, PARENT=EMPLOYEE, PROCOPT=GI
6 PSBGEN         LANG=PL/1, PSBNAME= PERSON_PSB
7 END
```

Figure 23.9   PCB definition of a type1 view of the COMPANY
physical database

pendents. The latter requires the hierarchical sequence key of DEPENDENT, and hence knowledge of the parent EMPLOYEE segment is mandatory.

This view facility accomplishes the usual objectives of selective access to only the relevant portion of a database and provides a certain amount of security. When the PRO-COPT specification allows updates, the corresponding change allows updates to the "base" physical record. This is governed by a complicated set of rules in IMS and may lead to inconsistencies if not done properly. The PCB is included in a program specification block named in the PSBGEN macro statement. Thus one PSB for a given application may include several PCBs that correspond to several type 1 views.

Type 2 Views in IMS over Multiple Physical Databases

This facility in IMS is a true view facility in that it allows one to create views that are virtual hierarchies. A **virtual hierarchy** consists of segments, some of which are connected by *logical parent-child relationships* (an IMS term)—we called them virtual parent-child relationships (VPCRs) in Chapter 10. By setting up logical relationships among segments from different physical databases it is possible to create a complex network. The type 2 view facility allows us to carve out any hierarchies from such a network. In Figure 23.10 we show two virtual hierarchies based on the hierarchies of Figure 10.10.

Type 2 views must be defined explicitly in IMS as logical databases (LDBs) using the DBD macro and with ACCESS = LOGICAL (see Figure 23.11).

In Figure 23.11 we define the virtual hierarchy called Manager_View of Figure 23.10a as a logical database. A pointer segment type in IMS corresponds to the pointer record type of Chapter 10. A pointer segment concatenated with its logical parent is declared as if it is a single segment of the virtual hierarchy. We assume that D_HIERARCHY and E_HIERARCHY are the names of the corresponding physical databases. The segment definitions in statements 3 and 4 describe how the DEPT and MGR segments in the logical database are composed from the original (SOURCE =) segment(s) from the respective databases. The logical parent-child relationships may be implemented using a variety of pointer options, which are mentioned while defining the original physical database.

Various rules govern logical parent-child relationships and the construction of logical databases from physical databases. Among the more important ones are:

1. The root of an LDB must be the root of some PDB.

2. A logical child segment must have one physical and only one logical parent. As a consequence, a root segment *cannot* be a logical child segment.

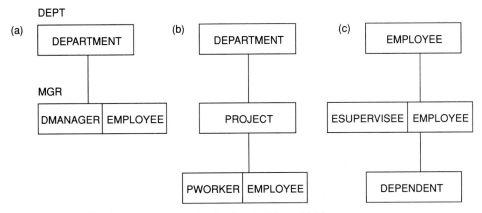

Figure 23.10 Type2 views in IMS on the database in Figure 10.10.
(a) Manager_View. (b) Project_View. (c) Dependent_View.

3. A physical child of a logical parent may appear as a dependent of a concatenated (logical child/logical parent) segment in the LDB. By virtue of this facility we can create a logical database from Figure 10.10 as shown in Figure 23.10c, which shows the use of an EMPLOYEE segment type twice (once as a supervisor and once as a supervisee) in the same logical database. This makes the tracking of currencies of segments even more difficult than we indicated in Section 10.4. This feature is a very powerful one in IMS and expands the scope of generating new hierarchies a great deal.

4. A logical parent segment type may have multiple logical child segment types. This is already seen for the EMPLOYEE segment in Figure 10.10.

Views in IMS versus Views in Relational Systems

We saw two types of view definitions or external schema facilities in IMS. Type 1 allowed views over single hierarchies; type 2 allowed views over multiple hierarchies. Let us compare this view facility with the views in relational systems:

1. A relational view does not have to be contemplated at the time of defining a conceptual schema or a set of base relations. In contrast, the definition of PDBs

```
1 DBD  NAME = MANAGER_VIEW   ACCESS = LOGICAL
2 DATASET LOGICAL
3 SEGM  NAME = DEPT, SOURCE = (DEPARTMENT, D_HIERARCHY)
4 SEGM  NAME = MGR, PARENT = DEPT,
  SOURCE = ((DMANAGER, D_HIERARCHY),
  (EMPLOYEE, E_HIERARCHY))
5 DBDGEN
6 FINISH
7 END
```

Figure 23.11 Database Description (DBD) of a Logical Database
MANAGER_VIEW from Figure 23.10

is determined by what LDBs need to use them. The IMS type 2 views are therefore not purely external schemas; they influence and determine the definition of the conceptual schema. The spirit of the three-schema architecture (see Section 2.2.1) is thus *not* fully maintained.

2. Relational views do not assume any physical access structure to support the views. IMS type 2 views, in contrast, require explicit definitions of pointers to link segments from multiple PDBs. The feasible LDBs are restricted by the types of pointers declared in the physical database(s).

3. The definition of a type 1 view is compulsory for an application to access a physical (or a logical) database. Even if the entire physical database is accessed by one application, a PCB (type 1 view) must be defined for it. In fact, a PCB is still required on top of an LDB to access it. There is no corresponding requirement in relational systems.

The type 2 view facility is a useful feature that extends the capabilities of IMS as follows:

- It allows a limited network facility by allowing two segments to have an M:N relationship via a common child pointer segment. N-ary relationships with N > 2 are *not* possible, unlike the situation in the network model.

- It reduces redundant storage of data. Correspondingly, updates may also be saved.

- Most important, it allows users to view the data in a variety of hierarchical ways besides the rigidly defined physical database hierarchies. This is done by combining segments from multiple existing hierarchies.

Unfortunately, the physical and logical database definitions, different types of pairing of segments—physical and virtual—in "bidirectional relationships," coupled with the complicated loading procedures for logical databases make type 2 views a very complex feature of IMS. We have left out a number of details in this discussion. It appears that some IMS installations do without the use of logical databases and are satisfied with just using physical databases.

23.2.4   *Data Manipulation in* IMS

Data manipulation operations in IMS closely parallel the HDML operations of Chapter 10. DL/1 includes the data manipulation language (DML) of IMS as well as the data definition language (DDL). We will not describe the detailed language syntax here. Instead we will show how DL/1 applications interface with IMS and will point out a few special features of DL/1.

Calls to DL/1 are embedded in an IMS application program written in COBOL, PL/1, System 360/370 basic assembly language, or FORTRAN. This call has the following syntax:

CALL <procedure name> (<parameter list>).

The procedure name to be called varies depending on the language in which the application program is written. A PL/1 program must use the name PL1TDL1 (for PL/1 to DL/1), which is fixed. Suppose we need to obtain the following information in IMS by using the PCB in Figure 23.9:

Query: "Obtain a list of dependents born after JAN-01-1980 for the employees in the departments with DNUMBER = 4".

A call to DL/1 would be coded as

CALL PL1TDL1 (SIX, GU, PCB_1, DEPND_IO_AREA, DEPT,D_SSA, EMPL_SSA, DEPND_SSA.)

This call appears in the application program assumed to be in PL/1. The parameter list is interpreted as follows:

- SIX refers to a variable containing the string 'SIX'. It indicates the number of remaining parameters in the list. Different queries can have different numbers of parameters.

- GU represents a variable containing the string 'GU', which stands for the operation to be performed—in this case, "get unique."

- PCB_1 is the name of the structure defined in the PL/1 program that acts as a mask to address an area called the program communication block (PCB). It is the common area through which information is passed back and forth between IMS and the application program. Among other things, it includes a hierarchy level indicator, the processing options in effect (based on the PROCOPT key word in the PCB; see Figure 23.9), the current segment name, the current hierarchical sequence key (this is the database record indicator of section 10.4.2), and the number of sensitive segments for the corresponding PCB definition. The internal structure of the various components within the PCB area is fixed.

- DEPND_IO_AREA is a 25-byte input-output area reserved in the program to receive the entire DEPENDENT segment as defined in the PCB of Figure 23.9, line 5.

- D_SSA, EMPL_SSA, and DEPND_SSA are segment search arguments, one per query. They stand for variable-containing strings that specify the search conditions for that statement. In our example the three strings would contain 'DEPARTMENT (DNUMBER = '000004')', 'EMPLOYEE', and 'DEPENDENT(BDATE > 'JAN-01-1980')', respectively.

As an IMS application program can have a number of PCBs, a separate PCB area would be defined in the program to address the information in each PCB. Observe that the PCB refers to the definition in DL/1 as shown in Figure 23.9, which represents the application's view of a database. The PCB communication area is defined as a part of the application program with a name; PCB_1 is the name of such area in the above call. Unfortunately, both of these are referred to as PCBs in IMS usage. At run time, IMS passes appropriate pointers to the relevant PCBs to a given program, which then becomes addressable by a name the program uses in making calls to DL/1.

In the HDML language of Chapter 10, the effect of the above CALL would be to do the following query:

GET FIRST PATH DEPARTMENT, EMPLOYEE, DEPENDENT
WHERE DNUMBER = '000004' AND DEPENDENT.BDATE > 'JAN-01-1980'

The only difference is that in HDML we assumed that this would retrieve data for each of the segments; in IMS, with the Get Unique command, *only* the DEPENDENT segment (the terminal node of the path) is fetched into memory.

CALL Interface versus Embedded Query Language Interface

The above scenario demonstrates the use of a parameterized 'CALL interface' between a high-level programming language such as PL/1 and the DBMS. This should be contrasted with the embedded query language interface exemplified by the use of SQL in relational systems (see Section 7.6 and 23.1.4). The advantages of a CALL interface are:

1. The compiler for the host language remains unchanged; hence no precompilation is necessary.
2. The application program looks homogeneous; there is no intervention of any foreign syntax.

The main disadvantages are:

1. The positional parameters in a CALL can easily be interchanged or omitted.
2. By looking at a CALL statement, it is impossible to judge the embedded data retrieval update operations. Hence application programs become difficult to read.
3. There are no semantic checks on the parameters in a CALL. Hence errors may surface later at execution time without being detected at compile time.

In our opinion the CALL interface may be convenient for the implementer but it is not desirable for application development.

Table 23.2 summarizes the correspondence between the operations proposed in HDML and those that exist in DL/1. The DL/1 operations are invoked using the CALL facility described above. In Chapter 10 we used a different notation where the HDML commands were embedded in PASCAL programs and the search conditions were written with a WHERE clause. This distinction must be kept in mind while reading this table. We offer below a few additional explanations corresponding to the notes in Table 23.2.

- *Note 1:* Each time a hierarchy is processed, in general, IMS requires that the first command be a Get Unique (GU), which must address a hierarchical path in the hierarchy starting with the root. Accessing segments within the hierarchy directly is not possible. (Exceptions exist but are beyond the scope of this discussion.)

- *Note 2:* Get Unique in DL/1 is used to account for GET FIRST as well as GET FIRST PATH of HDML. For Examples 1, 2, and 3 of Section 10.4, GU of DL/1 would work exactly like GET FIRST of HDML. Example 4 of Chapter 10 is shown in DL/1 plus a host language below (in a pseudosyntax *without* coding as an exact CALL). This query retrieves employee-dependent pairs where both have the first name John. The segment search arguments (e.g., "EMPLOYEE*D (FNAME = 'JOHN')") are shown next to the operation for notational convenience.

```
GU EMPLOYEE *D (FNAME = 'JOHN')
    DEPENDENT (DEPNAME = 'JOHN')
   while DB_STATUS = 'segment found' do
```

Table 23.2   Operations Proposed in HDML (Chapter 10) and Those Existing in IMS DL/1

HDML Operation	DL/1 Operation	Meaning
Get First (GF)	Get Unique (GU)	Get the first occurrence of a specified record (*see Note 1*)
Get Next (GN)	Get Next (GN)	Get the next occurrence of a specified record
Get First Path	Get Unique (GU) plus command code *D	Get the first occurrence of all records along a hierarchical path (*see Note 2*)
Get Next Path	Get Next within Parent (GNP) or Get Next (GN)	Get the next occurrence of a specified hierarchical path (*see Note 3*)
Get Next within Parent	Get Next within Parent (GNP)	Get the next child occurrence for the current parent occurrence
Get Next within Virtual Parent	No special operation	Get the next child occurrence for the current virtual parent occurrence (*see Note 3*)
INSERT	INSERT (ISRT)	Insert new record occurrence
DELETE	DELETE (DLET)	Delete old record occurrence
REPLACE	REPLACE (REPL)	Replace current record occurrence with a new occurrence
Get with Hold	Get Unique with Hold (GHU) Get Next with Hold (GHN) Get Next within Parent with Hold (GHNP)	Perform a corresponding GET operation with a hold on the record so that it can be subsequently replaced or deleted

```
begin
     WRITE EMPLOYEE NAME, EMPLOYEE BIRTHDATE, DEPENDENT
          BIRTHDATE
     GN EMPLOYEE *D (FNAME = 'JOHN')
          DEPENDENT (DEPNAME = 'JOHN')
end;
```

The *D for data in the above example is called a **command code**. Note that Get Next with a *D produces the same effect as Get Next Path in HDML. It would be possible in DL/1 to code the above without using *D. In that case, instead of the entire path, only the terminal segment (DEPENDENT in the above example) would be retrieved.

- *Note 3:* There are no special commands in IMS for processing the virtual ("logical" in IMS) parent-child relationships, because virtual relationships *cannot be processed directly without defining a logical database.*

A few additional observations comparing DL/1 with HDML are in order. The hold option was demonstrated for HDML in Example 10 of Section 10.4. It applies to all forms of the GET operation in IMS. We did not introduce the idea of defining new (virtual) hierarchies out of predefined hierarchies connected by virtual parent-child relationships in Chapter 10. We showed how the VPCRs may be processed directly in HDML. That entire discussion does *not* apply to IMS. It is *mandatory* to create logical databases in order to process logical parent-child relationships in IMS. The processing of retrievals for an LDB is the same as for a PDB. However, insertions and modifications to LDBs are more involved as they affect the underlying PDBs. We shall not discuss them here.

The while .. do .. end loops shown in the PASCAL plus HDML examples in Section 10.4 were controlled by a DB-STATUS code. Loops must be explicitly coded in the same way in the host language for IMS. Status code is available as part of the PCB area.

IMS provides a command code *F that allows an application to search in the hierarchy to determine whether a condition is satisfied and then move back to a previous named segment within the same physical database record and retrieve data. The *V command code is used to position the retrieval processing in the current of a particular segment type (see Section 10.4.2). With these command codes it is possible to change the normal forward direction of processing through the linearized hierarchical sequences.

An IMS application program can open several PCBs or type 1 views and process them concurrently. Currency of segment types within each PCB is maintained by the system. Each CALL includes one parameter referring to a specific PCB.

23.2.5   *Storage of Databases in* IMS

We shall review the different types of file organizations available to store physical databases in IMS without going into details. In IMS these are referred to as access methods. Compared to most DBMSs, IMS provides by far the widest array of access methods. We mention all of them here.

- Each physical database in IMS is a stored database. The logical databases are virtual hierarchical databases that may be viewed as such, but in storage they do not represent separate data. Logical databases consist of the physical databases plus linkages provided by pointer structures.

- Each stored segment contains stored data fields plus a prefix (not visible to user programs) containing a segment type code, pointers, a delete flag, and other control information.

- Regardless of the access method, a stored database is always stored as a sequence of occurrence trees, called **physical database records**, where each occurrence tree contains a preorder sequence of segments (see Sections 10.1.3 and 10.1.4). It is owned by a specific root segment. For brevity, we shall sometimes refer to an occurrence tree as a **tree**.

- Various IMS access methods differ in terms of how the sequence of segments is "tied together" within a physical database record and what type of access structure

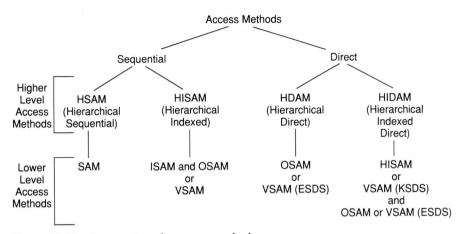

Figure 23.12   An overview of IMS access methods

is provided to locate the physical database record or individual segment occurrences within it.

- Based on the type of access provided to the physical database records, two types
  of structures are provided in IMS: **hierarchical sequential** (HS) and **hierarchical direct** (HD). They are further divided into HSAM, HISAM, HDAM, and HIDAM as shown
  in Figure 23.12.

We will discuss the basic properties of each organization shortly. The IMS access
methods may be regarded as high-level ones. IMS provides routines for HISAM, HDAM, etc.
that in turn use the lower-level access methods called SAM (sequential access method),
OSAM (overflow sequential access method), and ISAM (indexed sequential access method). A combination of files at the lower-level access method is used by the higher-level
access method (see Figure 23.12). For example, a database in HISAM consists of two files
maintained and accessed via two different access methods. HIDAM goes one step further,
since it uses a HISAM database underneath for an index. Each file is organized as a series
of fixed-length blocks.

HSAM

HSAM ties together the segments within a tree by *physical contiguity*. The trees themselves
are placed in physical sequence in storage. Suppose the database in Figure 10.5 was
stored as a physical database in IMS. Figure 10.6 shows an occurrence tree, and its linearized representation is shown in Figure 10.7. Using HSAM, the data in Figure 10.6
would constitute one physical database record. HSAM would "string out" these records
sequentially in order of the sequence key of the root segment with a fixed block size.
This organization is "tapelike" and is of academic importance only, since it supports no
updating. However, it can be used for dumping and transporting databases. Once a
database is loaded using ISRT commands, only the GET operations (excluding GET HOLD)
are allowed. To do modification/deletion/insertion of data, the old database is read
in and an entire new copy is written out. This organization is used to process data that
remains fixed over a period of time.

HISAM

In the HISAM organization, the database consists of two files or storage areas or data sets: one file (prime area) contains root segments (plus some additional segments that fit within the record in that file), another file (overflow area) contains the remaining tail portion of each linearized tree. Figure 23.13 shows how the physical database record corresponding to Figure 10.7 would be stored in IMS using HISAM. It shows how a record is split into two files and how fixed-length blocks are linked together within the overflow.

Both files have fixed-length records. Hence, because of the uneven lengths of segments, some space is wasted at the end of records. The first file is either an ISAM or a prime VSAM area that is accessible via an index on the sequence field of the root segment.

Deletion of segments is handled by setting a deletion flag in the segment prefix. The subtree of a deleted segment is considered to be deleted. With ISAM, deleted segments still physically reside in the database but are marked deleted; with VSAM, segments are actually deleted in most cases. Insertion of segments is more involved. All insertions after the initial loading of the database are placed in the overflow area, including new root segments. To maintain hierarchical sequence, data must be moved; however, cascading of the moves is avoided by creating new segments in the overflow area. The ex-

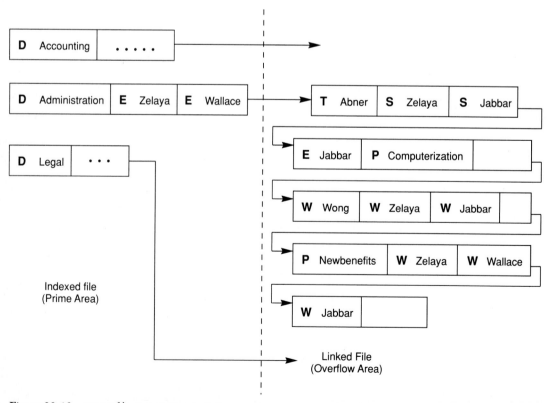

Figure 23.13   HISAM file organization in IMS

ample in Figure 23.13 amply illustrates that the record lengths of the prime and overflow areas are important performance parameters. The DBA must judiciously choose these record types.

HDAM

An HDAM database consists of a single OSAM or VSAM file. In both HD structures, the root segment is accessed by a hash on the sequence field; segments are stored independently and linked using two types of pointers:

- *Hierarchical pointers:* Figure 23.14 shows the use of hierarchic pointers. Each segment points to the next in hierarchical sequence, except for the last dependent segment in the hierarchy, which does not bear a pointer. This is essentially the preorder threading of the tree.

- *Child/twin pointers:* Figure 23.15 shows the use of child/twin pointers. Each segment type has a *designated number* of child pointers equal to the number of children segment types defined in the database definition and has *one* twin pointer. For a given tree, the child pointer in a segment can be (a) a null value if it has no child segment of the corresponding type (e.g., no DEPENDENT for Zelaya or Jabbar in Figure 23.15) or (b) the location of the first child segment of the corresponding type. Children of the same parent are linked using a twin pointer. The twin pointer of the last child is a null.

Note that the HDAM organization provides no sequential access on the root segment. It can be provided by means of a secondary index (see Section 23.2.5). Backward pointers can be created in addition to forward pointers. Declaration of pointers is done as part of the database definition.

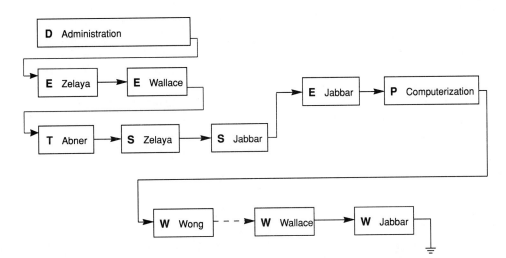

Figure 23.14 HDAM with hierarchic pointers in IMS

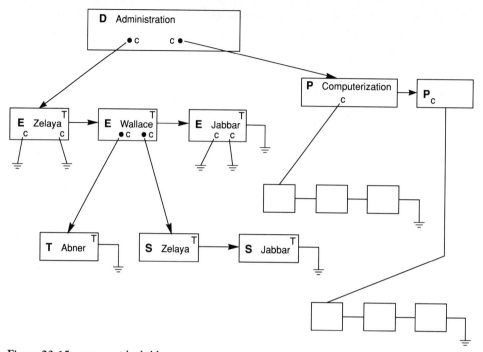

Figure 23.15   HDAM with child-twin pointers in IMS

From a performance standpoint, hierarchical pointers are favored when requirements dictate direct access to the root coupled with sequential access on dependent segments, as in producing reports, where a variety of different segments must be listed. Child/twin pointers are favored when quick access to lower levels in the hierarchy or to the right bottom part of the tree is desired.

HDAM differs from the other three access methods in that the initial loading of the database can be done in any (random) sequence, a tree at a time. Inserting a segment requires no data to be moved (as needed in HISAM in most cases); new segments are allocated in free space wherever it occurs. Segments once stored are never moved. Deletion is also more efficient than in HISAM since segments are actually deleted and the space freed up. A GET NEXT (GN) used on the root segment in HDAM returns the *next root segment in storage* regardless of the sequence field value. To further improve performance of an HDAM database, the address space in the file is divided into two parts: records 1 to R are designated as the root-addressable area; the rest of the records, R + 1 to N, are the non-root-addressable or overflow area. Parameter R is specified in the DBD by the DBA.

HIDAM

A HIDAM database consists of two parts: an index database and a "data" database. The data database is a single OSAM or VSAM (entry-sequenced data set) file consisting of fixed-length records that are initially loaded in hierarchical sequence. It is treated as an HDAM database by itself. Either hierarchic or child/twin pointer schemes are used to link segments.

The INDEX database is a HISAM database where the hierarchy consists of only one type of segment, an index segment. Each index segment contains a root sequence field value as its key and the pointer to that root segment in the data database as its data field. Figure 23.16 schematically shows a HIDAM database. D1, D2, D3, and D4 refer to the root segments of the first four departments in the database of Figure 10.5. Details of pointer schemes in the data database are suppressed. The index database is much smaller than the data database. If VSAM is used, a single key-sequenced data set suffices as the index database. Deletions are handled by freeing the space for reuse as in HDAM and adjusting pointers appropriately. Insertion of a new segment requires no shifting of existing segments; they are allocated in the available space. Space utilization of the index database is more efficient with VSAM than with ISAM/OSAM. HIDAM databases are popular because they combine the advantages of HISAM and HDAM. Direct access to the root segments in the database is provided by using the root sequence key as a hash key; indexed access is available by going through the index database.

Other IMS Storage Structures

Besides the access methods described above, IMS provides the following additional storage structures:

1. **Simple HSAM and simple HISAM** (SHSAM, SHISAM) are variants of HSAM and HISAM, respectively, where a database contains only one segment type (the root segment). No prefixes are stored in segments.

2. **The fast path feature** in IMS is designed for on-line transaction systems with high transaction rates and relatively simple processing. It provides data communication facilities and two special database structures:

    a. Main storage databases (MSDBs): An MSDB is a root-only database. It is kept in

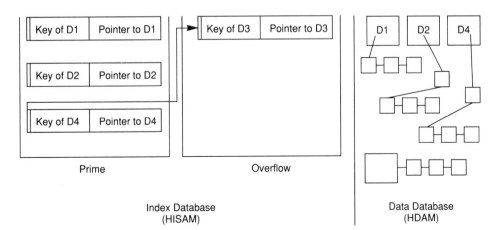

Prime   Overflow

Index Database
(HISAM)

Data Database
(HDAM)

Figure 23.16   HIDAM organization in IMS (Schematic diagram)

primary memory throughout system operation. Small reference tables such as conversion tables and timetables are good candidates for MSDBs.

b. Data entry databases (DEDBs): A DEDB is a special form of HDAM database for better availability and performance. It is a restricted form of hierarchy with only two levels and may be partitioned into up to 240 areas. The leftmost segment at the second level, called the sequential dependent segment type, is given special treatment. Each area is a separate VSAM data set and each database record (root plus all dependents) is wholly contained in the area. The partitioning is not visible to the application.

3. **Secondary data set groups** (DSGs): A HISAM, HDAM, or HIDAM database can be partitioned into groups of segment types. One primary data set group and nine secondary data set groups can be created. The primary DSG contains the root segment. Each secondary DSG is a separate database containing all segment occurrences for the type of segments that belong to it. In HISAM, the secondary DSG must contain a subhierarchy drawn from the original hierarchy with a second-level segment as the root. However, in HDAM and HIDAM a segment can be in any DSG regardless of its position in the hierarchy; choice of appropriate partitions of the hierarchy becomes another physical design parameter at the disposal of the DBA. An appropriate choice can lead to performance improvements with faster access to segments at lower levels and to the right of the hierarchy. It also reduces storage fragmentation in case of HDAM and HIDAM databases, which can occur with different-sized segments. For example, consider an HD database with segments of 100 and 40 bytes. A 60-byte free space cannot be used for a 100-byte segment; if it is used for a 40-byte segment, the remaining 20 bytes are wasted. Creating two separate DSGs for 40-and 100-byte segments would be a solution.

Secondary Indexing in IMS

In Chapter 5 we saw the importance of secondary indexes for improving access times in various types of files. In the last subsection we outlined some features of IMS like the secondary data set groups that can potentially give improved performance. Our discussion of IMS's internal storage organization would be incomplete if we did not mention its secondary indexing facilities. Since we are dealing with hierarchical data instead of a "flat" collection of records in a file, many types of secondary indexing are meaningful. However, IMS provides only the following two types:

1. An index that provides access to a root or a dependent segment based on the value of any field in it.

2. An index that indexes a given segment on the basis of a field in some *segment at a lower level*. For our database of Figures 10.5 and 23.7 with the designated sequence fields some of the secondary indexes it would be possible to create are:

   A. An index to DEPARTMENT by department name (DNAME).
   B. An index on DEPENDENT by birthdate (BIRTHDATE).
   C. An index on DEPARTMENT by location of project in that department (PLOCATION in PROJECT).

There are two shortcomings with secondary index processing in IMS:

1. The DL/1 code must refer explicitly to an index if it is to be used; otherwise processing is done *without* the index.

2. When a field in a lower-level segment in the hierarchy is used for indexing, the hierarchy is visualized as if it is restructured with that segment as the root.

Both of these directly violate the objective of data independence (see Section 2.2) whereby a user's external view is insulated from the internal organization of the database.

RESTRUCTURING OF THE HIERARCHY DUE TO SECONDARY INDEXING: We illustrate the restructuring of the hierarchy with index B suggested above. Suppose DEPENDENTs are indexed on birthdate (BDATE) in our example database of Figure 23.7 via an index called XBDATE. *Just for this example*, let us assume that there is a PET segment underneath DEPENDENT in the original database. If the user chooses to specify a secondary processing sequence (an IMS term that means process in order by secondary index key) corresponding to this index in the PCB, IMS effectively restructures the schema and presents the user with a restructured view as follows:

- The indexed segment becomes the new root.
- The schema tree is "lifted" by this root and the hierarchical path leading up to it "falls down," creating a left branch; segments that were originally its ancestors now appear as the leftmost descendents of the new root on this branch in reverse order.
- The original dependents of the indexed segment remain as before, except they are to the right of this new (left) branch.
- All other segments are excluded.

Thus, we get the secondary data structure (an IMS term) shown in Figure 23.17 (with PET added in to illustrate the third point). Notice that the original segments SUPERVISEE, PROJECT, WORKER, etc. (see Figure 10.5) have disappeared from this view. The present view is not exactly a type 1 view although it arises from a PCB and a secondary index definition (which we did not show explicitly).

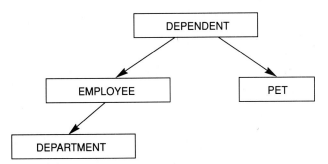

Figure 23.17   A restructured hierarchy produced by secondary indexing on DEPENDENT in IMS

A secondary index in IMS is a database in its own right and may be processed independently of the data it indexes. Thus, it is possible to ignore the main database and just process an index to compute counts or to find that a certain value exists and so on. To improve the usefulness of this index, certain fields from the original indexed segment may be repeated in the index. IMS automatically maintains these duplicate fields and updates them whenever the corresponding data in the source segment is updated.

23.3   A Network System—IDMS

23.3.1   Introduction

In this section we survey a popular DBMS based on the network model of Chapter 11 called the Integrated Database Management System (IDMS). In fact, the network model has had the greatest number of major commercial DBMS implementations: IDS II of Honeywell, DMS II of Burroughs (now UNISYS), DMS 1100 of UNIVAC (now UNISYS), DBMS 10 and 11 of Digital Equipment, IMAGE of Hewlett-Packard, and IDMS of Cullinet Software. All of these systems (with the exception of the original IDS) were developed following the 1971 CODASYL DBTG report (DBTG 1971) and implemented the concepts specified in that report. As pointed out in Chapter 11, the DBTG report was revised in 1978 and 1981, adding some concepts and deleting some. For example, data structure descriptions or views over multiple record types were added in the 1978 report, which we did not discuss in Chapter 11. LOCATION MODE for record type definition and the AREA concept from the original report were dropped, which we did not discuss either. When we analyze any particular CODASYL system (sometimes called DBTG system), we should typically explore most of the features of the network model in Chapter 11. Otherwise, the CODASYL DBTG classification of the system becomes questionable. Minor variations exist, some of which can be attributed to the DBTG report updates of 1978 and 1981.

DMS II of UNISYS is not a true CODASYL DBTG implementation as it does not follow the network data model strictly. It supports embedded record types and hence can be considered as hierarchical as well as network. The TOTAL system of CINCOM also does *not* follow the DBTG concepts. It represents data in terms of two types of record types, called master and variable. Relationships can be defined from any master record type to any variable record type, but no relationships are possible among variable record types.

The DBTG proposed three languages:

- Schema DDL—to describe a network-structured database. This is equivalent to the ANSI/SPARC conceptual schema (Section 2.2).

- Subschema DDL—to describe the part of the database relevant to one application. This corresponds to the ANSI/SPARC external schema.

- DML—data manipulation language for processing the data defined by the above two languages. The DML in DBTG (1971) was proposed to be used in conjunction with COBOL and hence was called COBOL DML.

All network model implementations have their own syntax for these three languages. Our DML syntax in Chapter 11 is quite close to that in IDMS. All systems use the concept of user work areas (UWAs) and currency indicators as shown in Figure 11.12. Some DBMSs including IDMS also use a device media control language (DMCL), which defines the physical characteristics of the storage media such as buffer sizes and page sizes to which the schema definition is mapped. We will describe it briefly in Section 23.3.3.

IDMS is an implementation of the CODASYL DBTG concepts by Cullinet Software. It is designed to run on IBM mainframes under all standard operating systems. The name of the product was officially changed to **IDMS/R** (IDMS/Relational) in 1983, when relational facilities were added on top of the base product. In this section we concentrate on the basic network-oriented facilities of IDMS/R that correspond to IDMS. The relational extensions are discussed briefly in Sections 23.3.7 and 23.3.8. IDMS is closely integrated with a dictionary product called **Integrated Data Dictionary** (IDD). We will not describe IDD further.

23.3.2 Basic Architecture of IDMS

The IDMS family of products provides a variety of facilities based on the central DBMS and the IDD. The IDD stores a variety of entities (an IDD term). Basic entities include users, systems, files, data items, reports, transactions, programs, and program entry points. The teleprocessing entities include messages, screens, display formats, queues, destinations, lines, terminals, and encoding tables. A number of relationships and cross-references among these entities are also stored.

Data definition facilities include three compilers that compile the schema DDL, the subschema DDL, and the DMCL. IDMS (like IMS) is invoked by a CALL interface for data manipulation. Users do not code the calls in their programs (unlike IMS). Instead, they use a set of DML statements similar to those in Table 11.2. A **DML preprocessor** translates the DML statements into calling sequences appropriate to the host language. IDMS provides DML facilities within the following host languages: COBOL, PL/1, FORTRAN, and IBM System/370 assembler language. The relational extensions in IDMS/R include the Automatic System Facility (ASF), which is a menu-driven front end to the system. It allows a set of form-based functions to define and manipulate relational views in the form of logical records. The Logical Record Facility (LRF) creates a view of the underlying database as virtual tables for relational processing.

Cullinet also provides a set of supporting products for use with IDMS. Besides IDD, they include the following:

- *Application generator* (Application Development System/On-Line Application Generator—ADSA): With this tool, an application developer defines the application functions and responses to the dictionary. It acts as a prototype tool and enables the user to have an on-line preview of the application.

- *On-line query* (OLQ): This interface allows users to ask ad hoc queries against the database or obtain formatted reports using predefined queries.

- *On-line English:* This is the INTELLECT product (see Section 22.1.3) marketed in conjunction with IDMS as a natural language interface.

- *Report writer* (CULPRIT): This is a parameter-driven report writer. It actively uses the definition stored in the dictionary to generate reports. Report definitions can be stored in the dictionary and invoked by just supplying the report name and parameters.

Using the above repertoire of facilities, the development of an IDMS application proceeds as follows:

1. Database schema, subschema, etc. are defined using interactive tools called IDD utilities.

2. The schemas are compiled using the schema compiler.

3. A DMCL description to define the physical characteristics of the database is compiled by the DMCL compiler.

4. Subschemas for various applications are compiled by the subschema compiler. The logical records or views are a part of the subschema in IDMS/R.

5. Application source programs are written in a host language with embedded DML statements and precompiled. The precompilers record in the dictionary the operations that each program performs on specific data. This information is automatically monitored by the IDD. Hence it is called an *active* dictionary.

23.3.3   Data Definition in IDMS

The schema is defined by using the schema DDL. The online schema compiler allows a free form syntax, incremental schema modification, and schema validation. The different parts of a schema are: schema description, file description, area description, record description, and set description. We will concentrate on the last two. The record and set type definitions to define the schema of Figure 11.10 that are shown in Figure 11.14 can be used with minor syntax variations in IDMS record definitions. We will not discuss the full syntax; instead we just highlight the differences between IDMS's DDL and the DDL in Section 11.2.2. The main differences are:

- A record type must be assigned to an AREA when it is defined, using the phrase "WITHIN AREA."

- A record type must have a LOCATION MODE specification.

An **area** is a DBTG concept that refers to a group of record types. An area is typically mapped to a physically contiguous storage space. This concept has physical overtones and compromises data independence. Hence it was removed from the 1981 DBTG report. The **location mode** for record type is a specification of how a new occurrence of that record should be stored and how existing occurrences should be retrieved. IDMS allows the following location modes:

- CALC—The record is stored by using a CALC key from within the record; this key is used for hashing to calculate a page address, and the record is stored in or near that page. The CALC key may be declared to be unique (DUPLICATES NOT ALLOWED).

- VIA—The VIA followed by a set type name means that a member record is stored physically as close as possible to the owner record (if they belong to the same area). If they are assigned to different areas, the member record is stored at the *same relative position* in the area as the owner in its area. This feature was valid up to release 10.0 of IDMS.

- VIA INDEX—In this option, available after release 10.0, a record is stored via a "system-owned index" providing a system owner record and a B^+-tree index. The system owner record contains the name of the index, and points to the B^+-tree which, in turn, points to the member records.

- DIRECT—A record is placed on or near a user-specified page.

Another option, called physical sequential, is also available. In Figure 23.18 we give sample definitions of record types EMPLOYEE and WORKS_ON from the database shown in Figure 11.10. Data items are defined in the style of COBOL. See the similarity of this definition to that in Figure 11.14. EMPLOYEE is accessed by the unique CALC key of SSN, whereas WORKS_ON is accessed using VIA E_WORKSON set type. To start searching a database directly at a record type, that record must have been declared with location

```
SCHEMA NAME IS COMPANY

RECORD NAME IS EMPLOYEE
LOCATION MODE IS CALC USING SSN
DUPLICATES NOT ALLOWED
WITHIN EMP_AREA
02 FNAME     PIC X(15)
02 MINIT     PIC X
02 LNAME     PIC X(15)
02 SSN       PIC 9(9)
02 BIRTHDATE PIC X(9)
02 ADDRESS   PIC X(30)
02 SEX       PIC X
02 SALARY    PIC 9(10)
02 DEPTNAME  PIC X(15)

RECORD NAME IS WORKS_ON
LOCATION MODE IS VIA E_WORKSON SET
WITHIN EMP_AREA
02 ESSN     PIC 9(9)
02 PNUMBER  PIC 999 USAGE COMP-3
02 HOURS    PIC 99  USAGE COMP-3

SET NAME IS WORKS_FOR
OWNER IS DEPARTMENT
MEMBER IS EMPLOYEE MANUAL OPTIONAL
ORDER IS SORTED
MODE IS CHAINED
ASCENDING KEY IS LNAME, FNAME
DUPLICATES ALLOWED
```

Figure 23.18 Sample record and set type definitions in IDMS schema DDL.

mode CALC or DIRECT. Another option is to use a system-owned set (Section 11.1.5) with that record type as a member.

IDMS also uses the concept of **database keys,** which we omitted in Chapter 11. IDMS assigns a unique identifier called a database key to each record occurrence when it is entered into the database. Its value corresponds to the absolute location address.

Set Definitions

IDMS set definitions differ from the set features described in Chapter 11 in the following ways:

1. The SET SELECTION clause is missing. Thus, to insert a record automatically into the set, an appropriate set occurrence must be selected by the program, making it current.

2. The FIXED set retention is not provided; only MANDATORY and OPTIONAL are allowed.

3. There is no CHECK facility to check that a member in a set satisfies a certain constraint before it is added into the set (see example of CHECK on the WORKS_FOR set in Figure 11.14b).

4. Set definition includes the choice of implementation by means of "MODE IS CHAINED or INDEXED." The former links up the members in every set occurrence by means of a circular linked list, whereas the latter sets up an index for each set occurrence (see Section 11.1.4).

5. It is possible to designate the order in which pointers such as next or prior pointers or owner pointers (see Section 11.1.4) should be allocated within the record. This is another example of how a low-level physical specification is done as part of the DDL in IDMS.

In Figure 23.18 we show how the set type WORKS_FOR in Figure 11.10 would be defined in the DDL.

Subschema Definition

A subschema in IDMS is a subset of the original schema obtained by omitting data items, record types, and set types. Whenever a record type is omitted, all set types in which it participates as an owner or member must be eliminated. Subschema definition has two data divisions—identification division and subschema data division. The latter specifies the areas, the record types or parts thereof, and the sets to be included. An on-line subschema compiler is available. Figure 23.19 shows a hypothetical subschema definition that includes a subset of the schema in Figure 11.10 related to employees, departments, and supervisors. Subschema definition can also include logical record and path-group statements. We will discuss them in Section 23.3.7.

There are some problems with the ERASE command when applied to a record in the subschema. The deletion can potentially propagate via set membership to a number of other records that may not be part of the subschema. The subschema designer must include all such record types to which a delete may propagate while defining the subschema.

```
ADD
     SUBSCHEMA NAME IS EMP_DEPT OF SCHEMA  NAME COMPANY
     DMCL NAME IS ED_DMCL
     PUBLIC ACCESS IS ALLOWED FOR DISPLAY
ADD
     AREA NAME IS EMP_AREA
     DEFAULT USAGE IS SHARED UPDATE
ADD
     AREA NAME IS DEP_AREA
ADD
     RECORD NAME IS EMPLOYEE
               ELEMENTS ARE ALL
ADD
     RECORD NAME IS SUPERVISOR
               ELEMENTS ARE ALL
ADD
     RECORD NAME IS DEPARTMENT
               ELEMENTS ARE NUMBER, NAME
ADD
     SET NAME IS IS_A_SUPERVISOR
ADD
     SET NAME IS SUPERVISEES
ADD
     SET NAME IS MANAGES
ADD
     SET NAME IS WORKS_FOR
```

Figure 23.19   Subschema definition for the schema in Figure 11.10
                 (details omitted).

Device Media Control Language (DMCL) Description

The DMCL allows a specification of the physical storage parameters that govern the mapping of the instances of data into storage for a given schema description. It specifies buffer size in terms of number of pages, and page size in bytes; it associates area names with names of buffer pools and finally states the names of journal files, specifying the types of device on which journal files will reside. We do not give any details of the syntax of DMCL here.

23.3.4   Data Manipulation in IDMS

The data manipulation language concepts introduced in Chapter 11 are applicable with minor changes to IDMS. All DML commands in Table 11.2 are available in some form. The variations are as follows:

Retrieval Commands

- The FIND CALC <record-type-name> is applicable when a key value is already supplied in the Calc-Key field.

- FIND <record-type-name> DBKEY is <dbkey-value> is a way of finding a record, given the database key value. This form can be used whether or not the location mode of that record is DIRECT. This requires that the program supply the database key value (absolute location id) of the record. This is normally done if a record that has been retrieved previously is to be retrieved again in the program. The DBKEY is saved and reused.

- To retrieve a record within a set type, or within an area, the following FIND is available:

FIND (FIRST | NEXT | PRIOR | LAST) <record-type-name> [WITHIN <set-type-name> | WITHIN <area-name>]

The available types of FINDs are summarized in Figure 23.20. IDMS also allows the verb OBTAIN in place of the FIND-GET combination.

- The fourth type of FIND in Figure 23.20 can be used not only within a set type but also within an area.

Update Commands

The STORE, ERASE, and MODIFY commands of Section 11.2.5 apply to IDMS. The IDMS ERASE has four options:

- ERASE—Deletes the CRU (current of run unit) record if it is not the owner of any nonempty set occurrence. The system takes into account all sets for which the record type is an owner.

- ERASE PERMANENT—Deletes the CRU record together with MANDATORY member occurrences of that record in any set type. OPTIONAL member occurrences are not deleted but are disconnected.

- ERASE SELECTIVE—Deletes the CRU record, the MANDATORY members, *and* the OPTIONAL members that do not participate in any other set occurrences of other set types.

- ERASE ALL—Deletes the CRU record and all members whether they are MANDATORY or OPTIONAL.

```
1  FIND ANY ( or CALC) <record-type-name>
   FIND DUPLICATE     <record-type-name>
2  FIND  <record-type-name> DBKEY IS <dbkey-value>
3  FIND CURRENT [ <record-type-name> | WITHIN <set-type-name> |
        WITHIN <area-name >]
4  FIND [ NEXT| PRIOR| FIRST| LAST| NTH ]   <record-type-name> WITHIN
        [<set-type-name> | WITHIN <area-name>]
5  FIND <record-type-name> WITHIN <set-type-name> USING
        <ordering-field-name>
```

Figure 23.20   Available types FIND in IDMS

In all of these options, deletion propagates recursively, that is, as if the member record that was deleted is itself an object of the ERASE command. IDMS CONNECT and DISCONNECT work as discussed in Section 11.2.5. There is no RECONNECT in IDMS.

23.3.5 Storage of Data in IDMS

In IDMS a database is logically composed of one or more areas, whereas physically it is composed of one or more physical files. The relationship among areas and files is many to many; that is, an area may be mapped to a number of files and vice versa. Note the similarity of this relationship to that between storage groups in IMS and spaces in DB2. This correspondence is stored as a part of schema description. Files are divided into fixed-length blocks called pages. Each record in a page has a prefix containing a line# (assigned from bottom of page), record-id, and record length. The record also includes pointers—a minimum of one per set type in which it is an owner or a member. The database key of a record on page 1051, line 3 is considered to be (1051,3).

Sets are implemented in two ways: as linked sets (MODE IS CHAIN) or as indexed sets (MODE IS INDEXED). A forward pointer is included for a set type in its owner and member record types. The designer may also request reverse pointers (LINKED TO PRIOR), which are assigned in both the owner and the member, and pointer to owner (LINKED TO OWNER), which is assigned to the member record.

In the indexed set representation, every set occurrence is represented by the owner and a small (local) index represented by a set of index records. Figure 23.21 shows the indexed set WORKS_FOR for the schema defined in Figure 23.18. The owner and the index records are linked along a linked list using next, prior, and owner pointers. Each member record points back to its index entry. Note that it is *not* necessary that an indexed set be ordered.

The system-owned sets are maintained as indexed sets. There the set-ordering specification is used to order the values of the ordering field. Each index record contains this value and the database key value. There is one occurrence of each set and the one index so created is equivalent to a clustering index. Note, however, that many system-owned sets can be defined with different set orderings for the same record type. The CALC

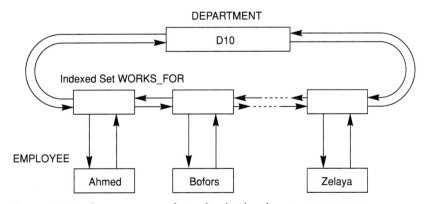

Figure 23.21 One occurrence of an ordered indexed set type WORKS_FOR.

option provides hashed access on a CALC key to a record type (in IMS it is available *only for root records*). With the VIA SET option, if that set is defined using MODE IS INDEX and ORDER IS SORTED, not only are the member records stored close to the owner (same page or a nearby page), but also the physical order of the member records closely approximates their logical order.

23.3.6   Internal Features of IDMS

IDMS provides extensive concurrency control, recovery, and security features. It is not our intent to cover all of them in detail. We will only highlight a few features.

Checkpoints

The word checkpoint in IDMS is equivalent to our concept of a **transaction**. Checkpoints are initiated with the READY command and terminated with COMMIT, FINISH, or ROLL-BACK. IDMS records the start and end of checkpoints in a journal file (system log).

COMMIT has two formats: COMMIT and COMMIT ALL. When a COMMIT (or COMMIT ALL) is executed, all changes to the database are written to the log and the changed pages are written to the database. After the operating system completes these two writes, a check-point message is written to the log. With COMMIT, all locks except those on current records are released; with COMMIT ALL, even the current records are released. The run unit then resumes processing. This COMMIT processing guarantees the synchronization between the database and the log for recovery purposes.

FINISH is used to signify the end of all transactions. All areas are closed from further processing and currency indicators are set to null. ROLLBACK is used to abort a trans-action. With a log on disk, changes made to the database during the current transaction are automatically rolled back. With a tape log file, a utility program must be run to do the rollback. Just ROLLBACK is equivalent to aborting the transaction followed by a FINISH to terminate processing; ROLLBACK CONTINUE rolls the current transaction back but resumes processing.

Locks for Concurrent Processing

IDMS allows locking at two levels of granularity: **area locks** and **record locks**. While preparing an area for processing, three options are allowed: retrieval, protected retrieval, and exclusive update. Protected or exclusive locks are issued as appropriate in the second and third cases. A **protected lock** allows other run units to retrieve data in the area but not update it; an **exclusive lock** allows neither retrieval nor update.

If the area itself is not locked, two types of locks are available to lock the records selectively within the area. They are called shared locks and exclusive locks; record locks are either *implicitly* placed by IDMS or *explicitly* specified by an application program. If implicit locking is used, a shared lock is placed on current of each record type, set type, area, and run unit. Shared locks are released when currency indicators change. An exclusive lock is placed on all modified records (STORE, ERASE, MODIFY, CONNECT, DISCONNECT). The exclusive lock will be held until a COMMIT or ROLLBACK or FINISH is issued. To obtain a lock explicitly, the KEEP command is used. It can also be used to place a LONGTERM lock.

Recovery

The recovery techniques used in IDMS are similar to those we discussed in Chapter 19. A transaction may issue a ROLLBACK and abort, or terminate due to error, or *time-out* when the maximum allowed time exceeds a predetermined time limit set at instruction time. The system uses "before images" to undo the changes to the database and rolls it back.

In the event of a system crash all checkpoints (transactions) in progress are rolled back and must be restarted. An application is supposed to be written in a way such that any checkpoint can be restarted. Since the log (JOURNAL in IDMS terms) and the database are synchronized at each commit point, every afterimage of a changed page is guaranteed to be in the database before the commit log entry is made. This makes recovery simpler. IDMS maintains a LOG file which is used for collecting system statistics and program abend information.

To recover from selective physical database damages, a saved copy is used to restore the database, and afterimages of all transactions since saving the last copy are applied to the database. The backup operation can be applied to individual areas of the database.

Security

All security features are optional. There is no user authorization mechanism as far as access to application programs is concerned. However, the processing of schema and sub-schema descriptions is restricted. Users are identified by a user-id and given specific permissions to create, modify, delete, and display the schema and subschemas. The data dictionary can be used to store authorization information for restricting access to certain parts of the database.

There is a program registration feature that allows only the registered programs to access a valid subschema; the subschemas are themselves registered in the dictionary. When subschemas are defined, an authorization specification establishes the type of operations that can be performed against areas, record types, set types, etc. It is possible to write external security checking procedures called **database procedures** that are referenced within the DDL. During the processing of the corresponding data, control automatically transfers to this procedure for authorization verification.

23.3.7 Relational Views in IDMS/R

IDMS/R is an enhancement of the basic IDMS system that is supposed to allow relational processing of the underlying network data. This is made possible by the **logical record facility (LRF)** of IDMS/R. The LRF mechanism is comparable to the view mechanism in the relational data model and type 2 views in IMS. It results in generating "logical records", which are virtual collections of items derived from the underlying physical records (compare with logical and physical databases in IMS).

We do not intend to give the detailed syntax associated with the definition and processing of logical records in IDMS/R. The facility works as follows:

1. A **logical record** is defined as a relation over a number of related record types. For example, using the network schema of Figure 11.10, the WORKS_ON1 view that we defined in Section 7.4.2 can be defined by involving record types EMPLOYEE, WORKS_ON, and PROJECT, together with set types E_WORKSON and P_WORKSON:

    WORKS_ON1(FNAME, LNAME, PNAME, HOURS)

2. The normal DML to process the network database is different from the **view-DML** (VDML—this is *not* an IDMS term) used to process the logical records. The VDML is used by the DBA to define a view and to define how the DML operations of OBTAIN, STORE, ERASE, and MODIFY will work on the logical record. Users use a modified form of the DML to obtain data and to update data in the views. It can contain a WHERE clause, which can take many complex forms. For example, consider the modified DML command OBTAIN NEXT WORKS1 WHERE FULLTIME. Here FULLTIME may be a DBA-defined keyword that stands for some complex condition on PNAME and HOURS. We shall refer to the modified DML, containing the modified versions of OBTAIN, STORE, ERASE, and MODIFY, as just DML.

3. To define a view in VDML, the DBA has to write one or more procedures. Although the resulting views are comparable to relational views created by using SQL or QUEL, not all views possible in SQL can be defined in VDML. Views are basically projections of Cartesian products of the underlying record types. Most select/project/join-based views can be defined. Views involving the union operator and those using built-in functions or the join of a logical record with itself cannot be defined. Several forms of OUTER JOIN can be defined, however.

4. The DBA has to provide procedures (**"path groups"** in IDMS/R) to tell the system how it should perform certain normal DML operations on the defined views. For example, to list the employees and their hours for those who work on the project with PNAME = x, a procedure would be written:

```
PATH-GROUP NAME IS OBTAIN PROJ_LISTING
OBTAIN CALC PROJECT
WHERE PNAME = x
PATH-GROUP NAME IS MODIFY EMP_PROJ_HOURS
```

Each time an operation OBTAIN PROJ_LISTING is issued, the above procedure would be invoked. For a given view, a number of different OBTAIN or MODIFY procedures may be written. Another such procedure called MODIFY EMP_PROJ_HOURS is shown above but is not expanded. For a given LRF view and a user request, the procedures are sequentially scanned to see if a match is found; otherwise, the request is rejected. This idea of predefining all possible procedures against a view is similar to the encapsulation of methods with objects in the object-oriented model (see Section 15.4.1). But object-oriented systems such as Vbase, discussed in Section 23.4, take advantage of encapsulation by following it throughout the system. In IDMS/R it is used only within the LRF portion of the system.

5. There is no notion of query optimization for the above procedures. For a logical record to be materialized, several options can be considered. It is the responsibility of the DBA to choose an optimal way to implement each operation against a view. The DBA must choose from the indexes defined and access methods available to retrieve appropriate records from those defined in the schema definition and order the record types and set types optimally to "collect" the relevant data in the view.

6. To implement the LRF mechanism, the network DBMS must deal with the important problem of currency. Users are advised not to mix view processing with normal DML processing. Otherwise, unpredictable errors might occur.

We offer the following comments to compare the LRF against relations and relational views (see Section 7.4) and sometimes against the IMS view mechanism (Section 23.2.3).

- A logical record *cannot* be called a relation in a strict sense. There are no relational operators available to generate new relations; moreover, the following characteristics of relations are *not necessarily* observed: no duplicate tuples, ordering of tuples is insignificant, no multivalued domains.

- The view facility is further limited in that views on views cannot be defined as in the relational model. Note that even IMS type 2 views called logical databases do not have this limitation so rigidly. It is possible to define several type 1 views (subset of hierarchies) over a type 2 view (logical database).

- As opposed to relational views, updates are possible on views involving joins provided the DBA can define an appropriate procedure (PATH-GROUP) for it. There is no standard way to update or process views. All procedures are ad hoc and are left to the discretion of the DBA.

23.3.8   Automatic System Facility in IDMS/R

This facility is claimed to be the source of the relational nature of IDMS. It is provided as a layer on top of the logical record facility LRF. The purpose of ASF is to define, create, and support *new* relational databases. It not only acts as a relational view mechanism over existing network data but also provides for creating new relations. We highlight a few features of this facility:

- ASF provides a set of form-based interfaces to allow the definition and manipulation of relations. It runs under the IDMS's data communication subsystem IDMS/DC.

- The interactive access to relations is available via On-line query (OLQ), which is strictly a query language and does not support any updating or joins.

- Application programs can be written in the modified DML against relations as described in Section 23.3.7 because relations are implemented as logical records.

- Batched access to relations for report generation is provided via the CULPRIT report writer or On-line query.

The new stored relations in ASF are called basic stored tables. They are created as follows:

- Using forms to define new basic stored tables, the user supplies a table name, field names, data types, key specifications, and integrity constraints.

- A generate command creates the above table and adds it to the internal stored description of relations. It automatically generates indexed sets for each defined key.

- A generate command *automatically creates a subschema* with the defined relation as a logical record (in LRF) and also automatically generates OBTAIN, STORE, ERASE, MODIFY procedures to retrieve and update that relation. Indexes are used whenever appropriate.

The user is then able to perform single-table retrievals (SELECT, PROJECT) in OLQ and also perform STORE, ERASE, and MODIFY on the table. ASF allows creation of views on top of the basic tables where up to six tables can be joined and no duplicates are eliminated. These views are updatable according to the update specifications that work via procedures (similar to PATH-GROUP in LRF). As of release 10.2, the user can join multiple ASF tables, DBA defined logical records, and network record types from multiple subschemas.

ASF also allows modification of basic tables, which can involve deleting tables, adding and deleting columns, adding and deleting keys, and modifying integrity constraints. View definitions can also be modified. New table definitions are generated each time such changes are made. The *user is responsible* for modifying or recompiling old application programs to conform to the changed definitions of tables.

23.4   An Object-oriented DBMS—Vbase

A very recent arrival on the commercial DBMS scene is the Vbase integrated object-oriented System of Ontologic, Inc.* Compared to the first three systems we described in this chapter, this system is still undergoing development and has not yet reached its full intended functionality. We include it as a representative of the emerging direction in the commercial DBMS market—the object-oriented DBMSs. The description given here is based on the information available at the time of writing. Other commercial object-oriented DBMSs available now include GEMSTONE/OPAL of Serviologic and ORION of Microelectronics and Computer Technology Corporation (available on a restricted basis). Our purpose in including the Vbase discussion is to highlight the salient features and the departure from the three conventional implementations described earlier in this chapter. The following account is by no means complete.

23.4.1   Introduction to Vbase and Its Salient Features

The Vbase system was released commercially in early 1988. The current version (1.0)** runs on Sun3 workstations under the Sun OS 3.2 UNIX operating system. The product is also available on Digital VAX machines under the VMS operating system. This product claims to provide tight integration among data management and programming language facilities. The ultimate aim is to provide an environment where users can think of their problem and the "miniworld" of their application in terms of various objects of interest and where the system does not bog them down in the details of procedural language programming.

The Vbase philosophy is consistent with the principles of object-oriented data models covered in Section 15.4.1. All concepts and the accompanying advantages apply to Vbase. In the following, object-oriented is abbreviated as **o-o**. The salient features of Vbase are the following:

1. Vbase is influenced by the **abstract data type** paradigm and the CLU programming language development at Massachusetts Institute of Technology (Liskov

---

*We have drawn heavily from Andrews and Harris (1987) in introducing Vbase.

**Version 1.2 of Vbase has recently been announced. Detailed information was not available at the time of writing.

et al. 1981). The object behavior is elicited by a combination of properties and operations. The GEMSTONE/OPAL system, on the other hand, follows an object/ message paradigm that was pioneered by the SMALLTALK-80 language (Goldberg and Robson 1983).

2. **Strong typing** is evident throughout the system. In the commercial database environment, where objects of interest are known to have certain value constraints and fixed behavioral properties, typing is very advantageous. This is in contrast to the SMALLTALK-based o-o systems. The advantages of strong typing are:

   a. Resolution of errors at compile time as opposed to run time.

   b. Less reliance on user-enforced naming and other constraints to convey typing information.

   c. Improved system performance due to superior analysis of specification at compile time.

3. Vbase follows a **layered approach** to system architecture. A flexible architecture is achieved with a clear separation of specification and implementation. The language layer provides for the specification of objects in terms of what they are and what they can do. The abstraction layer provides essential modeling features of the o-o approach, the representation layer provides the semantics of the mapping to stored objects, and the lowest storage layer is responsible for object persistence essential to data management. Interestingly, each layer was implemented using Vbase, thus bootstrapping the system to higher levels.

4. While maintaining its desirable o-o characteristics, the system also provides the traditional DBMS characteristics. They include sharing of object data among multiple processes and users, handling large object storage spaces (in hundreds of megabytes), and providing transaction support in terms of concurrency control and recovery.

23.4.2   Basic Architecture of Vbase

The layered architecture of Vbase was already pointed out above. The compile time and run time components of the system are shown in Figure 23.22. The run time system consists of an object manager, which is called on by an application program to provide services related to data objects. There are two primary languages—TDL (type definition language), which is roughly a data definition language, and COP (C object processor), which is an object-oriented extension of the programming language C. Compilers are provided for TDL and COP.

The COP language provides access to the database by providing METHODS, the code units to implement operations on the database. It also provides for writing APPLICATIONS, executable programs that access the database using the operations. TDL includes type definitions with which the user describes his or her application environment. TDL compiler does rigid type checking of the user-defined types in the context of system-defined data types and objects.

The query language Object SQL is also supported as a report generation tool. It allows SELECT .. FROM .. WHERE queries that can directly access instances of object types.

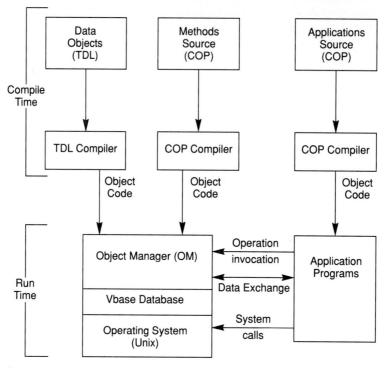

Figure 23.22 Compile and Run-Time architecture in Vbase
(Source: Ontologic, Inc.)

Vbase proposes to provide in the future a graphic subsystem for which CIRCLE, LINE, ARC, RECTANGLE, etc. are simply another set of built-in primitive object data types with very well defined properties. The image composition level of the system can structure images hierarchically and can merge vector-based pictures into single images. The integrated tool set (ITS) includes a source browser, a database browser, and a debugger. Further forms-oriented as well as graphic interface tools are under development. The storage manager is a run time subsystem that provides space management functions for the object databases.

23.4.3   Data Modeling Concepts and Data Definition in Vbase

Vbase has an object-oriented data model. It supports the basic characteristics of the o-o approach in terms of:

- **Encapsulation of data and procedures:** This creates a class of abstract objects that is supported by means of type definitions in the system. The system has approximately 65 predefined types. The user adds new types via TYPE definitions in TDL.

- **Object identity:** The system creates a unique system-defined identifier called OID for each object.

- **Inheritance:** Subtypes inherit both the properties and the behavior of their super-types; they can be further refined in the subtype.
- **Complex objects:** Complex object types are created by using hierarchies (defined below).

The system comes with a type library that has two primary uses. First, the user may want to create direct instances of system library types, retrieve property values for them, and perform operations on them. Second, the user may want to *extend* the library of types; the new types must be integrated into the existing hierarchy.

The hierarchy of types in the system type library is shown in Figure 23.23. The type Entity heads the hierarchy in Vbase; Aggregate and its subtypes are uninstantiable types. They essentially define a hierarchy of different types of domains. For example, Number has subtypes Real and Integer. The type Type has as instance all types in the system library as well as user-defined types. TDL is used to create instances of type Type. The library types form a *subtype hierarchy*; any new type must be integrated into the hierarchy. There is no type called OBJECT in the model. Objects mean instances.

Data structures such as strings, lists, sets, bags, queues, and arrays are subtypes of the aggregate type. The relationships among types and instances are summarized in Figure 23.24. We see that the abstractions of data we described in Section 15.3 are supported in this figure. The association abstraction (or relationship among objects) is provided via properties. The (name of the) property within a type can be used to relate it to another type as in the functional data model; its value is the OID of the associated object. The unique OIDs in the model support the identification abstraction of Section 15.3.

Exception types are generated to provide for error handling at run time. They form a type (generalization) hierarchy of their own. Methods, a type in their own right, are

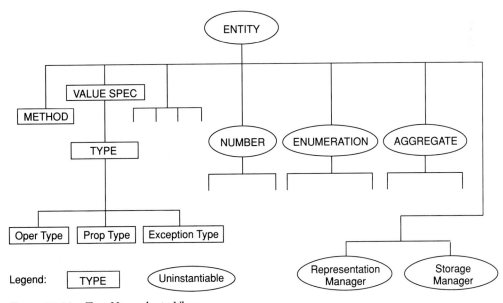

Figure 23.23 Type Hierarchy in Vbase

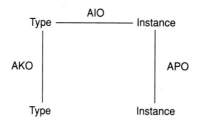

AKO: A-kind-of (Generalization/Specialization)

APO: A-part-of   (Aggregation)

AIO: An-instance-of   (Classification)

Figure 23.24 Support of different data abstractions in Vbase.
(Source: Ontologic, Inc.)

procedures in COP that are used to implement operations. The same abstract operation, such as print, may be implemented by different methods for different types. The relationship between methods and operations invoked by COP application programs is many to many.

The application developer has a full set of types visible to him or her. Only the top few types are shown in Figure 23.23. Using TDL, the application developer builds a schema that adds to the type hierarchy shown. For our COMPANY database in Figure 6.5, sample definitions of types PERSON, EMPLOYEE, and WORKS_ON as well as Sex, Month, Date, and Address are shown in Figure 23.25.

In Figure 23.25 we defined each type as a subtype of Entity. Properties correspond to attributes in the ER or relational models. They describe static behavior. Note that properties can have the following additional specification:

- Optional or required (required is the default).
- Single-valued or distributed (meaning multivalued).
- Protection against access or change.
- Inverses.
- Refinement or constraints over inherited properties.

If a type is supposed to have no instances, the specification "Is Instantiable = $ False;" is added to the definition of the type. Vbase supports **inverse relationships** via properties. For example, notice a property called Works_On in Employee with an inverse specification; there is a corresponding property Employee in Works_On with an inverse specification. The Employee-to-Works_On relationship is defined as one to many by virtue of the distributed set (multivalued) specification. Whenever an instance is modified on one side of an inverse relationship, the other side is *automatically* modified.

In the Person type definition we show an example of an operation called Person_age. Operations are procedures or functions bound to an object. Operations are called from application programs by name and are passed a list of arguments. The operation Person_age returns an integer result; it "raises" a possible exception called Bad_date,

(a) **define type** Person
      supertypes = { Entity };
      properties =
          {   Fname   : String;
                    MInit   : Character;
                    SSN   : Integer;
                    Lname   : String;
                    BDate   : Date;
                    Address   : Address;
                    Sex   : Sex;
          };

      operations =
          {   Person_age (p: Person, d: Date);
                    returns (Integer);
                    raises (BadDate);
                    method (Person_age_method);
          };
    end Person;

define Unordered Dictionary Person_Catalog
        Member_Spec = Person;
        Index_Spec   = Integer;
end Person_Catalog;

define type Employee
      supertypes = { Person };
      properties =
          {   Salary   : Integer;
                    Works_for   : Department inverse Department$Employs;
                    Has_Dependent : optional distributed Set[Dependent] inverse Dependent$Depends_On;
                    Works_On   : distributedSet[Works_on] inverse Works_On$Employees;
                    Manages   : optional Department inverse Department$Manager;
                    Supervises : optional distributed Set[Employee]inverse Employee$Supervised_By;
                    Supervised_By : Employee inverse Employee$Supervises;
          };
    end Employee;

define type Works_On
      supertypes = { Entity };
      properties =
          { Employee   : Employee inverse Employee$Works_On;
            Project   : Project inverse Project$Has_Emp;
            Hours   : Integer;
          };
    end Works_On;

define type Sex
      is enum
          (Male, Female);

define type Month
      is enum
          (Jan, Feb, Mar, Apr, May, Jun, Jul, Aug, Sep, Oct, Nov, Dec);

(continued on next page)

```
define type Date
      supertypes = { Entity };
      properties =
            {         Day               : Integer;
                      Month             : Month;
                      Year              : Integer;
            };
end Date;

define type Address
      supertypes = { Entity };
      properties =
            { Str_Number               : Integer;
              Street                    : String;
              City                      : String;
              State                     : String;
              Zip                       : Integer;
            };
end Address;

(b) define exceptiontype Bad_date
      supertypes = { Exception };
      properties  =
                  {
                  Date: Date;
                  };
end Bad_date;
```

Figure 23.25   *(continued)* Sample data definition. (a) Sample definition of
types Person, Employee and Works_On. (b) Definition
of Exception Type Bad_date.

which is itself a type and is therefore separately defined, as shown with the supertype
Exception in Figure 23.25b. A subtype inherits the operations of its supertype. It may define additional operations of its own and refine any of the inherited operations. Operations are implemented by methods. We will explain methods further in Section 23.4.4.

The dictionary is part of the object database. All types are instances of the system
type called Type, all properties are instances of the system type called PropType, and all
operations are instances of the system type OperType. Vbase thus provides uniform treatment of data and meta-data.

The Person_Catalog type definition included in Figure 23.25a shows that an index
to the instances of Person type is maintained in the dictionary. This index will be assigned integer values by the application as new instances are created, in no particular
order, and is accessible by using GetElement, which is a system-defined operation. As
shown in Figure 23.3, the representation and storage layers are themselves defined via
types. They can be further extended via subtypes.

23.4.4   Data Manipulation in Vbase

Manipulation of the object database is accomplished by means of methods. Two kinds of
methods are used—base methods and triggers. **Base methods** are used to perform the
general part of the operation and may be common to a number of types. **Triggers** are
written as customizing functions which exhibit behavior specific to a type while sharing
the base method with a number of types.

As we saw in the TDL definition of Person in Figure 23.25, operations are defined on types by giving an operation name, an argument list, and a call list of methods (including base and trigger methods). The return value data type, if any, is listed, and so are any exception types raised. (Compare this with the CALL statement in an IMS application program given in Section 23.2.4.) Here, it occurs as part of data definition.

The COP (C object processor) language, which is a strict superset of the C language, is used for two purposes in Vbase. First, it is used to build methods that are executed internally within the DBMS; second, it is used to build application modules that will access the database. The COP compiler works in conjunction with the system catalog; it can bind the application to data and/or operations at compile time rather than at run time. This optimization is controlled by the programmer, who is in a better position to understand the semantics of such binding. A COP program is able to access names and named objects directly from the database; the symbol table of a COP program is viewed in its "global" database context.

An application program written in COP dispatches operations against one or more objects in the database. Operations are called from application programs by name and are passed a list of arguments. A type may execute a method corresponding to its own special function and may invoke its supertype's operation. Method combination occurs when a refined method invokes its original method automatically (Vbase uses $$ for this purpose corresponding to SMALLTALK's "super" pseudovariable). Refinements of the inherited specification are verified by the TDL compiler. The execution sequence of an operation involving the refined base methods, base methods, and trigger methods is determined by the specification of the operation in the type definition in TDL. We do not cover that detail here. Another interesting feature is the *assert statement* in a method. It defers type checking until run time, thereby giving some needed flexibility to the programmer.

Another data manipulation option available in Vbase is **Object SQL**. It is provided as an ad hoc query language as well as a report generation tool. With the standard SQL syntax of SELECT .. FROM .. WHERE, the query uses object names in the FROM clause and retrieves property lists in the SELECT clause. Property chains are a handy naming mechanism allowed in the SELECT clause; a **property chain** consists of a list of property names (separated by periods) obtained by traversing properties to visit related objects. Thus:

```
SELECT   Fname, Lname, SupervisedBy. SupervisedBy. Lname
FROM     $ EMPLOYEE
WHERE    Salary > 50000
```

gives a list of employees' first and last names together with the second-level supervisor's last name for those with a salary exceeding $50,000. The SQL SELECT clause can also reference operations defined on the objects in their TDL definition. This lends a powerful capability. Joins and nested queries are supported. At the time of writing, SQL is implemented as a basic query facility without any optimization. Other than the feature of being able to reference the operations on objects and using path names, it is a subset of the SQL described in Chapter 7.

23.4.5   Storage of Data in Vbase

Each type in Vbase has an associated **create** operation by which an instance of the object is created. When an object is created, the user can specify whether or not the object is to persist, that is, whether or not it should be saved permanently in secondary storage. This is done by specifying the value of the *storagemanager* argument to the create operation. The assignment StorageManager:OK Storage indicates object kernel; in this case the object is stored and managed by object kernel. Alternatively, StorageManager:$PlO Storage means "process local storage"; such objects do not persist. Persistent objects are assigned unique identifiers.

The object database is stored in UNIX files or "raw" disk partitions. The storage is visualized at two levels—the secondary storage on disk and an "area cache" in the virtual address space in the user's program. Physical units called **segments** are units of transfer between disk and database cache.

For large objects, the constraint is that a segment must fit into the available main memory; however, objects can span segments. Persistent objects that are likely to be accessed together can be clustered in storage. To cluster the instances of a type, the key word arguments "where: Entity" and "hownear: Clustering" should be included as part of the create procedure. The type **clustering** is an enumerated type with three instances: $segment, $area, and $chunk, each of which is a unit of storage on a disk. To store an object of type TWO in the segment where objects of type ONE are stored, the procedure Create for object TWO must specify "where: ONE" and "hownear: $segment". This results in keeping objects of types ONE and TWO clustered in secondary storage. The $chunk option is not implemented in version 1.0.

The delete operation is used to make an object inaccessible. Delete is not allowed on universal objects; for example, it is not possible to delete the number 100. Delete is also suspended when the resources to perform the delete are unavailable (e.g., a device may be down). In Vbase, references to an entity may exist even after it is deleted. It is the programmer's responsibility to unset or reset references to deleted entities or properties. This is accomplished by refining the Entity$Delete operation by adding triggers.

23.4.6   Other Features of Vbase

The integrated tool set (ITS) is a single tool that performs three functions:

- Browsing of the source COP programs.
- Browsing of the database to display and modify database objects.
- Debugging of COP application programs by a controlled execution.

There is a uniform interface called the event manager for input and display manager for output. The debugger can manipulate methods and application programs. It can manage program text and execution. The applications' run time environment and COP source text can be viewed and manipulated through the debugger. The modification made via the debugger takes effect immediately. Details of concurrency control, recovery, and other internal features are given in Vbase manuals.

23.4.7   Closing Remarks on Vbase

In this section we briefly review the features and facilities of the Vbase integrated object system. This recent product is still under development; we have provided a summary of the essential concepts contributing to its design. Some performance data on this product is available. In conclusion, we wish to highlight the following:

- A basic philosophy behind Vbase design is strong typing. It provides several advantages and contributes to the ease of application development with resulting productivity gains.

- The system has an extensible data model with more than 60 predefined types. A user's database design consists of defining further types in the context of the system hierarchy of types. The benefits of object-oriented models (Section 15.4.1) accrue to this system; it supports all the data abstractions of Section 15.3.

- One drawback is the lack of a diagrammatic notation to go with the data model.

- The static behavior is captured by properties and the dynamic behavior by operations. Inverse properties make it easy to represent many-to-many relationships.

- The sytem follows the philosophy of invoking operations of objects rather than passing messages to objects. This is a departure from the SMALLTALK philosophy.

- The C object processor (COP) language works uniformly both to write methods for types and to write application programs. The iterate statement precludes the necessity for writing loops. C program variables and object variables can be combined arbitrarily. The COP processor works in conjunction with the object type definitions and is able to read and build database objects as needed. This results in an integrated environment combining a procedural object-oriented language and a persistent object base.

- The system provides a uniform interface to both data and meta-data storage. This is also accomplished in the DB2 system, where everything is stored as relations and is accessible to SQL.

- "Every object is a first-class object" is the philosophy that is maintained. However, Integer, Character, and Boolean also define special representation and storage manager types. As such, they can be implemented in a special way to accommodate the hardware and operating system characteristics. This capability can also be used to transfer data between an external database and Vbase.

- Access methods for storage and retrieval of objects have not yet been exhaustively developed in object-oriented DBMSs. We can contrast this with the variety of techniques for the storage of data as well as indexing and hashing structures available for the IMS system (Section 23.2.5) and the DB2 system (Section 23.1.5).

Overall, it remains to be seen how the object-oriented DBMSs will perform for traditional large databases with sizes of the order of hundreds of megabytes. They seem to be geared for nonconventional applications such as engineering design, spatial data management, and image databases that we discussed in Chapter 22.

Appendix to Chapter 23

E. F. Codd, the originator of the relational data model, published a two-part article in *Computerworld* (Codd 1985) that lists 12 rules* for how to determine whether a DBMS is

---

*The rules in the appendix are derived from two papers by Ted Codd that appeared in *Computerworld*: "Is your DBMS really relational" (October 14, 1985) and "Does your DBMS run by the rules?" (October 12, 1985), copyright © 1988 by CW Publishing, Inc.

relational and to what extent it is relational (see also Codd {1986}). We list these here because they provide a very useful yardstick for evaluating a relational system. Codd also mentions that, according to these rules, no fully relational system is available so far. In particular, rules 6, 9, 10, 11, and 12 are demanding and hence difficult to satisfy.

Rule 1: The Information Rule

All information in a relational database is represented explicitly at the logical level in exactly one way—by values in tables.

Rule 2: Guaranteed Access Rule

Each and every datum (atomic value) in a relational database is guaranteed to be logically accessible by resorting to a combination of table name, primary key value, and column name.

Rule 3: Systematic Treatment of Null Values

Null values (distinct from the empty character string or a string of blank characters and distinct from zero or any other number) are supported in the fully relational DBMS for representing missing information in a systematic way, independent of data type.

Rule 4: Dynamic On-Line Catalog Based on the Relational Model

The database description is represented at the logical level in the same way as ordinary data, so that authorized users can apply the same relational language to its interrogation as they apply to regular data.

Rule 5: Comprehensive Data Sublanguage Rule

A relational system may support several languages and various modes of terminal use (for example, the fill-in-the-blanks mode). However, there must be at least one language whose statements are expressible, per some well-defined syntax, as character strings and that is comprehensive in supporting all of the following items: data definition, view definition, data manipulation (interactive and by program), integrity constraints, and transaction boundaries (begin, commit and rollback).

Rule 6: View Updating Rule

All views that are theoretically updatable are also updatable by the system.

Rule 7: High-Level Insert, Update, and Delete

The capability of handling a base relation or a derived relation as a single operand applies not only to the retrieval of data but also to the insertion, update and deletion of data.

Rule 8: Physical Data Independence

Application programs and terminal activities remain logically unimpaired whenever any changes are made in either storage representation or access methods.

Rule 9: Logical Data Independence

Application programs and terminal activities remain logically unimpaired when information-preserving changes of any kind that theoretically permit unimpairment are made to the base tables.

Rule 10: Integrity Independence

Integrity constraints specific to a particular relational database must be definable in the relational data sublanguage and storable in the catalog, not in the application programs.

A minimum of the following two integrity constraints must be supported:

1. Entity integrity: No component of a primary key is allowed to have a null value.

2. Referential integrity: For each distinct non-null foreign key value in a relational database, there must exist a matching primary key value from the same domain.

Rule 11: Distribution Independence

A relational DBMS has distribution independence. Distribution independence implies that users should not have to be aware of whether or not a database is distributed.

Rule 12: Nonsubversion Rule

If a relational system has a low-level (single-record-at-a-time) language, that low-level language cannot be used to subvert or bypass the integrity rules or constraints expressed in the higher level relational language (multiple-records-at-a-time).

There is a rider to these 12 rules known as **Rule Zero:** "For any system that is claimed to be a relational database management system, that system must be able to manage data entirely through its relational capabilities."

On the basis of the above rules, there is no fully relational DBMS available today.

Selected Bibliography

DB2 is described in detail by Date and White (1988). SQL/DS, which is a similar relational DBMS of IBM, is described in Date and White (1988a). System R, which was a forerunner of DB2, is described by Astrahan et al. (1976). Chamberlin et al. (1981) give a historical account and an evaluation of System R. Blasgen et al. (1981) give an architectural overview. A number of manuals describing DB2 are available. A few important ones are listed below:

- IBM Database 2 General Information (IBM Form No. GC26-4073).
- IBM Database 2 Introduction to SQL (IBM Form No. GC26-4082).
- Query Management Facility (QMF): General Information (IBM Form No. GC26-4071).
- Data Extract: General Information (IBM Form No. GC26-4070).

The IMS system is described in full detail in Date (1977, 2nd edition). The hierarchical data model with specific reference to IMS is discussed in Tsichritzis and Lochovsky (1976). McGee (1977) has a comprehensive article on IMS. The book by Kapp and Leben (1978) is entirely devoted to IMS.

The IMS system is described in various IBM manuals. Some of the more important ones are:

- IMS/VS Version 1 General Information Manual (GH20-1260-12).
- IMS/VS Database Administration Guide (SH20-9025).
- IMS/VS Application Programming: Design and Coding (SH20-9025).
- IMS/VS Fast Path Feature General Information Manual (GH20-9069).

- IMS/VS Utilities Reference Manual (SH20-9029).
- IMS/VS Application Programming CICS/VS Users (SH20-9210).

The IDMS system is described by Date (1986) and by Kroenke and Dolan (1988). Important IDMS manuals include:

- IDMS System Overview (IDDB-0180-05502).
- IDMS/R DDL Reference.
- IDMS/R Database Operations (TDDB-0220-10000).
- Integrated Data Dictionary (IDD) User's Guide (TDID-0310-3001).
- Application Development System /On Line Reference Guide (TDAO-0330-11P0).
- IDMS Utilities (TDDB-0230-5330).
- CULPRIT User's Guide (TACU-0310-6102).

A report published by ANSI (1986a) proposes the new standards for network definition called network definition language (NDL).

The Vbase system concepts are described in Andrews and Harris (1987). Liskov et al. (1981) describe the CLU project at MIT that inspired the development of Vbase. Another object-oriented system, GEMSTONE/OPAL, is described in Maier et al. (1986). Its origin, SMALLTALK-80 language, and its implementation are described in Goldberg and Robson (1983). Kim et al. (1987) describe the ORION system of Microelectronics and Computer Technology Corporation. Vbase documentation includes:

- Vbase Programmer's Guide.
- TDL Language Reference Manual.
- COP Language Reference Manual.
- System Type Library.
- ITS Development Tools.

Among relational systems, INGRES has already been referenced in connection with QUEL in Chapter 9, and its query optimization based on decomposition was described in Chapter 18. Some of its facilities (QBF, in Section 22.1.3) were also referenced. The papers from the INGRES research project at the University of California, Berkeley are compiled in Stonebraker (1986). The commercial version of INGRES is marketed by RTI, from which the Ingres Documentation Set (by Relational Technology Inc., 1080 Marina Village Parkway, Alameda, CA 94501) is available.

ORACLE is documented in manuals from Oracle Corporation for different types of hardware ranging from personal computers to minis to mainframes.

System 2000, a hierarchical DBMS, has different sets of manuals for different operating systems (under IBM, Sperry, and CDC NOS). The following are of interest:

- System 2000 Language Specification Manual for the DEFINE language (No. 1010).
- System 2000 Getting Started with Create (No. 221139).
- System 2000 Language Specification Manual for the COBOL Programming Language Extension (PLEX) (No. 1020).

- System 2000 Language Specification Manual for QUEST Language (No. 221126).
- Language Specification Manual for the Administrative Facilities (No. 1013).

A comprehensive description of System 2000 can also be found in Cardenas (1985). Kroenke (1983) describes this system briefly.

A number of books have been written on microcomputer DBMSs. Simpson (1989), Prague and Hammit (1985), and Ross (1986) describe dBase, and Harrington (1987) describes ORACLE. Rbase, dBase, Informix, Paradox, etc. are described in their respective manuals.

A recent book by Valduriez and Gardarin (1989) compares a number of relational database systems.

APPENDIX A

Parameters of Disks

The most important disk parameter is the time it takes to locate an arbitrary disk block, given its block address, and then to transfer the block between the disk and a main memory buffer. This is the **random access time** for accessing a disk block. There are three time components to consider:

1. **Seek time** s: This is the time needed to mechanically position the read/write head on the correct track for movable-head disks. (For fixed-head disks, it is the time to electronically switch to the appropriate read/write head.) For movable-head disks this time varies, depending on the distance between the current track under the read/write head and the track specified in the block address. Usually, the disk manufacturer provides an average seek time in milliseconds. The typical range of average seek time is 10 to 60 msec. This is the main "culprit" for the delay involved in transferring blocks between disk and memory.

2. **Rotational delay** rd: Once the read/write head is at the correct track, it is necessary to wait for the beginning of the required block to rotate into a position under the read/write head. On the average, this will take about the time for half a revolution of the disk, but it will actually range from immediate access, if the start of the required block is in position under the read/write head right after the seek, up to a full disk revolution, if the start of the required block just passed the read/write head after the seek. If the speed of disk rotation is p revolutions per minute (rpm), then the average rotational delay rd is given by

$$rd = (1/2)*(1/p) \text{ min} = (60*1000)/(2*p) \text{ msec}$$

A typical value for p is 3600 rpm, which gives a rotational delay of rd = 8.33 msec. For fixed-head disks, where the seek time is negligible, this component causes the most delay when transferring a disk block.

3. **Block transfer time** btt: Once the read/write head is at the beginning of the required block, some time is needed to transfer the data in the block. This is the block transfer time and depends on the block size, track size, and rotational

speed. If the **transfer rate** for the disk is tr bytes/msec and the block size is B bytes, then

$$btt = B/tr \text{ msec}$$

If we have a track size of 50 Kbytes and p is 3600 rpm, then the transfer rate in bytes/msec would be

$$tr = (50*1000)/(60*1000/3600) = 3000 \text{ bytes/msec}$$

In this case, btt = B/3000 msec, where B is the block size in bytes.

The average time needed to find and transfer a block, given its block address, is estimated by

$$(s + rd + btt) \text{ msec}$$

This holds for either reading or writing a block. The principal method of reducing this time is to transfer several blocks that are stored on one or more tracks of the same cylinder; then the seek time is required only for the first block. To transfer consecutively k *noncontiguous* blocks that are on the *same cylinder*, we need approximately

$$s + (k * (rd + btt)) \text{ msec}$$

In this case, we will need two or more buffers in main storage, because we are continuously reading or writing the k blocks, as we discussed in Section 4.3. The transfer time per block is reduced even further when transferring *consecutive blocks* on the same track or cylinder. This eliminates the rotational delay for all but the first block, so the estimate for transferring k consecutive blocks is

$$s + rd + (k * btt) \text{ msec}$$

A more accurate estimate for transferring consecutive blocks takes into account the interblock gap discussed in Section 4.2.1. This interblock gap includes the information that enables the read/write head to determine which block it is about to read. Usually, the disk manufacturer provides a **bulk transfer rate** btr that takes the gap size into account when reading consecutively stored blocks. If the gap size is G bytes, then

$$btr = (B/(B + G)) * tr \text{ bytes/msec}$$

The bulk transfer rate is the rate of transferring *useful bytes* in the data blocks. The disk read/write head must go over all bytes on a track as the disk rotates, including the bytes in the interblock gaps, which store control information but not real data. When using the bulk transfer rate, the time to transfer the useful data in one block out of several consecutive blocks is B/btr. Hence, the estimated time to read k blocks consecutively stored on the same cylinder becomes

$$s + rd + (k * (B/btr)) \text{ msec}$$

Another parameter of disks is the **rewrite time**. This is useful in cases when we read a block from the disk into a main memory buffer, update the buffer, then write the buffer back to the same disk block on which it was stored. In many cases, the time to update the buffer in main memory is less than the time for one disk revolution. If we know that the buffer will be ready for rewriting, the system can keep the disk heads on the same track, and during the next disk revolution the updated buffer is rewritten back to the disk block. Hence, the rewrite time T_{rw} is usually estimated to be the time for one disk revolution:

$T_{rw} = 2 * rd$ msec

To summarize, here is a list of the parameters we discussed and the symbols we use for them:

seek time: s msec

rotational delay: rd msec

block transfer time: btt msec

rewrite time: T_{rw} msec

transfer rate: tr bytes/msec

bulk transfer rate: btr bytes/msec

block size: B bytes

interblock gap size: G bytes

APPENDIX **B**

Strengths and Weaknesses of SQL

The following remarks are mainly directed toward the SQL language currently supported in its major implementations. A new relational data language standard based on SQL has been proposed by ANSI (1986), but it leaves the basic shortcomings of the SQL language largely unresolved. For a more complete discussion the reader is referred to Date (1984), on which the following summary is based.

B.1   Strengths of SQL

The following strengths of SQL should be noted:

- SQL supports a simple data structure, namely tables. It does not explicitly support any links among tables. This latter point can also be considered a weakness, as discussed below.

- SQL supports the relational algebra operators of PROJECT, SELECT, and JOIN and operates on entire relations to generate new relations.

- SQL provides physical data independence to a large extent. Indexes may be added and deleted freely. There is also logical data independence for users in the sense that they can concentrate on data of interest to them by defining appropriate SQL views.

- SQL combines table creation, querying and updating, and view definition into a uniform syntax.

- SQL can be used both as a stand-alone query language and within a general-purpose programming language by embedding it within a host language.

- The language can be optimized and compiled or may be interpreted and executed on line. Since this is more of an implementation feature, it may not necessarily be considered a strong point of the language.

B.2 Weaknesses of SQL

The language leaves a number of shortcomings without satisfactory solutions. It also has a fair number of idiosyncrasies:

- SQL does *not* provide a means of declaring the primary key of a relation. In addition, candidate keys *cannot* be declared independently of a physical index, hence confusing a logical concept (specifying a key constraint) with a physical access path (declaring an index).

- SQL does *not* address the notion of foreign keys and the related notion of referential integrity at all. It is easily possible to leave a database in an inconsistent state by using foreign key values that do not obey the constraint.

- SQL does *not* show the meaningful relationships among tables to the user, such as those specifying referential integrity constraints; rather, all such relationships must explicitly be specified as join conditions in an SQL query. Users may overlook specifying join conditions that are semantically obvious, leading to incorrectly specified queries.

- SQL provides no mechanism for specifying strategies for view updates. Systems like DB2 have settled for simple rules such as "allow a view update only if it is on a single table consisting of some (or all) of its columns and a subset of rows," which are just not adequate. DB2 SQL does not even declare primary keys of tables and hence does not account for them during view updating.

- Although SQL is somewhat based on the relational calculus, the universal quantifiers (see Section 8.2) are not satisfactorily handled. There is no easy way to accomplish the DIVISION operation of relational algebra (see Section 6.2.5) in SQL.

- SQL has no easy-to-use facility for saving temporary results of queries and reusing them. It forces one to nest subqueries to accomplish passing of results.

- Set operators in SQL are restricted and sometimes look unnatural. For example, to take a union of the two tables:

      EE_STUDENTS (Student#, Name)
      CS_STUDENTS (Student#, Name)

  one is required to say:

  ```
  SELECT   *
  FROM     EE_STUDENTS
  UNION
  SELECT   *
  FROM     CS_STUDENTS
  ```

- In many instances, the user ends up specifying how to get the result rather than stating what the desired result is. This counters the philosophy of a relational calculus-based language. For example, to list the employees who have more than three dependents, writing

```
SELECT   EMPSSN
FROM     DEPENDENT
WHERE    COUNT (DEPENDENT_NAME) > 3
```

does not work. Instead, we have to write

```
SELECT     EMPSSN
FROM       DEPENDENT
GROUP BY   EMPSSN
HAVING     COUNT(*) > 3
```

Here the process of grouping and counting is almost procedurally indicated.

- Set operators like UNION are given a restricted treatment that makes the language like neither calculus nor algebra, but a mixture of the two. (For example, try computing the sum of the elements in the union of two columns in the tables).

- The useful extensions to relational algebra such as a variety of OUTER JOIN operations (see Section 6.3.3) are *not* supported in SQL.

- The treatment of built-in functions such as AVG or SUM is not cleanly handled. Placing them outside a SELECT .. FROM .. WHERE block may be more desirable than embedding them within the SELECT clause. For example, to assign a programming variable X the average salary of employees from department D3, it would be better to say

```
X := AVG (  SELECT   SALARY
            FROM     EMPLOYEE
            WHERE    DNO = D3 )
```

rather than first computing the scalar value using

```
SELECT   AVG (SALARY)
FROM     EMPLOYEE
WHERE    DNO = D3
```

The latter especially leads to problems in dealing with a null result when the set of tuples of the employees in department D3 is a null set. Current SQL implementations arbitrarily return the "not found" error condition or a null value as the result, depending on the context.

- NULL values are always eliminated from the argument of built-in functions such as SUM or AVG, whereas COUNT(*) counts rows including duplicates and all null rows. This is reasonable but arbitrary and it would be desirable to have some user-specified options available.

- Embedded SQL does not exploit the control structures or exception-handling capabilities of the host languages.

Because of the above and a host of other weaknesses, SQL cannot be considered a very well designed and deficiency-free language. The new RDL standard adds some features but fails to address some of the basic shortcomings pointed out above.

Performance Analysis
of Various Access Paths

In this appendix we use an example to analyze quantitatively the performance of different access paths. This will give us a better understanding of how these access paths compare and under which circumstances we should choose each. We first present our example file and disk parameters. We show how to estimate the storage requirements for the file and its access paths in Section C.1. In Section C.2 we discuss how to estimate the performance of record retrieval for various access paths. We estimate the performance of update operations in Section C.3. Section C.4 compares the performance of various access paths.

We will use the following values for disk parameters. These are not parameters for any particular disk unit but are typical values. Refer to Appendix A and Section 4.2.1 for an explanation of these parameters.

(average) seek time s = 20 msec

(average) rotational delay rd = 9.5 msec

block size B = 512 bytes

interblock gap size G = 106 bytes

transfer rate tr = 1024 bytes/msec

block transfer time btt = B/tr = 0.5 msec

bulk transfer rate btr = tr * (B/(B + G)) = 848 bytes/msec

rewrite time T_{rw} = 2 * rd = 19 msec

block pointer size P = 5 bytes

record pointer size Pr = 6 bytes

Our example file is an EMPLOYEE file with the following fields: SSN (9 chars), NAME (30 chars), BIRTHDATE (8 chars), DEPARTMENT (9 chars), ADDRESS (30 chars), and PHONE (10 chars). The file has r = 30,000 records, and the record format is fixed length and unspanned. A 1-byte deletion marker per record is used for marking deleted records. For this file the record size R, the blocking factor bfr, and the number of file blocks b are calculated as follows:

$$R = (9 + 30 + 8 + 9 + 30 + 10) + 1 = 97 \text{ bytes}$$
$$bfr = \lfloor (B/R) \rfloor = \lfloor (512/97) \rfloor = 5 \text{ records per block}$$
$$b = \lceil (r/bfr) \rceil = \lceil (30,000/5) \rceil = 6000 \text{ blocks}$$

C.1   Storage Requirements

We now show how to estimate the storage capacity required by a file and the storage overhead that each file incurs because of access paths, record blocking, pointers, etc. There are various storage overheads for a file. First, a file header or descriptor is needed for each file to keep track of where the file blocks are stored on disk, information concerning the record formats and access paths defined for the file, record blocking information, protection information, etc. Second, any indexing, hashing, or other access structures for the file themselves require additional storage. Third, the method of record blocking and the interblock gaps also incur storage overhead. We will discuss the overhead due to record blocking and interblock gaps first, then estimate storage overhead for indexing and hashing.

By choosing **unspanned record blocking** in the above example, we use up (or "waste") W_B bytes per block, where

$$W_B = B - (R * bfr) = 512 - (97*5) = 27 \text{ bytes per block}$$

This makes each record *effectively* use $R_E = (B/bfr) = (512/5) = 102.4$ bytes of storage even though a record is *actually* 97 bytes long—a storage overhead of $R_E - R = 5.4$ bytes per record. In addition, the **interblock gap** uses up $G = 106$ bytes per block, which adds an overhead of $G/bfr = 106/5 = 21.2$ bytes per record.

If we had chosen **spanned blocking** (see Section 4.4.3) with a 1-byte record separator field and a block pointer in each block to point to the next file block, we would have used up $P = 5$ bytes per block for the block pointer, plus 1 byte per record for the separator character. The file would need $b' = \lceil ((r * (R + 1))/(B - P)) \rceil = \lceil ((30,000 * (97 + 1))/(512 - 5)) \rceil = 5799$ blocks. In this case the effective record size is $R_E = (B * b')/r = (512 * 5799)/30,000 = 98.96$ bytes—an overhead of $R_E - R = 1.96$ bytes per record.

The use of spanning effectively requires 3.44 fewer bytes per record than unspanned blocking. In terms of blocks, spanning would require $b - b' = 201$ fewer blocks to store our example file. However, spanned blocking makes records start at arbitrary locations within a block rather than at known fixed locations. In addition, some records (approximately one in five) would be stored on two blocks. These factors complicate record retrieval, making unspanned blocking the favored technique with fixed-length records in spite of its higher storage requirements. In general, the file system takes care of blocking decisions and the programmer does not have to be concerned with these details. However, it is useful to understand these techniques to get good estimates for the storage requirements of a file.

Next, consider the storage overhead due to the different types of *indexes*. We consider a primary multilevel index on the SSN field of our example file (Index1), a secondary index on SSN that is organized as a B^+-tree (Index2), and a clustering index on the DEPARTMENT field of the file (Index3).

For Index1, the primary index on SSN, the file records are physically ordered by SSN. Block anchors and an overflow file organized using chaining are used as discussed in Section 5.1.1. A pointer to a linked list of overflow records is maintained in each file block—to those overflow records whose SSN values make them belong to this block. Hence, we need to recalculate the blocking factor bfr for the file as bfr = $\lfloor((B - Pr)/R)\rfloor$ = $\lfloor((512 - 6)/97)\rfloor$ = 5 records per block. For this example, we get the same blocking factor, although in general, we could have gotten a smaller blocking factor because of the extra pointer in each block.

For Index1, each index entry consists of an index field value of size V_{SSN} = 9 bytes and a block pointer of size P = 5 bytes. Hence, the index entry size is R_{I1} = $(V_{SSN} + P)$ = $(9 + 5)$ = 14 bytes. The index blocking factor is bfr_{I1} = $\lfloor(B/R_{I1})\rfloor$ = $\lfloor(512/14)\rfloor$ = 36 index entries per block. At the first index level, we will have one index entry for *each file block*. Hence, the numbers of first-level index entries r_1 and first-level index blocks b_1 are r_1 = b = 6000 entries and b_1 = $\lceil(r_1/bfr_{I1})\rceil$ = $\lceil(6000/36)\rceil$ = 167 blocks.

The numbers of second-level index entries r_2 and second-level index blocks b_2 are r_2 = b_1 = 167 entries and b_2 = $\lceil(r_2/bfr_{I1})\rceil$ = $\lceil(167/36)\rceil$ = 5 blocks. The numbers of third-level index entries r_3 and third-level index blocks b_3 are r_3 = b_2 = 5 entries and b_3 = $\lceil(r_3/bfr_{I1})\rceil$ = $\lceil(5/36)\rceil$ = 1 block. Because b_3 = 1, level 3 is the top level of the index, so Index1 will have x_{I1} = 3 levels. The total number of blocks for Index1 is b_{I1} = b_1 + b_2 + b_3 = 167 + 5 + 1 = 173 blocks. Each record in the file is now effectively using up additional space W_{I1} = $(b_{I1} * B)/r$ = (173 * 512) / 30,000 = 2.95 bytes per record

For Index2 we have one first-level index entry *for each record* in the file, so we have r = 30,000 entries in level 1 of the index. This is because we now assume the file is not ordered by SSN so block anchors cannot be used. Because we assume the index is a B^+-tree, we must calculate the maximum number of pointers p and the average number of pointers k in a B^+-tree node as discussed in Section 5.3.2. For nodes of the tree, we can get at most p block pointers and p − 1 index values in a node (disk block), so we get

$(p * P) + ((p - 1) * V_{SSN}) \le B$, or
$(5 * p) + (9 * (p - 1)) \le 512$, which gives $14 * p \le 521$, so p = 37.

On the average, the node in a B^+-tree is 69% full, so the average number of pointers in a node (average fan-out) will be approximately k = 0.69 * p = 0.69 * 37 = 25.53 pointers per block.

On the average, each leaf-level node will point to k − 1 records. Hence, the average number of leaf-level nodes (first-level blocks) b_1 = $\lceil(r/(k - 1))\rceil$ = $\lceil(30,000/24.53)\rceil$ = 1223 blocks.

At the second and subsequent levels, the internal nodes of a B^+-tree will each point to, on the average, k blocks at the next lower level. Hence, the numbers of blocks b_i at level i, for i > 1, are b_2 = $\lceil(b_1/k)\rceil$ = $\lceil(1223/25.53)\rceil$ =48 blocks, b_3 = $\lceil(b_2/k)\rceil$ = $\lceil(48/25.53)\rceil$ = 2 blocks, and b_4 = ceiling(b_3/k) = $\lceil(2/25.53)\rceil$ =1 block. Hence, the number of levels of Index2 is x_{I2} = 4 levels, and the total number of blocks needed for the index—on average under the 0.69 occupancy assumption—is b_{I2} = b_1 + b_2 + b_3 + b_4 =

$1223 + 48 + 2 + 1 = 1274$ blocks. This means that each record in the file is now effectively using up additional space $W_{I2} = (b_{I2} * B)/r = (1274 * 512)/30,000 = 21.74$ bytes per record.

For the clustering index Index3 on the DEPARTMENT field, we assume the file records are physically ordered by the DEPARTMENT field. The number of index entries in the first level of a clustering index does not depend on the number of records r, nor does it depend on the number of blocks b of the file. Rather, it is determined by the *number of distinct values* that the indexing field has. If we know that the company that maintains our example file has 100 distinct departments, then the DEPARTMENT field will have 100 distinct values. Hence, the first level of Index3 will have 100 entries—one for each distinct value. Note that this may change if the number of departments increases or decreases. Each index entry contains one DEPARTMENT value and a pointer to the first block in a sequence of blocks that contain records with that value. Hence, the index entry size is $R_{I3} = (V_{\text{DEPARTMENT}} + P) = (9 + 5) = 14$ bytes and the blocking factor for the index is $bfr_{I3} = \lfloor (B/R_{I3}) \rfloor = \lfloor (512/14) \rfloor = 36$ index entries per block.

The number of first-level index blocks $b_1 = \lceil (100/bfr_{I3}) \rceil = \lceil (100/36) \rceil = 3$ blocks. The numbers of second-level index entries r_2 and second-level index blocks b_2 are $r_2 = b_1 = 3$ entries and $b_2 = \lceil (r_2/bfr_{I3}) \rceil = \lceil (3/36) \rceil = 1$ block. Hence, Index3 will have $x_{I3} = 2$ levels, and the total number of blocks it uses $b_{I3} = b_1 + b_2 = 3 + 1 = 4$ blocks. This means that each record in the file is now effectively using up additional space $W_{I3} = (b_{I3} * B)/r = (4 * 512)/30,000 = 0.07$ bytes per record.

Table C.1 summarizes the storage requirements for the various indexes in our example and compares indexing with other access paths in terms of storage requirements. In general, a secondary index will use more storage than a primary index and may have a higher number of levels. The storage overhead of a clustering index depends on the number of *distinct values* of the indexing field, but a clustering index will generally use less storage space and have fewer index levels than either of the other two. Note that in many cases the top-level index block has a small number of entries; in our example, the top levels of Index1, Index2, and Index3 have 5, 2, and 3 entries, respectively. These top-level entries are usually copied and kept in memory when the file is opened for processing, thus reducing the number of levels by one.

It is much harder to estimate accurately the storage overhead due to hashing because the hash function, number of overflow records, and method of handling overflow all affect the storage requirements. We will make certain assumptions here and consider only the static hashing technique described in Section 4.8.2. We assume that buckets are used that are of size one block each and that overflow is handled by chaining. Hence, the number of records m that can be stored in each bucket is $m = \lfloor ((B - Pr)/R) \rfloor = \lfloor ((512 - 6)/97) \rfloor = 5$ records per block. To keep the file approximately 90% full, we choose the number of buckets M to be a *prime number* close to $(b/0.9) = (6000/0.9) = 6667$. We choose the prime number 6661, so $M = 6661$ buckets (blocks). Let us assume that $r_O = 1000$ of the $r = 30,000$ records were placed in overflow blocks by chaining them to the bucket to which they hashed. Each overflow record will need a record pointer, so the size of an overflow record R_O and the number of overflow blocks b_O, assuming spanned blocking, are $R_O = R + Pr = 97 + 6 = 103$ bytes and $b_O = \lceil ((r_O * R_O)/(B - P)) \rceil = \lceil ((1000 * 103)/(512 - 5)) \rceil = 204$ blocks.

Table C.1   Comparing the Storage Space Needed by Various Access Paths for Our Example File

		Number of Blocks	Additional Space per Record (in bytes)	Number of Index Levels
Effect of interblock gap	Unspanned		21.2	
	Spanned		20.49	
Effect of blocking of records	Unspanned	6000	5.4	
	Spanned	5799	1.96	
Hash file		6865	20.16	
Primary index (Index1)		173	2.95	3
Secondary B$^+$-tree index (Index2)		1274	21.74	4
Clustering index (Index3)		4	0.07	2

Each record effectively uses $((M + b_O) * B)/r = ((6661 + 204) * 512)/30,000 = 117.16$ bytes, which is $(117.95 - 97) = 20.16$ more bytes per record. The total number of blocks used by hashing in this example is $M + b_O = 6865$. Table C.1 compares the storage requirements for hashing with other access paths *for this particular example*.

C.2   Performance of Retrieval Operations

In this section we estimate the performance of retrieving records under some of the different storage structures and access paths discussed in Chapters 4 and 5. Retrieval involves searching for and finding a record or records that satisfy a certain **search criterion** or **condition**. Consider two cases for the condition that is used to find records in a file:

1. Equality condition on a key (unique) field of the file.
2. Equality condition on a nonkey (nonunique) field.

In case 1, either we find a single record that satisfies the criterion or no record is found. In case 2, numerous records may satisfy the condition. For a condition on a key field, we consider the following cases:

1a. Finding a record in a file given its key field value.
1b. Finding the next record (from the last record found) in order of the key field.

For a condition on a nonkey field, we consider the following cases:

2a. Finding the first record in a file having a given nonkey field value.

2b. Finding all the records in the file having a given nonkey field value.

We denote the time for finding the first record by t_F and the number of blocks accessed to find that record by ba_F. For the next record we use the notation t_N and ba_N, whereas for finding all records we use the notation t_A and ba_A. We consider the following access structures: unordered file, ordered file with binary search, primary index, secondary index, clustering index, and hashing. We use the disk parameters and example file specified in the beginning of this appendix.

C.2.1   Condition on a Key Field

For a condition on a key field, such as SSN = '123456789', we can estimate the number of block accesses and time to find the record for various access paths. First, for an *unordered file*, or if *no access path exists* on the search key field, we must do a **linear search**. On the average, this requires us to search half the file blocks when the record is found and all the file blocks if the record is not found. Hence, we get $ba_F = b/2 = 6000/2 = 3000$ block accesses on the average. The access time depends on whether or not the file blocks are stored contiguously. If not, we get $t_F = (s + rd + btt) * (b/2) = 30 * 3000 = 90{,}000$ msec = 90 sec = 1.5 min (!). If the blocks are *stored contiguously*, and assuming we use buffering to speed up the disk access, we can use the bulk transfer rate, so we get $t_F = s + rd + ((b/2) * (B/btr)) = 20 + 9.5 + (3000 * (512/848)) = 29.5 + 1811.32 = 1840.82$ msec = 1.84 sec. Note the vast improvement in linear search time when the file is stored in consecutive blocks and buffering is used to speed up the search.

Finding the next record in order of the key field requires searching the whole file once again if we *do not know* the next value. This gives $ba_N = 2 * ba_F$ and $t_N = 2 * t_F$. If we *do know* the next value, we will search only half the file on the average, so we get $ba_N = ba_F$ and $t_N = t_F$.

Next, suppose the file records are *ordered* by SSN but no primary index exists. We can do a **binary search** on the blocks, so the number of block accesses and the access time become approximately $ba_F = \log_2(b) = \log2(6000) = 8.7$ block accesses and $t_F = \log_2(b) * (s + rd + btt) = 8.7 * 30 = 261$ msec = 0.261 sec.

To find the next record we do not have to go far. In most cases, the next record will be in the same block as the current record so no more block accesses are needed. In approximately 1/bfr of the cases, we have to access another block. Hence, on the average, we get $ba_N = (1/bfr) = 1/5 = 0.2$ block accesses and $t_N = (1/bfr) * (s + rd + btt) = 0.2 * 30 = 6$ msec= 0.006 sec.

If we have a **primary index** on SSN, such as Index1 of Section C.1, we must access one block at each index level plus one block from the file itself. To simplify our discussion, we ignore overflow records. The number of block accesses and the access time for this case are $ba_F = (x_{I1} + 1) = (3 + 1) = 4$ block accesses and $t_F = (x_{I1} + 1) * (s + rd + btt) = 4 * 30 = 120$ msec = 0.12 sec. Note that if all blocks of an index are stored on the same cylinder, as is often the case, we save the seek time during all but the first index block access and the file block access, so we get $t_F = (s + rd + btt) + ((x_{I1} - 1) * (rd +$

btt)) + (s + rd + btt) = 30 + 2 * 10 + 30 = 80 msec = 0.08 sec. If, in addition, the top-level index block is stored in memory, we get $ba_F = (x_{I1} + 1 - 1) = 3$ block accesses and $t_F = (s + rd + btt) + ((x_{I1} - 2) * (rd + btt)) + (s + rd + btt) = 30 + 1 * 10 + 30 = 70$ msec = 0.07 sec. (The latter equation assumes that an index has at least two levels.) Finding the next record on a primary index is the same as the case for ordered records, because the records are ordered by the indexing field.

For a **secondary index** on SSN, such as Index2 of Section C.1, we also must access one block at each index level plus one block from the file itself. The number of block accesses and the access time for this case are $ba_F = (x_{I2} + 1) = (4 + 1) = 5$ block accesses and $t_F = (x_{I2} + 1) * (s + rd + btt) = 5 * 30 = 150$ msec = 0.15 sec. If all blocks of an index are stored on the same cylinder, we get $t_F = (s + rd + btt) + ((x_{I2} - 2) * (rd + btt))$ + (s + rd + btt) = 30 + (3 * 10) + 30 = 90 msec = 0.09 sec. If, in addition, the top-level index block is stored in memory, we get $ba_F = (x_{I2} + 1 - 1) = 4$ block accesses and $t_F = (s + rd + btt) + ((x_{I2} - 2) * (rd + btt)) + (s + rd + btt) = 30 + (2 * 10) + 30 = 80$ msec = 0.08 sec. (The latter equation assumes that an index has at least two levels.)

To find the next record using the B+-tree secondary index, we assume that the leaf-level index block used to retrieve the current record is kept in memory. In approximately $(1/(k - 1))$ of the cases, we need to retrieve the next leaf-level index block. We must also retrieve, in $(b - 1)/b$ of the cases, another file block to locate the record. Hence, we get, on the average $ba_N = (1/(k - 1)) + ((b - 1)/b) = (1/24.53) + (5999/6000) = 1.04$ block accesses and $t_N = ((1/(k - 1)) * (s + rd + btt)) + (((b - 1)/b) * (s + rd + btt)) = 1.04 * 30$ = 31.2 msec = 0.0312 sec.

Finally, consider the case of a **hash file,** with hash key on SSN. To find a record in the file given the value of its hash key field, we will need one block access in most cases. A more accurate estimate is to take into account the possibility of having to go to overflow. If we assume that the records are equally likely to be accessed, then the probability of accessing an overflow record p_O is r_O/r, where r_O is the number of overflow records. The average length of each chain (linked list) of overflow records is r_O/M if we assume that the overflow records are evenly distributed among the M buckets. On the average, we will search half a chain before we find the overflow record. Hence, we get $ba_F = 1 + (p_O * (1/2) * (r_O/M))$ and $t_F = (s + rd + btt) + (p_O * (1/2) * (r_O/M) * (s + rd + btt))$. In our example, the average chain length is less than one so we approximate it to one. This is so because each time we go to the overflow we will access at least one extra block. Hence, for our example file, we get $t_F = (s + rd + btt) + (p_O * (s + rd + btt)) = 30 +$ ((1000/30,000) * 30) = 31 msec = 0.031 sec.

With hashing, finding the next record in order of the key field is very inefficient if we *do not know* the value of the next key field, since we will have to search all the records of the file. Hence, we must read and search $(M + b_O)$ blocks. If we *do know* the value of the next key field in the file, then we can use the hash key to retrieve the record, and $t_N = t_F$.

Table C.2 shows a summary of the retrieval performance for finding a record on a key field for our example file. Table C.3 shows the performance for retrieving the next record from the current one. It is clear that hashing is best for random retrieval. However, because (static) hashing creates problems with file expansion and because it does not support finding the next record in key order, indexing is often given preference over hashing.

Table C.2   Comparing the Performance of Retrieving a Random Record on the Key Field for Various Access Paths for Our Example File

		Estimated Average Number of Block Accesses	Estimated Average Retrieval Time (in msec)
Linear search (unordered records)		3,000	1,840.82 (contiguous) 90,000 (noncontiguous)
Binary search (ordered records)		8.7	261
Primary index	(top index block not in main memory)	4	120 80 (same cylinder)
	(top index block in main memory)	3	90 70 (same cylinder)
Secondary index (B^+-tree)	(top index block not in main memory)	5	150 90 (same cylinder)
	(top index block in main memory)	4	120 80 (same cylinder)
Hash file		1.03	31

Table C.3   Comparing the Performance of Retrieving the Next Record from the Current Record for Various Access Paths for Our Example File

		Estimated Average Number of Block Accesses	Estimated Average Retrieval Time (in msec)
Linear search (unordered records)	(value not known) (value known)	6,000 3,000	180,000 90,000
Binary search (ordered records)		0.2	6
Primary index		0.2	6
Secondary index		1.04	31.2
Hash file	(value not known) (value known)	6,000 1.03	180,000 31

C.2.2   Condition on a Nonkey Field

For a condition on a nonkey field, such as DEPARTMENT='Research', several records may satisfy the search criterion. If a clustering index is defined on the field, then the records are physically ordered and the records with DEPARTMENT='Research' are clustered together on disk blocks. Otherwise, the records for each department are scattered all over the file.

We first consider the latter case of an **unordered file,** where the records are *not clustered* by value of DEPARTMENT. Finding the first of the records satisfying the search criterion will, on the average, take fewer block accesses than if the condition was on a key field. Suppose n records out of the r records in the file satisfy the condition DEPARTMENT='Research'. The ratio (n/r) is called the **selection factor** of the search criterion. If we assume the records are uniformly distributed in the file and that $n < b$, then on the average it will take $(1/2) * (b/n)$ block accesses to find the first record satisfying the criterion and another (b/n) block accesses to find each of the next records satisfying the same criterion. For our file, we assumed that there were 100 distinct departments. If we further assume that each department has approximately the same number of employees, then we get n = r/100 = 30,000/100 = 300 records per distinct value. Hence, we get $ba_F = (1/2) * (b/n) = 0.5 * (6000/300) = 0.5 * 20 = 10$ block accesses and $t_F = (1/2) * (b/n) * (s + rd + btt) = 10 * 30 = 300$ msec = 0.3 sec. If we assume the file blocks are *stored contiguously*, we get $t_F = s + rd + ((baF - 1) * (B/btr)) = 20 + 9.5 + (9 * (512/848)) = 34.93$ msec.

To find all records with a given value, we have to search through the whole file, so we get $ba_A = b = 6000$ block accesses and $t_A = b * (s + rd + btt) = 6000 * 30 = 180,000$ msec = 180 sec. If we assume the file blocks are stored contiguously, we get $t_A = s + rd + (b * (B/btr)) = 20 + 9.5 + (6000 * (512/848)) = 29.5 + 3622.64 = 3652.14$ msec = 3.65 sec.

Next, consider the case of a **clustering index,** such as Index3 of Section C.1. In this case we access one block at each level of the index, which leads us to the first file block that contains one of the desired records. We can then access the n records that are stored contiguously in approximately another (n/bfr) block accesses. Hence, we get $ba_F = x_{I3} + 1 = 2 + 1 = 3$ block accesses, $t_F = (x_{I3} + 1) * (s + rd + btt) = 3 * 30 = 90$ msec = 0.09 sec, $ba_A = x_{I3} + (n/bfr) = 2 + (300/5) = 62$ block accesses, and $t_A = (x_{I3} + (n/bfr)) * (s + rd + btt) = 62 * 30 = 1860$ msec = 1.86 sec. If we assume that the blocks of a cluster are *contiguously allocated*, we get $t_A = (x_{I3} * (s + rd + btt)) + s + rd + ((n/bfr) * (B/btr)) = (2 * 30) + 29.5 + (60 * (512/848)) = 60 + 29.5 + 36.2 = 125.7$ msec = 0.1257 sec.

There is another option for an access structure on a nonkey field, which is to have a two-level secondary index similar to the clustering index, Index3, but with the records themselves not physically clustered by the index field. In this case, the pointer P in each first-level index entry <V, P> points to a disk block or a linked list of disk blocks that contain pointers to all the records with index field value equal to V (see Figure 5.5). If we assume in our example that these blocks contain record pointers, then each block can hold $\lfloor ((B - P)/Pr)\rfloor = \lfloor ((512 - 5)/6)\rfloor = 84$ record pointers. We would need approximately $\lceil (r/84)\rceil = \lceil (30,000/84)\rceil = 358$ such blocks, so the index and the pointer blocks would require a total of $358 + b_{I3} = 358 + 4 = 362$ disk blocks. In this case, finding the first record satisfying the search criterion would require $ba_F = x_{I3} + 2 = 2 + 2 = 4$ block accesses and $t_F = ba_F * (s + rd + btt) = 4 * 30 = 120$ msec = 0.12 sec.

Table C.4   Comparing the Performance of Retrieving the First Record Satisfying a Search Criterion on a Nonkey Field

		Estimated Average Number of Block Accesses	Estimated Average Retrieval Time (in msec)
Linear search	(noncontiguous)	10	300
(unordered records)	(contiguous)	10	35.54
Clustering index (ordered records)		3	90
Secondary index (unordered records)		4	12

Table C.5   Comparing the Performance of Retrieving All the Records Satisfying a Search Criterion on a Nonkey Field

		Estimated Average Number of Block Accesses	Estimated Average Retrieval Time (in msec)
Linear search	(noncontiguous)	6,000	180,000
(unordered records)	(contiguous)	6,000	3,652.14
Clustering index	(noncontiguous)	62	1,860
(ordered records)	(contiguous)	62	125.7
Secondary index		308	9,240
(unordered records)	(same cylinder)	308	3,100

Finding all the records satisfying the search criterion would require accessing approximately 300 records, where each may be on a separate block. In addition, we must access x_{I3} index blocks, plus $\lceil (300/84) \rceil = 4$ pointer blocks. Hence, we get $ba_A = x_{I3} + 4 + 300 = 308$ block accesses and $t_A = ba_F * (s + rd + btt) = 308 * 30 = 9240$ msec = 9.24 sec. If we assume that the file, index, and pointer blocks are on the same cylinder, the above time can be reduced to $t_A = s + (ba_F * (rd + btt)) = 20 + (308 * 10) = 3100$ msec = 3.1 sec.

Tables C.4 and C.5 summarize the results of retrieval on a nonkey field.

C.3   Performance of Update Operations

There are three main types of update operations: inserting a record, deleting a record, and modifying a record. Deletion and modification are straightforward to analyze. We must first find and retrieve the block containing the record, modify the record in memory, and write it—along with its block—back to disk. In the case of deletion, the deletion marker is changed. In the case of modification, the fields whose values are to be modified are changed. Most file systems will find and read the block that contains the record into a buffer, modify the record in the buffer, and rewrite the buffer back to disk during the next disk rotation. Hence, for our example file, we get delete time t_D and modify time t_M of $t_D = t_M = t_F + T_{rw} = t_F + 19$ msec.

Inserting a new record depends on the file organization. Insertion is most straightforward for the case of an unordered file, where we place the new record at the end of the file. In this case we retrieve the last file block, add a record to it, and then rewrite the block back to disk. Hence, we get $t_I = (s + rd + btt) + T_{rw}$. If the unordered file has one or more secondary indexes, then an index entry must be added to each such index to point to the new record. If the index is implemented as a B^+-tree, we usually need to find the appropriate leaf-level block and place the new index entry in it. This will require approximately $x * (s + rd + btt) + T_{rw}$ msec if no splitting occurs.

Insertion is very expensive for an ordered file unless we use a separate overflow (or transaction) file. For hashing, insertion is quite efficient except for the case where a collision occurs. We will not analyze these cases here but leave them for the reader as exercises.

C.4 Summary

As we can see from the example analyzed here, having no access structures on the field that specifies the record selection criterion makes it very expensive in time to find and retrieve that record. Having access structures on the search field drastically improves the performance of record retrieval. The cost for most access structures is the use of additional storage and the higher cost of record insertions. The trade-off is to improve the retrieval time performance at the cost of additional storage and higher insertion time.

Hashing gives the best performance for finding a record on the key field but does not, in general, support the finding of the next record. The next best access structure for arbitrary record access on a key field is a primary index, which makes it very efficient both to find an arbitrary record and to retrieve the records in order of the key field. This makes it ideally suited for both selection conditions and equijoin conditions on a file. Secondary indexes improve finding both the first and next records, but they require more storage space than primary indexes. However, because they do not require that the file records be physically sorted on the indexing field, it is possible to have several secondary indexes on different fields of the same file. This is the main reason for the popularity of secondary indexes.

For retrieval on a nonkey field, a clustering index gives a very efficient mechanism for retrieving all the records that satisfy a selection criterion on the indexing field. In addition, the clustering index does not usually use up much space unless the indexing field has very many distinct field values. However, the clustering index does require that the records be physically ordered by the indexing field. If this is not possible, a secondary index with pointer blocks can be used instead of the clustering index. This is substantially slower than the clustering index for retrieving all records satisfying the search criterion, but it is better than no access path at all.

APPENDIX D

Summary of Relational Algebra Transformations

In this appendix we give a summary of transformations on the operations of the relational algebra involving selection, projection, join, Cartesian product, union, set intersection, and set difference. The tables show which transformations are not permitted and which transformations hold only under certain qualifying conditions. The tables are based on similar tables in Ceri and Pelagatti (1984a).

Notation:

Y: Operation holds.

N: Operation does not hold.

C_i: Selection condition i.

A_i: Set of attributes.

JC: Join condition.

Attr(X): Set of attributes in X.

Q_i: Qualification i, which states a condition under which the operation holds.

D.1 Idempotence of the Unary Operations SELECT and PROJECT

A = a set of attributes
C = a conditional expression

a. $\pi_A(R) \Rightarrow \pi_A(\pi_{A1}(R))$ if $A \subseteq A1$.
b. $\sigma_C(R) \Rightarrow \sigma_{C1}(\sigma_{C2}(R))$ if C = C1 and C2.

In the following, the formulae are valid after replacing the @-sign by appropriate entries from the column headers. The Q_i's are qualification conditions under which the transformation would be valid.

D.2   Commutativity of the Unary Operations SELECT and PROJECT

	$@ = \sigma_{C2}$	$@ = \pi_{A2}$
$\sigma_{C1}(@(R)) \Rightarrow @(\sigma_{C1}(R))$	Y	Y
$\pi_{A1}(@(R)) \Rightarrow @(\pi_{A1}(R))$	Q1	Q2

Q1: if (the attributes involved in the condition C2) $\subseteq$ A1
Q2: $\pi_{A1}(\pi_{A2}(R) \Rightarrow \pi_{A1}(R)$ if A1 $\subseteq$ A2, undefined otherwise

D.3   Commutativity and Associativity of Binary Operations

	$@ = \bowtie_{JC}$	$@ = X$	$@ = \cup$	$@ = \cap$	$@ = -$
$R @ S \Rightarrow S @ R$	Y	Y	Y	Y	N
$(R @ S) @ T \Rightarrow R @ (S @ T)$	Q2	Y	Y	Y	N

Q2: $(R \bowtie_{JC1} S) \bowtie_{JC2} T \Rightarrow R \bowtie_{JC1}(S \bowtie_{JC2} T)$ only if Attr(JC2) $\subseteq$ Attr(S) $\cup$ Attr(T)

D.4   Distributivity of Unary Operations over Binary Operations

	$@ = \bowtie_{JC}$	$@ = X$
$\sigma_C(R@S) \Rightarrow$		
$\quad \sigma_{CR}(R)@\sigma_{CS}(S)$	Q3	Q3
$\pi_A(R@S) \Rightarrow$		
$\quad \pi_{AR}(R)@\pi_{AS}(S)$	Q4	Y
	AR = A − S	AR = A − S
	AS = A − R	AS = A − R

	$@ = \cup$	$@ = \cap$	$@ = -$
$\sigma_C(R@S) \Rightarrow$	Y	Y	Y
$\quad \sigma_{CR}(R)@\sigma_{CS}(S)$	CR = C	CR = C	CR = C
	CS = C	CS = C	CS = C
$\pi_A(R@S) \Rightarrow$	Y	Y	N
$\quad \pi_{AR}(R)@\pi_{AS}(S)$	AR = A	AR = A	
	AS = A	AS = A	

Q3: C = CR and CS and Attr(CR) $\subseteq$ R and Attr(CS) $\subseteq$ S
Q4: Attr(JC) $\subseteq$ A

D.5   Factoring SELECT and PROJECT from Binary Operations

	@ = $\bowtie$	@ = X
$\sigma_{CR}(R)@\sigma_{CS}(S)$	Y	Y
$\Rightarrow \sigma_C(R@S)$	C = CR and CS	C = CR and CS
$\pi_{AR}(R)@\pi_{AS}(S)$	Y	Y
$\Rightarrow \pi_A(R@S)$	A = AR $\cup$ AS	A = AR $\cup$ AS

	@ = $\cup$	@ = $\cap$	@ = $-$
$\sigma_{CR}(R)@ \sigma_{CS}(S)$	Q: CR = CS	Q: CR = CS	Q: CR $\Rightarrow$ CS
$\Rightarrow \sigma_C(R@S)$	C = CR = CS	C = CR = CS	C = CR
$\pi_{AR}(R)@\pi_{AS}(S)$	Q: R = S	Q: R = S	N
$\Rightarrow \pi_A(R@S)$	A = AR = AS	A = AR = AS	

Selected Bibliography

Abbreviations Used in the Bibliography

ACM: Association for Computing Machinery.

AFIPS: American Federation of Information Processing Societies.

CACM: Communications of the ACM (journal).

DE Conference: Proceedings of the IEEE CS International Conference on Data Engineering.

EDS: Proceedings of the International Conference on Expert Database Systems.

ER Conference: Proceedings of the International Conference on Entity-Relationship Approach.

IEEE: Institute of Electrical and Electronics Engineers.

IEEE Computer: Computer magazine (journal) of the IEEE CS.

IEEE CS: IEEE Computer Society.

IFIP: International Federation for Information Processing.

JACM: Journal of the ACM.

NCC: Proceedings of the National Computer Conference (published by AFIPS).

OOPSLA: Proceedings of the ACM Conference on Object-Oriented Programming Systems, Languages, and Applications.

PODS: Proceedings of the ACM Symposium on Principles of Database Systems.

SIGMOD: Proceedings of the ACM SIGMOD International Conference on Management of Data.

TOCS: ACM Transactions on Computer Systems (journal).

TODS: ACM Transactions on Database Systems (journal).

TOOIS: ACM Transactions on Office Information Systems (journal).

TSE: IEEE Transactions on Software Engineering (journal).

VLDB: Proceedings of the International Conference on Very Large Data Bases (issues after 1981 available from Morgan Kaufmann, Menlo Park, California).

Format for Bibliographic Citations

Book titles are in boldface; for example, **Database Computers**. Conference proceedings names are in italics; for example, NCC or *Proceedings of the ACM Pacific Conference*. Journal names are in boldface; for example, **TODS** or **Information Systems**. For journal citations, we give the volume number:issue number (within the volume, if any) and date of issue. For example "**TODS,** 3:4, December 1978" refers to the December 1978 issue of ACM Transactions on Database Systems, which is Volume 3, Number 4. Articles that appear in books or conference proceedings that are themselves cited in the bibliography are referenced as "in" these references; for example, "in VLDB [1978]" or "in Rustin [1974]". For citations with more than four authors, we will give the first author only followed by et al. In our selected bibliography at the end of each chapter, we use et al. if there are more than two authors. All author names are given with *a single initial* (for example, Codd, E. instead of Codd, E.F.).

Bibliographic References

Abbott, R. and Garcia-Molina, H. [1988] "Scheduling Real-Time Transactions: A Performance Evaluation," in VLDB [1988].

Abrial, J. [1974] "Data Semantics", in Klimbie and Koffeman [1974].

Afsarmanesh, H., McLeod, D., Knapp, D., and Parker, A. [1985] "An Extensible Object-Oriented Approach to Databases for VLSI/CAD", in VLDB [1985].

Aho, A., Beeri, C., and Ullman, J. [1979] "The Theory of Joins in Relational Databases", TODS, 4:3, September 1979.

Aho, A., Sagiv, Y., and Ullman, J. [1979a] "Efficient Optimization of a Class of Relational Expressions", TODS, 4:4, December 1979.

Akl, S. [1983] "Digital Signatures: A Tutorial Survey", IEEE **Computer**, 16:2, February 1983.

Albano, A., Cardelli, L., and Orsini, R. [1985] "GALILEO: A Strongly-Typed Interactive Conceptual Language", TODS, 10:2, June 1985.

Albano, A., de Antonellis, V., and di Leva, A. (editors) [1985a] **Computer-Aided Database Design: The DATAID Project,** North-Holland, 1985.

Allen, F., Loomis, M., and Mannino, M. [1982] "The Integrated Dictionary/Directory System", ACM **Computing Surveys,** 14:2, June 1982.

Andrews, T. and Harris, C. [1987] "Combining Language and Database Advances in an Object-Oriented Development Environment", OOPSLA, 1987.

ANSI [1975] American National Standards Institute Study Group on Data Base Management Systems: Interim Report, FDT, 7:2, ACM, 1975.

ANSI [1986] American National Standards Institute: The Database Language SQL, Document ANSI X3.135, 1986.

ANSI [1986a] American National Standards Institute: The Database Language NDL, Document ANSI X3.133, 1986.

ANSI [1989] American National Standards Institute: Information Resource Dictionary Systems, Document ANSI X3.138, 1989.

Apers, P., Hevner, A., and Yao, S. [1983] "Optimization Algorithms for Distributed Queries", TSE, 9:1, January 1983.

Armstrong, W. [1974] "Dependency Structures of Data Base Relationships", *Proceedings of the IFIP Congress*, 1974.

Astrahan, M. et al. [1976] "System R: A Relational Approach to Data Base Management", TODS, 1:2, June 1976.

Atre, S. [1980] **Structured Techniques for Design, Performance, and Management,** Wiley, 1980.

Bachman, C. [1969] "Data Structure Diagrams", **Data Base** (Bulletin of ACM SIGFIDET), 1:2, March 1969.

Bachman, C. [1973] "The Programmer as a Navigator", CACM, 16:1, November 1973.

Bachman, C. [1974] "The Data Structure Set Model", in Rustin [1974].

Bachman, C. and Williams, S. [1964] "A General Purpose Programming System for Random Access Memories", *Proceedings of the Fall Joint Computer Conference*, AFIPS, 26, 1964.

Badal, D. and Popek, G. [1979] "Cost and Performance Analysis of Semantic Integrity Validation Methods", in SIGMOD [1979].

Banerjee, J. et al. [1987] "Data Model Issues for Object-Oriented Applications", TOOIS, 5:1, January 1987.

Banerjee, J., Kim, W., Kim, H., and Korth, H. [1987a] "Semantics and Implementation of Schema Evolution in Object-Oriented Databases", in SIGMOD [1987].

Baroody, A. and DeWitt, D. [1981] "An Object-Oriented Approach to Database System Implementation", TODS, 6:4, December 1981.

Bassiouni, M. [1988] "Single-Site and Distributed Optimistic Protocols for Concurrency Control", TSE, 14:8, August 1988.

Batini, C., Ceri, S., and Navathe, S. [1989] **Database Design: An Entity-Relationship Approach,** Benjamin/Cummings (forthcoming).

Batini, C., Lenzerini, M., and Navathe, S. [1987] "A Comparative Analysis of Methodologies for Database Schema Integration", ACM **Computing Surveys,** 18:4, December 1986.

Batory, D. and Buchmann, A. [1984] "Molecular Objects, Abstract Data Types, and Data Models: A Framework", in VLDB [1984].

Batory, D. et al. [1986] "GENESIS: An Extensible Database Management System", TSE, 14:11, November 1988.

Bayer, R., Graham, M., and Seegmuller, G. (editors) [1978] **Operating Systems: An Advanced Course,** Springer-Verlag, 1978.

Bayer, R. and McCreight, E. [1972] "Organization and Maintenance of Large Ordered Indexes", **Acta Informatica,** 1:3, February 1972.

Beck, H., Gala, S., and Navathe, S. [1989] "Classification as a Query Processing Technique in the CANDIDE Semantic Data Model", in DE Conference [1989].

Beeri, C., Fagin, R., and Howard, J. [1977] "A Complete Axiomatization for Functional and Multivalued Dependencies", in SIGMOD [1977].

Ben-Zvi, J. [1982] "The Time Relational Model", Ph.D. Thesis, University of California, Los Angeles, 1982.

Bernstein, P. [1976] "Synthesizing Third Normal Form Relations from Functional Dependencies", TODS, 1:4, December 1976.

Bernstein, P., Blaustein, B., and Clarke, E. [1980] "Fast Maintenance of Semantic Integrity Assertions Using Redundant Aggregate Data", in VLDB [1980].

Bernstein, P. and Goodman, N. [1980] "Timestamp-Based Algorithms for Concurrency Control in Distributed Database Systems", in VLDB [1980].

Bernstein, P. and Goodman, N. [1981] "The Power of Natural Semijoins", SIAM **Journal of Computing,** 10:4, December 1981.

Bernstein, P. and Goodman, N. [1981a] "Concurrency Control in Distributed Database Systems", ACM **Computing Surveys,** 13:2, June 1981.

Bernstein, P. and Goodman, N. [1984] "An Algorithm for Concurrency Control and Recovery in Replicated Distributed Databases", TODS, 9:4, December 1984.

Bernstein, P., Hadzilacos, V., and Goodman, N. [1988] **Concurrency Control and Recovery in Database Systems**, Addison-Wesley, 1988.

Bhargava, B. (editor) [1987] **Concurrency and Reliability in Distributed Systems,** Van Nostrand-Reinhold, 1987.

Bhargava, B. and Reidl, J. [1988] "A Model for Adaptable Systems for Transaction Processing", in DE Conference [1988].

Biller, H. [1979] "On the Equivalence of Data Base Schemas—A Semantic Approach to Data Translation", **Information Systems, 4**:1, 1979.

Bjork, A. [1973] "Recovery Scenario for a DB/DC System", *Proceedings of the* ACM *National Conference*, 1973.

Bjorner, D. and Lovengren, H. [1982] "Formalization of Database Systems and a Formal Definition of IMS", in VLDB [1982].

Blasgen, M. and Eswaran, K. [1976] "On the Evaluation of Queries in a Relational Database System", **IBM Systems Journal, 16**:1, January 1976.

Blasgen, M., et al. [1981] "System R: An Architectural Overview", **IBM Systems Journal, 20**:1, January 1981.

Bleier, R. and Vorhaus, A. [1968] "File Organization in the SDC TDMS", *Proceedings of the IFIP Congress*, 1968.

Bocca, J. [1986] "EDUCE—A Marriage of Convenience: Prolog and a Relational DBMS", *Proceedings of the Third International Conference on Logic Programming*, Springer-Verlag, 1986.

Bocca, J. [1986a] "On the Evaluation Strategy of EDUCE", in SIGMOD [1986].

Borkin, S. [1978] "Data Model Equivalence", in VLDB [1978].

Boyce, R., Chamberlin, D., King, W., and Hammer, M. [1975] "Specifying Queries as Relational Expressions", **CACM,** 18:11, November 1975.

Bracchi, G., Paolini, P., and Pelagatti, G. [1976] "Binary Logical Associations in Data Modelling", in Nijssen [1976].

Bracchi, G. and Pernici, B. [1984] "The Design Requirements of Office Systems", **TOOIS,** 2:2, April 1984.

Bracchi, G. and Pernici, B. [1987] "Decision Support in Office Information Systems", in Holsapple and Whinston [1987].

Brachman, R. and Levesque, H. [1984] "What Makes a Knowledge Base Knowledgeable? A View of Databases from the Knowledge Level", in EDS [1984].

Bradley, J. [1978] "An Extended Owner-Coupled Set Data Model and Predicate Calculus for Database Management", **TODS,** 3:4, December 1978.

Bray, O. [1988] **Computer Integrated Manufacturing—The Data Management Strategy,** Digital Press, 1988.

Brodie, M., Mylopoulos, J., and Schmidt, J. (editors) [1984] **On Conceptual Modeling,** Springer-Verlag, 1984.

Brosey, M. and Shneiderman, B. [1978] "Two Experimental Comparisons of Relational and Hierarchical Database Models", **International Journal of Man-Machine Studies,** 1978.

Bubenko, J., Berild, S., Lindercrona-Ohlin, E., and Nachmens, S. [1976] "From Information Requirements to DBTG Data Structures", *Proceedings of the ACM SIGMOD/SIGPLAN Conference on Data Abstraction*, 1976.

Bubenko, J., Langefors, B., and Solvberg, A. (editors) [1971] **Computer-Aided Information Systems Analysis and Design,** Studentlitteratur, Lund, Sweden, 1971.

Buneman, P. and Frankel, R. [1979] "FQL: A Functional Query Language", in SIGMOD [1979].

Bush, V. [1945] "As We May Think", *The Atlantic Monthly*, 176:1, January 1945 (reprinted in Kochen, M. (editor) **The Growth of Knowledge,** Wiley, 1967).

Campbell, D., Embley, D., and Czejdo, B. [1985] "A Relationally Complete Query Language for the Entity-Relationship Model", in ER Conference [1985].

Cardenas, A. [1985] **Data Base Management Systems,** Second Edition, Allyn and Bacon, 1985.

Carey, M. et al. [1986] "The Architecture of the EXODUS Extensible DBMS", in Dittrich and Dayal [1986].

Carey, M., DeWitt, D., Richardson, J. and Shekita, E. [1986a] "Object and File Management in the EXODUS Extensible Database System", in VLDB [1986].

Carey, M., DeWitt, D., and Vandenberg, S. [1988] "A Data Model and Query Language for Exodus", in SIGMOD [1988].

Carlis, J. [1986] "HAS, a Relational Algebra Operator or Divide Is Not Enough to Conquer", in DE Conference [1986].

Carlis, J. and March, S. [1984] "A Descriptive Model of Physical Database Design Problems and Solutions", in DE Conference [1984].

Casanova, M., Fagin, R., and Papadimitriou, C. [1981] "Inclusion Dependencies and Their Interaction with Functional Dependencies", *PODS*, 1981.

Casanova, M. and Vidal, V. [1982] "Toward a Sound View Integration Method", *PODS*, 1982.

Ceri, S. (editor) [1983] **Methodology and Tools for Database Design,** North-Holland, 1983.

Ceri, S., Navathe, S., and Wiederhold, G. [1983] "Distribution Design of Logical Database Schemas", TSE, 9:4, July 1983.

Ceri, S., Negri, M., and Pelagatti, G. [1982] "Horizontal Data Partitioning in Database Design", in SIGMOD [1982].

Ceri, S. and Owicki, S. [1983] "On the Use of Optimistic Methods for Concurrency Control in Distributed Databases", *Proceedings of the Sixth Berkeley Workshop on Distributed Data Management and Computer Networks*, February 1983.

Ceri, S. and Pelagatti, G. [1984] "Correctness of Query Execution Strategies in Distributed Databases", TODS, 8:4, December 1984.

Ceri, S. and Pelagatti, G. [1984a] **Distributed Databases: Principles and Systems,** McGraw-Hill, 1984.

Ceri, S. and Tanka, L. [1987] "Optimization of Systems of Algebraic Equations for Evaluating Datalog Queries", in VLDB [1987].

Chamberlin, D. and Boyce, R. [1974] "SEQUEL: A Structured English Query Language", in SIGMOD [1984].

Chamberlin, D., et al. [1976] "SEQUEL 2: A Unified Approach to Data Definition, Manipulation, and Control", IBM **Journal of Research and Development,** 20:6, November 1976.

Chamberlin, D., et al. [1981] "A History and Evaluation of System R", CACM, 24:10, October 1981.

Chandy, K., Browne, J., Dissley, C., and Uhrig, W. [1975] "Analytical Models for Rollback and Recovery Strategies in Database Systems", TSE, 1:1, March 1975.

Chang, C. and Walker, A. [1984] "PROSQL: A Prolog Programming Interface with SQL/DS", in EDS [1984].

Chang, N. and Fu, K. [1981] "Picture Query Languages for Pictorial Databases", IEEE **Computer,** 14:11, November 1981.

Chang, S., Lin, B., and Walser, R. [1979] "Generalized Zooming Techniques for Pictorial Database Systems", NCC, AFIPS, 48, 1979.

Chen, P. [1976] "The Entity Relationship Mode—Toward a Unified View of Data", TODS, 1:1, March 1976.

Childs, D. [1968] "Feasibility of a Set Theoretical Data Structure—A General Structure Based on a Reconstituted Definition of Relation", *Proceedings of the IFIP Congress*, 1968.

Chin, F. [1978] "Security in Statistical Databases for Queries with Small Counts", TODS, 3:1, March 1978.

Chin, F. and Ozsoyoglu, G. [1981] "Statistical Database Design", TODS, 6:1, March 1981.

Christodoulakis, S. et al. [1984] "Development of a Multimedia Information System for an Office Environment", in VLDB [1984].

Christodoulakis, S. and Faloutsos, C. [1986] "Design and Performance Considerations for an Optical Disk-Based Multimedia Object Server", IEEE **Computer,** 19:12, December 1986.

Chu, W. and Hurley, P. [1982] "Optimal Query Processing for Distributed Database Systems", IEEE **Transactions on Computers,** 31:9, September 1982.

Ciborra, C., Migliarese, P., and Romano, P. [1984] "A Methodological Inquiry of Organizational Noise in Socio Technical Systems", **Human Relations,** 37:8, 1984.

Claybrook, B. [1983] **File Management Techniques,** Wiley, 1983.

Clifford, J. and Tansel, A. [1985] "On an Algebra for Historical Relational Databases: Two Views", in SIGMOD [1985].

CODASYL [1978] Data Description Language Journal of Development, Canadian Government Publishing Centre, 1978.

Codd, E. [1970] "A Relational Model for Large Shared Data Banks", CACM, 13:6, June 1970.

Codd, E. [1971] "A Data Base Sublanguage Founded on the Relational Calculus", *Proceedings of the ACM SIGFIDET Workshop on Data Description, Access, and Control*, November 1971.

Codd, E. [1972] "Relational Completeness of Data Base Sublanguages", in Rustin [1972].

Codd, E. [1972a] "Further Normalization of the Data Base Relational Model", in Rustin [1972].

Codd, E. [1974] "Recent Investigations in Relational Database Systems", *Proceedings of the IFIP Congress*, 1974.

Codd, E. [1978] "How About Recently? (English Dialog with Relational Data Bases Using Rendezvous Version 1)", in Shneiderman [1978].

Codd, E. [1979] "Extending the Database Relational Model to Capture More Meaning", TODS, 4:4, December 1979.

Codd, E. [1982] "Relational Database: A Practical Foundation for Productivity", CACM, 25:2, December 1979.

Codd, E. [1985] "Is Your DBMS Really Relational?" and "Does Your DBMS Run By the Rules", COMPUTER WORLD, October 14 and October 21, 1985.

Codd, E. [1986] "An Evaluation Scheme for Database Management Systems That Are Claimed to be Relational", in DE Conference [1986].

Comer, D. [1979] "The Ubiquitous B-tree", ACM **Computing Surveys,** 11:2, June 1979.

Curtice, R. [1981] "Data Dictionaries: An Assessment of Current Practice and Problems", in VLDB [1981].

Czejdo, B., Elmasri, R., Rusinkiewicz, M., and Embley, D. [1987] "An Algebraic Language for Graphical Query Formulation Using an Extended Entity-Relationship Model", *Proceedings of the ACM Computer Science Conference*, 1987.

Dahl, R. and Bubenko, J. [1982] "IDBD: An Interactive Design Tool for CODASYL DBTG Type Databases", in VLDB [1982].

Dahl, V. [1984] "Logic Programming for Constructive Database Systems", in EDS [1984].

Date, C. [1977] **An Introduction to Database Systems,** Second Edition, Addison-Wesley, 1977.

Date, C. [1983] **An Introduction to Database Systems,** Volume 2, Addison-Wesley, 1983.

Date, C. [1983a] "The Outer Join", *Proceedings of the Second International Conference on Databases (ICOD-2)*, 1983.

Date, C. [1984] "A Critique of the SQL Database Language", ACM SIGMOD **Record,** 14:3, November 1984.

Date, C. [1986] **An Introduction to Database Systems,** Volume 1, Fourth Edition, Addison-Wesley, 1986.

Date, C. and White, C. [1988] **A Guide to DB2,** Second Edition, Addison-Wesley, 1988.

Date, C. and White, C. [1988a] **A Guide to SQL/DS,** Addison-Wesley, 1988.

Davies, C. [1973] "Recovery Semantics for a DB/DC System", *Proceedings of the* ACM *National Conference*, 1973.

Dayal, U. and Bernstein, P. [1978] "On the Updatability of Relational Views", in VLDB [1978].

Dayal, U. et al. [1987] "PROBE Final Report", Technical Report CCA-87-02, Computer Corporation of America, December 1987.

DBTG [1971] Report of the CODASYL Data Base Task Group, ACM, April 1971.

DE Conference [1984] *Proceedings of the* IEEE CS *International Conference on Data Engineering*, Berra, P. (editor), Los Angeles, California, April 1984.

DE Conference [1986] *Proceedings of the* IEEE CS *International Conference on Data Engineering*, Wiederhold, G. (editor), Los Angeles, California, February 1986.

DE Conference [1987] *Proceedings of the* IEEE CS *International Conference on Data Engineering*, Wah, B. (editor), Los Angeles, California, February 1987.

DE Conference [1988] *Proceedings of the* IEEE CS *International Conference on Data Engineering*, Carlis, J. (editor), Los Angeles, California, February 1988.

DE Conference [1989] *Proceedings of the* IEEE CS *International Conference on Data Engineering*, Shuey, R. (editor), Los Angeles, California, February 1989.

DeMarco, T. [1979] **Structured Analysis and System Specification,** Prentice-Hall Yourdan Inc., 1979.

Denning, D. [1980] "Secure Statistical Databases with Random Sample Queries", TODS, 5:3, September 1980.

Denning, D. and Denning, P. [1979] "Data Security", ACM **Computing Surveys,** 11:3, September 1979.

Devor, C. and Weeldreyer, J. [1980] "DDTS: A Testbed for Distributed Database Research", *Proceedings of the* ACM *Pacific Conference*, 1980.

DeWitt, D. et al. [1984] "Implementation Techniques for Main Memory Databases", in SIGMOD [1984].

Diffie, W. and Hellman, M. [1979] "Privacy and Authentication", **Proceedings of the** IEEE, 67:3, March 1979.

Dittrich, K. [1986] "Object-Oriented Database Systems: The Notion and the Issues", in Dittrich and Dayal [1986].

Dittrich, K. and Dayal, U. (editors) [1986] *Proceedings of the International Workshop on Object-Oriented Database Systems*, IEEE CS, Pacific Grove, California, September 1986.

Dodd, G. [1969] "APL—A Language for Associative Data Handling in PL/I", *Proceedings of the Fall Joint Computer Conference*, AFIPS, 29, 1969.

Dodd, G. [1969] "Elements of Data Management Systems", ACM **Computing Surveys,** 1:2, June 1969.

Dos Santos, C., Neuhold, E., and Furtado, A. [1979] "A Data Type Approach to the Entity-Relationship Model", in ER Conference [1979].

Du, H. and Ghanta, S. [1987] "A Framework for Efficient IC/VLSI CAD Databases", in DE Conference [1987].

Dumas, P. et al. [1982] "MOBILE-Burotique: Prospects for the Future", in Naffah [1982].

Dumpala, S. and Arora, S. [1983] "Schema Translation Using the Entity-Relationship Approach", in ER Conference [1983].

Dwyer, S. et al. [1982] "A Diagnostic Digital Imaging System", *Proceedings of the IEEE CS Conference on Pattern Recognition and Image Processing*, June 1982.

Eastman, C. [1987] "Database Facilities for Engineering Design", **Proceedings of the IEEE**, 69:10, October 1981.

EDS [1984] **Expert Database Systems,** Kerschberg, L. (editor), (*Proceedings of the First International Workshop on Expert Database Systems*, Kiawah Island, South Carolina, October 1984), Benjamin/Cummings, 1986.

EDS [1986] **Expert Database Systems,** Kerschberg, L. (editor), (*Proceedings of the First International Conference on Expert Database Systems*, Charleston, South Carolina, April 1986), Benjamin/Cummings, 1987.

EDS [1988] **Expert Database Systems,** Kerschberg, L. (editor), (*Proceedings of the Second International Conference on Expert Database Systems*, Tysons Corner, Virginia, April 1988), Benjamin/Cummings (forthcoming).

Eick, C. and Lockemann, P. [1985] "Acquisition of Terminological Knowledge Using Database Design Techniques", in SIGMOD [1985].

ElAbbadi, A. and Toueg, S. [1988] "The Group Paradigm for Concurrency Control", in SIGMOD [1988].

Ellis, C. and Nutt, G. [1980] "Office Information Systems and Computer Science", **ACM Computing Surveys,** 12:1, March 1980.

Elmagarmid, A. and Helal, A. [1988] "Supporting Updates in Heterogeneous Distributed Databases Systems", in DE Conference [1988].

Elmasri, R. and Larson, J. [1985] "A Graphical Query Facility for ER Databases", in ER Conference [1985].

Elmasri, R., Larson, J., and Navathe, S. [1986] "Schema Integration Algorithms for Federated Databases and Logical Database Design", Honeywell CSDD, Technical Report CSC-86-9: 8212, January 1986.

Elmasri, R. and Navathe, S. [1984] "Object Integration in Logical Database Design", in DE Conference [1984].

Elmasri, R., Srinivas, P., and Thomas, G. [1987] "Fragmentation and Query Decomposition in the ECR Model", in DE Conference [1987].

Elmasri, R., Weeldreyer, J., and Hevner, A. [1985] "The Category Concept: An Extension to the Entity-Relationship Model", **International Journal on Data and Knowledge Engineering,** 1:1, May 1985.

Elmasri, R. and Wiederhold, G. [1979] "Data Model Integration Using the Structural Model", in SIGMOD [1979].

Elmasri, R. and Wiederhold, G. [1980] "Structural Properties of Relationships and Their Representation", NCC, AFIPS, 49, 1980.

Elmasri, R. and Wiederhold, G. [1981] "GORDAS: A Formal, High-Level Query Language for the Entity-Relationship Model", in ER Conference [1981].

Engelbart, D. and English, W. [1968] "A Research Center for Augmenting Human Intellect", *Proceedings of the Fall Joint Computer Conference*, AFIPS, December 1968.

Epstein, R., Stonebraker, M., and Wong, E. [1978] "Distributed Query Processing in a Relational Database System", in SIGMOD [1978].

ER Conference [1979] **Entity-Relationship Approach to Systems Analysis and Design,** Chen, P. (editor), (*Proceedings of the First International Conference on Entity-Relationship Approach*, Los Angeles, California, December 1979), North-Holland, 1980.

ER Conference [1981] **Entity-Relationship Approach to Information Modeling and Analysis**, Chen, P. (editor), (*Proceedings of the Second International Conference on Entity-Relationship Approach*, Washington, D.C., October 1981), Elsevier Science, 1981.

ER Conference [1983] **Entity-Relationship Approach to Software Engineering,** Davis, C., Jajodia, S., Ng, P., and Yeh, R. (editors), (*Proceedings of the Third International Conference on Entity-Relationship Approach*, Anaheim, California, October 1983), North-Holland, 1983.

ER Conference [1985] *Proceedings of the Fourth International Conference on Entity-Relationship Approach*, Liu, J. (editor), Chicago, Illinois, October 1985, IEEE CS.

ER Conference [1986] *Proceedings of the Fifth International Conference on Entity-Relationship Approach*, Spaccapietra, S. (editor), Dijon, France, November 1986, Express-Tirages.

ER Conference [1987] *Proceedings of the Sixth International Conference on Entity-Relationship Approach*, March, S. (editor), New York, New York, November 1987.

ER Conference [1988] *Proceedings of the Seventh International Conference on Entity-Relationship Approach*, Batini, C. (editor), Rome, Italy, November 1988.

Eswaran, K. and Chamberlin, D. [1975] "Functional Specifications of a Subsystem for Database Integrity", in VLDB [1975].

Eswaran, K., Gray, J., Lorie, R., and Traiger, I. [1976] "The Notions of Consistency and Predicate Locks in a Data Base System", CACM, 19:11, November 1976.

Everett, G., Dissly, C., and Hardgrave, W. [1971] RFMS User Manual, TRM-16, Computing Center, University of Texas at Austin, 1981.

Fagin, R. [1977] "Multivalued Dependencies and a New Normal Form for Relational Databases", TODS, 2:3, September 1977.

Fagin, R. [1979] "Normal Forms and Relational Database Operators", in SIGMOD [1979].

Fagin, R. [1981] "A Normal Form for Relational Databases That is Based on Domains and Keys", TODS, 6:3, September 1981.

Fagin, R., Nievergelt, J., Pippenger, N., and Strong, H. [1979] "Extendible Hashing—A Fast Access Method for Dynamic Files", TODS, 4:3, September 1979.

Fernandez, E., Summers, R., and Wood, C. [1981] **Database Security and Integrity,** Addison-Wesley, 1981.

Ferrier, A. and Stangret, C. [1982] "Heterogeneity in the Distributed Database Management System SIRIUS-DELTA", in VLDB [1982].

Fishman, D. et al. [1986] "IRIS: An Object-Oriented DBMS", TOOIS, 4:2, April 1986.

Fry, J. and Sibley, E. [1976] "Evolution of Data-Base Management Systems", ACM **Computing Surveys,** 8:1, March 1976.

Furtado, A. [1978] "Formal Aspects of the Relational Model", **Information Systems,** 3:2, 1978.

Gadia, S. [1988] "A Homogeneous Relational Model and Query Language for Temporal Databases", TODS, 13:4, December 1988.

Gait, J. [1988] "The Optical File Cabinet: A Random-Access File System for Write-Once Optical Disks", IEEE **Computer,** 21:6, June 1988.

Gallaire, H. and Minker, J. (editors) [1978] **Logic and Databases,** Plenum Press, 1978.

Gallaire, H., Minker, J., and Nicolas, J. [1984] "Logic and Databases: A Deductive Approach", ACM **Computing Surveys,** 16:2, June 1984.

Gamal-Eldin, M., Thomas, G., and Elmasri, R. [1988] "Integrating Relational Databases with Support for Updates", *Proceedings of the International Symposium on Databases in Parallel and Distributed Systems,* IEEE CS, December 1988.

Gane, C. and Sarson, T. [1977] **Structured Systems Analysis: Tools and Techniques,** Improved Systems Technologies Inc., 1977.

Garcia-Molina, H. [1978] "Performance Comparison of Two Update Algorithms for Distributed Databases", *Proceedings of the Berkeley Workshop on Distributed Data Management and Computer Networks,* IEEE CS, February 1978.

Garcia-Molina, H. [1982] "Elections in Distributed Computing Systems", IEEE **Transactions on Computers,** 31:1, January 1982.

Garcia-Molina, H. [1983] "Using Semantic Knowledge for Transaction Processing in a Distributed Database", TODS, 8:2, June 1983.

Gerritsen, R. [1975] "A Preliminary System for the Design of DBTG Data Structures", CACM, 18:10, October 1975.

Ghosh, S. [1984] "An Application of Statistical Databases in Manufacturing Testing", in DE Conference [1984].

Ghosh, S. [1986] "Statistical Data Reduction for Manufacturing Testing", in DE Conference [1986].

Gifford, D. [1979] "Weighted Voting for Replicated Data", *Proceedings of the Seventh* ACM *Symposium on Operating Systems Principles,* 1979.

Goldberg, A. and Robson, D. [1983] **Smalltalk-80: The Language and Its Implementation,** Addison-Wesley, 1983.

Goldfine, A. and Konig, P. [1988] A Technical Overview of the Information Resource Dictionary System (IRDS), Second Edition, NBS IR 88-3700, National Bureau of Standards.

Gotlieb, L. [1975] "Computing Joins of Relations", in SIGMOD [1975].

Graefe, G. and DeWitt, D. [1987] "The EXODUS Optimizer Generator", in SIGMOD [1987].

Gray, J. [1978] "Notes on Data Base Operating Systems", in Bayer, Graham, and Seegmuller [1978].

Gray, J. [1981] "The Transaction Concept: Virtues and Limitations", in VLDB [1981].

Gray, J., Lorie, R., and Putzulo, G. [1975] "Granularity of Locks and Degrees of Consistency in a Shared Data Base", in Nijssen [1976].

Gray, J., McJones, P., and Blasgen, M. [1981] "The Recovery Manager of the System R Database Manager", ACM **Computing Surveys,** 13:2, June 1981.

Griffiths, P. and Wade, B. [1976] "An Authorization Mechanism for a Relational Database System", TODS, 1:3, September 1976.

Guttman, A. [1984] "R-Trees: A Dynamic Index Structure for Spatial Searching", in SIGMOD [1984].

Haerder, T. and Rothermel, K. [1987] "Concepts for Transaction Recovery in Nested Transactions", in SIGMOD [1987].

Hall, P. [1976] "Optimization of a Single Relational Expression in a Relational Data Base System", IBM **Journal of Research and Development,** 20:3, May 1976.

Hammer, M. and McLeod, D. [1975] "Semantic Integrity in a Relational Data Base System", in VLDB [1975].

Hammer, M. and McLeod, D. [1981] "Database Description with SDM: A Semantic Data Model", TODS, 6:3, September 1980.

Hammer, M. and Sarin, S. [1978] "Efficient Monitoring of Database Assertions", in SIGMOD [1978].

Hardgrave, W. [1974] "BOLT: A Retrieval Language for Tree-Structured Database Systems", in Tou [1984].

Hardgrave, W. [1980] "Ambiguity in Processing Boolean Queries on TDMS Tree Structures: A Study of Four Different Philosophies", TSE, 6:4, July 1980.

Harrington, J. [1987] **Relational Database Management for Microcomputer: Design and Implementation,** Holt Rinehart Winston, 1987.

Harris, L. [1978] "The ROBOT System: Natural Language Processing Applied to Data Base Query", *Proceedings of the* ACM *National Conference*, December 1978.

Haskin, R. and Lorie, R. [1982] "On Extending the Functions of a Relational Database System", in SIGMOD [1982].

Hayes-Roth, F., Waterman, D., and Lenat, D. (editors) [1983] **Building Expert Systems,** Addison-Wesley, 1983.

Held, G. and Stonebraker, M. [1978] "B-Trees Reexamined", CACM, 21:2, February 1978.

Herot, C. [1980] "Spatial Management of Data", TODS, 5:4, December 1980.

Hevner, A. and Yao, S. [1979] "Query Processing in Distributed Database Systems", TSE, 5:3, May 1979.

Hoffer, J. [1982] "An Empirical Investigation with Individual Differences in Database Models", *Proceedings of the Third International Information Systems Conference*, December 1982.

Holsapple, C. and Whinston, A. (editors) [1987] **Decisions Support Systems Theory and Application,** Springer-Verlag, 1987.

Hsu, A. and Imielinsky, T. [1985] "Integrity Checking for Multiple Updates", in SIGMOD [1985].

Hull, R. and King, R. [1987] "Semantic Database Modeling: Survey, Applications, and Research Issues", ACM **Computing Surveys,** 19:3, September 1987.

IBM [1978] QBE Terminal Users Guide, Form Number SH20-2078-0.

IBM [1978a] QBE Quick Reference Card, Form Number JX20-2030-0.

IGES [1983] International Graphics Exchange Specification Version 2, National Bureau of Standards, U.S. Depertment of Commerce, January 1983.

Imielinski, T. and Lipski, W. [1981] "On Representing Incomplete Information in a Relational Database", in VLDB [1981].

Ioannidis, Y. and Wong, E. [1988] "Transforming Non-Linear Recursion to Linear Recursion", in EDS [1988].

Iossophidis, J. [1979] "A Translator to Convert the DDL of ERM to the DDL of System 2000", in ER Conference [1979].

Irani, K., Purkayastha, S., and Teorey, T. [1979] "A Designer for DBMS-Processable Logical Database Structures", in VLDB [1979].

Jajodia, S. and Mutchler, D. [1987] "Dynamic Voting", in SIGMOD [1987].

Jajodia, S., Ng, P., and Springsteel, F. [1983] "The Problem of Equivalence for Entity-Relationship Diagrams", TSE, 9:5, September, 1983.

Jardine, D. (editor) [1977] **The ANSI/SPARC DBMS Model,** North-Holland, 1977.

Jarke, M. and Koch, J. [1984] "Query Optimization in Database Systems", ACM **Computing Surveys,** 16:2, June 1984.

Kamel, N. and King, R. [1985] "A Model of Data Distribution Based on Texture Analysis", in SIGMOD [1985].

Kapp, D. and Leben, J. [1978] IMS **Programming Techniques,** Van Nostrand-Reinhold, 1978.

Katz, R. [1985] **Information Management for Engineering Design,** Surveys in Computer Science, Springer-Verlag, 1985.

Katz, R. and Wong, E. [1982] "Decompiling CODASYL DML into Relational Queries", TODS, 7:1, March 1982.

Kedem, Z. and Silberschatz, A. [1980] "Non-Two Phase Locking Protocols with Shared and Exclusive Locks", in VLDB [1980].

Keller, A. [1982] "Updates to Relational Database Through Views Involving Joins", in Scheuermann [1982].

Kemper, A., Lockemann, P., and Wallrath, M. [1987] "An Object-Oriented Database System for Engineering Applications", in SIGMOD [1987].

Kemper, A. and Wallrath, M. [1987] "An Analysis of Geometric Modeling in Database Systems", **ACM Computing Surveys,** 19:1, March 1987.

Kent, W. [1978] **Data and Reality,** North-Holland, 1978.

Kent, W. [1979] "Limitations of Record-Based Information Models", TODS, 4:1, March 1979.

Kerschberg, L., Ting, P., and Yao, S. [1982] "Query Optimization in Star Computer Networks", TODS, 7:4, December 1982.

Kifer, M. and Lozinskii, E. [1986] "A Framework for an Efficient Implementation of Deductive Databases", *Proceedings of the Sixth Advanced Database Symposium*, Tokyo, Japan, August 1986.

Kim, W. [1982] "On Optimizing an SQL-like Nested Query", TODS, 3:3, September 1982.

Kim, W., Reiner, D., and Batory, D. (editors) [1985] **Query Processing in Database Systems,** Springer-Verlag, 1985.

Kim, W. et al. [1987] "Features of the ORION Object-Oriented Database System", Microelectronics and Computer Technology Corporation, Technical Report ACA-ST-308-87, September 1987.

King, J. [1981] "QUIST: A System for Semantic Query Optimization in Relational Databases", in VLDB [1981].

Klimbie, J. and Koffeman, K. (editors) [1974] **Data Base Management,** North-Holland, 1974.

Klug, A. [1982] "Equivalence of Relational Algebra and Relational Calculus Query Languages Having Aggregate Functions", JACM, 29:3, July 1982.

Knuth, D. [1973] **The Art of Computer Programming,** Volume 3: **Sorting and Searching,** Addison-Wesley, 1973.

Kohler, W. [1981] "A Survey of Techniques for Synchronization and Recovery in Decentralized Computer Systems", **ACM Computing Surveys,** 13:2, June 1981.

Konsynski, B., Bracker, L., and Bracker, W. [1982] "A Model for Specification of Office Communications", IEEE **Transactions on Communications,** 30:1, January 1982.

Korth, H. [1983] "Locking Primitives in a Database System", JACM, 30:1, January 1983.

Korth, H. and Silberschatz, A. [1986] **Database System Concepts,** McGraw-Hill, 1986.

Kroenke, D. [1983] **Database Processing,** Second Edition, Science Research Associates, 1983.

Kroenke, D. and Dolan, K. [1988] **Database Processing,** Third Edition, Science Research Associates, 1983.

Kumar, A. and Stonebraker, M. [1987] "Semantics Based Transaction Management Techniques for Replicated Data", in SIGMOD [1987].

Kung, H. and Robinson, J. [1981] "Optimistic Concurrency Control", TODS, 6:2, June 1981.

Kunii, T. and Harada, M. [1980] "SID: A System for Interactive Design", NCC, AFIPS, 49, June 1980.

Lacroix, M. and Pirotte, A. [1977] "Domain-Oriented Relational Languages", in VLDB [1977].

Lacroix, M. and Pirotte, A. [1977a] "ILL: An English Structured Query Language for Relational Data Bases", in Nijssen [1977].

Lafue, G. and Smith, R. [1984] "Implementation of a Semantic Integrity Manager with a Knowledge Representation System", in EDS [1984].

Lamport, L. [1978] "Time, Clocks, and the Ordering of Events in a Distributed System", CACM, 21:7, July 1978.

Larson, J. [1983] "Bridging the Gap Between Network and Relational Database Management Systems", IEEE **Computer,** 16:9, September 1983.

Larson, J., Navathe, S., and Elmasri, R. [1989] "Attribute Equivalence and its Use in Schema Integration", to appear in TSE.

Larson, P. [1978] "Dynamic Hashing", BIT, 18, 1978.

Larson, P. [1981] "Analysis of Index-Sequential Files with Overflow Chaining", TODS, 6:4, December 1981.

Lehman, P. and Yao, S. [1981] "Efficient Locking for Concurrent Operations on B-Trees", TODS, 6:4, December 1981.

Leiss, E. [1982] "Randomizing, A Practical Method for Protecting Statistical Databases Against Compromise", in VLDB [1982].

Leiss, E. [1982a] **Principles of Data Security,** Plenum Press, 1982.

Lenzerini, M. and Santucci, C. [1983] "Cardinality Constraints in the Entity Relationship Model", in ER Conference [1983].

Lien, E. and Weinberger, P. [1978] "Consistency, Concurrency, and Crash Recovery", in SIGMOD [1978].

Lilien, L. and Bhargava, B. [1985] "Database Integrity Block Construct: Concepts and Design Issues", TSE, 11:9, September 1985.

Lindsay, B. et al. [1984] "Computation and Communication in R*: A Distributed Database Manager", TOCS, 2:1, January 1984.

Lipski, W. [1979] "On Semantic Issues Connected with Incomplete Information", TODS, 4:3, September 1979.

Liskov, B. and Zilles, S. [1975] "Specification Techniques for Data Abstractions", TSE, 1:1, March 1975.

Liskov, B. et al. [1981] CLU Reference Manual, Lecture Notes in Computer Science, Springer-Verlag, 1981.

Litwin, W. [1978] "Virtual Hashing: A Dynamically Changing Hashing", in VLDB [1978].

Litwin, W. [1980] "Linear Hashing: A New Tool for File and Table Addressing", in VLDB [1980].

Liu, K. and Sunderraman, R. [1988] "On Representing Indefinite and Maybe Information in Relational Databases", in DE Conference [1988].

Livadas, P. [1989] **File Structures: Theory and Practice,** Prentice-Hall, 1989.

Lockemann, P. and Knutsen, W. [1968] "Recovery of Disk Contents after System Failure", CACM, 11:8, August 1968.

Lorie, R. [1977] "Physical Integrity in a Large Segmented Database", TODS, 2:1, March 1977.

Lorie, R. and Plouffe, W. [1983] "Complex Objects and Their Use in Design Transactions", in SIGMOD [1983].

Lozinskii, E. [1986] "A Problem-Oriented Inferential Database System", TODS, 11:3, September 1986.

Lu, H., Mikkilineni, K., and Richardson, J. [1987] "Design and Evaluation of Algorithms to Compute the Transitive Closure of a Database Relation", in DE Conference [1987].

Maier, D. [1983] **The Theory of Relational Databases,** Computer Science Press, 1983.

Maier, D., Stein, J., Otis, A., and Purdy, A. [1986] "Development of an Object-Oriented DBMS", OOPSLA, 1986.

Malley, C. and Zdonick, S. [1986] "A Knowledge-Based Approach to Query Optimization", in EDS [1986].

Mannino, M. and Effelsberg, W. [1984] "Matching Techniques in Global Schema Design", in DE Conference [1984].

March, S. and Severance, D. [1977] "The Determination of Efficient Record Segmentations and Blocking Factors for Shared Files", TODS, 2:3, September 1977.

Markowitz, V. and Raz, Y. [1983] "ERROL: An Entity-Relationship, Role Oriented, Query Language", in ER Conference [1983].

Maryanski, F. [1980] "Backend Database Machines", ACM **Computing Surveys,** 12:1, March 1980.

McFadden, F. and Hoffer, J. [1988] **Database Management,** Second Edition, Benjamin/ Cummings, 1988.

McGee, W. [1977] "The Information Management System IMS/VS, Part I: General Structure and Operation", IBM **Systems Journal,** 16:2, June 1977.

McLeod, D. and Heimbigner, D. [1985] "A Federated Architecture for Information Systems", **TOOIS,** 3:3, July 1985.

Menasce, D., Popek, G., and Muntz, R. [1980] "A Locking Protocol for Resource Coordination in Distributed Databases", TODS, 5:2, June 1980.

Mendelzon, A. and Maier, D. [1979] "Generalized Mutual Dependencies and the Decomposition of Database Relations", in VLDB [1979].

Mikkilineni, K. and Su, S. [1988] "An Evaluation of Relational Join Algorithms in a Pipelined Query Processing Environment", TSE, 14:6, June 1988.

Miller, N. [1987] **File Structures Using PASCAL,** Benjamin/Cummings, 1987.

Minoura, T. and Wiederhold, G. [1981] "Resilient Extended True-Copy Token Scheme for a Distributed Database", TSE, 8:3, May 1981.

Missikoff, M. and Wiederhold, G. [1984] "Toward a Unified Approach for Expert and Database Systems", in EDS [1984].

Morgan, H. and Levin, K. [1977] "Optimal Program and Data Locations in Computer Networks", **CACM,** 20:5, May 1977.

Morris, K., Ullman, J., and VanGelden, A. [1986] "Design Overview of the NAIL! System", *Proceedings of the Third International Conference on Logic Programming,* Springer-Verlag, 1986.

Morris, R. [1968] "Scatter Storage Techniques", CACM, 11:1, January 1968.

Moss, J. [1982] "Nested Transactions and Reliable Distributed Computing", *Proceedings of the Symposium on Reliability in Distributed Software and Database Systems,* IEEE CS, July 1982.

Motro, A. [1987] "Superviews: Virtual Integration of Multiple Databases", TSE, 13:7, July 1987.

Mylopolous, J., Bernstein, P., and Wong, H. [1980] "A Language Facility for Designing Database-Intensive Applications", TODS, 5:2, June 1980.

Naffah, N. (editor) [1982] **Office Information Systems,** North-Holland, 1982.

Naish, L. and Thom, J. [1982] "The MU-PROLOG Deductive Database", Technical Report 83/10, Department of Computer Science, University of Melbourne, 1983.

Navathe, S. [1980] "An Intuitive View to Normalize Network-Structured Data", in VLDB [1980].

Navathe, S. [1985a] "Important Issues in Database Design Methodologies and Tools", in Albano et al. [1985].

Navathe, S. and Ahmed, R. [1988] "A Temporal Relational Model and Query Language", **Information Sciences** (to appear).

Navathe, S., Ceri, S., Wiederhold, G., and Dou, J. [1984] "Vertical Partitioning Algorithms for Database Design", TODS, 9:4, December 1984.

Navathe, S., Elmasri, R., and Larson, J. [1986] "Integrating User Views in Database Design", IEEE **Computer**, 19:1, January 1986.

Navathe, S. and Gadgil, S. [1982] "A Methodology for View Integration in Logical Database Design", in VLDB [1982].

Navathe, S. and Kerschberg, L. [1986] "Role of Data Dictionaries in Database Design", **Information and Management,** 10:1, January 1986.

Navathe, S. and Pillalamarri, M. [1988] "Toward Making the ER Approach Object-Oriented", in ER Conference [1988].

Navathe, S., Sashidhar, T., and Elmasri, R. [1984a] "Relationship Merging in Schema Integration", in VLDB [1984].

Navathe, S. and Schkolnick, M. [1978] "View Representation in Logical Database Design", in SIG-MOD [1978].

Ng, P. [1981] "Further Analysis of the Entity-Relationship Approach to Database Design", TSE, 7:1, January 1981.

Nicolas, J. [1978] "Mutual Dependencies and Some Results on Undecomposable Relations", in VLDB [1978].

Nievergelt, J. [1974] "Binary Search Trees and File Organization", ACM **Computing Surveys,** 6:3, September 1974.

Nijssen, G. (editor) [1976] **Modelling in Data Base Management Systems,** North-Holland, 1976.

Nijssen, G. (editor) [1977] **Architecture and Models in Data Base Management Systems,** North-Holland, 1977.

Obermarck, R. [1982] "Distributed Deadlock Detection Algorithms", TODS, 7:2, June 1982.

Ohsuga, S. [1982] "Knowledge Based Systems as a New Interactive Computer System of the Next Generation", in **Computer Science and Technologies,** North-Holland, 1982.

Olle, T. [1978] **The CODASYL Approach to Data Base Management,** Wiley, 1978.

Olle, T., Sol, H., and Verrijn-Stuart, A. (editors) [1982] **Information System Design Methodology,** North-Holland, 1982.

Onuegbe, E., Rahimi, S., and Hevner, A. [1983] "Local Query Translation and Optimization in a Distributed System", NCC, AFIPS, 52, 1983.

Orenstein, J. [1986] "Spatial Query Processing in an Object Oriented Database System", in SIGMOD [1986].

Osborn, S. [1979] "Towards a Universal Relation Interface", in VLDB [1979].

Ozsoyoglu, G., Ozsoyoglu, Z., and Matos, V. [1985] "Extending Relational Algebra and Relational Calculus with Set Valued Attributes and Aggregate Functions", TODS, 12:4, December 1987.

Ozsoyoglu, Z. and Yuan, L. [1987] "A New Normal Form for Nested Relations", TODS, 12:1, March 1987.

Palermo, F. [1974] "A Database Search Problem", in Tou [1974].

Papadimitriou, C. [1979] "The Serializability of Concurrent Database Updates", JACM, 26:4, October 1979.

Papadimitriou, C. [1986] **The Theory of Database Concurrency Control,** Computer Science Press, 1986.

Papadimitriou, C. and Kanellakis, P. [1979] "On Concurrency Control by Multiple Versions", TODS, 9:1, March 1974.

Parent, C. and Spaccapietra, S. [1985] "An Algebra for a General Entity-Relationship Model", TSE, 11:7, July 1985.

Paris, J. [1986] "Voting with Witnesses: A Consistency Scheme for Replicated Files", in DE Conference [1986].

Paul, H. et al. [1987] "Architecture and Implementation of the Darmstadt Database Kernel System", in SIGMOD [1987].

Pillalamarri, M., Navathe, S., and Papachristidis, A. [1988] "Understanding the Power of Semantic Data Models", Working Paper, Database Systems R & D Center, University of Florida.

Prague, C. and Hammit, J. [1985] **Programming with dBase III,** Tab Books, 1985.

Ramamoorthy, C. and Wah, B. [1979] "The Placement of Relations on a Distributed Relational Database", *Proceedings of the First International Conference on Distributed Computing Systems,* IEEE CS, 1979.

Reed, D. [1983] "Implementing Atomic Actions on Decentralized Data", TOCS, 1:1, February 1983.

Reisner, P. [1977] "Use of Psychological Experimentation as an Aid to Development of a Query Language", TSE, 3:3, May 1977.

Reisner, P. [1981] "Human Factors Studies of Database Query Languages: A Survey and Assessment", ACM **Computing Surveys,** 13:1, March 1981.

Ries, D. [1979] "The Effect of Concurrency Control on the Performance of a Distributed Database Management System", *Proceedings of the Berkeley Workshop on Distributed Data Management and Computer Networks,* IEEE CS, February 1979.

Ries, D. and Stonebraker, M. [1977] "Effects of Locking Granularity in a Database Management System", TODS, 2:3, September 1977.

Rissanen, J. [1977] "Independent Components of Relations", TODS, 2:4, December 1977.

Rivest, R., Shamir, A., and Adelman, L. [1978] "On Digital Signatures and Public Key Cryptosystems", CACM, 21:2, February 1978.

Ross, S. [1986] **Understanding and Using dBase III,** West Publishing, 1986.

Roth, M. and Korth, H. [1987] "The Design of Non-1NF Relational Databases into Nested Normal Form", in SIGMOD [1987].

Rothnie, J. [1975] "Evaluating Inter-Entry Retrieval Expressions in a Relational Data Base Management System", NCC, AFIPS, 44, 1975.

Rothnie, J. et al. [1980] "Introduction to a System for Distributed Databases (SDD-1)", TODS, 5:1, March 1980.

RTI [1983] INGRES Reference Manual, Relational Technology Inc., 1983.

Rusinkiewicz, M. et al. [1988] "Query Processing in OMNIBASE—A Loosely-Coupled Multi-Database System", Computer Science Department, University of Houston, Technical Report UH-CS-88-05, February 1988.

Rustin, R. (editor) [1972] **Data Base Systems,** Prentice-Hall, 1972.

Rustin, R. (editor) [1974] *Proceedings of the* ACM SIGMOD *Debate on Data Models: Data Structure Set Versus Relational,* 1974.

Sacca, D. and Zaniolo, C. [1987] "Implementation of Recursive Queries for a Data Language Based on Pure Horn Clauses", *Proceedings of the Fourth International Conference on Logic Programming,* MIT Press, 1986.

Sadri, F. and Ullman, J. [1982] "Template Dependencies: A Large Class of Dependencies in Relational Databases and Its Complete Axiomatization", JACM, 29:2, April 1982.

Sagiv, Y. and Yannakakis, M. [1981] "Equivalence among Relational Expressions with the Union and Difference Operators", JACM, 27:4, November 1981.

Sakai, H. [1980] "Entity-Relationship Approach to Conceptual Schema Design", in SIGMOD [1980].

Sammut, C. and Sammut, R. [1983] "The Implementation of UNSW-PROLOG", **The Australian Computer Journal,** May 1983.

Schenk, H. [1974] "Implementation Aspects of the DBTG Proposal", *Proceeding of the IFIP Working Conference on Database Management Systems*, 1974.

Scheuermann, P. (editor) [1982] **Improving Database Usability and Responsiveness,** Academic Press, 1982.

Scheuermann, P., Schiffner, G., and Weber, H. [1979] "Abstraction Capabilities and Invariant Properties Modeling within the Entity-Relationship Approach", in ER Conference [1979].

Schkolnick, M. [1978] "A Survey of Physical Database Design Methodology and Techniques", in VLDB [1978].

Schlageter, G. [1981] "Optimistic Methods for Concurrency Control in Distributed Database Systems", in VLDB [1981].

Schmidt, J. and Swenson, J. [1975] "On the Semantics of the Relational Model", in SIGMOD [1975].

Schwarz, P. et al. [1986] "Extensibility in the Starburst Database System", in Dittrich and Dayal [1986].

Sciore, E. [1982] "A Complete Axiomatization for Full Join Dependencies", JACM, 29:2, April 1982.

Selinger, P. et al. [1979] "Access Path Selection in a Relational Database Management System", in SIGMOD [1979].

Senko, M. [1975] "Specification of Stored Data Structures and Desired Output in DIAM II with FORAL", in VLDB [1975].

Senko, M. [1980] "A Query Maintenance Language for the Data Independent Accessing Model II", **Information Systems,** 5:4, 1980.

Sheth, A., Larson, J., Cornelio, A., and Navathe, S. [1988] "A Tool for Integrating Conceptual Schemas and User Views", in DE Conference [1988].

Shipman, D. [1981] "The Functional Data Model and the Data Language DAPLEX", TODS, 6:1, March 1981.

Shneiderman, B. (editor) [1978] **Databases: Improving Usability and Responsiveness,** Academic Press, 1978.

Sibley, E. [1976] "The Development of Database Technology", ACM **Computing Surveys,** 8:1, March 1976.

Sibley, E. and Kerschberg, L. [1977] "Data Architecture and Data Model Considerations", NCC, AFIPS, 46, 1977.

SIGMOD [1974] *Proceedings of the ACM SIGMOD-SIGFIDET Conference on Data Description, Access, and Control*, Rustin, R. (editor), May 1974.

SIGMOD [1975] *Proceedings of the 1975 ACM SIGMOD International Conference on Management of Data*, King, F. (editor), San Jose, California, May 1975.

SIGMOD [1976] *Proceedings of the 1976 ACM SIGMOD International Conference on Management of Data*, Rothnie, J. (editor), Washington, D.C., June 1976.

SIGMOD [1977] *Proceedings of the 1977 ACM SIGMOD International Conference on Management of Data*, Smith, D. (editor), Toronto, Canada, August 1977.

SIGMOD [1978] *Proceedings of the 1978 ACM SIGMOD International Conference on Management of Data,* Lowenthal, E. and Dale, N. (editors), Austin, Texas, May/June 1978.

SIGMOD [1979] *Proceedings of the 1979 ACM SIGMOD International Conference on Management of Data,* Bernstein, P. (editor), Boston, Massachusetts, May/June 1979.

SIGMOD [1980] *Proceedings of the 1980 ACM SIGMOD International Conference on Management of Data,* Chen, P. and Sprowls, R. (editors), Santa Monica, California, May 1980.

SIGMOD [1981] *Proceedings of the 1981 ACM SIGMOD International Conference on Management of Data,* Lien, Y. (editor), Ann Arbor, Michigan, April/May 1981.

SIGMOD [1982] *Proceedings of the 1982 ACM SIGMOD International Conference on Management of Data,* Schkolnick, M. (editor), Orlando, Florida, June 1982.

SIGMOD [1983] *Proceedings of the 1983 ACM SIGMOD International Conference on Management of Data,* DeWitt, D. and Gardarin, G. (editors), San Jose, California, May 1983.

SIGMOD [1984] *Proceedings of the 1984 ACM SIGMOD International Conference on Management of Data,* Yormark, B. (editor), Boston, Massachusetts, June 1984.

SIGMOD [1985] *Proceedings of the 1985 ACM SIGMOD International Conference on Management of Data,* Navathe, S. (editor), Austin, Texas, May 1985.

SIGMOD [1986] *Proceedings of the 1986 ACM SIGMOD International Conference on Management of Data,* Zaniolo, C. (editor), Washington, D.C., May 1986.

SIGMOD [1987] *Proceedings of the 1987 ACM SIGMOD International Conference on Management of Data,* Dayal, U. and Traiger, I. (editors), San Francisco, California, May 1987.

SIGMOD [1988] *Proceedings of the 1988 ACM SIGMOD International Conference on Management of Data,* Boral, H. and Larson, P. (editors), Chicago, Illinois, June 1988.

Simpson, A. [1989] **dBase Programmers Reference Guide,** SYBEX Inc., 1989.

Sirbu, M., Schoichet, S., Kunin, J., and Hammer, M. [1981] "OAM: An Office Analysis Methodology", Massachusetts Institute of Technology Office Automation Group, Memo OAM-016, 1981.

Skeen, D. [1981] "Non-Blocking Commit Protocols", in SIGMOD [1981].

Smith, J. and Chang, P. [1975] "Optimizing the Performance of a Relational Algebra Interface", **CACM,** 18:10, October 1975.

Smith, J. and Smith, D. [1977] "Database Abstractions: Aggregation and Generalization", **TODS,** 2:2, June 1977.

Smith, J. et al. [1981] "MULTIBASE: Integrating Distributed Heterogeneous Database Systems", NCC, AFIPS, 50, 1981.

Smith, P. and Barnes, G. [1987] **Files & Databases: An Introduction,** Addison-Wesley, 1987.

Snodgrass, R. and Ahn, I. [1985] "A Taxonomy of Time in Databases", in SIGMOD [1985].

Stonebraker, M. [1975] "Implementation of Integrity Constraints and Views by Query Modification", in SIGMOD [1975].

Stonebraker, M. (editor) [1986] **The INGRES Papers,** Addison-Wesley, 1986.

Stonebraker, M., Hanson, E., and Hong, C. [1987] "The Design of the POSTGRES Rules System", in DE Conference [1987].

Stonebraker, M. and Rowe, L. [1986] "The Design of POSTGRES", in SIGMOD [1986].

Stonebraker, M., Rubenstein, B., and Guttman, A. [1983] "Application of Abstract Data Types and Exact Indices to CAD Databases", in SIGMOD [1983].

Stonebraker, M. and Wong, E. [1974] "Access Control in a Relational Database Management System by Query Modification", *Proceedings of the ACM Annual Conference,* 1974.

Stonebraker, M., Wong, E., Kreps, P. and Held, G. [1976] "The Design and Implementation of IN-GRES", TODS, 1:3, September 1976.

Su, S. [1985] "A Semantic Association Model for Corporate and Scientific-Statistical Databases", **Information Science,** 29, 1983.

Su, S. [1988] **Database Computers,** McGraw-Hill, 1988.

Su, S., Krishnamurthy, V., and Lam, H. [1988] "An Object-Oriented Semantic Association Model (OSAM*)", in **AI in Industrial Engineering and Manufacturing: Theoretical Issues and Applications,** American Institute of Industrial Engineers, 1988.

Tanenbaum, A. [1981] **Computer Networks,** Prentice-Hall, 1981.

Taylor, R. and Frank, R. [1976] "CODASYL Data Base Management Systems", ACM **Computing Surveys,** 8:1, March 1976.

Teorey, T. and Fry, J. [1982] **Design of Database Structures,** Prentice-Hall, 1982.

Teorey, T., Yang, D., and Fry, J. [1986] "A Logical Design Methodology for Relational Databases Using the Extended Entity-Relationship Model", ACM **Computing Surveys,** 18:2, June 1986.

Thomas, J. and Gould, J. [1975] "A Psychological Study of Query By Example", NCC, AFIPS, **44,** 1975.

Thomas, R. [1979] "A Majority Consensus Approach to Concurrency Control for Multiple Copy Data Bases", TODS, 4:2, June 1978.

Todd, S. [1976] "The Peterlee Relational Test Vehicle—A System Overview", IBM **Systems Journal,** 15:4, December 1976.

Tou, J. (editor) [1984] **Information Systems COINS-IV,** Plenum Press, 1984.

Tsichritzis, D. [1982] "Forms Management", CACM, 25:7, July 1982.

Tsichritzis, D. and Klug, A. (editors) [1978] **The ANSI/X3/SPARC DBMS Framework,** AFIPS Press, 1978.

Tsichritzis, D., and Lochovsky, F. [1976] "Hierarchical Data-base Management: A Survey", ACM **Computing Surveys,** 8:1, March 1976.

Tsichritzis, D. and Lochovsky, F. [1982] **Data Models,** Prentice-Hall, 1982.

Uhrowczik, P. [1973] "Data Dictionary/Directories", IBM **Systems Journal,** 12:4, December 1973.

Ullman, J. [1982] **Principles of Database Systems,** Second Edition, Computer Science Press, 1982.

Ullman, J. [1985] "Implementation of Logical Query Languages for Databases", TODS, 10:3, September 1985.

Valduriez, P. and Gardarin, G. [1989] **Analysis and Comparison of Relational Database Systems,** Addison-Wesley, 1989.

Vassiliou, Y. [1980] "Functional Dependencies and Incomplete Information", in VLDB [1980].

Verheijen, G. and VanBekkum, J. [1982] "NIAM: An Information Analysis Method", in Olle et al. [1982].

Verhofstadt, J. [1978] "Recovery Techniques for Database Systems", ACM **Computing Surveys,** 10:2, June 1978.

Vielle, L. [1988] "From QSQ Towards QoSaQ: Global Optimization of Recursive Queries", in EDS [1988].

VLDB [1975] *Proceedings of the First International Conference on Very Large Data Bases,* Kerr, D. (editor), Framingham, Massachusetts, September 1975.

VLDB [1976] **Systems For Large Databases,** Lockemann, P. and Neuhold, E. (editors) (*Proceedings of the Second International Conference on Very Large Data Bases,* Brussels, Belgium, July 1976), North-Holland, 1977.

VLDB [1977] *Proceedings of the Third International Conference on Very Large Data Bases*, Merten, A. (editor), Tokyo, Japan, October 1977.

VLDB [1978] *Proceedings of the Fourth International Conference on Very Large Data Bases*, Bubenko, J. and Yao, S. (editors), West Berlin, Germany, September 1978.

VLDB [1979] *Proceedings of the Fifth International Conference on Very Large Data Bases*, Furtado, A. and Morgan, H. (editors), Rio de Janeiro, Brazil, October 1979.

VLDB [1980] *Proceedings of the Sixth International Conference on Very Large Data Bases*, Lochovsky, F. and Taylor, R. (editors), Montreal, Canada, October 1980.

VLDB [1981] *Proceedings of the Seventh International Conference on Very Large Data Bases*, Zaniolo, C. and Delobel, C. (editors), Cannes, France, September 1981.

VLDB [1982] *Proceedings of the Eighth International Conference on Very Large Data Bases*, McLeod, D. and Villasenor, Y. (editors), Mexico City, Mexico, September 1982.

VLDB [1983] *Proceedings of the Ninth International Conference on Very Large Data Bases*, Schkolnick, M. and Thanos, C. (editors), Florence, Italy, October/November 1983.

VLDB [1984] *Proceedings of the Tenth International Conference on Very Large Data Bases*, Dayal, U., Schlageter, G., and Seng, L. (editors), Singapore, August 1984.

VLDB [1985] *Proceedings of the Eleventh International Conference on Very Large Data Bases*, Pirotte, A. and Vassiliou, Y. (editors), Stockholm, Sweden, August 1985.

VLDB [1986] *Proceedings of the Twelfth International Conference on Very Large Data Bases*, Chu, W., Gardarin, G., and Ohsuga, S. (editors), Kyoto, Japan, August 1986.

VLDB [1987] *Proceedings of the Thirteenth International Conference on Very Large Data Bases*, Stocker, P., Kent, W., and Hammersley, P. (editors), Brighton, England, September 1987.

VLDB [1988] *Proceedings of the Fourteenth International Conference on Very Large Data Bases*, Bancilhon, F. and DeWitt, D. (editors), Los Angeles, California, August/September 1988.

Vorhaus, A. and Mills, R. [1967] "The Time-Shared Data Management System: A New Approach to Data Management", System Development Corporation, Report SP-2634, 1967.

Weldon, J. [1981] **Data Base Administration,** Plenum Press, 1981.

Whang, K. [1985] "Query Optimization in Office By Example", IBM Research Report RC 11571, December 1985.

Whang, K. and Navathe, S. [1987] "An Extended Disjunctive Normal Form Approach for Processing Recursive Logic Queries in Loosely Coupled Environments", in VLDB [1987].

Whang, K., Wiederhold, G., and Sagalowicz, D. [1982] "Physical Design of Network Model Databases Using the Property of Separability", in VLDB [1982].

Wiederhold, G. [1983] **Database Design,** Second Edition, McGraw-Hill, 1983.

Wiederhold, G. [1984] "Knowledge and Database Management", IEEE **Software,** January 1984.

Wiederhold, G., Beetem, A., and Short, G. [1982] "A Database Approach to Communication in VLSI Design", IEEE **Transactions on Computer-Aided Design of Integrated Circuits and Systems,** 1:2, April 1982.

Wiederhold, G. and Elmasri, R. [1979] "The Structural Model for Database Design", in ER Conference [1979].

Wilson, B. and Navathe, S. [1986] "An Analytical Framework for Limited Redesign of Distributed Databases", *Proceedings of the Sixth Advanced Database Symposium*, Tokyo, Japan, August 1986.

Wirth, N. [1972] **Algorithms + Data Structures = Programs,** Prentice-Hall, 1972.

Wong, E. [1983] "Dynamic Rematerialization-Processing Distributed Queries Using Redundant Data", TSE, 9:3, May 1983.

Wong, E., and Youssefi, K. [1976] "Decomposition—A Strategy for Query Processing", TODS, 1:3, September 1976.

Wong, H. [1984] "Micro and Macro Statistical/Scientific Database Management", in DE Conference [1984].

Yao, S. [1979] "Optimization of Query Evaluation Algorithms", TODS, 4:2, June 1979.

Yao, S. (editor) [1985] **Principles of Database Design,** Volume 1: **Logical Organizations,** Prentice-Hall, 1985.

Youssefi, K. and Wong, E. [1979] "Query Processing in a Relational Database Management System", in VLDB [1979].

Zadeh, L. [1983] "The Role of Fuzzy Logic in the Management of Uncertainty in Expert Systems", **Fuzzy Sets and Systems,** 11, North-Holland, 1983.

Zaniolo, C. [1976] "Analysis and Design of Relational Schemata for Database Systems", Ph.D. Thesis, University of California, Los Angeles, 1976.

Zaniolo, C. et al. [1986] "Object-Oriented Database Systems and Knowledge Systems", in EDS [1984].

Zloof, M. [1975] "Query By Example", NCC, AFIPS, 44, 1975.

Zloof, M. [1982] "Office By Example: A Business Language That Unifies Data, Word Processing, and Electronic Mail", IBM **Systems Journal,** 21:3, 1982.

Zook, W. et al. [1977] INGRES **Reference Manual,** Department of EECS, University of California at Berkeley, 1977.

Zvieli, A. [1986] "A Fuzzy Relational Calculus", in EDS [1986].

Technical Terms Index

Author Index

797

Reiner, D. 762
Reisner, P. 210, 352, 766
Richardson, J. 755, 764
Ries, D. 585, 633, 766
Rissanen, J. 408, 766
Rivest, R. 606, 766
Robinson, J. 585, 763
Robson, D. 717, 728, 760
Romano, P. 756
Ross, S. 729, 766
Roth, M. 173, 766
Rothermel, K. 585, 760
Rothnie, J. 533, 634, 766, 767, 768
Rowe, L. 660, 769
Rubenstein, B. 769
Rusinkiewicz, M. 634, 657, 756, 767
Rustin, R. 767, 768

Sacca, D 660, 767
Sadri, F. 408, 767
Sagalowicz, D. 770
Sagiv, Y. 534, 752, 767
Sakai, H. 352, 767
Sammut, C. 653, 767
Sammut, R. 653, 767
Santucci, C. 64, 763
Sarin, S. 607, 761
Sarson, T. 485, 760
Sashidhar, T. 765
Schenk, H. 325, 767
Scheuermann, P. 451, 767
Schiffner, G. 767
Schkolnick, M. 451, 485, 765, 767, 768, 770
Schlageter, G. 633, 767, 770
Schmidt, J. 19, 64, 451, 606, 754, 767
Schwarz, P. 767
Sciore, E. 408, 767
Seegmuller, G. 753
Selinger, P. 534, 767
Seng, L. 770
Senko, M. 64, 451, 452, 767
Severance, D. 485, 764
Shamir, A. 766
Shekita, E. 755
Sheth, A. 485, 657, 767
Shipman, D. 451, 648, 767
Shneiderman, B. 352, 754, 768
Short, G. 771
Shuey, R. 757
Sibley, E. 21, 451, 759, 768

Silberschatz, A. 21, 36, 279, 585, 762
Simpson, A. 729, 768
Sirbu, M. 646, 768
Skeen, D. 634, 768
Smith, D. 637, 768
Smith, J. 451, 533, 634, 637, 768
Smith, P. 99, 132, 451, 769
Smith, R. 660, 763
Snodgrass, R. 173, 769
Sol, H. 765
Solvberg, A. 754
Spaccapietra, S. 452, 759, 766
Springsteel, F. 352, 762
Sprowls, R. 768
Srinivas, P. 758
Stangret, C. 634, 759
Stein, J. 764
Stocker, P. 770
Stonebraker, M. 132, 224, 251, 585, 606, 634,
    644, 660, 729, 759, 761, 763, 766, 769
Strong, H. 759
Su, S. 452, 534, 633, 644, 647, 764, 769
Summers, R. 758
Sunderraman, R. 660, 763
Swenson, J. 64, 451, 606, 767

Tanenbaum, A. 769
Tanka, L. 660, 755
Tansel, A. 173, 650, 756
Taylor, R. 325, 769, 770
Teorey, T. 451, 485, 761, 769
Thanos, C. 770
Thom, J. 653, 765
Thomas, G. 758, 760
Thomas, J. 251, 769
Thomas, R. 633, 769
Ting, P. 762
Todd, S. 173, 769
Tou, J. 769
Toueg, S. 633, 758
Traiger, I. 759, 768
Tsichritzis, D. 25, 36, 279, 352, 451, 607, 660,
    728, 769

Uhrig, W. 755
Uhrowczik, P. 36, 769
Ullman, J. 21, 36, 132, 219, 222, 224, 279, 385,
    392, 394, 408, 534, 585, 660, 752, 764,
    767, 769